Investigating American Democracy

Investigating American Democracy

Readings on Core Questions

Edited by

Thomas K. Lindsay, Ph.D.

Former Deputy Chairman of the National Endowment for the Humanities

Gary D. Glenn

Distinguished Teaching Professor Emeritus
Northern Illinois University

With an Introductory Essay and Commentary by

Thomas K. Lindsay

New York Oxford
OXFORD UNIVERSITY PRESS

Oxford University Press, Inc., publishes works that further
Oxford University's objective of excellence
in research, scholarship, and education.

Oxford New York
Auckland Cape Town Dar es Salaam Hong Kong Karachi
Kuala Lumpur Madrid Melbourne Mexico City Nairobi
New Delhi Shanghai Taipei Toronto

With offices in
Argentina Austria Brazil Chile Czech Republic France Greece
Guatemala Hungary Italy Japan Poland Portugal Singapore
South Korea Switzerland Thailand Turkey Ukraine Vietnam

For titles covered by Section 112 of the US Higher Education Opportunity Act, please visit www.oup.com/us/he for the latest information about pricing and alternate formats.

Published by Oxford University Press, Inc.
198 Madison Avenue, New York, New York 10016
http://www.oup.com

Library of Congress Cataloging-in-Publication Data

Lindsay, Thomas K.
Investigating American democracy : core questions / Thomas K. Lindsay, Gary D. Glenn.
p. cm.
Includes bibliographical references and index.
ISBN 978-0-19-539211-1
1. United States—Politics and government—Textbooks. 2. United States—Politics and government—Philosophy—Textbooks. 3. Democracy—United States—Textbooks. I. Glenn, Gary Dean, 1941- II. Title.
JK276.L56 2012
320.473—dc23
2012012978

BRIEF CONTENTS

CONTENTS

ACKNOWLEDGMENTS

For many years now, Gary Glenn has organized and taught an honors course at Northern Illinois University titled "Democracy in America." Thomas Lindsay employed his syllabus for this same course later in his own teaching, as did a number of Glenn's students at colleges and universities across the country. Glenn's syllabus has provided the indispensable outline for this book.

Thomas Lindsay is grateful to the Aequus Institute, which provided him generous financial support during the revisions stage of the project.

The editors would like to express their deep gratitude for the thoughtful guidance on this project provided by Jennifer Carpenter, politics editor at Oxford University Press. Over the course of the three-plus years from the book's inception to its completion, Jennifer's prudent, patient editing was key. We are also grateful to Maegan Sherlock, assistant editor at Oxford, for her steady hand and generous care in preparing the manuscript for production.

The editors thank Erik Boneff who, in the summer of 2009, gave helpful editorial assistance with the collection and organization of a number of the readings. The editors would also like to thank the following reviewers for their feedback: Claudia Bryant, Western Carolina University; Therese Cingranelli, Binghamton University; Clement Fatovic, Florida International University; Richard Herrera, Arizona State University; Dwight C. Kiel, University of Central Florida; James Matthew Wilson, Southern Methodist University; A. Lanethea Mathews-Gardner, Muhlenberg College; Maria Sampanis, California State University, Sacramento; Lois T. Vietri, Rowan University; Paul L. DeBole, Lasell College and Bentley University; Mack Mariani, Xavier University; Harvey D. Palmer, University at Buffalo, SUNY; and Michael Reinhard, Millsaps College.

PREFACE

Investigating American Democracy can be variously employed to serve a number of purposes. It can stand, and has stood, alone as a text in American government courses whose approach is political, historical, and cultural. Alternatively, it can serve as a supplemental text. In the latter case, it can complement a textbook that focuses on institutional framework and/or political research findings. Given the range of topics that it addresses and the manner in which it does so, it can also serve as a supplement to courses in both American public law and American political thought.

Investigating American Democracy makes use of a number of devices designed to enhance its readability for undergraduates. First, and most important, it employs, when appropriate, a back-and-forth, point-counterpoint format in order to draw students into the debates over the core questions regarding the scope and purpose of American democracy. Normally, each chapter highlights at least one instance of such direct disagreement; for example, chapter two pits Frederick Douglass's arguments against those of Alexander Stephens on the meaning of the proposition "All men are created equal" and its relationship to the practice of chattel slavery. Chapter six presents the face-off between Hamilton and Jefferson on the question of the independence of the federal judiciary and the propriety of judicial review.

Furthermore, for each and every reading we include a section with guiding questions that employ the point-counterpoint approach to invite students to reflect on how the current selection reacts to, agrees with, or seeks to rebut the previous reading(s). Test-bank question also are provided for the instructor in a supplemental volume. In this manner, and to the extent that a book can be "interactive," *Investigating American Democracy* encourages students not only to digest but to compare the conflicting opinions on certain key questions, with the view to enhancing their capacities to critically evaluate the positions of the various camps whose clashes have driven and continue to drive the debate over the meaning and direction of American democracy.

To this end, each discrete reading begins with an introduction titled "Why this Reading?" Each introduction provides the historical background needed to appreciate more fully the reading's place and purpose. Through no fault of their own, many students come to college today with little substantive instruction in American government and history. Within the attainable limits of a single textbook, *Investigating American Democracy* attempts to remedy this deficiency. Because no one text can accomplish everything, we hope that instructors will, depending on their areas of interest and expertise, either include an additional textbook and/or provide further context in classroom discussion.

One potential obstacle to our approach is the difficulty that students have understanding word usage as it was practiced at the time of the Founding. *The Federalist* is a key example of this. Although the 85 newspaper essays written by Hamilton, Madison, and Jay were intended for a general audience, the language employed in 1787–1788 can occasionally appear strange and distant to today's students. Instructors are thus confronted with the following dilemma: Although there is no single source that better explains the meaning and purpose of the original Constitution, assigning *The Federalist* to those who have difficulty understanding it runs the risk of demoralizing and turning off such students.

To remedy this, we have annotated *The Federalist* essays reprinted in this text. We have also annotated a number of other contemporaneous readings here. Specifically, key words and phrases are explained or defined (in brackets) after their first appearance in the readings. The terms that have meanings in brackets were chosen on the basis of classroom experience over the last two decades. In this we have erred on the side of caution: We expect that nearly all of the students will know at least some of these terms. We are encouraged if some of the students know all of the terms, but experience has shown that all of the students will not know all of the terms. In any event, by "updating" the terminology of historical readings and providing historical background, we seek to make students' entrance into these important texts less burdensome and more illuminating.

It is the editors' view that employing core questions to provide students access to primary texts is the best way to inform as well as engage them. Doubtless, American government textbooks provide a great deal of valuable context, but, unavoidably, they do so at the price of removing students from the debates and arguments that have shaped American democracy. By approaching the primary texts in search of the competing answers to America's deepest and most persistent questions, students have the opportunity to place their engagement—and their political perspectives—within the great sweep of debate that has taken place over the course of American history. In so doing, they are more likely to situate themselves actively in these debates and thus reflect on the questions posed in a more serious and comprehensive fashion.

At the same time, such an approach as ours carries the price of presenting a surface appearance of "unevenness." That is to say, *Investigating American Democracy* examines the writings and speeches of thinkers such as Tocqueville, of politician-theorists such as Jefferson, Madison, Hamilton, and Lincoln, as well as of everyday politicians. The arguments of this last group are rarely, if ever, as insightful as those of the former, nor do they offer the same quality of prose. Although such intellectual and stylistic unevenness is unavoidable, what matters most is that the meaning and direction of American democracy since the Revolution has been the product of the writings, speeches, and official acts of members of *all* these groups. Moreover, students will quickly come to see the influence of earlier theorists and politician-theorists on current thoughts and deeds, even when this influence is perhaps unknown to or, at least, unattributed by everyday politicians.

In taking this approach, the editors are guided by the spirit of John Maynard Keynes's observation in *The General Theory of Employment, Interest and Money*: "Practical men, who believe themselves to be quite exempt from any intellectual influences, are usually the slaves of some defunct economist."

Investigating American Democracy

CHAPTER 1

Introduction: Why a "core questions" approach to the study of American democracy, and why should such study include the examination of "old books"?

> "The unexamined life is not worth living for a living being."
> –Socrates
>
> —Plato,
> *Apology of Socrates*

> We have besides these men descended by blood from our ancestors-among us perhaps half our people who are not descendants at all of these men, . . . if they look back through this history to trace their connection with those days by blood, they find they have none, . . . but when they look through that old Declaration of Independence they find that those old men say that We hold these truths to be self-evident, that all men are created equal, and then they feel that moral sentiment taught in that day evidences their relation to those men, that it is the father of all moral principle in them, and that they have a right to claim it as though they were blood of blood, and flesh of the flesh of the men who wrote that Declaration, ***and so they are.***
>
> –Abraham Lincoln
> Speech in Chicago, 1858 (emphasis supplied)

What is American democracy, and what does it mean to be an American citizen? For Abraham Lincoln, any serious attempt on our part to address these fundamental questions must begin at the beginning, with the justification for America's existence: the Declaration of Independence. Its claims are meant to be universal, addressed not only to King George III, but also, it informs us, to the "opinions of mankind." The Declaration, whose primary author was Thomas Jefferson, argues that, in the new American order, blood, creed, and national origin—the constituents of citizenship throughout history—have been dethroned. Instead, U.S. citizenship entails adherence to certain moral and political principles, the truth of which, according to the Declaration, is "self-evident" to those who reason rightly about what it means to be a human being. These principles, which form what has been called the "American theory of justice," argue for human equality; for the inalienable rights to life, liberty, and the pursuit of happiness; for government established by popular consent; and for the right of the people to rebel should government cease to fulfill the purposes for which it was instituted. On this basis, Lincoln's basis, the United States is more than its geography, more than its history, and more than its demographics. It is, in its essence, an *idea*.

Of course, the United States is also its geography, history, and demographics. But the point here is that, precisely because this country was the first in history to ground its identity not in "blood and soil," but in political principles, it is incumbent on those investigating American democracy to take account of these principles—what they are, how they have been interpreted from the Founding to the present day, and, in turn, how they have influenced the practice of American politics.

This uniqueness of American democracy lends itself particularly to the approach championed by the Greek philosopher Socrates, who argues that our quest for knowledge of the whole of existence cannot take place in a vacuum. It requires that we simultaneously examine our act of examining. That is to say, it requires that we study the context in which we pursue knowledge. This is why, Socrates tells us, he shifted his primary focus from what we call the"natural sciences" to the study of "human things," politics chief among them. Simply put, the particular study of the intellectual and moral foundations of the American republic is not merely an exercise in antiquarianism or filial piety, but rather an essential element in our attempt to live the "examined life."

For Alexis de Tocqueville, such an approach promises a benefit beyond intellectual understanding. It can also have the effect of supporting the health of American democracy. In *Democracy in America*, Tocqueville argues that, in the democratic marketplace of free and equal citizens, the opinion of the majority takes on a power previously unimaginable, threatening us with a new form of despotism—"soft" or "sweet" despotism. "Soft" despotism is not imposed by force but rather submitted to, almost without being noticed. In the absence of any authority outside the majority, it becomes increasingly difficult for the solitary democratic "individual" to conceive of ways of life contrary to those esteemed in popular opinion. We acknowledge the force of Tocqueville's diagnosis when we reflect on the immense power that public opinion surveys hold over us today. This hold hinders the development of intellectual freedom—the freedom from unexamined assumptions—that is the *sine qua non* of the Socratic examined life.

How might the freedom of the mind be protected from the tendency of democratic conformism to swallow it whole? Socratic-inspired education, and perhaps it alone, has the capacity to play the role of liberator of the mind from unthinking slavery to majority opinion. Part and parcel of such conformism is its unending thralldom to the demands of commerce and utility. This is understandable. The Founders and their intellectual forefathers—Locke, Montesquieu, and Bacon, among them—understood these demands to be important to ensuring individual liberty and domestic tranquility, as well as prosperity. A people whose government limited itself largely to physical security and material comfort (the "relief of man's estate," as Bacon has it) would, it was hoped, be less likely to fall prey to the civil strife that had devastated Europe and caused a number of its inhabitants to emigrate to the new American colonies in the first place.

But this very focus on utility, so valuable from the perspective of domestic peace, tends to lower our gaze from attention to the highest and deepest—what Socrates deems the truly human—questions (e.g., "What is a noble life, and how might I achieve it?").

In short, modern democracy urgently requires asylum from the merely urgent. It needs an island where it can transcend and therewith place in proper perspective its endemic attention to narrowly practical concerns in order to ask the most important questions, the questions the examination of which, says Socrates, makes life worth living. Questioning this country's core principles promises to help us declare our independence from the tyranny of utility and the seductions of conformism.

To this end, my hope is to demonstrate in the course of this textbook that there are certain core questions regarding American democracy that all students need to seriously ponder. I seek also to show that this text's initial emphasis on the Founding documents springs not from mystical, "filial piety," but rather from the requirements of the examined life. Indeed, filial piety is contrary to what the Founders themselves intended. The Declaration's appeal to the "opinions of mankind" makes no demands based on the tenets of faith, the ties of tradition, or the tracing of bloodlines. Instead, it asks us to reason about—to investigate and argue with—its assertions that human equality and individual liberty are the true grounds of justice.

By examining the questions and sources contained herein, we continue the debate proposed by the Founders. Socrates argues that human goodness, at its peak, may well consist primarily in investigating the question "What is human goodness?" Socrates taught Plato, who in turn taught Aristotle. In his *Nicomachean Ethics*, Aristotle honors both Plato and Socrates when he takes his teacher Plato to task: "Plato," writes his best student, "is dear to me, but dearer still is truth." In a like manner, we pay tribute to the Founders when we subject their radical reinterpretation of citizenship to the most searching scrutiny. Such tribute is far from filial piety; it is instead the quest demanded by the desire to know ourselves.

This is why we turn, in part, to "old books." Today's students can be expected to ask, "But what do the texts of the Founding, written more than two centuries ago, have to do with me?" The late political scientist Martin Diamond sought to address this question in his *The Founding of the Democratic Republic*:

> Many mistakenly think of the Constitution of 1787 as belonging to a rustic America now rendered remote by changes in American society. But think how remote 1787 is to other nations. The study of, say, modern Russian, Chinese, or Ghanaian government doubtless profits by some reference to the late eighteenth-century politics of those countries, but in 1787, Catherine the Great ruled in Russia, a Manchu emperor ruled in China, and Ghana did not exist. Catherine and the Manchu would find their countries incomprehensible today; in comparison, James Madison would be practically at his ease in modern America. The Constitution of 1787 is still the fundamental document of the American polity; it still embodies its fundamental principles; it still is the legal source of its basic institutions and powers, and it still influences the politics of their operation.

Accordingly, Diamond concludes, "Despite enormous *social* and *economic* change, the constitutional system imparts to America a remarkable *political* continuity. Therefore, it is not mere filial piety but sound political science to study carefully the Convention at which the Constitution was framed" (1981, pp. 15–16).

In light of the preceding reflections, *Investigating American Democracy* examines the political and social institutions of the United States primarily through the writings and speeches of three categories of persons: (1) the nation's founders, that is, those who framed the Declaration of Independence and the U.S. Constitution and therewith established the framework within which political controversies have been fashioned through subsequent generations; (2) officeholders who bore responsibility for dealing with these controversies and who both changed and preserved constitutional institutions and democratic thought and practice; and (3) other influential non-officeholders whose thought helped shape public opinion, social change, and law, and continues to provide insight into both the strengths and weaknesses of American democracy.

Emphasis is placed on the Constitution because, as the central legitimating symbol of American political life, students and citizens need to understand how it frames political controversy, as well as the manner in which it influences political and social change.

Core questions address the following issues, among others:

- whether and why the country required a national government, separate from the governments of the several states, and how the Framers thought that the national government might be kept from endangering individual liberty and the proper functioning of the governments of the states;
- disputes over the political and economic conditions that make American democracy possible;
- successive waves of contentious disagreement over suffrage (voting rights) and its expansion;
- whether the Founders' Constitution was democratic;
- whether it was a slave or a free Constitution;
- whether it recognized the humanity of Negroes, as African-Americans were then called;
- whether the national government should regulate the economy and provide for the welfare of individuals;
- disputes over what democratic representation is;
- whether separation of powers stifles democracy—dooming it to what today is called "gridlock"—or makes possible the first self-moderating democracy in history;
- whether religion is a useful political institution or a persistent political problem;
- what makes one a "citizen";
- what law-abidingness means and whether it is or is not a duty;
- what the relationship of women is to democratic government and society; and
- what lessons can America's experience with democracy provide for those countries struggling to attain it?

The persistent and overarching theme of the book is the disputed question "What is American democracy?" In keeping with this disputed nature, the book provides a range of conflicting answers to the issues listed above. Why these questions and not others? The questions have been selected because they point us to the principled foundations of American political life. Fully to investigate American democracy, one has to come to grips with the role that debate over these questions has played in this country's history and in defining who we are today. To this end, when appropriate, *Investigating American Democracy* proceeds in a point-counterpoint mode, enabling the student to reflect on and participate in the contested meanings of American democracy.

Considerable attention is given to the perennial dispute over whether democracy, in its most humanly relevant and ennobling sense, is possible primarily through local institutions—as maintained in the American political tradition by the anti-Federalists as well as Alexis de Tocqueville—or whether it is possible primarily through national institutions—as has been argued by the Progressives, the New Deal, and the Great Society. This dispute turns on whether democracy is understood to mean primarily "*self*-government"—in that one's self and one's neighbors are primarily responsible for solving the day-to-day problems of living together—or whether democracy is understood to be primarily the central direction of the nation's economy and political life to (1) rectify what is perceived as the free-market economy's maldistribution of wealth and (2) enforce uniform national standards respecting legally enforceable rights.

In point of fact, this dispute over the meaning of self-government undergirds and thus illuminates most, if not all, of today's political controversies, and certainly all of the interesting ones. One need think only of the 2010 national health care bill ("Patient Protection and Affordable Care Act") and the ongoing challenges it faces in the federal courts, challenges whose merits will be decided, yea or nay, on an interpretation of the powers granted to Congress under the U.S. Constitution.

Finally, both this overarching theme and the nature of the readings present a distinctive approach to the study of American politics. The approach is historical, cultural, and philosophic, with an emphasis on the mutual dependence of governmental and social institutions. It is further distinguished by the fact that, in the process of introducing students to the subfields of American government and American political thought, as well as to the discipline of political science generally, it cannot help but have the effect of deepening *citizens'* understanding and awareness of persistent issues, arguments, and themes in American democracy's development.

This effect simultaneously explains our inclusion of Alexis de Tocqueville, one of but a very few thinkers included here who was neither a Founder, an officeholder, nor an American citizen. Yet, perhaps no one in his day, or since, has treated America's soul with such depth—even, and especially, in those instances in which he challenges our assumptions and provokes our sensibilities. Such thoughtful provocation as Tocqueville offers may well be indispensable to our quest to live the examined life. If so, he must be counted a friend to those who would seek the roots in investigating American democracy.

CHAPTER 2

Core Question: What is American democracy? Over two centuries of dispute about our national identity

The readings begin with an examination of the core question "What is American democracy?" Some scholars argue that it should be considered a permanent aspect of the American identity that citizens, politicians, and other opinion leaders—from the Founding to the present day—regularly question the very meaning of American democracy.

This chapter tracks the course of the most influential debates over American identity as they have occurred throughout our history. We begin with James Madison's famous treatment, in *The Federalist*, of whether America is a democracy or a republic. On first encountering the writings of Madison, known as the "The Father of the Constitution," students are understandably shocked to read his praise of republics and criticism of democracy. Indeed, Madison's arguments have sometimes been used to advance the claim that the Constitution was not originally intended to be democratic at all, but rather republican. But closer examination shows this to be a misleading dichotomy. Next, we turn to Thomas Jefferson's views on the essential characteristics of American democracy, which he outlines in his First Inaugural Address in 1801. Jefferson, the author of the Declaration of Independence (1776), became the country's third president in 1801, after winning a hotly contested election against the incumbent, John Adams. In the course of his address, he offers a defense of states' rights that is echoed to some extent today by political conservatives. To give Jefferson's account needed context—historical, theoretical, and sociological—we conclude this first section of the chapter with an examination of Alexis de Tocqueville's presentation of the demographics of American equality, as well as the manner in which the American version of equality was translated into majority rule and individual rights at the time of the Founding.

No examination of the American identity would be complete without a serious attempt to come to grips with the core principles animating the struggle over slavery. As we shall read, the first and creedal "self-evident truth" of the Declaration of Independence is its proposition that "all men are created equal." If the Founders meant what they said, how are we to square the principle of human equality with the practice of chattel slavery, which was not eradicated until 1865, with the passage of the 13th Amendment. Three years later would come the 14th Amendment, which, among other things, guaranteed the "equal protection of the laws" to the newly freed slaves. In 1870, the 15th Amendment would guarantee this group the right to vote. Given the centrality of the slavery battle to the question of the American identity, we present and contrast the opinions of a large number of interlocutors here: Jefferson, William Lloyd Garrison, Frederick Douglass, Alexander Stephens, and Abraham Lincoln.

We turn next to the question of whether American democracy requires for its fulfillment the institution of what has been labeled "economic democracy." By the phrase economic democracy, we refer to the general view (noting that there are many variations on the economic-democracy theme) that genuine political equality requires the broad expansion of economic equality. That is, proponents of economic democracy regard as unjust what they argue is the overwhelming concentration of wealth in the hands of a relatively few corporations and their shareholders. Capitalism, in this account, efficiently solves the production problem, but, left to its own devices, inequitably addresses the distribution issue, resulting in severe poverty for some in what is otherwise a land of plenty. To remedy this, proponents argue that economic decision-making should be made more democratic, in the manner that political decision-making is. How this general theory applies to the American experiment in democracy we shall see when we investigate the views of three 20th century American presidents: Theodore Roosevelt, Franklin D. Roosevelt, and Lyndon B. Johnson.

Finally, we turn to the dispute over the proper scope and purpose of civil liberties and civil rights in American democracy. The term "civil liberties" generally refers to freedoms guaranteed under the Constitution (e.g., freedom of speech, religion, press, etc.). Here, we examine three statements on civil liberties so understood: the 1943 Supreme Court opinion, *West Virginia v. Barnette*, and the post-9/11 debate over the "Patriot Act" between then-U.S. Senator Russ Feingold (D-WI) and then-U.S. Attorney General John Ashcroft. In the wake of the 9/11 attacks, the Bush administration secured the passage of the "USA Patriot Act," a set of measures designed to combat terrorism. Senator Feingold opposed the Act, arguing that the Bush White House had sacrificed civil liberties in the name of national security. Attorney General Ashcroft defends the Act as essential to the maintenance of "ordered liberty."

The term "civil rights" refers to the right not to suffer unequal treatment based on certain traits (race, sex, etc.) in pursuits such as employment. On this theme, we begin with the Reverend Doctor Martin Luther King Jr.'s famous "I Have a Dream Speech," delivered on the National Mall in Washington, D.C., in 1963. King argues for expanding the national government's power to ensure the protection of the civil rights of minorities. We conclude this chapter with the Supreme Court's opinion in the civil-rights case of *Grutter v. Bollinger* (2003). Here, the Court upheld the University of Michigan Law School's "narrowly tailored use of race in admissions" in language that echoes King's civil-rights vision.

N.B.: As *Investigating American Democracy* goes to press, the Supreme Court is hearing *Fisher* v. *University of Texas*, which seeks to overturn or delineate exceptions to the ruling in *Grutter.*

At the Founding: Was America founded as a democracy or a republic? The confusion regarding the Founders' intentions

JAMES MADISON, EXCERPT FROM *THE FEDERALIST, NO. 10* (1787)

Written by Alexander Hamilton, James Madison, and John Jay under the pseudonym (pen name) "Publius," *The Federalist* is a collection of 85 essays that appeared in New York newspapers from 1787–1788. The essays' purpose was to defend the proposed new Constitution against its critics (later dubbed the "anti-Federalists") and, therewith, to persuade the state ratifying conventions. For the new Constitution to become the law of the land, it needed to be ratified by nine of the 13 then-existing states.

WHY THIS READING?

Thomas Jefferson, in recommending texts to be used in teaching government at the University of Virginia (which Jefferson founded), referred to *The Federalist* as "an authority to which appeal is habitually made by all, and rarely declined or denied by any as evidence of the general opinion of those who framed, and of those who accepted the Constitution of the United States" (*Minutes of the Board of Visitors*, University of Virginia, March 4, 1825).

In this excerpt from *Federalist 10*, one of the most famous of the 85 essays, Madison-as-Publius explains why the new American republic (by which he means what we would call representative democracy) will better protect individual liberty and promote competent government than did prior experiments in democracy (by which he means "pure" or "direct" democracy). This essay has given rise to confusion regarding the Founders' purposes, confusion that persists to some extent to the present day. It is therefore necessary to clarify this crucial point at the outset of our investigation. Some point to Madison's criticisms of democracy to argue that the American Constitution, as originally written, was not democratic, but rather republican. As you will read, the democracies that Madison criticizes are the small, direct democracies of antiquity, not the representative democracy enshrined in the Constitution that he helped to draft.

Questions to guide you as you read:

- What is a "faction"? How does Madison trace factions to human nature itself?
- Given advances in modern information technology, it is conceivable that "direct democracy" (all citizens participating in legislation) could be possible today. In fact, Ross Perot, who ran for President as a third-party candidate in both 1992 and 1996, proposed a project along these very lines. Based on this reading, what would be Madison's objections to such a proposal?

To the People of the State of New York:

Among the numerous advantages promised by a well constructed Union, none deserves to be more accurately developed than its tendency to break and control the violence of faction. The friend of popular governments never finds himself so much alarmed for their character and fate, as when he contemplates their propensity to this dangerous vice. He will not fail, therefore, to set a due value on any plan which, without violating the principles to which he is attached, provides a proper cure for it. The instability, injustice, and confusion introduced into the public councils, have, in truth, been the mortal diseases under which popular governments have everywhere perished; as they continue to be the favorite and fruitful topics from which the adversaries to liberty derive their most specious declamations [theatrical speeches]. The valuable improvements made by the American constitutions on the popular models, both ancient and modern, cannot certainly be too much admired; but it would be an unwarrantable partiality, to contend that they have as effectually [effectively] obviated [averted] the danger on this side, as was wished and expected. Complaints are everywhere heard from our most considerate and virtuous citizens, equally the friends of public and private faith, and of public and personal liberty, that our governments are too unstable, that the public good is disregarded in the conflicts of rival parties, and that measures are too often decided, not according to the rules of justice and the rights of the minor party, but by the superior force of an interested and overbearing majority. However anxiously we may wish that these complaints had no foundation, the evidence, of known facts will not permit us to deny that they are in some degree true. It will be found, indeed, on a candid review of our situation, that some of the distresses under which we labor have been erroneously charged on the operation of our governments; but it will be found, at the same time, that other causes will not alone account for many of our heaviest misfortunes; and, particularly, for that prevailing and increasing distrust of public engagements, and alarm for private rights, which are echoed from one end of the continent to the other. These must be chiefly, if not wholly, effects of the unsteadiness and injustice with which a factious spirit has tainted our public administrations.

By a faction, I understand a number of citizens, whether amounting to a majority or a minority of the whole, who are united and actuated [motivated to action] by some common impulse of passion, or of interest, adverse to the rights of other citizens, or to the permanent and aggregate interests of the community.

There are two methods of curing the mischiefs of faction: the one, by removing its causes; the other, by controlling its effects.

There are again two methods of removing the causes of faction: the one, by destroying the liberty which is essential to its existence; the other, by giving to every citizen the same opinions, the same passions, and the same interests.

It could never be more truly said than of the first remedy, that it was worse than the disease. Liberty is to faction what air is to fire, an aliment [something that nourishes] without which it instantly expires. But it could not be less folly to abolish liberty, which is essential to political life, because it nourishes faction, than it would be to wish the annihilation of air, which is essential to animal life, because it imparts to fire its destructive agency.

The second expedient is as impracticable as the first would be unwise. As long as the reason of man continues fallible, and he is at liberty to exercise it, different opinions will be formed. As long as the connection subsists between his reason and his self-love, his opinions and his passions will have a reciprocal influence on each other; and the former will be objects to which the latter will attach themselves. The diversity in the faculties of men, from which the rights of property originate, is not less an insuperable obstacle to a uniformity of interests. The protection of these faculties is the first object of government. From the protection of different and unequal faculties of acquiring property, the possession of different degrees and kinds of property immediately results; and from the influence of these on the sentiments and views of the respective proprietors, ensues a division of the society into different interests and parties.

The latent [present but not visible] causes of faction are thus sown in the nature of man; and we see them everywhere brought into different degrees of activity, according to the different circumstances of civil society. A zeal for different opinions concerning religion, concerning government, and many other points, as well of speculation as of practice; an attachment to different leaders ambitiously contending for pre-eminence and power; or to persons of other descriptions whose fortunes have been interesting to the human passions, have, in turn, divided mankind into parties, inflamed them with mutual animosity, and rendered them much more disposed to vex and oppress each other than to co-operate for their common good. So strong is this propensity of mankind to fall into mutual animosities, that where no substantial occasion presents itself, the most frivolous and fanciful distinctions have been sufficient to kindle their unfriendly passions and excite their most violent conflicts. But the most common and durable source of factions has been the various and unequal distribution of property. Those who hold and those who are without property have ever formed distinct interests in society. Those who are creditors, and those who are debtors, fall under a like discrimination. A landed interest, a manufacturing interest, a mercantile interest, a moneyed interest, with many lesser interests, grow up of necessity in civilized nations, and divide them into different classes, actuated by different sentiments and views. The regulation of these various and interfering interests forms the principal task of modern legislation, and involves the spirit of party [partisanship] and faction in the necessary and ordinary operations of the government.

No man is allowed to be a judge in his own cause, because his interest would certainly bias his judgment, and, not improbably, corrupt his integrity. With equal, nay with greater reason, a body of men are unfit to be both judges and parties at the same time; yet what are many of the most important acts of legislation, but so many judicial determinations, not indeed concerning the rights of single persons, but concerning the rights of large bodies of citizens? And what are the different classes of legislators but advocates and parties to the causes which they determine? Is a law proposed concerning private debts? It is a question to which the creditors are parties on one side and the debtors on the other. Justice ought to hold the balance between them. Yet the parties are, and must be, themselves the judges; and the most numerous party, or, in other words, the most powerful faction must be expected to prevail. Shall domestic manufactures be encouraged, and in what degree, by restrictions on foreign manufactures? are questions which would be differently decided by the landed and the manufacturing classes, and probably by neither with a sole regard to justice and the public good. The apportionment of taxes on the various descriptions of property is an act which seems to require the most exact impartiality; yet there is, perhaps, no legislative act in which greater opportunity and temptation are given to a predominant party to trample on the rules of justice. Every shilling with which they overburden the inferior number, is a shilling saved to their own pockets.

It is in vain to say that enlightened statesmen will be able to adjust these clashing interests, and render them all subservient to the public good. Enlightened statesmen will not always be at the helm. Nor, in many cases, can such an adjustment be made at all without taking into view indirect and remote considerations, which will rarely prevail over the immediate interest which one party may find in disregarding the rights of another or the good of the whole.

The inference to which we are brought is, that the causes of faction cannot be removed, and that relief is only to be sought in the means of controlling its effects.

If a faction consists of less than a majority, relief is supplied by the republican principle, which enables the majority to defeat its sinister views by regular vote. It may clog the administration, it may convulse the society; but it will be unable to execute and mask its violence under the forms of the Constitution. When a majority is included in a faction, the form of popular government, on the other hand, enables it to sacrifice to its ruling passion or interest both the public good and the rights of other citizens. To secure the public good and private rights against the danger of such a faction, and at the same time to preserve the spirit and the form of popular government, is then the great object to which our inquiries are directed. Let me add that it is the great desideratum [hoped-for goal] by which this form of government can be rescued from the opprobrium [bad reputation] under which it has so long labored, and be recommended to the esteem and adoption of mankind.

By what means is this object attainable? Evidently by one of two only. Either the existence of the same passion or interest in a majority at the same time must be prevented, or the majority, having such coexistent passion or interest, must be rendered, by their number and local situation, unable to concert and carry into effect schemes of oppression. If the impulse and the opportunity be suffered to coincide, we well know that neither moral nor religious motives can be relied on as an adequate control. They are not found to be such on the injustice and violence of individuals, and lose their efficacy in proportion to the number combined together, that is, in proportion as their efficacy becomes needful.

From this view of the subject it may be concluded that a pure democracy, by which I mean a society consisting of a small number of citizens, who assemble and administer the government in person, can admit of no cure for the mischiefs of faction. A common passion or interest will, in almost every case, be felt by a majority of the whole; a communication and concert result from the form of government itself; and there is nothing to check the inducements to sacrifice the weaker party or an obnoxious individual. Hence it is that such democracies have ever been spectacles of turbulence and contention; have ever been found incompatible with personal security or the rights of property; and have in general been as short in their lives as they have been violent in their deaths. Theoretic politicians, who have patronized this species of government, have erroneously supposed that by reducing mankind to a perfect equality in their political rights, they would, at the same time, be perfectly equalized and assimilated in their possessions, their opinions, and their passions.

A republic, by which I mean a government in which the scheme of representation takes place, opens a different prospect, and promises the cure for which we are seeking....

JAMES MADISON, *THE FEDERALIST, NO. 39* (1788)

In this essay, Madison-as-Publius first champions the republican (representative-democratic) character of the proposed Constitution and then defends it against his opponents' accusation that it abandons federalism ("a Confederacy of sovereign states") in favor of a "national government, which regards the Union as a consolidation [combination into a single mass] of the States." In response to this charge, he argues that the new Constitution is in fact neither wholly national nor merely federal, "but a composition of both."

For the proposed Constitution to become law, the Federalists "went over the heads" of the state legislatures. The decision whether to adopt the new Constitution was mandated to come from the various state ratifying conventions, the members of which would be elected by the citizens of each state, rather than by the state legislatures. Why was this change in procedure so crucial? Had the proposed Constitution required ratification by the state legislatures, this likely would have doomed its passage, for state legislators knew well that they stood to lose political power under the provisions of the new Constitution. Moreover, Madison understood that, even in the unlikely event that the state legislatures themselves were to approve the Constitution, this would create the impression ever after that the national government was the creation of the states, and hence subordinate to them.

WHY THIS READING?

As will be seen in the pages to follow, the debate over the powers of the "national" (which is now used synonymously with "federal") government versus those of the individual states did not end with the ratification of the Constitution. It continues today with, for example, the debate over the constitutionality of the national health care bill ("Patient Protection and Affordable Care Act") passed in 2010. Opponents of the bill argue, among other things, that it unconstitutionally expands the power of the national government at the expense of state and local governments. At this writing, 26 states have joined the suit challenging the constitutionality of the law. In November 2011, the U.S. Supreme Court agreed to hear the case. Its decision is expected to come down in the summer of 2012.

Questions to guide you as you read:

- What elements does Madison identify as distinctive of the republican (representative-democratic) form of government?
- To what extent does Madison insist that the new government is federal? What does he mean by "federal"? In what way does his presentation help to illuminate competing principles underlying the current debate over the 2010 Health Care Bill?

To the People of the State of New York:

The last paper having concluded the observations which were meant to introduce a candid survey of the plan of government reported by the convention, we now proceed to the execution of that part of our undertaking.

The first question that offers itself is, whether the general form and aspect of the government be strictly republican. It is evident that no other form would be reconcilable with the genius [spirit] of the people of America; with the fundamental principles of the Revolution; or with that honorable determination which animates every votary [dedicated follower] of freedom, to rest all our political experiments on the capacity of mankind for self-government. If the plan of the convention, therefore, be found to depart from the republican character, its advocates must abandon it as no longer defensible.

What, then, are the distinctive characters of the republican form? Were an answer to this question to be sought, not by recurring to principles, but in the application of the term by political writers, to the constitution of different States, no satisfactory one would ever be found. Holland, in which no particle of the supreme authority is derived from the people, has passed almost universally under the denomination of a republic. The same title has been bestowed on Venice, where absolute power over the great body of the people is exercised, in the most absolute manner, by a small body of hereditary nobles. Poland, which is a mixture of aristocracy and of monarchy in their worst forms, has been dignified with the same appellation. The government of England, which has one republican branch only, combined with an hereditary aristocracy and monarchy, has, with equal impropriety, been frequently placed on the list of republics. These examples, which are nearly as dissimilar to each other as to a genuine republic, show the extreme inaccuracy with which the term has been used in political disquisitions.

If we resort for a criterion to the different principles on which different forms of government are established, we may define a republic to be, or at least may bestow that name on, a government which derives all its powers directly or indirectly from the great body of the people, and is administered by persons holding their offices during pleasure, for a limited period, or during good behavior. It is essential to such a government that it be derived from the great body of the society, not from an inconsiderable proportion, or a favored class of it; otherwise a handful of tyrannical nobles, exercising their oppressions by a delegation of their powers, might aspire to the rank of republicans, and claim for their government the honorable title of republic. It is sufficient for such a government that the persons administering it be appointed, either directly or indirectly, by the people; and that they hold their appointments by either of the tenures just specified; otherwise every government in the United States, as well as every other popular government that has been or can be well organized or well executed, would be degraded from the republican character. According to the constitution of every State in the Union, some or other of the officers of government are appointed indirectly only by the people. According to most of them, the chief magistrate himself is so appointed. And according to one, this mode of appointment is extended to one of the co-ordinate branches of the legislature. According to all the constitutions, also, the tenure of the highest offices is extended to a definite period, and in many instances, both within the legislative and executive departments, to a period of years. According to the provisions of most of the constitutions, again, as well as according to the most respectable and received opinions on the subject, the members of the judiciary department are to retain their offices by the firm tenure of good behavior.

On comparing the Constitution planned by the convention with the standard here fixed, we perceive at once that it is, in the most rigid sense, conformable to it. The House of Representatives, like that of one branch at least of all the State legislatures, is elected immediately by the great body of the people. The Senate, like the present Congress, and the Senate of Maryland, derives its appointment indirectly from the people. The President is indirectly derived from the choice of the people, according to the example in most of the States. Even the judges, with all other officers of the Union, will, as in the several States, be the choice, though a remote choice, of the people themselves, the duration of the appointments is equally conformable to the republican standard, and to the model of State constitutions The House of Representatives is periodically elective, as in all the States; and for the period of two years, as in the State of South Carolina. The Senate is elective, for the period of six years; which is but one year more than the period of the Senate of Maryland, and but two more than that of the Senates of New York and Virginia. The President is to continue in office for the period of four years; as in New York and Delaware, the chief magistrate is elected for three years, and in South Carolina for two years. In the other States the election is annual. In several of the States, however, no constitutional provision is made for the impeachment of the chief magistrate. And in Delaware and Virginia he is not impeachable till out of office. The President of the United States is impeachable at any time during his continuance in office. The tenure by which the judges are to hold their places, is, as it unquestionably ought to be, that of good behavior. The tenure of the ministerial offices generally, will be a subject of legal regulation, conformably to the reason of the case and the example of the State constitutions.

Could any further proof be required of the republican complexion of this system, the most decisive one might be found in its absolute prohibition of titles of nobility, both under the federal and the State governments; and in its express guaranty of the republican form to each of the latter.

"But it was not sufficient," say the adversaries of the proposed Constitution, "for the convention to adhere to the republican form. They ought, with equal care, to have preserved the federal form, which regards the Union as a Confederacy of sovereign states; instead of which, they have framed a national government, which regards the Union as a consolidation of the States." And it is asked by what authority this bold and radical innovation was undertaken? The handle which has been made of this objection requires that it should be examined with some precision.

Without inquiring into the accuracy of the distinction on which the objection is founded, it will be necessary to a just estimate of its force, first, to ascertain the real character of the government in question; secondly, to inquire how far the convention were authorized to propose such a government; and thirdly, how far the duty they owed to their country could supply any defect of regular authority.

First. In order to ascertain the real character of the government, it may be considered in relation to the foundation on which it is to be established; to the sources from which its ordinary powers are to be drawn; to the operation of those powers; to the extent of them; and to the authority by which future changes in the government are to be introduced.

On examining the first relation, it appears, on one hand, that the Constitution is to be founded on the assent and ratification of the people of America, given by deputies elected for the special purpose; but, on the other, that this assent and ratification is to be given by the people, not as individuals composing one entire nation, but as composing the distinct and independent States to which they respectively belong. It is to be the assent and ratification of the several States, derived from the supreme authority in each State, the authority of the people themselves. The act, therefore, establishing the Constitution, will not be a national, but a federal act.

That it will be a federal and not a national act, as these terms are understood by the objectors; the act of the people, as forming so many independent States, not as forming one aggregate nation, is obvious from this single consideration, that it is to result neither from the decision of a majority of the people of the Union, nor from that of a majority of the States. It must result from the unanimous assent of the several States that are parties to it, differing no otherwise from their ordinary assent than in its being expressed, not by the legislative authority, but by that of the people themselves. Were the people regarded in this transaction as forming one nation, the will of the majority of the whole people of the United States would bind the minority, in the same manner as the majority in each State must bind the minority; and the will of the majority must be determined either by a comparison of the individual votes, or by considering the will of the majority of the States as evidence of the will of a majority of the people of the United States. Neither of these rules have been adopted. Each State, in ratifying the Constitution, is considered as a sovereign body, independent of all others, and only to be bound by its own voluntary act. In this relation, then, the new Constitution will, if established, be a federal, and not a national constitution.

The next relation is, to the sources from which the ordinary powers of government are to be derived. The House of Representatives will derive its powers from the people of America; and the people will be represented in the same proportion, and on the same principle, as they are in the legislature of a particular State. So far the government is national, not federal. The Senate, on the other hand, will derive its powers from the States, as political and coequal societies; and these will be represented on the principle of equality in the Senate, as they now are in the existing Congress. So far the government is federal, not national. The executive power will be derived from a very compound source. The immediate election of the President is to be made by the States in their political characters. The votes allotted to them are in a compound ratio, which considers them partly as distinct and coequal societies, partly as unequal members of the same society. The eventual election, again, is to be made by that branch of the legislature which consists of the national representatives; but in this particular act they are to be thrown into the form of individual delegations, from so many distinct and coequal bodies politic. From this aspect of the government it appears to be of a mixed character, presenting at least as many federal as national features.

The difference between a federal and national government, as it relates to the operation of the government, is supposed to consist in this, that in the former the powers operate on the political bodies composing the Confederacy, in their political capacities; in the latter, on the individual citizens composing the nation, in their individual capacities. On trying the Constitution by this criterion, it falls under the national, not the federal character; though perhaps not so completely as has been understood. In several cases, and particularly in the trial of controversies to which States may be parties, they must be viewed and proceeded against in their collective and political capacities only. So far the national countenance of the government on this side seems to be disfigured by a few federal features. But this blemish is perhaps unavoidable in any plan; and the operation of the government on the people, in their individual capacities, in its ordinary and most essential proceedings, may, on the whole, designate it, in this relation, a national government.

But if the government be national with regard to the operation of its powers, it changes its aspect again when we contemplate it in relation to the extent of its powers. The idea of a national government involves in it, not only an authority over the individual citizens, but an indefinite supremacy over all persons and things, so far as they are objects of lawful government. Among a people consolidated into one nation, this supremacy is completely vested in the national legislature. Among communities united for particular purposes, it is vested partly in the general and partly in the municipal legislatures. In the former case, all local authorities are subordinate to the supreme; and may be controlled, directed, or abolished by it at pleasure. In the latter, the local or municipal authorities form distinct and independent portions of the supremacy, no more subject, within their respective spheres, to the general authority, than the general authority is subject to them, within its own sphere. In this relation, then, the proposed government cannot be deemed a national one; since its jurisdiction extends to certain enumerated objects only, and leaves to the several States a residuary and inviolable sovereignty over all other objects. It is true that in controversies relating to the boundary between the two jurisdictions, the tribunal which is ultimately to decide, is to be established under the general government. But this does not change the principle of the case. The decision is to be impartially made, according to the rules of the Constitution; and all the usual and most effectual precautions are taken to secure this impartiality. Some such tribunal is clearly essential to prevent an appeal to the sword and a dissolution of the compact; and that it ought to be established under the general rather than under the local governments, or, to speak more properly, that it could be safely established under the first alone, is a position not likely to be combated.

If we try the Constitution by its last relation to the authority by which amendments are to be made, we find it neither wholly national nor wholly federal. Were it wholly national, the supreme and ultimate authority would reside in the majority of the people of the Union; and this authority would be competent at all times, like that of a majority of every national society, to alter or abolish its established government. Were it wholly federal, on the other hand, the concurrence of each State in the Union would be essential to every alteration that would be binding on all. The mode provided by the plan of the convention is not founded on either of these principles. In requiring more than a majority, and particularly in computing the proportion by States, not by citizens, it departs from the national and advances towards the federal character; in rendering the concurrence of less than the whole number of States sufficient, it loses again the federal and partakes of the national character.

The proposed Constitution, therefore, is, in strictness, neither a national nor a federal Constitution, but a composition of both. In its foundation it is federal, not national; in the sources from which the ordinary powers of the government are drawn, it is partly federal and partly national; in the operation of these powers, it is national, not federal; in the extent of them, again, it is federal, not national; and, finally, in the authoritative mode of introducing amendments, it is neither wholly federal nor wholly national.

PUBLIUS

What is Jeffersonian Democracy, and what is its contemporary relevance?

THOMAS JEFFERSON, "FIRST INAUGURAL ADDRESS" (1801)

The 1800 presidential election resulted in the young country's first transfer of power from one party (the Federalists) to another (the Democratic-Republicans). The incumbent, President John Adams, had defeated Jefferson in the presidential election of 1796, but in the election of 1800, Adams's bid for reelection would fail. He received 65 votes in the Electoral College, while both Jefferson and Aaron Burr, Jefferson's running mate, received 73 electoral votes. Consequently, the House of Representatives met in special session to resolve the impasse resulting from no one candidate having a majority of electoral votes (as required by the Constitution, Article II, Section 1). But the House of Representatives was dominated by Federalists, many of whom detested Jefferson and were inclined to vote for Burr as the "lesser of evils." Alexander Hamilton, though he also was no friend to Jefferson, used his influence with his fellow Federalists to help Jefferson prevail. After more than 30 hours of debate and balloting, Jefferson emerged as president, and Burr as vice president. To prevent a recurrence of these electoral difficulties, the Twelfth Amendment to the Constitution was ratified in 1804. Under its provisions, electors would be supplied with separate Electoral College ballots for president and vice president.

In this speech, Jefferson held out an olive branch to his political enemies. Inviting them to bury the partisanship of the past and to unite now as Americans, he said "we are all Republicans, we are all Federalists."

WHY THIS READING?

Jefferson's First Inaugural Address answers the question "What is American democracy?" with an emphasis on "the support of the State governments in all their rights, as the most competent administrations for our domestic concerns and the surest bulwarks [strongholds] against anti-republican [democratic] tendencies. . . . " In his emphasis on the rights of the states against the national or federal government, Jefferson, along with James Madison, set himself against Alexander Hamilton, who voiced a more expansive interpretation of the powers granted to the national government under the Constitution. An emphasis on states' rights and a concomitant distrust of the federal or national government continue to the present day. It has been carried on largely by political conservatives, as we shall see later in this text, when we examine speeches by Ronald Reagan and Lamar Alexander.

Questions to guide you as you read:

- What does Jefferson regard as the "essential principles" of American democracy? Why does he deem them essential?
- What is Jefferson's case for what today is called "states' rights"?

FRIENDS AND FELLOW-CITIZENS,

Called upon to undertake the duties of the first executive office of our country, I avail myself of the presence of that portion of my fellow-citizens which is here assembled to express my grateful thanks for the favor with which they have been pleased to look toward me, to declare a sincere consciousness that the task is above my talents, and that I approach it with those anxious and awful presentiments [premonition] which the greatness of the charge and the weakness of my powers so justly inspire. A rising nation, spread over a wide and fruitful land, traversing [going across] all the seas with the rich productions of their industry, engaged in commerce with nations who feel power and forget right, advancing rapidly to destinies beyond the reach of mortal eye—when I contemplate [consider] these transcendent [surpassing others] objects, and see the honor, the happiness, and the hopes of this beloved country committed to the issue and the auspices

[omen] of this day, I shrink from the contemplation, and humble myself before the magnitude [greatness] of the undertaking. Utterly [completely], indeed, should I despair did not the presence of men, whom I here see remind me that in the other high authorities provided by our Constitution I shall find resources of wisdom, of virtue, and of zeal [enthusiasm] on which to rely under all difficulties. To you, then, gentlemen, who are charged with the sovereign [supreme] functions of legislation, and to those associated with you, I look with encouragement for that guidance and support which may enable us to steer with safety the vessel in which we are all embarked amidst the conflicting elements of a troubled world.

During the contest of opinion through which we have passed the animation [vigor] of discussions and of exertions has sometimes worn an aspect [appearance] which might impose on strangers unused to think freely and to speak and to write what they think; but this being now decided by the voice of the nation, announced according to the rules of the Constitution, all will, of course, arrange themselves under the will of the law, and unite in common efforts for the common good. All, too, will bear in mind this sacred principle, that though the will of the majority is in all cases to prevail [win], that will to be rightful must be reasonable; that the minority possess their equal rights, which equal law must protect; and to violate would be oppression. Let us, then, fellow-citizens unite with one heart and one mind. Let us restore to social intercourse that harmony and affection without which liberty and life itself are but dreary things. And let us reflect that, having banished [exiled] from our land that religious intolerance under which mankind so long bled and suffered, we have yet gained little if we countenance [express approval] a political intolerance as despotic, as wicked, and capable of as bitter and bloody persecutions. During the throes [spasms] and convulsions of the ancient world, during the agonizing spasms of infuriated man, seeking through blood and slaughter his long-lost liberty, it was not wonderful that the agitation of the billows [large waves] should reach even this distant and peaceful shore; that this should be more felt and feared by some and less by others, and should divide opinions as to measures of safety. But every difference of opinion is not a difference of principle. We have called by different names brethren of the same principle. We are all Republicans we are all Federalists. If there be any among us who would wish to dissolve this Union or to change its republican form, let them stand undisturbed as monuments of the safety with which error of opinion may be tolerated where reason is left free to combat it. I know, indeed, that some honest men fear that a republican government can not be strong, that this Government is not strong enough; but would the honest patriot, in the full tide of successful experiment, abandon a government which has so far kept us free and firm on the theoretic and visionary fear that this Government, the world's best hope, may by possibility want energy to preserve itself? I trust not. I believe this, on the contrary, the strongest Government on earth. I believe it the only one where every man, at the call of the law, would fly to the standard of the law, and would meet invasions of the public order as his own personal concern. Sometimes it is said that man cannot be trusted with the government of himself. Can he, then, be trusted with the government of others? Or have we found angels in the forms of kings to govern him? Let history answer this question.

Let us, then, with courage and confidence pursue our own Federal and Republican principles, our attachment to union and representative government. Kindly separated by nature and a wide ocean from the exterminating havoc of one quarter of the globe; too high-minded to endure the degradations [lowering] of the others; possessing a chosen country, with room enough for our descendants to the thousandth and thousandth generation; entertaining a due sense of our equal right to the use of our own faculties, to the acquisitions of our own industry, to honor and confidence from our fellow-citizens, resulting not from birth, but from our actions and their sense of them; enlightened by a benign [gentle] religion, professed, indeed, and practiced in various forms, yet all of them inculcating honesty, truth, temperance [self-restraint], gratitude, and the love of man; acknowledging and adoring an overruling Providence, which by all its dispensations [indulgences] proves that it delights in the happiness of man here and his greater happiness hereafter-with all these blessings, what more is necessary to make us a happy and a prosperous people? Still one thing more, fellow-citizens, a wise and frugal Government, which shall restrain men from injuring one another, shall leave them otherwise free to regulate their own pursuits of industry and improvement, and shall not take from the mouth of labor the bread it has earned. This is the sum of good government, and this is necessary to close the circle of our felicities [things that cause happiness].

About to enter, fellow-citizens, on the exercise of duties, which comprehend everything dear and valuable to you, it is proper you should understand what I deem the essential principles of our Government, and consequently those, which ought to shape its Administration. I will compress them within the narrowest compass they will bear, stating the general principle, but not all its limitations. Equal and exact justice to all men, of whatever state or persuasion, religious or political; peace, commerce, and honest friendship with all nations, entangling alliances with none; the support of the State governments in all their rights, as the most competent administrations for our domestic concerns and the surest bulwarks [defenses] against anti-republican tendencies; the preservation of the General Government in its whole constitutional vigor [strength], as the sheet anchor [emergency anchor] of our peace at home and safety abroad; a jealous care of the right of election by the people-a mild and safe corrective of abuses which are lopped [cut off] by the sword of revolution where peaceable remedies are unprovided; absolute acquiescence in the decisions of the majority, the vital principle of republics, from which is no appeal but to force, the vital [animating] principle and immediate parent of despotism[1] [absolute power]; a well-disciplined militia, our best reliance in peace and for the first moments of war till regulars may relieve them; the supremacy of the civil over the military authority; economy in the public expense, that labor may be lightly burthened [burdened], the honest payment of our debts and sacred preservation of the public faith; encouragement of agriculture, and of commerce as its handmaid [servant]; the diffusion of information and arraignment of all abuses at the bar of the public reason; freedom of religion; freedom of the press, and freedom of person under the protection of the habeas corpus,[2] and trial by juries impartially selected. These principles form the bright constellation [gathering of related things], which has gone before us and guided our steps through an age of revolution and reformation. The wisdom of our sages and blood of our heroes have been devoted to their attainment. They should be the creed of our political faith, the text of civic instruction, the touchstone [criterion] by which to try the services of those we trust; and should we wander from them in moments of error or of alarm, let us hasten to retrace our steps and to regain the road which alone leads to peace, liberty, and safety.

I repair [go], then, fellow-citizens, to the post you have assigned me. With experience enough in subordinate [lower] offices to have seen the difficulties of this the greatest of all, I have learnt to expect that it will rarely fall to the lot of imperfect man to retire from this station with the reputation and the favor, which bring him into it. Without pretensions [claim] to that high confidence you reposed in our first and greatest revolutionary character, whose preeminent services had entitled him to the first place in his country's love and destined for him the fairest page in the volume of faithful history, I ask so much confidence only as may give firmness and effect to the legal administration of your affairs. I shall often go wrong through defect of judgment. When right, I shall often be thought wrong by those whose positions will not command a view of the whole ground. I ask your indulgence [forgiveness] for my own errors, which will never be intentional, and your support against the errors of others, who may condemn what they would not if seen in all its

1. Despotism: a government or political system in which the ruler exercises absolute power.

2. *Habeas corpus*: the name given to a variety of writs having as their object to bring a party before a court or judge.

parts. The approbation [praise] implied by your suffrage is a great consolation to me for the past, and my future solicitude [concern] will be to retain the good opinion of those who have bestowed it in advance, to conciliate [regain] that of others by doing them all the good in my power, and to be instrumental to the happiness and freedom of all.

Relying, then, on the patronage of your good will, I advance with obedience to the work; ready to retire from it whenever you become sensible how much better choice it is in your power to make. And may that Infinite Power which rules the destinies of the universe lead our councils to what is best, and give them a favorable issue for your peace and prosperity.

The demographics of American political equality: Early-American democracy, according to Tocqueville

Equality of conditions

ALEXIS DE TOCQUEVILLE, *DEMOCRACY IN AMERICA,* AUTHOR'S INTRODUCTION (1833)

Alexis de Tocqueville (1805–1859) was a Frenchman of aristocratic birth who visited the United States for nine months in 1831–1832. The result of his visit, *Democracy in America*, was published in two volumes in 1835 and 1840.

WHY THIS READING?

Although *Democracy in America* was written over 170 years ago, it is still consulted frequently today by political scientists and theorists who want to understand the wealth of insights behind its ambitious project to educate modern democratic citizens in the "the art of being [or living] free." Despite his aristocratic lineage, Tocqueville sees in the demise of aristocracy and the rise of democratic equality the hand of "Providence."

Tocqueville's many praises of American democracy do not prevent him from having serious concerns over its future as well as that of the emerging democracies in Europe. Chief among his fears is that this new form of government might give rise to a new form of despotism: "soft" or "sweet" despotism, under which democratic citizens would, for the sake of ever-greater equality, come to vote away their political and intellectual liberty. Contemporary echoes of this concern can be heard to some extent from those commentators who criticize the "nanny-state" and "political correctness."

In this reading, Tocqueville explains why, during his time in America, no single fact "struck him more forcibly" than the "general equality of condition among the people." Indeed, he finds in the last 700 years of European history, an irresistible movement toward such "equality of condition" (equal economic and social status.) He identifies a number of factors at play in this centuries-long democratic revolution. Among them are the role of the clergy; the rise of commerce [democratic capitalism]; the dissemination of knowledge made possible through the invention of the printing press; the invention of firearms; and the democratic nature of Protestantism.

Convinced that democratic equality is unstoppable, he calls for the need to "educate democracy" through a "new science of politics."

Questions to guide you as you read:

- Why is Tocqueville convinced that the movement toward equality is irresistible? In the 170 years since he made this statement, has history borne him out?
- What role does the spread of commerce play in the growth of equality, according to Tocqueville?

Among the novel objects that attracted my attention during my stay in the United States, nothing struck me more forcibly than the general equality of condition among the people. I readily discovered the prodigious influence that this primary fact exercises on the whole course of society; it gives a peculiar direction to public opinion and a peculiar tenor to the laws; it imparts new maxims to the governing authorities and peculiar habits to the governed.

I soon perceived that the influence of this fact extends far beyond the political character and the laws of the country, and that it has no less effect on civil society than on the government; it creates opinions, gives birth to new sentiments, founds novel customs, and modifies whatever it does not produce. The more I advanced in the study of American society, the more I perceived that this equality of condition is the fundamental fact from which all others seem to be derived and the central point at which all my observations constantly terminated.

I then turned my thoughts to our own hemisphere, and thought that I discerned there something analogous to the spectacle which the New World presented to me. I observed that equality of condition, though it has not there reached the extreme limit which it seems to have attained in the United States, is constantly approaching it; and that the democracy which governs the American communities appears to be rapidly rising into power in Europe.

Hence I conceived the idea of the book that is now before the reader.

It is evident to all alike that a great democratic revolution is going on among us, but all do not look at it in the same light. To some it appears to be novel but accidental, and, as such, they hope it may still be checked; to others it seems irresistible, because it is the most uniform, the most ancient, and the most permanent tendency that is to be found in history.

I look back for a moment on the situation of France seven hundred years ago, when the territory was divided among a small number of families, who were the owners of the soil and the rulers of the inhabitants; the right of governing descended with the family inheritance from generation to generation; force was the only means by which man could act on man; and landed property was the sole source of power.

Soon, however, the political power of the clergy was founded and began to increase: the clergy opened their ranks to all classes, to the poor and the rich, the commoner and the noble; through the church, equality penetrated into the government, and he who as a serf must have vegetated in perpetual bondage took his place as a priest in the midst of nobles, and not infrequently above the heads of kings....

...While the kings were ruining themselves by their great enterprises, and the nobles exhausting their resources by private wars, the lower orders were enriching themselves by commerce. The influence of money began to be perceptible in state affairs. The transactions of business opened a new road to power, and the financier rose to a station of political influence in which he was at once flattered and despised.

Gradually enlightenment [reason and science] spread, a reawakening of taste for literature and the arts became evident; intellect and will contributed to success; knowledge became an attribute of government, intelligence a social force; the educated man took part in affairs of state.

The value attached to high birth declined just as fast as new avenues to power were discovered. In the eleventh century, nobility was beyond all price; in the thirteenth, it might be purchased. Nobility was first conferred by gift in 1270, and equality was thus introduced into the government by the aristocracy itself.

In the course of these seven hundred years it sometimes happened that the nobles, in order to resist the authority of the crown or to diminish the power of their rivals, granted some political power to the common people. Or, more frequently, the king permitted the lower orders to have a share in the government, with the intention of limiting the power of the aristocracy.

In France the kings have always been the most active and the most constant of levelers [those who make the people more equal]. When they were strong and ambitious, they spared no pains to raise the people to the level of the nobles; when they were temperate and feeble, they allowed the people to rise above themselves....

...As soon as land began to be held on any other than a feudal [aristocratic] tenure, and personal property could in its turn confer influence and power, every discovery in the arts, every improvement in commerce of manufactures, created so many new elements of equality among men. Henceforward every new invention, every new want [desire] which it occasioned, and every new desire which craved satisfaction were steps towards a general leveling. The taste for luxury, the love of war, the rule of fashion, and the most superficial as well as the deepest passions of the human heart seemed to co-operate to enrich the poor and to impoverish the rich.

From the time when the exercise of the intellect became a source of strength and of wealth, we see that every addition to science, every fresh truth, and every new idea became a germ of power placed within the reach of the people. Poetry, eloquence, and memory, the graces of the mind, the fire of imagination, depth of thought, and all the gifts which Heaven scatters at a venture turned to the advantage of democracy; and even when they were in the possession of its adversaries, they still served its cause by throwing into bold relief the natural greatness of man. Its conquests spread, therefore, with those of civilization and knowledge; and literature became an arsenal open to all, where the poor and the weak daily resorted for arms.

In running over the pages of our history, we shall scarcely find a single great event of the last seven hundred years that has not promoted equality of condition.

The Crusades and the English wars decimated the nobles and divided their possessions: the municipal corporations introduced democratic liberty into the bosom of feudal monarchy; the invention of firearms equalized the vassal and the noble on the field of battle; the art of printing opened the same resources to the minds of all classes; the post brought knowledge alike to the door of the cottage and to the gate of the palace; and Protestantism proclaimed that all men are equally able to find the road to heaven. The discovery of America opened a thousand new paths to fortune and led obscure adventurers to wealth and power....

...The noble has gone down the social ladder, and the commoner has gone up; the one descends as the other rises. Every half-century brings them nearer to each other, and they will soon meet.

Nor is this peculiar to France. Wherever we look, we perceive the same revolution going on throughout the Christian world.

The various occurrences of national existence have everywhere turned to the advantage of democracy: all men have aided it by their exertions, both those who have intentionally labored in its cause and those who have served it unwittingly; those who have fought for it and even those who have declared themselves its opponents have all been driven along in the same direction, have all labored to one end; some unknowingly and some despite themselves, all have been blind instruments in the hands of God.

The gradual development of the principle of equality is, therefore, a providential [guidance believed to be provided by God] fact. It has all the chief characteristics of such a fact: it is universal, it is lasting, it constantly eludes all human interference,

and all events as well as all men contribute to its progress....

...Whither, then, are we tending? No one can say, for terms of comparison already fail us. There is greater equality of condition in Christian countries at the present day than there has been at any previous time, in any part of the world, so that the magnitude of what already has been done prevents us from foreseeing what is yet to be accomplished.

The whole book that is here offered to the public has been written under the influence of a kind of religious awe produced in the author's mind by the view of that irresistible revolution which has advanced for centuries in spite of every obstacle and which is still advancing in the midst of the ruins it has caused....

...The Christian nations of our day seem to me to present a most alarming spectacle; the movement which impels them is already so strong that it cannot be stopped, but it is not yet so rapid that it cannot be guided. Their fate is still in their own hands; but very soon they may lose control.

The first of the duties that are at this time imposed upon those who direct our affairs is to educate democracy, to reawaken, if possible, its religious beliefs; to purify its morals; to mold its actions; to substitute a knowledge of statecraft for its inexperience, and an awareness of its true interest for its blind instincts, to adapt its government to time and place, and to modify it according to men and to conditions. A new science of politics is needed for a new world.

Majority rule

ALEXIS DE TOCQUEVILLE, *DEMOCRACY IN AMERICA,* "THE PRINCIPLE OF THE SOVEREIGNTY OF THE PEOPLE IN NORTH AMERICA"; "THE OMNIPOTENCE OF THE MAJORITY IN THE UNITED STATES AND ITS EFFECTS" (1835)

WHY THIS READING?

In this reading, Tocqueville argues that "the people [the majority] reign in the American political world as the Deity does in the universe." But this "omnipotence of the majority" is, he argues, a cause for alarm, because "unlimited power is in itself a bad and dangerous thing," whether held by a monarch, an aristocracy, or the people.

Tocqueville regards as especially pernicious the deadening effect on thought that is exercised by the power of the majority. So all-encompassing is the majority's power—"physical and moral at the same time"—that he is forced to conclude: "I know of no country in which there is so little independence of mind and real freedom of discussion as in America." As you read his arguments, consider the power that public opinion polls hold over your own opinions—and over your willingness to express them when you find that your opinion is in the minority.

Tocqueville next describes what he deems the antidote to the unchecked power enjoyed by the majority in the United States: Although this country has a centralized government, it lacks centralized administration. This lack Tocqueville applauds, for with centralized administration, "freedom would soon be banished from the New World." By this he can be understood to mean that the dictates of the federal government are moderated by the fact that they are administered by a multitude of smaller governments—states, counties, and cities. These smaller units, because they are closer to the people over whom they govern, are likely to know better the people's particular needs and sensibilities. On this basis, their administration of the laws is likely to be less oppressive. More important still for Tocqueville, local administration of the laws provides greater opportunity for more citizens to be involved in the political process. Such participation, he argues, has an elevating or ennobling effect on the soul.

Questions to guide you as you read:

- Since Tocqueville wrote, the course of American history has moved toward greater control of administration by the national government. What would be his view of this historical development?
- We tend to think of democracy as the opposite of despotism. Why does Tocqueville argue that a regime can be simultaneously democratic *and* despotic?

The Principle of the Sovereignty of the People in North America

...In America the principle of the sovereignty of the people is neither barren nor concealed, as it is with some other nations; it is recognized by the customs and proclaimed by the laws; it spreads freely, and arrives without impediment at its most remote consequences. If there is a country in the world where the doctrine of the sovereignty of the people can be fairly appreciated, where it can be studied in its application to the affairs of society, and where its dangers and its advantages may be judged, that country is assuredly America.

I have already observed that, from their origin, the sovereignty of the people was the fundamental principle of most of the British colonies in America. It was far, however, from then exercising as much influence on the government of society as it now does. Two obstacles, the one external, the other internal, checked its invasive progress.

It could not ostensibly [openly] disclose [reveal] itself in the laws of colonies which were still forced to obey the mother country; it was therefore obliged to rule secretly in the provincial assemblies, and especially in the townships....

...The American Revolution broke out, and the doctrine of the sovereignty of the people came out of the townships and took possession of the state. Every class was enlisted in its cause; battles were fought and victories obtained for it; it became the law of laws.

A change almost as rapid was effected in the interior of society, where the law of inheritance completed the abolition of local influences.

As soon as this effect of the laws and of the Revolution became apparent to every eye, victory was irrevocably pronounced in favor of the democratic cause. All power was, in fact, in its hands, and resistance was no longer possible. The higher orders submitted without a murmur and without a struggle to an evil that was thenceforth inevitable. The ordinary fate of falling powers awaited them: each of their members followed his own interest; and as it was impossible to wring the power from the hands of a people whom they did not detest sufficiently to brave, their only aim was to secure its goodwill at any price. The most democratic laws were consequently voted by the very men whose interests they impaired: and thus, although the higher classes did not excite the passions of the people against their order, they themselves accelerated the triumph of the new state of things; so that, by a singular change, the democratic impulse was found to be most irresistible in the very states where the aristocracy had the firmest hold. The state of Maryland, which had been founded by men of rank, was the first to proclaim universal suffrage and to introduce the most democratic forms into the whole of its government.

When a nation begins to modify the elective qualification, it may easily be foreseen that, sooner or later, that qualification will be entirely abolished. There is no more invariable rule in the history of society: the further electoral rights are extended, the greater is the need of extending them; for after each concession the strength of the democracy increases, and its demands increase with its strength. The ambition of those who are below the appointed rate is irritated in exact proportion to the great number of those who are above it. The exception at last becomes the rule, concession follows concession, and no stop can be made short of universal suffrage.

At the present day the principle of the sovereignty of the people has acquired in the United States all the practical development that the imagination can conceive. It is unencumbered by those fictions that are thrown over it in other countries, and it appears in every possible form, according to the exigency of the occasion. Sometimes the laws are made by the people in a body, as at Athens [an ancient Greek democracy]; and sometimes its representatives, chosen by universal suffrage, transact business in its name and under its immediate supervision.

In some countries a power exists which, though it is in a degree foreign to the social body, directs it, and forces it to pursue a certain track. In others the ruling force is divided, being partly within and partly without the ranks of the people. But nothing of the kind is to be seen in the United States; there society governs itself for itself. All power centers in its bosom, and scarcely an individual is to be met with who would venture to conceive or, still less, to express the idea of seeking it elsewhere. The nation participates in the making of its laws by the choice of its legislators, and in the execution of them by the choice of the agents of the executive government; it may almost be said to govern itself, so feeble and so restricted is the share left to the administration, so little do the authorities forget their popular origin and the power from which they emanate. The people reign in the American political world as the Deity does in the universe. They are the cause and the aim of all things; everything comes from them, and everything is absorbed in them.

The Omnipotence of the Majority in the United States and its Effects

The very essence of democratic government consists in the absolute sovereignty of the majority; for there is nothing in democratic states that is capable of resisting it. Most of the American constitutions have sought to increase this natural strength of the majority by artificial means.

Of all political institutions, the legislature is the one that is most easily swayed by the will of the majority. The Americans determined that the members of the legislature should be elected by the people directly, and for a very brief term, in order to subject them, not only to the general convictions, but even to the daily passions, of their constituents. The members of both houses are taken from the same classes in society and nominated in the same manner; so that the movements of the legislative bodies are almost as rapid, and quite as irresistible, as those of a single assembly.

It is to a legislature thus constituted that almost all the authority of the government has been entrusted.

At the same time that the law increased the strength of those authorities which of themselves were strong, it enfeebled more and more those which were naturally weak. It deprived the representatives of the executive power of all stability and independence; and by subjecting them completely to the caprices of the legislature, it robbed them of the slender influence that the nature of a democratic government might have allowed them to exercise. In several states the judicial power was also submitted to the election of the majority and in all of them its existence was made to depend on the pleasure of the legislative authority, since the representatives were empowered annually to regulate the stipend of the judges.

Custom [tradition] has done even more than law. A proceeding is becoming more and more general in the United States which will, in the end, do away with the guarantees of representative government: it frequently happens that the voters, in electing a delegate, point out a certain line of conduct to him and impose upon him certain positive obligations that he is pledged to fulfill. With the exception of the tumult [commotion], this comes to the same thing as if the majority itself held its deliberations in the market-place.

Several particular circumstances combine to render the power of the majority in America not only preponderant, but irresistible. The moral authority of the majority is partly based upon the notion that there is more intelligence and wisdom in a number of men united than in a single individual, and that the number of the legislators is more important than their quality. The theory of equality is thus applied to the intellects of men; and human pride is thus assailed in its last retreat by a doctrine which the minority hesitate to admit, and to which they will but slowly assent [acquiesce]. Like all other powers, and perhaps more than any other, the authority of the many requires the sanction of time in order to appear legitimate. At first it enforces obedience by constraint; and its laws are not respected until they have been long maintained.

The right of governing society, which the majority supposes itself to derive from its superior intelligence, was introduced into the United States by the first settlers; and this idea, which of itself would be sufficient to create a free nation, has now been amalgamated with the customs of the people and the minor incidents of social life.

The French under the old monarchy held it for a maxim that the king could do no wrong; and if he did do wrong, the blame was imputed to his advisers. This notion made obedience very easy; it enabled the subject to complain of the law without ceasing to love and honor the lawgiver. The Americans entertain the same opinion with respect to the majority.

The moral power of the majority is founded upon yet another principle, which is that the interests of the many are to be preferred to those of the few.... When a nation is divided into several great irreconcilable interests, the privilege of the majority is often overlooked, because it is intolerable to comply with its demands.

If there existed in America a class of citizens whom the legislating majority sought to deprive of exclusive privileges which they had possessed for ages and to bring down from an elevated station to the level of the multitude, it is probable that the minority would be less ready to submit to its laws. But as the United States was colonized by men holding equal rank, there is as yet no natural or permanent disagreement between the interests of its different inhabitants.

There are communities in which the members of the minority can never hope to draw the majority over to their side, because they must then give up the very point that is at issue between them. Thus an aristocracy can never become a majority while it retains its exclusive privileges, and it cannot cede its privileges without ceasing to be an aristocracy.

In the United States, political questions cannot be taken up in so general and absolute a manner; and all parties are willing to recognize the rights of the majority, because they all hope at some time to be able to exercise them to their own advantage. The majority in that country, therefore, exercise a prodigious [extraordinary] actual authority, and a power of opinion which is nearly as great; no obstacles exist which can impede or even retard its progress, so as to make it heed the complaints of those whom it crushes upon its path. This state of things is harmful in itself and dangerous for the future.

I hold it to be an impious and detestable maxim that, politically speaking, the people have a right to do anything; and yet I have asserted that all authority originates in the will of the majority. Am I, then, in contradiction with myself?

A general law, which bears the name of justice, has been made and sanctioned, not only by a majority of this or that people, but by a majority of mankind. The rights of every people are therefore confined within the limits of what is just. A nation may be considered as a jury which is empowered to represent society at large and to apply justice, which is its law. Ought such a jury, which represents society, to have more power than the society itself whose laws it executes?

When I refuse to obey an unjust law, I do not contest the right of the majority to command, but I simply appeal from the sovereignty of the people to the sovereignty of mankind. Some have not feared to assert that a people can never outstep the boundaries of justice and reason in those affairs which are peculiarly its own; and that consequently full power may be given to the majority by which it is represented. But this is the language of a slave.

A majority taken collectively is only an individual, whose opinions, and frequently whose interests, are opposed to those of another individual, who is styled a minority. If it be admitted that a man possessing absolute power may misuse that power by wronging his adversaries, why should not a majority be liable to the same reproach? Men do not change their characters by uniting with one another; nor does their patience in the presence of obstacles increase with their strength. For my own part, I cannot believe it; the power to do everything, which I should refuse to one of my equals, I will never grant to any number of them....

...I am therefore of the opinion that social power superior to all others must always be placed somewhere; but I think that liberty is endangered when this power finds no obstacle which can retard its course and give it time to moderate its own vehemence.

Unlimited power is in itself a bad and dangerous thing. Human beings are not competent to exercise it with discretion. God alone can be omnipotent, because his wisdom and his justice are always equal to his power. There is no power on earth so worthy of honor in itself or clothed with rights so sacred that I would admit its uncontrolled and all-predominant authority. When I see that the right and the means of absolute command are conferred on any power whatever, be it called a people or a king, an aristocracy or a democracy, a monarchy or a republic, I say there is the germ of tyranny, and I seek to live elsewhere, under other laws.

In my opinion, the main evil of the present democratic institutions of the United States does not arise, as is often asserted in Europe, from their weakness, but from their irresistible strength. I am not so much alarmed at the excessive liberty which reigns in that country as at the inadequate securities which one finds there against tyranny. An individual or a party is wronged in the United States, to whom can he apply for redress? If to public opinion, public opinion constitutes the majority; if to the legislature, it represents the majority and implicitly obeys it; if to the executive power, it is appointed by the majority and serves as a passive tool in its hands. The public force consists of the majority under arms; the jury is the majority invested with the right of hearing judicial cases; and in certain states even the judges are elected by the majority. However iniquitous or absurd the measure of which you complain, you must submit to it as well as you can.

If, on the other hand, a legislative power could be so constituted as to represent the majority without necessarily being the slave of its passions, an executive so as to retain a proper share of authority, and a judiciary so as to remain independent of the other two powers, a government would be formed which would still be democratic while incurring scarcely any risk of tyranny.

I do not say that there is a frequent use of tyranny in America at the present day; but I maintain that there is no sure barrier against it, and that the causes which mitigate [moderate] the government there are to be found in the circumstances and the manners of the country more than in its laws.

It is in the examination of the exercise of thought in the United States that we clearly perceive how far the power of the majority surpasses all the powers with which we are acquainted in Europe. Thought is an invisible and subtle power that mocks all the efforts of tyranny. At the present time the most absolute monarchs in Europe cannot prevent certain opinions hostile to their authority from circulating in secret through their dominions and even in their courts. It is not so in America; as long as the majority is still undecided, discussion is carried on; but as soon as its decision is irrevocably pronounced, everyone is silent, and the friends as well as the opponents of the measure unite in assenting to its propriety. The reason for this is perfectly clear: no monarch is so absolute as to combine all the powers of society in his own hands and to conquer all opposition, as a majority is able to do, which has the right both of making and of executing the laws.

The authority of a king is physical and controls the actions of men without subduing their will. But the majority possesses a power that is physical and moral at the same time, which acts upon the will as much as upon the actions and represses not only all contest, but all controversy.

I know of no country in which there is so little independence of mind and real freedom of discussion as in America. In any constitutional state in Europe every sort of religious and political theory may be freely preached and disseminated; for there is no country in Europe so subdued by any single authority as not to protect the man who raises his voice in the cause of truth from the consequences of his hardihood. If he is unfortunate enough to live under an absolute government, the people are often on his side; if he inhabits a free country, he can, if necessary, find a shelter behind the throne. The aristocratic part of society supports him in some countries, and the democracy in others. But in a nation where democratic institutions exist, organized like those of the United States, there is but one authority, one element of strength and success, with nothing beyond it.

In America the majority raises formidable barriers around the liberty of opinion; within these barriers an author may write what he pleases, but woe to him if he goes beyond them. Not that he is in danger of an auto-da-fé [a death sentence], but he is exposed to continued obloquy [public humiliation] and persecution. His political career is closed forever, since he has offended the only authority that is able to open it. Every sort of compensation, even that of celebrity, is refused to him. Before making public his opinions he thought he had sympathizers; now it seems to him that he has none any more since he has revealed himself to everyone; then those who blame him criticize loudly and those who think as he does keep quiet and move away without courage. He yields at length, overcome by the daily effort which he has to make, and subsides into silence, as if he felt remorse for having spoken the truth.

Fetters [chains] and headsmen [public executioners who beheaded prisoners] were the coarse instruments that tyranny formerly employed; but the civilization of our age has perfected despotism itself, though it seemed to have nothing to learn. Monarchs had, so to speak, materialized oppression; the democratic republics of the present day have rendered it as entirely an affair of the mind as the will which it is intended to coerce. Under the absolute sway of one man the body was attacked in order to subdue the soul; but the soul escaped the blows which were directed against it and rose proudly superior. Such is not the course adopted by tyranny in democratic republics; there the body is left free, and the soul is enslaved. The master no longer says: "You shall think as I do or you shall die"; but he says: "You are free to think differently from me and to retain your life, your property, and all that you possess; but you are henceforth a stranger among your people. You may retain your civil rights, but they will be useless to you, for you will never be chosen by your fellow citizens if you solicit their votes; and they will affect to scorn you if you ask for their esteem. You will remain among men, but you will be deprived of the rights of mankind. Your fellow creatures will shun you like an impure being; and even those who believe in your innocence will abandon you, lest they should be shunned in their turn. Go in peace! I have given you your life, but it is an existence worse than death."

Absolute monarchies had dishonored despotism; let us beware lest democratic republics should reinstate it and render it less odious [hateful] and degrading in the eyes of the many by making it still more onerous [burdensome] to the few.

...[T]he ruling power in the United States is not to be made game of. The smallest reproach irritates its sensibility, and the slightest joke that has any foundation in truth renders it indignant, from the forms of its language up to the solid virtues of its character, everything must be made the subject of encomium [high praise]. No writer, whatever be his eminence, can escape paying this tribute of adulation [adoration] to his fellow citizens. The majority lives in the perpetual utterance of self-applause, and there are certain truths which the Americans can learn only from strangers or from experience.

If America has not as yet had any great writers, the reason is given in these facts; there can be no literary genius without freedom of opinion, and freedom of opinion does not exist in America. The Inquisition has never been able to prevent a vast number of anti-religious books from circulating in Spain. The empire of the majority succeeds much better in the United States, since it actually removes any wish to publish them. Unbelievers are to be met with in America, but there is no public organ of infidelity. Attempts have been made by some governments to protect morality by prohibiting licentious [immoral] books. In the United States no one is punished for this sort of books, but no one is induced to write them; not because all the citizens are immaculate in conduct, but because the majority of the community is decent and orderly....

...I have already pointed out the distinction between a centralized government and a centralized administration. The former exists in America, but the latter is nearly unknown there. If the directing power of the American communities had both these instruments of government at its disposal and united the habit of executing its commands to the right of commanding; if, after having established the general principles of government, it descended to the details of their application; and if, having regulated the great interests of the country, it could descend to the circle of individual interests, freedom would soon be banished from the New World.

But in the United States the majority, which so frequently displays the tastes and the propensities of a despot, is still destitute of the most perfect instruments of tyranny.

In the American republics the central government has never as yet busied itself except with a small number of objects, sufficiently prominent to attract its attention. The secondary affairs of society have never been regulated by its authority; and nothing has hitherto betrayed its desire of even interfering in them. The majority has become more and more absolute, but has not increased the prerogatives of the central government; those great prerogatives have been confined to a certain sphere; and although the despotism of the majority may be galling upon one point, it cannot be said to extend to all. However the predominant party in the nation may be carried away by its passions, however ardent it may be in the pursuit of its projects, it cannot oblige all the citizens to comply with its desires in the same manner and at the same time throughout the country. When the central government which represents that majority has issued a decree, it must entrust the execution of its will to agents over whom it frequently has no control and whom it cannot perpetually direct. The townships, municipal bodies, and counties form so many concealed breakwaters, which check or part the tide of popular determination. If an oppressive law were passed, liberty would still be protected by the mode of executing that law; the majority cannot descend to the details and what may be called the puerilities [childish or immature acts] of administrative tyranny. It does not even imagine that it can do so, for it has not a full consciousness of its authority. It knows only the extent of its natural powers, but is unacquainted with the art of increasing them.

This point deserves attention; for if a democratic republic, similar to that of the United States, were ever founded in a country where the power of one man had previously established a centralized administration and had sunk it deep into the habits and the laws of the people, I do not hesitate to assert that in such a republic a more insufferable despotism would prevail than in any of the absolute monarchies of Europe; or, indeed, than any that could be found on this side of Asia.

The "House Divided"—What the battle over slavery reveals about America's core principles

THOMAS JEFFERSON, *NOTES ON THE STATE OF VIRGINIA,* "QUERY XVIII" (1784)

WHY THIS READING?

Notes on the State of Virginia, the only book Jefferson ever published, was written as a response to questions, or queries, regarding the state of Virginia posed to him by a Frenchman "of distinction." Written in 1781–1782 and published in 1787, Jefferson's *Notes* include thoughts on a wide variety of subjects. In the excerpt below, Jefferson, himself a slaveholder, offers his famous critique of slavery: "Indeed I tremble for my country when I reflect that God is just...." By this he apparently means that the evil of slavery was so monstrous that he could not help but fear that it would someday call down an awful, divine punishment. Many in the anti-slavery movement would later come to regard the Civil War (1861–1865), the bloodiest war in American history, as the retribution that Jefferson feared.

Questions to guide you as you read:

- What does Jefferson regard as the natural and inevitable effect of slaveholding on the characters of masters?
- How should the fact that Jefferson owned slaves during his entire adult life affect our understanding of what he wrote in the Declaration of Independence, namely, that "all men are created equal"? If he did believe in human equality, why would he have held slaves? If he did not believe in equality, why would he have written that human beings are created equal?

Manners

It is difficult to determine on the standard by which the manners of a nation may be tried, whether catholic, or particular. It is more difficult for a native to bring to that standard the manners of his own nation, familiarized to him by habit. There must doubtless be an unhappy influence on the manners of our people produced by the existence of slavery among us. The whole commerce between master and slave is a perpetual exercise of the most boisterous passions, the most unremitting despotism on the one part, and degrading submissions on the other. Our children see this, and learn to imitate it; for man is an imitative animal. This quality is the germ of all education in him. From his cradle to his grave he is learning to do what he sees others do. If a parent could find no motive either in his philanthropy [love of humanity] or his self-love, for restraining the intemperance of passion towards his slave, it should always be a sufficient one that his child is present. But generally it is not sufficient. The parent storms [rages], the child looks on, catches the lineaments [facial features] of wrath, puts on the same airs in the circle of smaller slaves, gives a loose to his worst of passions, and thus nursed, educated, and daily exercised in tyranny, cannot but be stamped by it with odious [detestable] peculiarities. The man must be a prodigy who can retain his manners and morals undepraved [uncorrupted] by such circumstances. And with what execration [curses] should the statesman be loaded, who permitting one half the citizens thus to trample on the rights of the other, transforms those into despots, and these into enemies, destroys the morals of the one part, and the *amor patriae* [love of country] of the other. For if a slave can have a country in this world, it must be any other in preference to that in which he is born to live and labour for another: in which he must lock up the faculties [abilities] of his nature, contribute as far as depends on his individual endeavours to the evanishment [disappearance] of the human race, or entail his own miserable condition on the endless generations proceeding from him. With the morals of the people, their industry also is destroyed. For in a warm climate, no man will labour for himself who can make another labour for him. This is so true, that of the proprietors of slaves a very small proportion indeed are ever seen to labour. And can the liberties of a nation be thought secure when we have removed their only firm basis, a conviction in the minds of the people that these liberties are of the gift of God? That they are not to be violated but with his wrath? Indeed I tremble for my country when I reflect that God is just: that his justice cannot sleep for ever: that considering numbers, nature and natural means only, a revolution of the wheel of fortune, an exchange of situation, is among possible events: that it may become probable by supernatural interference! The Almighty has no attribute which can take side with us in such a contest. But it is impossible to be temperate and to pursue this subject through the various considerations of policy, of morals, of history natural and civil. We must be contented to hope

they will force their way into every one's mind. I think a change already perceptible, since the origin of the present revolution. The spirit of the master is abating [waning], that of the slave rising from the dust, his condition mollifying, the way I hope preparing, under the auspices of heaven [with the support of heaven], for a total emancipation, and that this is disposed, in the order of events, to be with the consent of the masters, rather than by their extirpation [annihilation].

FREDERICK DOUGLASS, "THE MEANING OF THE FOURTH OF JULY FOR THE NEGRO" (1852)

Douglass (1818–1895) was a former slave, abolitionist, writer, and orator. He was the most prominent black abolitionist of the 19th century, serving as an advisor on two occasions to President Lincoln. His three autobiographies (1845, 1855, and 1881) are recognized today as classics of American literature.

WHY THIS READING?

Although Douglass consistently opposed slavery throughout his distinguished career, in the 1850s he broke away from the uncompromising calls for abolition led by William Lloyd Garrison. At the 1843 meeting of the Massachusetts Anti-Slavery Society, Garrison secured passage of the following resolution: "Resolved, that the compact which exists between the North and the South [the Constitution] is 'a covenant with death and an agreement with hell' —involving both parties in atrocious criminality—and should be immediately annulled [declared null and void]."

In the famous address below, Douglass clarifies his differences and similarities with Garrison. Douglass had been invited to speak about the meaning of the Fourth of July. He used the opportunity to deliver a memorable and at times fiery meditation on how the promise of the Declaration of Independence had not yet been extended to blacks. On the question "What is American democracy?," he reminded the audience that "The blessings in which you, this day, rejoice, are... shared by you, not by me."

Questions to guide you as you read:

- Does Douglass agree with Garrison's view that the Declaration and the Constitution are pro-slavery documents?
- What would have been the likely result had slavery been outlawed—over the South's objections—in 1843, as Garrison demanded? How many slaves would in fact have been freed? Why?
- What are Douglass's criticisms of the American church of the time?

On the 2nd of July 1776, the old Continental Congress,[3] to the dismay of the lovers of ease, and the worshipers of property, clothed that dreadful idea [revolution] with all the authority of national sanction. They did so in the form of a resolution; and as we seldom hit upon resolutions, drawn up in our day, whose transparency is at all equal to this, it may refresh your minds and help my story if I read it.

3. The Continental Congress to which Douglass here refers is the Second Continental Congress that took the final step toward separation from England by adopting the Declaration of Independence on July 4, 1776.

"Resolved, That these united colonies are, and of right, ought to be free and Independent States; that they are absolved from all allegiance to the British Crown; and that all political connection between them and the State of Great Britain is, and ought to be, dissolved."

Citizens, your fathers made good that resolution. They succeeded; and today you reap the fruits of their success. The freedom gained is yours; and you, therefore, may properly celebrate this anniversary. The 4th of July is the first great fact in your nation's history—the very ringbolt [a bolt with a ring attached for fitting a chain or rope to it] in the chain of your yet undeveloped destiny.

Pride and patriotism, not less than gratitude, prompt you to celebrate and to hold it in perpetual remembrance. I have said that the Declaration of Independence is the ringbolt to the chain of your nation's destiny; so, indeed, I regard it. The principles contained in that instrument are saving principles. Stand by those principles, be true to them on all occasions, in all places, against all foes, and at whatever cost....

...The coming into being of a nation, in any circumstances, is an interesting event. But, besides general considerations, there were peculiar circumstances which make the advent of this republic an event of special attractiveness....

...Fellow Citizens, I am not wanting in respect for the fathers of this republic. The signers of the Declaration of Independence were brave men. They were great men, too—great enough to give frame to a great age. It does not often happen to a nation to raise, at one time, such a number of truly great men. The point from which I am compelled to view them is not, certainly, the most favorable; and yet I cannot contemplate their great deeds with less than admiration. They were statesmen, patriots and heroes, and for the good they did, and the principles they contended for, I will unite with you to honor their memory.

They loved their country better than their own private interests; and, though this is not the highest form of human excellence, all will concede that it is a rare virtue, and that when it is exhibited it ought to command respect. He who will, intelligently, lay down his life for his country is a man whom it is not in human nature to despise. Your fathers staked their lives, their fortunes, and their sacred honor,[4] on the cause of their country. In their admiration of liberty, they lost sight of all other interests.

They were peace men; but they preferred revolution to peaceful submission to bondage. They were quiet men; but they did not shrink from agitating against oppression. They showed forbearance; but that they knew its limits. They believed in order; but not in the order of tyranny. With them, nothing was "settled" that was not right. With them, justice, liberty and humanity were "final"; not slavery and oppression. You may well cherish the memory of such men. They were great in their day and generation. Their solid manhood stands out the more as we contrast it with these degenerate times.

How circumspect, exact and proportionate were all their movements! How unlike the politicians of an hour! Their statesmanship looked beyond the passing moment, and stretched away in strength into the distant future. They seized upon eternal principles,[5] and set a glorious example in their defense. Mark them!

Fully appreciating the hardships to be encountered, firmly believing in the right of their cause, honorably inviting the scrutiny of an on-looking world, reverently appealing to heaven to attest their sincerity, soundly comprehending the solemn responsibility they were about to assume, wisely measuring the terrible odds against them, your fathers, the fathers of this republic, did, most deliberately, under the inspiration of a glorious patriotism, and with a sublime faith in the great principles of justice and freedom, lay deep, the cornerstone[6] of the national super-structure, which has risen and still rises in grandeur around you.

---

4. This passage is a quotation from the final paragraph of the Declaration of Independence.
5. The "eternal principles" are most likely the self-evident truths of the Declaration of Independence.
6. The "cornerstone" is the Declaration of Independence.

Of this fundamental work,[7] this day is the anniversary. Our eyes are met with demonstrations of joyous enthusiasm. Banners and pennants wave exultingly on the breeze.... The causes which led to the separation of the colonies from the British crown have never lacked for a tongue. They have all been taught in your common schools, narrated at your firesides, unfolded from your pulpits, and thundered from your legislative halls, and are as familiar to you as household words. They form the staple of your national poetry and eloquence....

...I leave, therefore, the great deeds of your fathers to other gentlemen whose claim to have been regularly descended will be less likely to be disputed than mine!

My business, if I have any here today, is with the present. The accepted time with God and His cause is the ever-living now....

...To all inspiring motives, to noble deeds which can be gained from the past, we are welcome. But now is the time, the important time. Your fathers have lived, died, and have done their work, and have done much of it well. You live and must die, and you must do your work. You have no right to enjoy a child's share in the labor of your fathers, unless your children are to be blest by your labors. You have no right to wear out and waste the hard-earned fame of your fathers to cover your indolence [laziness]....

...Fellow-citizens, pardon me, allow me to ask, why am I called upon to speak here today? What have I, or those I represent, to do with your national independence? Are the great principles of political freedom and of natural justice, embodied in that Declaration of Independence, extended to us?...

...Would to God, both for your sakes and ours, that an affirmative answer could be truthfully returned to these questions! Then would my task be light, and my burden easy and delightful....

...But such is not the state of the case. I say it with a sad sense of the disparity between us. I am not included within the pale [boundary] of this glorious anniversary! Your high independence only reveals the immeasurable distance between us. The blessings in which you, this day, rejoice, are not enjoyed in common. The rich inheritance of justice, liberty, prosperity and independence, bequeathed by your fathers, is shared by you, not by me. The sunlight that brought light and healing to you, has brought stripes [blows from a whip] and death to me. This Fourth July is yours, not mine. You may rejoice, I must mourn....

...Fellow-citizens, above your national, tumultuous [noisy] joy, I hear the mournful wail [cry] of millions! Whose chains, heavy and grievous yesterday, are, to-day, rendered more intolerable by the jubilee [joyful] shouts that reach them.... To forget them, to pass lightly over their wrongs, and to chime in with the popular theme, would be treason most scandalous and shocking, and would make me a reproach before God and the world. My subject, then, fellow-citizens, is American slavery. I shall see this day and its popular characteristics from the slave's point of view. Standing there identified with the American bondman, making his wrongs mine, I do not hesitate to declare, with all my soul, that the character and conduct of this nation never looked blacker to me than on this 4th of July! Whether we turn to the declarations of the past, or to the professions of the present, the conduct of the nation seems equally hideous and revolting. America is false to the past, false to the present, and solemnly binds herself to be false to the future standing with God and the crushed and bleeding slave on this occasion, I will, in the name of humanity which is outraged, in the name of liberty which is fettered [chained], in the name of the constitution and the Bible which are disregarded and trampled upon, dare to call in question and to denounce, with all the emphasis I can command, everything that serves to perpetuate [make everlasting] slavery—the great sin and shame of America!...

...For the present, it is enough to affirm the equal manhood of the Negro race. Is it not astonishing that, while we are ploughing, planting, and reaping, using all kinds of mechanical tools, erecting houses, constructing bridges, building ships, working in metals of brass, iron, copper, silver and gold; that, while we are reading, writing and

7. The "fundamental work" is the Declaration of Independence.

ciphering, acting as clerks, merchants and secretaries, having among us lawyers, doctors, ministers, poets, authors, editors, orators and teachers; that, while we are engaged in all manner of enterprises common to other men, digging gold in California, capturing the whale in the Pacific, feeding sheep and cattle on the hill-side, living, moving, acting, thinking, planning, living in families as husbands, wives and children, and, above all, confessing and worshiping the Christian's God, and looking hopefully for life and immortality beyond the grave, we are called upon to prove that we are men!

Would you have me argue that man is entitled to liberty? That he is the rightful owner of his own body? You have already declared it. Must I argue the wrongfulness of slavery? Is that a question for Republicans? Is it to be settled by the rules of logic and argumentation, as a matter beset with great difficulty, involving a doubtful application of the principle of justice, hard to be understood? How should I look today, in the presence of Americans, dividing, and subdividing a discourse, to show that men have a natural right to freedom? Speaking of it relatively and positively, negatively and affirmatively. To do so, would be to make myself ridiculous, and to offer an insult to your understanding.—There is not a man beneath the canopy [cover] of heaven that does not know that slavery is wrong *for him.*

What, am I to argue that it is wrong to make men brutes [animals], to rob them of their liberty, to work them without wages, to keep them ignorant of their relations to their fellow men, to beat them with sticks, to flay their flesh with the lash [whip], to load their limbs with irons, to hunt them with dogs, to sell them at auction, to sunder [separate] their families, to knock out their teeth, to burn their flesh, to starve them into obedience and submission to their masters? Must I argue that a system thus marked with blood, and stained with pollution, is *wrong?* No! I will not. I have better employment for my time and strength than such arguments would imply.

What, then, remains to be argued? Is it that slavery is not divine; that God did not establish it; that our doctors of divinity are mistaken? There is blasphemy in the thought. That which is inhuman, cannot be divine! *Who* can reason on such a proposition? They that can, may; I cannot. The time for such argument is passed....

...What, to the American slave, is your 4th of July? I answer; a day that reveals to him, more than all other days in the year, the gross injustice and cruelty to which he is the constant victim. To him, your celebration is a sham; your boasted liberty, an unholy license; your national greatness, swelling vanity; your sounds of rejoicing are empty and heartless; your denunciation of tyrants, brass fronted impudence [disrespect]; your shouts of liberty and equality, hollow mockery; your prayers and hymns, your sermons and thanksgivings, with all your religious parade and solemnity, are, to Him, mere bombast [pomposity], fraud, deception, impiety, and hypocrisy—a thin veil to cover up crimes which would disgrace a nation of savages. There is not a nation on the earth guilty of practices more shocking and bloody than are the people of the United States, at this very hour.

Go where you may, search where you will, roam through all the monarchies and despotisms[8] of the Old World, travel through South America, search out every abuse, and when you have found the last, lay your facts by the side of the everyday practices of this nation, and you will say with me, that, for revolting barbarity and shameless hypocrisy, America reigns without a rival.

Take the American slave-trade, which we are told by the papers, is especially prosperous just now. Ex-Senator Benton tells us that the price of men was never higher than now. He mentions the fact to show that slavery is in no danger. This trade is one of the peculiarities of American institutions. It is carried on in all the large towns and cities in one-half of this confederacy; and millions are pocketed every year by dealers in this horrid traffic. In several states this trade is a chief source of wealth. It is called (in contradistinction to the foreign slave-trade) *"the internal slave-trade."* It is, probably, called so, too, in order to divert from it the horror with which the foreign slave-trade is contemplated. That trade has

8. Despotism is a synonym for tyranny.

long since been denounced by this government as piracy....[9]

...Behold the practical operation of this internal slave-trade, the American slave-trade, sustained by American politics and American religion. Here you will see men and women reared like swine for the market. You know what is a swine-drover [herder of swine]? I will show you a man-drover [herder of men]. They inhabit all our Southern States. They perambulate [walk from place to place] the country, and crowd the highways of the nation, with droves of human stock. You will see one of these human flesh jobbers, armed with pistol, whip, and Bowie knife, driving a company of a hundred men, women, and children, from the Potomac to the slave market at New Orleans. These wretched people are to be sold singly, or in lots, to suit purchasers. They are food for the cotton-field and the deadly sugar-mill. Mark the sad procession, as it moves wearily along, and the inhuman wretch who drives them. Hear his savage yells and his blood-curdling oaths, as he hurries on his affrighted captives! There, see the old man with locks thinned and gray. Cast one glance, if you please, upon that young mother, whose shoulders are bare to the scorching sun, her briny [water filled with salt] tears falling on the brow of the babe in her arms. See, too, that girl of thirteen, weeping, *yes!* Weeping as she thinks of the mother from whom she has been torn!... Tell me, citizens, where, under the sun, you can witness a spectacle more fiendish and shocking. Yet this is but a glance at the American slave-trade, as it exists, at this moment in the ruling part of the United States.

I was born amid such sights and scenes. To me the American slave trade is a terrible reality. When a child, my soul was often pierced with a sense of its horrors....

...In the deep, still darkness of midnight, I have been often aroused by the dead, heavy footsteps, and the piteous cries of the chained gangs that passed our door. The anguish of my boyish heart was intense; and was often consoled, when speaking to my mistress in the morning, to hear her say that the custom was very wicked; that she hated to hear the rattle of the chains and the heart-rending cries. I was glad to find one who sympathized with me in my horror.

Fellow-citizens, this murderous traffic is, to-day, in active operation in this boasted republic. In the solitude of my spirit I see clouds of dust raised on the highways of the South; I see the bleeding footsteps; I hear the doleful wail of fettered humanity on the way to the slave-markets, where the victims are to be sold like horses, sheep, and swine, knocked to the highest bidder....

But a still more inhuman, disgraceful, and scandalous state of things remains to be presented. By an act of the American Congress, not yet two years old, slavery has been nationalized in its most horrible and revolting form.[10] By that act, Mason and Dixon's line has been obliterated; New York has become as Virginia; and the power to hold, hunt, and sell men, women and children, as slaves, remains no longer a mere state institution, but is now an institution of the whole United States. The power is co-extensive with the star-spangled banner, and American Christianity. Where these go, may also go the merciless slave-hunter. Where these are, man is not sacred. He is a bird for the sportsman's gun. By that most foul and fiendish of all human decrees, the liberty and person of every man are put in peril. Your broad republican domain is hunting ground for *men*. *Not* for thieves and robbers, enemies of society, merely, but for men guilty of no crime. Your law-makers have commanded all good citizens to engage in this hellish sport.... Not fewer than forty Americans have, within the

9. According to the U.S. Constitution, Art. I, Sec. 9, the U.S. Congress as of 1808 has the right to prohibit the migration or importation of slaves from abroad into the United States. According to the U.S. Constitution, the U.S. Congress also has the right to define for itself and punish piracy.

10. Douglass refers here to the Fugitive Slave Law, which was the most controversial part of the Compromise of 1850. It called for warrants to be issued to help catch runaway slaves. Accused runaways were often denied both a jury trial and the right to testify on their own behalf. Northern blacks were often torn from their families and forced into slavery.

past two years, been hunted down and, without a moment's warning, hurried away in chains, and consigned to slavery and excruciating torture. Some of these have had wives and children, dependent on them for bread; but of this, no account was made. The right of the hunter to his prey stands superior to the right of marriage, and to *all* rights in this republic, the rights of God included! For black men there is neither law nor justice, humanity nor religion. The Fugitive Slave Law makes mercy to them a crime; and bribes the judge who tries them. An American judge gets ten dollars for every victim he consigns to slavery, and five when he fails to do so. The oath of any two villains is sufficient, under this hell-black enactment, to send the most pious and exemplary black man into the remorseless jaws of slavery! His own testimony is nothing. He can bring no witnesses for himself. The minister of American justice is bound by the law to hear but one side; and that side is the side of the oppressor. Let this damning fact be perpetually [always] told....

In glaring violation of justice, in shameless disregard of the forms of administering law, in cunning arrangement to entrap the defenseless, and in diabolical intent this Fugitive Slave Law stands alone in the annals [records] of tyrannical legislation....

...I take this law to be one of the grossest infringements of Christian Liberty, and, if the churches and ministers of our country were not stupidly blind, or most wickedly indifferent, they, too, would so regard it.

At the very moment that they are thanking God for the enjoyment of civil and religious liberty, and for the right to worship God according to the dictates of their own consciences, they are utterly silent in respect to a law which robs religion of its chief significance and makes it utterly worthless to a world lying in wickedness....The fact that the church of our country (with fractional exceptions) does not esteem [regard] the Fugitive Slave Law as a declaration of war against religious liberty, implies that that church regards religion simply as a form of worship, an empty ceremony, and *not* a vital principle, requiring active benevolence, justice, love, and good will towards man. It esteems sacrifice above mercy; psalm-singing above right doing; solemn meetings above practical righteousness. A worship that can be conducted by persons who refuse to give shelter to the houseless, to give bread to the hungry, clothing to the naked, and who enjoin obedience to a law forbidding these acts of mercy is a curse, not a blessing to mankind....

But the church of this country is not only indifferent to the wrongs of the slave, it actually takes sides with the oppressors. It has made itself the bulwark [defensive wall] of American slavery, and the shield of American slave-hunters. Many of its most eloquent Divines [priests, ministers, and theologians], who stand as the very lights of the church, have shamelessly given the sanction of religion and the Bible to the whole slave system. They have taught that man may, properly, be a slave; that the relation of master and slave is ordained of God;...

...For my part, I would say, welcome infidelity! Welcome atheism! Welcome anything! In preference to the gospel, ***as preached by those Divines!*** They convert the very name of religion into an engine of tyranny and barbarous cruelty, and serve to confirm more infidels [unbelievers in religion], in this age, than all the infidel writings of Thomas Paine, Voltaire, and Bolingbroke put together have done! These ministers make religion a cold and flinty-hearted thing, having neither principles of right action nor bowels of compassion. They strip the love of God of its beauty and leave the throne of religion a huge, horrible, repulsive form. It is a religion for oppressors, tyrants, man-stealers, and ***thugs. It is*** not that ***"pure and undefiled religion"*** which is from above, and which is ***"first pure, then peaceable, easy to be entreated,*** full of mercy and good fruits, ***without partiality, and without hypocrisy."*** But a religion which favors the rich against the poor; which exalts the proud above the humble; which divides mankind into ***two*** classes, tyrants and slaves; which says to the man in chains, ***stay there;*** and ***to*** the oppressor, ***oppress on....***

...The American church is guilty, when viewed in connection with what it is doing to uphold slavery; but it is superlatively [of the highest quality or degree] guilty when viewed in its connection with its ability to abolish slavery.

The sin of which it is guilty is one of omission [an action that has not been committed] as well as of commission [an action that has been committed]. Albert Barnes but uttered what the common sense of every man at all observant of the actual state of the case will receive as truth, when he declared that "There is no power out of the church that could sustain slavery an hour, if it were not sustained in it."

Let the religious press, the pulpit, the Sunday School, the conference meeting, the great ecclesiastical, missionary, Bible and tract association of the land array [combine] their immense powers against slavery, and slave-holding and the whole system of crime and blood would be scattered to the winds and that they do not do this involves them in the most awful responsibility of which the mind can conceive.

In prosecuting the anti-slavery enterprise, we have been asked to spare the church, to spare the ministry; but *how,* we ask, could such a thing be done? We are met on the threshold of our efforts for the redemption of the slave, by the church and ministry of the country, in battle arrayed against us; and we are compelled to fight or flee. From *what* quarter, I beg to know, has proceeded a fire so deadly upon our ranks, during the last two years, as from the Northern pulpit? As the champions of oppressors, the chosen men of American theology have appeared—men honored for their so-called piety, and their real learning. The Lords of Buffalo, the Springs of New York, the Lathrops of Auburn, the Coxes and Spencers of Brooklyn, the Gannets and Sharps of Boston, the Deweys of Washington, and other great religious lights of the land have, in utter denial of the authority of *Him* by whom they professed to be called to the ministry, deliberately taught us, against the example of the Hebrews, and against the remonstrance of the Apostles, *that we ought to obey man's law before the law of God.* My spirit wearies of such blasphemy [impious talk]; and how such men can be supported, as the "standing types and representatives of Jesus Christ," is a mystery which I leave others to penetrate. In speaking of the American church, however, let it be distinctly understood that I mean the *great mass* of the religious organizations of our land. There are exceptions, and I thank God that there are. Noble men may be found, scattered all over these Northern States....

...Americans! Your republican politics, not less than your republican religion, are flagrantly inconsistent. You boast of your love of liberty, your superior civilization, and your pure Christianity, while the whole political power of the nation (as embodied in the two great political parties) is solemnly pledged to support and perpetuate the enslavement of three millions of your countrymen. You hurl your anathemas [curses] at the crowned headed tyrants of Russia and Austria and pride yourselves on your Democratic institutions, while you yourselves consent to be the *mere tools* and *body-guards* of the tyrants of Virginia and Carolina. You invite to your shores fugitives of oppression from abroad, honor them with banquets, greet them with ovations, cheer them, toast them, salute them, protect them, and pour out your money to them like water; but the fugitives from your own land you advertise, hunt, arrest, shoot, and kill. You glory in your refinement and your universal education; yet you maintain a system as barbarous [barbarian-like] and dreadful as ever stained the character of a nation—a system begun in avarice [greed], supported in pride, and perpetuated in cruelty....

You profess to believe "that, of one blood, God made all nations of men to dwell on the face of all the earth," and hath commanded all men everywhere, to love one another; yet you notoriously hate (and glory in your hatred) all men whose skins are not colored like your own. You declare before the world, and are understood by the world to declare that you *"hold these truths to be self-evident, that all men are created equal and are endowed by their Creator with certain inalienable rights; and that among these are, life, liberty, and the pursuit of happiness,"* and yet you hold securely, in a bondage which, according to your own Thomas Jefferson, *"is worse than ages of that which your fathers rose in rebellion to oppose," a seventh part* of the inhabitants of your country.

Fellow-citizens, I will not enlarge further on your national inconsistencies. The existence of slavery in this country brands your republicanism as a sham, your humanity as a base pretense, and your Christianity as a lie. It destroys your moral power abroad: It corrupts your politicians at home. It saps the foundation of religion; it makes your name a hissing and a bye-word to a mocking earth. It is the antagonistic force in your government, the only thing that seriously disturbs and endangers your *Union*. It fetters [enchains or imprisons] your progress; it is the enemy of improvement; the deadly foe of education; it fosters pride; it breeds insolence [disrespect]; it promotes vice; it shelters crime; it is a curse to the earth that supports it; and yet you cling to it as if it were the sheet anchor of all your hopes. Oh! Be warned! Be warned!...

...But it is answered in reply to all this, that precisely what I have now denounced is, in fact, guaranteed and sanctioned by the Constitution of the United States; that, the right to hold, and to hunt slaves is a part of that Constitution framed by the illustrious Fathers of this Republic.

Then, I dare to affirm, notwithstanding all I have said before, your fathers stooped, basely stooped

> *To palter with us in a double sense:*
> *And keep the word of promise to the ear,*
> *But break it to the heart.*

And instead of being the honest men I have before declared them to be, they were the veriest impostors that ever practiced on mankind. This is the inevitable conclusion, and from it there is no escape; but I differ from those who charge this baseness on the framers of the Constitution of the United States. It is a slander upon their memory, at least, so I believe. There is not time now to argue the constitutional question at length; nor have I the ability to discuss it as it ought to be discussed. The subject has been handled with masterly power by Lysander Spooner, Esq., by William Goodell, by Samuel E. Sewall, Esq., and last, though not least, by Gerrit Smith, Esq. These gentlemen have, as I think, fully and clearly vindicated the Constitution from any design to support slavery for an hour.

Fellow-citizens! There is no matter in respect to which the people of the North have allowed themselves to be so ruinously imposed upon as that of the pro-slavery character of the Constitution. In that instrument I hold there is neither warrant, license, nor sanction of the hateful thing[11]; but interpreted, as it ought to be interpreted, the Constitution is a glorious liberty document. Read its preamble, consider its purposes. Is slavery among them? Is it at the gateway? Or is it in the temple? It is neither. While I do not intend to argue this question on the present occasion, let me ask, if it be not somewhat singular that, if the Constitution were intended to be, by its framers and adopters, a slaveholding instrument, why neither slavery, slaveholding, nor slave can anywhere be found in it? What would be thought of an instrument, drawn up, legally drawn up, for the purpose of entitling the city of Rochester to a tract of land, in which no mention of land was made? Now, there are certain rules of interpretation for the proper understanding of all legal instruments. These rules are well established. They are plain, commonsense rules, such as you and I, and all of us, can understand and apply, without having passed years in the study of law. I deny the idea that the question of the constitutionality, or unconstitutionality of slavery, is not question for the people. I hold that every American citizen has a right to form an opinion of the Constitution, and to propagate [broadcast] that opinion, and to use all honorable means to make his opinion the prevailing one. Without this right, the liberty of an American citizen would be as insecure that of a Frenchman. Ex-Vice-President Dallas tells us that the constitution is an object to which no American mind can be too attentive, and no American heart too devoted. He further says, the Constitution, in its words, is plain and intelligible, and is meant for the home-bred, unsophisticated understandings of our fellow-citizens. Senator Berrien tells us that the Constitution is the fundamental law,[12] that which controls all others. The charter of our liberties, which every citizen has a personal interest in understanding thoroughly.... Now, take the

11. The "hateful thing" is slavery.
12. See the U.S. Constitution, Art. VI. The U.S. Constitution is here called "the supreme Law of the Land.

Constitution according to its plain reading, and I defy the presentation of a single pro-slavery clause in it. On the other hand, it will be found to contain principles and purposes, entirely hostile to the existence of slavery....

...Allow me to say, in conclusion, notwithstanding the dark picture I have this day presented, of the state of the nation, I do not despair of this country. There are forces in operation which must inevitably work the downfall of slavery. "The arm of the Lord is not shortened," and the doom of slavery is certain. I, therefore, leave off where I began, with hope. While drawing encouragement from the Declaration of Independence, the great principles it contains, and the genius of American Institutions, my spirit is also cheered by the obvious tendencies of the age. Nations do not now stand in the same relation to each other that they did ages ago. No nation can now shut itself up from the surrounding world and trot round in the same old path of its fathers without interference. The time was when such could be done.... Knowledge was then confined and enjoyed by the privileged few, and the multitude walked on in mental darkness. But a change has now come over the affairs of mankind.... The arm of commerce has borne away the gates of the strong city. Intelligence is penetrating the darkest corners of the globe. It makes its pathway over and under the sea, as well as on the earth. Wind, steam, and lightning are its chartered agents. Oceans no longer divide, but link nations together. From Boston to London is now a holiday excursion. Space is comparatively annihilated. Thoughts expressed on one side of the Atlantic are distinctly heard on the other.

ALEXANDER STEPHENS, "CORNERSTONE SPEECH" (1861)

Alexander Stephens (1812–1883) served as vice president of the Confederate States of America (1861–1865). Prior to that, he was a Georgia member of the U.S. House of Representatives, a post to which he returned after the Civil War, as well as governor of Georgia from 1882 until his death in 1883.

WHY THIS READING?

In this speech, Stephens make clear what he perceives to be the chief causes of contention between the North and the secessionist Southern states. Although he lists a number of divisive issues related to taxes, etc., he unambiguously identifies slavery as both the chief cause of sectional strife, as well as the foundation of the Southern way of life. He takes direct aim at the Declaration of Independence's assertion that "all men are created equal." His defense of race-based inequality calls into question the argument made by some that the South seceded over a concern with "states' rights" primarily, rather than over the slavery question. On this point, Stephens is unequivocal: "[A]gitating questions relating to our peculiar [our own] institution African slavery" formed "the immediate cause of the late rupture and present revolution."

Questions to guide you as you read:

- Does Stephens believe that Jefferson, the author of the Declaration, meant to include blacks in his pronouncement that "all men are created equal"?
- What does Stephens argue was the view of the majority of the Founding generation regarding the moral status of slavery? Does he agree or disagree with what he takes to be the Founders' view?

...I was remarking that we are passing through one of the greatest revolutions in the annals of the world. Seven States have within the last three months thrown off an old government and formed a new. This revolution has been signally marked, up to this time, by the fact of its having been accomplished without the loss of a single drop of blood.

This new constitution or form of government, constitutes the subject to which your attention will be partly invited. In reference to it, I make this first general remark: it amply secures all our ancient rights, franchises, and liberties. All the great principles of Magna Charta [established in 1215, it is regarded as the basis of political liberty in England] are retained in it. No citizen is deprived of life, liberty, or property, but by the judgment of his peers under the laws of the land. The great principle of religious liberty, which was the honor and pride of the old constitution, is still maintained and secured. All the essentials of the old constitution, which have endeared it to the hearts of the American people, have been preserved and perpetuated. Some changes have been made. Some of these I should have preferred not to have seen made; but other important changes do meet my cordial approbation. They form great improvements upon the old constitution. So, taking the whole new constitution, I have no hesitancy in giving it as my judgment that it is decidedly better than the old.

Allow me briefly to allude to some of these improvements. The question of building up class interests, or fostering one branch of industry to the prejudice of another under the exercise of the revenue power, which gave us so much trouble under the old constitution, is put at rest forever under the new. We allow the imposition of no duty with a view of giving advantage to one class of persons, in any trade or business, over those of another. All, under our system, stand upon the same broad principles of perfect equality. Honest labor and enterprise are left free and unrestricted in whatever pursuit they may be engaged. This old thorn of the tariff, which was the cause of so much irritation in the old body politic, is removed forever from the new.

...But not to be tedious in enumerating the numerous changes for the better, allow me to allude to one other though last, not least. The new constitution has put at rest, forever, all the agitating questions relating to our peculiar institution African slavery as it exists amongst us the proper status of the negro in our form of civilization. This was the immediate cause of the late rupture and present revolution. Jefferson in his forecast, had anticipated this, as the "rock upon which the old Union would split." He was right. What was conjecture with him, is now a realized fact. But whether he fully comprehended the great truth upon which that rock stood and stands, may be doubted. The prevailing ideas entertained by him and most of the leading statesmen at the time of the formation of the old constitution, were that the enslavement of the African was in violation of the laws of nature; that it was wrong in principle, socially, morally, and politically. It was an evil they knew not well how to deal with, but the general opinion of the men of that day was that, somehow or other in the order of Providence, the institution would be evanescent [short-lived] and pass away. This idea, though not incorporated in the constitution, was the prevailing idea at that time. The constitution, it is true, secured every essential guarantee to the institution while it should last, and hence no argument can be justly urged against the constitutional guarantees thus secured, because of the common sentiment of the day. Those ideas, however, were fundamentally wrong. They rested upon the assumption of the equality of races. This was an error. It was a sandy foundation, and the government built upon it fell when the "storm came and the wind blew."

Our new government is founded upon exactly the opposite idea; its foundations are laid, its corner-stone rests, upon the great truth that the negro is not equal to the white man; that slavery subordination to the superior race is his natural and normal condition. This, our new government, is the first, in the history of the world, based upon this great physical, philosophical, and moral truth. This truth has been slow in the process of its development, like all other truths in the various departments of science. It has been so even amongst us. Many who hear me, perhaps, can recollect well, that this truth was not generally admitted, even within their day.

The errors of the past generation still clung to many as late as twenty years ago. Those at the North, who still cling to these errors, with a zeal [enthusiasm] above knowledge, we justly denominate fanatics. All fanaticism springs from an aberration of the mind from a defect in reasoning. It is a species of insanity. One of the most striking characteristics of insanity, in many instances, is forming correct conclusions from fancied or erroneous premises; so with the anti-slavery fanatics. Their conclusions are right if their premises were. They assume that the negro is equal, and hence conclude that he is entitled to equal privileges and rights with the white man. If their premises were correct, their conclusions would be logical and just but their premise being wrong, their whole argument fails. I recollect once of having heard a gentleman from one of the northern States, of great power and ability, announce in the House of Representatives, with imposing effect, that we of the South would be compelled, ultimately, to yield upon this subject of slavery, that it was as impossible to war successfully against a principle in politics, as it was in physics or mechanics. That the principle would ultimately prevail. That we, in maintaining slavery as it exists with us, were warring against a principle, a principle founded in nature, the principle of the equality of men. The reply I made to him was, that upon his own grounds, we should, ultimately, succeed, and that he and his associates, in this crusade against our institutions, would ultimately fail. The truth announced, that it was as impossible to war successfully against a principle in politics as it was in physics and mechanics, I admitted; but told him that it was he, and those acting with him, who were warring against a principle. They were attempting to make things equal which the Creator had made unequal.

In the conflict thus far, success has been on our side, complete throughout the length and breadth of the Confederate States. It is upon this, as I have stated, our social fabric is firmly planted; and I cannot permit myself to doubt the ultimate success of a full recognition of this principle throughout the civilized and enlightened world.

As I have stated, the truth of this principle may be slow in development, as all truths are and ever have been, in the various branches of science. It was so with the principles announced by Galileo it was so with Adam Smith and his principles of political economy. It was so with Harvey, and his theory of the circulation of the blood. It is stated that not a single one of the medical profession, living at the time of the announcement of the truths made by him, admitted them. Now, they are universally acknowledged. May we not, therefore, look with confidence to the ultimate universal acknowledgment of the truths upon which our system rests? It is the first government ever instituted upon the principles in strict conformity to nature, and the ordination of Providence, in furnishing the materials of human society. Many governments have been founded upon the principle of the subordination and serfdom of certain classes of the same race; such were and are in violation of the laws of nature. Our system commits no such violation of nature's laws. With us, all of the white race, however high or low, rich or poor, are equal in the eye of the law. Not so with the negro. Subordination is his place. He, by nature, or by the curse against Canaan [a Biblical prophecy of condemnation to slavery; see Genesis 9, 18–29], is fitted for that condition which he occupies in our system. The architect, in the construction of buildings, lays the foundation with the proper material—the granite; then comes the brick or the marble. The substratum [bedrock] of our society is made of the material fitted by nature for it, and by experience we know that it is best, not only for the superior, but for the inferior race, that it should be so. It is, indeed, in conformity with the ordinance of the Creator. It is not for us to inquire into the wisdom of His ordinances, or to question them. For His own purposes, He has made one race to differ from another, as He has made "one star to differ from another star in glory." The great objects of humanity are best attained when there is conformity to His laws and decrees, in the formation of governments as well as in all things else. Our confederacy is founded upon principles in strict conformity with these laws. This stone which was rejected by the first builders "is become the chief of the corner" the real "corner-stone" in our new edifice. I have been asked, what of the future? It has been apprehended by some that we would have arrayed against us the civilized world. I care not who or how many they may be against us, when we stand upon the eternal principles of truth, if we are true to ourselves and the principles for which we contend, we are obliged to, and must triumph.

Thousands of people who begin to understand these truths are not yet completely out of the shell; they do not see them in their length and breadth. We hear much of the civilization and Christianization of the barbarous tribes of Africa. In my judgment, those ends will never be attained, but by first teaching them the lesson taught to Adam, that "in the sweat of his brow he should eat his bread," and teaching them to work, and feed, and clothe themselves.

But to pass on: Some have propounded the inquiry whether it is practicable for us to go on with the confederacy without further accessions? Have we the means and ability to maintain nationality among the powers of the earth? On this point I would barely say, that as anxiously as we all have been, and are, for the border States, with institutions similar to ours, to join us, still we are abundantly able to maintain our position, even if they should ultimately make up their minds not to cast their destiny with us. That they ultimately will join us be compelled to do it is my confident belief; but we can get on very well without them, even if they should not.

We have all the essential elements of a high national career. The idea has been given out at the North, and even in the border States, that we are too small and too weak to maintain a separate nationality. This is a great mistake. In extent of territory we embrace five hundred and sixty-four thousand square miles and upward. This is upward of two hundred thousand square miles more than was included within the limits of the original thirteen States. It is an area of country more than double the territory of France or the Austrian empire. France, in round numbers, has but two hundred and twelve thousand square miles. Austria, in round numbers, has two hundred and forty-eight thousand square miles. Ours is greater than both combined. It is greater than all France, Spain, Portugal, and Great Britain, including England, Ireland, and Scotland, together. In population we have upward of five millions, according to the census of 1860; this includes white and black. The entire population, including white and black, of the original thirteen States, was less than four millions in 1790, and still less in 76, when the independence of our fathers was achieved. If they, with a less population, dared maintain their independence against the greatest power on earth, shall we have any apprehension of maintaining ours now?

In point of material wealth and resources, we are greatly in advance of them. The taxable property of the Confederate States cannot be less than twenty-two hundred millions of dollars! This, I think I venture but little in saying, may be considered as five times more than the colonies possessed at the time they achieved their independence. Georgia, alone, possessed last year, according to the report of our comptroller-general, six hundred and seventy-two millions of taxable property. The debts of the seven confederate States sum up in the aggregate less than eighteen millions, while the existing debts of the other of the late United States sum up in the aggregate the enormous amount of one hundred and seventy-four millions of dollars. This is without taking into account the heavy city debts, corporation debts, and railroad debts, which press, and will continue to press, as a heavy incubus upon the resources of those States. These debts, added to others, make a sum total not much under five hundred millions of dollars. With such an area of territory as we have—with such an amount of population—with a climate and soil unsurpassed by any on the face of the earth—with such resources already at our command—with productions which control the commerce of the world—who can entertain any apprehensions as to our ability to succeed, whether others join us or not?

It is true, I believe I state but the common sentiment, when I declare my earnest desire that the border States should join us. The differences of opinion that existed among us anterior to secession, related more to the policy in securing that result by co-operation than from any difference upon the ultimate security we all looked to in common.

These differences of opinion were more in reference to policy than principle, and as Mr. Jefferson said in his inaugural, in 1801, after the heated contest preceding his election, that there might be differences of opinion without differences on principle, and that all, to some extent, had been Federalists and all Republicans; so it may now be said of us, that whatever differences of opinion as to the best policy in having a co-operation with our border sister slave States, if the worst came to the worst, that as we were all co-operationists, we are now all for independence, whether they come or not.

In this connection I take this occasion to state, that I was not without grave and serious apprehensions, that if the worst came to the worst, and cutting loose from the old government should be the only remedy for our safety and security, it would be attended with much more serious ills than it has been as yet. Thus far we have seen none of those incidents which usually attend revolutions. No such material as such convulsions usually throw up has been seen. Wisdom, prudence, and patriotism, have marked every step of our progress thus far. This augurs [portends] well for the future, and it is a matter of sincere gratification to me, that I am enabled to make the declaration. Of the men I met in the Congress at Montgomery, I may be pardoned for saying this, an abler, wiser, a more conservative, deliberate, determined, resolute, and patriotic body of men, I never met in my life. Their works speak for them; the provisional government speaks for them; the constitution of the permanent government will be a lasting monument of their worth, merit, and statesmanship.

But to return to the question of the future. What is to be the result of this revolution? Will every thing, commenced so well, continue as it has begun? In reply to this anxious inquiry, I can only say it all depends upon ourselves. A young man starting out in life on his majority, with health, talent, and ability, under a favoring Providence, may be said to be the architect of his own fortunes. His destinies are in his own hands. He may make for himself a name, of honor or dishonor, according to his own acts. If he plants himself upon truth, integrity, honor and uprightness, with industry, patience and energy, he cannot fail of success. So it is with us. We are a young republic, just entering upon the arena of nations; we will be the architects of our own fortunes. Our destiny, under Providence, is in our own hands. With wisdom, prudence, and statesmanship on the part of our public men, and intelligence, virtue and patriotism on the part of the people, success, to the full measures of our most sanguine hopes, may be looked for. But if unwise counsels prevail if we become divided if schisms arise if dissentions spring up if factions are engendered if party spirit, nourished by unholy personal ambition shall rear its hydra [a nine-headed monster of Greek myth] head, I have no good to prophesy for you. Without intelligence, virtue, integrity, and patriotism on the part of the people, no republic or representative government can be durable or stable.

We have intelligence, and virtue, and patriotism. All that is required is to cultivate and perpetuate these. Intelligence will not do without virtue. France was a nation of philosophers. These philosophers become Jacobins. They lacked that virtue, that devotion to moral principle, and that patriotism which is essential to good government Organized upon principles of perfect justice and right-seeking amity and friendship with all other powers—I see no obstacle in the way of our upward and onward progress. Our growth, by accessions from other States, will depend greatly upon whether we present to the world, as I trust we shall, a better government than that to which neighboring States belong. If we do this, North Carolina, Tennessee, and Arkansas cannot hesitate long; neither can Virginia, Kentucky, and Missouri. They will necessarily gravitate to us by an imperious law. We made ample provision in our constitution for the admission of other States; it is more guarded, and wisely so, I think, than the old constitution on the same subject, but not too guarded to receive them as fast as it may be proper. Looking to the distant future, and, perhaps, not very far distant either, it is not beyond the range of possibility, and even probability, that all the great States of the north-west will gravitate this way, as well as Tennessee, Kentucky, Missouri, Arkansas, etc. Should they do so, our doors are wide enough to receive them, but not until they are ready to assimilate with us in principle.

The process of disintegration in the old Union may be expected to go on with almost absolute certainty if we pursue the right course. We are now the nucleus of a growing power which, if we are true to ourselves, our destiny, and high mission, will become the controlling power on this continent. To what extent accessions will go on in the process of time, or where it will end, the future will determine. So far as it concerns States of the old Union, this process will be upon no such principles of reconstruction as now spoken of, but upon reorganization and new assimilation. Such are some of the glimpses of the future as I catch them.

...As to whether we shall have war with our late confederates, or whether all matters of differences between us shall be amicably settled, I can only say that the prospect for a peaceful adjustment is better, so far as I am informed, than it has been. The prospect of war is, at least, not so threatening as it has been. The idea of coercion, shadowed forth in President Lincoln's inaugural, seems not to be followed up thus far so vigorously as was expected. Fort Sumter, it is believed, will soon be evacuated. What course will be pursued toward Fort Pickens, and the other forts on the gulf, is not so well understood. It is to be greatly desired that all of them should be surrendered. Our object is peace, not only with the North, but with the world. All matters relating to the public property, public liabilities of the Union when we were members of it, we are ready and willing to adjust and settle upon the principles of right, equity, and good faith. War can be of no more benefit to the North than to us. Whether the intention of evacuating Fort Sumter is to be received as an evidence of a desire for a peaceful solution of our difficulties with the United States, or the result of necessity, I will not undertake to say. I would feign hope the former. Rumors are afloat, however, that it is the result of necessity. All I can say to you, therefore, on that point is, keep your armor bright and your powder dry.

The surest way to secure peace, is to show your ability to maintain your rights. The principles and position of the present administration of the United States the republican party present some puzzling questions. While it is a fixed principle with them never to allow the increase of a foot of slave territory, they seem to be equally determined not to part with an inch "of the accursed soil." Notwithstanding their clamor against the institution, they seemed to be equally opposed to getting more, or letting go what they have got. They were ready to fight on the accession of Texas, and are equally ready to fight now on her secession. Why is this? How can this strange paradox be accounted for? There seems to be but one rational solution and that is, notwithstanding their professions of humanity, they are disinclined to give up the benefits they derive from slave labor. Their philanthropy yields to their interest. The idea of enforcing the laws, has but one object, and that is a collection of the taxes, raised by slave labor to swell the fund necessary to meet their heavy appropriations. The spoils is what they are after though they come from the labor of the slave.

That as the admission of States by Congress under the constitution was an act of legislation, and in the nature of a contract or compact between the States admitted and the others admitting, why should not this contract or compact be regarded as of like character with all other civil contracts liable to be rescinded by mutual agreement of both parties? The seceding States have rescinded it on their part, they have resumed their sovereignty. Why cannot the whole question be settled, if the north desire peace, simply by the Congress, in both branches, with the concurrence of the President, giving their consent to the separation, and a recognition of our independence?

ABRAHAM LINCOLN, "ADDRESS DELIVERED AT THE DEDICATION OF THE CEMETERY AT GETTYSBURG" (GETTYSBURG ADDRESS) (1863)

This short but influential speech was given in Gettysburg, Pennsylvania, some four months after the Union armies had scored a decisive victory over Robert E. Lee's Confederate forces there.

WHY THIS READING?

Despite his modest assertion that "the world will little note, nor long remember what we say here," Lincoln's Gettysburg Address remains powerful to this day owing to the fact that he uses the occasion of this pivotal Union victory to explain the Civil War as a great test of whether American democracy, "dedicated to the proposition that all men are created equal...can long endure."

Questions to guide you as you read:

- Does Lincoln's address place him closer to William Lloyd Garrison or to Frederick
- Douglass in regard to the question of the Founders' view of slavery?
- What is the "new birth of freedom" for America to which Lincoln refers?

Four score and seven years ago our fathers brought forth on this continent a new nation, conceived in Liberty, and dedicated to the proposition that all men are created equal.

Now we are engaged in a great civil war, testing whether that nation, or any nation, so conceived and so dedicated, can long endure. We are met on a great battle-field of that war. We have come to dedicate a portion of that field, as a final resting place for those who here gave their lives that that nation might live. It is altogether fitting and proper that we should do this.

But, in a larger sense, we can not dedicate...we can not consecrate...we can not hallow this ground. The brave men, living and dead, who struggled here, have consecrated it, far above our poor power to add or detract. The world will little note, nor long remember what we say here, but it can never forget what they did here. It is for us the living, rather, to be dedicated here to the unfinished work which they who fought here have thus far so nobly advanced. It is rather for us to be here dedicated to the great task remaining before us—that from these honored dead we take increased devotion to that cause for which they gave the last full measure of devotion—that we here highly resolve that these dead shall not have died in vain—that this nation, under God, shall have a new birth of freedom—and that government: of the people, by the people, for the people, shall not perish from the earth.

Critiquing the Founders' vision: The progressives' argument that a genuine political democracy requires "economic democracy"

THEODORE ROOSEVELT, "TWO NOTEWORTHY BOOKS ON DEMOCRACY" (1914)

Theodore Roosevelt (1858–1919) was the 26th president of the United States (1901–1909). Prior to becoming president, he served as the Republican governor of New York.

His presidency was marked by his work as a "trust-buster," conservationist, and as the driving force behind the construction of the Panama Canal, which provided a more direct route between the Atlantic and Pacific Oceans. In 1912, Roosevelt reentered national politics when he ran again, unsuccessfully, for president—not as a Republican—but on a progressive ticket. Roosevelt was guided by the view that the president has the right and duty to enact what he deems necessary for the common good, as long as such enactments do not run counter to the clear intentions of the Constitution.

WHY THIS READING?

Roosevelt was a progressive. Progressivism is both an academic and a political movement that seeks to give people more direct power over the government and to give the government more power over the economy, thereby promoting "economic democracy." Roosevelt's efforts at political and economic reform were an attempt to deal with new problems created by industrialization. These efforts were guided by an answer to this chapter's question "What is American democracy?" that focuses more on the threat to liberty posed by "big business," rather than by "big government." Here he reviews new books by two of the progressive movement's foremost thinkers and publicists, Herbert Croly and Walter Lippmann. (See also the introduction to this chapter.)

Questions to guide you as you read:

- What arguments does Roosevelt offer to substantiate his opinion that the original Constitution was insufficiently democratic?
- What does Roosevelt offer as the best means to remedy what he deems are undemocratic elements in the U.S. Constitution? What political arguments today echo Roosevelt's vision?

There are books of which it is impossible to make an epitome [short summary], and which therefore it is impossible to review save in the way of calling attention to their excellence. Bryce's "American Commonwealth," Lowell's "Study of Representative Government in Europe," Thayer's "Study of Cavour," illustrate what is meant by this statement. Two new volumes, "Progressive Democracy," by Herbert Croly, and "Drift and Mastery," by Walter Lippmann, come in this category. No man who wishes seriously to study our present social, industrial, and political life with the view of guiding his thought and action so as to work for national betterment in the future can afford not to read these books through and through and to ponder and digest them. They worthily carry forward the argument contained in the authors' previous works—"The Promise of American Life," by Mr. Croly, and "A Preface to Politics," by Mr. Lippmann....

Mr. Croly explicitly points out that the position which American conservatism has elected to defend arouses on the part of its defenders a sincere and admirable loyalty of conviction. He recognizes that our traditional constitutional system has had a long and honorable career, and has contributed enormously to American political and social prosperity, giving stability, order, and security to a new political experiment undertaken in a new country under peculiarly hazardous and trying conditions. He also gives the wise warning that in order to attack the old system progressivism must not occupy a position...of mere destruction; that it must not represent wild-eyed and unbalanced seeking after an impossible millennium; and, furthermore, that it must be constructive rather than restorative. In his book he poses the two questions: (1) Whether any substitute is needed for the traditional system, and (2) whether the progressive creed offers what can fairly be considered such a working substitute. He answers both questions in the affirmative; but the value of his book, although it consists partly in the working out of the definite conclusions he reaches, consists even more in the spirit in which he has attempted to reach these conclusions.

Mr. Croly strikes at the root of the difficulties encountered by men who seriously strive for a juster [more just] economic and social life when he points out that the chief obstacles to securing the needed betterment are found in the legalism with which we have permitted our whole government to be affected, and in the extreme difficulty of amending the Constitution. As for the latter point, objection to an easier method of amending the Constitution can be reasonably advanced only by those who sincerely and frankly disbelieve in the fitness of the people for self-government. Government under a Constitution which in actual practice can be amended only on the terms which formerly permitted the Polish Parliament to legislate, and under a system of court procedure which makes the courts the ultimate irresponsible interpreters of the Constitution, and therefore ultimately the irresponsible makers of the law under the Constitution—such government really represents a system as emphatically undemocratic as government by a hereditary aristocracy. As Mr. Croly says, what is needed is not to increase the power of Congress at the expense of the judiciary, or to conserve the power of the judiciary at the expense of Congress or of the Executive, but to increase popular control over all the organs of government; and this can be accomplished only by the increase of direct popular power over the Constitution.

No less admirable is Mr. Croly's showing of the damage done to justice and to the whole democratic ideal by the saturation of our government with legalism.[13] As he points out, the final outcome of this effort was to make the paralyzing of administration by law an everyday spectacle. Under such conditions the ship of state merely drifted round and round. In practice the public welfare was sedulously [constantly] sacrificed to this theory of government by litigation [lawsuits]. The law continually prevented the correction of abuses and continually shielded officials who had gone wrong, but it never helped to make things go right. Corruption increased and special privilege was fostered. In practice the equal protection of the laws meant very unequal opportunity to bring lawsuits, and government by law was turned into government by corporations and political bosses. This continued until observers of vision finally became convinced that democracy and legalism were incompatible....

The adoption of direct government may in the end accomplish most of its purposes by reinvigorating representative government; and not the least interesting part of Mr. Croly's book is a study of the method proposed in Oregon for achieving this result. Mr. Croly emphatically believes in nationalizing our democracy, but this does not in the least mean mere centralization of power.... It is eminently desirable that we should keep in State and in city vigorous forms of local self-government. What is meant by the nationalization of the democratic method is the giving to the whole people themselves the power to do those things that are essential in the interest of the whole people....

Mr. Lippmann sees clearly, as does Mr. Croly, that democracy cannot possibly be achieved save among a people fit for democracy. There can be no real political democracy unless there is something approaching an economic democracy. A democracy must consist of men who are intellectually, morally, and materially fit to be their own masters. There can be neither political nor industrial democracy unless people are reasonably well-to-do, and also reasonably able to achieve the difficult task of self-mastery. As Mr. Lippmann says, the first item in any rational program for a democratic State must be the insistence on a reasonably high minimum standard of life, and therefore of pay, for the average worker.

It is not possible even for reformers of lofty vision and fine and sane judgment to treat of everything. Neither of these two books dwells sufficiently upon, although both of them hint at, certain vital facts which are connected with a further fundamental fact, that there must be ample prosperity

13. Here, "legalism" refers to a strict interpretation of or adherence to a law or code, with no attention to the potential political consequences.

in the nation. Public welfare depends upon general public prosperity, and the reformer whose reforms interfere with the general prosperity will accomplish little.

We cannot pay for what the highest type of democracy demands unless there is a great abundance of prosperity. A business that does not make money necessarily pays bad wages and renders poor service. Merely to change the ownership of the business without making it yield increased profits will achieve nothing. In practice this means that when the nation suffers from hard times. Wage-workers will concern themselves, and must concern themselves, primarily with a return to good times, and not with any plan for securing social and industrial justice. If women cannot get any work, and nevertheless have to live, they will be far more concerned with seeing a factory opened in which they can work at night or work twelve hours every day than they are concerned with the abolition of night work or the limitation of hours of labor. Exactly the same is true of men. In the recent election in Pennsylvania the majority of the miners and wage-workers generally voted for the Republican machine, although this Republican machine had just defeated a workmen's compensation act, a child-labor law, a minimum wage for women law, and various other bits of very desirable labor legislation. The attitude of the wage-workers was perfectly simple. They wished employment. They wished a chance to get a job. They believed that they had more chance if the candidates of the Republican machine were elected than they would otherwise have. Personally I very strongly believe that they were in error; but it was their belief that counted. The average voter usually sees what he is voting about in very simple form. He does not regard the political picture as an etching and follow out the delicate tracery. He treats it as a circus poster, in which the colors are in very vivid contrast and are laid on with a broad brush. When the average man feels the pinch of poverty, the only things he sees in the political picture are the broad, vivid colors which in his mind deal with that particular matter. He wishes to have his material condition improved at the present time or in the immediate future; and for the moment questions of ultimate betterment, and especially of moral betterment, sink into abeyance. This attitude is in no way peculiar to the laboring man or the farmer. It is just as evident in the big business man and in his college-bred son, and in the wealthy clubs of which these two make up most of the membership.

Finally, it is imperative to count the cost of all reforms, and therefore to remember that only a wealthy state can spend money sufficient to embody the reform into law. There is no point in having prosperity unless there can be an equitable [fair] division of prosperity. But there can be no equitable division of prosperity until the prosperity is there to divide. All reformers with any wisdom will keep this fact steadily in mind, and will realize that it is their duty in all legislation to work for the general prosperity of the community; and this in spite of the further fact that no good comes from the performance of this first duty unless some system of equity and justice is built upon the prosperity thus secured.

FRANKLIN D. ROOSEVELT, "COMMONWEALTH CLUB CAMPAIGN SPEECH" (1932)

Franklin Roosevelt was the 32nd president of the United States. Prior to becoming president, Roosevelt served as governor of New York. He was a fifth cousin to Theodore Roosevelt, but, unlike Theodore, a Republican, Franklin was a Democrat. He was elected to an unprecedented four presidential terms (1933–1945) over a period that included the Great Depression and World War II. (Subsequently, the 22nd Amendment, ratified in 1951, would limit presidents to two terms.) Early in the first year of his fourth term (April 1945), Roosevelt died. He was succeeded in office by then-Vice President Harry Truman.

WHY THIS READING?

In this address to business leaders, Roosevelt discusses the changing face of the American economic system. Specifically, he notes a growing concentration of property ownership in ever-fewer hands and proposes that the federal government mitigate the effects of this greater concentration of wealth. He declares it time for "new terms of the old social contract." That is, what he terms "the old social contract,"—as stated in the Declaration of Independence—promises political democracy but not the economic democracy that is, for progressives, essential to full justice. (See also the introduction to this chapter.)

Questions to guide you as you read:

- What is the basis of Roosevelt's disagreement with Thomas Jefferson? How does their disagreement parallel arguments at play in American democracy today?
- What does Franklin Roosevelt believe were Theodore Roosevelt's strengths and weaknesses in addressing the challenges that arose with industrialization?

I count it a privilege to be invited to address the Commonwealth Club. It has stood in the life of this city and state, and it is perhaps accurate to add, the nation, as a group of citizen leaders interested in fundamental problems of government, and chiefly concerned with achievement of progress in government through non-partisan means. The privilege of addressing you, therefore, in the heat of a political campaign, is great. I want to respond to your courtesy in terms consistent with your policy.

I want to speak not of politics but of government. I want to speak not of parties, but of universal principles. They are not political, except in that larger sense in which a great American once expressed a definition of politics, that nothing in all of human life is foreign to the science of politics....

The issue of government has always been whether individual men and women will have to serve some system of government and economics, or whether a system of government and economics exists to serve individual men and women. This question has persistently dominated the discussion of government for many generations. On questions relating to these things men have differed, and for time immemorial it is probable that honest men will continue to differ.

The final word belongs to no man; yet we can still believe in change and in progress. Democracy, as a dear old friend of mine in India, Meredith Nicholson, has called it, is a quest, a never-ending seeking for better things, and in the seeking for these things and the striving for them, there are many roads to follow. But, if we map the course of these roads, we find that there are only two general directions.

When we look about us, we are likely to forget how hard people have worked to win the privilege of government. The growth of the national governments of Europe was a struggle for the development of a centralized force in the nation, strong enough to impose peace upon ruling barons. In many instances the victory of the central government, the creation of a strong central government, was a haven of refuge to the individual. The people preferred the master far away to the exploitation and cruelty of the smaller master near at hand.

But the creators of national government were perforce ruthless men. They were often cruel in their methods, but they did strive steadily toward something that society needed and very much wanted, a strong central state, able to keep the peace, to stamp out civil war, to put the unruly nobleman in his place, and to permit the bulk of individuals to live safely. The man of ruthless force had his place in developing a pioneer country, just as he did in fixing the power of the central government in the development of nations. Society paid him well for his services and its development. When the development among the nations of Europe, however, has been completed, ambition, and ruthlessness, having served its term, tended to overstep its mark.

There came a growing feeling that government was conducted for the benefit of a few who thrived unduly at the expense of all. The people sought a balancing—a limiting force. There came gradually, through town councils, trade guilds, national parliaments, by constitution and by popular participation and control, limitations on arbitrary power.

Another factor that tended to limit the power of those who ruled, was the rise of the ethical conception that a ruler bore a responsibility for the welfare of his subjects.

The American colonies were born in this struggle. The American Revolution was a turning point in it. After the revolution the struggle continued and shaped itself in the public life of the country. There were those who because they had seen the confusion which attended the years of war for American independence surrendered to the belief that popular government was essentially dangerous and essentially unworkable. They were honest people, my friends, and we cannot deny that their experience had warranted some measure of fear. The most brilliant, honest and able exponent of this point of view was Hamilton. He was too impatient of slow moving methods. Fundamentally he believed that the safety of the republic lay in the autocratic strength of its government, that the destiny of individuals was to serve that government, and that fundamentally a great and strong group of central institutions, guided by a small group of able and public spirited citizens could best direct all government.

But Mr. Jefferson, in the summer of 1776, after drafting the Declaration of Independence turned his mind to the same problem and took a different view. He did not deceive himself with outward forms. Government to him was a means to an end, not an end in itself; it might be either a refuge and a help or a threat and a danger, depending on the circumstances. We find him carefully analyzing the society for which he was to organize a government. "We have no paupers. The great mass of our population is of laborers, our rich who cannot live without labor, either manual or professional, being few and of moderate wealth. Most of the laboring class possess property, cultivate their own lands, have families and from the demand for their labor, are enabled to exact from the rich and the competent such prices as enable them to feed abundantly, clothe above mere decency, to labor moderately and raise their families."

These people, he considered, had two sets of rights, those of personal competency and those involved in acquiring and possessing property. By "personal competency" he meant the right of free thinking, freedom of forming and expressing opinions, and freedom of personal living each man according to his own lights. To insure the first set of rights, a government must so order its functions as not to interfere with the individual. But even Jefferson realized that the exercise of the property rights might so interfere with the rights of the individual that the government, without whose assistance the property rights could not exist, must intervene, not to destroy individualism but to protect it.

You are familiar with the great political duel which followed, and how Hamilton, and his friends, building towards a dominant centralized power were at length defeated in the great election of 1800, by Mr. Jefferson's party. Out of that duel came the two parties, Republican and Democratic, as we know them today.

So began, in American political life, the new day, the day of the individual against the system, the day in which individualism was made the great watchword of American life. The happiest of economic conditions made that day long and splendid. On the Western frontier, land was substantially free. No one, who did not shirk the task of earning a living, was entirely without opportunity to do so. Depressions could, and did, come and go; but they could not alter the fundamental fact that most of the people lived partly by selling their labor and partly by extracting their livelihood from the soil, so that starvation and dislocation were practically impossible. At the very worst there was always the possibility of climbing into a covered wagon and moving west where the untilled prairies afforded a haven for men to whom the East did not provide a place. So great were our natural resources that we could offer this relief not only to our own people, but to the distressed of all the world; we could invite immigration from Europe, and welcome it with open arms. Traditionally, when a depression came, a new section of land was opened in the West; and even our temporary misfortune served our manifest destiny.

It was the middle of the 19th century that a new force was released and a new dream created. The force was what is called the industrial revolution, the advance of steam and machinery and the rise of the forerunners of the modern industrial plant. The dream was the dream of an economic machine, able to raise the standard of living for everyone; to bring luxury within the reach of the humblest; to annihilate distance by steam power and later by electricity, and to release everyone from the drudgery of the heaviest manual toil. It was to be expected that this would necessarily affect government. Heretofore, government had merely been called upon to produce conditions within which people could live happily, labor peacefully, and rest secure. Now it was called upon to aid in the consummation of this new dream. There was, however, a shadow over the dream. To be made real, it required use of the talents of men of tremendous will, and tremendous ambition, since by no other force could the problems of financing and engineering and new developments be brought to a consummation [a satisfying conclusion].

So manifest [clear to see] were the advantages of the machine age, however, that the United States fearlessly, cheerfully, and, I think, rightly, accepted the bitter with the sweet. It was thought that no price was too high to pay for the advantages which we could draw from a finished industrial system. The history of the last half century is accordingly in large measure a history of a group of financial Titans, whose methods were not scrutinized with too much care, and who were honored in proportion as they produced the results, irrespective of the means they used. The financiers who pushed the railroads to the Pacific were always ruthless, we have them today. It has been estimated that the American investor paid for the American railway system more than three times over in the process; but despite that fact the net advantage was to the United States. As long as we had free land; as long as population was growing by leaps and bounds; as long as our industrial plants were insufficient to supply our needs, society chose to give the ambitious man free play and unlimited reward provided only that he produced the economic plant so much desired.

During this period of expansion, there was equal opportunity for all and the business of government was not to interfere but to assist in the development of industry. This was done at the request of businessmen themselves. The tariff was originally imposed for the purpose of fostering our infant industry, a phrase I think the older among you will remember as a political issue not so long ago. The railroads were subsidized, sometimes by grants of money, oftener by grants of land; some of the most valuable oil lands in the United States were granted to assist the financing of the railroad which pushed through the Southwest. A nascent [embryonic] merchant marine was assisted by grants of money, or by mail subsidies, so that our steam shipping might ply the seven seas. Some of my friends tell me that they do not want the Government in business. With this I agree; but I wonder whether they realize the implications of the past. For while it has been American doctrine that the government must not go into business in competition with private enterprises, still it has been traditional particularly in Republican administrations for business urgently to ask the government to put at private disposal all kinds of government assistance.

The same man who tells you that he does not want to see the government interfere in business—and he means it, and has plenty of good reasons for saying so—is the first to go to Washington and ask the government for a prohibitory tariff on his product. When things get just bad enough—as they did two years ago—he will go with equal speed to the United States government and ask for a loan; and the Reconstruction Finance Corporation is the outcome of it. Each group has sought protection from the government for its own special interest, without realizing that the function of government must be to favor no small group at the expense of its duty to protect the rights of personal freedom and of private property of all its citizens.

In retrospect we can now see that the turn of the tide came with the turn of the century. We were reaching our last frontier; there was no more free land and our industrial combinations had become great uncontrolled and irresponsible units of power within the state. Clear-sighted men saw with fear the danger that opportunity would no longer be equal; that the growing corporation, like the feudal baron of old, might threaten the economic freedom of individuals to earn a living. In that hour, our antitrust laws were born. The cry was raised against the great corporations. Theodore Roosevelt, the first great Republican progressive, fought a Presidential campaign on the issue of trust busting and talked freely about malefactors of great wealth. If the government had a policy it was rather to turn the clock back, to destroy the large combinations and to return to the time when every man owned his individual small business.

This was impossible; Theodore Roosevelt, abandoning the idea of trust busting, was forced to work out a difference between good trusts and bad trusts. The Supreme Court set forth the famous "rule of reason" by which it seems to have meant that a concentration of industrial power was permissible if the method by which it got its power, and the use it made of that power, was reasonable.

Woodrow Wilson, elected in 1912, saw the situation more clearly. Where Jefferson had feared the encroachment of political power on the lives of individuals, Wilson knew that the new power was financial. He saw, in the highly centralized economic system, the despot of the twentieth century, on whom great masses of individuals relied for their safety and their livelihood, and whose irresponsibility and greed (if it were not controlled) would reduce them to starvation and penury [poverty]. The concentration of financial power had not proceeded so far in 1912 as it has today; but it had grown far enough for Mr. Wilson to realize fully its implications. It is interesting, now, to read his speeches.

What is called "radical" today (and I have reason to know whereof I speak) is mild compared to the campaign of Mr. Wilson. "No man can deny," he said, "that the lines of endeavor have more and more narrowed and stiffened; no man who knows anything about the development of industry in this country can have failed to observe that the larger kinds of credit are more and more difficult to obtain unless you obtain them upon terms of uniting your efforts with those who already control the industry of the country, and nobody can fail to observe that every man who tries to set himself up in competition with any process of manufacture which has taken place under the control of large combinations of capital will presently find himself either squeezed out or obliged to sell and allow himself to be absorbed."

Had there been no World War—had Mr. Wilson been able to devote eight years to domestic instead of to international affairs—we might have had a wholly different situation at the present time. However, the then distant roar of European cannon, growing ever louder, forced him to abandon the study of this issue. The problem he saw so clearly is left with us as a legacy; and no one of us on either side of the political controversy can deny that it is a matter of grave concern to the government.

A glance at the situation today only too clearly indicates that equality of opportunity as we have known it no longer exists. Our industrial plant is built; the problem just now is whether under existing conditions it is not overbuilt. Our last frontier has long since been reached, and there is practically no more free land. More than half of our people do not live on the farms or on lands and cannot derive a living by cultivating their own property. There is no safety valve in the form of a Western prairie to which those thrown out of work by the Eastern economic machines can go for a new start. We are not able to invite the immigration from Europe to share our endless plenty. We are now providing a drab living for our own people.

Our system of constantly rising tariffs has at last reacted against us to the point of closing our Canadian frontier on the north, our European markets on the east, many of our Latin American markets to the south, and a goodly proportion of our Pacific markets on the west, through the retaliatory tariffs of those countries. It has forced many of our great industrial institutions who exported their surplus production to such countries, to establish plants in such countries within the tariff walls. This has resulted in the reduction of the operation of their American plants, and opportunity for employment.

Just as freedom to farm has ceased, so also the opportunity in business has narrowed. It still is true that men can start small enterprises, trusting to native shrewdness and ability to keep abreast of competitors; but area after area has been preempted altogether by the great corporations, and even in the fields which still have no great concerns, the small man starts with a handicap. The unfeeling statistics of the past three decades show that the independent business man is running a losing race. Perhaps he is forced to the wall; perhaps he cannot command credit; perhaps he is "squeezed out," in Mr. Wilson's words, by highly organized corporate competitors, as your corner grocery man can tell you.

Recently a careful study was made of the concentration of business in the United States. It showed that our economic life was dominated by some six hundred odd corporations who controlled two-thirds of American industry. Ten million small business men divided the other third. More striking still, it appeared that if the process of concentration goes on at the same rate, at the end of another century we shall have all American industry controlled by a dozen corporations, and run by perhaps a hundred men. Put plainly, we are steering a steady course toward economic oligarchy, if we are not there already.

Clearly, all this calls for a re-appraisal of values. A mere builder of more industrial plants, a creator of more railroad systems, and organizer of more corporations, is as likely to be a danger as a help. The day of the great promoter or the financial Titan, to whom we granted anything if only he would build, or develop, is over. Our task now is not discovery or exploitation of natural resources, or necessarily producing more goods. It is the soberer, less dramatic business of administering resources and plants already in hand, of seeking to reestablish foreign markets for our surplus production, of meeting the problem of under consumption, of adjusting production to consumption, of distributing wealth and products more equitably, of adapting existing economic organizations to the service of the people. The day of enlightened administration has come.

Just as in older times the central government was first a haven of refuge, and then a threat, so now in a closer economic system the central and ambitious financial unit is no longer a servant of national desire, but a danger. I would draw the parallel one step farther. We did not think because national government had become a threat in the 18th century that therefore we should abandon the principle of national government. Nor today should we abandon the principle of strong economic units called corporations, merely because their power is susceptible of easy abuse. In other times we dealt with the problem of an unduly ambitious central government by modifying it gradually into a constitutional democratic government. So today we are modifying and controlling our economic units.

As I see it, the task of government in its relation to business is to assist the development of an economic declaration of rights, an economic constitutional order. This is the common task of statesman and business man. It is the minimum requirement of a more permanently safe order of things.

Every man has a right to life; and this means that he has also a right to make a comfortable living. He may by sloth [a dislike of work] or crime decline to exercise that right; but it may not be denied him. We have no actual famine or death; our industrial and agricultural mechanism can produce enough and to spare. Our government formal and informal, political and economic, owes to every one an avenue to possess himself of a portion of that plenty sufficient for his needs, through his own work.

Every man has a right to his own property; which means a right to be assured, to the fullest extent attainable, in the safety of his savings. By no other means can men carry the burdens of those parts of life which, in the nature of things afford no chance of labor; childhood, sickness, old age. In all thought of property, this right is paramount; all other property rights must yield to it. If, in accord with this principle, we must restrict the operations of the speculator, the manipulator, even the financier, I believe we must accept the restriction as needful, not to hamper [restrict] individualism but to protect it.

These two requirements must be satisfied, in the main, by the individuals who claim and hold control of the great industrial and financial combinations which dominate so large a part of our industrial life. They have undertaken to be, not business men, but princes—princes of property. I am not prepared to say that the system which produces them is wrong. I am very clear that they must fearlessly and competently assume the responsibility which goes with the power. So many enlightened business men know this that the statement would be little more that a platitude, were it not for an added implication.

This implication is, briefly, that the responsible heads of finance and industry instead of acting each for himself, must work together to achieve the common end. They must, where necessary, sacrifice this or that private advantage; and in reciprocal self-denial must seek a general advantage. It is here that formal government—political government, if you choose, comes in. Whenever in the pursuit of this objective the lone wolf, the unethical competitor, the reckless promoter, the Ishmael or Insull[14] whose hand is against every man's, declines to join in achieving an end recognized as being for the public welfare, and threatens to drag the industry back to a state of anarchy, the government may properly be asked to apply restraint.[15] Likewise, should the group ever use its collective power contrary to public welfare, the government must be swift to enter and protect the public interest.

The government should assume the function of economic regulation only as a last resort, to be tried only when private initiative, inspired by high responsibility, with such assistance and balance as government can give, has finally failed. As yet there has been no final failure, because there has been no attempt, and I decline to assume that this nation is unable to meet the situation.

The final term of the high contract was for liberty and the pursuit of happiness. We have learnt a great deal of both in the past century. We know that individual liberty and individual happiness mean nothing unless both are ordered in the sense that one man's meat is not another man's poison. We know that the old "rights of personal competency"—the right to read, to think, to speak to choose and live a mode of life, must be respected at all hazards. We know that liberty to do anything which deprives others of those elemental rights is outside the protection of any compact; and that government in this regard is the maintenance of a balance, within which every individual may have a place if he will take it; in which every individual may find safety if he wishes it; in which every individual may attain such power as his ability permits, consistent with his assuming the accompanying responsibility....

Faith in America, faith in our tradition of personal responsibility, faith in our institutions, faith in ourselves demands that we recognize the new terms of the old social contract. We shall fulfill them, as we fulfilled the obligation of the apparent Utopia which Jefferson imagined for us in 1776, and which Jefferson, Roosevelt and Wilson sought to bring to realization. We must do so, lest a rising tide of misery engendered by our common failure, engulf us all. But failure is not an American habit; and in the strength of great hope we must all shoulder our common load.

14. "Ishmael" is apparently a reference to Genesis, chapters 16, 17, and 21, which tell the story of Ishmael's "mocking" of his half-brother Isaac. For this act, their father Abraham sent Ishmael away.

15. Samuel Insull (1859–1938) was a utilities magnate who was indicted for larceny, embezzlement, and mail fraud during the Great Depression. Though never convicted, he was publicly regarded as partly to blame for the deepening of the Depression.

FRANKLIN D. ROOSEVELT, "MESSAGE ON THE STATE OF THE UNION" (THE ECONOMIC BILL OF RIGHTS) (1944)

In his 1944 State of the Union Address, President Franklin D. Roosevelt asks Congress to work toward the implementation of what he terms a "second" Bill of Rights.

WHY THIS READING?

FDR's "Economic Bill of Rights" addresses the question "What is American democracy?" by proposing to empower the national government to secure certain economic goods deemed necessary if our "inalienable political rights" are to "assure us equality in the pursuit of happiness." The inalienable right to the pursuit of happiness is one of the "self-evident truths" listed in the Declaration of Independence.

Although Roosevelt's plan for an Economic Bill of Rights was never adopted by Congress, his address was influential in forming the provisions for economic equality in the United Nation's 1948 Universal Declaration of Human Rights. Articles 22 and 23 of the U.N. Declaration state: "Everyone, as a member of society, has the right to social security and is entitled to realization, through national effort and international co-operation and in accordance with the organization and resources of each State, of the economic, social and cultural rights indispensable for his dignity and the free development of his personality. Everyone has the right to work, to free choice of employment, to just and favourable conditions of work and to protection against unemployment."

Questions to guide you as you read:

- Does Roosevelt's call to expand the powers of the national government conflict with Madison's presentation of the constitutional limits on power presented in *Federalist 39*? If so, why? If not, why not?
- How does Franklin Roosevelt's version of economic democracy differ from that of Theodore Roosevelt?

...It is our duty now to begin to lay the plans and determine the strategy for the winning of a lasting peace and the establishment of an American standard of living higher than ever before known. We cannot be content, no matter how high that general standard of living may be, if some fraction of our people, whether it be one-third or one-fifth or one-tenth, is ill-fed, ill-clothed, ill-housed, and insecure.

This Republic had its beginning, and grew to its present strength, under the protection of certain inalienable political rights—among them the right of free speech, free press, free worship, trial by jury, freedom from unreasonable searches and seizures. They were our rights to life and liberty.

As our Nation has grown in size and stature, however—as our industrial economy expanded—these political rights proved inadequate to assure us equality in the pursuit of happiness.

We have come to a clear realization of the fact that true individual freedom cannot exist without economic security and independence. "Necessitous [needy] men are not free men." People who are hungry and out of a job are the stuff of which dictatorships are made.

In our day these economic truths have become accepted as self-evident. We have accepted, so to speak, a second Bill of Rights under which a new basis of security and prosperity can be established for all—regardless of station, race, or creed.

Among these are:

The right to a useful and remunerative [paying] job in the industries or shops or farms or mines of the Nation;

The right to earn enough to provide adequate food and clothing and recreation;

The right of every farmer to raise and sell his products at a return which will give him and his family a decent living;

The right of every businessman, large and small, to trade in an atmosphere of freedom from unfair competition and domination by monopolies at home or abroad;

The right of every family to a decent home;

The right to adequate medical care and the opportunity to achieve and enjoy good health;

The right to adequate protection from the economic fears of old age, sickness, accident, and unemployment;

The right to a good education.

All of these rights spell security.... And after this war is won we must be prepared to move forward, in the implementation of these rights, to new goals of human happiness and well-being....

America's own rightful place in the world depends in large part upon how fully these and similar rights have been carried into practice for our citizens. For unless there is security here at home there cannot be lasting peace in the world....

I ask the Congress to explore the means for implementing this economic bill of rights—for it is definitely the responsibility of the Congress so to do. Many of these problems are already before committees of the Congress in the form of proposed legislation. I shall from time to time communicate with the Congress with respect to these and further proposals. In the event that no adequate program of progress is evolved, I am certain that the Nation will be conscious of the fact.

Our fighting men abroad—and their families at home—expect such a program and have the right to insist upon it. It is to their demands that this Government should pay heed rather than to the whining demands of selfish pressure groups who seek to feather their nests while young Americans are dying.

The foreign policy that we have been following—the policy that guided us at Moscow, Cairo, and Teheran—is based on the common sense principle which was best expressed by Benjamin Franklin on July 4, 1776: "We must all hang together, or assuredly we shall all hang separately."

I have often said that there are no two fronts for America in this war. There is only one front. There is one line of unity which extends from the hearts of the people at home to the men of our attacking forces in our farthest outposts. When we speak of our total effort, we speak of the factory and the field, and the mine as well as of the battleground—we speak of the soldier and the civilian, the citizen and his Government.

Each and every one of us has a solemn obligation under God to serve this Nation in its most critical hour—to keep this Nation great—to make this Nation greater in a better world.

LYNDON B. JOHNSON, "THE GREAT SOCIETY" (1964)

Lyndon Johnson (1908–1973), a Democrat, served as the 36th president of the United States from 1963 to 1969. He was vice president from 1961 to 1963, becoming president after John F. Kennedy was assassinated. In 1964, he was elected to a full term as president by the largest popular margin in history. He decided not to seek reelection in 1968. Prior to becoming vice president, he served as both a Texas member of the U.S. House of Representatives and, later, of the U.S. Senate, where he attained the rank of Senate majority leader.

WHY THIS READING?

During his tenure in office, Johnson presided over the buildup of American forces in the Vietnam War, pushed forward civil-rights legislation, and ushered in the Great Society programs. The Great Society agenda centered on a "War on Poverty" and consisted of numerous social welfare programs offered to the economically disadvantaged. These programs included assistance with health care, urban development, housing, and food stamps. In this speech, given at the University of Michigan on May 22, 1964, Johnson introduces his justification for the Great Society programs.

Questions to guide you as you read:

- Is the "Great Society" advanced by Johnson different from or similar to the "soft despotism" described by Tocqueville? Why? What would Johnson's rejoinder to Tocqueville be?
- Is the increase in national power that Johnson deems necessary to end poverty consistent with Madison's description in *Federalist 39* of the constitutional limits on the national government? If so, why? If not, why not?

President Hatcher, Governor Romney, Senators McNamara and Hart, Congressmen Meader and Staebler, and other members of the fine Michigan delegation, members of the graduating class, my fellow Americans:

It is a great pleasure to be here today. This university has been coeducational since 1870, but I do not believe it was on the basis of your accomplishments that a Detroit high school girl said (and I quote), "In choosing a college, you first have to decide whether you want a coeducational school or an educational school." Well, we can find both here at Michigan, although perhaps at different hours. I came out here today very anxious to meet the Michigan student whose father told a friend of mine that his son's education had been a real value. It stopped his mother from bragging about him.

I have come today from the turmoil of your capital to the tranquility of your campus to speak about the future of your country. The purpose of protecting the life of our Nation and preserving the liberty of our citizens is to pursue the happiness of our people. Our success in that pursuit is the test of our success as a Nation.

For a century we labored to settle and to subdue a continent. For half a century we called upon unbounded invention and untiring industry to create an order of plenty for all of our people. The challenge of the next half century is whether we have the wisdom to use that wealth to enrich and elevate our national life, and to advance the quality of our American civilization.

Your imagination and your initiative and your indignation will determine whether we build a society where progress is the servant of our needs, or a society where old values and new visions are buried under unbridled growth. For in your time we have the opportunity to move not only toward the rich society and the powerful society, but upward to the Great Society.

The Great Society rests on abundance and liberty for all. It demands an end to poverty and racial injustice, to which we are totally committed in our time. But that is just the beginning.

The Great Society is a place where every child can find knowledge to enrich his mind and to enlarge his talents. It is a place where leisure is a welcome chance to build and reflect, not a feared cause of boredom and restlessness. It is a place where the city of man serves not only the needs of the body and the demands of commerce but the desire for beauty and the hunger for community. It is a place where man can renew contact with nature. It is a place which honors creation for its own sake and for what is adds to the understanding of the race. It is a place where men are more concerned with the quality of their goals than the quantity of their goods.

But most of all, the Great Society is not a safe harbor, a resting place, a final objective, a finished work. It is a challenge constantly renewed, beckoning us toward a destiny where the meaning of our lives matches the marvelous products of our labor.

So I want to talk to you today about three places where we begin to build the Great Society—in our cities, in our countryside, and in our classrooms.

Many of you will live to see the day, perhaps 50 years from now, when there will be 400 million Americans—four-fifths of them in urban areas. In the remainder of this century urban population will double, city land will double, and we will have to build homes and highways and facilities equal to all those built since this country was first settled. So in the next 40 years we must re-build the entire urban United States.

Aristotle said: "Men come together in cities in order to live, but they remain together in order to live the good life." It is harder and harder to live the good life in American cities today. The catalog of ills is long: there is the decay of the centers and the despoiling of the suburbs. There is not enough housing for our people or transportation for our traffic. Open land is vanishing and old landmarks are violated. Worst of all expansion is eroding these precious and time honored values of community with neighbors and communion with nature. The loss of these values breeds loneliness and boredom and indifference.

And our society will never be great until our cities are great. Today the frontier of imagination and innovation is inside those cities and not beyond their borders. New experiments are already going on. It will be the task of your generation to make the American city a place where future generations will come, not only to live, but to live the good life. And I understand that if I stayed here tonight I would see that Michigan students are really doing their best to live the good life.

This is the place where the Peace Corps was started.

It is inspiring to see how all of you, while you are in this country, are trying so hard to live at the level of the people.

A second place where we begin to build the Great Society is in our countryside. We have always prided ourselves on being not only America the strong and America the free, but America the beautiful. Today that beauty is in danger. The water we drink, the food we eat, the very air that we breathe, are threatened with pollution. Our parks are overcrowded, our seashores overburdened. Green fields and dense forests are disappearing.

A few years ago we were greatly concerned about the "Ugly American." Today we must act to prevent an ugly America.

For once the battle is lost, once our natural splendor is destroyed, it can never be recaptured. And once man can no longer walk with beauty or wonder at nature his spirit will wither and his sustenance be wasted.

A third place to build the Great Society is in the classrooms of America. There your children's lives will be shaped. Our society will not be great until every young mind is set free to scan the farthest reaches of thought and imagination. We are still far from that goal. Today, 8 million adult Americans, more than the entire population of Michigan, have not finished 5 years of school. Nearly 20 million have not finished 8 years of school. Nearly 54 million—more than one quarter of all America—have not even finished high school.

Each year more than 100,000 high school graduates, with proved ability, do not enter college because they cannot afford it. And if we cannot educate today's youth, what will we do in 1970 when elementary school enrollment will be 5 million greater than 1960? And high school enrollment will rise by 5 million. And college enrollment will increase by more than 3 million.

In many places, classrooms are overcrowded and curricula are outdated. Most of our qualified teachers are underpaid and many of our paid teachers are unqualified. So we must give every child a place to sit and a teacher to learn from. Poverty must not be a bar to learning, and learning must offer an escape from poverty.

But more classrooms and more teachers are not enough. We must seek an educational system which grows in excellence as it grows in size. This means better training for our teachers. It means preparing youth to enjoy their hours of leisure as well as their hours of labor. It means exploring new techniques of teaching, to find new ways to stimulate the love of learning and the capacity for creation.

These are three of the central issues of the Great Society. While our Government has many programs directed at those issues, I do not pretend that we have the full answer to those problems. But I do promise this: We are going to assemble the best thought and the broadest knowledge from all over the world to find those answers for America.

I intend to establish working groups to prepare a series of White House conferences and meetings—on the cities, on natural beauty, on the quality of education, and on other emerging challenges. And from these meetings and from this inspiration and from these studies we will begin to set our course toward the Great Society.

The solution to these problems does not rest on a massive program in Washington, nor can it rely solely on the strained resources of local authority. They require us to create new concepts of cooperation, a creative federalism, between the National Capital and the leaders of local communities.

Woodrow Wilson once wrote: "Every man sent out from his university should be a man of his Nation as well as a man of his time."

Within your lifetime powerful forces, already loosed, will take us toward a way of life beyond the realm of our experience, almost beyond the bounds of our imagination.

For better or for worse, your generation has been appointed by history to deal with those problems and to lead America toward a new age. You have the chance never before afforded to any people in any age. You can help build a society where the demands of morality, and the needs of the spirit, can be realized in the life of the Nation.

So, will you join in the battle to give every citizen the full equality which God enjoins and the law requires, whatever his belief, or race, or the color of his skin?

Will you join in the battle to give every citizen an escape from the crushing weight of poverty?

Will you join in the battle to make it possible for all nations to live in enduring peace—as neighbors and not as mortal enemies?

Will you join in the battle to build the Great Society, to prove that our material progress is only the foundation on which we will build a richer life of mind and spirit?

There are those timid souls that say this battle cannot be won; that we are condemned to a soulless wealth. I do not agree. We have the power to shape the civilization that we want. But we need your will and your labor and your hearts, if we are to build that kind of society.

Those who came to this land sought to build more than just a new country. They sought a new world. So I have come here today to your campus to say that you can make their vision our reality. So let us from this moment begin our work so that in the future men will look back and say: It was then, after a long and weary way, that man turned the exploits of his genius to the full enrichment of his life.

Thank you. Good-bye.

The rise of "civil-liberties democracy"

Are courts, or the people and their representatives, the best guardians of liberty?

JUSTICE ROBERT JACKSON, OPINION OF THE COURT IN *WEST VIRGINIA STATE BOARD OF EDUCATION V. BARNETTE* (1943)

This case addresses a 1940 law passed by the West Virginia state legislature. The law required students to study the Founding documents and American history in order to support the "teaching, fostering, and perpetuating [of] the ideals, principles and spirit of Americanism, and increasing the knowledge of the organization and machinery of government." As a result, the state Board of Education required students to salute the American flag at the beginning of each school day. A number of Jehovah's Witness families brought suit against this requirement, arguing that it violated their First Amendment guarantee of the free exercise of their religion. According to their faith, they argued, saluting the American flag was tantamount to worshiping "graven images." The Court decided in their favor.

WHY THIS READING?

Note the difference between "civil rights" and "civil liberties." Civil liberties generally refer to freedoms guaranteed under the Constitution, for example, freedom of speech, press, the right to a fair trial, etc. (see Bill of Rights, below). Civil rights center on the right not to suffer unequal treatment based on certain traits (race, sex, etc.) in activities such as employment.

"Civil-liberties democracy" is the name given by this textbook to the profound change that occurred in the course taken by American democracy as a result of the Supreme Court's introduction of the idea of civil liberties to constitutional law.

The essence of this change is contained in Justice Robert Jackson's opinion for the Court in *West Virginia State Board of Education v. Barnette* (1943). Jackson's pronouncement that the provisions of the Bill of Rights are both "beyond the reach of majorities" and "legal principles to be applied by the courts" may be said to put the High Court effectively in the business of governing through the exclusive right to interpret the Bill of Rights. According to *Barnette*, only the Court may define of what the freedoms of the Bill of Rights consist. The people and its elected and removable representatives are either prohibited from doing so, or, at the least, are subordinated to the Court in doing so. As you read earlier in this chapter, prohibiting the people from defining what their liberties are is a dramatically different idea of democracy than what had preceded it. It constitutes, some argue, a movement in the direction of "judicial preeminence," not merely in relation to the legislative and executive branches of the national government, but also in relation to the people. To the extent that this transformation moves American democracy in the direction of rule by the judiciary, rather than government by the people, it is considered by some a "regime change"—that is, a fundamental change in the form and purposes of American government.

Questions to guide you as you read:

- Is Justice Jackson's depiction of the Constitution in Barnette consistent with Lincoln's notion of American democracy as government "of the people, by the people, [and] for the people"? If not, why not?
- According to Jackson, which branch of the federal government is responsible for defining and protecting civil liberties? Based on your earlier reading, which branch of the government would you say the Founders thought would define liberty?
- Since the *Barnette* case, has the Supreme Court become more or less involved in defining the people's liberties?

...The very purpose of a Bill of Rights was to withdraw certain subjects from the vicissitudes [sudden changes] of political controversy, to place them beyond the reach of majorities and officials and to establish them as legal principles to be applied by the courts. One's right to life, liberty, and property, to free speech, a free press, freedom of worship and assembly, and other fundamental rights may not be submitted to vote; they depend on the outcome of no elections....

What is the proper balance between individual liberty and national security?

U.S. SENATOR RUSS FEINGOLD, "ON THE ANTI-TERRORISM BILL" (2001)

On the morning of September 11, 2001, Islamic extremists hijacked four commercial airliners, crashing two of them into the World Trade Center in New York City and another into the Pentagon in Arlington, Virginia. On the fourth hijacked plane, a group of passengers overcame their captors and rushed the cockpit in an effort to prevent the plane from being used to attack yet another target (believed to have been either Congress or the White House). In the ensuing struggle, the plane crashed in a field in Shanksville, Pennsylvania, killing all aboard. The attacks that day took nearly 3,000 American lives. In the weeks that followed, the legislative and executive branches cooperated in crafting the "USA Patriot Act," which aimed to combat terrorism.

WHY THIS READING?

The Patriot Act gives federal officials increased power to intercept communications, both for law-enforcement and foreign-intelligence-gathering purposes. The Act also seeks to close America's borders to foreign terrorists, as well as to capture and remove those currently found to be within the country's borders. The Act was signed by President George W. Bush on October 26, 2001. Critics of the law, such as U.S. Senator Russ Feingold (D-WI), held that it violates civil liberties in the name of national security. Immediately following, then-Attorney General John Ashcroft offers the counterpoint to Feingold's thesis.

Questions to guide you as you read:

- What does Senator Feingold say is his standard for judging whether the demands of national security and civil liberties have been balanced properly? How might his standard apply to current concerns over, for example, the regulation of the Internet?
- What historical examples does Feingold present of instances in which, in his view, concerns with national security have endangered civil liberties?

Mr. President [of the U.S. Senate], I have asked for this time to speak about the anti-terrorism bill before us, H.R. 3162. As we address this bill, we are especially mindful of the terrible events of September 11 and beyond, which led to the bill's proposal and its quick consideration in the Congress....

...[W]e must continue to respect our Constitution and protect our civil liberties in the wake of the attacks. As the chairman of the Constitution Subcommittee of the Judiciary Committee, I recognize that this is a different world with different technologies, different issues, and different threats.

Yet we must examine every item that is proposed in response to these events to be sure we are not rewarding these terrorists and weakening ourselves by giving up the cherished freedoms that they seek to destroy....

...During those first few hours after the attacks, I kept remembering a sentence from a case I had studied in law school. Not surprisingly, I didn't remember which case it was, who wrote the opinion, or what it was about, but I did remember these words: "While the Constitution protects against invasions of individual rights, it is not a suicide pact." I took these words as a challenge to my concerns about civil liberties at such a momentous time in our history; that we must be careful to not take civil liberties so literally that we allow ourselves to be destroyed.

But upon reviewing the case itself...I found that Justice Arthur Goldberg had made this statement but then ruled in favor of the civil liberties position in the case, which was about draft evasion. He elaborated:

> It is fundamental that the great powers of Congress to conduct war and to regulate the Nation's foreign relations are subject to the constitutional requirements of due process. The imperative necessity for safeguarding these rights to procedural due process under the gravest of emergencies has existed throughout our constitutional history, for it is then, under the pressing exigencies of crisis, that there is the greatest temptation to dispense with fundamental constitutional guarantees which, it is feared, will inhibit governmental action. The Constitution of the United States is a law for rulers and people, equally in war and peace, and covers with the shield of its protection all classes of men, at all times, and under all circumstances....In no other way can we transmit to posterity unimpaired the blessings of liberty, consecrated by the sacrifices of the Revolution.

I have approached the events of the past month and my role in proposing and reviewing legislation relating to it in this spirit. I believe we must, we must redouble our vigilance. We must redouble our vigilance to ensure our security and to prevent further acts of terror. But we must also redouble our vigilance to preserve our values and the basic rights that make us who we are. The Founders who wrote our Constitution and Bill of Rights exercised that vigilance even though they had recently fought and won the Revolutionary War. They did not live in comfortable and easy times of hypothetical enemies. They wrote a Constitution of limited powers and an explicit Bill of Rights to protect liberty in times of war, as well as in times of peace.

There have been periods in our nation's history when civil liberties have taken a back seat to what appeared at the time to be the legitimate exigencies of war. Our national consciousness still bears the stain and the scars of those events: The Alien and Sedition Acts, the suspension of habeas corpus during the Civil War, the internment of Japanese-Americans, German-Americans, and Italian-Americans during World War II, the blacklisting of supposed communist sympathizers during the McCarthy era, and the surveillance and harassment of antiwar protesters, including Dr. Martin Luther King Jr., during the Vietnam War. We must not allow these pieces of our past to become prologue.

Mr. President, even in our great land, wartime has sometimes brought us the greatest tests of our Bill of Rights. For example, during the Civil War, the government arrested some 13,000 civilians, implementing a system akin to martial law. President Lincoln issued a proclamation ordering the arrest and military trial of any persons "discouraging volunteer enlistments, or resisting militia drafts...."

...During World War II, President Roosevelt signed orders to incarcerate more than 110,000 people of Japanese origin, as well as some roughly 11,000 of German origin and 3,000 of Italian origin....

...Now some may say, indeed we may hope, that we have come a long way since those days of infringements on civil liberties. But there is ample reason for concern. And I have been troubled in the past six weeks by the potential loss of commitment in the Congress and the country to traditional civil liberties.

...As it seeks to combat terrorism, the Justice Department is making extraordinary use of its power to arrest and detain individuals, jailing hundreds of people on immigration violations and arresting more than a dozen "material witnesses" not charged with any crime. Although the government has used these authorities before, it has not done so on such a broad scale. Judging from government announcements, the government has not brought any criminal charges related to the attacks with regard to the overwhelming majority of these detainees....

...Even as America addresses the demanding security challenges before us, we must strive mightily also to guard our values and basic rights. We must guard against racism and ethnic discrimination against people of Arab and South Asian origin and those who are Muslim....

...Of course, there is no doubt that if we lived in a police state, it would be easier to catch terrorists. If we lived in a country that allowed the police to search your home at any time for any reason; if we lived in a country that allowed the government to open your mail, eavesdrop on your phone conversations, or intercept your email communications; if we lived in a country that allowed the government to hold people in jail indefinitely based on what they write or think, or based on mere suspicion that they are up to no good, then the government would no doubt discover and arrest more terrorists.

But that probably would not be a country in which we would want to live. And that would not be a country for which we could, in good conscience, ask our young people to fight and die. In short, that would not be America.

Preserving our freedom is one of the main reasons that we are now engaged in this new war on terrorism. We will lose that war without firing a shot if we sacrifice the liberties of the American people.

That is why I found the antiterrorism bill originally proposed by Attorney General Ashcroft and President Bush to be troubling.

The Administration's proposed bill contained vast new powers for law enforcement, some seemingly drafted in haste and others that came from the FBI's wish list that Congress has rejected in the past. You may remember that the Attorney General announced his intention to introduce a bill shortly after the September 11 attacks. He provided the text of the bill the following Wednesday, and urged Congress to enact it by the end of the week....

It is one thing to shortcut the legislative process in order to get federal financial aid to the cities hit by terrorism. We did that, and no one complained that we moved too quickly. It is quite another to press for the enactment of sweeping new powers for law enforcement that directly affect the civil liberties of the American people without due deliberation by the peoples' elected representatives.

Fortunately, cooler heads prevailed at least to some extent, and while this bill has been on a fast track, there has been time to make some changes and reach agreement on a bill that is less objectionable than the bill that the Administration originally proposed.

As I will discuss in a moment, I have concluded that this bill still does not strike the right balance between empowering law enforcement and protecting civil liberties. But that does not mean that I oppose everything in the bill. Indeed many of its provisions are entirely reasonable, and I hope they will help law enforcement more effectively counter the threat of terrorism....

...Now, I am pleased that the final version of the legislation includes a few improvements over the bill that passed the Senate. In particular, the bill would require the Attorney General to review the detention decision every six months and would allow only the Attorney General or Deputy Attorney General, not lower level officials, to make that determination. While I am pleased these provisions are included in the bill, I believe it still falls short of meeting even basic constitutional standards of due process and fairness....

...And speaking of the First Amendment, under this bill, a lawful permanent resident who makes a controversial speech that the government deems to be supportive of terrorism might be barred from returning to his or her family after taking a trip abroad....

...When concerns of this kind have been raised with the Administration and supporters of this bill they have told us, "don't worry, the FBI would never do that." I call on the Attorney General and the

Justice Department to ensure that my fears are not borne out....

...Protecting the safety of the American people is a solemn duty of the Congress; we must work tirelessly to prevent more tragedies like the devastating attacks of September 11th....But the Congress will fulfill its duty only when it protects *both* the American people and the freedoms at the foundation of American society. So let us preserve our heritage of basic rights. Let us practice as well as preach that liberty. And let us fight to maintain that freedom that we call America.

U.S. ATTORNEY GENERAL JOHN ASHCROFT, "ADDRESS BEFORE THE FEDERALIST SOCIETY" (2003)

In 2001, John Ashcroft was appointed by President George W. Bush to serve as U.S. attorney general, the nation's highest law-enforcement post. He remained in the position until 2005. Prior to that, he was a U.S. senator from Missouri.

WHY THIS READING?

In this speech, Ashcroft defends the constitutionality of the Patriot Act (you have just read Senator Russ Feingold's criticism of the Act). Against the charge made by Feingold and others that the Act unconstitutionally violates civil liberties, Ashcroft defends the law as nothing less than indispensable to what George Washington labeled "ordered liberty." Moreover, the Act, says Ashcroft, "honors Madison's first principles [regarding separation of powers], giving each branch of government a role in ensuring both the lives and the liberties of American citizens are protected."

Questions to guide you as you read:

- What, according to Ashcroft, is "ordered liberty"? What constitutional evidence does he provide for his conclusion that this is the chief goal of the American Constitution? Does Ashcroft's constitutional interpretation recognize any possible conflicts between order—in this instance, national security—and liberty? If so, what standard does he supply for resolving such conflicts?
- Based on your reading of Feingold's speech, how might he reply to Ashcroft's thesis?

...The notion that the law can enhance, not diminish, freedom is an important one, and it is an old one. John Locke said, "The end of law is not to abolish or restrain, but to preserve and enlarge freedom." George Washington called this "ordered liberty."

There are some voices in this discussion of how best to preserve freedom that reject the idea that law can enhance freedom. They think that passage and enforcement of any law is necessarily an infringement of liberty. Ordered liberty is the reason we are most open, and that we are not only the most open but the most secure society in the world. Ordered liberty is a guiding principle. It is not a stumbling block to security.

When the first societies passed and enforced the first laws against murder, against theft and rape, the men and women of those societies unquestionably were more free as a result of the law, not less free as a result of the law. A test of a law, then, is this: Does it honor or degrade or devalue liberty? Does it enhance or diminish freedom?

The founders provided the mechanism to protect our liberties and preserve the safety and security of the republic. It's more than a mechanism; it's a framework—the Constitution of the United States. It is a document that safeguards security, but not at the expense of freedom. It celebrates freedom, but not at the expense of security. It protects us and our way of life.

Since September 11, 2001, the Department of Justice has fought for, and Congress has created, and the judiciary has upheld, legal tools, tools that honor the Constitution, tools that make America safer while enhancing American freedom. It is a compliment to all who worked on the PATRIOT Act to say that it is not constitutionally innovative. These are not new ideas. The Act used and uses court-tested safeguards and time-honored ideas to aid the War against Terrorism, at the same time protecting the rights and the lives of citizens.

Madison noted in 1792 that the greatest threat to our liberty was centralized power. "Such focused power," he wrote, "is liable to abuse." That's why he included a distribution of power into separate departments as a first principle of free government. The PATRIOT Act honors Madison's first principles, giving each branch of government a role in ensuring both the lives and the liberties of American citizens are protected. The PATRIOT Act grants the executive branch critical tools in the War on Terrorism. It provides the legislative branch with extensive oversight. It honors the judicial branch with court supervision over the Act's most important powers....

...We are using the tough tools provided in the U.S. PATRIOT Act to defend American lives and liberty from those who have shed blood and decimated lives in other parts of the world. The PATRIOT Act does three basic things. It closes, first, gaping holes in the law enforcement community's ability to collect vital intelligence information on terrorist enterprises. It allows law enforcement to use proven tactics, long used in the fight against organized crime and drug dealers. Second, the PATRIOT Act updates our anti-terrorism laws to meet the challenges of new technology and new threats. And third, with these critical new investigative tools created by the PATRIOT Act, law enforcement can share information and cooperate better with other law enforcement agencies. From prosecutors to intelligence agents, the Act allows law enforcement to connect the dots and uncover terrorist plots before they are launched....

...One thing the PATRIOT Act does not do is to allow the investigation of individuals "solely on the basis of activities protected by the First Amendment to the Constitution of the United States." We know that it does not do that. And even if the law did not prohibit it, the Justice Department has neither the time nor the inclination to delve into the reading habits or other First Amendment activities of our citizens. Despite all the hoopla to the contrary, for example, the PATRIOT Act, which allows for court-approved requests for business records, including library records, has never been used to obtain records from the library. Not once. Senator Diane Feinstein [D-CA] said, "I have never had a single abuse of the PATRIOT Act reported to me." I'll go on to quote her more extensively. "My staff," she said, "emailed the ACLU [American Civil Liberties Union] and asked them for instances of actual abuses. They emailed back and said they have none...."

...Legislative oversight of the Executive Branch is critical to ordered liberty. I spent some time in the legislature. I understand how important it is for the representatives of the people to understand the way the laws which they enact are being implemented. That oversight ensures that the laws are administered in ways that respect the rights and liberties of the citizens.

There has not been a major terrorist attack within our borders in this time. Time and again, Congress has found the PATRIOT Act to be effective against terrorist threats and respectful and protective of citizens' liberties. The Constitution has been honored; it has not been degraded.

Finally...[t]he PATRIOT Act provides for close judicial supervision of the Executive Branch's use of PATRIOT Act authorities. The act allows the government to utilize many long-standing, well-accepted law enforcement tools in the fight against terror. These tools include delayed notification, judicially supervised, of searches....

...Now, many of you have heard the hue and cry of critics of the PATRIOT Act who allege that liberty has been eroded. But more telling is what you have

not heard. You have not heard of one single case in which a judge has found an abuse of the PATRIOT Act because, again, there have been no abuses. It is also important to consider what we have not seen: no major terrorist attacks on our soil over the past two years. The PATRIOT Act's record demonstrates that we are protecting the American people while honoring the Constitution and preserving the liberties we hold dear....

...Time and again, the spirit of our nation has been renewed and our greatness as a people has been strengthened by our dedication to the cause of liberty, to the rule of law, and to the primacy and dignity of each individual. I know we'll keep alive these noble aspirations that are at the base of the hearts of all of our fellow citizens and for which our young men and women at this moment are fighting and making the supreme sacrifice....

Extending the national government's reach to ensure protection of minorities: The movement toward "civil-rights democracy"

This textbook employs the term "civil-rights democracy" to describe what Dr. Martin Luther King's "I Have a Dream" speech stands for and, in part, inaugurates. King's speech does not call for and constitute a "regime change" in the manner that, according to some, "civil-liberties democracy" does. At the same time, Dr. King offers a significantly different answer to the core question of this chapter. On the one hand, he echoes earlier answers to this question in his call for a renewed commitment to racial equality. On the other, his vision gives rise to more than this by articulating a great strengthening of the central or national government in an effort to better secure such equality. Similarly, he calls for a transfer of power away from legislatures and presidents to the courts. His vision anticipates, in certain respects, what three years later would be given the name "affirmative action," which, over time, developed into giving preferences, under certain conditions, to minorities in hiring by "federal contractors" and, later, in other areas. After King's speech, we will read Justice O'Connor's majority opinion in the recent Supreme Court case, *Grutter v. Bollinger*, which echoes aspects of King's vision.

As you read King's speech, please take note of another aspect of his vision of civil-rights democracy. Dr. King here envisions something more than mere political equality. He issues a call for what might be described as "brotherhood and sisterhood." Up to this point in the textbook, American democracy has been presented as grounded in self-interest and operating with the view to regulating conflict among such interested selves (see, e.g., *Federalist 10*, previously in this chapter). That is to say (recalling Tocqueville), American democracy had been understood to aim at no more than "self-interest rightly understood" (rational selfishness), not brother- or sisterhood.

REV. DR. MARTIN LUTHER KING JR., "I HAVE A DREAM" (1963)

Dr. Martin Luther King Jr. (1929–1968) was a world-renowned civil-rights leader and an advocate of nonviolent social change. In Montgomery, Alabama, in the wake of the 1955–1956 boycotts that followed Rosa Parks's refusal to move to the back of the bus,

Dr. King gained fame for his courage and eloquence on the theme of racial equality. In 1957, he became president of the Southern Christian Leadership Conference, a national organization formed to organize the growing civil-rights movement. He wrote numerous books and articles (later in this text, we shall read his "Letter from a Birmingham Jail"). He was consulted by both Presidents Kennedy and Johnson. In 1963, he was named *Time* magazine's Man of the Year. He was the youngest man ever to receive the Nobel Peace Prize.

However, his civil-rights stance also brought harassment, numerous arrests, and physical assaults. In April 1968, he was struck down by an assassin's bullet in Memphis, Tennessee.

WHY THIS READING?

After the Supreme Court declared Alabama's segregation laws [laws enforcing the separation of blacks and whites] unconstitutional, King turned to the issue of African-American voting rights. In 1963, clashes between unarmed black demonstrators and violent police officers in the South led to a planned march on Washington, D.C., on August 28, 1963, which attracted more than 250,000 protestors. Here, speaking on the steps of the Lincoln Memorial in the National Mall, King delivered his famous "I Have a Dream" speech.

Questions to guide you as you read:

- Dr. King's defense of "civil-rights democracy" envisions the transcendence of partisan conflict and the transformation of political society into something resembling the familial relationship. Based on your reading of *Federalist 10*, how does this differ from Madison's understanding of human nature and the purposes of government?
- Does Dr. King agree or disagree with William Lloyd Garrison's reading of the Declaration's and Constitution's view of slavery? Why?

Five score years ago[16] a great American, in whose symbolic shadow we stand, signed the Emancipation Proclamation.[17] This momentous decree came as a great beacon light of hope to millions of Negro slaves who had been seared [burned] in the flames of withering injustice. But one hundred years later, we must face the tragic fact that the Negro is still not free. One hundred years later, the life of the Negro is still sadly crippled by the manacles [handcuffs] of segregation and the chains of discrimination. One hundred years later, the Negro lives on a lonely island of poverty in the midst of a vast ocean of material prosperity. One hundred years later, the Negro is still languishing in the corners of American society and finds himself an exile in his own land. So we have come here today to dramatize an appalling condition.

In a sense we have come to our nation's Capital to cash a check. When the architects of our republic wrote the magnificent words of the Constitution and the Declaration of Independence, they were signing a promissory note to which every American was to fall heir. This note was a promise that all men would be guaranteed the unalienable rights of life, liberty, and the pursuit of happiness.

16. Compare the beginning of Lincoln's Gettysburg Address (above).

17. The Emancipation Proclamation, issued by Lincoln, took effect on January 1, 1863. Lincoln argued that freeing the slaves was necessary in order to save the Union.

It is obvious today that America has defaulted [failed to pay] on this promissory note insofar as her citizens of color are concerned. Instead of honoring this sacred obligation, America has given the Negro people a bad check; a check which has come back marked 'insufficient funds.' But we refuse to believe that the bank of justice is bankrupt.... So we have come to cash this check—a check that will give us upon demand the riches of freedom and the security of justice. We have also come to this hallowed [sacred] spot to remind America of the urgency of *now*. This is no time to engage in the luxury of cooling off or to take the tranquilizing drug of gradualism [gradual improvement]. *Now is* the time to make real the promises of Democracy. *Now* is the time to rise from the dark and desolate valley of segregation to the sunlit path of racial justice. *Now is* the time to open the doors of opportunity to all of God's children. *Now* is the time to lift our nation from the quicksand of racial injustice to the solid rock of brotherhood....

But there is something that I must say to my people who stand on the warm threshold [point of entry] which leads into the palace of justice. In the process of gaining our rightful place we must not be guilty of wrongful deeds. Let us not seek to satisfy our thirst for freedom by drinking from the cup of bitterness and hatred. We must forever conduct our struggle on the high plane of dignity and discipline. We must not allow our creative protest to degenerate into physical violence. Again and again we must rise to the majestic heights of meeting physical force with soul force. The marvelous new militancy [warfare in support of a political cause] which has engulfed the Negro community must not lead us to a distrust of all white people, for many of our white brothers, as evidenced by their presence here today, have come to realize that their destiny is tied up with our destiny....

There are those who are asking the devotees of civil rights, 'when will you be satisfied?' We can never be satisfied as long as the Negro is the victim of the unspeakable horrors of police brutality. We can never be satisfied as long as our bodies, heavy with the fatigue of travel, cannot gain lodging in the motels of the highways and the hotels of the cities. We cannot be satisfied as long as the Negro's basic mobility is from a smaller ghetto to a larger one. We can never be satisfied as long as a Negro in Mississippi cannot vote and a Negro in New York believes he has nothing to vote for.

I say to you today, my friends, that in spite of the difficulties and frustrations of the moment I still have a dream. It is a dream deeply rooted in the American dream. I have a dream that one day this nation will rise up and live out the true meaning of its creed: 'We hold these truths to be self-evident—that all men are created equal.' I have a dream that one day on the red hills of Georgia the sons of former slaves and the sons of former slave owners will be able to sit down together at the table of brotherhood. I have a dream that one day even the state of Mississippi, a desert state sweltering with the heat of injustice and oppression, will be transformed into an oasis of freedom and justice. I have a dream that my four little children will one day live in a nation where they will not be judged by the color of their skin by the content of their character.

I have a dream today. I have a dream that one day the state of Alabama, whose Governor's lips are presently dripping with the words of interposition and nullification, will be transformed into a situation where little black boys and black girls will be able to join hands with little white boys and white girls and walk together as sisters and brothers.

I have a *dream* today. I have a dream that one day every valley shall be exalted, every hill and mountain shall be made low, the rough places will be made plain, and the crooked places will be made straight, and the glory of the Lord shall be revealed, and all flesh shall see it together.

This is our hope. This is the faith I shall return to the South with. With this faith we will be able to hew [cut] out of the mountain of despair a stone of hope. With this faith we will be able to transform the jangling discords of our nation into a beautiful symphony of brotherhood. With this faith we will be able to work together, pray together, struggle together, go to jail together, stand up for freedom together, knowing that we will be free one day.

This will be the day when all of God's children will be able to sing with new meaning 'My country 'tis of thee, sweet land of liberty of thee I sing. Land

where my fathers died, land of the pilgrims pride, from every mountainside let freedom ring.' And if America is to be a great nation this must become true. So let freedom ring from the prodigious [enormous] hilltops of New Hampshire. Let freedom ring from the mighty mountains of New York. Let freedom ring from the heightening Alleghenies of Pennsylvania.... But not only that; let freedom ring from Stone Mountain of Georgia. Let freedom ring from Lookout Mountain of Tennessee. Let freedom ring from every hill and mole hill of Mississippi. From every mountaintop, let freedom ring.

When we let freedom ring, when we let it ring from every village and every hamlet, from every state and every city, we will be able to speed up that day when all of God's children, black men and white men, Jews and Gentiles, Protestants and Catholics, will be able to join hands and sing in the words of the old Negro spiritual, 'Free at last! Free at last! Thank God almighty, we are free at last!'

JUSTICE SANDRA DAY O'CONNOR, OPINION OF THE COURT IN *GRUTTER V. BOLLINGER* (2003)

In this civil-rights case dealing with affirmative action, the Supreme Court upheld the constitutionality of the University of Michigan Law School's use of race in admissions to "achieve student body diversity." Affirmative action refers to the process by which a governmental agency or private business grants a preference in hiring, or advancement, or, as in the *Grutter* case, in university admissions, to select minorities and women in an effort to remediate past discrimination against these groups. For governmental agencies and those private entities that receive federal funds, individuals with disabilities and select veterans are also included. Affirmative action has brought with it intense controversy, with critics arguing, as you will read in the *Grutter* case, that it results in what they term "reverse discrimination"—that is, in discrimination against whites.

WHY THIS READING?

Grutter, a white female with a 3.8 cumulative grade point average in college, and a 161 LSAT (Law School Admissions Test) score, was denied admission to the University of Michigan Law School. She filed suit, charging discrimination based on race, in violation of the 14th Amendment. The Court upheld the Law School's "narrowly tailored use of race in admissions" on the grounds that it furthered a "compelling interest in obtaining the educational benefits that flow from a diverse student body." In his dissent, Justice Thomas, citing the abolitionist Frederick Douglass, raises the question of whether the Constitution is meant to apply to "individuals" or to "groups," in this case, races. This group-versus-individual debate over the meaning of the Constitution constitutes a core issue in the investigation of America democracy; accordingly, it receives further treatment in chapter five.

N.B.: As *Investigating American Democracy* goes to press, the Supreme Court is hearing *Fisher* v. *University of Texas,* which seeks to overturn or delineate exceptions to the ruling in *Grutter.*

Questions to guide you as you read:

- In her opinion for the majority, Justice O'Connor writes that the 14th Amendment "protects *persons* not *groups.*" How, then, does the Court go on to uphold the use of race in university admissions?
- In his dissent, Justice Thomas argues that the Court's opinion sanctions "faddish racial discrimination." Where does he find this "racial discrimination"? What does he mean by describing it as "faddish"?

The [University] policy aspires to "achieve that diversity which has the potential to enrich everyone's education and thus make a law school class stronger than the sum of its parts...."

...The Equal Protection Clause provides that no State shall "deny to any person within its jurisdiction the equal protection of the laws." Because the Fourteenth Amendment "protect[s] *persons*, not *groups*," all "governmental action based on race—a *group* classification long recognized as in most circumstances irrelevant and therefore prohibited—should be subjected to detailed judicial inquiry to ensure that the *personal* right to equal protection of the laws has not been infringed...." It follows from that principle that "government may treat people differently because of their race only for the most compelling reasons."

...We have held that all racial classifications imposed by government "must be analyzed by a reviewing court under strict scrutiny...." This means that such classifications are constitutional only if they are narrowly tailored to further compelling governmental interests...."

...With these principles in mind, we turn to the question whether the Law School's use of race is justified by a compelling state interest. Before this Court, as they have throughout this litigation, respondents [the University] assert only one justification for their use of race in the admissions process: obtaining "the educational benefits that flow from a diverse student body...." In other words, the Law School asks us to recognize, in the context of higher education, a compelling state interest in student body diversity....

...The Law School's educational judgment that such diversity is essential to its educational mission is one to which we defer....

...To be narrowly tailored, a race-conscious admissions program cannot use a quota system—it cannot "insulat[e] each category of applicants with certain desired qualifications from competition with all other applicants." Instead, a university may consider race or ethnicity only as a "'plus' in a particular applicant's file," without "insulat[ing] the individual from comparison with all other candidates for the available seats...." In other words, an admissions program must be "flexible enough to consider all pertinent elements of diversity in light of the particular qualifications of each applicant, and to place them on the same footing for consideration, although not necessarily according them the same weight."

We find that the Law School's admissions program bears the hallmarks of a narrowly tailored plan....

...The Law School's goal of attaining a critical mass of underrepresented minority students does not transform its program into a quota....

...What is more, the Law School actually gives substantial weight to diversity factors besides race. The Law School frequently accepts nonminority applicants with grades and test scores lower than underrepresented minority applicants (and other nonminority applicants) who are rejected....This shows that the Law School seriously weighs many other diversity factors besides race that can make a real and dispositive difference for nonminority applicants as well. By this flexible approach, the Law School sufficiently takes into account, in practice as well as in theory, a wide variety of characteristics besides race and ethnicity that contribute to a diverse student body....

...[I]n the context of its individualized inquiry into the possible diversity contributions of all applicants, the Law School's race-conscious admissions program does not unduly harm nonminority applicants.

We are mindful, however, that "[a] core purpose of the Fourteenth Amendment was to do away with all governmentally imposed discrimination based on race." Accordingly, race-conscious admissions policies must be limited in time. This requirement reflects that racial classifications, however compelling their goals, are potentially so dangerous that they may be employed no more broadly than the interest demands. Enshrining a permanent justification for racial preferences would offend this fundamental equal protection principle. We see no reason to exempt race-conscious admissions programs from the requirement that all governmental use of race must have a logical end point. The Law School, too, concedes that all "race-conscious programs must have reasonable durational limits...."

...We expect that 25 years from now, the use of racial preferences will no longer be necessary to further the interest approved today....

...In summary, the Equal Protection Clause does not prohibit the Law School's narrowly tailored use of race in admissions decisions to further a compelling interest in obtaining the educational benefits that flow from a diverse student body....

JUSTICE CLARENCE THOMAS, CONCURRING IN PART AND DISSENTING IN PART

Frederick Douglass, speaking to a group of abolitionists almost 140 years ago, delivered a message lost on today's [Supreme Court] majority:

"[I]n regard to the colored people, there is always more that is benevolent, I perceive, than just, manifested towards us. What I ask for the negro is not benevolence, not pity, not sympathy, but simply *justice*. The American people have always been anxious to know what they shall do with us....I have had but one answer from the beginning. Do nothing with us! Your doing with us has already played the mischief with us. Do nothing with us! If the apples will not remain on the tree of their own strength, if they are worm-eaten at the core, if they are early ripe and disposed to fall, let them fall!...And if the negro cannot stand on his own legs, let him fall also. All I ask is, give him a chance to stand on his own legs! Let him alone!... [Y]our interference is doing him positive injury...."

...Like Douglass, I believe blacks can achieve in every avenue of American life without the meddling of university administrators. Because I wish to see all students succeed whatever their color, I share, in some respect, the sympathies of those who sponsor the type of discrimination advanced by the University of Michigan Law School (Law School). The Constitution does not, however, tolerate institutional devotion to the status quo in admissions policies when such devotion ripens into racial discrimination. Nor does the Constitution countenance the unprecedented deference the Court gives to the Law School, an approach inconsistent with the very concept of "strict scrutiny."

No one would argue that a university could set up a lower general admission standard and then impose heightened requirements only on black applicants. Similarly, a university may not maintain a high admission standard and grant exemptions to favored races. The Law School, of its own choosing, and for its own purposes, maintains an exclusionary admissions system that it knows produces racially disproportionate results. Racial discrimination is not a permissible solution to the self-inflicted wounds of this elitist admissions policy.

The majority upholds the Law School's racial discrimination not by interpreting the people's Constitution, but by responding to a faddish slogan of the cognoscenti. Nevertheless, I concur in part in the Court's opinion. First, I agree with the Court insofar as its decision, which approves of only one racial classification, confirms that further use of race in admissions remains unlawful. Second, I agree with the Court's holding that racial discrimination in higher education admissions will be illegal in 25 years. I respectfully dissent from the remainder of the Court's opinion and the judgment, however, because I believe that the Law School's current use of race violates the Equal Protection Clause and that the Constitution means the same thing today as it will in 300 months....

...The Constitution abhors classifications based on race, not only because those classifications can harm favored races or are based on illegitimate motives, but also because every time the government places citizens on racial registers and makes race relevant to the provision of burdens or benefits, it demeans us all. "Purchased at the price of immeasurable human suffering, the equal protection principle reflects our Nation's understanding that such classifications ultimately have a destructive impact on the individual and our society."

...The proffered interest that the majority vindicates today, then, is not simply "diversity." Instead the Court upholds the use of racial discrimination as a tool to advance the Law School's interest in offering a marginally superior education while maintaining an elite institution. Unless each constituent part of this state interest is of pressing public necessity, the Law School's use of race is unconstitutional. I find each of them to fall far short of this standard....

...[T]he Court's decision today rest on the fundamentally flawed proposition that racial discrimination can be contextualized so that a goal, such as classroom aesthetics, can be compelling in one context but not in another. This "we know it when we see it" approach to evaluating state interests is not capable of judicial application. Today, the Court insists on radically expanding the range of permissible uses of race to something as trivial (by comparison) as the assembling of a law school class. I can only presume that the majority's failure to justify its decision by reference to any principle arises from the absence of any such principle....

...The Court bases its unprecedented deference to the Law School—a deference antithetical to strict scrutiny—on an idea of "educational autonomy" grounded in the First Amendment....In my view, there is no basis for a right of public universities to do what would otherwise violate the Equal Protection Clause....

...Putting aside the absence of any legal support for the majority's reflexive deference, there is much to be said for the view that the use of tests and other measures to "predict" academic performance is a poor substitute for a system that gives every applicant a chance to prove he can succeed in the study of law. The rallying cry that in the absence of racial discrimination in admissions there would be a true meritocracy ignores the fact that the entire process is poisoned by numerous exceptions to "merit." For example, in the national debate on racial discrimination in higher education admissions, much has been made of the fact that elite institutions utilize a so-called "legacy" preference to give the children of alumni an advantage in admissions. This, and other, exceptions to a "true" meritocracy give the lie to protestations that merit admissions are in fact the order of the day at the Nation's universities. The Equal Protection Clause does not, however, prohibit the use of unseemly legacy preferences or many other kinds of arbitrary admissions procedures. What the Equal Protection Clause does prohibit are classifications made on the basis of race. So while legacy preferences can stand under the Constitution, racial discrimination cannot. I will not twist the Constitution to invalidate legacy preferences or otherwise impose my vision of higher education admissions on the Nation. The majority should similarly stay its impulse to validate faddish racial discrimination the Constitution clearly forbids.

...Similarly no modern law school can claim ignorance of the poor performance of blacks, relatively speaking, on the Law School Admissions Test (LSAT). Nevertheless, law schools continue to use the test and then attempt to "correct" for black underperformance by using racial discrimination in admissions so as to obtain their aesthetic student body. The Law School's continued adherence to measures it knows produce racially skewed results is not entitled to deference by this Court....

...The Court will not even deign to make the Law School try other methods, however, preferring instead to grant a 25-year license to violate the Constitution. And the same Court that had the courage to order the desegregation of all public schools in the South now fears, on the basis of platitudes rather than principle, to force the Law School to abandon a decidedly imperfect admissions regime that provides the basis for racial discrimination....

...The Law School is not looking for those students who, despite a lower LSAT score or undergraduate grade point average, will succeed in the study of law. The Law School seeks only a facade—it is sufficient that the class looks right, even if it does not perform right.

The Law School tantalizes unprepared students with the promise of a University of Michigan degree and all of the opportunities that it offers. These overmatched students take the bait, only to find that they cannot succeed in the cauldron of competition. And this mismatch crisis is not restricted to elite institutions. Indeed, to cover the tracks of the aestheticists, this cruel farce of racial discrimination must continue—in selection for the Michigan Law Review, and in hiring at law firms and for judicial clerkships—until the "beneficiaries" are no longer tolerated. While these students may graduate with law degrees, there is no evidence that they have received a qualitatively better legal education (or become better lawyers) than if they had gone to a less "elite" law school for which they were better prepared. And the aestheticists will never address the real problems facing "underrepresented minorities," instead continuing their social experiments on other people's children....

...It is uncontested that each year, the Law School admits a handful of blacks who would be admitted in the absence of racial discrimination.... Who can differentiate between those who belong and those who do not? The majority of blacks are admitted to the Law School because of discrimination, and because of this policy all are tarred as undeserving. This problem of stigma does not depend on determinacy as to whether those stigmatized are actually the "beneficiaries" of racial discrimination. When blacks take positions in the highest places of government, industry, or academia, it is an open question today whether their skin color played a part in their advancement. The question itself is the stigma—because either racial discrimination did play a role, in which case the person may be deemed "otherwise unqualified," or it did not, in which case asking the question itself unfairly marks those blacks who would succeed without discrimination....

...The Court's civics lesson presents yet another example of judicial selection of a theory of political representation based on skin color—an endeavor I have previously rejected. The majority appears to believe that broader utopian goals justify the Law School's use of race, but "[t]he Equal Protection Clause commands the elimination of racial barriers, not their creation in order to satisfy our theory as to how society ought to be organized."

...For the immediate future, however, the majority has placed its *imprimatur* [official approval] on a practice that can only weaken the principle of equality embodied in the Declaration of Independence and the Equal Protection Clause. "Our Constitution is color-blind, and neither knows nor tolerates classes among citizens." It has been nearly 140 years since Frederick Douglass asked the intellectual ancestors of the Law School to "[d]o nothing with us!" and the Nation adopted the Fourteenth Amendment. Now we must wait another 25 years to see this principle of equality vindicated. I therefore respectfully dissent from the remainder of the Court's opinion and the judgment.

CHAPTER 3

Core Question: What political–economic conditions and character in the American people might best allow American democracy to balance both liberty and equality?

No political order exists in a vacuum: All originate from, promote, and in turn depend, to some extent, on a variety of economic, social, and geographic conditions, as well as political and moral principles. This chapter examines the most pressing perennial questions that have animated the American debate on this subject since the Founding.

We focus initially on the early debates over these questions, because, as we shall see, these debates provide the principled foundations that illuminate our contemporary disputes. We begin with the debate between the Federalists and the anti-Federalists over the question of whether democracy fares better in a large or a small country. The accepted wisdom up to the time of the Founding was that democratic liberty could be preserved only in a relatively small country, such as was the case with the *polis* ("city-state") of Greek antiquity. You will better understand the anti-Federalists' opposition to ratification of the proposed Constitution when you understand the ramifications of the issue of size. In the following excerpt from *Federalist 10*, James Madison's "Publius" argues that a clear-eyed examination of the history of all past attempts at democratic government reveals that they failed precisely **because** they were small.

In contrast, the anti-Federalists feared that the very largeness on which Madison and Hamilton insisted would inevitably destroy liberty in democracy. A large country, to be properly administered, requires greater power in the central or national government than does a small one. According to one anti-Federalist, writing under the pen-name "Brutus" (whom we shall read in this chapter), this inevitable increase in the power of the national government must come at the expense of state and local governments. But state and local governments, argue the anti-Federalists, are closer to their citizens, better know their needs, and are therefore less likely to oppress them. Such oppression can, but need not, take the form of the "iron fist." A powerful centralized bureaucracy in Washington, D.C., precisely because it is so large and remote, can "oppress" everyday citizens in a "softer" fashion—through its ignorance of and/or indifference to local concerns. (We continue to hear echoes of this anti-Federalist concern today in complaints about the mistreatment and/or neglect of citizens by bureaucracies such as the Internal Revenue Service and the Environmental Protection Agency.) Further corollaries of the anti-Federalists' fear over the size of the new republic were their objections that both the executive and legislative branches would possess too much power and their concern over the national government's posting of an army during peacetime. Finally, the anti-Federalists criticized the lack of a bill of rights in the proposed Constitution. This final criticism gave rise to the agreement that a bill of rights would be added as the first order of business of the new government. To fulfill this agreement, the first ten amendments to the Constitution were ratified in 1791.

The debate concerning whether American democracy is best served by decentralized local government or centralized federal (national) government is still powerfully present today. We investigate this question further in this chapter by reading the arguments on behalf of decentralized locally oriented government offered by Thomas Jefferson, Alexis de Tocqueville, and Republican politician Lamar Alexander. Alexander Hamilton provides the counterpoint (in *Federalist* 9).

Moreover, the battle over large versus small democracy is, as we shall see, linked to the question of whether the health of American democracy requires that it be situated primarily in an agrarian or agricultural society or in one that is industrial–technological. On this issue, Jefferson and Hamilton again square off. Jefferson's concern over the moral health of the American people leads him to support this country's remaining an agriculture-based democracy. Hamilton's concern that America offer opportunities for economic and social mobility, among other reasons, leads him to support the case for the country becoming largely industrial. Tocqueville finds the argument already largely settled: Americans, he argues, by virtue of their love of equality, will inevitably be drawn ever more away from farms and small towns and toward industrial callings in the big cities. Time has proven the accuracy of Tocqueville's prediction.

The debates over large versus small, agricultural versus industrial, and decentralized local government versus centralized federal government are inextricably intertwined with the issue of "federalism." Federalism refers to the division of powers between the national and state governments. On the place, power, and history of federalism in American democracy, we contrast the opinions of Tocqueville, Madison's Publius, then-President Ronald Reagan, and the Supreme Court (in its 1985 decision, *Garcia v. San Antonio*).

We conclude this chapter with a further exploration of Tocqueville's dissection of the American soul and the effect on it of the "the love of equality." The love of equality is so powerful in America, he argues, that it may someday lead Americans to sacrifice even their liberties. Tocqueville's attempt, in *Democracy in America*, to provide an "education for democracy" seeks first and foremost to help Americans retain **both** equality *and* liberty. In his view, the challenge to reconcile the at-times competing claims of equality and liberty is, has been, and likely always will be the analytical key for those investigating American democracy.

The earlier argument over "small" versus "large" democracy, and why it still matters today

Democracy can succeed only in a large country

JAMES MADISON, EXCERPT FROM *THE FEDERALIST, NO. 10* (1787)

In the previous chapter, we read the first section of *Federalist 10*, which differentiates a "democracy" from a "republic." We examine a later excerpt from the essay.

WHY THIS READING?

Picking up from where we left it in chapter two, the remainder of *Federalist 10* calls for a large, commercial (free-market or capitalist) democracy. American democracy must be large, argues Madison's Publius, because largeness is necessary for a thriving commercial economy. Why? A small country is more likely to offer its citizens only a few economic pursuits and will therefore be relatively static. Largeness, on the other hand, makes it possible to have a "multiplicity" of occupations and economic "interests" (ways of making a living), providing for a dynamic, growing economy that is more likely to focus citizens on local economic pursuits rather than the fatal politics of struggle between the nation's rich and poor. Hence, largeness is necessary because a commercial economy is necessary, and a commercial economy is necessary to combat the "mortal disease" of "faction," to which all previous democracies had succumbed.

Questions to guide you as you read:

- According to Publius, how will largeness combat the "mortal disease" of democracy?
- Does Publius believe that largeness can serve as a remedy to the causes or effects of faction?

...Let us examine [further] the points in which it [a republic] varies from pure democracy, and we shall comprehend both the nature of the cure and the efficacy [usefulness] which it must derive from the Union.

The two great points of difference between a democracy and a republic are: first, the delegation of the government, in the latter, to a small number of citizens elected by the rest; secondly, the greater number of citizens, and greater sphere of country, over which the latter may be extended.

The effect of the first difference is, on the one hand, to refine and enlarge the public views, by passing them through the medium of a chosen body of citizens, whose wisdom may best discern the true interest of their country, and whose patriotism and love of justice will be least likely to sacrifice it to temporary or partial considerations. Under such a regulation, it may well happen that the public voice, pronounced by the representatives of the people, will be more consonant to the public good than if pronounced by the people themselves, convened for the purpose. On the other hand, the effect may be inverted. Men of factious [inclined to injustice] tempers, of local prejudices, or of sinister designs, may, by intrigue, by corruption, or by other means, first obtain the suffrages, and then betray the interests, of the people. The question resulting is, whether small or extensive republics are more favorable to the election of proper guardians of the public weal; and it is clearly decided in favor of the latter by two obvious considerations.

In the first place, it is to be remarked that, however small the republic may be, the representatives must be raised to a certain number, in order to guard against the cabals of a few; and that, however large it may be, they must be limited to a certain number, in order to guard against the confusion of a multitude. Hence, the number of representatives in the two cases not being in proportion to that of the two constituents, and being proportionally greater in the small republic, it follows that, if the proportion of fit characters be not less in the large than in the small republic, the former will present a greater option, and consequently a greater probability of a fit choice.

In the next place, as each representative will be chosen by a greater number of citizens in the large than in the small republic, it will be more difficult for unworthy candidates to practice with success the vicious arts by which elections are too often carried; and the suffrages of the people being more free, will be more likely to centre in men who possess the most attractive merit and the most diffusive and established characters.

It must be confessed that in this, as in most other cases, there is a mean, on both sides of which inconveniences will be found to lie. By enlarging too much the number of electors, you render the representatives too little acquainted with all their local circumstances and lesser interests; as by reducing it too much, you render him unduly attached to these, and too little fit to comprehend and pursue great and national objects. The federal Constitution forms a happy combination in this respect; the great and aggregate interests being referred to the national, the local and particular to the State legislatures.

The other point of difference is, the greater number of citizens and extent of territory which may be brought within the compass of republican than of democratic government; and it is this circumstance principally which renders factious combinations less to be dreaded in the former than in the latter. The smaller the society, the fewer probably will be the distinct parties and interests composing it; the fewer the distinct parties and interests, the more frequently will a majority be found of the same party; and the smaller the number of individuals composing a majority, and the smaller the compass within which they are placed, the more easily will they concert and execute their plans of oppression. Extend the sphere, and you take in a greater variety of parties and interests; you make it less probable that a majority of the whole will have a common motive to invade the rights of other citizens; or if such a common motive exists, it will be more difficult for all who feel it to discover their own strength, and to act in unison with each other. Besides other impediments, it may be remarked that, where there is a consciousness of unjust or dishonorable purposes, communication is always checked by distrust in proportion to the number whose concurrence is necessary.

Hence, it clearly appears, that the same advantage which a republic has over a democracy, in controlling the effects of faction, is enjoyed by a large over a small republic,—is enjoyed by the Union over the States composing it. Does the advantage consist in the substitution of representatives whose enlightened views and virtuous sentiments render them superior to local prejudices and schemes of injustice? It will not be denied that the representation of the Union will be most likely to possess these requisite endowments. Does it consist in the greater security afforded by a greater variety of parties, against the event of any one party being able to outnumber and oppress the rest? In an equal degree does the increased variety of parties comprised within the Union, increase this security. Does it, in fine, [in conclusion] consist in the greater obstacles opposed to the concert and accomplishment of the secret wishes of an unjust and interested majority? Here, again, the extent of the Union gives it the most palpable [obvious] advantage.

The influence of factious leaders may kindle a flame within their particular States, but will be unable to spread a general conflagration [fire, disturbance] through the other States. A religious sect may degenerate into a political faction in a part of the Confederacy; but the variety of sects dispersed over the entire face of it must secure the national councils against any danger from that source. A rage for paper money, for an abolition of debts, for an equal division of property, or for any other improper or wicked project, will be less apt to pervade the whole body of the Union than a particular member of it; in the same proportion as such a malady is more likely to taint a particular county or district, than an entire State.

In the extent and proper structure of the Union, therefore, we behold a republican remedy for the diseases most incident to republican government. And according to the degree of pleasure and pride we feel in being republicans, ought to be our zeal in cherishing the spirit and supporting the character of Federalists.

PUBLIUS

Democracy can succeed only in a small country

"BRUTUS I" (1787)

Anti Federalist

Opponents of the proposed Constitution, known as the anti-Federalists, included well-known politicians such as Samuel Adams and Patrick Henry. They and others voiced a number of concerns, primary among which were the charges that the Constitution erected a consolidated national government, thereby unjustly infringing on the sovereignty of the states, and that it violated genuine republicanism through its oligarchic features [oligarchy is the unjust rule by the wealthy few]. In addition, and tied to their concern over the power of the states, the anti-Federalists objected that the proposed Constitution lacked a bill of rights. To win over opponents, the Federalists promised that, following ratification of the Constitution, they would draft and secure passage of a bill of rights during the First Congress, which sat from 1789–1791. The first ten amendments were ratified in 1791.

WHY THIS READING?

"Brutus I" confronts squarely and in some detail the very largeness that we have just seen Madison defend. From their point-counterpoint, we see much of what is contested in the debate today over, for example, the expansion of the national government under the 2010 Health Care Reform Bill.

Questions to guide you as you read:

- Although Madison remains confident that largeness will combat democracy's tendency toward faction, Brutus sees a quite different result. What is it, and why?
- Article I, Section 8 of the Constitution declares that "Congress shall have Power To... make all Laws which shall be necessary and proper for carrying into Execution the foregoing Powers, and all other Powers vested by this Constitution in the Government of the United States...." What does Brutus fear will be the logical and natural consequence of this "Necessary and Proper Clause"?

To the Citizens of the State of New York:

When the public is called to investigate and decide upon a question in which not only the present members of the community are deeply interested, but upon which the happiness and misery of generations yet unborn is in great measure suspended, the benevolent mind cannot help feeling itself peculiarly interested in the result.

In this situation, I trust the feeble efforts of an individual, to lead the minds of the people to a wise and prudent determination, cannot fail of being acceptable to the candid and dispassionate part of the community. Encouraged by this consideration, I have been induced to offer my thoughts upon the present important crisis of our public affairs.

Perhaps this country never saw so critical a period in their political concerns. We have felt the feebleness of the ties by which these United-States are held together, and the want of sufficient energy in our present confederation, to manage, in some instances, our general concerns. Various expedients have been proposed to remedy these evils, but none have succeeded. At length a Convention of the states has been assembled, they have formed a constitution which will now, probably, be submitted to the people to ratify or reject, who are the fountain of all power, to whom alone it of right belongs to make or unmake constitutions, or forms of government, at their pleasure. The most important question that was ever proposed to your decision, or to the decision of any people under heaven, is before you, and you are to decide upon it by men of your own election, chosen specially for this purpose. If the constitution, offered to your acceptance, be a wise one, calculated to preserve the invaluable blessings of liberty, to secure the inestimable rights of mankind, and promote human happiness, then, if you accept it, you will lay a lasting foundation of happiness for millions yet unborn; generations to come will rise up and call you blessed. You may rejoice in the prospects of this vast extended continent becoming filled with freemen, who will assert the dignity of human nature. You may solace yourselves with the idea, that society, in this favoured land, will fast advance to the highest point of perfection; the human mind will expand in knowledge and virtue, and the golden age be, in some measure, realised. But if, on the other hand, this form of government contains principles that will lead to the subversion of liberty—if it tends to establish a despotism, or, what is worse, a tyrannic aristocracy; then, if you adopt it, this only remaining asylum for liberty will be shut up, and posterity will execrate [detest] your memory.

Momentous then is the question you have to determine, and you are called upon by every motive which should influence a noble and virtuous mind, to examine it well, and to make up a wise judgment. It is insisted, indeed, that this constitution must be received, be it ever so imperfect. If it has its defects, it is said, they can be best amended when they are experienced. But remember, when the people once part with power, they can seldom or never resume it again but by force. Many instances can be produced in which the people have voluntarily increased the powers of their rulers; but few, if any, in which rulers have willingly abridged [reduced] their authority. This is a sufficient reason to induce you to be careful, in the first instance, how you deposit the powers of government.

With these few introductory remarks, I shall proceed to a consideration of this constitution:

The first question that presents itself on the subject is, whether a confederated government be the best for the United States or not? Or in other words, whether the thirteen United States should be reduced to one great republic, governed by one legislature, and under the direction of one executive and judicial; or whether they should continue thirteen confederated republics, under the direction and control of a supreme federal head for certain defined national purposes only?

This enquiry is important, because, although the government reported by the convention does not go to a perfect and entire consolidation, yet it approaches so near to it, that it must, if executed, certainly and infallibly terminate in it.

This government is to possess absolute and uncontrollable power, legislative, executive and judicial, with respect to every object to which it extends, for by the last clause of section 8th, article 1st, it is declared "that the Congress shall have power to make all laws which shall be *necessary and proper* for carrying into execution the foregoing powers, and all other powers vested by this constitution, in the government of the United States; or in any department or office thereof." And by the 6th article, it is declared "that this constitution, and the laws of the United States, which shall be made in pursuance thereof, and the treaties made, or which shall be made, under the authority of the United States, shall be the supreme law of the land; and the judges in every state shall be bound thereby, anything in the constitution, or law of any state to the contrary notwithstanding." It appears from these articles that there is no need of any intervention of the state governments, between the Congress and the people, to execute any one power vested in the general government, and that the constitution and laws of every state are nullified and declared void, so far as they are or shall be inconsistent with this constitution, or the laws made in pursuance of it, or with treaties made under the authority of the United States.—The government then, so far as it extends, is a complete one, and not a confederation. It is as much one complete government as that of New-York or Massachusetts, has as absolute and perfect powers to make and execute all laws, to appoint officers, institute courts, declare offences, and annex penalties, with respect to every object to which it extends, as any other in the world. So far therefore as its powers reach, all ideas of confederation are given up and lost. It is true this government is limited to certain objects, or to speak more properly, some small degree of power is still left to the states, but a little attention to the powers vested in the general government, will convince every candid man, that if it is capable of being executed, all that is reserved for the individual states must very soon be annihilated, except so far as they are barely necessary to the organization of the general government. The powers of the general legislature extend to every case that is of the least importance—there is nothing valuable to human nature, nothing dear to freemen, but what is within its power. It has authority to make laws which will affect the lives, the liberty, and property of every man in the United States; nor can the constitution or laws of any state, in any way prevent or impede the full and complete execution of every power given. The legislative power is competent to lay taxes, duties, imposts, and excises;—there is no limitation to this power, unless it be said that the clause which directs the use to which those taxes, and duties shall be applied, may be said to be a limitation: but this is no restriction of the power at all, for by this clause they are to be applied to pay the debts and provide for the common defence and general welfare of the United States; but the legislature have authority to contract debts at their discretion; they are the sole judges of what is necessary to provide for the common defence, and they only are to determine what is for the general welfare; this power therefore is neither more nor less, than a power to lay and collect taxes, imposts, and excises, at their pleasure; not only [is] the power to lay taxes unlimited, as to the amount they may require, but it is perfect and absolute to raise them in any mode they please. No state legislature, or any power in the state governments, have any more to do in carrying this into effect, than the authority of one state has to do with that of another. In the business therefore of laying and collecting taxes, the idea of confederation is totally lost, and that of one entire republic is embraced. It is proper here to remark, that the authority to lay and collect taxes is the most important of any power that can be granted; it connects with it almost all other powers, or at least will in process of time draw all other after it; it is the great mean of protection, security, and defence, in a good government, and the great engine of oppression and tyranny in a bad one. This cannot fail of being the case, if we consider the contracted limits which are set by this constitution, to the late [state] governments, on this article of raising money. No state can emit paper money—lay any duties, or imposts, on imports, or exports, but by consent of the Congress; and then the net produce shall be for the benefit of the United States: the only mean therefore left, for any state to support its government and discharge its debts, is by direct taxation; and the United States have also power to lay and collect taxes, in any way they please. Every one who has thought on the subject, must be convinced that but small sums of money can be collected in any country, by direct taxe[s], when the federal government begins to exercise the right of taxation in all its parts, the legislatures of the several states will find it impossible to raise monies to support their governments. Without money they cannot be supported, and they must dwindle away, and, as before observed, their powers absorbed in that of the general government.

It might be here shewn [shown], that the power in the federal legislative, to raise and support armies at pleasure, as well in peace as in war, and their control over the militia, tend, not only to a consolidation of the government, but the destruction of liberty.—I shall not, however, dwell upon these, as a few observations upon the judicial power of this government, in addition to the preceding, will fully evince the truth of the position.

The judicial power of the United States is to be vested in a supreme court, and in such inferior courts as Congress may from time to time ordain and establish. The powers of these courts are very extensive; their jurisdiction comprehends all civil causes, except such as arise between citizens of the same state; and it extends to all cases in law and equity arising under the constitution. One inferior court must be established, I presume, in each state, at least, with the necessary executive officers appendant [attached] thereto. It is easy to see, that in the common course of things, these courts will eclipse the dignity, and take away from the respectability, of the state courts. These courts will be, in themselves, totally independent of the states, deriving their authority from the United States, and receiving from them fixed salaries; and in the course of human events it is to be expected, that they will swallow up all the powers of the courts in the respective states.

How far the clause in the 8th section of the 1st article may operate to do away all idea of confederated states, and to effect an entire consolidation of the whole into one general government, it is impossible to say. The powers given by this article are very general and comprehensive, and it may receive a construction to justify the passing almost any law. A power to make all laws, which shall be *necessary and proper*, for carrying into execution, all powers vested by the constitution in the government of the United States, or any department or officer thereof, is a power very comprehensive and definite, and may, for ought I know, be exercised in a such manner as entirely to abolish the state legislatures. Suppose the legislature of a state should pass a law to raise money to support their government and pay the state debt, may the Congress repeal this law, because it may prevent the collection of a tax which they may think proper and necessary to lay, to provide for the general welfare of the United States? For all laws made, in pursuance of this constitution, are the supreme law of the land, and the judges in every state shall be bound thereby, any thing in the constitution or laws of the different states to the contrary notwithstanding.—By such a law, the government of a particular state might be overturned at one stroke, and thereby be deprived of every means of its support.

It is not meant, by stating this case, to insinuate that the constitution would warrant a law of this kind; or unnecessarily to alarm the fears of the people, by suggesting, that the federal legislature would be more likely to pass the limits assigned them by the constitution, than that of an individual state, further than they are less responsible to the people. But what is meant is, that the legislature of the United States are vested with the great and uncontrollable powers, of laying and collecting taxes, duties, imposts, and excises; of regulating trade, raising and supporting armies, organizing, arming, and disciplining the militia, instituting courts, and other general powers. And are by this clause invested with the power of making all laws, *proper and necessary*, for carrying all these into execution; and they may so exercise this power as entirely to annihilate all the state governments, and reduce this country to one single government. And if they may do it, it is pretty certain they will; for it will be found that the power retained by individual states, small as it is, will be a clog upon the wheels of the government of the United States; the latter therefore will be naturally inclined to remove it out of the way. Besides, it is a truth confirmed by the unerring experience of ages, that every man, and every body of men, invested with power, are ever disposed to increase it, and to acquire a superiority over every thing that stands in their way. This disposition, which is implanted in human nature, will operate in the federal legislature to lessen and ultimately to subvert the state authority, and having such advantages, will most certainly succeed, if the federal government succeeds at all. It must be very evident then, that what this constitution wants [lacks] of being a complete consolidation of the several parts of the union into one complete government, possessed of perfect legislative, judicial, and executive powers, to all intents and purposes, it will necessarily acquire in its exercise and operation.

Let us now proceed to enquire, as I at first proposed, whether it be best the thirteen United States should be reduced to one great republic, or not? It is here taken for granted, that all agree in this, that whatever government we adopt, it ought to be a free one; that it should be so framed as to secure the liberty of the citizens of America, and such an one as to admit of a full, fair, and equal representation of the people. The question then will be, whether a government thus constituted, and founded on such principles, is practicable, and can be exercised over the whole United States, reduced into one state?

If respect is to be paid to the opinion of the greatest and wisest men who have ever thought or wrote on the science of government, we shall be constrained to conclude, that a free republic cannot succeed over a country of such immense extent, containing such a number of inhabitants, and these increasing in such rapid progression as that of the whole United States. Among the many illustrious authorities which might be produced to this point, I shall content myself with quoting only two. The one is the baron de Montesquieu, spirit of laws, chap. xvi. vol. I [book VIII]. "It is natural to a republic to have only a small territory, otherwise it cannot long subsist. In a large republic there are men of large fortunes, and consequently of less moderation; there are trusts too great to be placed in any single subject; he has interest of his own; he soon begins to think that he may be happy, great and glorious, by oppressing his fellow citizens; and that he may raise himself to grandeur on the ruins of his country. In a large republic, the public good is sacrificed to a thousand views; it is subordinate to exceptions, and depends on accidents. In a small one, the interest of the public is easier perceived, better understood, and more within the reach of every citizen; abuses are of less extent, and of course are less protected." Of the same opinion is the marquis Beccarari.

History furnishes no example of a free republic, any thing like the extent of the United States. The Grecian republics were of small extent; so also was that of the Romans. Both of these, it is true, in process of time, extended their conquests over large territories of country; and the consequence was, that their governments were changed from that of free governments to those of the most tyrannical that ever existed in the world.

Not only the opinion of the greatest men, and the experience of mankind, are against the idea of an extensive republic, but a variety of reasons may be drawn from the reason and nature of things, against it. In every government, the will of the sovereign is the law. In despotic governments, the supreme authority being lodged in one, his will is law, and can be as easily expressed to a large extensive territory as to a small one. In a pure democracy the people are the sovereign, and their will is declared by themselves; for this purpose they must all come together to deliberate, and decide. This kind of government cannot be exercised, therefore, over a country of any considerable extent; it must be confined to a single city, or at least limited to such bounds as that the people can conveniently assemble, be able to debate, understand the subject submitted to them, and declare their opinion concerning it.

In a free republic, although all laws are derived from the consent of the people, yet the people do not declare their consent by themselves in person, but by representatives, chosen by them, who are supposed to know the minds of their constituents, and to be possessed of integrity to declare this mind.

In every free government, the people must give their assent [agreement] to the laws by which they are governed. This is the true criterion between a free government and an arbitrary one. The former are ruled by the will of the whole, expressed in any manner they may agree upon; the latter by the will of one, or a few. If the people are to give their assent to the laws, by persons chosen and appointed by them, the manner of the choice and the number chosen, must be such, as to possess, be disposed, and consequently qualified to declare the sentiments of the people; for if they do not know, or are not disposed to speak the sentiments of the people, the people do not govern, but the sovereignty is in a few. Now, in a large extended country, it is impossible to have a representation, possessing the sentiments, and of integrity, to declare the minds of the people, without having it so numerous and unwieldly [not easily handled or controlled], as to be subject in great measure to the inconveniency of a democratic government.

The territory of the United States is of vast extent; it now contains near three millions of souls, and is capable of containing much more than ten times that number. Is it practicable for a country, so large and so numerous as they will soon become, to elect a representation, that will speak their sentiments, without their becoming so numerous as to be incapable of transacting public business? It certainly is not.

In a republic, the manners, sentiments, and interests of the people should be similar. If this be not the case, there will be a constant clashing of opinions; and the representatives of one part will be continually striving against those of the other. This will retard the operations of government, and prevent such conclusions as will promote the public good. If we apply this remark to the condition of the United States, we shall be convinced that it forbids that we should be one government. The United States includes a variety of climates. The productions of the different parts of the union are very variant, and their interests, of consequence, diverse. Their manners and habits differ as much as their climates and productions; and their sentiments are by no means coincident. The laws and customs of the several states are, in many respects, very diverse, and in some opposite; each would be in favor of its own interests and customs, and, of consequence, a legislature, formed of representatives from the respective parts, would not only be too numerous to act with any care or decision, but would be composed of such heterogeneous and discordant principles, as would constantly be contending with each other.

The laws cannot be executed in a republic, of an extent equal to that of the United States, with promptitude.

The magistrates in every government must be supported in the execution of the laws, either by an armed force, maintained at the public expence for that purpose; or by the people turning out to aid the magistrate upon his command, in case of resistance.

In despotic governments, as well as in all the monarchies of Europe, standing armies are kept up to execute the commands of the prince or the magistrate, and are employed for this purpose when occasion requires: But they have always proved the destruction of liberty, and [are] abhorrent to the spirit of a free republic. In England, where they depend upon the parliament for their annual support, they have always been complained of as oppressive and unconstitutional, and are seldom employed in executing of the laws; never except on extraordinary occasions, and then under the direction of a civil magistrate.

A free republic will never keep a standing army to execute its laws. It must depend upon the support of its citizens. But when a government is to receive its support from the aid of the citizens, it must be so constructed as to have the confidence, respect, and affection of the people. Men who, upon the call of the magistrate, offer themselves to execute the laws, are influenced to do it either by affection to the government, or from fear; where a standing army is at hand to punish offenders, every man is actuated by the latter principle, and therefore, when the magistrate calls, will obey: but, where this is not the case, the government must rest for its support upon the confidence and respect which the people have for their government and laws. The body of the people being attached, the government will always be sufficient to support and execute its laws, and to operate upon the fears of any faction which may be opposed to it, not only to prevent an opposition to the execution of the laws themselves, but also to compel the most of them to aid the magistrate; but the people will not be likely to have such confidence in their rulers, in a republic so extensive as the United States, as necessary for these purposes. The confidence which the people have in their rulers, in a free republic, arises from their knowing them, from their being responsible to them for their conduct, and from the power they have of displacing them when they misbehave: but in a republic of the extent of this continent, the people in general would be acquainted with very few of their rulers: the people at large would know little of their proceedings, and it would be extremely difficult to change them. The people in Georgia and New-Hampshire would not know one another's mind, and therefore could not act in concert to enable them to effect a general change of representatives. The different parts of so extensive a country could not possibly be made acquainted with the conduct of their representatives, nor be informed of the reasons upon which measures were founded. The consequence will be, they will have no confidence in their legislature, suspect them of ambitious views, be jealous of every measure they adopt, and will not support the laws they pass. Hence the government will be nerveless and inefficient, and no way will be left to render it otherwise, but by establishing an armed force to execute the laws at the point of the bayonet—a government of all others the most to be dreaded.

In a republic of such vast extent as the United-States, the legislature cannot attend to the various concerns and wants of its different parts. It cannot be sufficiently numerous to be acquainted with the local condition and wants of the different districts, and if it could, it is impossible it should have sufficient time to attend to and provide for all the variety of cases of this nature, that would be continually arising.

In so extensive a republic, the great officers of government would soon become above the control of the people, and abuse their power to the purpose of aggrandizing themselves, and oppressing them. The trust committed to the executive offices, in a country of the extent of the United-States, must be various and of magnitude. The command of all the troops and navy of the republic, the appointment of officers, the power of pardoning offences, the collecting of all the public revenues, and the power of expending them, with a number of other powers, must be lodged and exercised in every state, in the hands of a few. When these are attended with great honor and emolument [salary], as they always will be in large states, so as greatly to interest men to pursue them, and to be proper objects for ambitious and designing men, such men will be ever restless in their pursuit after them. They will use the power, when they have acquired it, to the purposes of gratifying their own interest and ambition, and it is scarcely possible, in a very large republic, to call them to account for their misconduct, or to prevent their abuse of power.

These are some of the reasons by which it appears, that a free republic cannot long subsist over a country of the great extent of these states. If then this new constitution is calculated to consolidate the thirteen states into one, as it evidently is, it ought not to be adopted.

Though I am of opinion, that it is a sufficient objection to this government, to reject it, that it creates the whole union into one government, under the form of a republic, yet if this objection was obviated, there are exceptions to it, which are so material and fundamental, that they ought to determine every man, who is a friend to the liberty and happiness of mankind, not to adopt it. I beg the candid and dispassionate attention of my countrymen while I state these objections—they are such as have obtruded [imposed] themselves upon my mind upon a careful attention to the matter, and such as I sincerely believe are well founded. There are many objections, of small moment, of which I shall take no notice—perfection is not to be expected in any thing that is the production of man—and if I did not in my conscience believe that this scheme was defective in the fundamental principles—in the foundation upon which a free and equal government must rest—I would hold my peace.

"CENTINEL I" (1787)

"Centinel," the pen-name of another anti-Federalist writer, wrote a series of newspaper articles in opposition to the proposed Constitution that appeared in the Philadelphia press between 1787 and 1788.

WHY THIS READING?

Centinel I echoes and expands upon a number of the criticisms that you read in Brutus I. In this excerpt from his first essay on the subject, he argues that the U.S. Senate violates the principle of equality by allotting two senators to each state regardless of the state's population. He predicts that senators, whose terms run for six years and who have no term limits, will, in practice, serve for life. (It is worth noting here that, currently, more than 90 percent of incumbent senators, as well as incumbent members of the House of Representatives, are reelected.) Moreover, each member of the House, under the proposed Constitution, will represent 30,000 citizens. This number, writes Centinel, is too large for the people to sufficiently know their representative's deeds and thoughts, and for their representative to know the people's needs and opinions. The result, he predicts, will be a "permanent aristocracy." Fearing the influence under the new Constitution of the "wealthy and ambitious," he argues that a "republic or free government" requires both a "virtuous" citizenry and that property be "pretty equally divided." We will read contemporary reverberations of a number of these points in Lamar Alexander's speech.

Questions to guide you as you read:

- Centinel argues that democracy cannot survive without a virtuous people. What does he regard as the connection between popular virtue and "small" democracy? How would *Federalist 10* respond?
- Why does Centinel believe the proposed Constitution will create an "aristocracy"?

...The number of representatives (being only one for every 30,000 inhabitants) appears to be too few, either to communicate the requisite information of the wants, local circumstances, and sentiments of so extensive an empire, or to prevent corruption and undue influence in the exercise of such great powers. The term for which they are to be chosen is too long to preserve a due dependence and accountability to their constituents, and the mode and places of their election are not sufficiently ascertained; for as Congress have the control over both, they may govern the choice by ordering the representatives of a whole state to be elected in one place and that too may be the most inconvenient.

The senate, the great efficient body in this plan of government, is constituted on the most unequal principles. The smallest state in the union has equal weight with the great states of Virginia, Massachusetts, or Pennsylvania. The Senate, besides its legislative functions, has a very considerable share in the Executive; none of the principle appointments to office can be made without its advice or consent. The term and mode of its appointment will lead to permanency; the members are chosen for six years, the mode is under control of Congress, and as there is no exclusion by rotation, they may be continued for life, which, from their extensive means of influence, would follow of

course. The President, who would be a mere pageant of state, unless he coincides with the view of the Senate, would either become the head of the aristocratic junto [small controlling group (also spelled "junta")] in that body or its minion [slave]; besides, their influence being the most predominant could best secure his re-election to office....

From this investigation into the organization of this government, it appears that it is devoid of all responsibility or accountability to the great body of the people... it would be in practice a permanent ARISTOCRACY.

The framers of it, actuated by the true spirit of such a government, which ever abominates and suppresses all free inquiry and discussion, have no provision for the liberty of the press, that grand palladium [safeguard] of freedom and scourge of tyrants;...

A republican or free government can only exist where the body of the people are virtuous and where property is pretty equally divided; in such a government the people are the sovereign and their sense or opinion is the criterion of every public measure. When this ceases to be the case, the nature of the government is changed, and an aristocracy, monarchy or despotism will rise on its ruin. The highest responsibility is to be attained in a simple structure of government, for the great body of the people never steadily attend to the operations of government and for want [lack] of due information are liable to be imposed on. If you complicate the plan by various orders, the people will be perplexed and divided in their sentiments about the source of abuses or misconduct; some will impute it to the Senate, others to the House of Representatives, and so on, that the interposition of the people may be rendered imperfect or perhaps wholly abortive. But if imitating the constitution of Pennsylvania, you vest all of the legislative power in one body of men (separating the executive and judicial) elected for a short period, and necessarily excluded by rotation from permanency, and guarded from precipitancy [impulsiveness or rashness] and surprise by delays imposed on its proceedings, you will create the most perfect responsibility, for then whoever the people feel a grievance they cannot mistake the authors and will apply the remedy with certainty and effect, discarding them at the next election. This tie of responsibility will obviate all the dangers apprehended from a single legislature, and will best secure the rights of the people.

Having premised this much, I shall now proceed to the examination of the proposed plan of government, and I trust, shall make it appear to the meanest capacity, that it has none of the essential requisites of a free government....

The late revolution having effaced in a great measure all former habits and the present institutions are so recent that there exists not that great reluctance to innovation, so remarkable in old communities, and which accords with reason, for the most comprehensive mind cannot foresee the full operation of material changes on civil polity; it is the genius of the common law to resists innovation.

The wealthy and ambitious, who in every community think they have a right to lord it over their fellow creatures, have availed themselves very successfully to this favorable disposition; for the people thus unsettled in their sentiments have been prepared to accede to any extreme of government. All the distresses and difficulties they experience, proceeded from various causes, have been ascribed to the impotency of the present confederation, and thence they have been led to expect full relief from the adoption of the proposed system of government, and in the other event, immediate ruin and annihilation as a nation. These characters flatter themselves that they have lulled all distrust and jealousy of their new plan by gaining the concurrence of the two men in whom America has the highest confidence, and now triumphantly exult in the completion of their long meditated schemes of power and aggrandizement....

What competing notions of democracy drive our ongoing debate over decentralized local government versus centralized federal government?

THOMAS JEFFERSON, "ON CITIZENSHIP" (1824/1816/1814)

In this reading, which consists of three documents that Jefferson produced over a ten-year period late in his life, he distinguishes in some detail what he takes to be the proper division of the powers of the national government from those of state and local governments.

WHY THIS READING?

Jefferson's approach to this chapter's core question urges that the national government is, under the Constitution, empowered to provide only for national defense, and "administer foreign and federal relations," whereas legislation dealing with "civil rights, laws, police, and administration of what concerns the State generally" rightly belongs to state and local governments. We will read a contemporary echo of this argument in Ronald Reagan's 1982 State of the Union Address.

Questions to guide you as you read:

- What is the primary reason that Jefferson urges a comparatively narrow interpretation of the powers of the national or federal government?
- How, for Jefferson, does great wealth in the hands of a few affect a democratic people's capacity for self-government?

Federalism 101

...My own State...is now proposing to call a convention for amendment. Among other improvements, I hope they will adopt the subdivision of our counties into wards. The former may be estimated at an average of twenty-four miles square; the latter should be about six miles square each, and would answer to the hundreds of your Saxon Alfred.[1] In each of these might be: 1st. an elementary school; 2nd. a company of militia with its officers; 3rd. a justice of the peace and constable; 4th. each ward should take care of their own poor; 5th. their own roads; 6th. their own police; 7th. elect within themselves one or more jurors to attend the courts of justice; and, 8th. give in at their Folkhouse their votes for all functionaries [officeholders] reserved to their election. Each ward would thus be a small city within itself, and every man in the State would thus become an acting member of the Common government, transacting in person a great portion of its rights and duties, subordinate indeed, yet important, and entirely within his competence. The wit of man cannot devise a more solid basis for a free, durable, and well-administered republic.

...If it is believed that these elementary schools will be better managed by the governor and council, the commissioners of the literary fund, or any other general authority of the government, than by the parents within each ward, it is a belief against all experience. Try the principle one step further and amend the bill so as to commit to the governor and council the management of all our farms, our mills, and merchants' stores. No, my friend, the way to have good and safe government is not to trust it all to one but to divide it among the many, distributing to everyone exactly the functions he

1. Here Jefferson refers to the 9th century Anglo-Saxon King Alfred.

is competent to. Let the national government be entrusted with the defense of the nation and its foreign and federal relations; the State governments with the civil rights, laws, police, and administration of what concerns the State generally; the counties with the local concerns of the counties, and each ward direct the interests within itself. It is by dividing and subdividing these republics from the great national one down through all its subordinations until it ends in the administration of every man's farm by himself, by placing under everyone what his own eye may superintend, that all will be done for the best. What has destroyed liberty and the rights of man in every government, which has ever existed under the sun? The generalizing and concentrating all cares and powers into one body, no matter whether of the autocrats of Russia or France, or of the aristocrats of a Venetian senate. And I do believe that if the Almighty has not decreed that man shall never be free (and it is a blasphemy [impious act] to believe it), that the secret will be found to be in the making himself the depository of the powers respecting himself, so far as he is competent to them, and delegating only what is beyond his competence by a synthetical [made artificially] process to higher and higher orders of functionaries, so as to trust fewer and fewer powers in proportion as the trustees become more and more oligarchical.[2] The elementary republics of the wards, the county republics, the State republics, and the republic of the Union would form a gradation [systematic progression] of authorities, standing each on the basis of law, holding every one its delegated share of powers, and constituting truly a system of fundamental balances and checks for the government. Where every man is a sharer in the direction of his ward-republic, or of some of the higher ones, and feels that he is a participator in the government of affairs, not merely at an election one day in the year but every day; when there shall not be a man in the State who will not be a member of some one of its councils, great or small, he will let the heart be torn out of his body sooner than his power be wrested from him by a Caesar or a Bonaparte. How powerfully did we feel the energy of this organization in the case of embargo?...

...We have no paupers [extremely poor people].... The great mass of our population is of laborers; our rich, who can live without labor, either manual or professional, being few, and of moderate wealth. Most of the laboring class possess property, cultivate their own lands, have families, and from the demand for their labor are enabled to exact from the rich and the competent such prices as enable them to be fed abundantly, clothed above mere decency, to labor moderately and raise their families. They are not driven to the ultimate resources of dexterity [skill] and skill, because their wares will sell although not quite so nice as those of England. The wealthy, on the other hand, and those at their ease, know nothing of what the Europeans call luxury. They have only somewhat more of the comforts and decencies of life than those who furnish them. Can any condition of society be more desirable than this?...In England, happiness is the lot of the aristocracy only; and the proportion they bear to the laborers and paupers, you know better than I do. Were I to guess that they are four in every hundred, then the happiness of the nation would be to its misery as one in twenty-five. In the United States it is as eight millions to zero, or as all to none. But it is said they possess the means of defense, and that we do not. How so? Are we not men? Yes; but our men are so happy at home that they will not hire themselves to be shot at for a shilling a day. Hence we can have no standing armies for defense, because we have no paupers to furnish the materials. The Greeks and Romans had no standing armies, yet they defended themselves. The Greeks by their laws, and the Romans by the spirit of their people, took care to put into the hands of their rulers no such engine of oppression as a standing army. Their system was to make every man a soldier, and oblige him to repair to the standard of his country whenever that was reared. This made them invincible; and the same remedy will make us so. In the beginning of our government we were willing to introduce the least coercion possible on the will of the citizen.

2. Oligarchy: a form of government in which the exercise of power is restricted to a few wealthy people or families.

Hence a system of military duty was established too indulgent [lenient] to his indolence [laziness]. This is the first opportunity we have had of trying it, and it has completely failed; an issue foreseen by many, and for which remedies have been proposed. That of classing the militia according to age, and allotting each age to the particular kind of service to which it was competent, was proposed to Congress in 1805, and subsequently; and, on the last trial, was lost, I believe, by a single vote only. Had it prevailed, what has now happened would not have happened? Instead of burning our Capitol, we should have possessed theirs in Montreal and Quebec. We must now adopt it, and all will be safe.

ALEXIS DE TOCQUEVILLE, *DEMOCRACY IN AMERICA*, "THE AMERICAN SYSTEM OF TOWNSHIPS," "OF INDIVIDUALISM IN DEMOCRACIES," "HOW THE AMERICANS COMBAT THE EFFECTS OF INDIVIDUALISM BY FREE INSTITUTIONS" (1835)

In the passages below, Tocqueville praises "townships," or "municipal institutions," which, he argues, "constitute the strength of free nations." Political participation at the local level feeds the "spirit of liberty." Such participation combats the "individualism" (egoism) fostered by equality of conditions. With equality comes the habit of every citizen to "seek for his opinions within himself," causing him to "forget society at large...." This separation is precisely the social state desired by despots. Accordingly, "despotism...is more particularly to be feared in democratic ages."

WHY THIS READING?

The Americans, Tocqueville holds, combat the isolating tendencies of equality through "free institutions," by which he means political participation at the local level (such participation is possible for all but a few ***only*** at the local level). Local participation draws citizens to recognize their need for each other and, in turn, the existence of a truly common good. Political participation (what Tocqueville designates, "political freedom") educates democratic citizens away from the "individualism" that both follows from equality and threatens democracy with despotism. It is important to note that Tocqueville's concern with "despotism" differs in key respects from that voiced by present-day conservatives, who fear a large, strong national government primarily because of its capacity to act contrary to the wishes of the people. Tocqueville's concern is that the stripping away of meaningful opportunities for political participation at the local level will so atrophy citizens' political capacities that they will, in time, come to lose their freedom, not **contrary to**, but **in accordance with**, their wishes.

Questions to guide you as you read:

- How does Tocqueville's praise of townships square with Jefferson's support for dividing his state of Virginia into "wards"?
- What precisely does Tocqueville mean by the term "individualism," and why does he fear its effects on democratic self-government?

The American System of Townships

It is not without intention that I begin this subject with the township. The village or township is the only association which is so perfectly natural that, wherever a number of men are collected, it seems to constitute itself....

...[M]unicipal institutions constitute the strength of free nations. Town meetings are to liberty what primary schools are to science; they bring it within the people's reach, they teach men how to use and how to enjoy it. A nation may establish a free government, but without municipal institutions it cannot have the spirit of liberty. Transient [short-lived] passions, the interests of an hour, or the chance of circumstances may create the external forms of independence, but the despotic [tyrannical] tendency which has been driven into the interior of the social system will sooner or later reappear on the surface....

...The township and the county are not organized in the same manner in every part of the Union; it is easy to perceive, however, that nearly the same principles have guided the formation of both of them throughout the Union. I am inclined to believe that these principles have been carried further and have produced greater results in New England than elsewhere. Consequently they stand out there in higher relief and offer greater facilities to the observations of a stranger.

The township institutions of New England form a complete and regular whole; they are old; they have the support of the laws and the still stronger support of the manners of the community, over which they exercise a prodigious [exceptional] influence. For all these reasons they deserve our special attention.

Of Individualism in Democracies

I have shown how it is that in ages of equality every man seeks for his opinions within himself; I am now to show how it is that in the same ages all his feelings are turned towards himself alone. Individualism is a novel expression, to which a novel idea has given birth. Our fathers were only acquainted with egoism (selfishness). Selfishness is a passionate and exaggerated love of self, which leads a man to connect everything with himself and to prefer himself to everything in the world. Individualism is a mature and calm feeling, which disposes each member of the community to sever himself from the mass of his fellows and to draw apart with his family and his friends, so that after he has thus formed a little circle of his own, he willingly leaves society at large to itself. Selfishness originates in blind instinct; individualism proceeds from erroneous judgment more than from depraved feelings; it originates as much in deficiencies of mind as in perversity of heart.

Selfishness blights the germ of all virtue; individualism, at first, only saps the virtues of public life; but in the long run it attacks and destroys all others and is at length absorbed in downright selfishness. Selfishness is a vice as old as the world, which does not belong to one form of society more than to another; individualism is of democratic origin, and it threatens to spread in the same ratio as the equality of condition.

Among aristocratic nations, as families remain for centuries in the same condition, often on the same spot, all generations become, as it were, contemporaneous. A man almost always knows his forefathers and respects them; he thinks he already sees his remote descendants and he loves them....Men living in aristocratic ages are therefore almost always closely attached to something placed out of their own sphere, and they are often disposed to forget themselves. It is true that in these ages the notion of human fellowship is faint and that men seldom think of sacrificing themselves for mankind; but they often sacrifice themselves for other men. In democratic times, on the contrary, when the duties of each individual to the race are much more clear, devoted service to any one man becomes more rare; the bond of human affection is extended, but it is relaxed.

Among democratic nations new families are constantly springing up, others are constantly falling away, and all that remain change their condition; the woof [fabric] of time is every instant broken and the track of generations effaced [obliterated]. Those who went before are soon forgotten; of those who will come after, no one has any idea: the interest of man is confined to those in close propinquity [blood relationship] to himself. As each class gradually approaches others and mingles with them, its members become undifferentiated and lose their class identity for each other. Aristocracy had made a chain of all the members of the community, from the peasant to the king; democracy breaks that chain and severs every link of it.

As social conditions become more equal, the number of persons increases who, although they are neither rich nor powerful enough to exercise any great influence over their fellows, have nevertheless acquired or retained sufficient education and fortune to satisfy their own wants. They owe nothing to any man, they expect nothing from any man; they acquire the habit of always considering themselves as standing alone, and they are apt to imagine that their whole destiny is in their own hands.

Thus not only does democracy make every man forget his ancestors, but it hides his descendants and separates his contemporaries from him; it throws him back forever upon himself alone and threatens in the end to confine him entirely within the solitude of his own heart.

How Americans Combat the Effects of Individualism by Free Institutions

Despotism which by its nature is suspicious, sees in the separation among men the surest guarantee of its continuance, and it usually makes every effort to keep them separate. No vice of the human heart is so acceptable to it as selfishness: a despot easily forgives his subjects for not loving him, provided they do not love one another. He does not ask them to assist him in governing the state; it is enough that they do not aspire to govern it themselves. He stigmatizes as turbulent and unruly spirits those who would combine their exertions to promote the prosperity of the community; and, perverting the natural meaning of words, he applauds as good citizens those who have no sympathy for any but themselves.

Thus the vices which despotism produces are precisely those which equality fosters. These two things perniciously [maliciously] complete and assist each other. Equality places men side by side, unconnected by any common tie; despotism raises barriers to keep them asunder; the former predisposes them not to consider their fellow creatures, the latter makes general indifference a sort of public virtue.

Despotism, then, which is at all times dangerous, is more particularly to be feared in democratic ages. It is easy to see that in those same ages men stand most in need of freedom. When the members of a community are forced to attend to public affairs, they are necessarily drawn from the circle of their own interests and snatched at times from self-observation. As soon as a man begins to treat of public affairs in public, he begins to perceive that he is not so independent of his fellow men as he had at first imagined, and that in order to obtain their support he must often lend them his co-operation.

When the public govern, there is no man who does not feel the value of public goodwill or who does not endeavor to court it by drawing to himself the esteem and affection of those among whom he is to live. Many of the passions which congeal [harden] and keep asunder [apart] human hearts are then obliged to retire and hide below the surface. Pride must be dissembled [concealed through misleading speech or deeds]; disdain [contempt] dares not break out; selfishness fears its own self. Under a free government, as most public offices are elective, the men whose elevated minds or aspiring hopes are too closely circumscribed [restricted] in private life constantly feel that they cannot do without the people who surround them. Men learn at such times to think of their fellow men from ambitious motives; and they frequently find it, in a manner, their interest to forget themselves.

I may here be met by an objection derived from electioneering [unscrupulous campaigning for office], intrigues [scheming], the meanness of candidates, and the calumnies [malicious lies] of their opponents. These are occasions of enmity [hatred] which occur the oftener the more frequent elections become. Such evils are doubtless great, but they are transient; whereas the benefits that attend them remain. The desire of being elected may lead some men for a time to violent hostility; but this same desire leads all men in the long run to support each other; and if it happens that an election accidentally severs two friends, the electoral system brings a multitude of citizens permanently together who would otherwise always have remained unknown to one another. Freedom produces private animosities, but despotism gives birth to general indifference.

The Americans have combated by free institutions the tendency of equality to keep men asunder, and they have subdued it. The legislators of America did not suppose that a general representation of the whole nation would suffice to ward off a disorder at once so natural to the frame of democratic society and so fatal; they also thought that it would be well to infuse [fill, impart] political life into each portion of the territory in order to multiply to an infinite extent opportunities of acting in concert for all the members of the community and to make them constantly feel their mutual dependence. The plan was a wise one. The general affairs of a country engage the attention only of leading politicians, who assemble from time to time in the same places; and as they often lose sight of each other afterwards, no lasting ties are established between them. But if the object be to have the local affairs of a district conducted by the men who reside there, the same persons are always in contact, and they are, in a manner, forced to be acquainted and to adapt themselves to one another.

It is difficult to draw a man out of his own circle to interest him in the destiny of the state, because he does not clearly understand what influence the destiny of the state can have upon his own lot. But if it is proposed to make a road cross the end of his estate, he will see at a glance that there is a connection between this small public affair and his greatest private affairs; and he will discover, without its being shown to him, the close tie that unites private to general interest. Thus far more may be done by entrusting to the citizens the administration of minor affairs than by surrendering to them in the control of important ones, towards interesting them in the public welfare and convincing them that they constantly stand in need of one another in order to provide for it. A brilliant achievement may win for you the favor of a people at one stroke; but to earn the love and respect of the population that surrounds you, a long succession of little services rendered and of obscure good deeds, a constant habit of kindness, and an established reputation for disinterestedness will be required. Local freedom, then, which leads a great number of citizens to value the affection of their neighbors and of their kindred, perpetually brings men together and forces them to help one another in spite of the propensities that sever them.

In the United States the more opulent [wealthy] citizens take great care not to stand aloof [unfriendly and remote] from the people; on the contrary, they constantly keep on easy terms with the lower classes: they listen to them, they speak to them every day. They know that the rich in democracies always stand in need of the poor, and that in democratic times you attach a poor man to you more by your manner than by benefits conferred. The magnitude of such benefits, which sets off the difference of condition, causes a secret irritation to those who reap advantage from them, but the charm of simplicity of manners is almost irresistible; affability [sociability] carries men away, and even want [lack] of polish is not always displeasing. This truth does not take root at once in the minds of the rich. They generally resist it as long as the democratic revolution lasts, and they do not acknowledge it immediately after that revolution is accomplished. They are very ready to do good to the people, but they still choose to keep them at arm's length; they think that is sufficient, but they are mistaken. They might spend fortunes thus without warming the hearts of the population around them; that population does not ask them for the sacrifice of their money, but of their pride.

It would seem as if every imagination in the United States were upon the stretch to invent means of increasing the wealth and satisfying the wants of the public. The best-informed inhabitants of each district constantly use their information to discover new truths that may augment the general prosperity; and if they have made any such discoveries, they eagerly surrender them to the mass of the people.

When the vices and weaknesses frequently exhibited by those who govern in America are closely examined, the prosperity of the people occasions, but improperly occasions, surprise. Elected magistrates do not make the American democracy flourish; it flourishes because the magistrates are elective.

It would be unjust to suppose that the patriotism and the zeal that every American displays for the welfare of his fellow citizens are wholly insincere. Although private interest directs the greater part of human actions in the United States as well as elsewhere, it does not regulate them all. I must say that I have often seen Americans make great and real sacrifices to the public welfare; and I have noticed a hundred instances in which they hardly ever failed to lend faithful support to one another. The free institutions which the inhabitants of the United States possess, and the political rights of which they make so much use, remind every citizen, and in a thousand ways, that he lives in society. They every instant impress upon his mind the notion that it is the duty as well as the interest of men to make themselves useful to their fellow creatures; and as he sees no particular ground of animosity to them, since he is never either their master or their slave, his heart readily leans to the side of kindness. Men attend to the interests of the public, first by necessity, afterwards by choice; what was intentional becomes an instinct, and by dint [strength] of working for the good of one's fellow citizens, the habit and the taste for serving them are at length acquired.

Many people in France consider equality of condition as one evil and political freedom as a second. When they are obliged to yield to the former, they strive at least to escape from the latter But I contend that in order to combat the evils which equality may produce, there is only one effectual remedy: namely, political freedom [political participation].

LAMAR ALEXANDER, "CUT THEIR PAY AND SEND THEM HOME" (1994)

Alexander's public-service career included stints as governor of Tennessee, U.S. secretary of education, and U.S. senator. This address, given at The Heritage Foundation, a conservative–libertarian, Washington, D.C., think tank, was part of the lead-up to Alexander's unsuccessful bid for the 1996 Republican presidential nomination. Alexander lost the nomination to then-Senator Robert Dole (Kansas), who, in turn, lost in his effort to unseat the incumbent Democratic President Bill Clinton.

WHY THIS READING?

Alexander's speech takes place in the context of the national debate over then-President Bill Clinton's effort to pass comprehensive health care legislation. Clinton's plan, announced in September 1993, was withdrawn the following September without ever coming to a vote in Congress, despite the fact that at the time the Democrats held majorities in both the House and the Senate. The next attempt to pass such legislation occurred under President Barack Obama and was passed in 2010.

Here, Alexander argues that the federal government is too removed from the needs of individuals and local communities to make good decisions. In the course of advancing his case against what he labels Washington's "perceived arrogance," he champions what he takes to be the Founders' conception of the "citizen legislator."

Questions to guide you as you read:

- How does Alexander's view of Herbert Croly differ from that offered above by Theodore Roosevelt?
- What is Alexander's central concern with what he calls "big government"? How does this compare to Jefferson's?

...What I've Been Hearing

Let me start with what I have not been hearing. It struck me this morning as I read the Washington newspapers, consumed by Whitewater-gate and health care, that during the past three weeks on my drive I've probably heard seven minutes total about those two subjects. And all seven minutes have been on health care.

What I have heard about is crime. People are afraid to take walks in their neighborhoods, and not just in big cities....

Everyone has a welfare story. In Cassville, Missouri, I visited with a couple, both of whom are in their 20's and work on a production line, making $7.79 and $8.89 an hour. They know exactly what the federal benefits are in the Cassville area. They wonder why—when all the companies in the area are hiring—some of their friends make more not working than they do working....

...Talk of jobs usually leads to talk about schools. Parents worry about losing control of their schools to Washington, D.C. bureaucrats, social scientists, and Hollywood values. They worry about their child's safety. They worry about whether their children are learning enough to survive in the new job market.

There are two subjects, however, that by far I hear the most about. The first is a feeling ranging from bewilderment to outrage at the size, growth, and meddlesomeness of the government in Washington, D.C. The second is a sense—getting back to that grumpiness I mentioned a moment ago—that the country is seriously off track; it has wandered away from the principles and institutions that made it so remarkable in the first place....

...But my remarks today are about the first subject I've been hearing the most about—about the government in Washington, D.C. This is where we must start in order to help put the country back on track.

It's Washington, D.C., Stupid!

What has startled me in nearly three weeks so far of driving across America staying with people has been the depth and breadth of the sense of outrage and exasperation about the government in Washington—its spending, its growth, its meddling, its perceived arrogance....

...Here in Washington, D.C., everyone is talking about the crime bill Congress is trying to pass. I haven't run into anybody in three weeks who thinks it will make the street where they live safer. And I have run into only one law enforcement official who is for it. Now, there must be people who are for it, otherwise I'm sure the President and the Congress wouldn't be thinking about spending $30 billion on such a thing. That's $600 million or so in it for Tennessee. That's a lot of money.

In Baton Rouge, however, the Sheriff doesn't really want it, and probably won't hire any of the 100,000 police officers because he said, "in two years the money will be gone and I'll have the employees and I won't have any way to pay them." And then he said, "I've just gotten through with the Brady Bill. I've just had to hire two new employees and buy a bunch of fax machines, when my jail is overcrowded and we needed the money for that." During lunch, the District Attorney in Baton Rouge put it this way: "If they were cooking our dinner up there in Washington, even if they were good cooks, by the time it got here it would be cold and we'd be gone."

There are many more examples and stories. The government in Washington devours our paycheck, promises too much, delivers too little, pretends to do things we know very well it can't do, tells people to do things they don't want to do, and then tells us to pay for it ourselves. You can understand why Washington has come to be regarded as a company town that has grown too big for its britches.... The sense of outrage among mainstream Americans right now should not be underestimated. It is the stuff of which uprisings are made.

Why It's Different This Time

...Our country has become too focused on Washington. So has our Republican Party. At Southern Republican leadership meetings, it seemed all we would do was bring in well-respected people from Washington to talk about Washington issues. I became so exasperated that, in 1986, I helped form something called the Republican Exchange, so we could talk about how to create safe, clean communities where children could grow up healthy, go to a good school, and get a good job, which is what we were supposed to be working on.

In 1995, a group of Republican congressmen led by Newt Gingrich and several of us activist Republican Governors spent a weekend in the Tennessee mountains to see whether we were really in the same party and on the same song sheet. Of course, we quickly agreed that we were—that good Republican philosophy is to put a harness on the government in Washington, and do what needs to be done in communities and in the private sector.

So this is not a new subject for me. What is new is the number of Americans who want Washington out of their everyday lives and the strength of their feeling about it.

Why This Is the Issue

Why has this happened? I think it's important to go back almost to the beginning of the century to a book that has kept popping up ever since it was written. It's called *The Promise of American Life*, by Herbert Croly. The title is magnificent, the first chapter is also magnificent, but for our time, the rest of the book is wrong. Nevertheless, it's worth paying attention to, because in 1909 Croly wrote that what's unique about this country is the unlimited belief in America's future. That's what is different about America, together with the idea that any of us—from wherever we came—has the opportunity to have a piece of that future.

Croly argued that all of us just doing our own things in our communities didn't add up to enough, that we needed more of a national purpose and national identity. He liked what Lincoln had done and what Teddy Roosevelt was doing. So he argued for a stronger, more activist central government. He believed the federal government's role should be more than just national defense, monetary and commercial regulation, and the enforcement of our constitutional rights. He believed the government in Washington should get into the business of raising children, eradicating poverty, and creating opportunities and prosperity for all Americans.

This belief, which he articulated in a very compelling way, has been at the core of the near ceaseless expansion of the federal government, starting with the progressive era, through the New Deal and the Great Society, to today's supposedly "new" Democrats.

Just think of it: for over 80 years the federal government has been growing and growing, spending and spending, meddling and meddling. Particularly in the last 30 years, those numbers have grown into almost abstract figures. The number of federal employees has grown from just under 1 million in 1939 to almost 3 million today. Federal spending has gone from $715 million in 1913 to nearly $1.5 trillion today. We are now paying more in interest on the national debt than we are on national defense. The number of pages in the Federal Register has gone from 2,619 in 1936 to 61,000 in 1993. (The number of pages went down by over one-third during the Reagan Administration, but it is expected to be back up to 76,000 this year.)...

...All of this adds up to a very serious problem. Washington, D.C., is on a collision course with the people of this country, because the government here keeps doing things that most Americans know very well it should not be doing. The government in Washington just keeps growing and growing and meddling and meddling.

This continuous expansion is one reason for the surge of this exasperation with the government, but there is another fundamental one we ought to recognize. We have gone through a great divide and are entering a very different age. Back when Croly was advocating a large centralized government, it was the industrial age, when more centralization was the way to accomplish great things. It was a time, too, when we started to fall in love with the idea of single solutions to our problems. Expertise and resources from Washington, it was imagined, could solve almost anything.

Now we have entered the age of information, and as the big, centralized industries have discovered, centralized bureaucracy and decision-making don't work very well anymore. This is a time for being fast on your feet, having instant access to information, ideas, and expertise from around the country and the world, dealing with the unexpected, and tailoring activities to fit particular circumstances. A large, central bureaucracy can't do that.... Precisely because life is larger and so much more complicated, we need much less—not much more—government in Washington.

The information age has given Americans in all walks of life the tools and the flexibility to start making more of their own decisions, to share ideas, to develop their own ways of solving problems. The era of the search for a single best way, whether to educate children, to help the down and out, or to preserve natural resources, has given way to our natural inclinations as Americans toward pluralism [existence of different groups within society], creativity, and innovation. The lingering attitude here of "Washington knows best" and the efforts of the government in Washington to tell people in states and communities what to do run in exactly the wrong direction. This, too, adds to the exasperation with the federal government.

What We Need To Do

What can we do about this sense of exasperation?

Well, I think it is clear we need to take Herbert Croly's idea and roll it back in the other direction. We need to create a new promise of American life by getting the government in Washington out of the way....

Because the Democratic Party is so committed to the central government, so insistent on reinventing America from here, this creates an opening a mile wide for the Republican Party. But we have been timid about plowing through that opening. I believe that after 1996 the nation is likely to have a Republican government, that is, a Republican President and a Republican Congress—if for no other reason than because that is the only option that the voters have not yet tried. Republicans could advance that prospect by persuading the American people that, if they choose us, we will respond boldly by sending a good part of the federal government home. But between now and 1996 we must think strategically about this. We must decide upon, agree upon and advance big ideas that will actually work if we are given the opportunity to govern.

What I propose as a first step seems far-fetched, I'm sure, to many here. But I believe it is very mild compared to what may be coming down the pike during the rest of the 1990s.

Cut Their Pay and Send Them Home

We should cut the pay of Members of Congress and send them home. Here's how it would work. Congress could:

Convene on January 3rd, just as it now does, pass the authorization bills to help the government run, and go home early in the baseball season. Come back Labor Day, pass the appropriations bills and any other urgent legislation, and be home by Thanksgiving.

Cut the pay of Members in half and repeal the rules that keep them from holding real jobs and leading normal lives in their home towns. Pay Members adequate per diem for travel and expenses when they are Washington.

If Members of Congress would eat more of their meals in diners in Jennings, Louisiana, or in Nashville, or in Billings or in Hartford or anywhere in America, if they lived back in those places and had their roots there, then when these hare-brained ideas come up—turning health care over to the government to run, or reinventing welfare for the seventh time in Washington, or even drafting a rule about whether you can wear a cross or Star of David to work—these ideas would never see the light of day.

I am talking about an old idea, this idea of the citizen legislator, the idea that our political leadership is supposed to be us. The notion is that a part time Congress of community leaders makes a better government than a full-time Congress of career politicians. The country began with such a citizen legislature and operated that way for most of its existence.

Former U.S. Senate leader Howard Baker, not particularly known as a revolutionary, was the prime spokesman for the citizen legislature in the early 1980s. No one paid much attention even though Senator Baker at that time was selected by Republican and Democratic Senators as their most respected colleague. He thought this idea of cutting their pay and sending them home would dignify the Congress by forcing it to concentrate on the most urgent issues.

Senator Baker said the other day on our Republican Neighborhood Meeting broadcast, "I love the Congress, but I don't think it's essential to stay in Washington and be captured by the Federal

District. I'd like to see them in six months a year, and relieved of the total dependence on the federal paycheck. I'd like to see them once more become citizen legislators."

It is worth noting that Thomas Jefferson believed seven years was enough for any of America's diplomats to serve in another country. After that, he warned, "They'll cease to become citizens of the United States." The same thing applies to Members of Congress. If you move here, if you are forced by law to give up your normal job and income, if you put your kids in school here, it is very hard not to become a citizen of the District of Columbia and cease to be a citizen of the district you represent.

This idea—maybe more than any other—would begin to change the culture of the company town, and help to shift the focus away from Washington and back to communities.

Critics, of course, are apt to object by arguing that the business of the federal government has become too complicated and intricate to be handled by part-time legislators. I believe that one reason for this is because the work of Congress has expanded to fill the available time. Another reason is that Washington—with all its special interests and experts—also has a tendency to overcomplicate almost everything. Nobody I've seen on my drive has been jumping for joy over Congress's famous deficit reduction package and tax increases, or the 1,400 page health care reform bill. Regular Americans sitting around a kitchen table over a short period of time could come up with more fair, straight-forward, and effective answers. It is possible and usually better to deal with large matters in an uncomplicated way. A time limit would encourage just that....

Send the Bureaucracy Home, Too

Sending the Congress home deals with only one train that needs to be turned around and sent off in the opposite direction. So that we don't create imbalances in our system of government, we should send home chunks of the federal bureaucracy as well.

Senator Nancy Kassebaum's welfare proposal would be a good place to start. While everyone else seems to think the problems of welfare all across America can be solved from Washington, she proposes sending Aid to Families with Dependent Children, Food Stamps, and the Women, Infants and Children program back to the states along with the money to pay for them. That is $41 billion that states could decide what to do with. In exchange, the federal government would take over the states' share of Medicaid, which is plagued with problems that come from having two masters instead of just one. This is the one welfare reform proposal that would work.

What would happen with welfare? You would have all sorts of ideas and approaches springing up. I am certain Reverend Henry Delaney would know just what to do with that welfare money on 32nd Street in Savannah. And so would the Mayor of Henning. So would Father Hill and the Cherokee Chief I visited. So would most communities across this country.

Another obvious candidate for being sent home is job training. There are about 90 federal job training programs, spending about $25 billion. Rep. Bill Zeliff of New Hampshire believes most of these should be transferred to state and community and private sector control. He is right. Washington seems to have forgotten that the best training for work is work. Our national leadership spews out this invective that "entry level" jobs are demeaning. When I came along, entry level jobs were something you got patted on the back for doing. If you went to work sweeping or washing or waiting tables, you didn't have some Cabinet Secretary in Washington saying the country's going down the drain because everybody is doing entry level jobs. We were encouraged to do that, to sweep the store and dream of owning the store one day. That is how we learned to work.

We should also send home 150 federal elementary and secondary education programs that spend about $15 billion each year. Governor Voinovich of Ohio says his superintendents spend half their time filling out forms to get federal money that comprises 5 or 6 percent of their local school budgets. Parents and communities, not Washington, can do a better job deciding what's best for our children's future.

In choosing the strategies that are most likely to succeed in helping to send Washington home, high on the list also should go:

Term limits;
A balanced budget amendment;

Line-item veto for the President;
A systematic review of the rule-making authority of federal boards and agencies;
The election of a President who will veto legislation that imposes costs on state and local governments without paying for it;
Considering whether, in this telecommunications age, some of the federal departments and agencies might best be relocated outside the Beltway.

Focus the Presidency

We should not ignore the Presidency as we consider how to roll back the influence of the government in Washington, D.C. This is a topic that deserves an entire discussion of its own, but let me briefly offer a few thoughts.

The Presidency is the most unique and valuable institution our country has in a time of great change. More than any other institution, it can help us see who we are and where we are going and what we need to do to get there. It can set an agenda, make things happen. We ought to employ the Presidency in a more focused way.

When I became governor, a friend of mine gave me a book by Lyndon Johnson's former press secretary, George Reedy, called ***The Twilight of the Presidency.*** In it I found a definition of the Presidency that I thought also applied to the governorship, and so I used it for eight years.

Reedy wrote that aside from serving as commander in chief, what a President ought to do is three things: first, see the few most urgent needs facing the country; second, develop a strategy for dealing with each need; and third, persuade at least half the people he is right. That's good advice. And we should get the Presidency back into the position where that's what the President is trying to do.

It means first tending to responsibilities as commander in chief. In Baton Rouge, someone asked me what advice I would give President Clinton if he were suddenly to walk in the door. We had been talking about welfare, crime, schools, and jobs. I said this: "I would respectably suggest to the President that he assemble around him a town of men and women who know the world, understand national security and foreign policy issues, understand when to project our force and when not to. Then listen to their advice, make a decision, support the decision, and see it through to the end."

It is not so unusual to have a President who doesn't know everything about the world going in. It is unusual to have one who doesn't seem to know anybody else who does.

Focusing the Presidency means dispelling this notion that there can be a domestic President. There is no such thing. Everything about this world is too much intertwined. The President is the one American who can do the most to untangle it for all of us. George Shultz says that Ronald Reagan's most important act in foreign policy in his early years was the firing of the air traffic controllers. President Reagan said, "If you violate your oath, you will be fired." They did, and he did—and it sent a clear message to Qadhafi and people all around the world. Secretary of State Shultz said, "It made my job much easier."

Focusing the Presidency also means promising to do less for people through federal programs, while providing leadership to help people do for themselves more of what needs to be done. Margaret Thatcher used to talk about the "nanny state," and I believe the President should not act or be expected to act like the nation's nanny.

Focused presidential leadership would be useful right now in helping us as a country set some clear limits, both about our role in the world and our role at home. What we don't do can be as much an affirmation of policy as what we do do. And we haven't really come to terms with that. What we ***don't*** try to do from Washington, D.C., about crime in Savannah is policy. Every time we make a federal decision about what happens in a classroom, it takes away from the teacher, the parent, and the community the freedom to make that decision for themselves. If we do not invade Haiti, that is just as important a part of our policy—and part of a set of clear objectives—as was invading Kuwait.

The Challenge

Earlier this year, we began at the Hudson Institute a project called the New Promise of American Life, to examine how we might roll back the expansion of the federal government that Croly helped spark 80 years ago.

I would hope the Heritage and others might work with us to find chunks of the government in Washington that can be sent home, as long as Congress is going to be home more, and as long as the President is going to concentrate more of the Presidency on the most urgent needs facing the country. That would be step one toward renewing the promise of American life.

The second step, then is probably more difficult. It involves illustrating what happens with welfare, about schools, about safe streets if the federal government takes less of a role and communities have more in their hands. Such an approach represents a very unsatisfying set of answers for any disciple of Herbert Croly, because unless we have a federal program or a Washington, D.C., response, we're considered to be doing nothing.

I wish some of the people who feel that way had a chance to be with me these past few weeks and to see Henry Delaney on 32nd Street in Savannah. I wish they could have been with me on my visit with Reuben Greenberg, the police chief of Charleston, South Carolina, who has cut serious crime by very simple actions, like putting four police officers on the street to take to school any child under age 17 who is walking the street during school hours, or to take home any child under age 17 who is anywhere outside the home after midnight. Every school board ought to visit Becci Bookner, the teacher in Murfreesboro, Tennessee, who has helped to open the public schools 12 hours a day all year with academic programs at no extra cost to the taxpayer.

Most of the answers to the problems that trouble [*sic*] must spring up from the families and communities of America. The new promise of American life comes from communities. America had communities before it had a central government. The greatness of our country has always come from communities, and not from reinventing America in Washington, D.C.

Conclusion

...These are hard times. It is harder to be a parent, a teacher, a student, a policeman, a nurse. It seems harder to start a business, to find and keep a job. It is not easy to be a good political leader in such a troubled, cynical time. Despite all the impressive national statistics that can be mustered up, we are grumpy, troubled, and off track. One huge reason is that the government in Washington is suffocating so much of what we need to do. It has become a dead weight on our future.

If we can push the government out of the way, then we will at least be free to do something ourselves about the drift of our country away from principles that made it great to begin with and to repair institutions we have always depended upon—the family, the neighborhood, the church, the school—that have become broken. These we the greatest challenges we face in these hard times.

Cut their pay and send them home may be catchy phrase, but it is a catchy phrase for a serious idea. It's more than a bumper sticker. It's a plan to cut back on Washington's meddling—and to encourage community answers to community problems. It should become the centerpiece for a set of proposals that will send a good part of the government in Washington, D.C., home. It is probably the tip of the iceberg in the 1990s. It could help to give America a Republican national government by 1996. Most important it is the surest first step toward the new promise of American life.

Does it matter whether America is an agrarian or an industrial democracy?

THOMAS JEFFERSON, *NOTES ON THE STATE OF VIRGINIA* (1784)

In this response to a question from a Frenchman with whom Jefferson had been corresponding, our third president offers his famous defense of "agrarian [farming life's] virtue." "Those who labour in the earth," he argues, "are the chosen people of God, if ever he had a chosen people, whose breasts he has made his peculiar deposit for substantial and genuine virtue." For this reason, Jefferson hopes that "our work-shops [factories] remain in Europe." Jefferson's vision for American democracy would not be realized. In time, industrialization and, with it, big cities, would come to dominate much of American life; and these changes would, by the late 1800s, be accompanied by calls for a more active, interventionist national government.

WHY THIS READING?

Although Jefferson's vision did not come to fruition, his defense of agrarian virtue still finds echoes today. Some of those who defend government subsidies for agriculture argue that such support is needed to preserve the farming way of life and, with it, elements of character that are still essential to democratic health.

Jefferson's argument that democratic virtue requires a predominantly agricultural citizenry is compared with Hamilton's "Report on Manufactures," which provides the counterpoint.

Questions to guide you as you read:

- Why does Jefferson believe that farmers are the best human foundation for democracy?
- What virtues does he find in them? For what reasons does Jefferson regard these virtues as indispensable to both liberty and equality?

...The political economists of Europe have established it as a principle that every state should endeavor to manufacture for itself: and this principle, like many others, we transfer to America, without calculating the difference of circumstance which should often produce a difference of result. In Europe...Manufacture [manufacturing] must therefore be resorted to of necessity not of choice, to support the surplus of their people. But we have an immensity of land courting the industry of the husbandman [i.e., farmer]. Is it best then that all our citizens should be employed in its [i.e., the land's] improvement, or that one half should be called off from that to exercise manufactures and handicraft arts for the other? Those who labor in the earth are the chosen people of God, if ever He had a chosen people, whose breasts He has made his peculiar deposit for substantial and genuine virtue. It is the focus in which he keeps alive that sacred fire which otherwise might escape from the face of the earth. Corruption of morals in the mass of cultivators is a phenomenon of which no age nor nation has furnished an example. It [i.e., lack of corruption] is the mark set on those, who not looking up to heaven, to their own soil and industry, as does the husbandman, for their subsistence, depend for it on the casualties and caprice of customers. Dependence begets subservience and venality, suffocates the germ of virtue, and prepares fit tools for the designs of [political] ambition...generally speaking, the proportion which the aggregate of the other classes of citizens bears in any state to that of its husbandmen, is the proportion of its unsound to its healthy parts, and is a good-enough barometer whereby to measure its degree of corruption. While we have land to labour then, let us never wish to see our citizens occupied at a work-bench, or twirling a distaff...for the general operations of manufacture, let our work-shops remain in Europe. It is better to carry provisions and materials to workmen there, than bring them to the provisions and materials, with them their manners and principles. The loss by the transportation of commodities [goods] across the Atlantic will be made up in happiness and permanence of government. The mobs of great cities add just so

much to the support of pure government, as sores do to the strength of the human body. It is the manners and spirit of a people which preserve a republic in vigour. A degeneracy [deterioration] in these is a canker [ulcerous sore] which soon eats to the heart of its laws and constitution.

ALEXANDER HAMILTON, "REPORT ON MANUFACTURES" (1791)

Hamilton was George Washington's chief of staff during the Revolutionary War and later his secretary of the Treasury. He was best known for his fiscal policies settling the finances of the American Revolution, and for his role as the principal author of *The Federalist.* Throughout his political career, his overarching vision emphasized the need for a strong central government that would employ its power to create conditions to enhance individual opportunities. To this end, he championed "manufacturing" and technological improvement, opposed monopolies, and sought to use government power for the sake of building the economy through enhancing competition. This would create ambitious and talented citizens, who would in turn build a great and powerful nation.

WHY THIS READING?

The Report on Manufactures, designed to bolster the new country's economy, was submitted to Congress in 1791. The Report saw the encouragement of manufacturing as the chief expedient toward multiplying the number and variety of occupations, strengthening the economy and, in turn, attracting immigration. It also recommended subsidies to industry as well as a policy of tariffs (taxes on imported goods). Despite the opposition of Jefferson's Democratic-Republican Party, a good deal of the Report was adopted by Congress and, in time, Jefferson himself would ease his opposition to much of the Report. Moreover, its championing of tariffs would be carried on by the Whig Party's Henry Clay and later by the Whig-turned-Republican Abraham Lincoln.

The debate over tariffs remains with us to this day. Defenders argue, with Hamilton, that they serve to protect American industries and to raise money for the government. Opponents hold that American consumers, and thus the American economy, are hurt by tariffs, because they raise the price of tariff-burdened goods for domestic consumers.

Questions to guide you as you read:

- Although Jefferson associates "manufactures" (industry) with "corruption," Hamilton finds important virtues nurtured by industrial callings. What are these virtues, and how does manufacturing encourage them?
- Why does Hamilton believe that industry will spur immigration?

III. As to the additional employment of classes of the Community not ordinarily engaged in the particular business.

This is not among the least valuable of the means, by which manufacturing institutions contribute to augment [make greater] the general stock of industry and production. In places where those institutions prevail, besides the persons regularly engaged in them, they afford occasional and extra employment to industrious individuals and families, who

are willing to devote the leisure resulting from the intermissions [recess from] of their ordinary pursuits to collateral [parallel] labours, as a resource of multiplying their acquisitions or their employments. The husbandman [farmer] himself experiences a new source of profit and support from the increased industry of his wife and daughters; invited and stimulated by the demands of the neighboring manufactories.

Besides this advantage of occasional employment to classes having different occupations, there is another of a nature allied to it and of a similar tendency. This is the employment of persons who would otherwise be idle [not in use] and in many cases a burthen on the community, either from the bias of temper, habit, infirmity [weakness] of body, or some, other cause, indisposing [making unfit for], or disqualifying them for the toils [labor] of the Country. It is worthy of particular remark, that, in general, women and Children are rendered more useful and the latter more early useful by manufacturing establishments, than they would otherwise be. Of the number of persons employed in the cotton manufactories of Great Britain, it is computed that 4/7 nearly are women and children; of whom the greatest proportion are children and many of them of a very tender age.

And thus it appears to be one of the attributes to manufactures and one of no small consequence, to give occasion to the exertion of a greater quantity of Industry, even by the *same* number of persons, where they happen to prevail, than would exist, if there were no such establishments.

IV. As to the promoting of emigration from foreign Countries.

Men reluctantly quit one course of occupation and livelihood for another, unless invited to it by very apparent and proximate [very near] advantages. Many who would go from one country to another, if they had a prospect of continuing with more benefit the callings, to which they have been educated, will often not be tempted to change their situation, by the hope of doing better, in some other way. Manufacturers, who listening to the powerful invitations of a better price for their fabrics, or their labour of greater cheapness or provisions and raw materials, of an exemption from the chief part of the taxes burthens and restraints, which they endure in the old world, of greater personal independence and consequence, under the operation of a more equal government, and of what is far more precious than mere religious toleration a perfect equality of religious privileges; would probably flock from Europe to the United States to pursue their own trades or professions, if they were once made sensible of the advantages they would enjoy, and were inspired with an assurance of encouragement and employment, will, with difficulty, be induced to transplant themselves, with a view to becoming cultivators of land.

If it be true then, that it is the interest of the United States to open every possible [avenue to] emigration from abroad, it affords a weighty argument for the encouragement of manufactures; which for the reasons just assigned, will have the strongest tendency to multiply the inducements to it.

Here is perceived an important resource, not only for extending the population, and with it the useful and productive labour of the country, but likewise for the prosecution of manufactures, without deducting from the number of hands, which might otherwise be drawn to tillage; and even for the indemnification [protect against loss] of Agriculture for such as might happen to be diverted from it. Many, whom Manufacturing views would induce to emigrate, would afterwards yield to the temptations, which the particular situation of this Country holds out to Agricultural pursuits. And while Agriculture would in other respects derive many signal and unmingled advantages from the growth of manufactures, it is a problem whether it would gain or lose, as to...the number of persons employed in carrying it on.

V. As to the furnishing greater scope for the diversity of talents and dispositions [temperament], which discriminate men from each other.

This is a much more powerful means of augmenting the fund of national industry than may at first sight appear. It is a just observation, that minds of the strongest and most active powers...fall below mediocrity and labour without effect, if confined to uncongenial [not pleasing] pursuits. And it is thence to be inferred, that the results of human exertion may be immensely increased by diversifying its objects. When all the different kinds of industry obtain in a community, each individual can find his proper element, and can call into activity the whole vigour of his nature. And the community is benefitted by the services of its respective members, in the manner, in which each can serve it with most effect.

If there be anything in a remark often to be met with—namely that there is, in the genius of the people of this country, a peculiar aptitude for mechanic improvements, it would operate as a forcible reason for giving opportunities to the exercise of that species of talent by the propagation of manufactures.

VI. As to the affording a more ample and various field for enterprise.

This also is of greater consequence in the general scale of national exertion than might perhaps on a superficial view be supposed, and has effects not altogether dissimilar from those of the circumstance last noticed. To cherish and stimulate the activity of the human mind, by multiplying the objects of enterprise, is not among the least considerable of the expedients, by which the wealth of a nation may be promoted. Even things in themselves not positively advantageous sometimes become so, by their tendency to provoke exertion. Every new scene, which is opened to the busy nature of man to rouse and exert itself, is the addition of a new energy to the general stock of effort.

The spirit of enterprise, useful and prolific as it is, must necessarily be contracted or expanded in proportion to the simplicity or variety of the occupations and productions, which are to be found in a Society. It must be less in a nation of mere cultivators, than in a nation of cultivators and merchants; less in a nation of cultivators and merchants, than in a nation of cultivators, artificers [skilled workers] and merchants.

Federalism

What is the optimal relationship between the national and state governments with the view to enhancing both liberty and equality?

ALEXIS DE TOCQUEVILLE, *DEMOCRACY IN AMERICA,* "ADVANTAGES OF THE FEDERAL SYSTEM . . ." (1835)

Implicit and, at times, explicit in all of the prior readings in this chapter has been the issue of "federalism," which refers to the constitutional division of powers and responsibilities between the federal government and the state and local governments. In this reading, Tocqueville praises what he regards as the happy mix of national and state powers that was American federalism at the time (the 1830s). This "mix" was agreed to only after an intense and protracted debate at the Constitutional Convention in Philadelphia in 1787. Speaking for the anti-Federalists at the Convention on June 6, Sherman of Connecticut urged that there were but "few" . . . "objects of Union," chief among which were defending the country against foreign enemies and umpiring disputes between and among the states themselves. These alone, he said, made a "confederation of the States necessary." Everything else, including all "civil and criminal matters," belonged to and would be dealt with more justly and expeditiously by the states: "The people are more happy in small than large states."

Understanding better the historical background of this dispute—the most fundamental dispute at the Convention—helps us to grasp the terms of the debate today over federalism. Note that in the quotation above, Sherman refers to what makes a "confederation" necessary. Recall that this country's first governing document was titled the Articles of Confederation. Under the Articles, the national government was extremely weak; in many areas, final discretion lay with the individual states. (Think of the United Nations as a contemporary analogue.) At the time of the Convention, "confederal" was used synonymously with both "federal" and "purely federal." The anti-Federalists, as you have read, held that the proposed Constitution would fail to protect liberty and equality because it was insufficiently "federal"—that is, because it was too "national," or unitary, thereby unjustly depriving the states of their proper powers.

But if this is the case, why did the proponents of the new Constitution title their defense *The Federalist*? This was a clever rhetorical ploy of Alexander Hamilton, who sought through such "packaging" to persuade the undecided that the new Constitution was sufficiently federal to promote and protect republican government. So successful was this tack that today we use the terms "national government" and "federal government" interchangeably. Moreover, those who defended a "federal" system, as that term was understood at the Convention, have since come to be known as anti-Federalists.

In sum, "federalism" today is understood to refer to the mixture of national and state powers that resulted from the compromise on this question reached at the Constitutional Convention. As you read in the previous chapter, Madison, in *Federalist 39*, argues that the Convention produced a founding document that was "in strictness neither a national nor a federal Constitution, but a composition of both."

WHY THIS READING?

Like the anti-Federalists examined earlier in this chapter, Tocqueville fears that liberty is endangered in a large country: "[S]mall nations have... always been the cradle of political liberty." At the same time, he recognizes that smallness renders a regime comparatively weak and vulnerable. The American federal system, he argues, combines the advantages of largeness with those of smallness. "Congress regulates the principal [most important] measures of the national government, and all the details of the administration are reserved to the provincial [state and local] legislatures." In fact, Tocqueville fears that the federal system leaves the national government *too* weak, and that this weakness will reveal itself in the case of a long and protracted war. At the same time, because the country is so distant from hostile powers, such wars are "extremely improbable." Consider Tocqueville's remark—"[T]he federal government is hardly concerned with anything except foreign affairs; it is the state governments that really control American society"— in light of the great growth of the national government that has occurred since he published *Democracy in America*.

Questions to consider as you read:

- In what does Tocqueville discover, and criticize, what he labels the "relative weakness" of the national government under the Constitution?
- Why does Tocqueville regard the Constitution's delineation of the powers of the national and state governments to be less than clearly set forth in the Founding document? How do the Americans, in his view, mitigate the potentially troublesome effects of this lack of clarity?

"Why the Federal System is Not Practicable for All Citizens, and How the Anglo-Americans Were Enabled to Adopt It"

When, after many efforts, a legislator succeeds in exercising an indirect influence upon the destiny of nations, his genius is lauded by mankind, while, in point of fact, the geographical position of the country, which he is unable to change, a social condition which arose without his co-operation, customs and opinions which he cannot trace to their source, and an origin with which he is unacquainted exercise so irresistible an influence over the courses of society that he is himself borne away by the current after an ineffectual resistance. Like the navigator, he may direct the vessel which bears him, but he can neither change its structure, nor raise the winds, nor lull the waters that swell beneath him.

I have shown the advantages that the Americans derive from their federal system; it remains for me to point out the circumstances that enabled them to adopt it, as its benefits cannot be enjoyed by all nations. The accidental defects of the federal system which originate in the laws may be corrected by the skill of the legislator, but there are evils inherent in the system which cannot be remedied by any effort. The people must therefore find in themselves the strength necessary to bear the natural imperfections of their government. Two sovereignties are necessarily in presence of each other. The legislator may simplify and equalize as far as possible the action of these two sovereignties, by limiting each of them to a sphere of authority accurately defined; but he cannot combine them into one or prevent them from coming into collision at certain points. The federal system, therefore, rests upon a theory which is complicated at the best, and which demands the daily exercise of a considerable share of discretion on the part of those it governs.

A proposition must be plain, to be adopted by the understanding of a people. A false notion which is clear and precise will always have more power in the world than a true principle which is obscure or involved. Thus it happens that parties, which are like small communities in the heart of the nation, invariably adopt some principle or name as a symbol, which very inadequately represents the end they have in view and the means that they employ, but without which they could neither act nor exist. The governments that are founded upon a single principle or a single feeling which is easily defined are perhaps not the best, but they are unquestionably the strongest and the most durable in the world.

In examining the Constitution of the United States, which is the most perfect constitution that ever existed, one is startled at the variety of information and the amount of discernment [capacity for judgment] that it presupposes in the people whom it is meant to govern. The government of the Union depends almost entirely upon legal fictions; the Union is an ideal nation, which exists, so to speak, only in the mind, and whose limits and extent can only be discerned [taken note of] by the understanding.

After the general theory is comprehended, many difficulties remain to be solved in its application; for the sovereignty of the Union is so involved in that of the states that it is impossible to distinguish its boundaries at the first glance. The whole structure of the government is artificial and conventional, and it would be ill adapted to a people which has not been long accustomed to conduct its own affairs, or to one in which the science of politics has not descended to the humblest classes of society. I have never been more struck by the good sense and the practical judgment of the Americans than in the manner in which they elude the numberless difficulties resulting from their Federal Constitution. I scarcely ever met with a plain American citizen who could not distinguish with surprising facility the obligations created by the laws of Congress from those created by the laws of his own state, and who, after having discriminated between the matters which come under the cognizance of the Union and those which the local legislature is competent to regulate, could not point out the exact limit of the separate jurisdictions of the Federal courts and the tribunals of the state.

The Constitution of the United States resembles those fine creations of human industry which ensure wealth and renown to their inventors, but which are profitless in other hands. This truth is exemplified by the condition of Mexico at the present time. The

Mexicans were desirous of establishing a federal system, and they took the Federal Constitution of their neighbors, the Anglo-Americans, as their model and copied it almost entirely. But although they had borrowed the letter of the law, they could not carry over the spirit that gives it life. They were involved in ceaseless embarrassments by the mechanism of their dual government; the sovereignty of the states and that of the Union perpetually exceeded their respective privileges and came into collision; and to the present day Mexico is alternately the victim of anarchy and the slave of military despotism.

The second and most fatal of all defects, and that which I believe to be inherent in the federal system, is the relative weakness of the government of the Union. The principle upon which all confederations rest is that of a divided sovereignty. Legislators may render this partition less perceptible, they may even conceal it for a time from the public eye, but they cannot prevent it from existing; and a divided sovereignty must always be weaker than an entire one. The remarks made on the Constitution of the United States have shown with what skill the Americans, while restraining the power of the Union within the narrow limits of a federal government, have given it the semblance, and to a certain extent the force, of a national government. By this means the legislators of the Union have diminished the natural danger of confederations, but have not entirely obviated [avoided] it.

The American government, it is said, does not address itself to the states, but transmits its injunctions directly to the citizens and compels them individually to comply with its demands. But if the Federal law were to clash with the interests and the prejudices of a state, it might be feared that all the citizens of that state would conceive themselves to be interested in the cause of a single individual who refused to obey. If all the citizens of the state were aggrieved at the same time and in the same manner by the authority of the Union, the Federal government would vainly attempt to subdue them individually; they would instinctively unite in a common defense and would find an organization already prepared for them in the sovereignty that their state is allowed to enjoy. Fiction would give way to reality, and an organized portion of the nation might then contest the central authority.

The same observation holds good with regard to the Federal jurisdiction. If the courts of the Union violated an important law of a state in a private case, the real though not the apparent contest would be between the aggrieved state represented by a citizen and the Union represented by its courts of justice.

He would have but a partial knowledge of the world who should imagine that it is possible by the aid of legal fictions to prevent men from finding out and employing those means of gratifying their passions which have been left open to them. The American legislators, though they have rendered a collision between the two sovereignties less probable, have not destroyed the causes of such a misfortune. It may even be affirmed that, in case of such a collision, they have not been able to ensure the victory of the Federal element. The Union is possessed of money and troops, but the states have kept the affections and the prejudices of the people. The sovereignty of the Union is an abstract being, which is connected with but few external objects; the sovereignty of the states is perceptible by the senses, easily understood, and constantly active. The former is of recent creation, the latter is coeval with the people itself. The sovereignty of the Union is factitious, that of the states is natural and self-existent, without effort, like the authority of a parent. The sovereignty of the nation affects a few of the chief interests of society; it represents an immense but remote country, a vague and ill-defined sentiment. The authority of the states controls every individual citizen at every hour and in all circumstances; it protects his property, his freedom, and his life; it affects at every moment his well-being or his misery. When we recollect the traditions, the customs, the prejudices of local and familiar attachment with which it is connected, we cannot doubt the superiority of a power that rests on the instinct of patriotism, so natural to the human heart.

Since legislators cannot prevent such dangerous collisions as occur between the two sovereignties which coexist in the Federal system, their first object must be, not only to dissuade [argue against] the confederate states from warfare, but to encourage such dispositions as lead to peace. Hence it is that the Federal compact cannot be lasting unless there exists in the communities which are leagued together a certain number of inducements [motivations] to union which render their common dependence agreeable and the task of the government light. The Federal system cannot succeed without the presence of favorable circumstances added to the influence of good laws. All the nations that have ever formed a confederation have been held together by some common interests, which served as the intellectual ties of association.

But men have sentiments and principles as well as material interests. A certain uniformity of civilization is not less necessary to the durability of a confederation than a uniformity of interests in the states that compose it....

...The circumstance which makes it easy to maintain a Federal government in America is not only that the states have similar interests, a common origin, and a common language, but that they have also arrived at the same stage of civilization, which almost always renders a union feasible. I do not know of any European nation, however small, that does not present less uniformity in its different provinces than the American people, which occupy a territory as extensive as one half of Europe....

...The most important occurrence in the life of a nation is the breaking out of a war. In war a people act as one man against foreign nations in defense of their very existence. The skill of the government, the good sense of the community, and the natural fondness that men almost always entertain for their country may be enough as long as the only object is to maintain peace in the interior of the state and to favor its internal prosperity; but that the nation may carry on a great war the people must make more numerous and painful sacrifices; and to suppose that a great number of men will of their own accord submit to these exigencies is to betray an ignorance of human nature. All the nations that have been obliged to sustain a long and serious warfare have consequently been led to augment the power of their government. Those who have not succeeded in this attempt have been subjugated. A long war almost always reduces nations to the wretched alternative of being abandoned to ruin by defeat or to despotism by success. War therefore renders the weakness of a government most apparent and most alarming; and I have shown that the inherent defect of federal governments is that of being weak.

The federal system not only has no centralized administration, and nothing that resembles one, but the central government itself is imperfectly organized, which is always a great cause of weakness when the nation is opposed to other countries which are themselves governed by a single authority. In the Federal Constitution of the United States, where the central government has more real force than in any other confederation, this evil is still extremely evident. A single example will illustrate the case.

The Constitution confers upon Congress the right of "calling forth the militia to execute the laws of the Union, suppress insurrections, and repel invasions"; and another article declares that the President of the United States is the commander-in-chief of the militia. In the war of 1812 the President ordered the militia of the Northern states to march to the frontiers; but Connecticut and Massachusetts, whose interests were impaired by the war, refused to obey the command. They argued that the Constitution authorizes the Federal government to call forth the militia in case of insurrection or invasion; but in the present instance there was neither invasion nor insurrection. They added that the same Constitution which conferred upon the Union the right of calling the militia into active service reserved to the states that of naming the officers; and consequently (as they understood the clause) no officer of the Union had any right to command the militia, even during war, except the President in person: and in this case they were ordered to join an army commanded by another individual. These absurd and pernicious doctrines received the sanction not only of the governors and the legislative bodies, but also of the courts of justice in both states; and the Federal government was forced to raise elsewhere the troops that it required.

How does it happen, then, that the American Union, with all the relative perfection of its laws, is not dissolved by the occurrence of a great war? It is because it has no great wars to fear. Placed in the center of an immense continent, which offers a boundless field for human industry [diligence], the Union is almost as much insulated from the world as if all its frontiers were girt [bound] by the ocean....

...The great advantage of the United States does not, then, consist in a Federal Constitution which allows it to carry on great wars, but in a geographical position which renders such wars extremely improbable.

No one can be more inclined than I am to appreciate the advantages of the federal system, which I hold to be one of the combinations most favorable to the prosperity and freedom of man. I envy the lot of those nations which have been able to adopt it; but I cannot believe that any confederate people could maintain a long or an equal contest with a nation of similar strength in which the government is centralized. A people which, in the presence of the great military monarchies of Europe, should divide its sovereignty into fractional parts would, in my opinion, by that very act abdicate [renounce] its power, and perhaps its existence and its name. But such is the admirable position of the New World that man has no other enemy than himself, and that, in order to be happy and to be free, he has only to determine that he will be so.

In examining the federal Constitution we have seen that the lawgivers of the Union strove in the opposite direction. The result of their efforts has been to make the federal government more independent in its sphere than are the states in theirs. But the federal government is hardly concerned with anything except foreign affairs; it is the state governments which really control American society.

RONALD REAGAN, "STATE OF THE UNION ADDRESS" (1982)

Limited Government

Ronald Reagan, the 40th president of the United States, served two terms (1981–1989). Prior to that, he was the governor of California. In an effort to address the "stagflation" (the combination high inflation and high unemployment) that America experienced during the 1970s, Reagan, a Republican, championed "supply-side" economic policies—lower tax rates and a "tight" monetary policy (higher interest rates, which have the effect of reducing the money supply and, therewith, inflation).

WHY THIS READING?

In this address to Congress and the nation, Reagan describes the animating vision behind his policies, which, he asserts, is the principle of individual liberty and "the spirit of enterprise," upon which, he argues, the country was founded. According to Reagan, the growth of the national government signified that the country had fallen away from its core principles: "[G]overnment," he said, "is not the solution; government is the problem." What came to be called the "Reagan Revolution" refers to his efforts to scale back the size and scope of the national government and to return power and responsibilities to state and local governments. Most conservative politicians today appeal to Reagan's vision and example as they seek to promote and enact similar policies.

Questions to consider as you read:

- Note the extent to which Reagan's arguments for a smaller national government echo those of the anti-Federalists. Nevertheless, what differences do you find in Reagan's vision?
- In his remarks, Reagan laments what he deems is too high a tax burden on citizens. What does he posit as the connection between high taxation, on the one hand, and the preservation of liberty and equality, on the other?

Mr. Speaker, Mr. President, distinguished Members of the Congress, honored guests, and fellow citizens:

Once again, in keeping with time-honored tradition, I have come to report to you on the state of the Union, and I'm pleased to report that America is much improved, and there's good reason to believe that improvement will continue through the days to come.

You and I have had some honest and open differences in the year past. But they didn't keep us from joining hands in bipartisan cooperation to stop a long decline that had drained this nation's spirit and eroded its health. There is renewed energy and optimism throughout the land. America is back, standing tall, looking to the eighties with courage, confidence, and hope.

The problems we're overcoming are not the heritage of one person, party, or even one generation. It's just the tendency of government to grow, for practices and programs to become the nearest thing to eternal life we'll ever see on this Earth. And there's always that well-intentioned chorus of voices saying, "With a little more power and a little more money, we could do so much for the people." For a time we forgot the American dream isn't one of making government bigger; it's keeping faith with the mighty spirit of free people under God.

As we came to the decade of the eighties, we faced the worst crisis in our postwar history. In the seventies were years of rising problems and falling confidence. There was a feeling government had grown beyond the consent of the governed. Families felt helpless in the face of mounting inflation and the indignity of taxes that reduced reward for hard work, thrift, and risk-taking. All this was overlaid by an ever growing web of rules and regulations.

On the international scene, we had an uncomfortable feeling that we'd lost the respect of friend and foe. Some questioned whether we had the will to defend peace and freedom. But America is too great for small dreams. There was a hunger in the land for a spiritual revival; if you will, a crusade for renewal. The American people said: Let us look to the future with confidence, both at home and abroad. Let us give freedom a chance.

Americans were ready to make a new beginning, and together we have done it. We're confronting our problems one by one. Hope is alive tonight for millions of young families and senior citizens set free from unfair tax increases and crushing inflation. Inflation has been beaten down from 12.4 to 3.2 percent, and that's a great victory for all the people. The prime rate has been cut almost in half, and we must work together to bring it down even more.

Together, we passed the first across-the-board tax reduction for everyone since the Kennedy tax cuts. Next year, tax rates will be indexed so inflation can't push people into higher brackets when they get cost-of-living pay raises. Government must never again use inflation to profit at the people's expense.

Today a working family earning $25,000 has $1,100 more in purchasing power than if tax and inflation rates were still at the 1980 levels. Real after-tax income increased 5 percent last year. And economic deregulation of key industries like transportation has offered more chances—or choices, I should say, to consumers and new changes—or chances for entrepreneurs and protecting safety. Tonight, we can report and be proud of one of the best recoveries in decades. Send away the handwringers and the doubting Thomases. Hope is reborn for couples dreaming of owning homes and for risk-takers with vision to create tomorrow's opportunities.

The spirit of enterprise is sparked by the sunrise industries of high-tech and by small business people with big ideas—people like Barbara Proctor, who rose from a ghetto to build a multimillion-dollar advertising agency in Chicago; Carlos Perez, a Cuban refugee, who turned $27 and a dream into a successful importing business in Coral Gables, Florida.

People like these are heroes for the eighties. They helped 4 million Americans find jobs in 1983. More people are drawing paychecks tonight than ever before. And Congress helps—or progress helps everyone—well, Congress does too—everyone. In 1983 women filled 73 percent of all the new jobs in managerial, professional, and technical fields.

But we know that many of our fellow countrymen are still out of work, wondering what will come of their hopes and dreams. Can we love America and not reach out to tell them: You are not forgotten; we will not rest until each of you can reach as high as your God-given talents will take you?

The heart of America is strong; it's good and true. The cynics were wrong; America never was a sick society. We're seeing rededication to bedrock values of faith, family, work, neighborhood, peace, and freedom—values that help bring us together as one people, from the youngest child to the most senior citizen.

The Congress deserves America's thanks for helping us restore pride and credibility to our military. And I hope that you're as proud as I am of the young men and women in uniform who have volunteered to man the ramparts in defense of freedom and whose dedication, valor, and skill increases so much our chance of living in a world at peace.

People everywhere hunger for peace and a better life. The tide of the future is a freedom tide, and our struggle for democracy cannot and will not be denied. This nation champions peace that enshrines liberty, democratic rights, and dignity for every individual. America's new strength, confidence, and purpose are carrying hope and opportunity far from our shores. A world economic recovery is underway. It began here.

We've journeyed far, but we have much farther to go. Franklin Roosevelt told us 50 years ago this month: "Civilization cannot go back; civilization must not stand still. We have undertaken new methods. It is our task to perfect, to improve, to alter when necessary, but in all cases to go forward."

It's time to move forward again, time for America to take freedom's next step. Let us unite tonight behind four great goals to keep America free, secure, and at peace in the eighties together.

We can ensure steady economic growth. We can develop America's next frontier. We can strengthen our traditional values. And we can build a meaningful peace to protect our loved ones and this shining star of faith that has guided millions from tyranny to the safe harbor of freedom, progress, and hope.

Doing these things will open wider the gates of opportunity, provide greater security for all, with no barriers of bigotry or discrimination.

The key to a dynamic decade is vigorous economic growth, our first great goal. We might well begin with common sense in Federal budgeting: government spending no more than government takes in.

We must bring Federal deficits down. But how we do that makes all the difference.

We can begin by limiting the size and scope of government. Under the leadership of Vice President Bush, we have reduced the growth of Federal regulations by more than 25 percent and cut well over 300 million hours of government-required paperwork each year. This will save the public more than $150 billion over the next 10 years.

The Grace commission has given us some 2,500 recommendations for reducing wasteful spending, and they're being examined throughout the administration. Federal spending growth has been cut from 17.4 percent in 1980 to less than half of that today, and we have already achieved over $300 billion in budget savings for the period of 1982 to '86. But that's only a little more than half of what we sought. Government is still spending too large a percentage of the total economy.

Now, some insist that any further budget savings must be obtained by reducing the portion spent on defense. This ignores the fact that national defense is solely the responsibility of the Federal Government; indeed, it is its prime responsibility. And yet defense spending is less than a third of the total budget. During the years of President Kennedy and of the years before that, defense was almost half the total budget. And then came several years in which our military capability was allowed to deteriorate to a very dangerous degree. We are just now restoring, through the essential modernization of our conventional and strategic forces, our capability to meet our present and future security needs. We dare not shirk our responsibility to keep America free, secure, and at peace.

The last decade saw domestic spending surge literally out of control. But the basis for such spending had been laid in previous years. A pattern of overspending has been in place for half a century. As the national debt grew, we were told not to worry, that we owed it to ourselves.

Now we know that deficits are a cause for worry. But there's a difference of opinion as to whether taxes should be increased, spending cut, or some of both. Fear is expressed that government borrowing to fund the deficit could inhibit the economic recovery by taking capital needed for business and industrial expansion. Well, I think that debate is missing an important point. Whether government borrows or increases taxes, it will be taking the same amount of money from the private sector, and, either way, that's too much. Simple fairness dictates that government must not raise taxes on families struggling to pay their bills. The root of the problem is that government's share is more than we can afford if we're to have a sound economy.

We must bring down the deficits to ensure continued economic growth. In the budget that I will submit on February 1st, I will recommend measures that will reduce the deficit over the next 5 years. Many of these will be unfinished business from last year's budget.

Some could be enacted quickly if we could join in a serious effort to address this problem. I spoke today with Speaker of the House O'Neill, Senate Majority Leader Baker, Senate Minority Leader Byrd, and House Minority Leader Michel. I asked them if they would designate congressional representatives to meet with representatives of the administration to try to reach prompt agreement on a bipartisan deficit reduction plan. I know it would take a long, hard struggle to agree on a full-scale plan. So, what I have proposed is that we first see if we can agree on a down payment.

Now, I believe there is basis for such an agreement, one that could reduce the deficits by about a hundred billion dollars over the next 3 years. We could focus on some of the less contentious spending cuts that are still pending before the Congress. These could be combined with measures to close certain tax loopholes, measures that the Treasury Department has previously said to be worthy of support. In addition, we could examine the possibility of achieving further outlay savings based on the work of the Grace commission.

If the congressional leadership is willing, my representatives will be prepared to meet with theirs at the earliest possible time. I would hope the leadership might agree on an expedited timetable in which to develop and enact that down payment.

But a down payment alone is not enough to break us out of the deficit problem. It could help us start on the right path. Yet, we must do more. So, I propose that we begin exploring how together we can make structural reforms to curb the built-in growth of spending.

I also propose improvements in the budgeting process. Some 43 of our 50 States grant their Governors the right to veto individual items in appropriation bills without having to veto the entire bill. California is one of those 43 States. As Governor, I found this line-item veto was a powerful tool against wasteful or extravagant spending. It works in 43 States. Let's put it to work in Washington for all the people.

It would be most effective if done by constitutional amendment. The majority of Americans approve of such an amendment, just as they and I approve of an amendment mandating a balanced Federal budget. Many States also have this protection in their constitutions.

To talk of meeting the present situation by increasing taxes is a Band-Aid solution which does nothing to cure an illness that's been coming on for half a century—to say nothing of the fact that it poses a real threat to economic recovery. Let's remember that a substantial amount of income tax is presently owed and not paid by people in the underground economy. It would be immoral to make those who are paying taxes pay more to compensate for those who aren't paying their share.

There's a better way. Let us go forward with an historic reform for fairness, simplicity, and incentives for growth. I am asking Secretary Don Regan for a plan for action to simplify the entire tax code, so all taxpayers, big and small, are treated more fairly. And I believe such a plan could result in that underground economy being brought into the sunlight of honest tax compliance. And it could make the tax base broader, so personal tax rates could come down, not go up. I've asked that specific recommendations, consistent with those objectives, be presented to me by December 1984....

...[O]ur most precious resources, our greatest hope for the future, are the minds and hearts of our people, especially our children. We can help them build tomorrow by strengthening our community of shared values. This must be our third great goal. For us, faith, work, family, neighborhood, freedom, and peace are not just words; they're expressions of what America means, definitions of what makes us a good and loving people.

Families stand at the center of our society. And every family has a personal stake in promoting excellence in education. Excellence does not begin in Washington. A 600-percent increase in Federal spending on education between 1960 and 1980 was accompanied by a steady decline in Scholastic Aptitude Test scores. Excellence must begin in our homes and neighborhood schools, where it's the responsibility of every parent and teacher and the right of every child.

Our children come first, and that's why I established a bipartisan National Commission on Excellence in Education, to help us chart a commonsense course for better education. And already, communities are implementing the Commission's recommendations. Schools are reporting progress in math and reading skills. But we must do more to restore discipline to schools; and we must encourage the teaching of new basics, reward teachers of merit, enforce tougher standards, and put our parents back in charge.

I will continue to press for tuition tax credits to expand opportunities for families and to soften the double payment for those paying public school taxes and private school tuition. Our proposal would target assistance to low- and middle-income families. Just as more incentives are needed within our schools, greater competition is needed among our schools. Without standards and competition, there can be no champions, no records broken, no excellence in education or any other walk of life.

And while I'm on this subject, each day your Members observe a 200-year-old tradition meant to signify America is one nation under God. I must ask: If you can begin your day with a member of the clergy standing right here leading you in prayer, then why can't freedom to acknowledge God be enjoyed again by children in every schoolroom across this land?

America was founded by people who believed that God was their rock of safety. He is ours. I recognize we must be cautious in claiming that God is on our side, but I think it's all right to keep asking if we're on His side.

During our first 3 years, we have joined bipartisan efforts to restore protection of the law to unborn children. Now, I know this issue is very controversial. But unless and until it can be proven that an unborn child is not a living human being, can we justify assuming without proof that it isn't? No one has yet offered such proof; indeed, all the evidence is to the contrary. We should rise above bitterness and reproach, and if Americans could come together in a spirit of understanding and helping, then we could find positive solutions to the tragedy of abortion.

Economic recovery, better education, rededication to values, all show the spirit of renewal gaining the upper hand. And all will improve family life in the eighties. But families need more. They need assurance that they and their loved ones can walk the streets of America without being afraid. Parents need to know their children will not be victims of child pornography and abduction. This year we will intensify our drive against these and other horrible crimes like sexual abuse and family violence.

Already our efforts to crack down on career criminals, organized crime, drug-pushers, and to enforce tougher sentences and paroles are having effect. In 1982 the crime rate dropped by 4.3 percent, the biggest decline since 1972. Protecting victims is just as important as safeguarding the rights of defendants.

Opportunities for all Americans will increase if we move forward in fair housing and work to ensure women's rights, provide for equitable treatment in pension benefits and Individual Retirement Accounts, facilitate child care, and enforce delinquent parent support payments.

It's not just the home but the workplace and community that sustain our values and shape our future. So, I ask your help in assisting more communities to break the bondage of dependency.

Help us to free enterprise by permitting debate and voting "yes" on our proposal for enterprise zones in America. This has been before you for 2 years. Its passage can help high-unemployment areas by creating jobs and restoring neighborhoods.

A society bursting with opportunities, reaching for its future with confidence, sustained by faith, fair play, and a conviction that good and courageous people will flourish when they're free—these are the secrets of a strong and prosperous America at peace with itself and the world.

A lasting and meaningful peace is our fourth great goal. It is our highest aspiration. And our record is clear: Americans resort to force only when we must. We have never been aggressors. We have always struggled to defend freedom and democracy.

We have no territorial ambitions. We occupy no countries. We build no walls to lock people in. Americans build the future. And our vision of a better life for farmers, merchants, and working people, from the Americas to Asia, begins with a simple premise: The future is best decided by ballots, not bullets.

Governments which rest upon the consent of the governed do not wage war on their neighbors. Only when people are given a personal stake in deciding their own destiny, benefiting from their own risks, do they create societies that are prosperous, progressive, and free. Tonight, it is democracies that offer hope by feeding the hungry, prolonging life, and eliminating drudgery.

When it comes to keeping America strong, free, and at peace, there should be no Republicans or Democrats, just patriotic Americans. We can decide the tough issues not by who is right, but by what is right....

...How can we not believe in the greatness of America? How can we not do what is right and needed to preserve this last best hope of man on Earth? After all our struggles to restore America, to revive confidence in our country, hope for our future, after all our hard-won victories earned through the patience and courage of every citizen, we cannot, must not, and will not turn back. We will finish our job. How could we do less? We're Americans.

Carl Sandburg said, "I see America not in the setting sun of a black night of despair...I see America in the crimson light of a rising sun fresh from the burning, creative hand of God...I see great days ahead for men and women of will and vision."

I've never felt more strongly that America's best days and democracy's best days lie ahead. We're a powerful force for good. With faith and courage, we can perform great deeds and take freedom's next step. And we will. We will carry on the tradition of a good and worthy people who have brought light where there was darkness, warmth where there was cold, medicine where there was disease, food where there was hunger, and peace where there was only bloodshed.

Let us be sure that those who come after will say of us in our time, that in our time we did everything that could be done. We finished the race; we kept them free; we kept the faith.

Thank you very much. God bless you, and God bless America.

JUSTICE HARRY BLACKMUN, OPINION OF THE COURT IN *GARCIA V. SAN ANTONIO* (1985)

This Supreme Court case upheld the U.S. Department of Labor's ruling that local governments are subject to the provisions of the federal Fair Labor Standards Act. At issue was the question of the extent of the Tenth Amendment's protection of state sovereignty. The Tenth Amendment (1791) states, "The powers not delegated to the United States by the Constitution, nor prohibited by it to the States, are reserved to the States respectively, or to the people." The Tenth Amendment is often referred to as the "states' rights amendment." However, at the time of the debate over the language of the Amendment, leading anti-Federalists bitterly denounced it as a mere "truism," that is, as nothing more than a platitude that added nothing to the powers of the states than what they already possessed under the original Constitution. As you have read, these anti-Federalists regarded the powers that the states already possessed under the unamended Constitution to be insufficient, hence their call for an amendment—and their resulting bitterness.

WHY THIS READING?

As with Reagan's 1982 speech, this 1985 case reveals the perennial quality of debate in this country over the proper division of powers between the national and state governments. *Garcia* provides the counterpoint to the case for expanding the sovereignty of the states. Specifically, this case addresses the questions what are the "traditional government functions" of the states and whether Congress is empowered to regulate these functions under the Constitution's Commerce Clause. This Clause, found in Article I, Section 8 of the Constitution, states that "Congress shall have power to... regulate commerce... among the several states." It has been noted earlier that the very same question will be addressed again by the Supreme Court in the matter of the constitutionality of the 2010 health care bill.

Questions to guide you as you read:

- What degree of clear guidance on the subject of federalism does Blackmun find in the Constitution? How, for him, does this bear on contemporary efforts to strike a just balance between the national and state governments?
- Based on your prior reading in this chapter, what would Jefferson's rejoinder be to Blackmun's claims?

JUSTICE BLACKMUN delivered the opinion of the Court....

...[I]n *National League of Cities v. Usery* (1976),... this Court, by a sharply divided vote, ruled that the Commerce Clause does not empower Congress to enforce the minimum-wage and overtime provisions of the Fair Labor Standards Act (FLSA) against the States "in areas of traditional government functions."... *National League of Cities*... did not offer a general explanation of how a "traditional" function is to be distinguished from a "nontraditional" one.... In the present cases, a Federal District Court concluded that municipal ownership and operation of a mass-transit system is a traditional government function, and thus under *National League of Cities*, is exempt from the obligations imposed by the FLSA. Faced with the identical question, three Federal Courts of Appeals and one state appellate court have reached the opposite conclusion.

Our examination of this "function" standard applied in these and other cases over the last eight years now persuades us that the attempt to draw the boundaries of state regulatory immunity in terms of "traditional governmental function" is not only unworkable but is inconsistent with the established principles of federalism....

...We doubt that courts ultimately can identify principled constitutional limitations on the scope of Congress' Commerce Clause powers over the States merely by relying on *a priori* [known or assumed without reference to experience] definitions of state sovereignty. In part, this is because of the elusiveness of objective criteria for "fundamental" elements of state sovereignty, a problem we have witnessed in the search for "traditional governmental functions." There is, however, a more fundamental reason: the sovereignty of the States is limited by the Constitution itself....

...The fact that the States remain sovereign as to all powers not vested in Congress or denied them by the Constitution offers no guidance about where the frontier between state and federal power lies....

When we look for the States' "residuary and inviolable sovereignty," in the shape of the constitutional scheme rather than in predetermined notions of sovereign power, a different measure of state sovereignty emerges. Apart from the limitation on federal authority inherent in the delegated natures of Congress' Article I powers, the principal means chosen by the Framers to ensure the role of the States in the federal system lies in the structure of the Federal Government itself. It is no novelty to observe that the composition of the Federal Government was designed in large part to protect the States from overreaching by Congress. The Framers thus gave the States a role in the selection both of the Executive and the Legislative Branches of the Federal Government. The States were vested with indirect influence over the House of Representatives and the Presidency by their control of electoral qualifications and their role in presidential elections. They were given more direct influence in the Senate, where each State received equal representation and each Senator was to be selected by the legislature of his State. The significance attached to the States' equal representation in the Senate is underscored by the prohibition of any constitutional amendment divesting a State of equal representation without the State's consent.

The extent to which the structure of the Federal Government itself was relied on to insulate the interests of the States is evident in the view of the Framers. James Madison explained that the Federal Government "will partake sufficiently of the spirit [of the States], to be disinclined to invade the rights of the individual States, or the prerogatives of their governments." The Framers chose to rely on a federal system in which special restraints on federal power over the States inhered principally in the workings of the National Government itself, rather than in discrete limitations on the objects of federal authority. State sovereign interest, then, are more properly protected by procedural safeguards inherent in the structure of the federal system than by judicially created limitations on federal power....

We realize that changes in the structure of the Federal Government have taken place since 1789, not the least of which has been the substitution of popular elections of Senators by the adoption of the Seventeenth Amendment in 1913, and that these changes may work to alter the influence of the States in the federal political process. Nonetheless, against this background, we are convinced that the fundamental limitation that the constitutional scheme imposed on the Commerce Clause to protect the "States as States" is one of process rather than one of results....

JUSTICE LEWIS POWELL (WITH WHOM CHIEF JUSTICE BURGER, JUSTICE REHNQUIST, AND JUSTICE O'CONNOR JOIN, DISSENTING)

...Whatever effect the Court's decision may have in weakening the application of *stare decisis*, it is likely to be less important than what the Court has done to the Constitution itself. A unique feature of the United States is the federal system of government guaranteed by the Constitution and implicit in the very name of our country. Despite some genuflecting in the Court's opinion to the concept of federalism, today's decision effectively reduces the Tenth Amendment to meaningless rhetoric when Congress acts pursuant to the Commerce Clause....

Today's opinion does not explain how the States' role in the electoral process guarantees that particular exercises of the Commerce Clause power will not infringe on residual State sovereignty....

More troubling than the logical infirmities in the Court's reasoning is the result of its holding, i.e., that federal political officials, invoking the Commerce Clause, are the sole judges of the limits of their own power....

In our federal system, the States have a major role that cannot be preempted by the national government. As contemporaneous [of that period] writings and the debates at the ratifying conventions make clear, the States' ratification of the Constitution was predicated on this understanding of federalism. Indeed, the Tenth Amendment was adopted specifically to ensure that the important role promised the States by the proponents of the Constitution was realized....

JUSTICE SANDRA DAY O'CONNOR (WITH WHOM JUSTICE POWELL AND JUSTICE REHNQUIST JOIN, DISSENTING)

The court today surveys the battle scene of federalism and sounds a retreat....

...The true "essence" of federalism is that the States as States have legitimate interest which the National Government is bound to respect even though its laws are supreme.... If federalism so conceived and so carefully cultivated by the Framers of our Constitution is to remain meaningful, this Court cannot abdicate its constitutional responsibility to oversee the Federal Government's compliance with its duty to respect the legitimate interests of the States.

The Framers perceived the interstate commerce power to be important but limited, and expected that it would be used primarily if not exclusively to remove interstate tariffs and to regulate maritime affairs and large-scale mercantile enterprise.... This perception of a narrow commerce power is important not because it suggests that the commerce power should be as narrowly construed today. Rather, it explains why the Framers could believe the Constitution assured significant state authority even as it bestowed a range of powers, including the commerce power, on the Congress. In an era when interstate commerce represented a tiny fraction of economic activity and most goods and services were produced and consumed close to home, the interstate commerce power left a broad range of activities beyond the reach of Congress....

Might equality both make democratic liberty possible and then destroy it?

ALEXIS DE TOCQUEVILLE, *DEMOCRACY IN AMERICA,* "WHY DEMOCRATIC NATIONS SHOW A MORE ARDENT AND ENDURING LOVE FOR EQUALITY THAN FOR LIBERTY" (1835)

Tocqueville here explains in greater detail the basis for his fear that "the most intense passion that is produced by equality of condition" may, under certain circumstances, come to endanger political liberty itself. He locates this danger in the fact that "men cannot enjoy political liberty [political participation]" without "great exertions," whereas, in order to "taste" the pleasures of equality, "nothing is required but to live." Although he is convinced that democratic nations generally prefer "equality in freedom," he worries that, if they "cannot obtain" equality in freedom, they will "call for equality in slavery."

WHY THIS READING?

This chapter has examined a number of contrasting opinions regarding various conditions said to enable or to retard democracy's ability to successfully balance both equality and liberty. We conclude this examination with a reading in which Tocqueville analyzes the character of the American people as it bears on this issue, specifically, the effect that "the passion for equality" has on popular character. Although it is paradoxical on its face, especially to citizens in a democracy, nevertheless the principle of equality, argues Tocqueville, can bring despotism no less than liberty. Slaves, after all, "enjoy" equality among themselves. Yet, we might rejoin, "What of their master? Mastery, by definition, contradicts equality." But what if the population votes away its liberty, thus "consenting" to slavery? On the basis of the Declaration of Independence (which we examine later in this text), citizens do not have the right to enslave themselves. Why? Although the institution of government through the "consent of the governed" is deemed by the Declaration to be a necessary condition of political justice, it is not regarded as sufficient. Also required for justice is that government protect our "inalienable rights." What does the Declaration mean by "inalienable"? Clearly, it means that neither government nor our fellow citizens can alienate such rights, chief among them "life, liberty, and the pursuit of happiness." But it also means more than this. Neither can *we* alienate our own inalienable rights, because such rights inhere in human nature. We are not their authors. What we did not create, neither can we take away. So argues the Declaration. This, of course, is not to deny the plain fact that we have the ***power*** to commit suicide or even to surrender our freedom to another. But we can never have the ***right*** to do so. Were it otherwise, argues the Declaration, power, or might, "would make 'right.'"

But if the Declaration provides the ***principle*** governing the right use of political power, the question of how to ensure that this principle is realized in ***practice*** remains. It is this question to which Tocqueville turns.

Questions to guide you as you read:

- What does Tocqueville believe he sees in human nature that causes him to predict that democratic peoples "will endure poverty, servitude, [and] barbarism, but they will not endure aristocracy"?
- Based on Tocqueville's arguments, what might democratic "equality in slavery" look like? Which contemporary attitudes and practices can you find to contradict his thesis? Which would he deem confirms it?

The first and most intense passion that is produced by equality of condition is, I need hardly say, the love of that equality. My readers will therefore not be surprised that I speak of this feeling before all others.

Everybody has remarked that in our time, and especially in France, this passion for equality is every day gaining ground in the human heart. It has been said a hundred times that our contemporaries are far more ardently [passionately] and tenaciously [stubbornly or persistently] attached to equality than to freedom; but as I do not find that the causes of the fact have been sufficiently analyzed, I shall endeavor to point them out.

It is possible to imagine an extreme point at which freedom and equality would meet and blend. Let us suppose that all the people take a part in the government, and that each one of them has an equal right to take a part in it. As no one is different from his fellows, none can exercise a tyrannical power; men will be perfectly free because they are all entirely equal; and they will all be perfectly equal because they are entirely free. To this ideal state democratic nations tend. This is the only complete form that equality can assume upon earth; but there are a thousand others which, without being equally perfect, are not less cherished by those nations.

The principle of equality may be established in civil society without prevailing in the political world. There may be equal rights of indulging in the same pleasures, of entering the same professions, of frequenting the same places; in a word, of living in

the same manner and seeking wealth by the same means, although all men do not take an equal share in the government. A kind of equality may even be established in the political world though there should be no political freedom there. A man may be the equal of all his countrymen save one, who is the master of all without distinction and who selects equally from among them all the agents of his power....

...Although men cannot become absolutely equal unless they are entirely free, and consequently equality, pushed to its furthest extent, may be confounded with freedom, yet there is good reason for distinguishing the one from the other. The taste which men have for liberty and that which they feel for equality are, in fact, two different things; and I am not afraid to add that among democratic nations they are two unequal things.

Upon close inspection it will be seen that there is in every age some peculiar [distinctive] and preponderant [preeminent] fact with which all others are connected; this fact almost always gives birth to some pregnant [meaningful] idea or some ruling passion, which attracts to itself and bears away in its course all the feelings and opinions of the time....

Freedom has appeared in the world at different times and under various forms; it has not been exclusively bound to any social condition, and it is not confined to democracies. Freedom cannot, therefore, form the distinguishing characteristic of democratic ages. The peculiar and preponderant fact that marks those ages as its own is the equality of condition; the ruling passion of men in those periods is the love of this equality. Do not ask what singular charm the men of democratic ages find in being equal, or what special reasons they may have for clinging so tenaciously to equality rather than to the other advantages that society holds out to them: equality is the distinguishing characteristic of the age they live in....

But independently of this reason there are several others which will at all times habitually lead men to prefer equality to freedom.

If a people could ever succeed in destroying, or even in diminishing, the equality that prevails in its own body, they could do so only by long and laborious efforts. Their social condition must be modified, their laws abolished, their opinions superseded, their habits changed, their manners corrupted. But political liberty is more easily lost; to neglect to hold it fast is to allow it to escape. Therefore not only do men cling to equality because it is dear to them; they also adhere to it because they think it will last forever.

That political freedom in its excesses may compromise the tranquility, the property, the lives of individuals is obvious even to narrow and unthinking minds. On the contrary, none but attentive and clear-sighted men perceive the perils with which equality threatens us, and they commonly avoid pointing them out. They know that the calamities they apprehend are remote and flatter themselves that they will only fall upon future generations, for which the present generation takes but little thought. The evils that freedom sometimes brings with it are immediate; they are apparent to all, and all are more or less affected by them. The evils that extreme equality may produce are slowly disclosed; they creep gradually into the social frame; they are seen only at intervals; and at the moment at which they become most violent, habit already causes them to be no longer felt.

The advantages that freedom brings are shown only by the lapse of time, and it is always easy to mistake the cause in which they originate. The advantages of equality are immediate, and they may always be traced from their source.

Political liberty bestows exalted pleasures from time to time upon a certain number of citizens. Equality every day confers a number of small enjoyments on every man. The charms of equality are every instant felt and are within the reach of all; the noblest hearts are not insensible to them, and the most vulgar souls exult in them. The passion that equality creates must therefore be at once strong and general. Men cannot enjoy political liberty unpurchased by some sacrifices, and they never obtain it without great exertions. But the pleasures of equality are self-proffered [self-given]; each of the petty incidents of life seems to occasion them, and in order to taste them, nothing is required but to live.

Democratic nations are at all times fond of equality, but there are certain epochs at which the passion they entertain for it swells to the height of fury. This occurs at the moment when the old social system, long menaced, is overthrown after a severe internal struggle, and the barriers of rank are at length thrown down. At such times men pounce upon equality as their booty [plunder], and they cling to it as to some precious treasure which they fear to lose. The passion for equality penetrates on every side into men's hearts, expands there, and fills them entirely. Tell them not that by this blind surrender of themselves to an exclusive passion they risk their dearest interests; they are deaf. Show them not freedom escaping from their grasp while they are looking another way; they are blind, or rather they can discern but one object to be desired in the universe....

...I think that democratic communities have a natural taste for freedom; left to themselves, they will seek it, cherish it, and view any privation [deprivation] of it with regret. But for equality their passion is ardent, insatiable, incessant, invincible; they call for equality in freedom; and if they cannot obtain that, they still call for equality in slavery. They will endure poverty, servitude, barbarism, but they will not endure aristocracy.

This is true at all times, and especially in our own day. All men and all powers seeking to cope with this irresistible passion will be overthrown and destroyed by it. In our age freedom cannot be established without it, and despotism itself cannot reign without its support.

CHAPTER 4

Core Question: Who has the right to vote, on what, and why?

This chapter, along with the two that follow it, attempts to go to the roots of the questions regarding the political institutions essential to American democracy. Key among these institutions are voting and elections. Yet there is today a good deal of confusion regarding the original Constitution's stance toward the franchise. Because constitutional amendments gave African-Americans and women the right to vote across the country, it has been assumed that the original Constitution somehow, for some reason, excluded them from this. This is not the case. In fact, as you will read, the Constitution says *nothing* on the subject. Instead, following the design for the division of powers between the national and state governments, the Constitution left this to the discretion of the states.

The original Constitution addressed voting qualifications in only one place and for only one national office. The qualifications to vote for members of the House of Representatives, Article I, Section 2, states that "electors [voters] in each State shall have the Qualifications requisite for Electors of the most numerous Branch of the State Legislature." This meant that if one qualified to vote in elections for what is called the "lower house" in one's state, one could also vote in the election for one's local member of the House of Representatives. As you will read, at the time of the ratification of the Constitution, members of the U.S. House of Representatives were the only national legislators for whom citizens voted directly. U.S. senators were elected by their state legislatures. However, this method of electing senators did not stop the popular will from prevailing; in practice, state legislators ran on a platform that included their promise to vote for "U.S. Senator A" rather than "B" if elected to the statehouse. As you will read in this chapter, direct election of U.S. senators was secured with the ratification of the 17th Amendment in 1913.

If the original Constitution says nothing to exclude African-Americans or women from voting, leaving it instead to the discretion of the states, what was the practice during these early years of the Republic? In the case of African-Americans, the historical facts are likely to surprise today's student. In a later chapter, we examine the infamous Supreme Court case *Dred Scott v. Sandford* (1857). Writing for the majority in this case, Chief Justice Taney asserted that "Negroes" as they were then called, "had no rights which a white man was bound to respect." Two justices dissented from the opinion. One of them, Benjamin Curtis, provided as counter-evidence a detailed history proving that many African-Americans had in fact enjoyed the rights of citizenship at the time of the American Revolution, including the right to vote "on equal terms with other citizens." Beginning in 1776, state constitutions protected the right of blacks to vote in Delaware, Pennsylvania, and Maryland. New York (1777), Massachusetts (1780), and New Hampshire (1784) soon followed.

The historical evidence further demonstrates that these state constitutional provisions had teeth. As a result, wrote the historian John Hancock in his 1865 study *Essays on the Elective Franchise*, when the proposed Constitution was submitted to voters in 1787 and 1788, it was ratified by both African-Americans and whites in several states. In fact, during the early years of the Republic, cities such as Baltimore, Maryland, witnessed greater numbers of African-Americans voting in elections than whites. In addition to voting rights, African-Americans in New Hampshire, Massachusetts, and Pennsylvania could also hold elective office. Finally, during the period when America existed as colonies under Great Britain, these colonies were forbidden by the Crown from abolishing slavery. But, with the commencement of the Revolution, Pennsylvania, Massachusetts, Connecticut, Rhode Island, Vermont, New Hampshire, and New York—no longer colonies, but now states—all abolished slavery.

Needless to say, in no state could slaves vote. At the same time, the above historical facts, less well known to today's students, suggest that many among the Founding generation meant to include blacks in the Declaration's assertion that "all men are created equal." But if this was the case, such sentiments weakened in the period dating from the early Republic to the Civil War. In the South, pro-slavery passion only strengthened. In 1820, Congress passed the Missouri Compromise, which allowed the entry of new slave-holding states. Congress also passed the Fugitive Slave Law, which permitted Southern slaveholders to travel to the North to capture blacks whom they declared to be escaped slaves. In 1854, Congress passed the Kansas-Nebraska Act, which permitted slavery in the territories now known as the states of Colorado, Wyoming, Montana, Idaho, North Dakota, South Dakota, Kansas, and Nebraska. Further reversals of post-Revolution, egalitarian sentiment occurred in states such as Maryland, which in 1809, reversed its previous policy, now restricting voting to whites, and in North Carolina, which enacted a similar policy in 1835.

This growing passion in defense of racial inequality brought equally passionate opposition in the North. In 1854, it gave rise to a new political party, the Republican Party, which would elect its first president in 1860, Abraham Lincoln. Lincoln ran on a platform opposing the extension of slavery to any new territory or state. Because the country was expanding rapidly westward, Southern defenders of slavery knew that such a prohibition would spell the death of their political power in the Senate and, in time, they feared, the death of slavery. During the period between Lincoln's election and inauguration, 11 of the 15 slave-holding states seceded. The Civil War had begun; it would result in constitutional amendments abolishing slavery as well as guaranteeing equal rights, including the right to vote, to African-Americans.

However, for a century following the Civil War, racist elements in the South continued to conspire to deprive African-Americans of the franchise through a variety of tactics ranging from the devious—for example, the poll tax, literacy tests, the "Black Codes" (later known as "Jim Crow" laws), and compulsory segregation—to the violent—for example, cross-burnings, physical intimidation, and lynchings. These obstructions to the intent of the 14th and 15th Amendments were finally addressed by Congress in 1965, with the passage of the Voting Rights Act. In this chapter, we shall read President Lyndon B. Johnson's defense of the Act.

In the case of voting rights for women, we find that a number of states extended the franchise to women prior to the 1920 passage of the 19th Amendment. In 1837, Kentucky gave women the right to vote in school-board elections. Kansas followed suit in 1861, the year that it entered the Union. In 1869, the Constitution of the Wyoming territory gave women the right to vote as well as to hold public office. In 1870, the territory of Utah extended full voting rights to women. Colorado gave women the vote in 1893. In 1895, Utah followed suit. A year later, Idaho passed a constitutional amendment granting the vote to women. In 1902, Kentucky rescinded women's right to vote in school-board elections (New Jersey, the first state to grant women full voting rights, in 1776, repealed this in 1807, the same year that it repealed the right of African-Americans to vote). However, in 1912, Kentucky restored the right of women to vote in school-board elections. In 1910, the state of Washington extended the right to vote to women. California followed one year later. In 1912, Michigan, Kansas, Oregon, and Arizona ratified state constitutional amendments giving women the vote. That same year, Wisconsin failed to pass a proposed women's-vote amendment. In all, we find that 11 states or territories had granted women full voting rights prior to the passage of the 19th Amendment.

Grounded in the historical background provided above, we begin this chapter with an essay by James Madison (as *The Federalist's* Publius) that addresses the questions of why we vote and who should have the right to vote. In the course of so doing, we inquire into what the original Constitution provided on these questions. This leads to the subjects of how and why the vote has been extended to African-Americans, women, and 18-year-olds. A debate continues to this day over whether these extensions of the franchise represent a radical departure from, or the fulfillment of the letter and spirit of, the Declaration of Independence and the original Constitution. Tied to the above question is whether *any* principled limits on voting are consistent with American democracy. Here, we compare two takes on this question by Tocqueville and then-U.S. Senator Carol Moseley-Braun (D-IL, 1994).

Why do we hold elections?

JAMES MADISON, *THE FEDERALIST, NO. 52* (1788)

Here Madison-as-Publius addresses the issue of the "right of suffrage [voting]," which, he holds, "is very justly regarded as a fundamental article of republican government."

WHY THIS READING?

In this essay, Madison defends the proposed Constitution's requirement that members of the House of Representatives stand for reelection every two years (U.S. senators serve six-year terms). Biennial elections for Representatives, he argues, ensure that those elected will have "an immediate dependence on, and an intimate sympathy with, the people" who elect them.

Questions to guide you as you read:

- Under the original Constitution, what role do the individual states play in determining qualifications for voting?
- Why does Madison reject the argument that members of the U.S. House of Representatives should have terms shorter than two years? Would not shorter terms be more "democratic"? Why not, according to Madison?

To the People of the State of New York:

...The first view to be taken of this part of the government, relates to the qualifications of the electors and the elected. Those of the former are to be the same with those of the electors of the most numerous branch of the State Legislatures. The definition of the right of suffrage is very justly regarded as a fundamental article of republican government. It was incumbent [imposed as a duty] on the Convention therefore to define and establish this right, in the Constitution. To have left it open for the occasional regulation of the Congress, would have been improper for the reason just mentioned. To have submitted it to the legislative discretion of the States, would have been improper for the same reason; and for the additional reason, that it would have rendered too dependent on the State Governments, that branch of the Federal Government, which ought to be dependent on the people alone. To have reduced the different qualifications in the different States, to one uniform rule, would probably have been as dissatisfactory to some of the States, as it would have been difficult to the Convention. The provision made by the Convention appears therefore, to be the best that lay within their option. It must be satisfactory to every State; because it is conformable to the standard already established, or which may be established by the State itself. It will be safe to the United States; because, being fixed by the State Constitutions, it is not alterable by the State Governments, and it cannot be feared that the people of the States will alter this part of their Constitutions, in such a manner as to abridge the rights secured to them by the Federal Constitution....

...First. As it is essential to liberty that the government in general, should have a common interest with the people; so it is particularly essential that the branch of it under consideration should have an immediate dependence on, and an intimate sympathy with the people. Frequent elections are unquestionably the only policy by which this dependence and sympathy can be effectually [completely] secured. But what particular degree of frequency may be absolutely necessary for the purpose, does not appear to be susceptible of any precise calculation; and must depend on a variety of circumstances with which it may be connected. Let us consult experience, the guide that ought always to be followed, whenever it can be found.

The scheme of representation, as a substitute for a meeting of the citizens in person, being at most but very imperfectly known to ancient polity, it is in more modern times only that we are to expect instructive examples....

...The conclusion resulting from these examples will be not a little strengthened by recollecting three circumstances. The first is, that the federal legislature will possess a part only of that supreme legislative authority which is vested completely in the British Parliament; and which, with a few exceptions, was exercised by the colonial assemblies and the Irish legislature. It is a received and well-founded maxim, that where no other circumstances affect the case, the greater the power is, the shorter ought to be its duration; and, conversely, the smaller the power, the more safely may its duration be protracted. In the second place, it has, on another occasion, been shown that the federal legislature will not only be restrained by its dependence on its people, as other legislative bodies are, but that it will be, moreover, watched and controlled by the several collateral legislatures, which other legislative bodies are not. And in the third place, no comparison can be made between the means that will be possessed by the more permanent branches of the federal government for seducing, if they should be disposed to seduce, the House of Representatives from their duty to the people, and the means of influence over the popular branch possessed by the other branches of the government above cited. With less power, therefore, to abuse, the federal representatives can be less tempted on one side, and will be doubly watched on the other.

PUBLIUS

If everyone must have the right to vote in order for America to qualify as a democracy, when did it become a democracy? Voting eligibility under the original Constitution

EXCERPTS FROM THE U.S. CONSTITUTION ON VOTING ELIGIBILITY

Article I, Sec. 2, Clause 1: "The House of Representatives shall be composed of Members chosen every second Year by the People of the several States, and the Electors in each State shall have the Qualifications requisite for Electors of the most numerous Branch of the State Legislature."

Article I, Sec. 3, Clause 1: "The Senate of the United States shall be composed of two Senators from each State, chosen by the Legislature thereof, for six Years; and each Senator shall have one Vote."

EDITORS' NOTE: *Election of senators by their state legislatures was repealed by the 17th Amendment (1913), which established direct election by the people.*

CHANCELLOR KENT, "ON UNIVERSAL SUFFRAGE" (1821)

In 1821, a convention was called to reform the New York State Constitution with the purpose of broadening the right of suffrage (voting) for the New York State Senate. Kent wanted to limit universal suffrage so that the state senate would continue to represent those with a freehold estate, the so-called "landed interest."

WHY THIS READING?

Kent argues that "freeholders" [those who own "real property" such as a house or farm] are the "safest guardians of property and the laws." To give the right to vote for the state senate to those without land would be a "bold and hazardous experiment." Kent's view, while shocking to our modern ears, can be traced back over two millennia: The Greek philosopher Aristotle argues in *The Politics* (1295a25–1296b12) that those who possess neither property nor education are easy prey for manipulation by unscrupulous demagogues. Some degree of material and intellectual independence is requisite for making informed, rational choices in voting. Although this is in no way guaranteed by the possession of a moderate amount of property, nevertheless, such a requirement is deemed by Kent to be a necessary condition for the desired independence in voters. To support his view, he would ask us to consider the Constitution's requirement that one needs to be at least 35 years old to be president. Although age is no guarantee of the practical wisdom sought in those who occupy the office, such a requirement was viewed by the Founders as a necessary condition for the prudence sought in presidents.

Later in this chapter, we will read the counterpoint to Kent's position, as voiced by then-U.S. Senator Carol Moseley-Braun (D-IL), in her defense of the "Motor-Voter Bill."

Questions to guide you as you read:

- What advantages does Kent believe will follow from limiting the right to vote to those who possess at least a moderate amount of landed property?
- What disadvantages does Kent believe will follow from allowing the very poor to vote?

The Convention was debating a proposal to end the freehold (i.e., property) requirement to vote for the New York State Senate. An amendment was offered which would have retained that qualification.

I am in favor of the amendment which has been submitted by my honorable colleague from Albany; and I must beg leave to trespass for a few moments upon the patience of the committee, while I state the reasons which have induced me to wish that the senate should continue, as heretofore, the representative of the landed interest and exempted from the control of universal suffrage. I hope that I may have to say will be kindly received, for it will be well intended. But, if I thought otherwise, I should still prefer to hazard the loss of the little popularity, which I might have in this house, or out of it, than to hazard the loss of the approbation [praise] of my own conscience.

I have reflected upon the report of the select committee with attention and with anxiety. We appear to be disregarding the principles of the constitution, under which we have so long, and so happily lived and to be changing some of its essential institutions. I cannot but think that the considerable men, who have studied the history of republics or are read in lessons of experience, must look with concern upon our apparent disposition to vibrate [move] from a well-balanced government to the extremes of the democratic doctrines. Such a broad proposition as that contained in the report, at the distance of ten years past, would have struck the public mind with astonishment and terror. So rapid has been the career of our vibration.

Let us recall our attention, for a moment, to our past history.

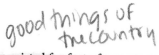

This state has existed for forty-four years under our present constitution, which was formed by those illustrious [famous] sages [wise persons] and patriots who adorned the revolution. It has wonderfully fulfilled all the great ends of civil government. During that long period we have enjoyed in an eminent degree the blessings of civil and religious liberty. We have had our lives, our privileges, and our property, protected. We have had a succession of wise and temperate legislatures. The code of our statute law has been again and again revised and corrected, and it may proudly bear a comparison with that of any other people. We have had, during that period, (though I am, perhaps not the fittest person to say it,) a regular, stable, honest, and enlightened administration of justice. All the peaceable pursuits of industry, and all the important interests of education and science, have been fostered and encouraged. We have trebled our numbers within the last twenty-five years, have displayed mighty resources, and have made unexampled [unparalleled] progress in the career of prosperity and greatness.

Our financial credit stands at an enviable height; and we are now successfully engaged in connecting the great lakes with the ocean by stupendous canals, which excite the admiration of our neighbors, and will make a conspicuous [easy to notice] figure even upon the map of the United States.

These are some of the fruits of our present government; and yet we seem to be dissatisfied with our condition, and we are engaged in the bold and hazardous experiment of remodeling the constitution. Is it not fit and discreet—I speak as to wise men—is it not fit and proper that we should pause in our career, and reflect well on the immensity of the innovation in contemplation. Discontent in the midst of so much prosperity, and with such abundant means of happiness, looks like ingratitude, and as if we were disposed to arraign [call before a court] the goodness of Providence [God]. Do we not expose ourselves to the danger of being deprived of the blessings we have enjoyed—when the husbandman has gathered in his harvest, and has filled his barns and his granaries [places to store grain] with the fruits of his industry, if he should then become discontented and unthankful, would we not have reason to apprehend that the Lord of the harvest might come in his wrath, and with his lightning destroy them?

The senate has hitherto been elected by the farmers of the state—by the free and independent lords of the soil—worth at least two hundred and fifty dollars in freehold estate, over and above all debts charged thereon. The governor has been chosen by the same electors, and we have hitherto elected citizens of elevated rank and character. Our assembly has been chosen by freeholders, possessing a freehold of the value of fifty dollars, or by persons renting a tenement of the yearly value of five dollars, and who have been rated and actually paid taxes to the state. By the report before us we propose to annihilate, at one stroke, all those property distinctions and to bow before the idol of universal suffrage. That extreme democratic principle, when applied to the legislative and executive departments of government, has been regarded with terror by the wise men of every age, because in every European republic, ancient and modern, in which it has been tried, it has terminated disastrously, and been productive of corruption, injustice, violence, and tyranny. And dare we flatter ourselves that we are a peculiar people, who can run the career of history exempted from the passions, which have disturbed and corrupted the rest of mankind? If we are like other races of men, with similar follies and vices, then I greatly fear that our posterity [future generations] will have reason to deplore [express sorrow over] in sackcloth [rags worn as a symbol of penitence] and ashes, the delusion of the day.

It is not my purpose at present to interfere with the report of the committee, so far as respects the qualifications of electors for governor and members of assembly. I shall feel grateful if we may be permitted to retain the stability and security of a senate, bottomed upon the freehold property of the state. Such a body, so constituted, may prove a sheet anchor amidst the future factions and storms of the republic. The great leading and governing interest of this state, is, at present, the agricultural; and what madness would it be to commit that interest to the winds. The great bodies of the people are now the owners and actual cultivators of the soil. With that wholesome population we always expect to find moderation, frugality [thriftiness], order, honesty, and a due sense of independence, liberty, and justice. It is impossible that any people can lose their liberties by internal fraud or violence, so long as the country is parceled out among freeholders of moderate possessions, and those freeholders have a sure and efficient control in the affairs of government. Their habits, sympathies, and employments, necessarily inspire them with a correct spirit of freedom and justice; they are the safest guardians of property and the laws: We certainly cannot too highly appreciate the value of the agricultural interest: It is the foundation of national wealth and power. According to the opinion of her ablest political economists, it is the surplus produce of the agriculture of England, that enables her to support her vast body of manufacturers, her formidable [awe-inspiring] fleets and armies, and the crowds of persons engaged in the liberal professions and the cultivation of the various arts.

Now, sir, I wish to present our senate as the representative of the landed interest. I wish those who have an interest in the soil, to retain the exclusive possession of a branch in the Legislature, as a stronghold in which they may find safety through all the vicissitudes [change], which the state may be destined, in the course of Providence, to experience. I wish them to be always enabled to say that their freeholds cannot be taxed without their consent. The men of no property, together with the crowds of dependents connected with great manufacturing and commercial establishments, and the motley [heterogeneous] and indefinable population of crowded ports, may, perhaps, at some future day, under skillful management, predominate in the assembly; and yet we should be perfectly safe if no laws could pass without the free consent of the owners of the soil. That security we at present enjoy; and it is that security which I wish to retain.

The apprehended danger from the experiment of universal suffrage applied to the whole legislative department is no dream of the imagination. It is too mighty an excitement for the moral constitution of men to endure. The tendency of universal suffrage is to jeopardize the rights of property, and the principles of liberty. There is a constant tendency in human society, and the history of every age proves it there is a tendency in the poor to covet and to share the plunder of the rich; in the debtor to relax or avert the obligation of contracts; in the majority to tyrannize over the minority, and trample down their rights; in the indolent [lazy] and the profligate [recklessly wasteful], to cast the whole burthens [burdens] of society upon the industrious and the virtuous; and ***there is a tendency in ambitious and wicked men to enflame these combustible materials.*** It requires a vigilant government, and a firm administration of justice, to counteract that tendency. Thou shalt not covet; thou shalt not steal; are divine injunctions induced by this miserable depravity of our nature. Who can undertake to calculate with any precision, how many millions of people this great state will contain in the course of this and the next century; and who can estimate the future extent and magnitude of our commercial ports? The disproportion between the men of property, and the men of no property, will be in every society in a ratio to its commerce, wealth, and population. We are no longer to remain plain and simple republics of farmers, like the New-England colonists, or the Dutch settlements on the Hudson. We are fast becoming a great nation, with great commerce, manufactures, population, wealth, luxuries, and with the vices and miseries that they engender [give rise to]. One seventh of the population of the city of Paris at this day subsists on charity, and one-third of the inhabitants of that city die in the hospitals; what would become of such a city with universal suffrage? France has upwards of four and England upwards of five millions of manufacturing and commercial laborers without property. Could these kingdoms sustain the weight of universal suffrage? The radicals in England, with the force of that mighty engine, would at once sweep away the property, the laws, and the liberties of that issued like a deluge.

The growth of the city of New-York is enough to startle and awaken those who are pursuing...

universal suffrage. In 1773 it had 21,000 souls. In 1801, 60,000. In 1806, 76,000. In 1820, 123,000.

It is rapidly swelling into the unwieldy population, and with the burdensome pauperism, of a European metropolis. New York is destined to become the future London of America; and in less than a century, that city, with the operation of universal suffrage, and under skillful direction, will govern the state.

The notion that every man that works a day on the road, or serves an idle hour in the militia, is entitled as of right to an equal participation in the whole power of the government, is most unreasonable, and has no foundation in justice. We had better at once discard from the report such a nominal [small] test of merit. If such persons have an equal share in one branch of the legislature, it is surely as much as they can in justice or policy demand. Society is an association for the protection of property as well as of life; and the individual who contributes only one cent to the common work, ought not to have the same power and influence in directing the property concerns of the partnership, as he who contributes his thousands. He will not have the same inducements to care, and diligence, and fidelity. His inducements and his temptation would be to divide the whole capital upon the principles of an agrarian law.

Liberty, rightly understood, is an inestimable blessing, but liberty without wisdom, and without justice, is no better than a wild and savage licentiousness. The danger, which we have hereafter to apprehend, is not the want, but the abuse, of liberty. We have to apprehend the oppression of minorities, and a disposition to encroach on private right to disturb chartered privileges and to weaken, degrade, and overawe the administration of justice; we have to apprehend the establishment of unequal, and consequently, unjust systems of taxation, and all the mischiefs of a crude and mutable [subject to change] legislation. A stable senate, exempted from the influence of universal suffrage, will powerfully check these dangerous propensities [tendencies], and such a check becomes the more necessary, since this convention has already determined to withdraw the watchful eye of the judicial department from the passage of laws.

We are destined to become a great manufacturing as well as commercial state. We have already numerous and prosperous factories of one kind or another, and one master capitalist with held his one hundredth apprentices, and journeymen, and agents, and dependants, will bear down at the polls an equal number of owners of small estates in his vicinity, who cannot safely unite for their common defense. Large manufacturing and mechanical establishments can act in an instant with the unity and efficacy [effectiveness] of disciplined troops. It is against such combinations, among others, that I think we ought to give the freeholders, or those who have interest in land one branch of the legislature for their asylum [safety] and their comfort. Universal suffrage once granted, is granted forever, and never can be recalled. There is no retrograde [move backward] step in the rear of democracy. However mischievous the precedent may be in its consequences, or however fatal in its effects, universal suffrage never can be recalled or checked, but by the strength of the bayonet. We stand, therefore, this moment, on the brink of fate, on the very edge of the precipice. If we let go our present hold on the senate, we commit our proudest hopes and our most precious interests to the waves.

It ought further to be observed, that the senate is a court of justice in the last resort. It is the last repository [place of safekeeping] of public and private rights; of civil and criminal justice. This gives the subject an awful consideration, and wonderfully increases the importance of securing that house from the inroads of universal suffrage. Our country freeholders are exclusively our jurors in the administration of justice, and there is equal reason that none but those who have an interest in the soil, should have any concern in the composition of that court. As long as the senate is safe, justice is safe, property is safe, and our liberties are safe. But when the wisdom, the integrity, and the independence of that court is lost, we may be certain that the freedom and happiness of the state are gone forever....

Extending the right to vote to women: Does the Declaration of Independence provide a principled basis for the equal rights of women?

"THE SENECA FALLS DECLARATION OF SENTIMENTS AND RESOLUTIONS" (1848)

Elizabeth Cady Stanton and Lucretia Mott, two American activists in the movement to abolish slavery, called the first conference to address women's-rights issues in Seneca Falls, New York, in 1848. Part of the reason for doing so was the fact that Mott had been refused permission to speak at the World Anti-Slavery Conference in London, even though she had been an official delegate.

WHY THIS READING?

Notice the parallel between the language of the Seneca Falls Declaration and that of the Declaration of Independence. Sixty-eight women and 32 men signed the Seneca Falls Declaration, which addresses this chapter's core question by insisting that women be allowed to exercise their "inalienable right to the elective franchise."

Questions to guide you as you read:

- Why do Stanton and Mott use the form and language of the Declaration of Independence to urge their claim that women should be allowed the right to vote?
- What does the original Constitution say about women's right to vote? Does it oppose it?

1. DECLARATION OF SENTIMENTS

When, in the course of human events, it becomes necessary for one portion of the family of man to assume among the people of the earth a position different from that which they have hitherto occupied, but one to which the laws of nature and of nature's God entitle them, a decent respect to the opinions of mankind requires that they should declare the causes that impel them to such a course.

We hold these truths to be self-evident: that all men and women are created equal; that they are endowed by their Creator with certain inalienable rights; that among these are life, liberty, and the pursuit of happiness; that to secure these rights governments are instituted, deriving their just powers from the consent of the governed. Whenever any form of government becomes destructive of these ends, it is the right of those who suffer from it to refuse allegiance to it, and to insist upon the institution of a new government, laying its foundation on such principles, and organizing its powers in such form, as to them shall seem most likely to effect their safety and happiness. Prudence, indeed, will dictate that governments long established should not be changed for light and transient causes; and accordingly all experience hath shown that mankind are more disposed to suffer while evils are sufferable, than to right themselves by abolishing the forms to which they are accustomed. But when a long train of abuses and usurpations [illegal seizures], pursuing invariably the same object, evinces [shows] a design to reduce them under absolute despotism, it is their duty to throw off such government, and to provide new guards for their future security. Such has been the patient sufferance of the women under this government, and such is now the necessity, which constrains them to demand the equal station to which they are entitled.

The history of mankind is a history of repeated injuries and usurpations on the part of man toward woman, having in direct object the establishment of an absolute tyranny over her. To prove this, let facts be submitted to a candid world.

He has never permitted her to exercise her inalienable right to the elective franchise.

He has compelled her to submit to laws, in the formation of which she had no voice.

He has withheld from her rights which are given to the most ignorant and degraded men both natives and foreigners.

Having deprived her of this first right of a citizen, the elective franchise, thereby leaving her without representation in the halls of legislation, he has oppressed her on all sides.

He has made her, if married, in the eye of the law, civilly dead.

He has taken from her all right in property, even to the wages she earns.

He has made her, morally, an irresponsible being, as she can commit many crimes with impunity [exemption from punishment], provided they be done in the presence of her husband. In the covenant [contract] of marriage, she is compelled to promise obedience to her husband, he becoming, to all intents and purposes, her master the law giving him power to deprive her of her liberty, and to administer chastisement [punish].

He has so framed the laws of divorce, as to what shall be the proper causes, and in case of separation, to whom the guardianship of the children shall be given, as to be wholly regardless of the happiness of women the law, in all cases, going upon a false supposition of the supremacy of man, and giving all power into his hands.

After depriving her of all rights as a married woman, if single, and the owner of property, he has taxed her to support a government, which recognizes her only when her property can be made profitable to it.

He has monopolized nearly all the profitable employments, and from those she is permitted to follow, she receives but a scanty [barely sufficient] remuneration [payment for services]. He closes against her all the avenues to wealth and distinction, which he considers most honorable to himself. As a Teacher of theology, medicine, or law, she is not known.

He has denied her the facilities for obtaining a thorough education, all colleges being closed against her.

He allows her in Church, as well as State, but a subordinate position, claiming apostolic authority for her exclusion from the ministry, and, with some exceptions, from any public participation in the affairs of the Church.

He has created a false public sentiment by giving to the world a different code of morals for men and women, by which moral delinquencies, which exclude women from society, are not only tolerated, but deemed of little account in man.

He has usurped the prerogative [exclusive right] of Jehovah [God] himself, claiming it as his right to assign for her a sphere of action, when that belongs to her conscience and to her God.

He has endeavored, in every way that he could, to destroy her confidence in her own powers to lessen her self-respect and to make her willing to lead a dependent and abject life.

Now, in view of this entire disfranchisement of one-half the people of this country, their social and religious degradation in view of the unjust laws above mentioned, and because women do feel themselves aggrieved, oppressed, and fraudulently deprived of their most sacred rights, we insist that they have immediate admission to all the rights and privileges which belong to them as citizens of the United States.

In entering upon the great work before us we anticipate no small amount of misconception, misrepresentation, and ridicule; but we shall use every instrumentality within our power to affect our object. We shall employ agents; circulate tracts, petition the State and National legislatures, and endeavor to enlist the pulpit and the press in our behalf. We hope this Convention will be followed by a series of Conventions embracing every part of the country.

2. RESOLUTIONS

WHEREAS, The great precept of nature is conceded to be, that "man shall pursue his own true and substantial happiness." Blackstone in his Commentaries remarks, that this law of Nature being coeval [existing during the same time] with mankind, and dictated by God himself, is of course superior in obligation to any other. It is binding over all the globe, in all countries and at all times; no human laws are of any validity if contrary to this, and such of them as are valid, derive all their force, and all their validity, and all their authority, mediately and immediately, from this original; therefore,

Resolved, That all laws which prevent woman from occupying such a station in society as her conscience shall dictate, or which place her in a position inferior to that of man, are contrary to the great precept [rule] of nature, and therefore of no force or authority.

Resolved, That woman is man's equal, was intended to be so by the Creator, and the highest good of the race demands that she should be recognized as such.

Resolved, That the women of this country ought to be enlightened in regard to the laws under which they live, that they may no longer publish their degradation by declaring themselves satisfied with their present position, nor their ignorance, by asserting that they have all the rights they want.

Resolved, That inasmuch as man, while claiming for himself intellectual superiority, does accord to woman moral superiority, it is pre-eminently [above all others] his duty to encourage her to speak and teach, as she has an opportunity, in all religious assemblies.

Resolved, That the same amount of virtue, delicacy, and refinement of behavior that is required of woman in the social state, should also be required of man, and the same transgressions should be visited with equal severity on both man and woman.

Resolved, That the objection of indelicacy and impropriety, which is so often brought against woman when she addresses a public audience, comes with a very ill-grace from those who encourage, by their attendance, her appearance on the stage, in the concert, or in feats of the circus.

Resolved, That woman has too long rested satisfied in the circumscribed limits [bounds] which corrupt customs and a perverted application of the Scriptures have marked out for her, and that it is time she should move in the enlarged sphere which her great Creator has assigned her.

Resolved, That it is the duty of the women *of* this country to secure to themselves their sacred right to the elective franchise.

Resolved, That the equality of human rights results necessarily from the fact of the identity of the race in capabilities and responsibilities.

Resolved, That the speedy success of our cause depends upon the zealous and untiring efforts of both men and women, for the overthrow of the monopoly of the pulpit, and for the securing to women an equal participation with men in the various trades, professions. And commerce.

Resolved, therefore, That, being invested by the creator with the same capabilities, and the same consciousness of responsibility for their exercise, it is demonstrably the right and duty of woman, equally with man, to promote every righteous cause by every righteous means; and especially in regard to the great subjects of morals and religion, it is self-evidently her right to participate with her brother in teaching them both in private and in public, by writing and by speaking, by any instrumentalities proper to be used, and in any assemblies proper to be held; and this being a self-evident truth growing out of the divinely implanted principles of human nature, any custom or authority adverse to it, whether modern or wearing the hoary [gray with age] sanction of antiquity, is to be regarded as a self-evident falsehood, and at war with mankind.

Jane Addams's argument for the practical benefits of extending the franchise

JANE ADDAMS, "WHY WOMEN SHOULD VOTE" (1910)

Jane Addams (1860–1931) founded Hull House in 1889 in Chicago, Illinois. Hull House served the needs of the underprivileged and came to serve as a national model for such work. She was also prominent in the cause of women's suffrage. She was elected vice president of the National Women's Suffrage Association in 1911. In 1931, her lifetime of service was recognized by being awarded the Nobel Peace Prize.

WHY THIS READING?

Here, Addams takes a different tack from that followed by Elizabeth Cady Stanton and Lucretia Mott. Addams does not deny Stanton and Mott's natural-rights argument for extending the vote to women; however, she chooses to focus here instead on the practical benefits of such extension.

Questions to guide you as you read:

- How does Addams respond to the argument that "woman's place is within the walls of her own home"?
- What key role does Addams envision women performing in American cities? Why does she think that women are especially needed for this task? In the 100-plus years that have passed since she wrote "Why Women Should Vote," has history confirmed her vision? In what ways?

For many generations it has been believed that woman's place is within the walls of her own home, and it is indeed impossible to imagine the time when her duty there shall be ended or to forecast any social change which shall release her from that paramount [chief] obligation.

This paper is an attempt to show that many women today are failing to discharge [perform] their duties to their own households properly simply because they do not perceive that as society grows more complicated it is necessary that woman shall extend her sense of responsibility to many things outside of her own home if she would continue to preserve the home in its entirety [wholly]. One could illustrate in many ways. A woman's simplest duty, one would say, is to keep her house clean and wholesome and to feed her children properly. Yet if she lives in a tenement [run-down] house, as so many of my neighbors do, she cannot fulfill these simple obligations by her own efforts because she is utterly dependent upon the city administration for the conditions, which render decent living possible. Her basement will not be dry, her stairways will not be fireproof, her house will not be provided with sufficient windows to give light and air, nor will it be equipped with sanitary plumbing, unless the Public Works Department sends inspectors who constantly insist that these elementary decencies be provided. Women who live in the country sweep their own dooryards and may either feed the refuse of the table to a flock of chickens or allow it innocently to decay in the open air and sunshine. In a crowded city quarter, however, if the street is not cleaned by the city authorities no amount of private sweeping will keep the tenement free from grime; if the garbage is not properly collected and destroyed a tenement-house mother may see her children sicken and die of diseases from which she alone is powerless to shield them, although her tenderness and devotion are unbounded. She cannot even secure untainted meat for her household, she cannot provide fresh fruit, unless the meat has been inspected by city officials, and the decayed fruit, which is so often placed upon sale in the tenement districts, has been destroyed in the interests of public health. In short, if woman would keep on with her old business of caring for her house and rearing her children she will have to have some conscience in regard to public affairs lying quite outside of her immediate household. The individual conscience and devotion are no longer effective....

If women follow only the lines of their traditional activities here are certain primary duties which belong to even the most conservative women, and which no one woman or group of women can adequately discharge unless they join the more general movements looking toward social amelioration [improvement] through legal enactment.

The first of these, of which this article has already treated, is woman's responsibility for the members of her own household that they may be properly fed and clothed and surrounded by hygienic [promoting health] conditions. The second is a responsibility for the education of children: (a) that they may be provided with good schools; (b) that they may be kept free from vicious influences on the street; that when working they may be protected by adequate child-labor legislation.

(a) The duty of a woman toward the schools, which her children attend, is so obvious that it is not necessary to dwell upon it. But even this simple obligation cannot be effectively carried out without some form of social organization as the mothers' school clubs and mothers' congresses testify, and to which the most conservative women belong because they feel the need of wider reading and discussion concerning the many problems of childhood. It is, therefore, perhaps natural that the public should have been more willing to accord a vote to women in school matters than in any other, and yet women have never been members of a Board of Education in sufficient numbers to influence largely actual school curricula. If they had been, kindergartens, domestic science courses and school playgrounds would be far more numerous than they are....

(b) But women are also beginning to realize that children need attention outside of school hours; that much of the petty vice in cities is merely the love of pleasure gone wrong, the over restrained boy or girl seeking improper recreation and excitement. It is obvious that a little study of the needs of children, a sympathetic understanding of the conditions under which they go astray, might save hundreds of them. Women traditionally have had an opportunity to observe the play of children and the needs of youth, and yet in Chicago, at least, they had done singularly little in this vexed [annoying] problem of juvenile delinquency until they helped to inaugurate the Juvenile Court movement a dozen years ago. The Juvenile Court Committee, made up largely of women, paid the salaries of the probation officers connected with the court for the first six years of its existence, and after the salaries were cared for by the county the same organization turned itself into a Juvenile Protective League, and through a score of paid officers are doing valiant service in minimizing some of the dangers of city life which boys and girls encounter.

This Protective League, however, was not formed until the women had had a civic training through their semi-official connection with the Juvenile Court. This is, perhaps, an illustration of our inability to see the duty "next to hand" until we have become alert through our knowledge of conditions in connection with the larger duties. We would all agree that social amelioration must come about through the efforts of many people who are moved thereto by the compunction and stirring of the individual conscience, but we are only beginning to understand that the individual conscience will respond to the special challenge largely in proportion as the individual is able to see the social conditions because he has felt responsible for their improvement.... The more extensively the modern city endeavors on the one hand to control and on the other hand to provide recreational facilities for its young people the more necessary it is that women should assist in their direction and extension.

...If woman's sense of obligation had enlarged as the industrial conditions changed she might naturally and almost imperceptibly have inaugurated the movements for social amelioration in the line of factory legislation and shop sanitation. That she has not done so is doubtless due to the fact that her conscience is slow to recognize any obligation outside of her own family circle, and because she was so absorbed in her own household that she failed to see what the conditions outside actually were.... After all, we see only those things to which our attention has been drawn; we feel responsibility for those things which are brought to us as matters of responsibility. If conscientious women were convinced that it was a civic duty to be informed in regard to these grave industrial affairs, and then to express the conclusions which they had reached by depositing a piece of paper in a ballot-box, one cannot imagine that they would shirk simply because the action ran counter to old traditions....

...Woman s traditional function has been to make her dwelling place both clean and fair. Is that dreariness in city life, that lack of domesticity, which the humblest farm dwelling presents, due to a withdrawal of one of the naturally cooperating forces? If women have in any sense been responsible for the gentler side of life, which softens and blurs some of its harsher conditions, may they not have a duty to perform in our American cities?

Why did an earlier Supreme Court deny that the 14th Amendment extends the vote to women?

CHIEF JUSTICE MORRISON WAITE, OPINION OF THE COURT IN *MINOR V. HAPPERSETT* (1875)

In 1872, the National Women's Suffrage Association urged women to attempt to vote in the upcoming elections, arguing that voting was a right of all U. S. citizens under the "privileges and immunities" clause of the 14th Amendment to the Constitution, which was ratified four years prior. Susan B. Anthony (1820–1906), a prominent leader in the suffragist movement in the 19th century, organized a group of women to try to vote in the 1872 elections, among them one Virginia Minor.

WHY THIS READING?

As you will read later in this text, judicial interpretation of the meaning of the 14th Amendment has broadened dramatically since 1868. In the matter of women's rights, this early case provides the counterpoint to that subsequent expansion. This case addresses Virginia Minor's claim that she was unconstitutionally denied entrance to the Missouri polls by registrar Reese Happersett. Happersett denied her admission on the grounds that the Missouri state constitution limited the voting franchise to males alone. Minor, along with her husband, sued Happersett, charging that her rights of citizenship under the 14th Amendment to the U.S. Constitution had been violated.

Questions to guide you as you read:

- On what basis does Chief Justice Waite, writing for the Court, deny that women are the subjects of the 14th Amendment?
- Why does the Court similarly deny that "men" generally are the subjects of the 14th Amendment? Who, then, are the precise "subjects" of the 14th Amendment, according to the Court?

The question is presented in this case, whether, since the adoption of the Fourteenth Amendment, a woman, who is a citizen of the United States and of the State of Missouri, is a voter in that State, notwithstanding the provision of the constitution and laws of the State, which confine the right of suffrage [voting] to men alone....

It is contended that the provisions of the Constitution and laws of the State of Missouri, which confined the right of suffrage and registration therefore to men, are in violation of the Constitution of the United States, and therefore void. The argument is, that as a woman, born or naturalized in the United States and subject to the jurisdiction thereof as a citizen of the United States and of the State in which she resides, she has the right of suffrage as one of the privileges and immunities of her citizenship, which the State cannot by its laws or constitution abridge.

There is no doubt that women may be citizens. They are persons, and by the Fourteenth Amendment "all persons born or naturalized in the United States and subject to the jurisdiction thereof" are expressly declared to be "citizens of the United States and of the State wherein they reside." But, in our opinion, it did not need this amendment to give them that position. Before its adoption the Constitution of the United States did not in terms prescribe who should be citizens of the United States or of the several States, yet there were necessarily such citizens without such provision....

For convenience it has been found necessary to give a name to this membership. The object is to designate by a title the person and the relation he bears to the nation. For this purpose the words "subject," "inhabitant," and "citizen" have been used, and the choice between them is sometimes made to, depend upon the form of the government. Citizen is now more commonly employed, however, and as it has been considered better suited to the description of one living under a republican government, it was adopted by nearly all of the States upon their separation from Great Britain, and was afterwards adopted in the Articles of Confederation and in the Constitution of the United States. When used in this sense it is understood as conveying the idea of membership of a nation, and nothing more....

...Sex has never been made one of the elements of citizenship in the United States. In this respect men have never had an advantage over women. The same laws precisely apply to both. The Fourteenth Amendment did not affect the citizenship of women any more than it did of men. In this particular, therefore, the rights of Mrs. Minor do not depend upon the amendment. She has always been a citizen from her birth, and entitled to all the privileges and immunities of citizenship....

If the right of suffrage is one of the necessary privileges of a citizen of the United States, then the constitution and laws of Missouri confining it to men are in violation of the Constitution of the United States, as amended, and consequently void. The direct question is, therefore, presented whether all citizens are necessarily voters.

The Constitution does not define the privileges and immunities of citizens. For that definition we must look elsewhere. In this case we need not determine what they are, but only whether suffrage is necessarily one of them.

It certainly is nowhere made so in express terms. The United States has no voters in the States of its own creation. The elective officers of the United States are all elected directly or indirectly by state voters....

The Amendment did not add to the privileges and immunities of a citizen. It simply furnished an additional guaranty for the protection of such as he already had. No new voters were necessarily made by it. Indirectly it may have had that effect, because it may have increased the number of citizens entitled to suffrage under the constitution and laws of the States, but it operates for this purpose, if at all, through the States and the state laws, and not directly upon the citizen.

It is clear therefore, we think, that the Constitution has not added the right of suffrage to the privileges and immunities of citizenship as they existed at the time it was adopted. This makes it proper to inquire whether suffrage was co-extensive with the citizenship of the States at the time of its adoption. If it was, then it may with force be argued that suffrage was one of the rights which belonged to citizenship, and in the enjoyment of which every citizen must be protected. But if it was not, the contrary may with propriety be assumed.

When the Federal Constitution was adopted, all the States, with the exception of Rhode Island and Connecticut, had constitutions of their own.... Upon an examination of these constitutions we find that in no State were all citizens permitted to vote....

In this condition of the law in respect to suffrage in the several States it cannot for a moment be doubted that if it had been intended to make all citizens of the United States voters, the framers of the Constitution would not have left it to implication....

It is true that the United States guarantees to every State a republican form of government.... The guaranty is of a republican form of government. No particular government is designated as republican, neither is the exact form to be guaranteed, in any manner especially designated. Here, as in other parts of the instrument, we are compelled to resort elsewhere to ascertain [find out] what was intended.

The guaranty necessarily implies a duty on the part of the States themselves to provide such a government All the States had governments when the Constitution was adopted. In all the people participated to some extent, through their representatives elected in the manner specially provided. These governments the Constitution did not change. They were accepted precisely as they were, and it is, therefore, to be presumed that they were such as it was the duty of the States to provide. Thus we have unmistakable evidence of what was republican in form, within the meaning of that term as employed in the Constitution.

As we have seen, all the citizens of the States were not invested with the right of suffrage. In all, save perhaps New Jersey, this right was only bestowed upon men and not upon all of them. Under these circumstances it is certainly now too late to contend that a government is not republican, within the meaning of this guaranty in the Constitution, because women are not made voters....

Certainly if the courts can consider any question settled this is one. For nearly ninety years the people have acted upon the idea that the Constitution, when it conferred [granted] citizenship, did not necessarily confer the right of suffrage....

Being unanimously of the opinion that the Constitution of the United States does not confer the right of suffrage upon any one, and that the constitutions and laws of the several States which commit that important trust to men alone are not necessarily void, we affirm the judgment.

19TH AMENDMENT TO THE U.S. CONSTITUTION (1920)

WHY THIS READING?

In 1872, "suffragists," as they were then called, began to mount legal challenges in the courts on the issue of women's right to vote. Immediately above, you read the Supreme Court's rejection of the claim that the 14th Amendment's "privileges and immunities' clause enfranchises women with the right to vote. As a result of this setback in the judicial arena, proponents of voting rights for women decided to turn to the political process. In 1878, a Constitutional amendment was proposed to give all women voting rights. It would not be until 1920 that the Congress approved and the states ratified the amendment (the 19th).

Question to guide you as you read:

- If all the states, individually, had amended their constitutions to allow women to vote, would this have violated the intent of the original Constitution?

"The right of citizens of the United States to vote shall not be denied or abridged by the United States or by any State on account of sex.

Congress shall have power to enforce this article by appropriate legislation."

Competing visions of sexual equality: "Complementarity" versus "sameness"

ALEXIS DE TOCQUEVILLE, *DEMOCRACY IN AMERICA*, "HOW THE AMERICAN VIEWS THE EQUALITY OF THE SEXES" (1835)

WHY THIS READING?

Here, Tocqueville offers his famous observation: "The singular prosperity and growing strength" of the American people are mainly to be attributed...to the superiority of their women." This superiority he finds to stem from the fact that the Americans treat sexual equality differently from the way it is treated in Europe. On the one hand, Europeans "confound together the different characteristics of the sexes [and] would make man and woman into beings not only equal but *alike* [emphasis supplied]." The Americans, on the other hand, understand sexual equality to consist in "complementarity," which means that men and women have natural differences, but those differences balance or harmonize with each other. Each is therefore incomplete without the other.

He next offers an argument that parallels his treatment of the place of religion in American democracy (which we examine in detail in chapter seven). Religion has immense power in the United States, he argues, because it does not share in political power. So situated, it can better direct the manners and fundamental opinions of the people. In a similar vein, women, who did not at the time participate in politics or business, can for this reason better serve as the guardians of morals. For Tocqueville, those who serve as the guardians of a nation's morals possess a power that is higher and deeper than political and economic power.

Questions to guide you as you read:

- Tocqueville's defense of sexual equality as complementarity is contrary to the contemporary sentiments of many. What precisely, then, does he mean when he observes that "nowhere" has he "seen woman occupy a loftier position" in society than in America? How can he make such a statement when women at the time did not participate in politics or business?
- Given that American society has moved toward the "European" understanding of sexual equality as "sameness," what would Tocqueville predict would be the effects on American democracy?

I have shown how democracy destroys or modifies the different inequalities that originate in society; but is this all, or does it not ultimately affect that great inequality of man and woman which has seemed, up to the present day, to be eternally based in human nature? I believe that the social changes that bring nearer to the same level the father and son, the master and servant, and, in general, superiors and inferiors will raise woman and make her more and more the equal of man. But here, more than ever, I feel the necessity of making myself clearly understood; for there is no subject on which the coarse and lawless fancies [imaginings] of our age have taken a freer range.

There are people in Europe who, confounding together the different characteristics of the sexes, would make man and woman into beings not only equal but alike. They would give to both the same functions, impose on both the same duties, and grant to both the same rights; they would mix them

in all things—their occupations, their pleasures, their business. It may readily be conceived that by thus attempting to make one sex equal to the other, both are degraded, and from so preposterous a medley of the works of nature nothing could ever result but weak men and disorderly women.

It is not thus that the Americans understand that species of democratic equality which may be established between the sexes. They admit that as nature has appointed such wide differences between the physical and moral constitution of man and woman, her manifest design was to give a distinct employment to their various faculties; and they hold that improvement does not consist in making beings so dissimilar do pretty nearly the same things, but in causing each of them to fulfill their respective tasks in the best possible manner. The Americans have applied to the sexes the great principle of political economy which governs the manufacturers of our age, by carefully dividing the duties of man from those of woman in order that the great work of society may be the better carried on.

In no country has such constant care been taken as in America to trace two clearly distinct lines of action for the two sexes and to make them keep pace one with the other, but in two pathways that are always different. American women never manage the outward concerns of the family or conduct a business or take a part in political life; nor are they, on the other hand, ever compelled to perform the rough labor of the fields or to make any of those laborious efforts which demand the exertion of physical strength. No families are so poor as to form an exception to this rule. If, on the one hand, an American woman cannot escape from the quiet circle of domestic employments, she is never forced, on the other, to go beyond it. Hence it is that the women of America, who often exhibit a masculine strength of understanding and a manly energy, generally preserve great delicacy of personal appearance and always retain the manners of women although they sometimes show that they have the hearts and minds of men.

Nor have the Americans ever supposed that one consequence of democratic principles is the subversion of marital power or the confusion of the natural authorities in families. They hold that every association must have a head in order to accomplish its object, and that the natural head of the conjugal association is man. They do not therefore deny him the right of directing his partner, and they maintain that in the smaller association of husband and wife as well as in the great social community the object of democracy is to regulate and legalize the powers that are necessary, and not to subvert all power.

This opinion is not peculiar to one sex and contested by the other; I never observed that the women of America consider conjugal [marital] authority as a fortunate usurpation of their rights, or that they thought themselves degraded by submitting to it. It appeared to me, on the contrary, that they attach a sort of pride to the voluntary surrender of their own will and make it their boast to bend themselves to the yoke [restraint], not to shake it off. Such, at least, is the feeling expressed by the most virtuous of their sex; the others are silent; and in the United States it is not the practice for a guilty wife to clamor for the rights of women while she is trampling on her own holiest duties.

It has often been remarked that in Europe a certain degree of contempt lurks even in the flattery which men lavish upon women; although a European frequently affects to be the slave of woman, it may be seen that he never sincerely thinks her his equal. In the United States men seldom compliment women, but they daily show how much they esteem them. They constantly display an entire confidence in the understanding of a wife and a profound respect for her freedom; they have decided that her mind is just as fitted as that of a man to discover the plain truth, and her heart as firm to embrace it; and they have never sought to place her virtue, any more than his, under the shelter of prejudice, ignorance, and fear.

It would seem in Europe, where man so easily submits to the despotic sway of women, that they are nevertheless deprived of some of the greatest attributes of the human species and considered as seductive but imperfect beings; and (what may well provoke astonishment) women ultimately look upon themselves in the same light and almost consider it as a privilege that they are entitled to show themselves futile, feeble, and timid. The women of America claim no such privileges.

Again, it may be said that in our morals we have reserved strange immunities to man, so that there is, as it were, one virtue for his use and another for the guidance of his partner, and that, according to the opinion of the public, the very same act may be punished alternately as a crime or only as a fault. The Americans do not know this iniquitous division of duties and rights; among them the seducer is as much dishonored as his victim.

It is true that the Americans rarely lavish upon women those eager attentions which are commonly paid them in Europe, but their conduct to women always implies that they suppose them to be virtuous and refined; and such is the respect entertained for the moral freedom of the sex that in the presence of a woman the most guarded language is used lest her ear should be offended by an expression. In America a young unmarried woman may alone and without fear undertake a long journey.

The legislators of the United States, who have mitigated almost all the penalties of criminal law, still make rape a capital [involving the death penalty] offense, and no crime is visited with more inexorable [unstoppable] severity by public opinion. This may be accounted for; as the Americans can conceive nothing more precious than a wsoman's honor and nothing which ought so much to be respected as her independence, they hold that no punishment is too severe for the man who deprives her of them against her will. In France, where the same offense is visited with far milder penalties, it is frequently difficult to get a verdict from a jury against the prisoner. Is this a consequence of contempt of decency or contempt of women? I cannot but believe that it is a contempt of both.

Thus the Americans do not think that man and woman have either the duty or the right to perform the same offices, but they show an equal regard for both their respective parts; and though their lot is different, they consider both of them as beings of equal value. They do not give to the courage of woman the same form or the same direction as to that of man, but they never doubt her courage; and if they hold that man and his partner ought not always to exercise their intellect and understanding in the same manner, they at least believe the understanding of the one to be as sound as that of the other, and her intellect to be as clear. Thus, then, while they have allowed the social inferiority of woman to continue, they have done all they could to raise her morally and intellectually to the level of man; and in this respect they appear to me to have excellently understood the true principle of democratic improvement.

As for myself, I do not hesitate to avow that although the women of the United States are confined within the narrow circle of domestic life, and their situation is in some respects one of extreme dependence, I have nowhere seen woman occupying a loftier position; and if I were asked, now that I am drawing to the close of this work, in which I have spoken of so many important things done by the Americans, to what the singular prosperity and growing strength of that people ought mainly to be attributed, I should reply: To the superiority of their women.

BARBARA JORDAN, "CHANGE: FROM WHAT TO WHAT?" KEYNOTE ADDRESS AT THE DEMOCRATIC NATIONAL CONVENTION (1992)

Barbara Jordan (1936–1996) was the first African-American woman from the Deep South to be elected to the U.S. House of Representatives, representing a district in Texas from 1973 to 1979. She also chaired the President's Commission on Immigration Reform and, at the time of this speech, was special counsel to the governor of Texas on ethics. The theme of this address is that of political and social change. Given four years before her death, it was the second time that she provided the keynote address at a Democratic National Convention (the first was in 1976).

WHY THIS READING?

Jordan offers the counterpoint to Tocqueville's sexual-equality-as-complementary argument. As you will read, she defends the position that equality between men and women requires that all have the same opportunities to perform the same tasks in both business and politics. Interestingly, in praising the increase in the number of women running for elective office at the time, she quotes Tocqueville's statement that the "prosperity and growing strength" of the American people is due to the "superiority of [its] women." Although she concurs with Tocqueville's praise, their agreement on matters of sexual equality ends there.

Questions to guide you as you read:

- Although Jordan quotes Tocqueville in her defense of sexual equality, the two in fact have different understandings of what sexual equality is. What are these differences?
- What is the primary area of disagreement between Jordan and Tocqueville on the question of the relationship of women to American democracy?

Change has become the watchword of this year's electioneering. Candidates contend with each other, arguing, debating which of them is the authentic agent of change. Each jostling acquires substance when we comprehend the public mind. There appears to be a general apprehension about the future which undermines our confidence in ourselves and each other. The American idea that tomorrow will be better than today has become destabilized by a stubborn, sluggish economy. Jobs lost have become permanent unemployment rather than cyclical unemployment. Public policy makers are held in low regard. Mistrust abounds. Given such an environment is it not understandable that the prevailing issue of this political season is identifying the catalyst for change that is required. I see that catalyst as: the Democratic Party and its nominee for President.

We are not strangers to change. We calmed the national interest in the wake of the Watergate abuses and we, the Democratic Party, can seize this moment. We know what is to be done and how to do it. We have been the monument of change in policies which impact education, human rights, civil rights, economic and social opportunity, and the environment. These are policies firmly imbedded in the soul of our party. We will do nothing to erode our stance. However, some things need to change. The Democratic Party is alive and well. It will change in order to fully serve the present and the future....

Change: From What to What? We will change from a party with a reputation of tax and spend to one of investment and growth. A growth economy is a must. We can mend the economy and at the same time sustain and even save our environment. When the economy is growing we are treating our air, water and soil kindly, all of us prosper. We all benefit from economic expansion. I certain do not mean the thinly disguised racism and elitism of their kind of trickle-down economics. I mean an economy where a young black woman or man from the Fifth Ward in Houston or south central Los Angeles, or a young person in the colonias [rural settlements along the U.S.-Mexican border] of the lower Rio Grande valley, can attend public schools and learn the skills that will enable her or him to prosper. We must have an economy that does not force the migrant worker's child to miss school in order to earn less than the minimum wage just so the family can have one meal a day. That is the moral bankruptcy that trickle-down economics is all about. We can change the direction of America's economic engine and become proud and competitive again. The American dream...is gasping for breath but it is not dead. However, there is no time to waste because the American Dream is slipping away from too many. It is slipping away from too many black and brown mothers and their children; from the homeless of every color and sex; from the immigrants living in communities without water and sewer systems. The American Dream is slipping away from the workers whose jobs are no longer there because we are better at building war equipment that sits in warehouses than we are at building decent housing; from the workers on indefinite layoffs while their chief executive officers are making bonuses that are more than the worker will take home in 10 or 20 or 30 years.

We need to change the decaying inner cities into places where hope lives. We should answer Rodney King's haunting question, "can we all get along?" with a resounding "YES." We must profoundly change from the deleterious environment of the Eighties, characterized by greed, selfishness, mega mergers and debt overhang to one characterized by devotion to the public interest and tolerance. And yes, love.

We are one, we Americans, and we reject any intruder who seeks to divide us by race or class. We honor cultural identity. However, separatism is not allowed. Separatism is not the American way. And we should not permit ideas like political correctness to become some fad that could reverse our hard won achievements in civil rights and human rights. Xenophobia has no place in the Democratic Party. We seek to unite people, not divide them and we reject both white racism and black racism. This party will not tolerate bigotry under any guise. America's strength is rooted in its diversity. Our history bears witness to that statement. *E Pluribus Unum* was a good motto in the early days of our country and it is a good motto today. From the many, one. It still identifies us, because we are Americans.

We must frankly acknowledge our complicity in the creation of the unconscionable budget deficit and recognize that to seriously address it will put entitlements at risk. The idea of justice between generations mandates such acknowledgment and more. The baby boomers and their progeny have a right to a secure future. We must be willing to sacrifice for growth, provided there is equity in sacrifice. Equity means all will sacrifice equally. That includes the retiree living on a fixed income, the day laborer, the corporate executive, the college professor, the Member of Congress... all means all.

One overdue change already underway is the number of women challenging the councils of political power dominated by white male policy makers. That horizon is limitless. What we see today is simply a dress rehearsal for the day and time we meet in convention to nominate... Madame President. This country can ill afford to continue to function using less than half of its human resources, brain power and kinetic energy. Our 19th century visitor from France, Tocqueville, observed in his work *Democracy in America,*

"If I were asked to what singular substance do I mainly attribute the prosperity and growing strength of the American people, I should reply: To the superiority of their women." The 20th century will not close without our presence being keenly felt....

Extending the right to vote to African-Americans

15TH AMENDMENT TO THE U.S. CONSTITUTION (1870)

The 15th Amendment was the last of the post-Civil War "Reconstruction Amendments" (the 13th through the 15th) to be ratified. Prior to its passage, the states bore full responsibility for determining the qualifications of voters. (See Federalist, No. 52.)

Questions to guide you as you read:

- Does the original Constitution deny African-Americans the right to vote?
- Does the original Constitution refer to African-Americans at all? Where?

1. The right of citizens of the United States to vote shall not be denied or abridged by the United States or by any State on account of race, color, or previous condition of servitude.
2. The Congress shall have power to enforce this article by appropriate legislation."

LYNDON B. JOHNSON, "VOTING RIGHTS ACT SPEECH" (1965)

Lyndon Baines Johnson (1908–1973), a Democrat, was the 36th president of the United States (1963–1969). As John F. Kennedy's vice president, he assumed the presidency upon Kennedy's assassination in November 1963. He was elected to a full term in 1964, defeating Republican challenger Barry Goldwater. He declined to seek reelection in 1968. His domestic program "The Great Society" followed in the tradition of Franklin D. Roosevelt's "New Deal," offering a package of social and economic programs that included the War on Poverty, numerous education bills, the Job Corps, and Head Start. On August 6th, 1965, President Johnson signed the Voting Rights Act, which prohibited racial discrimination in voting practices in the states. This legislation outlawed the infamous "literacy tests" and established federal officials to register qualified citizens to vote.

WHY THIS READING?

This marks the first time in our nation's history that the federal government gained legal authority to register citizens to vote. In this speech, President Johnson addresses this chapter's core question by defending the Voting Rights Act of 1965 as a necessary step in promoting the "dignity of man and the destiny of democracy."

Questions to guide you as you read:

- You have read that the original Constitution left the question of who qualifies to vote up to the states. Why was this overturned?
- Although it is not unreasonable to hope that all voters have some degree of education so that they might make informed choices, in what precisely did the "literacy tests," outlawed in 1965, consist?

I speak tonight for the dignity of man and the destiny of democracy. I urge every member of both parties, Americans of all religions and of all colors, from every section of this country, to join me in that cause.

At times history and fate meet at a single time in a single place to shape a turning point in man's unending search for freedom. So it was at Lexington and Concord. So it was a century ago at Appomattox. So it was last week in Selma, Alabama.[1]

There, long-suffering men and women peacefully protested the denial of their rights as Americans. Many were brutally assaulted. One good man, a man of God, was killed.

There is no cause for pride in what has happened in Selma. There is no cause for self-satisfaction in the long denial of equal rights of millions of Americans.

But there is cause for hope and for faith in our democracy in what is happening here tonight.

1. In March of 1965, civil rights activists, led by Martin Luther King Jr., marched from Selma, Alabama, to the state capital of Montgomery to protest Alabama's voter registration policies.

For the cries of pain and the hymns and protests of oppressed people, have summoned into convocation [assembly] all the majesty of this great government of the greatest nation on earth.

Our mission is at once the oldest and the most basic of this country: to right wrong, to do justice, to serve man.

In our time we have come to live with the moments of great crisis. Our lives have been marked with debate about great issues, issues of war and peace, issues of prosperity and depression. But rarely in any time does an issue lay bare the secret heart of America itself. Rarely are we met with a challenge, not to our growth or abundance, or our welfare or our security, but rather to the values and the purposes and the meaning of our beloved nation.

The issue of equal rights for American Negroes is such an issue. And should we defeat every enemy, and should we double our wealth and conquer the stars and still be unequal to this issue, then we will have failed as a people and as a nation.

For with a country as with a person, "What is a man profited, if he shall gain the whole world, and lose his own soul?"

There is no Negro problem. There is no Southern problem. There is no Northern problem. There is only an American problem. And we are met here tonight as Americans, not as Democrats or Republicans, we are met here as Americans to solve that problem.

This was the first nation in the history of the world to be founded with a purpose. The great phrases of that purpose still sound in every American heart, North and South: "All men are created equal," "government by consent of the governed," "give me liberty or give me death." Those are not just clever words. Those are not just empty theories. In their name Americans have fought and died for two centuries, and tonight around the world they stand there as guardians of our liberty, risking their lives.

Those words are a promise to every citizen that he shall share in the dignity of man. This dignity cannot be found in a man's possessions. It cannot be found in his power or in his position. It really rests on his right to be treated as a man equal in opportunity to all others. It says that he shall share in freedom, he shall choose his leaders, educate his children, provide for his family according to his ability and his merits as a human being.

To apply any other test, to deny a man his hopes because of his color or race, or his religion, or the place of his birth, is not only to do injustice, it is to deny America and to dishonor the dead who gave their lives for American freedom.

Our fathers believed that if this noble view of the rights of man was to flourish, it must be rooted in democracy. The most basic right of all was the right to choose your own leaders. The history of this country in large measure is the history of expansion of that right to all of our people.

Many of the issues of civil rights are very complex and most difficult. But about this there can and should be no argument. Every American citizen must have an equal right to vote. There is no reason which can excuse the denial of that right. There is no duty which weighs more heavily on us than the duty we have to ensure that right. Yet the harsh fact is that, in many places in this country, men and women are kept from voting simply because they are Negroes.

Every device of which human ingenuity is capable has been used to deny this right. The Negro citizen may go to register only to be told that the day is wrong, or the hour is late, or the official in charge is absent. And if he persists and if he manages to present himself to the registrar, he may be disqualified because he did not spell out his middle name or because he abbreviated a word on the application. And if he manages to fill out an application he is given a test. The registrar is the sole judge of whether he passes this test. He may be asked to recite the entire constitution, or explain the most complex provisions of state laws. And even a college degree cannot be used to prove that he can read and write.

For the fact is that the only way to pass these barriers is to show a white skin. Experience has clearly shown that the existing process of law cannot overcome systematic and ingenious discrimination. No law that we now have on the books, and I have helped to put three of them there, can ensure the right to vote when local officials are determined to deny it.

In such a case our duty must be clear to all of us. The Constitution says that no person shall be kept from voting because of his race or his color.

We have all sworn an oath before God to support and to defend that Constitution. We must now act in obedience to that oath.

Wednesday I will send to Congress a law designed to eliminate illegal barriers to the right to vote.

The broad principle of that bill will be in the hands of the Democratic and Republican leaders tomorrow. After they have reviewed it, it will come here formally as a bill. I am grateful for this opportunity to come here tonight at the invitation of the leadership to reason with my friends, to give them my views and to visit with my former colleagues.

I have had prepared a more comprehensive analysis of the legislation which I have intended to transmit to the clerks tomorrow, but which I will submit to the clerks tonight; but I want to really discuss with you now briefly the main proposals of this legislation.

This bill will strike down restrictions to voting in all elections, Federal, State, and local, which have been used to deny Negroes the right to vote.

This bill will establish a simple, uniform standard which cannot be used however ingenious the effort to flout our Constitution.

It will provide for citizens to be registered by officials of the United States government, if the state officials refuse to register them.

It will eliminate tedious, unnecessary lawsuits which delay the right to vote.

Finally, this legislation will ensure that properly registered individuals are not prohibited from voting.

I will welcome the suggestions from all of the members of Congress. I have no doubt that I will get some on ways and means to strengthen this law and to make it effective. But experience has plainly shown that this is the only path to carry out the command of the Constitution.

To those who seek to avoid action by their national government in their own communities, who want to and who seek to maintain purely local control over elections, the answer is simple.

Open your polling places to all your people.

Allow men and women to register and vote whatever the color of their skin.

Extend the rights of citizenship to every citizen of this land.

There is no constitutional issue here. The command of the Constitution is plain.

There is no moral issue. It is wrong to deny any of your fellow Americans the right to vote in this country.

There is no issue of states rights or national rights. There is only the struggle for human rights. I have not the slightest doubt what will be your answer.

But the last time a President sent a civil rights bill to the Congress it contained a provision to protect voting rights in Federal elections. That civil rights bill was passed after eight long months of debate. And when that bill came to my desk from the Congress for my signature, the heart of the voting provision had been eliminated.

This time, on this issue, there must be no delay, or no hesitation or no compromise with our purpose.

We cannot, we must not refuse to protect the right of every American to vote in every election that he may desire to participate in. And we ought not; we must not wait another eight months before we get a bill. We have already waited a hundred years and more and the time for waiting is gone.

So I ask you to join me in working long hours, nights, and weekends if necessary, to pass this bill. And I don't make that request lightly. Far from the window where I sit with the problems of our country, I recognize that from outside this chamber is the outraged conscience of a nation, the grave concern of many nations and the harsh judgment of history on our acts.

But even if we pass this bill, the battle will not be over. What happened in Selma is part of a far larger movement which reaches into every section and state of America. It is the effort of American Negroes to secure for themselves the full blessings of American life.

Their cause must be our cause too; because it is not just Negroes, but really it is all of us, who must overcome the crippling legacy of bigotry and injustice. And we shall overcome.

As a man whose roots go deeply into Southern soil I know how agonizing racial feelings are. I know how difficult it is to reshape the attitudes and the structure of our society.

But a century has passed, more than a hundred years, since the Negro was freed. And he is not fully free tonight.

It was more than a hundred years ago that Abraham Lincoln, the great President of the Northern party, signed the Emancipation Proclamation, but emancipation is a proclamation and not a fact.

A century has passed, more than a hundred years since equality was promised. And yet the Negro is not equal.

A century has passed since the day of promise. And the promise is unkept.

The time of justice has now come. I tell you that I believe sincerely that no force can hold it back. It is right in the eyes of man and God that it should come. And when it does, I think that day will brighten the lives of every American.

For Negroes are not the only victims. How many white children have gone uneducated, how many white families have lived in stark poverty, how many white lives have been scarred by fear because we wasted our energy and our substance to maintain the barriers of hatred and terror.

So I say to all of you here and to all in the nation tonight, that those who appeal to you to hold on to the past do so at the cost of denying you your future.

This great, rich, restless country can offer opportunity and education and hope to all, all black and white, all North and South, sharecropper, and city dweller. These are the enemies, poverty, ignorance, disease. They are enemies, not our fellow man, not our neighbor, and these enemies too, poverty, disease and ignorance, we shall overcome.

Now let none of us in any section look with prideful righteousness on the troubles in another section or the problems of our neighbors. There is really no part of America where the promise of equality has been fully kept. In Buffalo as well as in Birmingham, in Philadelphia as well as in Selma, Americans are struggling for the fruits of freedom.

This is one nation. What happens in Selma or in Cincinnati is a matter of legitimate concern to every American. But let each of us look within our own hearts and our own communities, and let each of us put our shoulder to the wheel to root out injustice wherever it exists.

As we meet here in this peaceful historic chamber tonight, men from the South, some of whom were at Iwo Jima, men from the North who have carried Old Glory to far corners of the world and brought it back without a stain on it, men from the East and West are all fighting together without regard to religion, or color, or region, in Vietnam, men from every region fought for us across the world twenty years ago. And now in these common dangers and these common sacrifices the South made its contribution of honor and gallantry no less than any other region of the great Republic; in some instances, a great many of them more. And I have not the slightest doubt that good men from everywhere in this country, from the Great Lakes to the Gulf of Mexico, from the Golden Gate to the harbors along the Atlantic, will rally now together in this cause to vindicate [defend as just] the freedom of all Americans. For all of us owe this duty; and I believe all of us will respond to it. Your President makes that request of every American.

The real hero of this struggle is the American Negro. His actions and protests, his courage to risk safety and even to risk his life, have awakened the conscience of this nation. His demonstrations have been designed to call attention to injustice, designed to provoke change, designed to stir reform. He has called upon us to make good the promise of America. And who among us can say that we would have made the same progress were it not for his persistent bravery and his faith in American democracy.

For at the real heart of battle for equality is a deep seated belief in the democratic process. Equality depends not on the force of arms or tear gas but depends upon the force of moral right, not on recourse to violence but on respect for law and order.

There have been many pressures upon your President and there will be others as the days come and go, but I pledge you tonight that we intend to fight this battle where it should be fought, in the courts, and in the Congress, and in the hearts of men.

We must preserve the right of free speech and the right of free assembly. But the right of free speech does not carry with it as has been said, the right to holler fire in a crowded theater. We must preserve the right to free assembly but free assembly does not carry with it the right to block public thoroughfares [streets] to traffic.

We do have a right to protest, and a right to march under conditions that do not infringe the Constitutional rights of our neighbors. I intend to protect all those rights as long as I am permitted to serve in this Office.

We will guard against violence, knowing it strikes from our hands the very weapons with which we seek progress, obedience to law, and belief in American values.

In Selma as elsewhere we seek and pray for peace. We seek order. We seek unity. But we will not accept the peace of stifled rights, or the order imposed by fear, or the unity that stifles protest. For peace cannot be purchased at the cost of liberty.

In Selma tonight, and we had a good day there, as in every city, we are working for just and peaceful settlement. We must all remember that after this speech I am making tonight, after the police and the FBI and the marshals have all gone, and after you have promptly passed this bill, the people of Selma and the other cities of the nation must still live and work together. And when the attention of the nation has gone elsewhere they must try to heal the wounds and to build a new community. This cannot be easily done on a battleground of violence as the history of the South itself shows. It is in recognition of this that men of both races have shown such an outstandingly impressive responsibility in recent days, last Tuesday, again today.

The bill that I am presenting to you will be known as a civil rights bill. But, in a larger sense, most of the program I am recommending is a civil right. Its object is to open the city of hope to all people of all races, because all Americans just must have the right to vote. And we are going to give them that right.

All Americans must have the privileges of citizenship regardless of race. And they are going to have those privileges of citizenship regardless of race.

But I would like to caution you and remind you that to exercise these privileges takes much more than just legal right. It requires a trained mind and a healthy body. It requires a decent home, and the chance to find a job, and the opportunity to escape from the clutches of poverty.

Of course people cannot contribute to the nation if they are never taught to read or write, if their bodies are stunted from hunger, if their sickness goes untended, if their life is spent in hopeless poverty just drawing a welfare check.

So we want to open the gates to opportunity. But we are also going to give all our people, black and white, the help that they need to walk through those gates.

My first job after college was as a teacher in Cotulla, Texas, in a small Mexican-American school. Few of them could speak English and I couldn't speak much Spanish. My students were poor and they often came to class without breakfast, hungry, and they knew even in their youth that pain of prejudice. They never seemed to know why people disliked them. But they knew it was so, because I saw it in their eyes. I often walked home late in the afternoon after the classes were finished, wishing there was more that I could do. But all I knew was to teach them the little that I knew, hoping that it might help them against the hardships that lay ahead.

Somehow you never forget what poverty and hatred can do when you see its scars on the hopeful face of a young child.

I never thought then in 1928 that I would be standing here in 1965. It never even occurred to me in my fondest dreams that I might have the chance to help the sons and daughters of those students and to help people like them all over this country. But now I do have that chance and I let you in on a secret, I mean to use it. And I hope that you will use it with me.

This is the richest and most powerful country which ever occupied this globe. The might of past empires is little compared to ours.

But I do not want to be the President who built empires, or sought grandeur, or extended dominion. I want to be the President who educated young children to the wonders of their world. I want to be the President who helped to feed the hungry and to prepare them to be taxpayers instead of taxeaters. I want to be the President who helped the poor to find their own way and who protected the right of every citizen to vote in every election. I want to be the President who helped to end hatred among his fellow men and who prompted love among the people of all races and all regions and all parties. I want to be the President who helped to end war among the brothers of this earth.

And so at the request of your beloved Speaker and Senator from Montana, the Majority Leader, the Senator from Illinois, the Minority Leader, Mr. McCulloch and other leaders of both parties, I came here tonight not as President Roosevelt came down one time in person to veto a bonus bill, not as President Truman came down one time to urge the passage of a railroad bill, but I came down here to ask you to share this task with me and to share it with the people that we both work for. I want this to be the Congress, Republicans and Democrats alike, which did all those things for all these people.

Beyond this great chamber, out yonder, the fifty states are the people we serve. Who can tell what deep and unspoken hopes are in their hearts tonight as they sit there and listen? We all can guess, from our own lives, how difficult they often find their own pursuit of happiness, how many problems each little family has. They look most of all to themselves for their futures. But I think that they also look to each of us.

Extending the right to vote to 18-year-olds: What was the chief argument employed to justify this extension?

26TH AMENDMENT TO THE U.S. CONSTITUTION (1971)

In his 1954 State of the Union address, President Dwight D. Eisenhower became the first president to publicly state his support for prohibiting age-based denials of suffrage for those 18 and older. A little over 16 years later, on June 22, 1970, President Richard Nixon signed a law that required the voting age to be 18 in all federal, state, and local elections. The Congress and the state legislatures felt increasing pressure to pass the constitutional amendment because of the Vietnam War, in which many who were too young to vote were conscripted to fight. "Old enough to fight, old enough to vote" was a common slogan used by proponents of lowering the voting age. The debate traces its roots back to World War II, when President Franklin D. Roosevelt lowered the military draft age to 18. The principle at work here was that those who were old enough to be drafted into the military should have a say in the selection of the civilian government that determines when and how military force is to be used. On March 10, 1971, the Senate voted 94–0 in favor of proposing a constitutional amendment to guarantee that the voting age could not be higher than 18. On March 23, 1971, the House of Representatives voted 401–19 in favor of the proposed amendment. Within months, the resolution was ratified by three-fourths of the state legislatures—more quickly than any other amendment in U.S. history.

Questions to guide you as you read:

- Is there a plausible case for insisting that one reach the age of 21 before being allowed to vote? How might such a restriction be thought to enhance the quality of democratic decision-making? (Recall that the Constitution requires that one be at least 25 to serve in the U.S. House of Representatives, 30 to serve in the U.S. Senate; and 35 to serve as president.)

1. The right of citizens of the United States, who are eighteen years of age or older, to vote shall not be denied or abridged by the United States or by any State on account of age.

2. The Congress shall have power to enforce this article by appropriate legislation."

Are any principled limits on the right to vote consistent with American democracy?

ALEXIS DE TOCQUEVILLE, *DEMOCRACY IN AMERICA,* "THE PEOPLE'S CHOICE AND THE INSTINCTS OF AMERICAN DEMOCRACY IN SUCH CHOICES" (1835)

In this reading, Tocqueville addresses the political and moral effects of universal "suffrage" (voting). He denies that it produces the choice of the best leaders. To the contrary, on visiting this country, he was "surprised to find so much distinguished talent among the citizens and so little among the heads of government." Periods of crisis are an exception to this rule. Then, the people, "alarmed by the perils of their situation, for a time forget their envious passions" and elect those whose extraordinary virtue is fully revealed in times of calamity. He goes on to assert that the "ablest" legislators are elected to the U.S. Senate, and this he attributes to the fact that senators are elected by the legislatures of their state. As you will read shortly, this practice was replaced with direct election of the Senate by the 17th Amendment (1913).

WHY THIS READING?

Tocqueville's reservations about direct election by the people serve as the counterpoint to contemporary confidence in the wisdom of *vox populi.* As you will read below, his hesitation to approve the untrammeled popular will leads him to assert that Americans may have chosen to hold elections too frequently, which has produced "instability in public affairs."

Questions to guide you as you read:

- Why does Tocqueville argue that the universal right to vote rarely yields the best leaders?
- Why does Tocqueville believe that the state legislatures, rather than the people of the states themselves, are better able to choose those most qualified to be U.S. senators? Is such a mode of election undemocratic? If so, why? If not, why not?

Any people in Europe are apt to believe without saying it, or to say without believing it, that one of the great advantages of universal suffrage is that it entrusts the direction of affairs to men who are worthy of the public confidence. They admit that the people are unable to govern of themselves, but they aver [assert] that the people always wish the welfare of the state and instinctively designate those who are animated by the same good will and who are the most fit to wield the supreme authority. I confess that the observations I made in America by no means coincide with these opinions. On my arrival in the United States I was surprised to find so much distinguished talent among the citizens and so little among the heads of the government. It is a constant fact that at the present day the ablest men in the United States are rarely placed at the head of affairs; and it must be acknowledged that such has been the result in proportion as democracy has exceeded all its former limits. The race of American statesmen has evidently dwindled most remarkably in the course of the last fifty years.

Several causes may be assigned for this phenomenon. It is impossible, after the most strenuous exertions, to raise the intelligence of the people above a certain level. Whatever may be the facilities of acquiring information, whatever may be the profusion of easy methods and cheap science, the human mind can never be instructed and developed without devoting considerable time to these objects.

The greater or lesser ease with which people can live without working is a sure index of intellectual progress. This boundary is more remote in some countries and more restricted in others, but it must exist somewhere as long as the people are forced to work in order to procure the means of subsistence; that is to say, as long as they continue to be the people. It is therefore quite as difficult to imagine a state in which all the citizens are very well informed as a state in which they are all wealthy; these two difficulties are correlative. I readily admit that the mass of the citizens sincerely wish to promote the welfare of the country; nay, more, I even grant that the lower classes mix fewer considerations of personal interest with their patriotism than the higher orders; but it is always more or less difficult for them to discern the best means of attaining the end which they sincerely desire. Long and patient observation and much acquired knowledge are requisite to form a just estimate of the character of a single individual. Men of the greatest genius often fail to do it, and can it be supposed that the common people will always succeed? The people have neither the time nor the means for an investigation of this kind. Their conclusions are hastily formed from a superficial inspection of the more prominent features of a question. Hence it often happens that mountebanks [deceivers] of all sorts are able to please the people, while their truest friends frequently fail to gain their confidence.

Moreover, democracy not only lacks that soundness of judgment which is necessary to select men really deserving of their confidence, but often have not the desire or the inclination to find them out. It cannot be denied that democratic institutions strongly tend to promote the feeling of envy in the human heart; not so much because they afford to everyone the means of rising to the same level with others as because those means perpetually disappoint the persons who employ them. Democratic institutions awaken and foster a passion for equality which they can never entirely satisfy. This complete equality eludes the grasp of the people at the very moment when they think they have grasped it, and "flies," as Pascal says, "with an eternal flight"; the people are excited in the pursuit of an advantage, which is more precious because it is not sufficiently remote to be unknown or sufficiently near to be enjoyed. The lower orders are agitated by the chance of success, they are irritated by its uncertainty; and they pass from the enthusiasm of pursuit to the exhaustion of ill success, and lastly to the acrimony of disappointment. Whatever transcends their own limitations appears to be an obstacle to their desires, and there is no superiority, however legitimate it may be, which is not irksome in their sight....

...In the United States the people do not hate the higher classes of society, but are not favorably inclined towards them and carefully exclude them from the exercise of authority. They do not fear distinguished talents, but are rarely fond of them. In general, everyone who rises without their aid seldom obtains their favor.

While the natural instincts of democracy induce [provoke] the people to reject distinguished citizens as their rulers, an instinct not less strong induces able men to retire from the political arena, in which it is so difficult to retain their independence, or to advance without becoming servile. This opinion has been candidly expressed by Chancellor Kent [previously in this chapter], who says, in speaking with high praise of that part of the Constitution which empowers the executive to nominate the judges: "It is indeed probable that the men who are best fitted to discharge the duties of this high office would have too much reserve in their manners, and too much austerity in their principles, for them to be returned by the majority at an election where universal suffrage is adopted." Such were the opinions which were printed without contradiction in America in the year 1830!

I hold it to be sufficiently demonstrated that universal suffrage is by no means a guarantee of the wisdom of the popular choice. Whatever its advantages may be, this is not one of them.

"Causes Which May Partly Correct These Tendencies of Democracy"

When serious dangers threaten the state, the people frequently succeed in selecting the citizens who are the most able to save it. It has been observed that man rarely retains his customary level in very critical circumstances; he rises above or sinks below his usual condition, and the same thing is true of nations.... [I]t is more common, with both nations and individuals, to find extraordinary virtues developed from the very imminence of the danger. Great characters are then brought into relief as the edifices [buildings] which are usually concealed by the gloom of night are illuminated by the glare of a conflagration [fire]. At those dangerous times genius no longer hesitates to come forward; and the people, alarmed by the perils of their situation, for a time forget their envious passions. Great names may then be drawn from the ballot box.

I have already observed that the American statesmen of the present day are very inferior to those who stood at the head of affairs fifty years ago. This is as much a consequence of the circumstances as of the laws of the country. When America was struggling in the high cause of independence to throw off the yoke of another country, and when it was about to usher a new nation into the world, the spirits of its inhabitants were roused to the height which their great objects required. In this general excitement distinguished men were ready to anticipate the call of the community, and the people clung to them for support and placed them at their head. But such events are rare, and it is from the ordinary course of affairs that our judgment must be formed....

...In New England, where education and liberty are the daughters of morality and religion, where society has acquired age and stability enough to enable it to form principles and hold fixed habits, the common people are accustomed to respect intellectual and moral superiority and to submit to it without complaint, although they set at naught all those privileges which wealth and birth have introduced among mankind. In New England, consequently, the democracy makes a more judicious choice than it does elsewhere.

But as we descend towards the South, to those states in which the constitution of society is more recent and less strong, where instruction is less general and the principles of morality, religion, and liberty are less happily combined, we perceive that talents and virtues become more rare among those who are in authority.

Lastly, when we arrive at the new Southwestern states, in which the constitution of society dates but from yesterday and presents only an agglomeration [jumbled mass] of adventurers and speculators, we are amazed at the persons who are invested with public authority, and we are led to ask by what force, independent of legislation and of the men who direct it, the state can be protected and society be made to flourish.

There are certain laws of a democratic nature which contribute, nevertheless, to correct in some measure these dangerous tendencies of democracy. On entering the House of Representatives at Washington, one is struck by the vulgar [crude, common] demeanor of that great assembly. Often there is not a distinguished man in the whole number.... In a country in which education is very general, it is said that the representatives of the people do not always know how to write correctly.

At a few yards' distance is the door of the Senate, which contains within a small space a large proportion of the celebrated men of America. Scarcely an individual is to be seen in it who has not had an active and illustrious career: the Senate is composed of eloquent advocates, distinguished generals, wise magistrates, and statesmen of note, whose arguments would do honor to the most remarkable parliamentary debates of Europe.

How comes this strange contrast, and why are the ablest citizens found in one assembly rather than in the other?... Both of these assemblies emanate [spring] from the people; both are chosen by universal suffrage; and no voice has hitherto been heard to assert in America that the Senate is hostile to the interests of the people. From what cause, then, does so startling a difference arise? The only reason which appears to me adequately to account for it is that the House of Representatives is elected by the people directly, while the Senate is elected by elected bodies. The whole body of the citizens name the legislature of each state, and the Federal Constitution converts these legislatures into so many electoral bodies, which return the members of the Senate. The Senators are elected by an indirect application of the popular vote; for the legislatures which appoint them are not aristocratic or privileged bodies, that elect in their own right, but they are chosen by the totality of the citizens; they are generally elected every year, and enough new members may be chosen every year to determine the senatorial appointments. But this transmission of the popular authority through an assembly of chosen men operates an important change in it by refining [elevating] its discretion [judgment] and improving its choice. Men who are chosen in this manner accurately represent the majority of the nation which governs them; but they represent only the elevated thoughts that are current in the community and the generous propensities that prompt its nobler actions rather than the petty passions that disturb or the vices that disgrace it.

The time must come when the American republics will be obliged more frequently to introduce the plan of election by an elected body into their system of representation or run the risk of perishing miserably among the shoals [underwater sandbanks] of democracy.

I do not hesitate to avow [declare] that I look upon this peculiar system of election as the only means of bringing the exercise of political power to the level of all classes of the people. Those who hope to convert this institution into the exclusive weapon of a party, and those who fear to use it, seem to me to be equally in error.

"Influence Which American Democracy Has Exercised on the Laws Relating to Elections"

When elections recur only at long intervals, the state is exposed to violent agitation every time they take place.... If, on the other hand, the legal struggle is soon to be repeated, the defeated parties take patience.

When elections occur frequently, their recurrence keeps society in a feverish excitement and gives a continual instability to public affairs. Thus, on the one hand, the state is exposed to the perils of a revolution, on the other to perpetual mutability [changeability]; the former system threatens the very existence of the government, the latter prevents any steady and consistent policy. The Americans have preferred the second of these evils to the first; but they were led to this conclusion by instinct more than by reason, for a taste for variety is one of the characteristic passions of democracy. Hence their legislation is strangely mutable.

Many Americans consider the instability of their laws as a necessary consequence of a system whose general results are beneficial. But no one in the United States affects to deny the fact of this instability or contends that it is not a great evil.

Hamilton, after having demonstrated the utility of a power that might prevent or at least impede the promulgation [spread] of bad laws adds: "It may perhaps be said, that the power of preventing bad laws includes that of preventing good ones, and may be used to the one purpose as well as to the other. But this objection will have little weight with those who can properly estimate the mischiefs of that inconstancy [fickleness] and mutability in the laws which form the greatest blemish in the character and genius of our governments."... Jefferson himself, the greatest democrat whom the democracy of America has as yet produced, pointed out the same dangers.

"The instability of our laws," said he, "is really a very serious inconvenience...."

U.S. SENATOR CAROL MOSELEY-BRAUN, "SPEECH ON THE MOTOR-VOTER BILL" (1994)

In 1993, Congress enacted the National Voter Registration Act (also known as the "NVRA" or "Motor-Voter Act"). Part of this legislation included a provision for "motor-voter registration," which was intended to make it easier for people to register to vote by allowing them to register while applying for or renewing their drivers' licenses.

WHY THIS READING?

Former Senator Carol Moseley-Braun (D-IL) was a co-sponsor of the Motor-Voter Act. Her speech in defense of the Act serves as the counterpoint to both Tocqueville and Chancellor Kent.

Questions to guide you as you read:

- Some democracies in other countries require by law that all citizens vote on every election day. Based on your reading of her remarks here, would Senator Moseley-Braun endorse this? If so, why? If not, why not?
- Based on what you have read in this chapter, what would be behind the argument that voting by all damages, rather than strengthens, democracy? How would Senator Moseley-Braun respond?

One of my colleagues in the Senate tells a story about an elderly African-American man attempting to register to vote somewhere in the South in the 1950s. The official at the registration office handed the man a newspaper printed in Chinese and asked him to read it. The old man turned it one way, then another, then totally upside down. "Well come on," the registrar said "tell me, what does it say? That's easy," the old man replied, "It says that I'm not going to be allowed to register to vote today."

Things have changed a lot since then, but what hasn't changed is the fundamental importance of making it possible for Americans to cast their ballots. Voting is the essence of our democracy, and it was that basic truth that led Congress to enact the Motor Voter Act.

What the act does is make it easier for people to qualify for voting by allowing them to register or change their registration by mail or in person when they are handling routine business with the government, such as getting a driver's license renewed.

But three states are resisting implementing the act, including, I am sad to say, the State of Illinois: Critics from these states argue that elections are state, not federal responsibilities; that the act is an unfunded mandate[2]; and that the act increases the risk of fraud. They are wrong on all counts.

First, the federal interest in expanding the opportunity to vote in federal elections could not be clearer. The Constitution contains four amendments designed to expand the voting franchise: the 15th Amendment, which forbids denying anyone the right to vote based on race; the 19th Amendment, which extends the right to vote to women; the 24th Amendment, which forbids states from using a poll tax or any other tax to prevent people from voting; and the 26th Amendment, which extends the vote to citizens above age 18. And a major component of the Civil Rights Movement, the demonstrations, the litigation [law suits] and the legislation it created, involved turning the promise of our democracy into an opportunity to vote.

The contention that the Motor Voter Act is some sort of major unfunded mandate imposed on states is equally without merit. The act is in compliance with the mandates bill passed by the Senate, although as a basic civil rights issue it might well be exempt from coverage under that legislation. As I stated in a letter to Illinois Gov. Jim Edgar, the Congressional Budget Office estimated total cost of about $20 million annually to all 50 states—well under the mandates bill's $50 million threshold. And the Motor Voter Act enables states to offset up to half of that cost through other savings and through postal subsidies.

Because the act will help keep voter registration rolls more up to date, it will likely reduce rather than increase the risk of voter fraud. The act also contains six anti-fraud provisions.

2. An "unfunded mandate" refers to an instance in which the general government requires a state to carry out some policy or project without providing that state with the necessary funding to do so. Thus, the full burden of funding the project falls upon the state.

But the real reason driving the opposition is that opponents are afraid it will work and that more people will register to vote. The act is already working—and working well—in the states that have not let their fear of new voters blind them to the core requirements of democracy. In Georgia, for example, more than 90,000 people have registered since that state implemented the act. In Kentucky, more than 10,000 new voters registered in the first 10 days and another 15,000 voters updated their registrations. In Florida, more than 5,000 people registered on the first day.

In November's elections 75 million Americans voted; another 112 million did not. The Senate and, the House passed from Democratic to Republican control based on the ballots of only 38.7 percent of eligible voters. More than six out of every ten eligible voters didn't vote.

The Motor Voter Act will change that. History tells us that up to 90 percent of registered voters, will actually vote on election day. By making registration easier and more convenient, the Motor Voter Act will increase participation in our democracy and that is what really motivates the opponents of this act.

The unstated concern of opponents of easier registration is that a majority of the new voters might not sympathize with their political views. However, that kind of rationale has no place in this debate. Moreover, it is wrong on the facts. The last two elections proved conclusively that elections belong to the voters—and that voters make their own decisions.

Motor Voter expansion of the right to vote is not a partisan political issue; it is an American issue...it is the duty of every elected official to ensure that Americans exercise the most basic of our democratic rights.

It is time for opponents of the Motor Voter Act to get on with it, to implement this act, to put away their fear of our own citizens and to embrace the core values of the democracy they profess to serve.

Who and what should voters have a right to vote for directly?

JAMES MADISON, *THE FEDERALIST, NO. 63* (1788)

In this essay, Madison-as-Publius defends six-year terms for U. S. senators, as well as the indirect election of senators by their state legislatures.

WHY THIS READING?

Senators, Madison argues, selected by the members of their state's legislatures and serving a lengthy term, will be more likely to provide the "due sense of national character" necessary to securing the "esteem of foreign powers." (The U.S. Senate, not the House of Representatives, has the power to ratify international treaties.) Because the U.S. House is a "numerous and changeable body," it is less likely to possess such a sense of national identity. Moreover, the senators' length of office and method of election will supply a "due responsibility in the government to the people." By this observation, which Publius grants is "paradoxical" on its face, he means that shorter terms of office would not provide senators the time needed to envision and implement "well-chosen and well-connected measures." In addition, longer terms of office will enable the Senate to ensure that the "cool and deliberate sense of the community" is more likely to prevail during those periods when popular passions run high. Finally, Publius is not worried—as are some of the proposed Constitution's critics—that a Senate so empowered will inevitably degenerate into a "tyrannical aristocracy," because the House of Representatives, the state legislatures, and the people themselves stand as tangible checks against any such imagined possibility.

Questions to guide you as you read:

- How does Madison respond to the charge that six-year terms for U.S. senators are undemocratic?
- What is the effect on American democracy of "staggering" senators' terms? (Staggering results in one-third of senators being up for reelection every two years.)

...The true distinction [difference] between these [ancient democracies] and the American Governments lies *in the total exclusion of the people in their collective capacity* from any share in the *latter* [American democracy], and not in the *total exclusion of representatives of the people,* from the administration of the *former.* The distinction however thus qualified must be admitted to leave a most advantageous superiority in favor of the United States. But to ensure to this advantage its full effect, we must be careful not to separate it from the other advantage, of an extensive territory. For it cannot be believed that any form of representative government, could have succeeded within the narrow limits occupied by the democracies of Greece.

In answer to all these arguments, suggested by reason, illustrated by examples, and enforced by our own experience, the jealous adversary of the constitution will probably content himself with repeating, that a senate appointed not immediately by the people, and for the term of six years, must gradually acquire a dangerous preeminence in the government, and finally transform it into a tyrannical aristocracy.

To this general answer the general reply ought to be sufficient; that liberty may be endangered by the abuses of liberty, as well as by the abuses of power; that there are numerous instances of the former as well as of the latter; and that the former rather than the latter is apparently most to be apprehended by the United States. But a more particular reply may be given.

Before such a revolution can be effected, the senate, it is to be observed, must in the first place corrupt itself, must next corrupt the state legislatures, must then corrupt the house of representatives, and must finally corrupt the people at large. It is evident that the senate must be first corrupted, before it can attempt an establishment of tyranny. Without corrupting the state legislatures, it cannot prosecute the attempt, because the periodical change of members would otherwise regenerate the whole body. Without exerting the means of corruption with equal success on the House of Representatives, the opposition of that co-equal branch of the government would inevitably defeat the attempt; and without corrupting the people themselves, a succession of new representatives would speedily restore all things to their pristine order. Is there any man who can seriously persuade himself that the proposed senate can, by any possible means within the compass of human address, arrive at the object of a lawless ambition, through all these obstructions?

17TH AMENDMENT TO THE U.S. CONSTITUTION (1913)

The 17th Amendment was passed by Congress in 1912 and ratified by the states in 1913. The Amendment supersedes Article I, Sections 2 and 3, of the Constitution.

Questions to guide you as you read:

- In chapter two, you read tracts from leaders of the Progressive movement. From those readings, what do you infer would have been their attitude toward the passing of the 17th Amendment? Why?

The Senate of the United States shall be composed of two Senators from each State, elected by the people thereof, for six years; and each Senator shall have one vote. The electors in each State shall have the qualifications requisite for electors of the most numerous branch of the State legislatures.

When vacancies happen in the representation of any State in the Senate, the executive authority of such State shall issue writs of election to fill such vacancies: *Provided,* That the legislature of any State may empower the executive thereof to make temporary appointments until the people fill the vacancies by election as the legislature may direct.

This amendment shall not be so construed as to affect the election or term of any Senator chosen before it becomes valid as part of the Constitution.

Presidential election through the Electoral College, rather than by direct popular election

U.S. CONSTITUTION: ART. II, SEC. 1 (1787)

Article II, Section 1, established the procedure for the election of the president and vice president. Under this constitutional provision, each elector could cast two votes. The candidate who received the vote from a majority of the electors won the election. The candidate who received the next-highest number of votes became vice president.

The 12th Amendment (below) provides that electors each have one vote on separate ballots for the election of the president and vice president. This amendment makes it less likely that an opponent of the winning candidate for president would be elected vice president. That is to say, the 12th Amendment establishes the election of the president and vice president as a single "ticket." (See the editors' introduction to Jefferson's 1801 *Inaugural Address* in chapter two.)

Questions to guide you as you read:

- You have read Madison's defense of indirect election of U.S. senators. Based on what you have read, do you think Madison would believe that election of the president through the Electoral College is more or less preferable than direct popular election? Why?

Each State shall appoint, in such Manner as the Legislature thereof may direct, a Number of Electors, equal to the whole Number of Senators and Representatives to which the State may be entitled in the Congress: but no Senator or Representative, or Person holding an Office of Trust or Profit under the United States, shall be appointed an Elector.

The Electors shall meet in their respective States, and vote by Ballot for two persons, of whom one at least shall not be an Inhabitant of the same State with themselves. And they shall make a List of all the Persons voted for, and of the Number of Votes for each; which List they shall sign and certify, and transmit sealed to the Seat of the Government of the United States, directed to the President of the Senate. The President of the Senate shall, in the Presence of the Senate and House of Representatives, open all the Certificates, and the Votes shall then be counted. The Person having the greatest Number of Votes shall be the President, if such Number be a Majority of the whole Number of Electors appointed; and if there be more than one who have such Majority, and have an equal Number of Votes, then the House of Representatives shall immediately chuse [choose] by Ballot one of them for President; and if no Person have a Majority, then from the five highest on the List the said House shall in like Manner chuse the President. But in chusing the President, the Votes shall be taken by States, the Representation from each State having one Vote; a quorum for this Purpose shall consist of a Member or Members from two-thirds of the States, and a Majority of all the States shall be necessary to a Choice. (In every Case, after the Choice of the President, the Person having the greatest Number of Votes of the Electors shall be the Vice President. But if there should remain two or more who have equal Votes, the Senate shall chuse from them by Ballot the Vice-President.) [This clause in parentheses was superseded by the 12th Amendment.]

The Congress may determine the Time of chusing [choosing] the Electors, and the Day on which they shall give their Votes; which Day shall be the same throughout the United States.

12TH AMENDMENT TO THE U.S. CONSTITUTION (1804)

The Electors shall meet in their respective states, and vote by ballot for President and Vice-President, one of whom, at least, shall not be an inhabitant of the same state with themselves; they shall name in their ballots the person voted for as President, and in distinct ballots the person voted for as Vice-President, and they shall make distinct lists of all persons voted for as President, and of all persons voted for as Vice-President and of the number of votes for each, which lists they shall sign and certify, and transmit sealed to the seat of the government of the United States, directed to the President of the Senate;

The President of the Senate shall, in the presence of the Senate and House of Representatives, open all the certificates and the votes shall then be counted;

The person having the greatest Number of votes for President, shall be the President, if such number be a majority of the whole number of Electors appointed; and if no person have such majority, then from the persons having the highest numbers not exceeding three on the list of those voted for as President, the House of Representatives shall choose immediately, by ballot, the President. But in choosing the President, the votes shall be taken by states, the representation from each state having one vote; a quorum for this purpose shall consist of a member or members from two-thirds of the states, and a majority of all the states shall be necessary to a choice. And if the House of Representatives shall not choose a President whenever the right of choice shall devolve upon them, before the fourth day of March next following, then the Vice-President shall act as President, as in the case of the death or other constitutional disability of the President.

The person having the greatest number of votes as Vice-President, shall be the Vice-President, if such number be a majority of the whole number of Electors appointed, and if no person have a majority, then from the two highest numbers on the list, the Senate shall choose the Vice-President; a quorum for the purpose shall consist of two-thirds of the whole number of Senators, and a majority of the whole number shall be necessary to a choice. But no person constitutionally ineligible to the office of President shall be eligible to that of Vice-President of the United States.

CHAPTER 5

Core Question: What is democratic representation meant to accomplish, and what is the role of race?

> The aim of every political constitution is, or ought to be, first to obtain for rulers men who possess most wisdom to discern, and most virtue to pursue, the common good of the society; and in the next place, to take the most effectual precautions for keeping them virtuous whilst they continue to hold their public trust. The elective mode of obtaining rulers is the characteristic policy of republican government.... Who are to be the objects of popular choice? Every citizen whose merit may recommend him to the esteem and confidence of his country. No qualification of wealth, of birth, of religious faith, or of civil profession is permitted to fetter the judgment or disappoint the inclination of the people.
>
> —JAMES MADISON,
> *as "Publius," Federalist 57*

As you have read, the Founders intended America to be a representative democracy. When Madison rejects a "pure democracy" in favor of a "republic" in *Federalist 10*, he means by the word "republic" a representative democracy. Recall that the ancient Greek democracies did not embrace representation. Instead, in these relatively small "city-states," public policy could be and was deliberated upon by all of the citizens. In contrast, even the smallest state in the Union was, by 1787, already much larger than any of the ancient democracies. Accordingly, such "town hall" deliberations were impossible, at least on a statewide basis. Democracy would be possible in such an expansive sphere only through representation. But recall also from your earlier reading that representation was, for the Founders, more than merely a "concession" to largeness. It was for them a blessing for liberty, because, in Madison and Hamilton's view, the ancient democracies disintegrated precisely *because* they were small. Smallness, and the static economy concomitant to smallness, exacerbated the always-present tension between the few rich and the many poor. As Hamilton's Publius states it:

> It is impossible to read the history of the petty republics of Greece and Italy without feeling sensations of horror and disgust at the distractions with which they were continually

agitated, and at the rapid succession of revolutions by which they were kept in a state of perpetual vibration between the extremes of tyranny and anarchy.

—*Federalist 9*

If "pure democracy" was not only impossible but also undesirable for the United States, and if representation was to substitute for "town hall meeting" democracy, what precisely did the Founders intend representation to accomplish, and by what means? These questions have not gone away with the Founding—far from it. Accordingly, in this chapter we begin with Hamilton and Tocqueville and then move on to examine a number of recent Supreme Court decisions addressing representation.

Of late, a far-reaching debate has arisen concerning whether democratic equality requires representation of specific groups, especially racial minorities. Here, Lani Guinier and former Supreme Court Justice Thurgood Marshall argue for such group representation. As you will read, for Guinier, "representation of racial groups is valid and desirable given our history and our acceptance of group representation in other forms...." As counterpoint, Robert Goldwin advances the case that representation of individuals, not groups, is both what the Founders intended and essential to maintaining the liberty of all: "The Constitution, he argues, finds rights inherent in individuals, not in the groups they belong to...we are all equal...no matter what our color, sex, national origin, or religion...." Accordingly, "it is not only unnecessary" for the Constitution "to mention race, sex, or religion, it is inconsistent and harmful."

Given its connection to the morally and politically charged issue of racial justice, it would be difficult to overstate the importance of the individual-based versus group-based conceptions of democratic representation. This schism informs some of the most strenuous debates taking place on the national stage today, as we shall see in the final two readings of the chapter: President Bill Clinton's 1995 speech on welfare reform and then-presidential candidate Senator Barack Obama's "Speech on Race in America" (2008).

Representation in the view of the Founders and Tocqueville

ALEXANDER HAMILTON, PUBLIUS LETTER III, "ON THE CHARACTER OF THE LEGISLATOR" (1778)

From Hamilton's scathing attack on a corrupt politician of his day comes his vision of the highest responsibilities of a true legislator.

WHY THIS READING?

Concern with politicians' ethics, or the lack thereof, is as old as politics itself. Recall the reading of *Federalist 10*, in which Hamilton's coauthor, James Madison, declares it "vain" to rely too much on wise and just officeholders to umpire democracy's "clashing" selfish "interests." Such "enlightened statesmen," Madison says delicately, "will not always be at the helm." No Pollyanna on this subject, Hamilton nonetheless insists that legislators be guided by "neither wealth, nor power, nor the temporary applause of a passionate, misguided majority...." Rather, "promoting human happiness" and "doing good to all mankind" should be their sole and constant concerns.

Questions to consider as you read:

- In this letter, Hamilton suggests that virtuous politicians will not follow the desires of their constituents when those desires are inconsistent with the common good. Does it violate democratic principles to place one's conscience above the dictates of those one has sworn to represent? If so, why? If not, why not?

...The station of a member of Congress is the most illustrious [famous] and important of any I am able to conceive. He is to be regarded not only as a legislator, but as the founder of an empire. A man of virtue and ability, dignified with so precious a trust, would rejoice that fortune had given him birth at a time, and placed him in circumstances so favourable for promoting human happiness. He would esteem [consider] it not more the duty, than the privilege and ornament of his office, to do good to mankind; from this commanding eminence [position of distinction], he would look down with contempt upon every mean [low in quality] or interested pursuit.

To form useful alliances abroad—to establish a wise government at home—to improve the internal resources, and finances of the nation would be the generous objects of his care. He would not allow his attention to be diverted from these to intrigue [secretly scheme] for personal connections, to confirm his own influence; nor would be able to reconcile it, either to the delicacy of his honour, or to the dignity of his pride, to confound in the same person the representative of the Commonwealth, and the little member of a trading company. Anxious for the permanent power and prosperity of the State, he would labour to perpetuate [prolong] the union and harmony of the several parts. He would not meanly court a temporary importance, by patronizing [supporting] the narrow views of local interest, or by encouraging dissensions either among the people or in Congress. In council, or debate, he would discover the candor [straightforwardness] of a statesman, zealous for truth, and the integrity of a patriot studious [in diligent study] of the public welfare; not the caviling [trivially objecting] petulance [ill-temper] of an attorney, contending for the triumph of an opinion, nor the perverse [perverted] duplicity [deceptiveness] of a partisan [one biased in support of], devoted to the service of a cabal [group of intriguers]. Despising the affectation of superior wisdom, he would prove the extent of his capacity, by foreseeing evils, and contriving [cleverly planning] expedients [means to an end] to prevent or remedy them. He would not expose the weak sides of the State, to find an opportunity of displaying his own discernment [recognition] by magnifying the follies and mistakes of others. In his transactions with individuals, whether foreigners or countrymen, his conduct would be guided by the sincerity of a man, and the politeness of a gentleman, not by the temporizing [acting evasively to gain time] flexibility of a courtier [one seeking favor], nor the fawning [using flattery] complaisance [complying willingly] of a sycophant [favor seeker]....

ALEXIS DE TOCQUEVILLE, *DEMOCRACY IN AMERICA*, EXCERPTS ON "PARTIES" AND "GOVERNANCE OF THE PEOPLE" (1835) ("WHY IT CAN STRICTLY BE SAID THAT THE PEOPLE GOVERN IN THE UNITED STATES," AND "PARTIES IN THE UNITED STATES")

Here, Tocqueville discusses the opposition between the Federalist and the Republican parties. The Jeffersonian-Republicans began calling themselves Democratic-Republicans in the mid-1790s; shortly thereafter, they shortened it to Republicans; during the Jacksonian era, they took the name of the Democratic Party, which they retain to this day. Today's Republican Party formed in the 1850s as a result of the slavery debate; the first Republican president was Abraham Lincoln, inaugurated in 1861.

WHY THIS READING?

The Federalist-Republican debate at the time of the Founding represents, for Tocqueville, "two opinions that are as old as the world... the one tending to limit, the other to extend indefinitely, the power of the people." The Federalists sought to limit the power of the people, and this, according to Tocqueville, explains why, in "the land of democracy," the Federalist Party soon withered and died.

Questions to guide you as you read:

- How likely does Tocqueville think it that Hamilton's model legislator will survive in office when conscience forces the choice of the common good over the desires of the voters?
- If Tocqueville is correct that those who seek to limit the power of the people are, like the Federalists, doomed politically, what sort of regime would you expect this country to become in time?

In America the people appoint the legislative and the executive power and furnish the jurors who punish all infractions of the laws. The institutions are democratic, not only in their principle, but in all their consequences; and the people elect their representatives directly, and for the most part annually, in order to ensure their dependence. The people are therefore the real directing power; and although the form of government is representative, it is evident that the opinions, the prejudices, the interests, and even the passions of the people are hindered by no permanent obstacles from exercising a perpetual influence on the daily conduct of affairs. In the United States the majority governs in the name of the people, as is the case in all countries in which the people are supreme. This majority is principally [chiefly] composed of peaceable citizens, who, either by inclination or by interest, sincerely wish the welfare of their country. But they are surrounded by the incessant agitation of parties, who attempt to gain their cooperation and support.

A great distinction must be made between parties. Some countries are so large that the different populations which inhabit them, although united under the same government, have contradictory interests, and they may consequently be in a perpetual state of opposition. In this case the different fractions of the people may more properly be considered as distinct nations than as mere parties; and if a civil war breaks out, the struggle is carried on by rival states rather than by factions in the same state.

But when the citizens entertain different opinions upon subjects which affect the whole country alike, such, for instance, as the principles upon which the government is to be conducted, then distinctions arise that may correctly be styled parties. Parties are a necessary evil in free governments; but they have not at all times the same character and the same propensities.

At certain periods a nation may be oppressed by such insupportable evils as to conceive the design of effecting a total change in its political constitution; at other times, the mischief lies still deeper and the existence of society itself is endangered. Such are the times of great revolutions and of great parties. But between these epochs of misery and confusion there are periods during which human society seems to rest and mankind to take breath. This pause is, indeed, only apparent, for time does not stop its course for nations any more than for men; they are all advancing every day towards a goal with which they are unacquainted. We imagine them to be stationary only when their progress escapes our observation, as men who are walking seem to be standing still to those who run....

...The political parties that I style great are those which cling to principles rather than to their consequences; to general and not to special cases; to ideas and not to men. These parties are usually distinguished by nobler features, more generous passions, more genuine convictions, and a more bold and open conduct than the others. In them private interest, which always plays the chief part in political passions, is more studiously veiled under the pretext of the public good; and it may even be sometimes concealed from the eyes of the very persons whom it excites and impels.

Minor parties, on the other hand, are generally deficient in political good faith. As they are not sustained or dignified by lofty purposes, they ostensibly [openly] display the selfishness of their character in their actions. They glow with a factitious [contrived and insincere] zeal [enthusiasm]; their language is vehement [passionate], but their conduct is timid and irresolute [indecisive]. The means which they employ are as wretched as the end at which they aim. Hence it happens that when a calm state succeeds a violent revolution, great men seem suddenly to disappear and the powers of the human mind to lie concealed. Society is convulsed by great parties, it is only agitated by minor ones; it is torn by the former, by the latter it is degraded; and if the first sometimes save it by a salutary perturbation, the last invariably disturb it to no good end.

America has had great parties, but has them no longer; and if her happiness is thereby considerably increased, her morality has suffered. When the War of Independence was terminated and the foundations of the new government were to be laid down, the nation was divided between two opinions—two opinions which are as old as the world and which are perpetually to be met with, under different forms and various names, in all free communities, the one tending to limit, the other to extend indefinitely, the power of the people. The conflict between these two opinions never assumed that degree of violence in America which it has frequently displayed elsewhere. Both parties of the Americans were agreed upon the most essential points; and neither of them had to destroy an old constitution or to overthrow the structure of society in order to triumph. In neither of them, consequently, were a great number of private interests affected by success or defeat: but moral principles of a high order, such as the love of equality and of independence, were concerned in the struggle, and these sufficed to kindle violent passions.

The party that desired to limit the power of the people, endeavored to apply its doctrines more especially to the Constitution of the Union, whence it derived its name of Federal. The other party, which affected to be exclusively attached to the cause of liberty, took that of Republican. America is the land of democracy, and the Federalists, therefore, were always in a minority; but they reckoned on their side almost all the great men whom the War of Independence had produced, and their moral power was very considerable. Their cause, moreover, was favored by circumstances. The ruin of the first Confederation had impressed the people with a dread of anarchy, and the Federalists profited by this transient disposition of the multitude. For ten or twelve years, they were at the head of affairs, and they were able to apply some, though not all, of their principles; for the hostile current was becoming from day to day too violent to be checked. In 1801 the Republicans got possession of the government: Thomas Jefferson was elected President; and he increased the influence of their party by the weight of his great name, the brilliance of his talents, and his immense popularity.

The means by which the Federalists had maintained their position were artificial, and their resources were temporary; it was by the virtues or the talents of their leaders, as well as by fortunate circumstances, that they had risen to power. When the Republicans attained that station in their turn, their opponents were overwhelmed by utter defeat. An immense majority declared itself against the retiring party, and the Federalists found themselves in so small a minority that they at once despaired of future success. From that moment the Republican or Democratic Party has proceeded from conquest to conquest, until it has acquired absolute supremacy in the country....

...The accession of the Federalists to power was, in my opinion, one of the most fortunate incidents that accompanied the formation of the great American Union: they resisted the inevitable propensities of their country and their age. But whether their theories were good or bad, they had the fault of being inapplicable, as a whole, to the society which they wished to govern, and that which occurred under the auspices of Jefferson must therefore have taken place sooner or later. But their government at least gave the new republic time to acquire a certain stability, and afterwards to support without inconvenience the rapid growth of the very doctrines which they had combated. A considerable number of their principles, moreover, were embodied at last in the political creed of their opponents; and the Federal Constitution, which subsists at the present day, is a lasting monument of their patriotism and their wisdom.

Great political parties, then, are not to be met with in the United States at the present time. Parties, indeed, may be found which threaten the future of the Union; but there is none which seems to contest the present form of government or the present course of society. The parties by which the Union is menaced do not rest upon principles, but upon material interests. These interests constitute, in the different provinces of so vast an empire, rival nations rather than parties. Thus, upon a recent occasion the North contended for the system of commercial prohibition, and the South took up arms in favor of free trade, simply because the North is a manufacturing and the South an agricultural community; and the restrictive system that was profitable to the one was prejudicial to the other.

In the absence of great parties the United States swarms with lesser controversies, and public opinion is divided into a thousand minute shades of difference upon questions of detail. The pains that are taken to create parties are inconceivable, and at the present day it is no easy task. In the United States there is no religious animosity, because all religion is respected and no sect is predominant; there is no jealousy of rank, because the people are everything and none can contest their authority; lastly, there is no public misery to serve as a means of agitation, because the physical position of the country opens so wide a field to industry that man only needs to be let alone to be able to accomplish prodigies [marvelous deeds]. Nevertheless, ambitious men will succeed in creating parties, since it is difficult to eject a person from authority upon the mere ground that this place is coveted by others. All the skill of the actors in the political world lies in the art of creating parties. A political aspirant in the United States begins by discerning his own interest, and discovering those other interests which may be collected around and amalgamated with it. He then contrives to find out some doctrine or principle that may suit the purposes of this new association, which he adopts in order to bring forward his party and secure its popularity.... This being done, the new party is ushered into the political world.

To a stranger all the domestic controversies of the Americans at first appear to be incomprehensible or puerile [childish], and he is at a loss whether to pity a people who take such arrant [outright] trifles in good earnest or to envy that happiness which enables a community to discuss them. But when he comes to study the secret propensities that govern the factions of America, he easily perceives that the greater part of them are more or less connected with one or the other of those two great divisions which have always existed in free communities. The deeper we penetrate into the inmost thought of these parties, the more we perceive that the object of the one is to limit and that of the other to extend the authority of the people. I do not assert that the ostensible purpose or even that the secret aim of American parties is to promote the rule of aristocracy or democracy in the country; but I affirm that aristocratic or democratic passions may easily be detected at the bottom of all parties, and that, although they escape a superficial observation, they are the main point and soul of every faction in the United States.

To quote a recent example, when President Jackson attacked the Bank of the United States, the country was excited, and parties were formed; the well-informed classes rallied round the bank, the common people round the President. But it must not be imagined that the people had formed a rational opinion upon a question which offers so many difficulties to the most experienced statesmen. By no means. The bank is a great establishment, which has an independent existence; and the people, accustomed to make and unmake whatsoever they please, are startled to meet with this obstacle to their authority. In the midst of the perpetual fluctuation of society, the community is irritated by so permanent an institution and is led to attack it, in order to see whether it can be shaken, like everything else.

Remains of the Aristocratic Party in the United States

It sometimes happens in a people among whom various opinions prevail that the balance of parties is lost and one of them obtains an irresistible preponderance [hold], overpowers all obstacles, annihilates its opponents, and appropriates all the resources of society to its own use. The vanquished despair of success, hide their heads, and are silent. The nation seems to be governed by a single principle, universal stillness prevails, and the prevailing party assumes the credit of having restored peace and unanimity to the country. But under this apparent unanimity still exist profound differences of opinion, and real opposition.

This is what occurred in America; when the democratic party got the upper hand, it took exclusive possession of the conduct of affairs, and from that time the laws and the customs of society have been adapted to its caprices [impulsive decisions]. At the present day the more affluent classes of society have no influence in political affairs; and wealth, far from conferring a right, is rather a cause of unpopularity than a means of attaining power. The rich abandon the lists, through unwillingness to contend, and frequently to contend in vain, against the poorer classes of their fellow citizens. As they cannot occupy in public a position equivalent to what they hold in private life, they abandon the former and give themselves up to the latter; and they constitute a private society in the state which has its own tastes and pleasures. They submit to this state of things as an irremediable evil, but they are careful not to show that they are galled [made angry] by its continuance; one often hears them laud the advantages of a republican government and democratic institutions when they are in public. Next to hating their enemies, men are most inclined to flatter them.

Mark, for instance, that opulent [wealthy] citizen, who is as anxious as a Jew of the Middle Ages to conceal his wealth. His dress is plain, his demeanor unassuming; but the interior of his dwelling glitters with luxury, and none but a few chosen guests, whom he haughtily styles his equals, are allowed to penetrate into this sanctuary. No European noble is more exclusive in his pleasures or more jealous of the smallest advantages that a privileged station confers. But the same individual crosses the city to reach a dark counting-house in the center of traffic, where everyone may accost him who pleases. If he meets his cobbler on the way, they stop and converse; the two citizens discuss the affairs of the state and shake hands before they part.

But beneath this artificial enthusiasm and these obsequious [submissive] attentions to the preponderating [dominant] power, it is easy to perceive that the rich have a hearty dislike of the democratic institutions of their country. The people form a power which they at once fear and despise. If the maladministration of the democracy ever brings about a revolutionary crisis and monarchical institutions ever become practicable in the United States, the truth of what I advance will become obvious....

Recent judicial concerns over representation

CHIEF JUSTICE EARL WARREN, OPINION OF THE COURT IN *REYNOLDS V. SIMS* (1964)

Chief Justice Earl Warren writes the majority opinion in *Reynolds,* a case challenging the constitutionality of apportionment in the Alabama state senate. The suit charged that voters in the more-populous urban areas were drastically underrepresented in the state senate, in violation of the principle of "one person, one vote."

WHY THIS READING?

For many years, the Supreme Court had held that the Constitution regarded issues of districting and apportionment (the delineation of voting districts and allocation of congressional seats) as "political questions"—to be decided by popularly elected legislatures—and not as "legal questions" to be decided by courts. But, in *Baker v. Carr* (1962), the Court declared apportionment to be "justiciable" (i.e., as a legal question to be decided by the court). This ushered in a series of apportionment cases. In this case, Warren addresses the meaning of the "Equal Protection Clause" of the 14th Amendment, ratified in 1868, which reads, "No state shall... deny to any person within its jurisdiction the equal protection of the laws" (Section 1). For Warren and the Court majority, the Equal Protection Clause mandates that districts be apportioned solely on the basis of population, ensuring that each and every person's vote is weighted equally.

In his dissenting opinion, which comes immediately after, Justice John Harlan II defends the traditional position that questions of districting and apportionment are best left to legislatures.

Questions to guide you as you read:

- As you have read, the Constitution allots to each state two seats in the U.S. Senate, regardless of the population of the state. This appears not to square with Chief Justice Warren's view that apportionment ought to be based on population alone. What use does Justice Harlan make of this fact in his dissent?

- The Court holds that "to the extent that a citizen's right to vote is debased, he is that much less a citizen." How does this view compare with the Seneca Falls Declaration, as well as with Lyndon B. Johnson's speech on the Voting Rights Act? How does it compare with the majority opinion in *Minor v. Happersett?*

A predominant consideration in determining whether a State's legislative apportionment scheme[1] constitutes an invidious [unjust] discrimination violative of rights asserted under the Equal Protection Clause[2] is that the rights allegedly impaired are individual and personal in nature.... While the result of a court decision in a state legislative apportionment controversy may be to require the restructuring of the geographical distribution of seats in a state legislature, the judicial focus must be concentrated upon ascertaining whether there has been any discrimination against certain of the State's citizens which constitutes an impermissible impairment of their constitutionally protected right to vote... such a case "touches a sensitive and important area of human rights," and "involves one of the basic civil rights of man," presenting questions of alleged "invidious discriminations... against groups or types of individuals in violation of the constitutional guaranty of just and equal laws.... Undoubtedly, the right of suffrage [voting] is a fundamental matter in a free and democratic society. Especially since the right to exercise the franchise [vote] in a free and unimpaired manner is preservative of other basic civil and political rights, any alleged infringement of the right of citizens to vote must be carefully and meticulously scrutinized [carefully examined]. Almost a century ago, in *Yick Wo v. Hopkins*... the Court referred to "the political franchise of voting" as "a fundamental political right, because preservative of all rights."

Legislators represent people, not trees or acres. Legislators are elected by voters, not farms or cities or economic interests. As long as ours is a representative form of government, and our legislatures are those instruments of government elected directly by and directly representative of the people, the right to elect legislators in a free and unimpaired fashion is a bedrock [foundation] of our political system. It could hardly be gainsaid that a constitutional claim had been asserted by an allegation that certain otherwise qualified voters had been entirely prohibited from voting for members of their state legislature. And, if a State should provide that the votes of citizens in one part of the State should be given two times, or five times, or 10 times the weight of votes of citizens in another part of the State, it could hardly be contended that the right to vote of those residing in the disfavored areas had not been effectively diluted. It would appear extraordinary to suggest that a State could be constitutionally permitted to enact a law providing that certain of the State's voters could vote two, five, or 10 times for their legislative representatives, while voters living elsewhere could vote only once. And it is inconceivable that a state law to the effect that, in counting votes for legislators, the votes of citizens in one part of the State would be multiplied by two, five, or 10, while the votes of persons in another area would be counted only at face value, could be constitutionally sustainable. Of course, the effect of state legislative districting schemes which give the same number of representatives to unequal numbers of constituents is identical. Overweighting and overvaluation of the votes of those living here has the certain effect of dilution [a watering-down] and undervaluation of the votes of those living there. The resulting discrimination against those individual voters living in disfavored areas is easily demonstrable mathematically. Their right to vote is simply not the same right to vote as that of those living in a favored

1. "Apportionment" here refers to the manner in which representative district lines are drawn. A "representative district" is the geographical area from which a public official is elected.

2. This is the "Equal Protection Clause" of the 14th Amendment, which holds that no state shall deny to any person within its jurisdiction the "equal protection of the laws."

part of the State. Two, five, or 10 of them must vote before the effect of their voting is equivalent to that of their favored neighbor. Weighting the votes of citizens differently, by any method or means, merely because of where they happen to reside, hardly seems justifiable. One must be ever aware that the Constitution forbids "sophisticated as well as simple-minded modes of discrimination...." As we stated in *Wesberry v. Sanders, supra:*

> We do not believe that the Framers of the Constitution intended to permit the same vote-diluting discrimination to be accomplished through the device of districts containing widely varied numbers of inhabitants. To say that a vote is worth more in one district than in another would...run counter to our fundamental ideas of democratic government....

State legislatures are, historically, the fountainhead [main source] of representative government in this country. A number of them have their roots in colonial times, and substantially antedate the creation of our Nation and our Federal Government. In fact, the first formal stirrings of American political independence are to be found, in large part, in the views and actions of several of the colonial legislative bodies. With the birth of our National Government, and the adoption and ratification of the Federal Constitution, state legislatures retained a most important place in our Nation's governmental structure. But representative government is in essence self-government through the medium of elected representatives of the people, and each and every citizen has an inalienable right to full and effective participation in the political processes of his State's legislative bodies. Most citizens can achieve this participation only as qualified voters through the election of legislators to represent them. Full and effective participation by all citizens in state government requires, therefore, that each citizen have an equally effective voice in the election of members of his state legislature. Modern and viable [workable] state government needs, and the Constitution demands, no less.

Logically, in a society ostensibly grounded on representative government, it would seem reasonable that a majority of the people of a State could elect a majority of that State's legislators. To conclude differently, and to sanction minority control of state legislative bodies, would appear to deny majority rights in a way that far surpasses any possible denial of minority rights that might otherwise be thought to result. Since legislatures are responsible for enacting laws by which all citizens are to be governed, they should be bodies which are collectively responsive to the popular will. And the concept of equal protection has been traditionally viewed as requiring the uniform treatment of persons standing in the same relation to the governmental action questioned or challenged. With respect to the allocation of legislative representation, all voters, as citizens of a State, stand in the same relation regardless of where they live. Any suggested criteria for the differentiation of citizens are insufficient to justify any discrimination, as to the weight of their votes, unless relevant to the permissible purposes of legislative apportionment. Since the achieving of fair and effective representation for all citizens is concededly the basic aim of legislative apportionment, we conclude that the Equal Protection Clause guarantees the opportunity for equal participation by all voters in the election of state legislators. Diluting the weight of votes because of place of residence impairs basic constitutional rights under the Fourteenth Amendment just as much as invidious discriminations based upon factors such as race...or economic status....Our constitutional system amply provides for the protection of minorities by means other than giving them majority control of state legislatures. And the democratic ideals of equality and majority rule, which have served this Nation so well in the past, are hardly of any less significance for the present and the future.

We are told that the matter of apportioning representation in a state legislature is a complex and many-faceted one. We are advised that States can rationally consider factors other than population in apportioning legislative representation. We are admonished not to restrict the power of the States to impose differing views as to political philosophy on their citizens. We are cautioned about the dangers of entering into political thickets and mathematical quagmires. Our answer is this: a denial of constitutionally protected rights demands judicial protection; our oath and our office require no less of us. As stated in *Gomillion v. Lightfoot, supra*:

> When a State exercises power wholly within the domain of state interest, it is insulated from federal judicial review. But such insulation is not carried over when state power is used as an instrument for circumventing [getting around] a federally protected right.

To the extent that a citizen's right to vote is debased [devalued], he is that much less a citizen. The fact that an individual lives here or there is not a legitimate reason for overweighting or diluting the efficacy of his vote. The complexions of societies and civilizations change, often with amazing rapidity. A nation once primarily rural in character becomes predominantly urban. Representation schemes once fair and equitable become archaic and outdated. But the basic principle of representative government remains, and must remain, unchanged—the weight of a citizen's vote cannot be made to depend on where he lives. Population is, of necessity, the starting point for consideration and the controlling criterion for judgment in legislative apportionment controversies. A citizen, a qualified voter, is no more nor no less so because he lives in the city or on the farm. This is the clear and strong command of our Constitution's Equal Protection Clause. This is an essential part of the concept of a government of laws and not men. This is at the heart of Lincoln's vision of "government of the people, by the people, [and] for the people." The Equal Protection Clause demands no less than substantially equal state legislative representation for all citizens, of all places as well as of all races.

We hold that, as a basic constitutional standard, the Equal Protection Clause requires that the seats in both houses of a bicameral [two-chamber] state legislature must be apportioned on a population basis. Simply stated, an individual's right to vote for state legislators is unconstitutionally impaired when its weight is in a substantial fashion diluted when compared with votes of citizens living in other parts of the State. Since, under neither the existing apportionment provisions nor either of the proposed plans was either of the houses of the Alabama Legislature apportioned on a population basis, the District Court correctly held that all three of these schemes were constitutionally invalid. Furthermore, the existing apportionment, and also to a lesser extent the apportionment under the Crawford-Webb Act, presented little more than crazy quilts, completely lacking in rationality, and could be found invalid on that basis alone. Although the District Court presumably found the apportionment of the Alabama House of Representatives under the 67-Senator Amendment to be acceptable, we conclude that the deviations from a strict population basis are too egregious to permit us to find that that body, under this proposed plan, was apportioned sufficiently on a population basis so as to permit the arrangement to be constitutionally sustained. Although about 43% of the State's total population would be required to comprise districts which could elect a majority in that body; only 39 of the 100 House seats were actually to be distributed on a population basis, a each of Alabama's 67 counties was given at least one representative, and population-variance ratios of close to 5-to-1 would have existed. While mathematical nicety is not a constitutional requisite, one could hardly conclude that the Alabama House, under the proposed constitutional amendment, had been apportioned sufficiently on a population basis to be sustainable under the requirements of the Equal Protection Clause. And none of the other apportionments of seats in either of the bodies of the Alabama Legislature, under the three plans considered by the District Court, came nearly as close to approaching the required constitutional standard as did that of the House of Representatives under the 67-Senator Amendment.

Legislative apportionment in Alabama is signally illustrative and symptomatic of the seriousness of this problem in a number of the State. At the time this litigation was commenced, there had been no reapportionment[3] of seats in the Alabama

---

3. "Reapportionment" means redrawing district lines in order to effectuate some desired proportion between the number or types of voters in a district and the offices to be elected.

Legislature for over 60 years. Legislative inaction, coupled with the unavailability of any political or judicial remedy, had resulted, with the passage of years, in the perpetuated scheme becoming little more than an irrational anachronism. Consistent failure by the Alabama Legislature to comply with state constitutional requirements as to the frequency of reapportionment and the bases of legislative representation resulted in a minority strangle hold on the State Legislature. Inequality of representation in one house added to the inequality in the other. With the crazy-quilt existing apportionment virtually conceded to be invalid, the Alabama Legislature offered two proposed plans for consideration by the District Court, neither of which was to be effective until 1966 and neither of which provided for the apportionment of even one of the two houses on a population basis. We find that the court below did not err in holding that neither of these proposed reapportionment schemes, considered as a whole, "meets the necessary constitutional requirements." And we conclude that the District Court acted properly in considering these two proposed plans, although neither was to become effective until the 1966 election and the proposed constitutional amendment was scheduled to be submitted to the State's voters in November 1962. Consideration by the court below of the two proposed plans was clearly necessary in determining whether the Alabama Legislature had acted effectively to correct the admittedly existing malapportionment and in ascertaining what sort of judicial relief, if any, should be afforded.

JUSTICE JOHN HARLAN, DISSENTING OPINION IN *REYNOLDS V. SIMS* (1964)

...Generalities cannot obscure the cold truth that cases of this type are not amenable [agreeable] to the development of judicial standards. No set of standards can guide a court which has to decide how many legislative districts a State shall have, or what the shape of the districts shall be, or where to draw a particular district line. No judicially manageable standard can determine whether a State should have single-member districts or multi-member districts[4] or some combination of both. No such standard can control the balance between keeping up with population shifts and having stable districts. In all these respects, the courts will be called upon to make particular decisions with respect to which a principle of equally populated districts will be of no assistance whatsoever. Quite obviously, there are limitless possibilities for districting consistent with such a principle. Nor can these problems be avoided by judicial reliance on legislative judgments so far as possible. Reshaping or combining one or two districts, or modifying just a few district lines, is no less a matter of choosing among many possible solutions, with varying political consequences, than reapportionment broadside.

The Court ignores all this, saying only that "what is marginally permissible in one State may be unsatisfactory in another, depending on the particular circumstances of the case,"...It is well to remember that the product of today's decisions will not be readjustment of a few districts in a few States which most glaringly depart from the principle of equally populated districts. It will be a redetermination, extensive in many cases, of legislative districts in all but a few States.

Although the Court—necessarily, as I believe—provides only generalities in elaboration of its main thesis, its opinion nevertheless fully demonstrates how far removed these problems are from fields of judicial competence. Recognizing that "indiscriminate districting" is an invitation to "partisan

4. In a "single-member district," only one person is elected to represent the entire district in the legislature. In a "multi-member district," more than one person is elected to represent the district in the legislature. Traditionally, multi-member districts are thought to be more conducive to achieving representation that is proportional to population.

gerrymandering,"[5]...the Court nevertheless excludes virtually every basis for the formation of electoral districts other than "indiscriminate districting." In one or another of today's opinions, the Court declares it unconstitutional for a State to give effective consideration to any of the following in establishing legislative districts: (1) history; (2) economic or other sorts of group interests; (3) area; (4) geographical considerations; (5) a desire to insure effective representation for sparsely settled areas; (6) availability of access of citizens to their representatives; (7) theories of bicameralism [two-chamber legislatures] (except those approved by the Court); (8) occupation; (9) an attempt to balance urban and rural power; (10) the preference of a majority of voters in the State.

So far as presently appears, the *only* factor which a State may consider, apart from numbers, is political subdivisions. But even "a clearly rational state policy" recognizing this factor is unconstitutional if "population is submerged as the controlling consideration...."

I know of no principle of logic or practical or theoretical politics, still less any constitutional principle, which establishes all or any of these exclusions. Certain it is that the Court's opinion does not establish them. So far as the Court says anything at all on this score, it says only that "legislators represent people, not trees or acres,"...; that "citizens, not history or economic interests, cast votes,"...; that "people, not land or trees or pastures, vote,"...All this may be conceded. But it is surely equally obvious, and, in the context of elections, more meaningful to note that people are not ciphers and that legislators can represent their electors only by speaking for their interests—economic, social, political—many of which do reflect the place where the electors live. The Court does not establish, or indeed even attempt to make a case for the proposition that conflicting interests within a State can only be adjusted by disregarding them when voters are grouped for purposes of representation.

With these cases the Court approaches the end of the third round set in motion by the complaint filed in *Baker v. Carr.* What is done today deepens my conviction that judicial entry into this realm is profoundly ill-advised and constitutionally impermissible. As I have said before, *Wesberry v. Sanders, supra,* at 48, I believe that the vitality of our political system, on which in the last analysis all else depends, is weakened by reliance on the judiciary for political reform; in time a complacent body politic may result.

These decisions also cut deeply into the fabric of our federalism. What must follow from them may eventually appear to be the product of state legislatures. Nevertheless, no thinking person can fail to recognize that the aftermath of these cases, however desirable it may be thought in itself, will have been achieved at the cost of a radical alteration in the relationship between the States and the Federal Government, more particularly the Federal Judiciary. Only one who has an overbearing impatience with the federal system and its political processes will believe that that cost was not too high or was inevitable.

Finally, these decisions give support to a current mistaken view of the Constitution and the constitutional function of this Court. This view, in a nutshell, is that every major social ill in this country can find its cure in some constitutional "principle," and that this Court should "take the lead" in promoting reform when other branches of government fail to act. The Constitution is not a panacea [remedy or solution] for every blot upon the public welfare, nor should this Court, ordained as a judicial body, be thought of as a general haven for reform movements. The Constitution is an instrument of government, fundamental to which is the premise

5. "Gerrymandering" refers to a certain type of malapportionment. When a census rolls around, the party that controls the legislature in a given state is responsible for redrawing the electoral districts. To "gerrymander" is to concentrate all of the opposing party's potential voters into just a few districts, leaving more votes for your own party in all the other districts. The term "gerrymander" dates back to 1812 and comes from Massachusetts governor Elbridge Gerry, who, in order to maximize his votes, constructed a long and winding district that looked like a salamander. Gerry's political opponents named the district "Gerry's Mander."

that in a diffusion of governmental authority lies the greatest promise that this Nation will realize liberty for all its citizens. This Court, limited in function in accordance with that premise, does not serve its high purpose when it exceeds its authority, even to satisfy justified impatience with the slow workings of the political process. For when, in the name of constitutional interpretation, the Court *adds* something to the Constitution that was deliberately excluded from it, the Court in reality substitutes its view of what should be so for the amending process.

I dissent in each of these cases, believing that in none of them have the plaintiffs stated a cause of action. To the extent that *Baker v. Carr,* expressly or by implication, went beyond a discussion of jurisdictional doctrines independent of the substantive issues involved here, it should be limited to what it in fact was: an experiment in venturesome constitutionalism.

CHIEF JUSTICE EARL WARREN, OPINION OF THE COURT IN *SOUTH CAROLINA V. KATZENBACH* (1966)

In the preceding chapter, you read President Lyndon B. Johnson's "Voting Rights Act Speech" (1965). The Act, which for the first time provided effective federal protection for African-Americans who wished to register and vote, resulted in increasing African-American registration throughout the South. The state of South Carolina sued to prevent enforcement of certain provisions of the Act, particularly, those suspending "literacy" and other tests; providing for federal voting examiners; enabling challenges to eligibility listings; and providing enforcement through criminal contempt suits.

WHY THIS READING?

This case squarely addresses this chapter's core question regarding the relationship of representation and race in American democracy. *Katzenbach's* primary constitutional question was whether various provisions of the 1965 Voting Rights Act were "appropriate" under the terms of the 15th Amendment (1870), which grants the U.S. Congress the power, through "appropriate legislation," to ensure that the right to vote "shall not be denied or abridged by the United States or by any State on account of race, color, or previous condition of servitude."

Question to guide you as you read:

- What historical and contemporary evidence does Chief Justice Warren point to in deeming the anti-discrimination measures taken by Congress "appropriate"?

...South Carolina has filed a bill of complaint, seeking a declaration that selected provisions of the Voting Rights Act of 1965 violate the Federal Constitution, and asking for an injunction against enforcement of these provisions by the Attorney General....

...The Voting Rights Act was designed by Congress to banish the blight of racial discrimination in voting, which has infected the electoral process in parts of our country for nearly a century. The Act creates stringent new remedies for voting discrimination where it persists on a pervasive scale, and in addition the statute strengthens existing remedies for pockets of voting discrimination elsewhere in the country. Congress assumed the power to prescribe these remedies from §2 of the Fifteenth Amendment, which authorizes the national legislature to effectuate by "appropriate" measures the constitutional prohibition against racial discrimination in voting. We hold that the sections of the Act which are properly before us are an appropriate means for carrying out Congress' constitutional responsibilities and are consonant with all other provisions of the Constitution. We therefore deny South Carolina's request that enforcement of these sections of the Act be enjoined.

The constitutional propriety of the Voting Rights Act of 1965 must be judged with reference to the historical experience which it reflects....

Two points emerge vividly from the voluminous legislative history of the Act contained in the committee hearings and floor debates. First, Congress felt itself confronted by an insidious and pervasive evil which had been perpetuated in certain parts of our country through unremitting and ingenious defiance of the Constitution. Second: Congress concluded that the unsuccessful remedies which it had prescribed in the past would have to be replaced by sterner and more elaborate measures in order to satisfy the clear commands of the Fifteenth Amendment....

According to the results of recent Justice Department voting suits,... discriminatory administration of voting qualifications has been found in all eight Alabama cases, in all nine Louisiana cases, and in all nine Mississippi cases which have gone to final judgment. Moreover, in almost all of these cases, the courts have held that the discrimination was pursuant to a widespread "pattern or practice." White applicants for registration have often been excused altogether from the literacy and understanding tests or have been given easy versions, have received extensive help from voting officials, and have been registered despite serious errors in their answers. Negroes, on the other hand have typically been required to pass difficult versions of all the tests, without any outside assistance and without the slightest error. The good morals requirement is so vague and subjective that it has constituted an open invitation to abuse at the hands of voting officials. Negroes obliged to obtain vouchers from registered voters have found it virtually impossible to comply in areas where almost no Negroes are on the rolls. In recent years, Congress has repeatedly tried to cope with the problem by facilitating case-by-case litigation against voting discrimination....

Despite the earnest efforts of the Justice Department and of many federal Judges, these new laws have done little to cure the problem of voting discrimination. According to estimates by the Attorney General during hearings on the Act, registration of voting age Negroes in Alabama rose only from 10.2% to 19.4% between 1958 and 1964; in Louisiana it barely inched ahead from 31.7% to 31.8% between 1956 and 1965; and in Mississippi it increased only from 4.4% to 6.4% between 1954 and 1964. In each instance, registration of voting age whites ran roughly 50 percentage points or more ahead of Negro registration.

The previous legislation has proved ineffective for a number of reasons. Voting suits are unusually onerous to prepare, sometimes requiring as many as 6,000 man-hours spent combing through registration records in preparation for trial. Litigation has been exceedingly slow, in part because of the ample opportunities for delay afforded voting officials and others involved in the proceedings. Even when favorable decisions have finally been obtained, some of the States affected have merely switched to discriminatory devices not covered by the federal decrees or have enacted difficult new tests designed to prolong the existing disparity between white and Negro registration. Alternatively, certain local officials have defied and evaded court orders or have simply closed their registration offices to freeze the voting rolls. The provision of the 1960 law authorizing registration by federal officers has had little impact on local mal-administration because of its procedural complexities.

During the hearings and debates on the Act, Selma, Alabama, was repeatedly referred to as the pre-eminent example of the ineffectiveness of existing legislation. In Dallas County, of which Selma is the seat, there were four years of litigation by the Justice Department and two findings by the federal courts of widespread voting discrimination. Yet in those four years, Negro registration rose only from 156 to 383, although there are approximately 15,000 Negroes of voting age in the county....

The Voting Rights Act of 1965 reflects Congress' firm intention to rid the country of racial discrimination in voting. The heart of the Act is a complex scheme of stringent remedies aimed at areas where voting discrimination has been most flagrant....

...The first of the remedies, contained in §4(a), b is the suspension of literacy tests and similar voting qualifications for a period of five years from the last occurrence of substantial voting discrimination. Section 5 prescribes a second remedy, the suspension of all new voting regulations pending review by federal authorities to determine whether their use would perpetuate voting discrimination. The third remedy...is the assignment of federal examiners by the Attorney General to list qualified applicants who are thereafter entitled to vote in all elections.... Section 8 authorizes the appointment of federal poll-watchers in places to which federal examiners have already been assigned. Section 10(d) excuses those made eligible to vote...from paying accumulated past poll taxes for state and local elections. Section 12(e) provides for balloting by persons denied access to the polls in areas where federal examiners have been appointed.

The remaining remedial portions of the Act are aimed at voting discrimination in any area of the country where it may occur....

These provisions of the Voting Rights Act of 1965 are challenged on the fundamental ground that they exceed the powers of Congress and encroach on an area reserved to the States by the Constitution. South Carolina and certain of the *amici curie* [plural of *amicus curiae:* those who provide information and arguments to a court during a case] also...argue that the coverage formula prescribed in §4(a)-(d) violates the principle of the equality of States, denies due process by employing an invalid presumption and by barring judicial review of administrative findings, constitutes a forbidden bill of attainder, and impairs the separation of powers by adjudicating guilt through legislation....

The ground rules for resolving this question are clear. The language and purpose of the Fifteenth Amendment, the prior decisions construing its several provisions, and the general doctrines of constitutional interpretation, all point to one fundamental principle. As against the reserved powers of the States, Congress may use any rational means to effectuate the constitutional prohibition of racial discrimination in voting....

Section I of the Fifteenth Amendment declares that "the right of citizens of the United States to vote shall not be denied or abridged by the United States or by any State on account of race, color, or previous condition of servitude." This declaration has always been treated as self-executing and has repeatedly been construed, without further legislative specification, to invalidate state voting qualifications or procedures which are discriminatory on their face or in practice....

We therefore reject South Carolina's argument that Congress may appropriately do no more than to forbid violations of the Fifteenth Amendment in general terms—that the task of fashioning specific remedies or of applying them to particular localities must necessarily be left entirely to the courts....

JUSTICE ANTHONY KENNEDY, OPINION OF THE COURT IN *MILLER V. JOHNSON* (1995)

Justice Anthony Kennedy writes the majority opinion in this 1995 case, which tackles the issues of affirmative action and "racial gerrymandering" in the context of the state of Georgia's redistricting plan. Racial gerrymandering refers to the practice of deliberately redrawing electoral districts to ensure that a particular racial minority has a majority vote within the geographical bounds of a district, for the purpose of guaranteeing that the racial minority has congressional representation by an individual of the same race.

WHY THIS READING?

At issue here is the interpretation of the phrase "equal protection of the laws" found in the 14th Amendment. Also at issue, and bearing directly on this chapter's concern with the relationship of representation and race, is the question of the extent to which equal treatment must be manifested in equal outcomes.

In declaring that the Georgia redistricting plan violated the 14th Amendment's Equal Protection Clause, Kennedy's opinion for the majority concludes that race was the primary criterion used by the Georgia General Assembly in creating the districts. This, argues Kennedy, is contrary to the Equal Protection Clause, whose "central mandate is race neutrality in governmental decision making."

Included here for your examination is also the dissenting opinion of Justice Ruth Bader Ginsburg. (Four of the nine Justices dissented.) Ginsburg's opinion for the minority argues that Georgia did not use racial factors as its principal criterion in the redistricting plan: "[T]raditional districting factors" also played a role. Ginsburg goes on to argue that, except in cases of gross abuse, redistricting should be left up to the states and local governments.

Questions to guide you as you read:

- In striking down the state of Georgia's redistricting plan, what arguments does Justice Kennedy derive from the 14th Amendment?
- What arguments does Justice Ginsburg employ in her dissenting opinion to defend the use of racial classifications with respect to voting?

The constitutionality of Georgia's congressional redistricting plan is at issue here. In *Shaw v. Reno*,...(1993), we held that a plaintiff states a claim under the Equal Protection Clause by alleging that, a state redistricting plan, on its face, has no rational explanation save as an effort to separate voters on the basis of race The question we now decide is whether Georgia's new Eleventh District gives rise to a valid equal protection claim under the principles announced in Shaw, and, if so, whether it can be sustained nonetheless as narrowly tailored to serve a compelling governmental interest.

The Equal Protection Clause of the Fourteenth Amendment provides that no State shall deny to any person within its jurisdiction the equal protection of the laws.... Its central mandate is racial neutrality in governmental decision making.... Though application of this imperative raises difficult questions, the basic principle is straightforward: Racial and ethnic distinctions of any sort are inherently suspect and thus call for the most exacting judicial examination.... This perception of racial and ethnic distinctions is rooted in our Nation's constitutional and demographic history.... This rule obtains with equal force regardless of the race of those burdened or benefited by a particular classification.... Laws classifying citizens on the basis of race cannot be upheld unless they are narrowly tailored to achieving a compelling state interest....

In *Shaw v. Reno, supra,* we recognized that these equal protection principles govern a State's drawing of congressional districts, though, as our cautious approach there discloses, application of these principles to electoral districting is a most delicate task. Our analysis began from the premise that laws that explicitly distinguish between individuals on racial grounds fall within the core of [the Equal Protection Clause's] prohibition.... This prohibition extends not just to explicit racial classifications, but also to laws neutral on their face but "unexplainable on grounds other than race...." Applying this basic Equal Protection analysis in the voting rights context, we held that "redistricting legislation that is so bizarre on its face that it is 'unexplainable on grounds other than race'... demands the same close scrutiny that we give other state laws that classify citizens by race...."

This case requires us to apply the principles articulated in *Shaw* to the most recent congressional redistricting plan enacted by the State of Georgia....

Shaw recognized a claim "analytically distinct from a vote dilution claim".... Whereas a vote dilution claim alleges that the State has enacted a particular voting scheme as a purposeful device to minimize or cancel out the voting potential of racial or ethnic minorities,... an action disadvantaging voters of a particular race, the essence of the equal protection claim recognized in *Shaw* is that the State has used race as a basis for separating voters into districts. Just as the State may not, absent extraordinary justification, segregate citizens on the basis of race in its public parks... golf courses... beaches... and schools... so did we recognize in *Shaw* that it may not separate its citizens into different voting districts on the basis of race. The idea is a simple one: "At the heart of the Constitution's guarantee of equal protection lies the simple command that the Government must treat citizens as individuals, not as simply components of a racial, religious, sexual or national class."

JUSTICE RUTH BADER GINSBURG, DISSENTING OPINION IN *MILLER V. JOHNSON (1995)*

To separate permissible and impermissible use of race in legislative apportionment, the Court orders strict scrutiny for districting plans predominantly motivated by race. No longer can a State avoid judicial oversight by giving—as in this case—genuine and measurable consideration to traditional districting practices. Instead, a federal case can be mounted whenever plaintiffs plausibly allege that other factors carried less weight than race. This invitation to litigate against the State seems to me neither necessary nor proper.

The Court derives its test from diverse opinions on the relevance of race in contexts distinctly unlike apportionment.... The controlling idea, the Court says, is "the simple command [at the heart of the Constitution's guarantee of equal protection] that the Government must treat citizens as individuals, not as simply components of a racial, religious, sexual or national class."...

In adopting districting plans, however, States do not treat people as individuals. Apportionment schemes, by their very nature, assemble people in groups. States do not assign voters to districts based on merit or achievement, standards States might use in hiring employees or engaging contractors. Rather, legislators classify voters in groups—by economic, geographical, political, or social characteristics—and then "reconcile the competing claims of [these] groups."...

That ethnicity defines some of these groups is a political reality.... Until now, no constitutional infirmity has been seen in districting Irish or Italian voters together, for example, so long as the delineation does not abandon familiar apportionment practices.... If Chinese-Americans and Russian-Americans may seek and secure group recognition in the delineation of voting districts, then African-Americans should not be dissimilarly treated. Otherwise, in the name of equal protection, we would shut out "the very minority group whose history in the United States gave birth to the Equal Protection Clause."...

Under the Court's approach, judicial review of the same intensity, i.e., strict scrutiny, is in order once it is determined that an apportionment is predominantly motivated by race. It matters not at all, in this new regime, whether the apportionment dilutes or enhances minority voting strength. As very recently observed, however, there is no moral or constitutional equivalence between a policy that is designed to perpetuate a caste system and one that seeks to eradicate racial subordination....

Special circumstances justify vigilant judicial inspection to protect minority voters—circumstances that do not apply to majority voters. A history of exclusion from state politics left racial minorities without clout to exact provisions for fair representation in the lawmaking forum.... The equal protection rights of minority voters thus could have remained unrealized absent the Judiciary's close surveillance. The majority, by definition, encounters no such blockage. White voters in Georgia do not lack means to exert strong pressure on their state legislators. The force of their numbers is itself a powerful determiner of what the legislature will do that does not coincide with perceived majority interests.

Should representation take account of individuals or groups, or both?

LANI GUINIER, "GROUPS, REPRESENTATION, AND RACE-CONSCIOUS DISTRICTING: A CASE OF THE EMPEROR'S CLOTHES" (1993)

Lani Guinier served as an attorney in the Justice Department during the Carter administration and as a professor of law at Harvard University.

WHY THIS READING?

What follows is an excerpt from an academic paper published by Guinier in 1992, in which she defends the position that minorities should be guaranteed their fair share of actual power, rather than merely formal equality of access to electoral opportunities. "Mathematical equality" in voting, she asserts, is merely a case of the "emperor's clothes." For Guinier, our current system of representation of geographic districts through a winner-take-all system produces the result that many votes are "wasted." To remedy this, she recommends that the winner-take-all system be replaced by cumulative voting, to guarantee "the right of protected minority groups to an equal opportunity to elect candidates of their choice."

Questions to guide you as you read:

- Guinier seeks to improve on Chief Justice Warren's "one man, one vote" interpretation of the meaning of democratic equality (*Reynolds v. Sims*). Why does she regard "one man, one vote" as insufficient for ensuring democratic representation?
- What does Guinier mean by "cumulative voting"? What does she mean by "one-vote, one-value"? Why does she believe that cumulative voting will more likely ensure "one-vote, one-value"?
- How would Madison's Publius, in *Federalist 10,* respond to Guinier? Specifically, would he regard the replacement of "winner-take-all" voting with "cumulative" voting as lessening the "mortal disease" of faction, or exacerbating it? Why?

...[T]he unit of representation [in this country] is geographic rather than political. Geographic constituencies, which are created through the use of single member districts, are a form of group representation in which common territory is a proxy for common interests. I argue that the representation of racial groups is valid and desirable given our history and our acceptance of group representation in other forms, although; as argued in previous essays, I claim that representation of either groups or individuals is not well accomplished by single-member districting. I also expand my exploration of cumulative voting, arguing that it is not only consistent with one-person, one-vote, but even better, it embodies one-person, one-vote, one-value in a way that districting systems do not. Yet, cumulative voting is not, in itself, the test for a grand moral theory of representation or even a panacea for across-the-board voting problems. Instead, I use the idea of cumulative voting as a way to explore and define the unfairness and incoherence of indirect representation of geographic constituencies within winner-take-all territorial units. This essay was written in 1992, and first published in 1993.

[N]ow that the first round of reapportionment has been accomplished, there is need to talk "one man-one vote" a little less and to talk a little more of "political equity," and of functional components of effective representation. A mathematically equal vote which is politically worthless because of gerrymandering or winner-take-all districting is as deceiving as "emperor's clothes."

With voices pitched in the high decibel range, critics of race-conscious districting are blasting the Voting Rights Act and its 1982 amendments. A recent *Wall Street Journal* headline declares that voting is now "rigged by race." Ethnic activists, the writer asserts, are collaborating with GOP operatives in an unholy political alliance to herd minorities into their own convoluted urban districts in order to improve GOP prospects in majority white suburban areas. According to such critics, this is a "political one night stand" made possible by misguided federal courts and Department of Justice officials construing the 1982 Act to create majority minority districts, the newest form of "racial packaging."

My students inform me that Cokie Roberts, as part of ABC News' election night coverage, dramatically illustrated the concerns of critics when she traced on a map of the Chicago area the "earmuff" district, allegedly carved out of two noncontiguous Chicago neighborhoods joined by a narrow rod to maximize the possibility that the Latino residents would be able to elect a representative of their choice to Congress. And in June 1993, the Supreme Court discovered a new constitutional right enabling white voters in North Carolina to challenge, based on its odd and irregular shapes, a "highway" district that narrowly tracks the path of an interstate, creating a swatch of voters on either side of the highway from one end of the state to the other. This fifty-four percent black district, the most integrated in the state, elected Melvin Watt, one of the first two blacks elected to Congress from that state in this century.

The Voting Rights Act codified the right of protected minority groups to an equal opportunity to elect candidates of their choice, although its language disclaims the right to racial representation by members of the racial group in direct proportion to population. The critics now claim this is special and unwarranted protection for racial and language minority groups. In the name of liberal individualism, these critics assert that the statute effected a radical transformation in the allocation and nature of representation.

Although race-conscious districting is their apparent target, these critics have fixed their aim on a deeper message—that pressing claims of racial identity and racial disadvantage diminish democracy. We all lose, the theory goes, when some of us identify in racial or ethnic group terms.

In my view, critics of race-conscious districting have misdirected their fire. Their emperor has no clothes. Their dissatisfaction with racial-group representation ignores the essentially group nature of political participation [and] representation...in a system of geographic districting. Perhaps unwittingly they also reveal a bias toward the representation of a particular racial group rather than their discomfort with group representation itself. In a society as deeply cleaved by issues of racial identity as ours, there is no one race. In the presence of such racial differences, a system of representation that fails to provide group representation loses legitimacy.

Yet these critics have, in fact, accurately identified a problem with a system of representation based on winner-take-all territorial district. There is an emperor wearing his clothes, but not as they describe. Rather than expressing a fundamental failure of democratic theory based on group representation per se, the critics have identified a problem with one particular solution. It is districting in general—not race-conscious districting in particular—that is the problem.

Winner-take-all territorial districting imperfectly distributes representation based on group attributes and disproportionately rewards those who win the representational lottery. Territorial districting uses an aggregating rule that inevitably groups people by virtue of some set of externally observed characteristics such as geographic proximity or racial identity. In addition, the winner-take-all principle inevitably wastes some votes. The dominant group within the district gets all the power; the votes of supporters of non-dominant groups or of disaffected voters within the dominant group are wasted. Their votes lose significance because they are consistently cast for political losers.

The essential unfairness of districting is a result, therefore, of two assumptions: (1) that a majority of voters within a given geographic community can be configured to constitute a 'group'; and (2) that incumbent politicians, federal courts, or some other independent set of actors can fairly determine which group to advantage by giving it all the power within the district. When either of these assumptions is not accurate, as is most often the case, the districting is necessarily unfair.

Another effect of these assumptions is gerrymandering, which results from the arbitrary allocation of disproportionate political power to one group. Districting breeds gerrymandering as a means of allocating group benefits; the operative principle is deciding whose votes get wasted. Whether it is racially or politically motivated, gerrymandering is the inevitable by-product of an electoral system that aggregates people by virtue of assumptions about their group characteristics and then inflates the winning group's power by allowing it to represent all voters in a regional unit. Given a system of winner-take-all territorial districts and working within the limitations of this particular election method, the courts have sought to achieve political fairness for racial minorities. As a result, there is some truth to the assertion that minority groups, unlike other voters, enjoy a special representational relationship under the Voting Rights Act's 1982 amendments to remedy their continued exclusion from effective political participation in some jurisdictions. But the proper response is not to deny minority voters that protection. The answer should be to extend that special relationship to all voters by endorsing the equal opportunity to vote for a winning candidate as a universal principle of political fairness.

I use the term "one-vote, one-value" to describe the principle of political fairness that as many votes as possible should count in the election of representatives. Each voter should be able to choose, by the way she casts her votes, who represents her. One-vote, one-value is realized when everyone's vote counts for someone's election. The only system with the potential to realize this principle for all voters is one in which the unit of representation is political rather than regional, and the aggregating rule is proportionality rather than winner-take-all. Semi-proportional systems, such as cumulative voting, can approximate the one-vote, one-value principle by minimizing the problem of wasted votes.

One-vote, one-value systems transcend the gerrymandering problem because each vote has an equal worth independent of decisions made by those who drew district lines. Votes are allocated based on decisions made by the voters themselves. These systems revive the connection between voting and representation, whether the participant consciously associates with a group of voters or chooses to participate on a fiercely individual basis.

Candidates are elected in proportion to the intensity of their political support within the electorate itself rather than as a result of decisions made by incumbent politicians or federal courts once every ten years....

For many liberal reformers, the one-person, one-vote principle is politically fair because its ideal of universal suffrage incorporates the respect due and the responsibilities owed to each citizen in a democracy. The one-person, one-vote cases attempt to equalize the purely formal opportunity to cast a ballot through a system of population-based apportionment. Under this rationale, each district contains approximately the same number of people; each person within the district has the same opportunity to vote for someone to represent the district; and each district representative represents the same number of constituents.

The one-person, one-vote principle thus assures all voters the right to cast a theoretically equal ballot. [However],... I argue that this theoretical possibility is unlikely to be realized in an electoral system using winner take-all districts. I further suggest that neither groups of voters nor individuals are fairly represented under such a system.

There are two issues at stake. One raises the question of whether voting is constitutionally protected because it implicates individual rights. If voting is an individual right, the second question asks whether the one-person, one-vote principles that operate within the confines of geographic districts adequately protect the right to vote. I concede that voting has garnered its highest constitutional protection when presented as an individual rights issue, but the widespread use of winner-take-all districts undermines the validity of this characterization. The fact that constitutional rules about voting evolved within a system of regional representation suggests that posing the problem as one of individual rather than group rights has been a distraction. I claim that the heavy reliance on one-person, one-vote jurisprudence to develop a theory of democracy fails both as a theory and as an adequate doctrinal protection of either individual or group rights.

A. One-Person, One-Vote and the Limits of Liberal Individualism

...[T]he assumption [is] that allocation of representatives through winner-take-all districting is a form of representation of individuals. The heart of this assumption is that citizenship is the ultimate reflection of individual dignity and autonomy and that voting is the means for individual citizens to realize this personal and social standing. Under this theory, voters realize the fullest meaning of citizenship by the individual act of voting for representatives who, once elected, participate on the voters' behalf in the process of self-government. Indeed the very terminology employed in the Supreme Court's one-person, one-vote constitutional principle suggests that voting is an individual right. For these reasons, some assume that the right at stake is the individual right to an equally weighted vote or an equally powerful vote.

The assumption is that constitutional protection for voting is exclusively about protecting an individual right, not necessarily about ensuring equal voting rights. At first, the connection between the two concepts seems plausible because every citizen has the right to vote and every citizen has the right to an equally weighted vote. But the one-person, one-vote principle of voting is primarily about equal, not individual, representation. Under this equality norm, the right to "fair and effective representation" subsumes concerns about equal voting and equal access. As the Court stated in one of its early reapportionment cases, the principle of equal representation for equal numbers of people is "designed to prevent debasement of voting power and diminution of access to elected representatives." Implicit in this equality norm is the moral proposition that every citizen has the right to equal legislative influence. This means an equal opportunity to influence legislative policy....

Proponents of the philosophy of individualism attempt to use the one-person, one-vote principle to locate voting in the status of individual or constituent. They rely on the fact that every individual has the opportunity to cast a potentially winning vote or to be represented vicariously by one who does. This approach camouflages the group nature of voting by emphasizing the personal aspects of representation.

Consistent with their prevailing political philosophy of individualism, some members of the Court have struggled mightily to use one-person, one-vote rules to avoid the concept of group representation. However, even where its nexus to group activity remains disguised, the principle of one-person, one-vote is as consistent with group as it is with individual representation. Similarly, the one-person, one-vote principle is consistent with semiproportional representation systems. Even if voters each were awarded five votes to plump as they choose, the one-person, one-vote principle would be satisfied, since each voter would have the same voting power or voting weight....

...[D]espite the efforts of some members of the Court to characterize representation as an exclusively individual notion, the concept of group representation became unavoidable for two reasons. The first...is that the concept of group voting was necessary to understand the political unfairness of excluding racial minorities in a racially polarized constituency. The second...is that the one-person, one-vote principle was conceived and articulated within a construction of constituencies based on geography. It is districting itself that merges individual representation with the representation of groups of individuals. Thus, it always has been necessary to acknowledge, at least implicitly, the relationship between districts and interests....

Group Representation and Territorial Districting

...[B]ecause of our explicit and implicit recognition of constituencies of geography, we have never actually employed a system of individual representation. Indeed, the use of geographic districts as the basis for establishing representational constituencies is at its very heart a system of group-based representation. Moreover, even where districts comply with principles of one-person, one-vote, such districts dilute the voting strength of both individuals and groups.

The concept of representation necessarily applies to groups: groups of voters elect representatives; individuals do not. Representation is more than the individual relationship between constituent and elected representative. Because representation is primarily about political influence, not political service, bottom-up representation becomes the essential link to a genuine voice in the process of self-government. Districting is a form of group-interest representation, albeit an imperfectly realized one.

Districting, by definition, assumes that each voter is a "'member' of a 'group' comprised of all the voters in her district." As Justice Stewart noted, "The very fact of geographic districting...carries with it an acceptance of the idea of legislative representation of regional needs and interests." Regardless of whether other Justices of the Warren Court ever consciously adopted the idea of interest representation, in working within territorial districts they assumed that interests reflect where people live.

The view that geography approximates political interests is not a new idea. Indeed, the idea that geographic units reflect a common or group identity is part of the historical explanation for the winner-take-all system of districts. The American system of winner-take-all districts was adapted from the system in Britain prior to 1832....

Group members also are more likely to be perceived by their constituents as representing them. This definition of representative as descriptive likeness or racial compatriot has a psychological component. Just as the flag stands for the nation, the presence of racial group members symbolizes inclusion of a previously excluded group. The symbolic role results from both the personal characteristics of the racial-group member and the assumption that, because of those characteristics, the racial-group member has had experiences in common with her constituents....Thus, many racial minorities do not feel represented unless members of their racial group are physically present in the legislature.

As a result, traditional voting rights advocates comfortably rely on race as a proxy for interests. For example, in conventional voting rights litigation, election contests between black and white candidates help define the degree of racial polarization, i.e., the degree to which blacks and whites vote differently. The idea is that the outcome would be different if elections were held only in one community or the other. The assumption of difference extends explicitly to the specific candidate elected, and implicitly to the issues that the candidate, once elected, would emphasize.

The assumption of this difference between races rests in part on the claim that where black candidates enjoy protection from electoral competition with whites, black voters can ratify their choices to hold their representatives accountable. In this way, the association between race and interests is modified to the extent that voters are given a meaningful choice in both initiating and terminating a representational relationship. Voting rights advocates assume that minority group sponsorship is critical. It is only where minority voters exercise electoral control, or have a meaningful opportunity to retire their representative, that race functions as a representational proxy. Thus, majority-black single-member districts take advantage of segregated housing patterns to use geography as a proxy for racial choice, racial control, and racial representation.

JUSTICE THURGOOD MARSHALL, "REMARKS AT THE ANNUAL SEMINAR OF THE SAN FRANCISCO PATENT AND TRADEMARK LAW ASSOCIATION" (1987)

Thurgood Marshall was the first African-American to serve on the U.S. Supreme Court. He was appointed by President Lyndon B. Johnson in 1967 and served until 1991. In 1954, working as a civil rights attorney, he successfully represented Linda Brown in the 1954 Supreme Court case, *Brown v. Board of Education*, which ruled that racial segregation in schools is a violation of the 14th Amendment's Equal Protection Clause.

WHY THIS READING?

In this speech, delivered in Hawaii in 1987 as part of the bicentennial celebration of the Constitution, Marshall argues that the original Constitution was "defective from the start," as evidenced by both the numerous amendments passed since its ratification in 1788 and the need for a civil war to settle finally the question of slavery. Justice Marshall finds in the original Constitution a series of what he deems to be unjustifiable compromises on the issue of inclusion of blacks and women. His passionate critique addresses the core question of this chapter head-on by denying that the Founders succeeded in 1787 in establishing a genuinely representative democracy.

Questions to guide you as you read:

- How does Justice Marshall interpret the "Three-Fifths" Clause of the original Constitution?
- Justice Marshall argues that the Constitution did not achieve the goal of political equality until the 14th Amendment was passed. Why?
- Later in this textbook, you will examine Chief Justice Taney's opinion for the majority in *Dred Scott v. Sandford* (1857), as well as Frederick Douglass's and Abraham Lincoln's critiques of that decision. What is Justice Marshall's interpretation of this decision, and what role does it play in his evaluation of the original Constitution?

1987 marks the 200th anniversary of the United States Constitution. A Commission has been established to coordinate the celebration. The official meetings, essay contests, and festivities have begun. The planned commemoration will span three years, and I am told 1987 is "dedicated to the memory of the Founders and the document they drafted in Philadelphia." We are to "recall the achievements of our Founders and the knowledge and experience that inspired them, the nature of the government they established, its origins, its character, and its ends, and the rights and privileges of citizenship, as well as its attendant responsibilities."

Like many anniversary celebrations, the plan for 1987 takes particular events and holds them up as the source of all the very best that has followed. Patriotic feelings will surely swell, prompting proud proclamations of the wisdom, foresight, and sense of justice shared by the Framers and reflected in a written document now yellowed with age. This is unfortunate—not the patriotism itself, but the tendency for the celebration to oversimplify, and overlook the many other events that have been instrumental to our achievements as a nation. The focus of this celebration invites a complacent belief that the vision of those who debated and compromised in Philadelphia yielded the "more perfect Union" it is said we now enjoy.

I cannot accept this invitation, for I do not believe that the meaning of the Constitution was forever "fixed" at the Philadelphia Convention. Nor do I find the wisdom, foresight, and sense of justice exhibited by the Framers particularly profound. To the contrary, the government they devised was defective from the start, requiring several amendments, a civil war, and momentous social transformation to attain the system of constitutional government, and its respect for the individual freedoms and human rights, we hold as fundamental today. When contemporary Americans cite "The Constitution," they invoke a concept that is vastly different from what the Framers barely began to construct two centuries ago.

For a sense of the evolving nature of the Constitution we need look no further than the first three words of the document's preamble: "We the People." When the Founding Fathers used this phrase in 1787, they did not have in mind the majority of America's citizens. "We the People" included, in the words of the Framers, "the whole Number of free Persons." On a matter so basic as the right to vote, for example, Negro slaves were excluded, although they were counted for representational purposes—at three-fifths each. Women did not gain the right to vote for over a hundred and thirty years.

These omissions were intentional. The record of the Framers' debates on the slave question is especially clear: The Southern States acceded to the demands of the New England States for giving Congress broad power to regulate commerce, in exchange for the right to continue the slave trade. The economic interests of the regions coalesced: New Englanders engaged in the "carrying trade" would profit from transporting slaves from Africa as well as goods produced in America by slave labor. The perpetuation of slavery ensured the primary source of wealth in the Southern States.

Despite this clear understanding of the role slavery would play in the new republic, use of the words "slaves" and "slavery" was carefully avoided in the original document. Political representation in the lower House of Congress was to be based on the population of "free Persons" in each State, plus three-fifths of all "other Persons." Moral principles against slavery, for those who had them, were compromised, with no explanation of the conflicting principles for which the American Revolutionary War had ostensibly been fought: the self-evident truths "that all men are created equal, that they are endowed by their Creator with certain unalienable Rights, that among these are Life, Liberty and the pursuit of Happiness."

It was not the first such compromise. Even these ringing phrases from the Declaration of Independence are filled with irony, for an early draft of what became that Declaration assailed the King of England for suppressing legislative attempts to end the slave trade and for encouraging slave rebellions. The final draft adopted in 1776 did not contain this criticism. And so again at the Constitutional Convention eloquent objections to the institution of slavery went unheeded, and its opponents eventually consented to a document which laid a foundation for the tragic events that were to follow.

Pennsylvania's Gouverneur Morris provides an example. He opposed slavery and the counting of slaves in determining the basis for representation in Congress. At the Convention he objected that "the inhabitant of Georgia [or] South Carolina who goes to the coast of Africa, and in defiance of the most sacred laws of humanity tears away his fellow creatures from their dearest connections and damns them to the most cruel bondages, shall have more votes in a Government instituted for protection of the rights of mankind, than the Citizen of Pennsylvania or New Jersey who views with a laudable horror, so nefarious a practice.

And yet Gouverneur Morris eventually accepted the three-fifths accommodation. In fact, he wrote the final draft of the Constitution, the very document the bicentennial will commemorate.

As a result of compromise, the right of the Southern States to continue importing slaves was extended, officially, at least until 1808. We know that it actually lasted a good deal longer, as the Framers possessed no monopoly on the ability to trade moral principles for self-interest. But they nevertheless set an unfortunate example. Slaves could be imported, if the commercial interests of the North were protected. To make the compromise even more palatable, customs duties would be imposed at up to ten dollars per slave as a means of raising public revenues.

No doubt it will be said, when the unpleasant truth of the history of slavery in America is mentioned during this bicentennial year, that the Constitution was a product of its times, and embodied a compromise which, under other circumstances, would not have been made. But the effects of the Framers' compromise have remained for generations. They arose from the contradiction between guaranteeing liberty and justice to all, and denying both to Negroes.

The original intent of the phrase, "We the People," was far too clear for any ameliorating construction. Writing for the Supreme Court in 1857, Chief Justice Taney penned the following passage in the *Dred Scott* case, on the issue whether, in the eyes of the Framers, slaves were "constituent members of the sovereignty," and were to be included among "We the People":

"We think they are not, and that they are not included, and were not intended to be included.... They had for more than a century before been regarded as beings of an inferior order, and altogether unfit to associate with the white race...; and so far inferior, that they had no rights which the white man was bound to respect; and that the Negro might justly and lawfully be reduced to slavery for his benefit.... Accordingly, a Negro of the African race was regarded... as an article of property, and held, and bought and sold as such.... [N] o one seems to have doubted the correctness of the prevailing opinion of the time."

And so, nearly seven decades after the Constitutional Convention, the Supreme Court reaffirmed the prevailing opinion of the Framers regarding the rights of Negroes in America. It took a bloody civil war before the 13th Amendment could be adopted to abolish slavery, though not the consequences slavery would have for future Americans.

While the Union survived the civil war, the Constitution did not. In its place arose a new, more promising basis for justice and equality, the 14th Amendment, ensuring protection of the life, liberty, and property of all persons against deprivations without due process, and guaranteeing equal protection of the laws. And yet almost another century would pass before any significant recognition was obtained of the rights of black Americans to share equally even in such basic opportunities as education, housing, and employment, and to have their votes counted, and counted equally. In the meantime, blacks joined America's military to fight its wars and invested untold hours working in its factories and on its farms, contributing to the development of this country's magnificent wealth and waiting to share in its prosperity.

What is striking is the role legal principles have played throughout America's history in determining the condition of Negroes. They were enslaved by law, emancipated by law, disenfranchised and segregated by law; and, finally, they have begun to win equality by law. Along the way, new constitutional principles have emerged to meet the challenges of a changing society. The progress has been dramatic, and it will continue.

The men who gathered in Philadelphia in 1787 could not have envisioned these changes. They could not have imagined, nor would they have accepted, that the document they were drafting would one day be construed by a Supreme Court to which had been appointed a woman and the descendent of an African slave. "We the People" no longer enslave, but the credit does not belong to the Framers. It belongs to those who refused to acquiesce in outdated notions of "liberty," "justice," and "equality," and who strived to better them. And so we must be careful, when focusing on the events which took place in Philadelphia two centuries ago, that we not overlook the momentous events which followed, and thereby lose our proper sense of perspective. Otherwise, the odds are that for many Americans the bicentennial celebration will be little more than a blind pilgrimage to the shrine of the original document now stored in a vault in the National Archives. If we seek, instead, a sensitive understanding of the Constitution's inherent defects, and its promising evolution through 200 years of history, the celebration of the "Miracle at Philadelphia" will, in my view, be a far more meaningful and humbling experience. We will see that the true miracle was not the birth of the Constitution, but its life, a life nurtured through two turbulent centuries of our own making, and a life embodying much good fortune that was not.

Thus, in this bicentennial year, we may not all participate in the festivities with flag-waving fervor. Some may more quietly commemorate the suffering, struggle, and sacrifice that has triumphed over much of what was wrong with the original document, and observe the anniversary with hopes not realized and promises not fulfilled. I plan to celebrate the bicentennial of the Constitution as a living document, including the Bill of Rights and the other amendments protecting individual freedoms and human rights.

ROBERT GOLDWIN, "WHY BLACKS, WOMEN, AND JEWS ARE NOT MENTIONED IN THE CONSTITUTION" (1987)

Robert A. Goldwin served in the Department of Defense during the Ford administration. He has written numerous articles and books on Constitutional rights, human rights, and education.

WHY THIS READING?

Serving as a counterpoint to the immediately preceding reading, Goldwin argues that Thurgood Marshall misreads the intentions of the Founders and is therefore mistaken in attributing to the original Constitution a "flawed" approach to the task of equal representation for women and minorities. The disagreement between Goldwin and Marshall focuses on what has become a crucial dividing line in today's debate over the justice of American democracy as it was founded. That debate centers on the meaning of the Constitution's "silence" regarding women and minorities. As you have read, Marshall blames this silence, interpreting it as moral acquiescence in racism and sexism. In contrast, Goldwin praises it—as the Founders' method of paving the way for the subsequent expansion of the protection of the rights of individuals, regardless of their race, class, gender, or religious beliefs.

Questions to guide you as you read:

- Goldwin regards the fact that the Constitution does not mention "blacks, women, and Jews" as essential to maintaining the freedom and equality of all. Why?
- What are Goldwin's differences with Marshall regarding the meaning of the "Three-Fifths Clause"? Why is understanding this disagreement indispensable to understanding the Founders' view of democracy?

The bicentennial we celebrate this year honors the Constitution written in 1787, that is, the original, unamended Constitution. Some well-meaning citizens have denounced celebrating or even praising that Constitution. They contend that its many severe defects should be considered a matter of national shame. For example, lacking the Thirteenth Amendment, the original Constitution permitted slavery to continue; lacking the Nineteenth Amendment, it did not secure the right of women to vote; and, lacking the First Amendment, it provided no protection for religious freedom, not to mention other rights. Why, they ask, should we celebrate a constitution that treated blacks as less than human, that left women out, and that did not combat religious intolerance?

These charges would be distressing if true, but fortunately they are false. They stem from a misreading of the document, a misreading that comes from not appreciating the importance of knowing how to read the original Constitution on subjects it does not mention.

Why bother with subjects not mentioned? Because, as a matter of fact, we have no choice. The list of unusually important subjects the Constitution does not mention is very long. The fact that they have not been mentioned has not prevented cases and controversies from arising, nor has it relieved courts and legislatures of the duty of determining what is constitutional with regard to them. The words "education" and "school," for example, do not occur in the Constitution, but even so the courts have been busy for decades deciding school controversies. There is no mention of labor unions, corporations, political parties, the air force, radio and television broadcasting, telecommunications, and so on, but the courts deliberate constitutional controversies on these subjects all the time. The list of subjects not mentioned in the text of the Constitution also includes words like "abortion," "contraceptives," and "sodomy," and phrases like "right to privacy," "substantive due process," and the "high wall separating church and state"—all matters on which the Supreme Court has pronounced.

The inescapable fact is that many subjects not mentioned in the Constitution must be interpreted, unavoidably, by anyone for whom the meaning of the Constitution is important. My argument is that there are valuable lessons to be learned about how we are constituted as a nation, and what in the original Constitution is worth celebrating, by devoting serious attention to subjects not mentioned in it. For that purpose, I propose close attention to three such subjects—blacks, women, and Jews.

Blacks

What to do about black slavery was a major concern in the Constitutional Convention; it was discussed at length in the debates, with frequent direct reference to both slavery and race. But neither term was mentioned when it came to the writing. No words indicating race or color, black, or white, occur in the text of the Constitution and neither do the words "slave" or "slavery." Circumlocutions [roundabout expressions or evasive talk] are used in the text to avoid the use of any form of the word "slave"; for example "person held to service or labor," and "such persons as any of the States now existing shall think proper to admit."

In fact, the word "slavery" entered the Constitution for the first time, after the Civil War, in the Thirteenth Amendment, which thereafter prohibited slavery anywhere in the United States. The words "race" and "color" were first used in the Fifteenth Amendment for the purpose of securing the right of all citizens to vote. The words "black" and "white" have never been part of the Constitution. What difference does it make, one may well ask, that the words were not used, if the ugly fact is that black slavery existed and was given constitutional status? Consider, for example, perhaps the most notorious and, I would contend, the most misunderstood constitutional provision relating to black slavery, the famous "three-fifths clause."

As Benjamin Hooks, executive director of the National Association for the Advancement of Colored People, put it recently in criticism of the original Constitution: "Article 1, section 2, clause 3 of the Constitution starts off with a quota: three-fifths. That is what black folks were in that original Constitution." Hooks is not alone in this view. The historian John Hope Franklin has written of this same clause that the Founders "degraded the human spirit by equating five black men with three white men"; and the constitutional-law professor Lino Graglia contends that the provision "that a slave was to be counted as three-fifths of a free person for purposes of representation" shows "how little the Constitution had to do with aspirations for brotherhood or human dignity."

These three agree in expressing the widely held view of this clause that, for the Founders blacks were less than human, somehow or other only a fraction of a human being. The constitutional clause they are referring to reads as follows:

> Representatives and direct taxes shall be apportioned among the several States...according to their respective numbers, which shall be determined by adding to the whole number of free persons, including those bound to service for a term of years, and excluding Indians not taxed, three-fifths of all other persons.

In short, count all of the free persons and indentured servants, do not count the Indians, and then add three-fifths of the slaves. The question is, what, if anything, does that provision tell us about what the Founders thought about slavery and about blacks as blacks and as human beings?

James Madison said, in the convention, that slavery was the central problem. Southern delegates emphasized that there was no chance of union including the South without accepting the long-established existence of slavery in the slave holding states. But slavery was a flat contradiction of the principles of the Declaration of Independence, the principles that are the bedrock foundation of the Constitution—the primacy of the rights of individuals, their equality with respect to their rights, and the consequence that the consent of the governed is the only legitimate source of political power. Almost all the delegates were fully aware that slavery profoundly contradicted these principles and therefore had no proper place in the Constitution.

If, on the one hand, the continuation of slavery was unavoidable, and, on the other hand, it was a contradiction of the most fundamental principles of the Constitution the delegates wanted and thought necessary, what could principled anti-slavery delegates do? One effective and consistent thing they could do was try to make the political base of slavery as weak as possible, to diminish its influence and improve the chances of eradicating it sometime in the future.

The struggle that took place in the convention was between Southern delegates trying to strengthen the constitutional supports for slavery and Northern delegates trying to weaken them. That issue—the initial and subsequent political strength of slavery—was in contention on the question of representation in the House of Representatives. It was agreed that every state, regardless of size, would have two Senators. But the number of representatives from any state would be apportioned according to its population, and that raised the question of whom to include in the count.

Slave-state delegates were in favor of including every slave, just as they would any other inhabitant. Madison's notes indicate that the delegates from South Carolina "insisted that blacks be included in the rule of representation, equally with the Whites."

On the other side, delegates from the non-slave states were opposed to counting the slaves, because it would give the South more votes and because it made a mockery of the principle of representation to count persons who had no influence whatsoever on the lawmaking process and who therefore were not "represented" in the legislature in any meaningful sense of the word. Counting the slaves for purposes of representation would also give the slave states an incentive to increase their slave population instead of decreasing it. In short, considering the chief purpose of this clause in the Constitution, it is obvious that an antislavery delegate would not want to count the slaves at all.

In the end, two things were done. First, it was agreed to use the census for two opposed purposes: representation and direct taxation. As the count of persons went up in any state, seats in Congress and direct taxes to be paid went up as well; as the count of persons went down, both the number of Congressmen and the direct taxes to be paid went down. Combining these two, and thereby establishing opposing incentives, seems clearly intended to provide a restraint on a state's either getting too much representation or avoiding paying a fair share of direct taxes. The additional compromise was that three-fifths of the slaves would be included in the population count, as the alternative to including all or none.

If none of the slaves had been included, as Northern delegates wanted, the slave states would have had only 41 percent of seats in the House. If all of the slaves had been included, as Southerners wanted, the slave states would have had 50 percent of the seats. By agreeing to include three fifths, the slave states ended up with 47 percent—not negligible, but still a minority likely to be outvoted on slavery issues.

However the slavery provisions look to us today, they had to be explained to concerned citizens in the South as well as the North. Charles Pinckney reported to the South Carolina ratifying convention that he thought they had "made the best terms for the security [of slavery] it was in our power to make. We would have made better if we could, but on the whole, I do not think them bad." Northern delegates were, at the same time, saying the opposite in a very similar fashion. James Wilson reported to the Pennsylvania ratifying convention that he thought they had succeeded in "laying the foundation for banishing slavery out of this country," but he regretted that "the period is more distant than I could wish."

In brief, both North and South, in trying to weaken or strengthen slavery, had sought more and gotten less than each had wanted, but for the sake of union had accepted a result that was "not bad."

The struggle between pro-slavery and antislavery forces for control of Congress, begun in the Constitutional Convention and continued relentlessly for more than seventy years thereafter was the major cause of the Civil War, and persisted long after that war and the constitutional amendments that followed it had ended slavery.

But to understand what the original Constitution had to say about blacks, the point is that the "three-fifths clause" had nothing at all to do with measuring the human worth of blacks. *Northern* delegates did not want black slaves included, not because they thought them unworthy of being counted, but because they wanted to weaken the slave holding power in Congress. *Southern* delegates wanted every slave to count "equally with the Whites," not because they wanted to proclaim that black slaves were human beings on an equal footing with free white persons, but because they wanted to increase the pro-slavery voting power in Congress. The humanity of blacks was not the subject of the three-fifths clause; voting power in Congress was the subject.

Thus, the three-fifths clause is irrelevant to the question of what the Founders thought of the slaves as human beings. What is relevant are two indisputable facts: in the original Constitution there is no mention of color, race, or slavery, and nowhere in it are slaves called anything but "persons."

There is nothing particularly new in the point that the original Constitution does not mention slavery. Luther Martin, a Maryland delegate to the Constitutional Convention who opposed ratification, explained to the Maryland legislature in 1787 that the authors of the Constitution did not use the word slave because they "anxiously sought to avoid the admission of expressions which might be odious in the ears of Americans." And Frederick Douglass, the great black leader and orator, commented on this silence in 1852, arguing against the "slander" on the memory of the Founders that the original Constitution was pro-slavery. "In that instrument," he said, "I hold there is neither warrant, license, nor sanction of the hateful thing." And a major element of his evidence is that "neither *slavery, slave holding,* nor *slave* can anywhere be found in it." "Now, take I the Constitution," he concluded, "according to its plain reading, and I defy the presentation of a single pro-slavery clause in it."

These two very different speakers, Luther Martin and Frederick Douglass, knew this fact about the silence of the Constitution about slavery, and so did many, many others. But apparently it needed to be pointed out in their times, and it needs to be pointed out today. And especially when we recall that there is an equal silence about race, do we see the importance of reminding ourselves about this point that seems to have been persistently forgotten by most Americans, even by unusually knowledgeable ones like Benjamin Hooks and John Hope Franklin.

Despite the existence of slavery and the persistence of it for seventy-five years more, the Founders left us with a constitutional document that has accommodated a very different order of things with regard to the place in our society of the descendants of former slaves. I do not contend that delegates foresaw the present-day consequences of emancipation, that the descendants of black slaves would become voting citizens and officeholders throughout the nation. But it is true that the Founders left in their text no obstacles to the profound improvements that have come about. In what remained in the text after the addition of the amendments abolishing slavery, there is no residue of racism, however much of it may remain in the society itself.

Therefore when the time came to terminate official segregation, we had to purge the racial provisions from federal regulations like those segregating the armed forces, and from state constitutions and state and local laws—but not from the Constitution of the United States. In fact, lawyers and judges were able to argue for profound changes by asserting that they were in accord with and demanded by the Constitution. We did not have to change it to fit new circumstances and times. Instead, the argument could be made, and was made, that conditions had to be changed to fit the Constitution. In that historic national effort, it spelled a very great difference that there was no racism in the original Constitution.

We must acknowledge that there was indeed strong and widespread racism among many Americans that helped to sustain for so long the vicious system of black slavery and its century-long aftermath of racial segregation, discrimination, persecution, and hatred. How best can we understand the meaning of the disjunction between the racism widespread in the society, and the absence of it in the written Constitution?

If a written constitution is not in close accord with the way the society itself is in fact constituted, it will be irrelevant to the everyday life of the people. But it must be more than an accurate depiction of how the society is constituted. A constitution will be a failure if it is no more than a beautiful portrait of an ugly society. A good constitution provides guidance and structure for the improvement of the society. A good constitution is designed to make the political society better than it is, and the citizens better persons. It must be close enough to the institutions and the people as they are to be relevant to the working of the society in its everyday activities, but it should also have what might be called formative features, a capacity to make us better if we live according to its provisions and adhere to its institutional arrangements. The constitutional goal for Americans would be to develop a nation of self-governing, liberty-loving citizens in a new kind of political society where the fundamental rights of all would be secure—and that would mean a society where slavery would have no place.

In that formative way of thinking about the task of constitution-writing, it seems entirely possible that the most foresighted and skillful of the Founders sought to make a constitution that —while accepting and even protecting slavery for a time, as an unavoidable evil, the price to pay for union—tried to make provisions for its ultimate extinction, and even gave thought to the constitutional preparations for a better society that would eventually be free of it. In that respect the original

Constitution was better than the political society it constituted.

We would face a very different situation in our own time if there had been in the original Constitution any evidence of the kind of thinking ascribed to the Founders by Chief Justice Taney in the *Dred Scott* case. Taney said that the Founders thought that blacks were not included in the declaration that "all men are created equal," and that blacks were "so far inferior, that they had no rights which the white man was bound to respect." But Taney was wrong; there is no such racism to be found in the Constitution, then or now, not a word of it. Those who wrongly now assert, however laudable their motives, that the "three-fifths clause" was racist, that it somehow denied the humanity of blacks, do a disservice to the truth, first of all, and also to the Constitution, to the nation, and to the cause of justice and equality for black Americans.

Women

The fact that blacks are not mentioned in the original Constitution requires some explanation because there are several provisions obviously concerning black slavery. But no such explanation is required in the case of women. Not only are women not mentioned in the original Constitution, there is no provision anywhere that applies to women as a distinct group. To the best of my knowledge, there is no evidence that the subject of women was ever mentioned in the Constitutional Convention.

This has led to the charge, heard frequently during the prolonged debate over the proposed Equal Rights Amendment, that "women were left out of the Constitution." The fact is, however, that women were not left out; they have always been included in all of the constitutional protections provided to all persons, fully and equally, without any basis in the text for discrimination on the basis of sex. How were they included without being mentioned?

The place to start is that famous provision we considered previously, Article I, section 2, clause 3, describing who will be counted for purposes of representation in the House of Representatives. The phrase "the whole number of free persons" is chiefly where the women are, but they are also among "those bound to service for a term of years," and even among taxed Indians and "all other persons." It is quite remarkable that they are not excluded from any one of these groups because, in 1787, women did not vote or hold office anywhere in the United States and were excluded from every level of government. What would be unremarkable, and typical of the time, would be a clear exclusion of women.

For example, in the Northwest Ordinance[6] we encounter provisions of this sort: So soon as there shall be five thousand free *male* inhabitants, of full age, in the district... they shall receive authority... to elect representatives... to represent them in the general assembly.... Provided also, that a freehold in fifty acres of land... shall be necessary to qualify a *man* as an elector of a representative. [emphasis added]

Under the terms of this famous ordinance, written in the same year as the Constitution and reaffirmed by the first Congress, which included James Madison and many other delegates to the Constitutional Convention, those who are counted for purposes of representation are men only, and voters are spoken of directly as men. That was, for the time, not at all exceptional. What is exceptional is the provision in the Constitution that everyone shall be counted. "The whole number of free persons" includes males and females. In the original Constitution, unlike the Northwest Ordinance, the words "man" or "male" do not occur, nor does any other noun or adjective denoting sex. By not mentioning women or men, speaking instead only of persons, the Constitution must mean that every right, privilege, and protection afforded to persons in the Constitution is afforded to female persons as well as male persons, equally. The terms used throughout the original Constitution are consistently what are now called non-sexist: for example, "electors," "citizens," "members," "inhabitants," "officers," "representatives," "persons." There are

6. Congress approved the Northwest Ordinance on July 13, 1787. It delineated rules for governing the Old Northwest, which lay north of the Ohio River and east of the Mississippi River. Among these rules, it specified that slavery was to be prohibited in the territory.

pronouns—"he," "his," and "himself"— but in the entire text of the original Constitution, there is not a single noun or adjective that denotes sex.

There are some who think that because of these pronouns, all masculine, the Founders meant that only men were to hold national office, and most certainly the Presidency. But it can be shown that the text itself presents no obstacle whatever to having a woman in the office of President or any other national office, because these pronouns can clearly be read as generic or neuter or genderless—or whatever we call a pronoun capable of denoting either sex.

The Constitution says of the President that "*He* shall hold *his* office during the term of four years" (the emphases here and throughout this section are all added). It says that when a bill passed by Congress is presented to the President, "if *he* approves *he* shall sign it, but if not *he* shall return it," etc. There are similar usages of the pronoun for the Vice President and for members of Congress, and the question is, are those pronouns exclusively masculine and therefore a definite indication that these offices are to be held by men only, or could they be genderless pronouns, leaving open the possibility that the antecedent is meant to be either a man or a woman? If the latter is the case, as is my contention, then there is no obstacle in the Constitution, and there never has been, to women occupying any office under the Constitution of the United States, including the Presidency, and every protection and every right extended to men by the Constitution is extended equally to women.

My argument rests on several provisions where the masculine pronouns must certainly be read as referring to women as well as men. Consider Article IV, section 2, clause 2, providing for the return of fugitives from justice. "A person" charged with a crime who flees from justice and is found in another state shall be delivered up on demand of the governor "of the State from which *he* fled...." If the "he" in this clause is assumed to mean men only, and not women, we get the absurd result that male fugitives from justice must be returned to face criminal charges, but not female fugitives.

We find similar examples in the amendments. The Fifth Amendment provides that "no person... shall be compelled in any criminal case to be a witness against *himself*." The Sixth Amendment provides that "in all criminal prosecutions, the accused shall enjoy the right...to be confronted with the witnesses against *him;* to have compulsory process for obtaining witnesses in *his* favor, and to have the assistance of counsel for *his* defense." Will anyone seriously contend, just because the masculine pronouns are used here, that just because the masculine pronouns are used here, that these protections were extended only to males accused in criminal prosecutions, and that the Constitution means that accused women cannot claim the same rights to confront their accusers, to compel the presence of witnesses, to be represented by a defense lawyer, and to be protected against self incrimination?

All these examples demonstrate the absurdity interpreting the masculine pronouns as applying to men only. And if the masculine pronouns of these provisions are genderless, then it is at least plausible that the same pronouns are genderless when used elsewhere in the same text. And they are, and since, in fact, there is not one adjective in the Constitution as ratified that in any way refers to sex, we must conclude that women are included in the Constitution, on equal footing with men, as persons, citizens, electors, etc.—and always have been.

We are speaking, of course, of a written document, the text of the original Constitution, which is not the same as asserting that women enjoyed political equality in practice in 1787, or for long time thereafter. Women's suffrage in United States seems to have begun...when women in Kentucky voted in school elections. Women voted on an equal basis with men for the first time anywhere in the United States in 1869, in the Wyoming Territory. But as late as 1914, only ten more states, in addition to the state of Wyoming, had accorded women the right to vote. It was not until the Nineteenth Amendment was ratified in 1920 that the right to vote was made secure for women. That amendment provides that: "The right of citizens of the United States to vote shall not be denied or abridged by the United States or by any State on account of sex."

First we must observe that this article is an addition to the Constitution, but it amends nothing and was intended to amend nothing in the Constitution of the United States. No provision in the text had to be changed or deleted, because there was never any provision the Constitution limiting or denying the right women to vote. The barriers to voting by women had always been in the state constitutions or laws.

It may very well be that the Founders never contemplated the possibility of a woman as President, or even women voting on an equal basis with men. Nevertheless, the text they adopted and the American people ratified presents no obstacle whatsoever to the changes that have occurred.

Jews

The significance of not being mentioned in the Constitution becomes clearest when we consider the last of the three unmentioned subjects—Jews. Most of us, when we think of the Constitution and freedom of religion, think of the security provided by the First Amendment, against "an establishment of religion" and for the "free exercise thereof." These protections were not, of course, part of the original Constitution. The original Constitution mentions religion just once, but that one provision is remarkable. Article VI, section 3, says simply that "no religious test shall ever be required as a qualification to any office or public trust under the United States."

Jews had suffered persecution almost everywhere in the world for millennia. Universally despised, they had been beaten, tortured, murdered, and hounded from country to country and even continent to continent. The best they enjoyed, here and there, now and then, was a kind of safeguarded second-class status, whereby one sort of decree or another they were permitted to engage in certain professions or businesses, or to live unmolested behind walls and gates in one or another section of a city. But these occasionally favorable arrangements were always precarious and often short-lived, never theirs by right but only by indulgence, not because they were entitled to decent treatment as citizens or subjects but because someone in authority had reason to protect them. Never did they have the security of political rights, not to mention the political power that comes with voting and holding office.

The question of religious tests was an old one in America and had been deliberated in every state from the moment of independence, and even before. At the time of the founding, almost every state had some form of religious test, but Jews were not the only target or even the main one. The chief concern was to bar Catholics in predominantly Protestant states, to bar some sects of Protestants in other states, and incidentally to exclude the very small numbers of "Jews, Turks, and infidels," as the saying went.

There were religious tests in the constitutions of at least eleven states, but the tests varied. Delaware required state officers to swear a Trinitarian oath; Georgia required that they be of the Protestant religion; Maryland demanded belief "in the Christian religion"—thus including Catholics as well as Protestants, but excluding Jews and nonbelievers; and New York discriminated against Catholics but was the only state in which Jews could hold office.

Against this background we see the history-making significance of the provision prohibiting religious tests in the Constitution. Religious toleration was amazingly prevalent in America, given the intensity of religious conviction observable everywhere, but political equality for members of different religious groups was rare. That is, provisions for the free exercise of religion were common in the state constitutions, but political equality was a different story. The free exercise of religion happened in church or synagogue; it did not assure the right to vote or hold office. Nevertheless, for whatever reasons, in a nation that had almost universal religious testing for state offices, the delegates proposed and the states ratified a constitution barring religious tests for holding national office.

Add to this one other fact, less easily discernible. That fact is that Jews are not mentioned in the Constitution. As we view things now, that Jews are not mentioned is no more remarkable than that Baptists or Roman Catholics or Muslims or any others are also not mentioned. But Jews had never been treated simply as "persons," let alone "citizens," anywhere in the world for more than 1500 years. By not mentioning them, that is, by not singling them out, the Constitution made Jews full citizens of a nation for the first time in all Diaspora [dispersion of the Jews among the Gentiles] history. By this silence, coupled with the prohibition of religious tests, the Founders "opened a door" to Jews and to all other sects as well.

The Constitution of the United States is unusual, and perhaps unique, among the constitutions of the world in the way that it protects the rights of the people. The unspoken principles—at least unspoken in the Constitution—are that rights are inherent in individuals, not in the groups they belong to; that we are all equal as human beings in the sense that no matter what our color, sex, national origin, or religion, we are equal in the possession of the rights that governments are instituted to protect; and, finally, that as a consequence, the only source of legitimate political power is the consent of the governed. Because these principles, all stemming from the primacy of individual rights, are the unmentioned foundation of the Constitution, it is not only unnecessary to mention race, sex, or religion, it is inconsistent and harmful.

In short, the reason no group of any sort included in the nation it founded is mentioned in the Constitution—originally and now—is that the Founders designed a better way to make sure that no one was left out, and that everyone was in on a basis of equality. To anyone who asks why we should celebrate the bicentennial of this Constitution, let that be the answer.

Recent presidential reflections on race and the Constitution

BILL CLINTON, "MEND IT, DON'T END IT" (1995)

Bill Clinton was the 42nd president of the United States. Elected in 1992 and again in 1996, Clinton served as president until January of 2001. Prior to becoming president, he served as governor of the state of Arkansas.

WHY THIS READING?

In this speech, Clinton argues that affirmative action needs to be mended, rather than abolished, as others had been urging. In the course of making his case, he addresses this chapter's core question by taking stock of the place of race in America. His reflections grow out of an interpretation of the intentions of the original Constitution that agrees fundamentally with that of Justice Marshall and disagrees with that of Robert Goldwin.

The debate among these three individuals is particularly illustrative of a larger debate in this country today between the political Left and Right regarding the justice, or lack thereof, of the country as founded. At stake in this debate is no less than the question of what degree of moral sway the Founders' Constitution deserves to exercise over Americans today. We shall return to this question later in this textbook when we examine both the Supreme Court's *Dred Scott* decision and its most prominent critiques.

Questions to guide you as you read:

- According to Clinton, can minorities "who seek to be a part of the American dream" succeed on their own without government's help?
- How would Goldwin respond to Clinton's interpretation of the three-fifths compromise?

In recent weeks I have begun a conversation with the American people about our fate and our duty to prepare our nation not only to meet the new century, but to live and lead in a world transformed to a degree seldom seen in all of our history. Much of this change is good, but it is not all good, and all of us are affected by it. Therefore, we must reach beyond our fears our divisions to a new time of great and common purpose. Our challenge is twofold: first, to restore the American dream opportunity and the American value of responsibility; and second, to bring our country together amid all our diversity in stronger community, so that we can find common ground to move forward as one.

More than ever, these two endeavors are inseparable. I am absolutely convinced that we cannot restore economic opportunity or solve our social problems unless we find a way to bring the American people together. And to bring our people together we must openly and honestly deal with the issues that divide us. Today I want to discuss one of those issues: affirmative action.

It is, in a way, ironic that this issue should be divisive today, because affirmative action began twenty-five years ago by a Republican president, with bipartisan support. It began simply as a means to an end of enduring national purpose—equal opportunity for all Americans. So let us today trace the roots of affirmative action in our never-ending search for equal opportunity. Let us determine what it is and what it isn't. Let us see where it's worked and where it hasn't, and ask ourselves what we need to do now. Along the way, let us remember always that finding common ground as we move toward the twenty-first century depends fundamentally on our shared commitment to equal opportunity for all Americans. It is a moral imperative [commandment], a constitutional mandate, and a legal necessity.

There could be no better place for this discussion than here at the National Archives, for within these walls are America's bedrocks of our common ground—the Declaration of Independence, the Constitution, the Bill of Rights. These documents are America's only crown jewels.

Beyond all else, our country is a set of convictions: We hold these truths to be self-evident, that all men are created equal; that they are endowed by their Creator with certain unalienable rights; that among these are life, liberty and the pursuit of happiness. Our whole history can be seen first as an effort to preserve these rights and then as an effort to make them real in the lives of all our citizens. We know that from the beginning there was a great gap between the plain meaning of our creed and the meaner [lower] reality of our daily lives. Back then, only white male property owners could vote. Black slaves were not even counted as whole people, and Native Americans were regarded as little more than an obstacle to our great national progress. No wonder Thomas Jefferson, reflecting on slavery, said he trembled to think that God is just.

On the two hundredth anniversary of our great Constitution, Justice Thurgood Marshall, the grandson of a slave, said, "The government our founders devised was defective from the start, requiring several amendments, a civil war, and momentous social transformation to attain the system of constitutional government and its respect for the individual freedoms and human rights we hold as fundamental today." Emancipation, women's suffrage, civil rights, voting rights, equal rights, the struggle for the rights of the disabled—all these and other struggles are milestones on America's often rocky but fundamentally righteous journey to close the gap between the ideals enshrined in these treasures here in the National Archives and the reality of our daily lives.

I first came to this very spot where I'm standing today thirty-two years ago this month. That was the summer that President Kennedy ordered Alabama National Guardsmen to enforce a court order to allow two young blacks to enter the University of Alabama. As he told our nation, "Every American ought to have the right to be treated as he would wish to be treated; as one would wish his children to be treated."

Later that same summer, on the steps of the Lincoln Memorial, Martin Luther King told Americans of his dream that one day the sons of former slaves and the sons of former slave owners would sit down together at the table of brother hood; that one day his four little children would be judged not "by the color of their skin, but by the content of their character." His words captured the hearts and steeled [steadied] the wills of millions of Americans....

...It's hard to believe where we were just three decades ago. My grandfather had a grade school education and ran a grocery store across the street from the cemetery in Hope [Arkansas]. Most of his customers were black, were poor, and were working people. As a child in that store, I saw that people of different races could treat each other with respect and dignity. But I also saw that the black neighborhood across the street was the only one in town where the streets weren't paved. And when I returned to that neighborhood in the late 1960s to see a woman who had cared for me as a toddler, the streets still weren't paved. As a child I never went to a movie where I could sit next to a black American. Blacks were always sitting upstairs.

In the 1960s, believe it or not, there were still a few courthouse squares in my state where the rest rooms were marked WHITE and COLORED. I graduated from a segregated high school seven years after President Eisenhower integrated Little Rock Central High School. And when President Kennedy carried my home state—barely—in 1960, the poll tax system was still alive and well there.

My experiences with discrimination are rooted in the South and in the legacy slavery left. I also lived with a working mother and a working grandmother when women's work was far rarer and far more circumscribed [limited] than it is today. But we all know there are millions of other stories—those of Hispanics, Asian-Americans, Native Americans, people with disabilities, and others at whom fingers have been pointed. Many of you have your own stories, and that's why you're here today—as people who at one time were denied the right to develop and use their full human potential. And this progress, too, is a part of our journey to make the reality of America consistent with the principles enshrined just behind me here.

Thirty years ago in this city, you didn't see many people of color or women making their way to work in the morning in business clothes, or serving in substantial numbers in powerful positions in Congress or at the White House, or making executive decisions every day in businesses. In fact, even the employment want ads were divided, men on one side and women on the other. It was extraordinary then to see women or people of color as television news anchors, or, even, believe it or not, in college sports. There were far fewer women and minorities working as job supervisors, or firefighters, or police officers, or doctors, or lawyers, or college professors, or in many other jobs that offer stability and honor and integrity to family life.

A lot has changed, and it did not happen as some sort of random evolutionary drift. It took hard work and sacrifices and countless acts of courage and conscience by millions of Americans. It took the political courage and statesmanship of Democrats and Republicans alike, the vigilance and compassion of courts and advocates, in and out of government, who were committed to the Constitution and to equal protection and to equal opportunity. It took the leadership of people in business who knew that in the end we would all be better off. It took the leadership of people in labor unions who knew that working people had to be reconciled.

Some people, like Congressman John Lewis of Georgia, put their lives on the line. Other people lost their lives. And millions of Americans changed their own lives and put hate behind them. As a result, today all our lives are better. Women have become a major force in business and political life, and far more able to contribute to their families' incomes. A true and growing black middle class has emerged. Higher education has literally been revolutionized, with women and racial and ethnic minorities attending once overwhelmingly white and sometimes all-male schools. In communities across our nation, police departments now better reflect the makeup of those whom they protect. A generation of professionals now serve as role models for young women and minority youth. Hispanics and newer immigrant populations are succeeding in making America stronger.

For an example of where the best of our future lies, just think about our space program and the stunning hookup with the Russian space station this month. Let's remember that that program, the world's finest, began with heroes like Alan Shepard and Senator John Glenn, but today it has American heroes like Sally Ride, Ellen Ochoa, Leroy Child, Guy Bluford, and other outstanding, completely qualified women and minorities.

How did this happen? Fundamentally, because we opened our hearts and minds and changed our ways. But not without pressure—the pressure of court decisions, legislation, and executive action as well as the power of examples in the public and private sector. Along the way we learned that laws alone do not change society; that old habits and thinking patterns are deeply ingrained and die hard; that more is required to really open the doors of opportunity. Our search to find ways to move more quickly to equal opportunity led to the development of what we now call affirmative action. The purpose of affirmative action is to give our nation a way to finally address the systematic exclusion of individuals of talent on the basis of their gender or race from opportunities to develop, perform, achieve, and contribute. Affirmative action is an effort to develop a systematic approach to open the doors of educational, employment, and business development opportunities to qualified individuals who happen to be members of groups that have experienced long-standing and persistent discrimination.

It is a policy that grew out of many years of trying to navigate between two unacceptable paths. One was to say simply that we have declared discrimination illegal, and that's enough. We saw that that way still relegated [forced] blacks with college degrees to jobs as railroad porters, and kept women with degrees under a glass ceiling, with lower paychecks. The other path was simply to try to impose change by leveling draconian [extremely harsh] penalties at employers who didn't meet certain imposed, ultimately arbitrary, and sometimes-unachievable quotas. That approach too was rejected out of a sense of fairness. So a middle ground was developed that would change an inequitable [unequal] status quo gradually but firmly by building the pool of qualified applicants for college, for contracts, for jobs, and giving more people the chance to learn, work, and earn. When affirmative action is done right it is flexible, it is fair, and it works.

I know some people are honestly concerned about the times affirmative action doesn't work, when it's done in the wrong way. And I know there are times when some employers don't use it in the right way. They may cut corners and treat a flexible goal as a quota. They may give opportunities to people who are unqualified instead of those who deserve them. They may, in so doing, allow a different kind of discrimination. When this happens, it is also wrong. But it isn't affirmative action, and it is not legal.

So when our administration finds cases of that sort, we will enforce the law aggressively. The Justice Department files hundreds of cases every year attacking discrimination in employment, including suits on behalf of white men. Most of these suits, however, affect women and minorities, for a simple reason: because the vast majority of discrimination in America is still discrimination against them.

Like many business executives and public servants, I owe it to you to say that my views on this subject are, more than anything else, the product of my personal experience. I have had experience with affirmative action, nearly twenty years of it now, and I know it works. When I was attorney general of my home state, I hired a record number of women and African-American lawyers—every one clearly qualified and exceptionally hardworking. As governor, I appointed more women to my cabinet and state boards than any other governor in the state's history, and more African-Americans than all the governors in the state's history combined. No one ever questioned their qualifications or performance. And our state was better and stronger because of their service.

In our administration, many government agencies are doing more business than ever before with qualified firms run by minorities and women. The Small Business Administration has reduced its budget by 40%, doubled its loan outputs, and dramatically increased the number of loans to women and minority small business people—all without reducing the number of loans to white business owners who happen to be male, and without changing the loan standards for a single, solitary application. Quality and diversity can go hand in hand, and they must.

Let me say that affirmative action has also done more than just open the doors of opportunity to individual Americans. Most economists who have studied this issue agree that affirmative action has also been important in closing gaps in economic opportunity in our society, thereby strengthening the entire economy.

Now there are those who say, my fellow Americans, that even good affirmative action programs are no longer needed; that it should be enough to resort to the courts or the Equal Employment Opportunity Commission in cases of actual, provable individual discrimination because there is no longer any systematic discrimination in our society. In deciding how to answer that, let us consider the facts.

The unemployment rate for African-Americans remains at twice that of whites. The Hispanic rate is still higher. Women have narrowed the earnings gap, but they still make only 72% as much as men do for comparable jobs. The average income for a Hispanic woman with a college degree is still less than the average income of a white man with a high school diploma.

According to the recently completed report of the Glass Ceiling Commission, sponsored by Republican members of Congress, in the nation's largest companies only 0.6% of senior management positions are held by African-Americans, 0.4% by Hispanic Americans, and 0.3% by Asian-Americans; women hold between 3 and 5% of these positions. White men make up 43% of our workforce, but they hold 95% of these jobs. Just last week, the Chicago Federal Reserve Bank reported that black home loan applicants are more than twice as likely to be denied credit as whites with the same qualifications, and that Hispanic applicants are more than one and a half times as likely to be denied loans as whites with the same qualifications.

Now let's deal with what I think is really behind so much of the current debate. There are a lot of people who oppose affirmative action today who supported it for a very long time. I believe they are responding to the sea change in the experiences that most Americans have in the world in which we live.

If you say you're now against affirmative action because the government or the private sector is using its power to help minorities at the expense of the majority, that gives you a way of explaining away the economic distress that a majority of Americans honestly feel. It gives you a way of turning resentment against minorities or against a particular government program, instead of having an honest debate about how we all got into the fix we're in and what we're all going to do together to get out of it.

That explanation, the affirmative action explanation for the fix we're in, is just wrong. It is just wrong. Affirmative action did not cause the great economic problems of the American middle class. And because most minorities and women are either members of the middle class or poor people who are struggling to get into it, we must also admit that affirmative action alone won't solve the problems of minorities and women who seek to be a part of the American Dream. To do that, we have to have an economic strategy that reverses the decline in wages and the growth of poverty among working people. Without that, women, minorities, and white men will all be in trouble in the future.

The job of ending discrimination in this country is not over. That should not be surprising. We had slavery for centuries before the passage of the Thirteenth, Fourteenth, and Fifteenth Amendments. We waited another hundred years for our civil rights legislation. Women have had the vote less than a hundred years. We have always had difficulty with these things, as most societies do. But we are making more progress than are many other countries.

Let me ask all Americans, whether they agree or disagree with what I have said today, to see this issue in the larger context of our times. President Lincoln said that we cannot escape our history. We cannot escape our future, either. And that future must be one in which every American has the chance to live up to his or her God-given capacities.

If properly done, affirmative action can help us come together, go forward and grow together. It is in our moral, legal, and practical interest to see that every person can make the most of his or her life. In the fight for the future, we need all hands on deck, and some of those hands still need a helping hand.

In our national community we're all different, yet we're all the same. We want liberty and freedom. We want the embrace of family and community. We want to make the most of our own lives, and we're determined to give our children a better one. Today there are voices of division who would say, Forget all that. But don't you dare. Remember that we're still closing the gap between our founders' ideals and our reality. But every step along the way has made us richer, stronger, and better. And the best is yet to come.

BARACK OBAMA, "A MORE PERFECT UNION" (2008), NATIONAL CONSTITUTION CENTER, PHILADELPHIA, PENNSYLVANIA

Barack Obama became the 44th president in 2009 after defeating the Republican nominee, Senator John McCain, in the 2008 presidential election. Prior to this, he served as a U.S. senator from the state of Illinois.

WHY THIS READING?

In the following speech, delivered in the midst of his battle for the Democratic Party's presidential nomination, then-Senator Obama addresses the role that race has played both in his presidential campaign and in American history. Note that the title of his speech, "A More Perfect Union," comes from the Preamble [prelude] to the Constitution, which states, "We the People of the United States, in Order to form a more perfect Union, establish Justice, insure domestic Tranquility, provide for the common defence, promote the general Welfare, and secure the Blessings of Liberty to ourselves and our Posterity, do ordain and establish this Constitution for the United States of America."

Questions to guide you as you read:

- When then-Senator Obama states that "the answer to the slavery question was already embedded within our Constitution," does this interpretation of the Founding correspond more closely with that shared by Justice Marshall and President Clinton, or with that offered by Robert Goldwin. Why?
- To which moral and political principles of American democracy does Obama point when he states that "in no other country on Earth is my story even possible."

"We the people, in order to form a more perfect union."

Two hundred and twenty one years ago, in a hall that still stands across the street, a group of men gathered and, with these simple words, launched America's improbable experiment in democracy. Farmers and scholars; statesmen and patriots who had traveled across an ocean to escape tyranny and persecution finally made real their declaration of independence at a Philadelphia convention that lasted through the spring of 1787.

The document they produced was eventually signed but ultimately unfinished. It was stained by this nation's original sin of slavery, a question that divided the colonies and brought the convention to a stalemate until the founders chose to allow the slave trade to continue for at least twenty more years, and to leave any final resolution to future generations.

Of course, the answer to the slavery question was already embedded within our Constitution—a Constitution that had at its very core the ideal of equal citizenship under the law; a Constitution that promised its people liberty, and justice, and a union that could be and should be perfected over time.

And yet words on a parchment would not be enough to deliver slaves from bondage, or provide men and women of every color and creed their full rights and obligations as citizens of the United States. What would be needed were Americans in successive generations who were willing to do their part—through protests and struggle, on the streets and in the courts, through a civil war and civil disobedience and always at great risk—to narrow that gap between the promise of our ideals and the reality of their time.

This was one of the tasks we set forth at the beginning of this campaign—to continue the long march of those who came before us, a march for a more just, more equal, more free, more caring and more prosperous America. I chose to run for the presidency at this moment in history because I believe deeply that we cannot solve the challenges of our time unless we solve them together—unless we perfect our union by understanding that we may have different stories, but we hold common hopes; that we may not look the same and we may not have come from the same place, but we all want to move in the same direction—towards a better future for our children and our grandchildren.

This belief comes from my unyielding faith in the decency and generosity of the American people. But it also comes from my own American story.

I am the son of a black man from Kenya and a white woman from Kansas. I was raised with the help of a white grandfather who survived a Depression to serve in Patton's Army during World War II and a white grandmother who worked on a bomber assembly line at Fort Leavenworth while he was overseas. I've gone to some of the best schools in America and lived in one of the world's poorest nations. I am married to a black American who carries within her the blood of slaves and slaveowners—an inheritance we pass on to our two precious daughters. I have brothers, sisters, nieces, nephews, uncles and cousins, of every race and every hue, scattered across three continents, and for as long as I live, I will never forget that in no other country on Earth is my story even possible.

It's a story that hasn't made me the most conventional candidate. But it is a story that has seared into my genetic makeup the idea that this nation is more than the sum of its parts—that out of many, we are truly one.

Throughout the first year of this campaign, against all predictions to the contrary, we saw how hungry the American people were for this message of unity. Despite the temptation to view my candidacy through a purely racial lens, we won commanding victories in states with some of the whitest populations in the country. In South Carolina, where the Confederate Flag still flies, we built a powerful coalition of African-Americans and white Americans.

This is not to say that race has not been an issue in the campaign. At various stages in the campaign, some commentators have deemed me either "too black" or "not black enough." We saw racial tensions bubble to the surface during the week before the South Carolina primary. The press has scoured every exit poll for the latest evidence of racial polarization, not just in terms of white and black, but black and brown as well.

And yet, it has only been in the last couple of weeks that the discussion of race in this campaign has taken a particularly divisive turn. On one end of the spectrum, we've heard the implication that my candidacy is somehow an exercise in affirmative action; that it's based solely on the desire of wide-eyed liberals to purchase racial reconciliation on the cheap. On the other end, we've heard my former pastor, Reverend Jeremiah Wright, use incendiary language to express views that have the potential not only to widen the racial divide, but views that denigrate both the greatness and the goodness of our nation; that rightly offend white and black alike....

...The fact is that the comments that have been made and the issues that have surfaced over the last few weeks reflect the complexities of race in this country that we've never really worked through—a part of our union that we have yet to perfect. And if we walk away now, if we simply retreat into our respective corners, we will never be able to come together and solve challenges like health care, or education, or the need to find good jobs for every American.

Understanding this reality requires a reminder of how we arrived at this point. As William Faulkner once wrote, "The past isn't dead and buried. In fact, it isn't even past." We do not need to recite here the history of racial injustice in this country. But we do need to remind ourselves that so many of the disparities that exist in the African-American community today can be directly traced to inequalities passed on from an earlier generation that suffered under the brutal legacy of slavery and Jim Crow.

Segregated schools were, and are, inferior schools; we still haven't fixed them, fifty years after *Brown v. Board of Education*, and the inferior education they provided, then and now, helps explain the pervasive achievement gap between today's black and white students.

Legalized discrimination—where blacks were prevented, often through violence, from owning property, or loans were not granted to African-American business owners, or black homeowners could not access FHA mortgages, or blacks were excluded from unions, or the police force, or fire departments—meant that black families could not amass any meaningful wealth to bequeath to future generations. That history helps explain the wealth and income gap between black and white, and the concentrated pockets of poverty that persist in so many of today's urban and rural communities.

A lack of economic opportunity among black men, and the shame and frustration that came from not being able to provide for one's family, contributed to the erosion of black families —a problem that welfare policies for many years may have worsened. And the lack of basic services in so many urban black neighborhoods—parks for kids to play in, police walking the beat, regular garbage pick-up and building code enforcement—all helped create a cycle of violence, blight and neglect that continue to haunt us.

This is the reality in which Reverend Wright and other African-Americans of his generation grew up. They came of age in the late fifties and early sixties, a time when segregation was still the law of the land and opportunity was systematically constricted. What's remarkable is not how many failed in the face of discrimination, but rather how many men and women overcame the odds; how many were able to make a way out of no way for those like me who would come after them.

But for all those who scratched and clawed their way to get a piece of the American Dream, there were many who didn't make it—those who were ultimately defeated, in one way or another, by discrimination. That legacy of defeat was passed on to future generations—those young men and increasingly young women who we see standing on street corners or languishing in our prisons, without hope or prospects for the future. Even for those blacks who did make it, questions of race, and racism, continue to define their worldview in fundamental ways. For the men and women of Reverend Wright's generation, the memories of humiliation and doubt and fear have not gone away; nor has the anger and the bitterness of those years. That anger may not get expressed in public, in front of white co-workers or white friends. But it does find voice in the barbershop or around the kitchen table. At times, that anger is exploited by politicians, to gin up [agitate] votes along racial lines, or to make up for a politician's own failings....

...In fact, a similar anger exists within segments of the white community. Most working- and middle-class white Americans don't feel that they have been particularly privileged by their race. Their experience is the immigrant experience—as far as they're concerned, no one's handed them anything, they've built it from scratch. They've worked hard all their lives, many times only to see their jobs shipped overseas or their pension dumped after a lifetime of labor. They are anxious about their futures, and feel their dreams slipping away; in an era of stagnant wages and global competition, opportunity comes to be seen as a zero sum game, in which your dreams come at my expense. So when they are told to bus their children to a school across town; when they hear that an African-American is getting an advantage in landing a good job or a spot in a good college because of an injustice that they themselves never committed; when they're told that their fears about crime in urban neighborhoods are somehow prejudiced, resentment builds over time.

Like the anger within the black community, these resentments aren't always expressed in polite company. But they have helped shape the political landscape for at least a generation. Anger over welfare and affirmative action helped forge the Reagan Coalition. Politicians routinely exploited fears of crime for their own electoral ends. Talk show hosts and conservative commentators built entire careers unmasking bogus claims of racism while dismissing legitimate discussions of racial injustice and inequality as mere political correctness or reverse racism....

This is where we are right now. It's a racial stalemate we've been stuck in for years. Contrary to the claims of some of my critics, black and white, I have never been so naïve as to believe that we can get beyond our racial divisions in a single election cycle, or with a single candidacy—particularly a candidacy as imperfect as my own.

But I have asserted a firm conviction—a conviction rooted in my faith in God and my faith in the American people—that working together we can move beyond some of our old racial wounds, and that in fact we have no choice if we are to continue on the path of a more perfect union.

For the African-American community, that path means embracing the burdens of our past without becoming victims of our past. It means continuing to insist on a full measure of justice in every aspect of American life. But it also means binding our particular grievances—for better health care, and better schools, and better jobs—to the larger aspirations of all Americans—the white woman struggling to break the glass ceiling, the white man who's been laid off, the immigrant trying to feed his family. And it means taking full responsibility for our own lives—by demanding more from our fathers, and spending more time with our children, and reading to them, and teaching them that while they may face challenges and discrimination in their own lives, they must never succumb to despair or cynicism; they must always believe that they can write their own destiny.

Ironically, this quintessentially American—and yes, conservative—notion of self-help found frequent expression in Reverend Wright's sermons. But what my former pastor too often failed to understand is that embarking on a program of self-help also requires a belief that society can change.

The profound mistake of Reverend Wright's sermons is not that he spoke about racism in our society. It's that he spoke as if our society was static; as if no progress has been made; as if this country—a country that has made it possible for one of his own members to run for the highest office in the land and build a coalition of white and black, Latino and Asian, rich and poor, young and old—is still irrevocably bound to a tragic past. But what we know—what we have seen—is that America can change. That is the true genius of this nation. What we have already achieved gives us hope—the audacity to hope—for what we can and must achieve tomorrow.

In the white community, the path to a more perfect union means acknowledging that what ails the African-American community does not just exist in the minds of black people; that the legacy of discrimination—and current incidents of discrimination, while less overt than in the past—are real and must be addressed. Not just with words, but with deeds—by investing in our schools and our communities; by enforcing our civil rights laws and ensuring fairness in our criminal justice system; by providing this generation with ladders of opportunity that were unavailable for previous generations. It requires all Americans to realize that your dreams do not have to come at the expense of my dreams; that investing in the health, welfare, and education of black and brown and white children will ultimately help all of America prosper.

In the end, then, what is called for is nothing more, and nothing less, than what all the world's great religions demand—that we do unto others as we would have them do unto us. Let us be our brother's keeper, Scripture tells us. Let us be our sister's keeper. Let us find that common stake we all have in one another, and let our politics reflect that spirit as well.

I would not be running for President if I didn't believe with all my heart that this is what the vast majority of Americans want for this country. This union may never be perfect, but generation after generation has shown that it can always be perfected. And today, whenever I find myself feeling doubtful or cynical about this possibility, what gives me the most hope is the next generation—the young people whose attitudes and beliefs and openness to change have already made history in this election....

CHAPTER 6

Core Question: Why does American democracy separate the powers of government?

Based on what we have read up to this point, we now have the historical and philosophical background necessary to fruitfully examine the fundamental institutional feature of American democracy: the separation of powers (legislative, executive, and judicial). Why should such separation be necessary? After all, in a democracy, as Thomas Jefferson argued in his First Inaugural Address: "[T]he will of the majority is in all cases to prevail." Sixty years later, Abraham Lincoln echoed and amplified this point in his First Inaugural Address: "Unanimity is impossible; the rule of a minority, as a permanent arrangement, is wholly inadmissible; so that, rejecting the majority principle, anarchy or despotism in some form is all that is left."

But if this is the case, are not the retarding effects of separation of powers on the will of the majority therefore "undemocratic"? Recall your reading of *Federalist* 9, in which Hamilton's Publius criticizes the "pure" democracies of antiquity. These regimes, which lacked any meaningful separation of powers, were "continually agitated," suffering a "rapid succession of revolutions by which they were kept in a state of perpetual vibration between the extremes of anarchy and tyranny." In sum, although democratic government requires obedience to the majority's will—quoting again from Jefferson's First Inaugural Address—"that will to be rightful must be reasonable."

With this Jefferson points us to the age-old dichotomy between might and right, between what the ruling authority—be it a monarch, an aristocratic body, or the people—has the power to do, versus what it ought to do. The challenge faced by the Founders was to find a means through which to incline the democratic will in the direction of the "rightful," but to do so without violating the majoritarian principle that serves to define democracy. Surveying the Founders' efforts, Tocqueville arrived at the conclusion that "social" (i.e., political) "power superior to all others must always be placed somewhere; but... liberty is endangered when this power finds no obstacle which can retard its course, and give it time to moderate its own vehemence."

To accomplish this task—of "moderating" democratic "vehemence"—the Constitution establishes separation of powers. The separation-of-powers doctrine is animated by the conviction that the exclusive possession of all political power must and will lead to despotism. As you will read shortly in *Federalist 47*, "The accumulation of all powers, legislative, executive, and judiciary, in the same hands, whether of one, a few, or many and whether hereditary, self-appointed, or elective, may justly be pronounced the very definition of tyranny." Accordingly, if liberty is to be protected, the powers of the three branches of government "should be separate." Under this plan, if one of the branches should advance a tyrannical agenda, the other two can resist it.

For example, if Congress should pass a law endangering liberty, the president, through the power of veto, can endeavor to nullify it. Under the Constitution, Congress needs a simple majority of both houses to pass ordinary legislation, whereas, for Congress to override a presidential veto requires the votes of two-thirds of both houses. This, in effect, gives the president one-sixth of the legislative power (one-sixth is the difference between two-thirds and a simple majority). Note that the president cannot simply negate, finally and forever, the popular will as expressed through the people's representatives, for this would be undemocratic. Although it is considerably more difficult for Congress to garner the votes needed to override a veto, it can and has been done. At most, then, the president can "slow down"—or, as Tocqueville stated it above, "moderate"—the Congress.

Moreover, if the president should acquiesce to and sign a tyrannical measure passed by Congress, the separation of powers offers citizens another chance at securing justice, through the vehicle of the federal courts. As you will read in this chapter, Hamilton's Publius, in *Federalist 78*, explains that the separation of powers aims to bolster to some extent the independence of not only the president but also of the judiciary. This has taken the form of "judicial review," which refers to the power of a federal court to strike down any law that it deems to be in violation of the Constitution. On the issue of judicial independence, we will read in this chapter two presidents who disagree fundamentally with Hamilton. Both Thomas Jefferson and Franklin D. Roosevelt advance the case that the judiciary's independence does not bolster, but rather endangers, democracy.

As is the case with the presidential veto, no pronouncement by a federal court, even the Supreme Court, can simply nullify, once and for all, measures championed by the elected branches of government. Should a decision by the Court sufficiently antagonize Congress, it can, under the Constitution (Art. III, Sect. 2), simply vote to remove the relevant category of cases from the federal courts' "appellate jurisdiction" (cases that the courts hear on appeal). More to the point, should Congress become sufficiently outraged with the decisions of one or more federal judges, it can vote to remove them from office. Congress has the same power to remove the president (Art. I, Sects. 2 and 3). In the course of American history, two presidents have been impeached. Neither was subsequently convicted at his impeachment trial (under the Constitution, the House votes to impeach, while the Senate actually tries impeachment cases).

It is fitting and proper in a democracy that, when "push comes to shove," the Congress has final power in practice compared to the other two branches. Of the three branches, the Congress is, after all, the closest to the people; and democracy is rule of the people. Of course, it is not the Congress, but the Constitution, and "laws made in Pursuance thereof," that constitute "the supreme Law of the Land" (Art. VI). And this observation returns us to where we began, to the question of why we have separation of powers, for it is through such separation that the Founders sought to ensure fidelity to the Constitution.

The original Constitution's design for the separation of powers

JAMES MADISON, *THE FEDERALIST*, NO. 47 (1788)

In this famous essay, Madison-as-Publius seeks to rebut the anti-Federalist charge that the proposed Constitution violates the separation-of-powers doctrine. According to these anti-Federalists, the proposed Constitution fails to protect liberty sufficiently because it fails to separate the powers of the legislative, executive, and judicial branches *completely*.

WHY THIS READING?

Examination of this debate between the Federalists and anti-Federalists enables us to better understand the scope and purpose of separation of powers, the fundamental institutional element of American national government. Madison begins by agreeing with his anti-Federalist critics that the separation of powers is indispensable to liberty: "The accumulation of all powers, legislative, executive, and judiciary, in the same hands... may justly be pronounced the very definition of tyranny." However, he denies the anti-Federalists' claim that the proposed Constitution's partial *mixing* of powers violates the separation of powers—far from it, he argues. Citing the authority of the "celebrated Montesquieu"(1689–1755)—a French political philosopher who deeply influenced the Founding generation, Federalists and anti-Federalists alike—he explains that a partial mixing of powers makes separation of powers effective in practice. He then goes on to demonstrate that the constitutions of the various states already, and rightly so, engage in a partial mixing of powers.

Questions to guide you as you read:

- Why does Madison believe that a *complete* separation of powers undermines the purposes it is meant to serve?
- What are some examples of the different powers enjoyed by the three branches that are intended to promote effective separation?

To the People of the State of New York:

Having reviewed the general form of the proposed government and the general mass of power allotted to it, I proceed to examine the particular structure of this government, and the distribution of this mass of power among its constituent parts.

One of the principal [key] objections inculcated [taught persistently] by the more respectable adversaries to the Constitution, is its supposed violation of the political maxim, that the legislative, executive, and judiciary departments ought to be separate and distinct. In the structure of the federal government, no regard, it is said, seems to have been paid to this essential precaution in favor of liberty. The several departments of power are distributed and blended in such a manner as at once to destroy all symmetry and beauty of form, and to expose some of the essential parts of the edifice to the danger of being crushed by the disproportionate weight of other parts.

No political truth is certainly of greater intrinsic [essential] value, or is stamped with the authority of more enlightened patrons of liberty, than that on which the objection is founded. The accumulation of all powers, legislative, executive, and judiciary, in the same hands, whether of one, a few, or many, and whether hereditary, self-appointed, or elective, may justly be pronounced the very definition of tyranny. Were the federal Constitution, therefore, really chargeable with the accumulation of power, or with a mixture of powers, having a dangerous tendency to such an accumulation, no further arguments would be necessary to inspire a universal reprobation of the system. I persuade myself, however, that it will be made apparent to everyone, that the charge cannot be supported, and that the maxim on which it relies has been totally misconceived and misapplied. In order to form correct ideas on this important subject, it will be proper to investigate the sense in which the preservation of liberty requires that the three great departments of power should be separate and distinct.

The oracle who is always consulted and cited on this subject is the celebrated Montesquieu. If he be not the author of this invaluable precept in the science of politics, he has the merit at least of displaying and recommending it most effectually to the attention of mankind. Let us endeavor, in the first place, to ascertain his meaning on this point.

The British Constitution was to Montesquieu what Homer has been to the didactic [instructive] writers on epic poetry. As the latter have considered the work of the immortal bard [poet] as the perfect model from which the principles and rules of the epic art were to be drawn, and by which all similar works were to be judged, so this great political critic appears to have viewed the Constitution of England as the standard, or to use his own expression, as the mirror of political liberty; and to have delivered, in the form of elementary truths, the several characteristic principles of that particular system. That we may be sure, then, not to mistake his meaning in this case, let us recur to the source from which the maxim was drawn.

On the slightest view of the British Constitution, we must perceive that the legislative, executive, and judiciary departments are by no means totally separate and distinct from each other. The executive magistrate forms an integral part of the legislative authority. He alone has the prerogative of making treaties with foreign sovereigns, which, when made, have, under certain limitations, the force of legislative acts. All the members of the judiciary department are appointed by him, can be removed by him on the address of the two Houses of Parliament, and form, when he pleases to consult them, one of his constitutional councils. One branch of the legislative department forms also a great constitutional council to the executive chief, as, on another hand, it is the sole depositary of judicial power in cases of impeachment, and is invested with the supreme appellate jurisdiction in all other cases. The judges, again, are so far connected with the legislative department as often to attend and participate in its deliberations, though not admitted to a legislative vote.

From these facts, by which Montesquieu was guided, it may clearly be inferred that, in saying "There can be no liberty where the legislative and executive powers are united in the same person, or body of magistrates," or, "if the power of judging be not separated from the legislative and executive powers," he did not mean that these departments ought to have no partial agency in, or no control over, the acts of each other. His meaning, as his own words import, and still more conclusively as illustrated by the example in his eye, can amount to no more than this, that where the whole power of one department is exercised by the same hands which possess the whole power of another department, the fundamental principles of a free constitution are subverted. This would have been the case in the constitution examined by him, if the king, who is the sole executive magistrate, had possessed also the complete legislative power, or the supreme administration of justice; or if the entire legislative body had possessed the supreme judiciary, or the supreme executive authority. This, however, is not among the vices of that constitution. The magistrate in whom the whole executive power resides cannot of himself make a law, though he can put a negative on every law; nor administer justice in person, though he has the appointment of those who do administer it. The judges can exercise no executive prerogative, though they are shoots [branches] from the executive stock; nor any legislative function, though they may be advised with by the legislative councils. The entire legislature can perform no judiciary act, though by the joint act of two of its branches the judges may be removed from their offices, and though one of its branches is possessed of the judicial power in the last resort. The entire legislature, again, can exercise no executive prerogative, though one of its branches constitutes the supreme executive magistracy, and another, on the impeachment of a third, can try and condemn all the subordinate officers in the executive department.

The reasons on which Montesquieu grounds his maxim are a further demonstration of his meaning. "When the legislative and executive powers are united in the same person or body," says he, "there can be no liberty, because apprehensions may arise lest the same monarch or senate should enact tyrannical laws to execute them in a tyrannical manner." Again: "Were the power of judging joined with the legislative, the life and liberty of the subject would be exposed to arbitrary control, for the judge would then be the legislator. Were it joined to the executive power, the judge might behave with all the violence of an oppressor." Some of these reasons are more fully explained in other passages; but briefly stated as they are here, they sufficiently establish the meaning which we have put on this celebrated maxim of this celebrated author.

If we look into the constitutions of the several States, we find that, notwithstanding the emphatical and, in some instances, the unqualified terms in which this axiom has been laid down, there is not a single instance in which the several departments of power have been kept absolutely separate and distinct. New Hampshire, whose constitution was the last formed, seems to have been fully aware of the impossibility and inexpediency of avoiding any mixture whatever of these departments, and has qualified the doctrine by declaring "that the legislative, executive, and judiciary powers ought to be kept as separate from, and independent of, each other *as the nature of a free government will admit; or as is consistent with that chain of connection that binds the whole fabric of the constitution in one indissoluble bond of unity and amity* [friendship]." Her constitution accordingly mixes these departments in several respects. The Senate, which is a branch of the legislative department, is also a judicial tribunal for the trial of impeachments. The President, who is the head of the executive department, is the presiding member also of the Senate; and, besides an equal vote in all cases, has a casting vote in case of a tie. The executive head is himself eventually elective every year by the legislative department, and his council is every year chosen by and from the members of the same department. Several of the officers of state are also appointed by the legislature. And the members of the judiciary department are appointed by the executive department.

The constitution of Massachusetts has observed a sufficient though less pointed caution, in expressing this fundamental article of liberty. It declares "that the legislative department shall never exercise the executive and judicial powers, or either of them; the executive shall never exercise the legislative and judicial powers, or either of them; the judicial shall never exercise the legislative and executive powers, or either of them." This declaration corresponds precisely with the doctrine of Montesquieu, as it has been explained, and is not in a single point violated by the plan of the convention. It goes no farther than to prohibit any one of the entire departments from exercising the powers of another department. In the very Constitution to which it is prefixed, a partial mixture of powers has been admitted. The executive magistrate has a qualified negative [veto] on the legislative body, and the Senate, which is a part of the legislature, is a court of impeachment for members both of the executive and judiciary departments. The members of the judiciary department, again, are appointable by the executive department, and removable by the same authority on the address of the two legislative branches. Lastly, a number of the officers of government are annually appointed by the legislative department. As the appointment to offices, particularly executive offices, is in its nature an executive function, the compilers of the Constitution have, in this last point at least, violated the rule established by themselves....

...The language of Virginia is still more pointed on this subject. Her constitution declares, "that the legislative, executive, and judiciary departments shall be separate and distinct; so that neither exercise the powers properly belonging to the other; nor shall any person exercise the powers of more than one of them at the same time, except that the justices of county courts shall be eligible to either House of Assembly." Yet we find not only this express exception, with respect to the members of the inferior courts, but that the chief magistrate, with his executive council, are appointable by the legislature; that two members of the latter are triennially displaced at the pleasure of the legislature; and that all the principal offices, both executive and judiciary, are filled by the same department. The executive prerogative of pardon, also, is in one case vested in the legislative department....

...In citing these cases, in which the legislative, executive, and judiciary departments have not been kept totally separate and distinct, I wish not to be regarded as an advocate for the particular organizations of the several State governments. I am fully aware that among the many excellent principles which they exemplify, they carry strong marks of the haste, and still stronger of the inexperience, under which they were framed. It is but too obvious that in some instances the fundamental principle under consideration has been violated by too great a mixture, and even an actual consolidation, of the different powers; and that in no instance has a competent provision been made for maintaining in practice the separation delineated on paper. What I have wished to evince is, that the charge brought against the proposed Constitution, of violating the sacred maxim of free government, is warranted neither by the real meaning annexed to that maxim by its author, nor by the sense in which it has hitherto been understood in America. This interesting subject will be resumed in the ensuing paper.

PUBLIUS

JAMES MADISON, *THE FEDERALIST*, NO. 48 (1788)

Here, Madison's Publius continues his explanation and defense (begun in *Federalist 47*, above) of how the separation-of-powers doctrine is expected to operate under the proposed Constitution.

WHY THIS READING?

In all, *The Federalist* devotes five essays (47–51) to the theme of separation of powers. This extended attention likely owes in good part to the fundamental, as well as novel, character of the separation of powers. At the same time, and by way of counterpoint, the very need for such lengthy explanations of this as well as other constitutional features was, for the anti-Federalist Patrick Henry (1736–1799) of Virginia, one of the chief reasons for his opposition to the proposed document. "A Constitution," said Henry, "ought to be, like a beacon, held up to the public eye, so as to be understood by every man." In contrast, the proposed "government is of such an intricate and complicated nature, that no man on this earth can know its real operation." Going further with this charge, Henry purports to detect malevolent intentions behind the proposed Constitution's opaqueness:

> What kind of government is this? Is this a Monarchy, like England—a compact between Prince and people; with checks on the former, to secure the liberty of the latter? Is this a Confederacy, like Holland—an association of a number of

independent States, each of which retain its individual sovereignty? It is not a democracy, wherein the people retain all their rights securely.

Madison responds here that, for the protection of the people's rights, mere "parchment" barriers are not sufficient. Rather, "the great problem to be solved," is how to secure separation in practice. In coming to grips with this problem, he reminds his readers that the enemy of liberty to be feared is no longer a hereditary monarch (such as King George III, the immediate addressee of the Declaration of Independence). Rather, because America is now a representative democracy, the legislature has become the predominant power; as such, it is now the branch of government with the greatest potential to dominate the other two branches and establish despotism. He then describes how precisely this type of legislative encroachment has already occurred in Virginia (Madison and Henry's home state) and Pennsylvania. For example, in Pennsylvania, he writes, the legislature has gone so far as to violate even its own state constitution by refusing to follow the constitutional requirement that "all bills of a public nature shall be previously printed for the consideration of the people."

Questions to guide you as you read:

- Why does Madison argue that, under the new Constitution, Congress (which he calls the "legislative department") poses the greatest threat to liberty?
- Why, according to Madison, is the legislature the most powerful branch of government under American democracy?

To the People of the State of New York:

It was shown in the last paper that the political apothegm [a general rule or principle] there examined does not require that the legislative, executive, and judiciary departments should be wholly unconnected with each other. I shall undertake, in the next place, to show that unless these departments be so far connected and blended as to give to each a constitutional control over the others, the degree of separation which the maxim requires, as essential to a free government, can never in practice be duly maintained.

It is agreed on all sides, that the powers properly belonging to one of the departments ought not to be directly and completely administered by either of the other departments. It is equally evident, that none of them ought to possess, directly or indirectly, an overruling influence over the others, in the administration of their respective powers. It will not be denied, that power is of an encroaching nature, and that it ought to be effectually restrained from passing the limits assigned to it. After discriminating, therefore, in theory, the several classes of power, as they may in their nature be legislative, executive, or judiciary, the next and most difficult task is to provide some practical security for each, against the invasion of the others. What this security ought to be, is the great problem to be solved.

Will it be sufficient to mark, with precision, the boundaries of these departments, in the constitution of the government, and to trust to these parchment barriers against the encroaching spirit of power? This is the security which appears to have been principally relied on by the compilers of most of the American constitutions. But experience assures us, that the efficacy of the provision has been greatly overrated; and that some more adequate defense is indispensably necessary for the more feeble, against the more powerful, members of the government. The legislative department is everywhere extending the sphere of its activity, and drawing all power into its impetuous [violent] vortex [a whirling mass].

The founders of our republics [the various states] have so much merit for the wisdom which they have displayed, that no task can be less pleasing than that of pointing out the errors into which they have fallen. A respect for truth, however, obliges us to remark, that they seem never for a moment to have turned their eyes from the danger to liberty from the overgrown and all-grasping prerogative of an hereditary magistrate, supported and fortified by an hereditary branch of the legislative authority. They seem never to have recollected the danger from legislative usurpations, which, by assembling all power in the same hands, must lead to the same tyranny as is threatened by executive usurpations.

In a government where numerous and extensive prerogatives are placed in the hands of an hereditary monarch, the executive department is very justly regarded as the source of danger, and watched with all the jealousy which a zeal for liberty ought to inspire. In a democracy, where a multitude of people exercise in person the legislative functions, and are continually exposed, by their incapacity for regular deliberation and concerted measures, to the ambitious intrigues of their executive magistrates, tyranny may well be apprehended, on some favorable emergency, to start up in the same quarter. But in a representative republic, where the executive magistracy is carefully limited; both in the extent and the duration of its power; and where the legislative power is exercised by an assembly, which is inspired, by a supposed influence over the people, with an intrepid [fearless] confidence in its own strength; which is sufficiently numerous to feel all the passions which actuate a multitude, yet not so numerous as to be incapable of pursuing the objects of its passions, by means which reason prescribes; it is against the enterprising ambition of this department that the people ought to indulge all their jealousy and exhaust all their precautions.

The legislative department derives a superiority in our governments from other circumstances. Its constitutional powers being at once more extensive, and less susceptible of precise limits, it can, with the greater facility, mask, under complicated and indirect measures, the encroachments which it makes on the co-ordinate departments. It is not unfrequently a question of real nicety [detail, refinement] in legislative bodies, whether the operation of a particular measure will, or will not, extend beyond the legislative sphere. On the other side, the executive power being restrained within a narrower compass, and being more simple in its nature, and the judiciary being described by landmarks still less uncertain, projects of usurpation by either of these departments would immediately betray and defeat themselves. Nor is this all: as the legislative department alone has access to the pockets of the people, and has in some constitutions full discretion, and in all a prevailing influence, over the pecuniary rewards of those who fill the other departments, a dependence is thus created in the latter, which gives still greater facility to encroachments of the former....

...[A]s a more concise, and at the same time equally satisfactory, evidence, I will refer to the example of two States, attested by two unexceptionable authorities.

The first example is that of Virginia, a State which, as we have seen, has expressly declared in its constitution, that the three great departments ought not to be intermixed. The authority in support of it is Mr. Jefferson, who, besides his other advantages for remarking the operation of the government, was himself the chief magistrate of it. In order to convey fully the ideas with which his experience had impressed him on this subject, it will be necessary to quote a passage of some length from his very interesting Notes on the State of Virginia, p. 195. "All the powers of government, legislative, executive, and judiciary, result to the legislative body. The concentrating these in the same hands, is precisely the definition of despotic government. It will be no alleviation, that these powers will be exercised by a plurality of hands, and not by a single one. One hundred and seventy-three despots would surely be as oppressive as one. Let those who doubt it, turn their eyes on the republic of Venice. As little will it avail us, that they are chosen by ourselves. An elective despotism [a despotism that has been elected by the people] was not the government we fought for; but one which should not only be founded on free principles, but in which the powers of government should be so divided and balanced among several bodies of magistracy, as that no one could transcend their legal limits, without being effectually checked and restrained by the others. For this reason, that convention which passed the ordinance [law] of government, laid its foundation on this basis, that the legislative, executive, and judiciary departments should be separate and distinct, so that no person should exercise the powers of more than one of them at the same time. But no barrier was provided between these several powers. The judiciary and the executive members were left dependent on the legislative for their subsistence in office, and some of them for their continuance in it. If, therefore, the legislature assumes executive and judiciary powers, no opposition is likely to be made; nor, if made, can be effectual; because in that case they may put their proceedings into the form of acts of Assembly, which will render them obligatory on the other branches. They have accordingly, in many instances, decided rights which should have been left to judiciary controversy, and the direction of the executive, during the whole time of their session, is becoming habitual and familiar."

The other State which I shall take for an example is Pennsylvania; and the other authority, the Council of Censors, which assembled in the years 1783 and 1784. A part of the duty of this body, as marked out by the constitution, was "to inquire whether the constitution had been preserved inviolate in every part; and whether the legislative and executive branches of government had performed their duty as guardians of the people, or assumed to themselves, or exercised, other or greater powers than they are entitled to by the constitution." In the execution of this trust, the council were necessarily led to a comparison of both the legislative and executive proceedings, with the constitutional powers of these departments; and from the facts enumerated, and to the truth of most of which both sides in the council subscribed, it appears that the constitution had been flagrantly violated by the legislature in a variety of important instances.

A great number of laws had been passed, violating, without any apparent necessity, the rule requiring that all bills of a public nature shall be previously printed for the consideration of the people; although this is one of the precautions chiefly relied on by the constitution against improper acts of legislature.

The constitutional trial by jury had been violated, and powers assumed which had not been delegated by the constitution.

Executive powers had been usurped....

...The conclusion which I am warranted in drawing from these observations is, that a mere demarcation [separation] on parchment of the constitutional limits of the several departments, is not a sufficient guard against those encroachments which lead to a tyrannical concentration of all the powers of government in the same hands.

PUBLIUS

How does separation of powers aim to secure liberty?

JAMES MADISON, *THE FEDERALIST, NO. 51* (1788)

WHY THIS READING?

In this essay, Madison-as-Publius completes his answer to the question of how to make separation of powers a safeguard of liberty, not only in theory but also in practice. In addition to the partial mixing of powers (e.g., the president's veto power over bills passed by Congress, the Senate's power to try impeachments of executive branch officers, and the federal courts' power to declare acts of Congress unconstitutional), he cites the necessity that members of all three branches have the "personal motives" (e.g., "ambition") to "resist encroachments of the others." Relying on "opposite and rival [selfish] interests" more than virtue, or public-spiritedness, is necessary due to "the defect [lack] of better motives" in political leaders, as well as in human nature generally. This is not to imply that Madison denies the existence of "better motives." Rather, he hopes to make American democracy more stable and just by depending on virtue less and on "interests" more.

Additional structural elements that he believes will serve to ensure liberty are bicameralism (the division of the legislative branch into two houses); the division of general powers between the national government and the states ("federalism," see chapter three); and, most important, the large size and diverse population of the Union. In the commercial republic of the United States, where there is a multitude of differing economic interests (ways of earning a living) and a multiplicity of religious denominations ("sects"), "society itself will be broken into so many parts... that the rights of individuals, or of the minority, will be in little danger from... the majority." This diversity of economic and geographic interests, as well as of religious viewpoints, will compel citizens and politicians to moderate their most extreme opinions if they hope to be able to cobble together a governing majority. As Publius states the case: "[A] coalition [combination] of a majority of the whole society could seldom take place on any other principles than those of justice and the general good." This is the deepest reason that he believes, contrary to the anti-Federalists, that liberty is best secured in a large and heterogeneous, rather than in a small and homogeneous, country.

Questions to guide you as you read:

- Why does Madison argue that "a dependence on the people" is primary but not sufficient for ensuring that the government will not endanger individual liberty?
- In relying on ambition to "counteract" ambition, what view of human nature does Madison presuppose? That is to say, what kind of human beings does Madison presuppose?

To the People of the State of New York:

To what expedient, then, shall we finally resort, for maintaining in practice the necessary partition of power among the several departments, as laid down in the Constitution? The only answer that can be given is, that as all these exterior provisions are found to be inadequate, the defect must be supplied, by so contriving the interior structure of the government as that its several constituent parts may, by their mutual relations, be the means of keeping each other in their proper places. Without presuming to undertake a full development of this important idea, I will hazard a few general observations, which may perhaps place it in a clearer light, and enable us to form a more correct judgment of the principles and structure of the government planned by the convention.

In order to lay a due foundation for that separate and distinct exercise of the different powers of government, which to a certain extent is admitted on all hands to be essential to the preservation of liberty, it is evident that each department should have a will of its own; and consequently should be so constituted that the members of each should have as little agency [activity] as possible in the appointment of the members of the others. Were this principle rigorously adhered to, it would require that all the appointments for the supreme executive, legislative, and judiciary magistracies should be drawn from the same fountain of authority, the people, through channels having no communication whatever with one another. Perhaps such a plan of constructing the several departments would be less difficult in practice than it may in contemplation appear. Some difficulties, however, and some additional expense would attend the execution of it. Some deviations, therefore, from the principle must be admitted. In the constitution of the judiciary department in particular, it might be inexpedient to insist rigorously on the principle: first, because peculiar qualifications being essential in the members, the primary consideration ought to be to select that mode of choice which best secures these qualifications; secondly, because the permanent tenure by which the appointments are held in that department, must soon destroy all sense of dependence on the authority conferring them.

It is equally evident, that the members of each department should be as little dependent as possible on those of the others, for the emoluments [salaries] annexed [attached] to their offices. Were the executive magistrate, or the judges, not independent of the legislature in this particular, their independence in every other would be merely nominal.

But the great security against a gradual concentration of the several powers in the same department [branch of government], consists in giving to those who administer each department the necessary constitutional means and personal motives to resist encroachments of the others. The provision for defense must in this, as in all other cases, be made commensurate to the danger of attack. Ambition must be made to counteract ambition. The interest of the man must be connected with the constitutional rights of the place. It may be a reflection on human nature, that such devices should be necessary to control the abuses of government. But what is government itself, but the greatest of all reflections on human nature? If men were angels, no government would be necessary. If angels were to govern men, neither external nor internal controls on government would be necessary. In framing a government which is to be administered by men over men, the great difficulty lies in this: you must first enable the government to control the governed; and in the next place oblige it to control itself. A dependence on the people is, no doubt, the primary control on the government; but experience has taught mankind the necessity of auxiliary precautions.

This policy of supplying, by opposite and rival interests, the defect [lack] of better motives, might be traced through the whole system of human affairs, private as well as public. We see it particularly displayed in all the subordinate distributions of power, where the constant aim is to divide and arrange the several offices in such a manner as that each may be a check on the other—that the private interest of every individual may be a sentinel over the public rights. These inventions of prudence cannot be less requisite in the distribution of the supreme powers of the State.

But it is not possible to give to each department an equal power of self-defense. In republican government, the legislative authority necessarily predominates. The remedy for this inconveniency is to divide the legislature into different branches; and to render them, by different modes of election and different principles of action, as little connected with each other as the nature of their common functions and their common dependence on the society will admit. It may even be necessary to guard against dangerous encroachments by still further precautions. As the weight of the legislative authority requires that it should be thus divided, the weakness of the executive may require, on the other hand, that it should be fortified. An absolute negative on the legislature appears, at first view, to be the natural defense with which the executive magistrate should be armed. But perhaps it would be neither altogether safe nor alone sufficient. On ordinary occasions it might not be exerted with the requisite firmness, and on extraordinary occasions it might be perfidiously [treacherously] abused. May not this defect of an absolute negative be supplied by some qualified connection between this weaker department and the weaker branch of the stronger department, by which the latter may be led to support the constitutional rights of the former, without being too much detached from the rights of its own department?

If the principles on which these observations are founded be just, as I persuade myself they are, and they be applied as a criterion to the several State constitutions, and to the federal Constitution it will be found that if the latter does not perfectly correspond with them, the former are infinitely less able to bear such a test.

There are, moreover, two considerations particularly applicable to the federal system of America, which place that system in a very interesting point of view.

First. In a single republic, all the power surrendered by the people is submitted to the administration of a single government; and the usurpations are guarded against by a division of the government into distinct and separate departments. In the compound republic of America, the power surrendered by the people is first divided between two distinct governments, and then the portion allotted to each subdivided among distinct and separate departments. Hence a double security arises to the rights of the people. The different governments will control each other, at the same time that each will be controlled by itself.

Second. It is of great importance in a republic not only to guard the society against the oppression of its rulers, but to guard one part of the society against the injustice of the other part. Different interests necessarily exist in different classes of citizens. If a majority be united by a common interest, the rights of the minority will be insecure. There are but two methods of providing against this evil: the one by creating a will in the community independent of the majority—that is, of the society itself; the other, by comprehending in the society so many separate descriptions of citizens as will render an unjust combination of a majority of the whole very improbable, if not impracticable. The first method prevails in all governments possessing an hereditary or self-appointed authority. This, at best, is but a precarious security; because a power independent of the society may as well espouse [support] the unjust views of the major, as the rightful interests of the minor party, and may possibly be turned against both parties. The second method will be exemplified in the federal republic of the United States. Whilst all authority in it will be derived from and dependent on the society, the society itself will be broken into so many parts, interests, and classes of citizens, that the rights of individuals, or of the minority, will be in little danger from interested combinations of the majority. In a free government the security for civil rights must be the same as that for religious rights. It consists in the one case in the multiplicity of interests, and in the other in the multiplicity of sects. The degree of security in both cases will depend on the number of interests and sects; and this may be presumed to depend on the extent of country and number of people comprehended under the same government. This view of the subject must particularly recommend a proper federal system to all the sincere and considerate friends of republican government, since it shows that in exact proportion as the territory of the Union may be formed into more circumscribed Confederacies, or States oppressive combinations of a majority will be facilitated: the best security, under the republican forms, for the rights of every class of citizens, will be diminished: and consequently the stability and independence of some member of the government, the only other security, must be proportionately increased. Justice is the end of government. It is the end of civil society. It ever has been and ever will be pursued until it be obtained, or until liberty be lost in the pursuit. In a society under the forms of which the stronger faction can readily unite and oppress the weaker, anarchy may as truly be said to reign as in a state of nature, where the weaker individual is not secured against the violence of the stronger; and as, in the latter state, even the stronger individuals are prompted, by the uncertainty of their condition, to submit to a government which may protect the weak as well as themselves; so, in the former state, will the more powerful factions or parties be gradually induced, by a like motive, to wish for a government which will protect all parties, the weaker as well as the more powerful.... In the extended republic of the United States, and among the great variety of interests, parties, and sects which it embraces, a coalition of a majority of the whole society could seldom take place on any other principles than those of justice and the general good; whilst there being thus less danger to a minor from the will of a major party, there must be less pretext, also, to provide for the security of

the former, by introducing into the government a will not dependent on the latter, or, in other words, a will independent of the society itself. It is no less certain than it is important, notwithstanding the contrary opinions which have been entertained, that the larger the society, provided it lie within a practical sphere, the more duly capable it will be of self-government. And happily for the republican cause, the practicable sphere may be carried to a very great extent, by a judicious modification and mixture of the federal principle.

PUBLIUS

JUSTICE LOUIS BRANDEIS, DISSENTING OPINION IN *MYERS V. U.S.* (1926)

An 1876 law stated that the president could neither appoint federal postmasters to, nor remove them from, office without the advice and consent of the Senate. In 1920, President Woodrow Wilson removed Mr. Myers, a postmaster, without the consent of the Senate. In fact, Wilson did not even seek such consent prior to acting. Myers sued, claiming that his termination was unlawful under the 1876 statute.

WHY THIS READING?

This case addresses this chapter's core question by the justification it provides for its ruling that the 1876 law unconstitutionally restricts the president's power to remove appointed officials. Basing his argument on the records of the debates over the appointment power that took place in the First Congress (1789–1791), Chief Justice Taft wrote the majority opinion. The deliberations of the First Congress hold special import in matters of constitutional interpretation, because the great majority of the members of the First Congress were actively present at the drafting of the proposed Constitution and/or the subsequent ratification debates in the states.

Taft's opinion for the majority held that the power to remove appointed officials resides in the president alone and that presidents must have this power to perform their constitutional duty of ensuring that the laws are "faithfully executed" (Art. II, Sect. 3). Taft argues that to wrest this power from the president would produce irreparable inefficiency in the executive branch. The excerpt below is from the dissent in the case, in which Justice Louis Brandeis argues that separation of powers was not intended to promote efficiency in government, but only to guard against the exercise of arbitrary power.

Questions to guide you as you read:

- Based on your prior reading of various *Federalist* essays, what would be Madison's rejoinder to Brandeis's interpretation of the meaning of the separation of powers?
- After the *Myers* decision, what other constitutional means are still available to Congress to block those presidential measures with which it disagrees?

The separation of the powers of government did not make each branch completely autonomous. It left each in some measure, dependent upon the others, as it left to each power to exercise, in some respects, functions in their nature executive, legislative and judicial. Obviously the President cannot secure full execution of the laws; if Congress denies to him adequate means of doing so! Full execution may be defeated because Congress declines to create offices indispensable for that purpose. Or, because

Congress, having created the office, declines to make the indispensable appropriation. Or, because Congress, having both created the office and made the appropriation, prevents, by restrictions which it imposes on the appointment of officials who in quality and character are indispensable to the efficient execution of the laws. If, in any such way, adequate means are denied to the President, the fault will lie with Congress. The President performs his full constitutional duty, if, with the means and instruments provided by Congress and within the limitations prescribed by it, he uses his best endeavors to secure the faithful execution of the laws enacted.

Checks and balances were established in order that there should be "a government of laws and not of men." As White said in the House, in 1789, an uncontrollable power of removal in the Chief Executive "is a doctrine not to be learned in American governments." Such power... had been denied in the thirteen States before the framing of the Federal Constitution. The doctrine of the separation of powers was adopted by the Convention of 1787, not to promote efficiency but to preclude the exercise of arbitrary power. The purpose was, not to avoid friction, but, by means of the inevitable friction incident to the distribution of the governmental powers among three departments, to save the people from autocracy. In order to prevent arbitrary executive action, the Constitution provided in terms that presidential appointments be made with the consent of the Senate, unless Congress should otherwise provide; and this clause was construed by Alexander Hamilton in *The Federalist*, No. 77, as requiring like consent to removals... [Hamilton's opinion is significant in view of the fact that it was he who on June 5, 1787, suggested the association of the Senate with the President in appointments as a compromise measure for dealing with the appointment of judges]. Limiting further executive prerogatives [recognized privileges] customary in monarchies, the Constitution empowered Congress to vest the appointment of inferior officers, "as they think proper, in the President alone, in the Courts of Law, or in the Heads of Departments." Nothing in support of the claim of uncontrollable power can be inferred from the silence of the Convention of 1787 on the subject of removal or the outstanding fact remains that every specific proposal to confer such uncontrollable power upon the President was rejected. In America, as in England, the conviction prevailed then that the people must look to representative assemblies for the protection of their liberties; and protection of the individual, even if he be an official, from the arbitrary or capricious [fickle] exercise of power was then believed to be an essential of free government.

How and why does separation of powers aim to make possible an "energetic" president who is "independent" of the legislature?

JAMES MADISON, *THE FEDERALIST*, NO. 37 (1788)

Here, Madison's Publius argues that the separation of powers, to achieve its intended effect, requires that the office of the president be granted sufficient "energy" in order to enable it to be independent of the legislature.

WHY THIS READING?

Since the publication of historian Arthur Schlesinger Jr.'s *The Imperial Presidency* (1973), and even long before that, fear over an unjust expansion of presidential power has been a feature of the American political landscape. Against such fears, some defenders of the growth of presidential power look to Madison in *Federalist 37* for the counterpoint.

By "energy," Madison means that executives must have an independent will, as well the power, to enable them to resist the legislature and, when needed, to act quickly and decisively. For him, the purpose of separation of powers is not solely to limit government for the sake of individual liberty, but also to provide for the competency of government. A government that is too weak or incompetent will be unable to protect liberty.

Questions to guide you as you read:

- Madison was one of the key delegates to the Constitutional Convention, held in Philadelphia in 1787. How does his interpretation of the intentions of the Framers at the Convention differ from that offered by Justice Brandeis in his dissenting opinion in *Myers*?
- What does Madison find to be the tension between providing "stability" and "energy" in government, on the one hand, and "the inviolable [sacred] attention due to liberty," on the other?

Among the difficulties encountered by the [Constitutional] Convention, a very important one must have lain in combining the requisite [necessary] stability and energy in Government, with the inviolable [not to be violated] attention due to liberty, and to the Republican form. Without substantially accomplishing this part of their undertaking, they would have very imperfectly fulfilled the object of their appointment, or the expectation of the public. Yet, that it could not be easily accomplished, will be denied by no one, who is unwilling to betray his ignorance of the subject. Energy in Government is essential to that security against external and internal danger, and to that prompt and salutary execution of the laws, which enter into the very definition of good Government. Stability in Government is essential to national character, and to the advantages annexed to it, as well as to that repose and confidence in the minds of the people, which are among the chief blessings of civil society. An irregular and mutable [often changing] legislation, is not more an evil in itself, than it is odious [repulsive] to the people; and it may be pronounced with assurance, that the people of this country, enlightened as they are, with regard to the nature, and interested, as the great body of them are, in the effects of good Government, will never be satisfied, till some remedy be applied to the vicissitudes [change of circumstances] and uncertainties, which characterize the State administrations. On comparing, however, these valuable ingredients with the vital principles of liberty, we must perceive at once, difficulty of mingling [mixing] them together in their due proportions. The genius of Republican liberty, seems to demand on one side, not only that all power should be derived from the people; but, that those entrusted with it should be kept in obedience to the people, by a short duration [length] of their appointments; and, that, even during this short period, the trust should be placed not in a few, but in a number of hands. Stability, on the contrary, requires, that the hands, in which power is lodged, should continue for a length of time, the same. A frequent change of men will result from a frequent return of electors, and a frequent change of measures, from a frequent change of men: whilst energy in Government requires not only a certain duration of power, but the execution of it by a single hand. How far the Convention may have succeeded in this part of their work, will better appear on a more accurate view of it. From the cursory [brief] view here taken, it must clearly appear to have been an arduous [difficult] part. Not less arduous must have been the task of marking the proper line of partition, between the authority of the general,[1] and that of the State Governments. Every man

1. Madison calls what is today labeled the "national" or "federal" government the "general" government.

will be sensible of this difficulty, in proportion, as he has been accustomed to contemplate and discriminate [distinguish between] objects, extensive and complicated in their nature.... Experience has instructed us that no skill in the science of Government has yet been able to discriminate and define, with sufficient certainty, its three great provinces, the Legislative, Executive and Judiciary; or even the privileges and powers of the different Legislative branches. Questions daily occur in the course of practice, which prove the obscurity [vagueness or haziness] which reigns in these subjects, and which puzzle the greatest adepts [experts] in political science....

ALEXANDER HAMILTON, *THE FEDERALIST*, NO. 70 (1788)

Recall that the country's previous experience with the "executive power" (the British King) had not been a happy one, to say the least. As the Declaration states it, "The history of the present King of Great Britain is a history of repeated injuries and usurpations, all having in direct object the establishment of an absolute Tyranny over these States." Still scarred from this experience, many of the anti-Federalists feared the power of the new executive under the proposed Constitution, charging, as you will read shortly, that its provision for a "vigorous Executive is inconsistent with the genius [spirit] of republican government." To the contrary, argues Hamilton's Publius, "Energy in the Executive is a leading character in the definition of good government."

WHY THIS READING?

Federalist 70 continues this chapter's investigation of the various means by which the Constitution seeks to give "teeth" to the doctrine of separation of powers. Here, Hamilton focuses on the need for "unity" in the executive to ensure the needed "energy." By "unity" he means that a single president, rather than two or more serving at the same time (he cites the example of the Consuls of ancient Rome) is to be preferred. He also rejects the calls made by some at the time for a single executive serving in conjunction with a "council." Such divisions of the executive power do not protect liberty and promote competent government; rather, he argues, they undermine both liberty and competent government by making it possible for each member of such a body to evade public responsibility for decisions by blaming any unpopular policies on the others. A single executive will be both more competent at governing and—because the executive cannot blame decisions on others—more closely watched and more accurately judged by the people.

Questions to guide you as you read:

- What are, for Hamilton, "the ingredients which constitute energy in the Executive"?
- Hamilton argues that one of the benefits of having a single executive consists in the superior ability of a lone ruler to maintain "secrecy." Is secrecy consistent with democracy? If so, why? If not, why not?

To the People of the State of New York:

There is an idea, which is not without its advocates, that a vigorous Executive is inconsistent with the genius of republican government. The enlightened well-wishers to this species of government must at least hope that the supposition is destitute of foundation; since they can never admit its truth, without at the same time admitting the condemnation of their own principles. Energy in the Executive is a leading character in the definition of good government. It is essential to the protection of the community against foreign attacks; it is not less essential to the steady administration of the laws; to the protection of property against those irregular and high-handed combinations which sometimes interrupt the ordinary course of justice; to the security of liberty against the enterprises and assaults of ambition, of faction, and of anarchy. Every man the least conversant in Roman history, knows how often that republic was obliged to take refuge in the absolute power of a single man, under the formidable title of Dictator, as well against the intrigues of ambitious individuals who aspired to the tyranny, and the seditions [rebellious acts] of whole classes of the community whose conduct threatened the existence of all government, as against the invasions of external enemies who menaced the conquest and destruction of Rome.

There can be no need, however, to multiply arguments or examples on this head. A feeble Executive implies a feeble execution of the government. A feeble execution is but another phrase for a bad execution; and a government ill executed, whatever it may be in theory, must be, in practice, a bad government.

Taking it for granted, therefore, that all men of sense will agree in the necessity of an energetic Executive, it will only remain to inquire, what are the ingredients which constitute this energy? How far can they be combined with those other ingredients which constitute safety in the republican sense? And how far does this combination characterize the plan which has been reported by the convention?

The ingredients which constitute energy in the Executive are, first, unity; secondly, duration; thirdly, an adequate provision for its support; fourthly, competent powers.

The ingredients which constitute safety in the republican sense are, first, a due dependence on the people, secondly, a due responsibility.

Those politicians and statesmen who have been the most celebrated for the soundness of their principles and for the justice of their views, have declared in favor of a single Executive and a numerous legislature. They have with great propriety, considered energy as the most necessary qualification of the former, and have regarded this as most applicable to power in a single hand, while they have, with equal propriety, considered the latter as best adapted to deliberation and wisdom, and best calculated to conciliate [win over] the confidence of the people and to secure their privileges and interests.

That unity is conducive to energy will not be disputed. Decision, activity, secrecy, and despatch [promptness and efficiency] will generally characterize the proceedings of one man in a much more eminent degree than the proceedings of any greater number; and in proportion as the number is increased, these qualities will be diminished.

This unity may be destroyed in two ways: either by vesting the power in two or more magistrates of equal dignity and authority; or by vesting it ostensibly [apparently] in one man, subject, in whole or in part, to the control and co-operation of others, in the capacity of counsellors to him. Of the first, the two Consuls of Rome may serve as an example; of the last, we shall find examples in the constitutions of several of the States. New York and New Jersey, if I recollect right, are the only States which have entrusted the executive authority wholly to single men. Both these methods of destroying the unity of the Executive have their partisans; but the votaries of an executive council are the most numerous. They are both liable, if not to equal, to similar objections, and may in most lights be examined in conjunction.

The experience of other nations will afford little instruction on this head. As far, however, as it teaches any thing, it teaches us not to be enamored of plurality in the Executive. We have seen that the Achaeans [the name used originally by Homer, in the Iliad, to refer to the Greeks in general who fought at Troy], on an experiment of two Praetors [a magistrate responsible for the administration of justice], were induced to abolish one. The Roman history records many instances of mischiefs to the republic from the dissensions between the Consuls, and between the military Tribunes, who were at times substituted for the Consuls. But it gives us no specimens of any peculiar advantages derived to the state from the circumstance of the plurality of those magistrates. That the dissensions between them were not more frequent or more fatal, is a matter of astonishment, until we advert [call attention] to the singular position in which the republic was almost continually placed, and to the prudent policy pointed out by the circumstances of the state, and pursued by the Consuls, of making a division of the government between them. The patricians engaged in a perpetual struggle with the plebeians for the preservation of their ancient authorities and dignities; the Consuls, who were generally chosen out of the former body, were commonly united by the personal interest they had in the defense of the privileges of their order. In addition to this motive of union, after the arms of the republic had considerably expanded the bounds of its empire, it became an established custom with the Consuls to divide the administration between themselves by lot—one of them remaining at Rome to govern the city and its environs, the other taking the command in the more distant provinces. This expedient must, no doubt, have had great influence in preventing those collisions and rival ships which might otherwise have embroiled the peace of the republic.

But quitting the dim light of historical research, attaching ourselves purely to the dictates of reason and good sense, we shall discover much greater cause to reject than to approve the idea of plurality in the Executive, under any modification whatever.

Wherever two or more persons are engaged in any common enterprise or pursuit, there is always danger of difference of opinion. If it be a public trust or office, in which they are clothed with equal dignity and authority, there is peculiar danger of personal emulation and even animosity. From either, and especially from all these causes, the most bitter dissensions are apt to spring. Whenever these happen, they lessen the respectability, weaken the authority, and distract the plans and operation of those whom they divide. If they should unfortunately assail the supreme executive magistracy of a country, consisting of a plurality of persons, they might impede or frustrate the most important measures of the government, in the most critical emergencies of the state. And what is still worse, they might split the community into the most violent and irreconcilable factions, adhering differently to the different individuals who composed the magistracy.

Men often oppose a thing, merely because they have had no agency in planning it, or because it may have been planned by those whom they dislike. But if they have been consulted, and have happened to disapprove, opposition then becomes, in their estimation, an indispensable duty of self-love. They seem to think themselves bound in honor, and by all the motives of personal infallibility, to defeat the success of what has been resolved upon contrary to their sentiments. Men of upright, benevolent tempers have too many opportunities of remarking, with horror, to what desperate lengths this disposition is sometimes carried, and how often the great interests of society are sacrificed to the vanity, to the conceit, and to the obstinacy of individuals, who have credit enough to make their passions and their caprices interesting to mankind. Perhaps the question now before the public may, in its consequences, afford melancholy proofs of the effects of this despicable frailty, or rather detestable vice, in the human character.

Upon the principles of a free government, inconveniences from the source just mentioned must necessarily be submitted to in the formation of the legislature; but it is unnecessary, and therefore unwise, to introduce them into the constitution of the Executive. It is here too that they may be most pernicious. In the legislature, promptitude of decision is oftener an evil than a benefit. The differences of opinion, and the jarrings [clashes] of parties in that department of the government, though they may sometimes obstruct salutary plans, yet often promote deliberation and circumspection, and serve to check excesses in the majority. When a resolution too is once taken, the opposition must be at an end. That resolution is a law, and resistance to it punishable. But no favorable circumstances palliate [alleviate] or atone [make amends] for the disadvantages of dissension in the executive department. Here, they are pure and unmixed. There is no point at which they cease to operate. They serve to embarrass and weaken the execution of the plan or measure to which they relate, from the first step to the final conclusion of it. They constantly counteract those qualities in the Executive which are the most necessary ingredients in its composition—vigor and expedition [efficient promptness], and this without any counterbalancing good. In the conduct of war, in which the energy of the Executive is the bulwark [support or protection] of the national security, everything would be to be apprehended from its plurality.

It must be confessed that these observations apply with principal weight to the first case supposed—that is, to a plurality of magistrates of equal dignity and authority, a scheme, the advocates for which are not likely to form a numerous sect; but they apply, though not with equal, yet with considerable weight to the project of a council, whose concurrence [agreement] is made constitutionally necessary to the operations of the ostensible Executive. An artful cabal [a secret group of plotters] in that council would be able to distract and to enervate [weaken] the whole system of administration. If no such cabal should exist, the mere diversity of views and opinions would alone be sufficient to tincture [stain] the exercise of the executive authority with a spirit of habitual feebleness and dilatoriness [tardiness].

But one of the weightiest objections to a plurality in the Executive, and which lies as much against the last as the first plan, is that it tends to conceal faults and destroy responsibility. Responsibility is of two kinds—to censure and to punishment. The first is the more important of the two, especially in an elective office. Man, in public trust, will much oftener act in such a manner as to render him unworthy of being any longer trusted, than in such a manner as to make him obnoxious to legal punishment. But the multiplication of the Executive adds to the difficulty of detection in either case. It often becomes impossible, amidst mutual accusations, to determine on whom the blame or the punishment of a pernicious measure, or series of pernicious measures, ought really to fall. It is shifted from one to another with so much dexterity [grace and skill], and under such plausible appearances, that the public opinion is left in suspense about the real author. The circumstances which may have led to any national miscarriage [failure of a project] or misfortune are sometimes so complicated that, where there are a number of actors who may have had different degrees and kinds of agency, though we may clearly see upon the whole that there has been mismanagement, yet it may be impracticable to pronounce to whose account the evil which may have been incurred [suffered] is truly chargeable.

"I was overruled by my council. The council were so divided in their opinions that it was impossible to obtain any better resolution on the point." These and similar pretexts are constantly at hand, whether true or false. And who is there that will either take the trouble or incur the odium, of a strict scrutiny into the secret springs of the transaction? Should there be found a citizen zealous enough to undertake the unpromising task, if there happen to be collusion between the parties concerned, how easy it is to clothe the circumstances with so much ambiguity, as to render it uncertain what was the precise conduct of any of those parties?

In the single instance in which the governor of this State is coupled with a council—that is, in the appointment to offices, we have seen the mischiefs of it in the view now under consideration. Scandalous appointments to important offices have been made. Some cases, indeed, have been so flagrant that ALL PARTIES have agreed in the impropriety of the thing. When inquiry has been made, the blame has been laid by the governor on the members of the council, who, on their part, have charged it upon his nomination; while the people remain altogether at a loss to determine, by whose influence their interests have been committed to hands so unqualified and so manifestly improper. In tenderness to individuals, I forbear [refrain] to descend to particulars.

It is evident from these considerations, that the plurality of the Executive tends to deprive the people of the two greatest securities they can have for the faithful exercise of any delegated power, first, the restraints of public opinion, which lose their efficacy, as well on account of the division of the censure attendant on bad measures among a number, as on account of the uncertainty on whom it ought to fall; and, second, the opportunity of discovering with facility and clearness the misconduct of the persons they trust, in order either to their removal from office or to their actual punishment in cases which admit of it.

In England, the king is a perpetual magistrate; and it is a maxim which has obtained for the sake of the public peace, that he is unaccountable for his administration, and his person sacred [set apart]. Nothing, therefore, can be wiser in that kingdom, than to annex [attach] to the king a constitutional council, who may be responsible to the nation for the advice they give. Without this, there would be no responsibility whatever in the executive department—an idea inadmissible in a free government. But even there the king is not bound by the resolutions of his council, though they are answerable for the advice they give. He is the absolute master of his own conduct in the exercise of his office, and may observe or disregard the counsel given to him at his sole discretion.

But in a republic, where every magistrate ought to be personally responsible for his behavior in office the reason which in the British Constitution dictates the propriety [correctness] of a council, not only ceases to apply, but turns against the institution. In the monarchy of Great Britain, it furnishes a substitute for the prohibited responsibility of the chief magistrate, which serves in some degree as a hostage to the national justice for his good behavior. In the American republic, it would serve to destroy, or would greatly diminish, the intended and necessary responsibility of the Chief Magistrate himself.

The idea of a council to the Executive, which has so generally obtained in the State constitutions, has been derived from that maxim of republican jealousy which considers power as safer in the hands of a number of men than of a single man. If the maxim should be admitted to be applicable to the case, I should contend that the advantage on that side would not counterbalance the numerous disadvantages on the opposite side. But I do not think the rule at all applicable to the executive power. I clearly concur in opinion, in this particular, with a writer whom the celebrated Junius [the pen name of an anonymous author critical of King George III] pronounces to be "deep, solid, and ingenious," that "the executive power is more easily confined when it is ONE"; that it is far more safe there should be a single object for the jealousy and watchfulness of the people; and, in a word, that all multiplication of the Executive is rather dangerous than friendly to liberty.

A little consideration will satisfy us, that the species of security sought for in the multiplication of the Executive, is unattainable. Numbers must be so great as to render combination difficult, or they are rather a source of danger than of security. The united credit and influence of several individuals must be more formidable to liberty, than the credit and influence of either of them separately. When power, therefore, is placed in the hands of so small a number of men, as to admit of their interests and views being easily combined in a common enterprise, by an artful leader, it becomes more liable to abuse, and more dangerous when abused, than if it be lodged in the hands of one man; who, from the very circumstance of his being alone, will be more narrowly watched and more readily suspected, and who cannot unite so great a mass of influence as when he is associated with others. The Decemvirs [a group of ten men appointed with sweeping powers over judicial or administrative matters] of Rome, whose name denotes their number, were more to be dreaded in their usurpation than any ONE of them would have been. No person would think of proposing an Executive much more numerous than that body; from six to a dozen have been suggested for the number of the council. The extreme of these numbers, is not too great for an easy combination; and from such a combination America would have more to fear, than from the ambition of any single individual. A council to a magistrate, who is himself responsible for what he does, are generally nothing better than a clog [hindrance] upon his good intentions, are often the instruments and accomplices of his bad and are almost always a cloak to his faults....

PUBLIUS

FRANKLIN D. ROOSEVELT, "INTERVIEW BY ARTHUR KROCK" (1937)

President Roosevelt presided over the "New Deal," a sweeping array of legislation and executive orders intended to rescue the economy from the Great Depression. Following his reelection to his second term in 1936, he was interviewed by Arthur Krock, a journalist for *The New York Times.*

WHY THIS READING?

Our examination of the debate over presidential power continues with this interview of one of the most powerful presidents in American history. Roosevelt was elected to an unprecedented four terms (1933–1945). In the original Constitution, no limit was put on the number of terms to which a president could be elected. However, a precedent of no more than two terms was informally established by virtue of the fact that our first president, George Washington, retired after serving two terms. The 22nd Amendment, ratified in 1951, limits presidents thenceforth to no more than two consecutive terms.

Here, Roosevelt discloses his plan to battle Supreme Court opposition to his New Deal agenda. Under what came to be called the "Court-packing" plan, Roosevelt intended to increase the Court's size (from 9 to 15 justices) and thereby give himself the opportunity to nominate six new members, who would go on to become part of a new—and New-Deal-friendly—majority. Under the Constitution, the number of Supreme Court Justices is not fixed. It is left to Congress to set the number. At the time, Roosevelt's party, the Democrats, enjoyed large majorities in both Houses. Accordingly, he hoped that Congress would cooperate in expanding the membership of the High Court. Ultimately, his plan failed. Nevertheless, the pressure it exerted on the Court led it to largely approve his programs for the remainder of his presidency.

Questions to guide you as you read:

- What are the constitutional arguments Roosevelt employs to justify the expansion of national power required to implement the New Deal?
- What is the substance of Roosevelt's critique of the Supreme Court? How would the Hamilton of *Federalist 78* respond?

"When I retire to private life on Jan. 20, 1941," the President this week has been saying to his friends, "I do not want to leave the country in the condition Buchanan left it to Lincoln. If I cannot, in the brief time given me to attack its deep and disturbing problems, solve those problems, I hope at least to have moved them well on the way to solution by my successor. It is absolutely essential that the solving process begin at once."

This is his answer to those who have contended that the President has a third term in mind, and would remake the Supreme Court majority for a period of submissive cooperation with the other Federal divisions that will exceed the precedental [having legal or ethical force as a past example for imitation] time for chief executives. And it is his answer also to those who insist that nothing in the present condition of the country calls for new haste in an attack on problems, and that nothing will be lost by awaiting the long process of a constitutional amendment. Doubtless he will make these responses in detail for himself before the argument about the Supreme Court is ended by triumph, defeat or compromise. Responses from him are expected, for, though it is only a few weeks since the Presidential election of 1936, the cry of "dictator" once more is

heard. The provocation is Mr. Roosevelt's recommendation to Congress of a statute whereby all Federal judges—including those of the Supreme Court—must retire at the age of 70 or have a judge of equal powers appointed to supplement them.

Since the effect of the President's proposal would be to supervene the present Supreme Court majority with his own appointees if judges eligible to retire refused to do so, or to nominate a new majority if they did, he has been widely accused of intending to supplant the Federal system of checks and balances with one-man government, assure decisions upholding any legislation he might propose and offer to some future dictator a precedent with which, with the approval of Congress, he could, by changing the age-limit, wholly remake the Supreme Court when he took office or increase it to the size—and reduce it to the futility—of a mass meeting.

In discussing with the President these charges and the proposals which produced them, the writer became conscious of Mr. Roosevelt's complete certainty that the accusations are all founded in a misconception of his aims and their consequences, in a total lack of understanding of the crisis which confronts the country and calls for drastic remedies, and in a failure to appreciate how sincere and sure is his labor to maintain democracy rather than to suspend it or undermine its future foundations.

In the President's view—and discussion with him makes it clearer—the Supreme Court issue is but part of a larger problem: how to make democracy work in a world where democracy has in many lands been subverted. He believes that within the American democratic machine are all the essential devices. He feels they must be boldly grasped and employed to save democracy itself. Far from agreeing that recourse to Statutes, within the plain permissions of the Constitution, to sweep away barriers to orderly progress and modern needs is an encouragement to future dictatorships, he is firm in the faith that this method stamps out the dictatorial seed. His belief is that legalistic or other obstructions to "action by our form of government on behalf of those who need help" are the real incentives to revolutions from which demagogues and dictators emerge. What he has done and is doing are to him the definite solvents of democracy.

The President believes it is necessary not only for the Federal Government to be able to regulate against overproduction and underproduction, to regulate against unsocial types of employment, and against the making of prices by speculation, but that it is also necessary for the Federal Government to have some authority to compel collective bargaining and to enforce the maintenance of contracts both by employers and employees. He feels that, today, there is real danger to the nation because any law passed by the Congress to provide national remedies is open to constitutional doubt if the language of the present Supreme Court majority is literally followed. In this connection, the President compared present conditions to a dead end street. The President, by dreading and observation, and by tried and unusual familiarity with the attitude of Americans toward their public men, sees a future far more dangerous if he is balked of his solutions than if they are adopted. He sees a growing belief among the underprivileged that judicial supremacy is certain to cancel the progressive and humanitarian efforts of Congress and the Executive. He sees this belief easily firing into a desperate conviction, and he does not doubt that, should this happen, a leader will arise to tread down democracy in the name of reform.

The President has not forgotten Huey P. Long. While he does not say so in precise words, he entertains the opinion that one important reason why the Louisiana dictator was not able to extend his dominion further during his lifetime was because he was fortunately co-existent with wiser and more sincere remedies for the conditions which produced Long. In other words, had public opinion against the Hoover administration not been sufficiently formed by the elections of 1932, and had Mr. Hoover therefore been reelected, the President believes that Huey Long would immediately have become a great menace to the democratic process.

Now, finding—from his viewpoint—essential, legal and democratic Federal action obstructed by the Supreme Court majority, or held in long uncertainty that has the effect of balking both preventive and remedial measures for what Mr. Roosevelt thinks ails the country, he sees the possibility at least that a new, more appealing and even more ruthless demagogue may arise to abolish American democracy for years. Whether a listener agrees with the President in his course and in his estimate of future menace, that listener notes in his words and tone no other primary objective than, as Mr. Roosevelt sees it, the preservation and the restoration of democracy.

Although there are many manifests of recovery, the number of the unemployed and the national relief bill impress the President with the certainty that much remains to be done if social dangers shall be averted and economic stability be attained. In averting social dangers and attaining economic stability, the President sees the assurance of continued democracy. That is what he is determined to assure, and he finds as natural attendant circumstances a better spread of income, steady work for the employable, a good standard of living, protection for the aged, opportunity for the young, and national action. The program to effect these benefits, which the President never thinks of save as human rights, is, to his mind, the program to keep American democracy working. At times the President is faced with this sort of problem in moving his program.

For one reason or another, a measure of national action which to him is essential to safeguard democracy comes newly into council and therefore has not been included in any specific mandate. Do the people expect him, and does fair dealing require, that he seek a popular referendum before proceeding?

If the President is convinced that the measure is effective, and that time is of its essence, he goes ahead. Since all such enterprises—this being a democracy—must first pass the Congressional test, the President sees in Congress itself a sufficient referendum in vital instances. It is true that Congress is made up of politicians, and, since 1932, that it has been dominated by members of the political group of which the President is party leader. But in conversation Mr. Roosevelt points out also that, being largely politicians, with district or State responsibility, members of Congress, if only for political self-preservation, submit his proposals to the test of public opinion, and to the further test of the democratic process. These tests, in conjunction with the full and free debate which is the privilege of the Senate, seem to the president to answer the charge that in any legislative request he ever tries "to put anything over" on the people.

He points out, for example, that many of his proposals to the Congress during the past four years have been either rejected by the Congress or have been so amended as to change them greatly—i.e., social security, bonus, $4,800,000,000 relief bill, etc.

He has been moving, through the medium of civil service reform, to withdraw political patronage from the Federal equation, and this will be well out of the sphere of Presidential influence over Congress if and when the government reorganization plan is adopted. Therefore, in the view of Mr. Roosevelt, the response of Congress to his recommendations is more and more a clear reflection of its free opinion as to the degree to which he represents wide and accredited popular leadership.

The President comes to the issue of the mandate with which he has been entrusted by the people with recent experience strongly in mind. He found it necessary, after taking office in 1933, to divert the course plotted by the party platform on which he was elected because of a change in conditions between June, 1932, and March, 1933—a change which all economic research and statistics reflect. In the Congressional campaign of 1934 this diversion was made an issue by the Republicans, and in return Democratic candidates for Congress offered the President himself as the only issue. "Shall Franklin D. Roosevelt's course thus far be approved and he be given a Congressional majority to proceed with the New Deal?" was the question as the people went to the polls in 1934. Overwhelming documentation of this is available in the political writings and oratory in that campaign. The answer was overwhelmingly in the affirmative.

In 1936 the President's diversion of course was again made an issue by the Republicans, who also pointed out that, if re-elected, he would probably have several new appointments to the Supreme Court. The age of many justices, if nothing else, was used to illustrate the certainty that, if re-elected, the opportunity to change the court majority would come to Mr. Roosevelt. . . . The Philadelphia convention had promised "a clarifying amendment" to the Constitution if problems arising in the Supreme Court could be disposed of in no other way. The President, in December, 1936, decided that the amendment process requires too much time for the country's needs and security He feels that, by the general permissions of 1934 and 1936, he was given ample mandate to attempt what upon mature consideration, and even altered method, he thinks does not forbid regulation of railroads or communications or trade practices and that, if the same rules were applied in the case of commodities of all sorts, unwieldy crop surpluses, starvation wages and unfair trade practices could be eliminated with the objective not only of improving social conditions but also of averring future panics. If newer and younger blood in the Federal courts does not result in decisions which accord with the views of the majority of the members of the legislative branch and the views of the President, he is then wholly willing to admit that a clarifying amendment to the Constitution will be necessary. In a time of public controversy, "so much," the President has said, "depends on what newspaper you read." Which is another way of saying that one's mental approach to an argument often forecloses the effect of that argument on one's conclusion—an indisputable fact. The President takes as an example of mental approach and inflection the wide use made on Feb. 22 of extracts from Washington's Farewell Address against his Supreme Court program. Suppose, he says, the reader begins his perusal with remembrance that Washington wrote the words in 1796 before the Supreme Court had attempted to override an act of Congress without specific warrant of the Constitution. It is best. Therefore, he does not for a moment believe that the majority which has supported him in full measure in three national elections shares the feeling that he has exceeded his permission. Nor does he consider that the American majority expected him to have been able, in what he views as a shifting and perilous time, to chart in detail and in advance the measures he might finally employ to achieve the end stated and, as he is certain, desired by the people.

Furthermore, the President by no means discards into finality "a clarifying amendment" as mentioned in the Democratic platform. Such an amendment, he argues, would be necessary if the problems cannot be disposed of otherwise. He takes the view that the great majority of both houses of the Congress, including many Republican members, believed in passing the New Deal bills of the past four years and that these bills were constitutional. He holds, as he stated in this year's annual message to the Congress, that the Constitution definitely permits the Congress to legislate in regard to the production of crops and the production of manufactured articles which enter generically as products into commerce between the States. It is his contention that the Constitution then, in his opinion wholly logical to read the warning words of the Father of His Country against usurpation as a criticism of the course the Supreme Court has followed in many decisions since it assumed the power of invalidating. Why, he asks, does not this passage more forcibly apply to the majority reasoning in the A[gricultural] A[djustment] A[ct] or Guffey Act cases (denounced by minority members of the court itself) than do any 'act' of the Executive since 1796:

It is important, likewise, that the habit of thinking in a free country should inspire caution, in those entrusted with its administration, to confine themselves within their respective constitutional spheres, avoiding in the exercise of the powers of one department to encroach upon another.

From the time he entered public life, the President has maintained as his goal the preservation of the American form of democracy. He thinks it still needs preserving, not from his forms or persuasions, but from those who have prospered most under it and returned least. He believes that his program stopped the descent of the capitalist system, threatened by enemies within and without. He wants to raise and firmly buttress it against the attacks of these enemies by the time he leaves office "on Jan. 20, 1941."

ALEXIS DE TOCQUEVILLE, *DEMOCRACY IN AMERICA*, "HOW AMERICAN DEMOCRACY CONDUCTS THE EXTERNAL AFFAIRS [FOREIGN POLICY] OF THE STATE" (1835)

Up to this point, we have examined the meaning and effects of separation-of-powers doctrine from the standpoint of domestic policy. Now we turn to foreign policy. Under the constitutional scheme, authority over key aspects of foreign affairs is delegated primarily to the president and the Senate. Here, Tocqueville examines the political effects of this division of authority. He argues that it "tends in some degree to detach the general foreign policy of the Union from the direct control of the people."

WHY THIS READING?

Although this arrangement is less purely democratic, such "detachment" is, he argues, beneficial, for he deems democracies "decidedly inferior" to other forms of government when it comes to the conduct of foreign policy. This may strike our contemporary ears as strange, because, as we discussed in the introduction to this chapter, we tend to believe in the unqualified rectitude of the democratic process. This sentiment was summed up famously by Alfred E. Smith (1873–1944), four-time New York governor and unsuccessful Democratic nominee for the presidency in 1928. As Smith put it, "All the ills of democracy can be cured by more democracy." This sentiment also has been attributed to President Woodrow Wilson's approach to international diplomacy. In negotiations between and among nations, Wilson, who served as president from 1913–1921, championed "open covenants of peace, openly arrived at."

Tocqueville provides the counterpoint to Wilson and Smith. Democracy, Tocqueville argues, finds it very difficult to "persevere in a fixed design" that requires both "secrecy" and "patience." We read a dramatic example of this debate in chapter two, in which we contrasted the views of Senator Russ Feingold with those of Attorney General John Ashcroft about the Patriot Act.

Questions to guide you as you read:

- What does Tocqueville argue were the views on foreign policy of Washington and Jefferson? What implications can be drawn from their foreign policy views regarding the separation of powers in American democracy?
- Why does Tocqueville think it helpful that foreign policy is somewhat "detached" from the "direct control of the people"? Is such detachment consistent with democracy? If so, why? If not, why not?

We have seen that the Federal Constitution entrusts the permanent direction of the external interests of the nation to the President and the Senate, which tends in some degree to detach the general foreign policy of the Union from the direct control of the people. It cannot, therefore, be asserted with truth that the foreign affairs of the state are conducted by the democracy.

There are two men who have imparted to American foreign policy a tendency that is still being followed today; the first is Washington and the second Jefferson. Washington said, in the admirable Farewell Address which he made to his fellow citizens, and which may be regarded as his political testament:

> The great rule of conduct for us in regard to foreign nations is, in extending our commercial relations, to have with them as little political connection as possible. So far as we have already formed engagements, let them be fulfilled with perfect good faith. Here let us stop....
>
> ...It is our true policy to steer clear of permanent alliances with any portion of the foreign world, so far, I mean, as we are now at liberty to do it; for let me not be understood as capable of patronizing infidelity to existing engagements. I hold the maxim no less applicable to public than to private affairs, that honesty is always the best policy. I repeat it, therefore, let those engagements be observed in their genuine sense; but in my opinion it is unnecessary, and would be unwise, to extend them.
>
> Taking care always to keep ourselves, by suitable establishments, in a respectable defensive posture, we may safely trust to temporary alliances for extraordinary emergencies....

...The political conduct of Washington was always guided by these maxims. He succeeded in maintaining his country in a state of peace while all the other nations of the globe were at war; and he laid it down as a fundamental doctrine that the true interest of the Americans consisted in a perfect neutrality with regard to the internal dissensions of the European powers.

Jefferson went still further and introduced this other maxim into the policy of the Union, that "the Americans ought never to solicit any privileges from foreign nations, in order not to be obliged to grant similar privileges themselves."

These two principles, so plain and just as to be easily understood by the people, have greatly simplified the foreign policy of the United States. As the Union takes no part in the affairs of Europe, it has, properly speaking, no foreign interests to discuss, since it has, as yet, no powerful neighbors on the American continent....

...The Union is free from all pre-existing obligations, it can profit by the experience of the old nations of Europe, without being obliged, as they are, to make the best of the past and to adapt it to their present circumstances. It is not, like them, compelled to accept an immense inheritance bequeathed by their forefathers an inheritance of glory mingled with calamities, and of alliances conflicting with national antipathies. The foreign policy of the United States is eminently expectant; it consists more in abstaining than in acting.

It is therefore very difficult to ascertain, at present, what degree of sagacity [practical wisdom] the American democracy will display in the conduct of the foreign policy of the country; upon this point its adversaries as well as its friends must suspend their judgment. As for myself I do not hesitate to say that it is especially in the conduct of their foreign relations that democracies appear to me decidedly inferior to other governments. Experience, instruction, and habit almost always succeed in creating in a democracy a homely [unattractive] species of practical wisdom and that science of the petty occurrences of life which is called good sense....

...Foreign politics demand scarcely any of those qualities which are peculiar to a democracy; they require, on the contrary, the perfect use of almost all those in which it is deficient. Democracy is favorable to the increase of the internal resources of a state, it diffuses [spreads] wealth and comfort, promotes public spirit [patriotism], and fortifies the respect for law in all classes of society: all these are advantages which have only an indirect influence over the relations which one people bears to another. But a democracy can only with great difficulty regulate the details of an important undertaking, persevere in a fixed design, and work out its execution in spite of serious obstacles. It cannot combine its measures with secrecy or await their consequences with patience. These are qualities which more especially belong to an individual or an aristocracy; and they are precisely the qualities by which a nation, like an individual, attains a dominant position....

...The propensity [inclination] that induces democracies to obey impulse rather than prudence, and to abandon a mature design for the gratification of a momentary passion, was clearly seen in America on the breaking out of the French Revolution. It was then as evident to the simplest capacity as it is at the present time that the interest of the Americans forbade them to take any part in the contest which was about to deluge Europe with blood, but which could not injure their own country. But the sympathies of the people declared themselves with so much violence in favor of France that nothing but the inflexible character of Washington and the immense popularity which he enjoyed could have prevented the Americans from declaring war against England. And even then the exertions which the austere [sober] reason of that great man made to repress the generous but imprudent passions of his fellow citizens nearly deprived him of the sole recompense which he ever claimed, that of his country's love. The majority reprobated [solemnly condemned] his policy, but it was afterwards approved by the whole nation.

If the Constitution and the favor of the public had not entrusted the direction of the foreign affairs of the country to Washington it is certain that the American nation would at that time have adopted the very measures which it now condemns....

How and why does separation of powers aim to make possible an independent judiciary?

ALEXANDER HAMILTON, *THE FEDERALIST,* NO. 78 (1788)

In this essay, Hamilton-as-Publius defends the proposed Constitution's provision for life tenure for federal judges.

WHY THIS READING?

In contrast to the president and members of Congress, the members of the judicial branch of the federal government—Supreme Court Justices, federal district court judges, and federal appellate court judges—are appointed by the Constitution, not for a fixed term of years, but during "good behavior." The constitutional provision for federal judges is found in Article III, Sect. 1: "The judicial power of the United States, shall be vested in one supreme Court, and in such inferior Courts as the Congress may from time to time ordain and establish. The Judges...shall hold their Offices during good Behaviour...." This provision, along with the sweeping jurisdiction of the national judiciary and the resulting reduction in the role of juries, led the anti-Federalist Brutus to "question whether the world ever saw, in any period of it, a court of justice invested with such immense powers, and yet placed in a situation so little responsible [to the will of the people]."

In opposition, Hamilton deems "good behavior" (effectively, life tenure) for judges an "excellent barrier to the encroachments and oppressions of the representative body." It is no less necessary to "secure a steady, upright, and impartial administration of the laws." Hamilton entertains no fears that life tenure will lead to an abuse of power. In his view, the judiciary is so constitutionally weak that it is the "least dangerous" branch of the federal government. While Congress has the power of the "purse [appropriations bills]" and the executive, the power of the "sword," the judiciary has neither "force" nor "will, but merely judgment." But another anti-Federalist, writing under the pen name, "The Federal Farmer," remained unconvinced: "[W]e are more in danger of sowing the seeds of arbitrary government in this department [the federal judiciary] than in any other."

Hamilton countered that the independence of the courts is essential if we are to preserve the limitations on governmental power found in the Constitution. For this reason, the power to nullify unconstitutional laws passed by Congress (later called "judicial review") must belong to the judicial branch: "The interpretation of the laws is the proper and peculiar province of the courts." But, without life tenure, judges would lack the constitutional means to stand up to Congress and enforce the Constitution.

Questions to guide you as you read:

- How does *Federalist* 78 provide the counterpoint to Franklin D. Roosevelt's criticism of the Supreme Court in the Krock interview?
- Regarding judicial review, Brutus argued that, should "the legislature pass any laws, inconsistent with the sense the judges put upon the constitution, they will declare it void; and therefore in this respect their power is superior to that of the legislature." To what constitutional power possessed by Congress would Hamilton point in an effort to rebut Brutus's prediction of judicial supremacy?

To the People of the State of New York:

We proceed now to an examination of the judiciary department of the proposed government.

In unfolding the defects of the existing Confederation, the utility and necessity of a federal judicature have been clearly pointed out. It is the less necessary to recapitulate the considerations there urged, as the propriety of the institution in the abstract is not disputed; the only questions which have been raised being relative to the manner of constituting it, and to its extent. To these points, therefore, our observations shall be confined.

The manner of constituting it seems to embrace these several objects: 1st. The mode of appointing the judges. 2d. The tenure by which they are to hold their places. 3d. The partition of the judiciary authority between different courts, and their relations to each other.

First. As to the mode of appointing the judges; this is the same with that of appointing the officers of the Union in general, and has been so fully discussed in the two last numbers, that nothing can be said here which would not be useless repetition.

Second. As to the tenure by which the judges are to hold their places; this chiefly concerns their duration in office; the provisions for their support; the precautions for their responsibility.

According to the plan of the convention, all judges who may be appointed by the United States are to hold their offices during good behavior; which is conformable to the most approved of the State constitutions and among the rest, to that of this State. Its propriety having been drawn into question by the adversaries of that plan, is no light symptom of the rage for objection, which disorders their imaginations and judgments. The standard of good behavior for the continuance in office of the judicial magistracy [judges], is certainly one of the most valuable of the modern improvements in the practice of government. In a monarchy it is an excellent barrier to the despotism of the prince; in a republic it is a no less excellent barrier to the encroachments and oppressions of the representative body. And it is the best expedient which can be devised in any government, to secure a steady, upright, and impartial administration of the laws.

Whoever attentively considers the different departments of power must perceive, that, in a government in which they are separated from each other, the judiciary, from the nature of its functions, will always be the least dangerous to the political rights of the Constitution; because it will be least in a capacity to annoy or injure them. The Executive not only dispenses the honors, but holds the sword of the community. The legislature not only commands the purse, but prescribes the rules by which the duties and rights of every citizen are to be regulated. The judiciary, on the contrary, has no influence over either the sword or the purse; no direction either of the strength or of the wealth of the society; and can take no active resolution whatever. It may truly be said to have neither FORCE nor WILL, but merely judgment; and must ultimately depend upon the aid of the executive arm even for the efficacy of its judgments.

This simple view of the matter suggests several important consequences. It proves incontestably, that the judiciary is beyond comparison the weakest of the three departments of power; that it can never attack with success either of the other two; and that all possible care is requisite to enable it to defend itself against their attacks. It equally proves, that though individual oppression may now and then proceed from the courts of justice, the general liberty of the people can never be endangered from that quarter; I mean so long as the judiciary remains truly distinct from both the legislature and the Executive. For I agree, that "there is no liberty, if the power of judging be not separated from the legislative and executive powers." And it proves, in the last place, that as liberty can have nothing to fear from the judiciary alone, but would have everything to fear from its union with either of the other departments; that as all the effects of such a union must ensue from a dependence of the former on the latter, notwithstanding a nominal and apparent separation; that as, from the natural feebleness of the judiciary, it is in continual jeopardy of being overpowered, awed, or influenced by its co-ordinate branches; and that as nothing can contribute so much to its firmness and independence as permanency in office, this quality may therefore be justly regarded as an indispensable ingredient in its constitution, and, in a great measure, as the citadel [stronghold] of the public justice and the public security.

The complete independence of the courts of justice is peculiarly essential in a limited Constitution. By a limited Constitution, I understand one which contains certain specified exceptions to the legislative authority; such, for instance, as that it shall pass no bills of attainder, no ex post facto laws, and the like. Limitations of this kind can be preserved in practice no other way than through the medium of courts of justice, whose duty it must be to declare all acts contrary to the manifest tenor of the Constitution void. Without this, all the reservations of particular rights or privileges would amount to nothing.

Some perplexity respecting the rights of the courts to pronounce legislative acts void, because contrary to the Constitution, has arisen from an imagination that the doctrine would imply a superiority of the judiciary to the legislative power. It is urged that the authority which can declare the acts of another void, must necessarily be superior to the one whose acts may be declared void. As this doctrine is of great importance in all the American constitutions, a brief discussion of the ground on which it rests cannot be unacceptable.

There is no position which depends on clearer principles, than that every act of a delegated authority, contrary to the tenor [intention] of the commission under which it is exercised, is void. No legislative act, therefore, contrary to the Constitution, can be valid. To deny this, would be to affirm, that the deputy is greater than his principal [chief officer]; that the servant is above his master; that the representatives of the people are superior to the people themselves; that men acting by virtue of powers, may do not only what their powers do not authorize, but what they forbid.

If it be said that the legislative body are themselves the constitutional judges of their own powers, and that the construction they put upon them is conclusive upon the other departments, it may be answered, that this cannot be the natural presumption, where it is not to be collected from any particular provisions in the Constitution. It is not otherwise to be supposed, that the Constitution could intend to enable the representatives of the people to substitute their will to that of their constituents. It is far more rational to suppose, that the courts were designed to be an intermediate body between the people and the legislature, in order, among other things, to keep the latter within the limits assigned to their authority. The interpretation of the laws is the proper and peculiar province of the courts. A constitution is, in fact, and must be regarded by the judges, as a fundamental law. It therefore belongs to them to ascertain its meaning, as well as the meaning of any particular act proceeding from the legislative body. If there should happen to be an irreconcilable variance between the two, that which has the superior obligation and validity ought, of course, to be preferred; or, in other words, the Constitution ought to be preferred to the statute, the intention of the people to the intention of their agents.

Nor does this conclusion by any means suppose a superiority of the judicial to the legislative power. It only supposes that the power of the people is superior to both; and that where the will of the legislature, declared in its statutes, stands in opposition to that of the people, declared in the Constitution, the judges ought to be governed by the latter rather than the former. They ought to regulate their decisions by the fundamental laws, rather than by those which are not fundamental.

This exercise of judicial discretion, in determining between two contradictory laws, is exemplified in a familiar instance. It not uncommonly happens, that there are two statutes existing at one time, clashing in whole or in part with each other, and neither of them containing any repealing clause or expression. In such a case, it is the province of the courts to liquidate [clarify] and fix their meaning and operation. So far as they can, by any fair construction, be reconciled to each other, reason and law conspire to dictate that this should be done; where this is impracticable, it becomes a matter of necessity to give effect to one, in exclusion of the other. The rule which has obtained in the courts for determining their relative validity is that the last in order of time shall be preferred to the first. But this is a mere rule of construction, not derived from any positive law, but from the nature and reason of the thing. It is a rule not enjoined [imposed] upon the courts by legislative provision, but adopted by themselves, as consonant to truth and propriety, for the direction of their conduct as interpreters of the law. They thought it reasonable, that between the interfering acts of an EQUAL authority, that which was the last indication of its will should have the preference.

But in regard to the interfering acts of a superior and subordinate authority, of an original and derivative power, the nature and reason of the thing indicate the converse of that rule as proper to be followed. They teach us that the prior act of a superior ought to be preferred to the subsequent act of an inferior and subordinate authority; and that accordingly, whenever a particular statute contravenes the Constitution, it will be the duty of the judicial tribunals to adhere to the latter and disregard the former.

It can be of no weight to say that the courts, on the pretense [charade] of a repugnancy [an inconsistency between two clauses of a law], may substitute their own pleasure to the constitutional intentions of the legislature. This might as well happen in the case of two contradictory statutes; or it might as well happen in every adjudication upon any single statute. The courts must declare the sense of the law; and if they should be disposed to exercise WILL instead of JUDGMENT, the consequence would equally be the substitution of their pleasure to that of the legislative body. The observation, if it prove any thing, would prove that there ought to be no judges distinct from that body.

If, then, the courts of justice are to be considered as the bulwarks [strong supports] of a limited Constitution against legislative encroachments, this consideration will afford a strong argument for the permanent tenure of judicial offices, since nothing will contribute so much as this to that independent spirit in the judges which must be essential to the faithful performance of so arduous a duty.

This independence of the judges is equally requisite to guard the Constitution and the rights of individuals from the effects of those ill humors, which the arts of designing men, or the influence of particular conjunctures, sometimes disseminate among the people themselves, and which, though they speedily give place to better information, and more deliberate reflection, have a tendency, in the meantime, to occasion dangerous innovations in the government, and serious oppressions of the minor party in the community. Though I trust the friends of the proposed Constitution will never concur with its enemies, in questioning that fundamental principle of republican government, which admits the right of the people to alter or abolish the established Constitution, whenever they find it inconsistent with their happiness, yet it is not to be inferred from this principle, that the representatives of the people, whenever a momentary inclination happens to lay hold of a majority of their constituents, incompatible with the provisions in the existing Constitution, would, on that account, be justifiable in a violation of those provisions; or that the courts would be under a greater obligation to connive at infractions [violations] in this shape, than when they had proceeded wholly from the cabals of the representative body. Until the people have, by some solemn and authoritative act, annulled or changed the established form, it is binding upon themselves collectively, as well as individually; and no presumption, or even knowledge, of their sentiments, can warrant their representatives in a departure from it, prior to such an act. But it is easy to see, that it would require an uncommon portion of fortitude in the judges to do their duty as faithful guardians of the Constitution, where legislative invasions of it had been instigated by the major voice of the community.

But it is not with a view to infractions of the Constitution only, that the independence of the judges may be an essential safeguard against the effects of occasional ill humors in the society. These sometimes extend no farther than to the injury of the private rights of particular classes of citizens, by unjust and partial laws. Here also the firmness of the judicial magistracy is of vast importance in mitigating the severity and confining the operation of such laws. It not only serves to moderate the immediate mischiefs of those which may have been passed, but it operates as a check upon the legislative body in passing them; who, perceiving that obstacles to the success of iniquitous intention are to be expected from the scruples of the courts, are in a manner compelled, by the very motives of the injustice they meditate, to qualify their attempts. This is a circumstance calculated to have more influence upon the character of our governments, than but few may be aware of. The benefits of the integrity and moderation of the judiciary have already been felt in more States than one; and though they may have displeased those whose sinister expectations they may have disappointed, they must have commanded the esteem and applause of all the virtuous and disinterested. Considerate men, of every description, ought to prize whatever will tend to beget or fortify that temper in the courts: as no man can be sure that he may not be to-morrow the victim of a spirit of injustice, by which he may be a gainer to-day. And every man must now feel, that the inevitable tendency of such a spirit is to sap the foundations of public and private confidence, and to introduce in its stead universal distrust and distress.

That inflexible and uniform adherence to the rights of the Constitution, and of individuals, which we perceive to be indispensable in the courts of justice, can certainly not be expected from judges who hold their offices by a temporary commission. Periodical appointments, however regulated, or by whomsoever made, would, in some way or other, be fatal to their necessary independence. If the power of making them was committed either to the Executive or legislature, there would be danger of an improper complaisance to the branch which possessed it; if to both, there would be an unwillingness to hazard the displeasure of either; if to the people, or to persons chosen by them for the special purpose, there would be too great a disposition to consult popularity, to justify a reliance that nothing would be consulted but the Constitution and the laws.

There is yet a further and a weightier reason for the permanency of the judicial offices, which is deducible from the nature of the qualifications they require. It has been frequently remarked, with great propriety, that a voluminous code of laws is one of the inconveniences necessarily connected with the advantages of a free government. To avoid an arbitrary discretion in the courts, it is indispensable that they should be bound down by strict rules and precedents, which serve to define and point out their duty in every particular case that comes before them; and it will readily be conceived from the variety of controversies which grow out of the folly and wickedness of mankind, that the records of those precedents must unavoidably swell to a very considerable bulk, and must demand long and laborious study to acquire a competent knowledge of them. Hence it is, that there can be but few men in the society who will have sufficient skill in the laws to qualify them for the stations of judges. And making the proper deductions for the ordinary depravity of human nature, the number must be still smaller of those who unite the requisite integrity with the requisite knowledge. These considerations apprise us, that the government can have no great option between fit character; and that a temporary duration in office, which would naturally discourage such characters from quitting a lucrative line of practice to accept a seat on the bench, would have a tendency to throw the administration of justice into hands less able, and less well qualified, to conduct it with utility and dignity. In the present circumstances of this country, and in those in which it is likely to be for a long time to come, the disadvantages on this score would be greater than they may at first sight appear; but it must be confessed, that they are far inferior to those which present themselves under the other aspects of the subject.

Upon the whole, there can be no room to doubt that the convention acted wisely in copying from the models of those constitutions which have established good behavior as the tenure of their judicial offices, in point of duration; and that so far from being blamable on this account, their plan would have been inexcusably defective, if it had wanted this important feature of good government. The experience of Great Britain affords an illustrious comment on the excellence of the institution.

PUBLIUS

THOMAS JEFFERSON, "AGAINST JUDICIAL SUPREMACY IN CONSTITUTIONAL INTERPRETATION" (1815)

WHY THIS READING?

In this correspondence, Jefferson addresses the question of whether or not federal judges have the "exclusive authority" to decide the constitutionality of a law. In answering, he makes reference to what the Constitution explicitly says, and does not say, regarding which branch of the government would have the power to make such decisions. In so doing, he finds that "there is not a word in the Constitution, which has given that power [to declare a law unconstitutional] to them [the federal judiciary] more than to the executive or legislative branches."

Five years later, in a letter to William Jarvis, Jefferson expands this point: "To consider the judges as the ultimate arbiters of all constitutional questions [is] a very dangerous doctrine indeed, and one which would place us under the despotism of an oligarchy. Our judges are as honest as other men and not more so. They have with others the same passions for party, for power, and the privilege of their corps. Their maxim is *boni judicis est ampliare jurisdictionem* [good justice is broad jurisdiction], and their power the more dangerous as they are in office for life and not responsible, as the other functionaries are, to the elective control. The Constitution has erected no such single tribunal, knowing that to whatever hands confided, with the corruptions of time and party, its members would become despots. It has more wisely made all the departments co-equal and co-sovereign within themselves."

Questions to guide you as you read:

- Earlier in this chapter, you read Franklin Roosevelt's criticism of judicial review. Where would you place Jefferson's critique in relation to Roosevelt's?
- Jefferson and Hamilton often found themselves on opposing sides of constitutional issues. What would Hamilton's rejoinder be to Jefferson in this case?

The...question, whether the judges are invested with exclusive authority to decide on the constitutionality of a law, has been heretofore a subject of consideration with me....Certainly there is not a word in the constitution, which has given that power to them more than to the executive or legislative branches. Questions of property, of character and of crime being ascribed to the judges, through a definite course of legal proceeding, laws involving such questions belong, of course, to them; and as they decide on them ultimately and without appeal, they of course decide for themselves. The constitutional validity of the law or laws again prescribing executive action, and to be administered by that branch ultimately and without appeal, the executive must decide for themselves also, whether, under the constitution, they are valid or not. So also as to laws governing the proceedings of the legislature, that body must judge for itself the constitutionality of the law, and equally without appeal or control from its coordinate branches. And, in general, that branch which is to act ultimately, and without appeal, on any law, is the rightful expositor [one who explains the meaning] of the validity of the law, uncontrolled by the opinions of the other coordinate authorities. It may be said that contradictory decisions may arise in such case, and produce inconvenience. This is possible, and is a necessary failing in all human proceedings. Yet the prudence of the public functionaries [officials], and authority of public opinion, will generally produce accommodation....So in the cases of Duane and of William Smith of South Carolina, whose characters of citizenship stood precisely on the same ground, the judges in a question of meum and tuum ["meum and tuum"—to fail to distinguish one's own property from that of others] which came before them, decided that Duane was not a citizen; and in a question of membership, the House of Representatives, under the same words of the same provision, adjudged William Smith to be a citizen. Yet no inconvenience has ensued from these contradictory decisions. This is what I believe myself to be sound. But there is another opinion entertained by some men of such Judgment and information as to lessen my confidence in my own. That is, that the legislature alone is the exclusive expounder of the sense of the constitution, in every part of it whatever. And they allege in its support, that this branch has authority to impeach and punish a member of either of the others acting contrary to its declaration of the sense of the constitution. It may indeed be answered, that an act may still be valid although the party is punished for it, right or wrong. However, this opinion which ascribes exclusive exposition to the legislature, merits respect for its safety, there being in the body of the nation a control over them, which, if expressed by rejection on the subsequent exercise of their elective franchise enlists public opinion against their exposition, and encourages a judge...on a future occasion to adhere to their former opinion. Between these two doctrines, everyone has a right to choose, and I know of no third meriting any respect....

Should the state courts enjoy the same independence afforded the federal courts?

THEODORE ROOSEVELT, "THE RECALL OF JUDICIAL DECISIONS" (1912)

Here, Roosevelt advances the case that the people should be given more direct control over judicial interpretation of the meaning of constitutions. While his explicit target is state constitutions, he was understood at the time to mean the federal constitution also.

WHY THIS READING?
Roosevelt's argument serves as a counterpoint to Tocqueville, who, as you have read, underscores democracy's tendency toward "tyranny of the majority." Roosevelt asserts that it is not tyranny by the majority that needs to be feared most, but rather tyranny over the majority—in this case, by courts acting to protect the special interests of corporations and/or wealthy individuals.

Questions to guide you as you read:

- In the absence of Roosevelt's proposed referendum to the people of "a certain class of cases of judicial decisions," what remedy in the original Constitution would Madison and Hamilton point to as constituting a sufficient check on judicial abuse of power? Why does Roosevelt find this inadequate?
- What form of tyranny does Roosevelt fear more than "tyranny of the majority," and why?

In the *New York World* of Thursday appears a detailed statement that some very eminent [well-respected] lawyers of New York have undertaken the formation of what they style the "Independent Judiciary Association." They propose, to use their own words, "to combat the spread of two ideas," namely, the recall[2] of judges, and the referendum[3] to the people of a certain class of cases of judicial decisions; and they assert, in President Taft's words, that these ideas "lay the axe at the root of the tree of well-ordered freedom." Many of the signers are distinguished men, standing high in their community; but we can gain a clew [clue] as to just what kind of well-ordered freedom they have in mind, the kind of "freedom" to the defense of which they are rushing, when we see among the signers of this call the names of attorneys for a number of corporations not distinguished for a high-keyed sense of civic duty, or for their disinterested conduct toward the public; such as, for instance, the Standard Oil Company, the Sugar Trust, the American Tobacco Company, the Metropolitan Traction Company of New York, and certain defunct corporations, the looting of which has passed into the history of financial and stock-jobbing [the buying and selling of high-risk securities with the intent of making quick profits] scandal, and forms one of its blackest chapters. I find also the name of one of the attorneys for the Northern Securities Company, which some years ago was dissolved at the suit of the government, instituted by my direction; I notice the name of the attorney for the New York Stock Exchange; and I do not overlook that of a member of the bar of New York who some years ago was denounced by

2. Here, by "recall," Roosevelt refers to the popular removal of judges. However, notice that the title of this piece is "The Recall of Judicial Decisions," which refers to the ability of the people to overturn state court decisions.
3. "Referendum" is the submission of proposed legislation or policy that has been passed upon by a legislature or convention to a vote of the people for ratification or rejection.

the very papers now applauding him and his associates, as a retained accelerator of public opinion in favor of certain measures of the Metropolitan Street Railway Company, which at the time were under general denunciation in New York as "traction grabs [corrupt efforts by the railroads (including bribery of government officials) to gain unmerited concessions from local governments]." The head of the association is announced to be Mr. Choate; and one of the members is Mr. Milburn, who in 1904 was the head of the Parker Constitution Club, a similar body, with a similar purpose, namely, to uphold privilege and sustain the special interests against the cause of justice and against the interest of the people as a whole.

I hold absolutely to my conviction that some basis of accommodation must be found between the declared policy of the States on matters of social justice within the proper scope of regulation in the interest of health, of decent living and working conditions, and of morals, and the attempt of the courts to substitute their own ideas on these subjects for the declarations of the people, made through their elected representatives in the several States....

...My proposal is for the exercise of the referendum by the people themselves in a certain class of decisions of constitutional questions in which the courts decide against the power of the people to do elementary justice. When men of trained intelligence call this "putting the axe to the tree of well-ordered freedom," it is quite impossible to reconcile their statements truth with good faith and with even reasonably full knowledge of the facts.

All that is necessary to do in order to prove the absolute correctness of the statement I have just made is to call your attention to the plain and obvious facts in the case. In the first place, consider the present practice in various countries in which there is substantially the same well-ordered freedom as in our own land. For instance, take the republic of France and the great English-speaking commonwealths of the British Empire, England, Canada, Australia, all of which are governed by the Parliaments in substantially the same manner that we are governed. In every country I have named the decision of the legislature on constitutional questions is absolute and not subject to action by the judiciary; and whenever the courts make a decision which the legislature regards as establishing a construction of the constitution which is unwarranted, the legislature, if it chooses, can by law override that construction and establish its own construction of the constitution. Not long ago this very method was adopted in England. On that occasion the courts held that labor-unions could be treated as corporations and sued and money taken from them by process of law. Parliament at once passed a law overriding the decision and summarily declared that the constitution should thereafter be construed by the courts in the directly opposite sense to the construction which they had adopted.

Now, Mr. Milburn is by birth an Englishman, and Mr. Choate has been ambassador to England, and it is quite impossible that they can be sincere in asserting that "well-ordered freedom" would be destroyed in this country by adopting a practice by no means as extreme (from the standpoint of giving the people instead of the courts the ultimate power to decide certain constitutional questions) as the practice which now obtains, and which always has obtained in England, in France since it was a republic, and just across our own border in Canada and in every province of Canada.

Either Messrs. Choate and Milburn hold that there is no "well-ordered freedom" in England, Scotland, in Australia, in Ontario, New Brunswick, or Manitoba, which is preposterous, or else they must admit that they are talking nonsense when they say that the adoption of my proposal would mean the destruction of "well-ordered freedom" in this country. There is no other alternative. If I could truthfully use less harsh language about the attitude of these gentlemen upon this question I would; the language I do use is merely descriptive.

Now, consider my proposal itself; and I shall illustrate it by two or three concrete cases which will show just what the attitude of these great corporation lawyers is on questions of fundamental justice as against special privilege. My proposal is merely to secure to the people the right which the Supreme Court, speaking through Mr. Justice Holmes, in the Oklahoma Bank Cases, says they undoubtedly should possess. My proposal is that the people shall have the power to decide for themselves, in the last resort, what legislation is necessary in exercising the police powers, the general welfare powers, so as to give expression to the general morality, the general opinion, of the people. In England, Canada, and the other countries I have mentioned, no one dreams that the court has a right to express an opinion in such matters as against the will of the people shown by the action of the legislature. I do not propose to go as far as this. I do not propose to do in these matters what England, Canada, Australia, and France have always done, that is, make the legislature supreme over the courts in these cases. I merely propose to make legislature and court alike responsible to the sober and deliberate judgment of the people, who are masters of both legislature and courts.

This proposal is precisely and exactly in line with Lincoln's attitude toward the Supreme Court in the *Dred Scott* case,[4] and with the doctrines he laid down for the rule of the people in his first inaugural as President. Messrs. Choate and Milburn well know that this is true; they well know that my position in no essential way differs from the principles laid down and acted upon by Abraham Lincoln in this matter. I am not dealing with any case of justice as between man and man, nor am I speaking of the Federal courts, which, because of the peculiar features of our Constitution, must be treated by themselves. Nor am I speaking of the recall of judges, a measure which I do not wish to see adopted in any community unless it proves impossible in any other way to get the judges to do justice—and I will add that nothing will so tend to strengthen the movement for the recall as action like this of Messrs. Choate and Milburn, and their associates, in seeking to buttress special privilege in the courts and to make them the bulwark of injustice instead of justice. I am seeking to introduce a system which will obviate the need of such a drastic measure as the recall. If in any case the legislature has passed a law under the police power for the purpose of promoting social and industrial justice and the courts declare it in conflict with the fundamental law of the State, the constitution as laid down by the people, then I propose that after due deliberation—for a period which could not be for less than two years after the passage of the original law—the people shall themselves have the right to declare whether or not the proposed law is to be treated as constitutional.

It is a matter of mere terminology whether this is called a method of construing or applying the Constitution, or a quicker method of getting the Constitution amended. It is certainly far superior to the ordinary method of getting the Constitution amended, because it will apply merely to the case at issue, and therefore would be definite and clear in its action; whereas, actual experience with the Fourteenth Amendment to the National Constitution, for instance, has shown us that an amendment passed by the people with one purpose may be given by the courts a construction which makes it apply to wholly different purposes and in a wholly different manner. The Fourteenth Amendment has been construed by the courts to apply to a multitude of cases to which it is positive the people who passed the amendment had not the remotest idea of applying it....

...The best way to test the merits of my proposal is to consider a few specimen [sample] cases to which it would apply. Within the last thirty years the court of appeals of New York has been one of the most formidable obstacles to social reform, one of the most formidable obstacles in the way of getting industrial justice, which men who strive for justice have had to encounter. Among very many other laws which this court has made abortive [imperfect or inoperative], or decided not to be laws on the ground that they conflicted with the Constitution, are the following:

1. The law for preventing the manufacture of tobacco in tenement-houses; the decision

4. The reference here is to *Dred Scott v. Sandford*, the infamous 1857 Supreme Court case that ruled that slaves were not included in the Declaration of Independence's phrase "all men are created equal," were not considered part of the Constitution's "We the people," and had no legal existence under the Constitution. Moreover, contrary to years of political practice, the Court ruled that Congress had no right to legislate with respect to slavery in the Western Territories. Lincoln vehemently disagreed with the decision and proposed that the new Republican Party do everything it could to have the decision overruled.

of the court in this case retarded by at least twenty years the work of tenement-house reform, and was directly responsible for causing hundreds of thousands of American citizens now alive to be brought up under conditions of reeking filth and squalor, which immeasurably decreased their chance of turning out to be good citizens. Yet his decision was rendered by perfectly well-meaning men who knew law, but who did not know life, and who, forsooth, based their decision on the ground that they would not permit legislation to interfere with the "sanctity of the home"—the home in question in many cases having precisely the "sanctity" that attaches to one room in which two large families, one with a boarder, live and work day and night, the tobacco they manufacture being surrounded with every kind of filth.

2. The courts held unconstitutional the law under which a girl was endeavoring to recover damages for the loss of her arm, taken off because dangerous machinery was not guarded. In this case the judges announced that they were "protecting the girl's liberty" to work where she would endanger life and limb if she chose! Of course, as the girl had no liberty save the "liberty" of starving or else of working under the dangerous conditions, the courts were merely protecting the liberty of her employer to endanger the lives of his employees, or kill or cripple them, with immunity to himself. I do not believe that in our entire history there is an instance in which a majority of the voters have showed such tyranny and such callous indifference to the suffering of a minority as were shown by these doubtless well-meaning judges in this case.

3. When the legislature of New York passed a law limiting the hours of labor of women in factories to ten hours a day for six days a week, and forbade their being employed after nine in the evening and before six in the morning, the New York court of appeals declared it unconstitutional, and a malign [evil] inspiration induced them to state in their opinion that the time had come for courts "fearlessly" to interpose [inject] a barrier against such legislation. Fearlessly! The court fearlessly condemned helpless women to be worked at inhuman toil for hours so long as to make it impossible that they should retain health or strength; and "fearlessly" upheld the right of big factory owners and small sweatshop owners to coin money out of the blood of the wretched women and girls whom they worked haggard for their own profit. To protect such wrongdoers was of course an outrage upon the decent and high-minded factory owners who did not wish to work the women and girls to an excessive degree, but who were forced to do so by the competition of the callous factory owners whom the court, by this decision, deliberately aided and abetted in their wrong-doing. Court after court in other States, including as conservative a State as Massachusetts, have declared such a law as this constitutional, yet the court of appeals in New York declared it unconstitutional. No popular majority vote could ever be more inconsistent with another popular majority vote than is the record of the court of appeals of New York in this matter when compared with the record of other courts in other States.

4. The Workmen's Compensation Act, but a year or two ago, was declared unconstitutional by the court of appeals of New York, although a directly reverse decision in precisely similar language had been rendered not only by the State courts of Iowa and Washington, but by the Supreme Court of the United States. Here again it is worth while to point out that no vote by popular majority could render the Constitution more uncertain of construction than the court of appeals of New York rendered it by making the decision it did in the teeth of the decision of the Supreme Court and of other State courts; and throughout our history no decision by a majority of the people in any State has shown more flagrant disregard

> of the elementary rights of a minority, no popular vote has ever in any State more flagrantly denied justice, than was the case in this decision by the highest court of the State of New York, but a year or two ago.

Now, in these cases in New York under the plan I propose, the people of the State of New York, after due deliberation, would have had an opportunity to decide for themselves whether the constitution which they themselves made should or should not be so construed as to prevent them from doing elementary justice in these matters. Remember also that in this case the conflict was not only between the New York legislature and the New York court. The New York court also took square issue, in its construction of constitutional provisions, with the position taken by State courts elsewhere in the Union, and with the position taken by the Supreme Court of the United States.

It would be an absolute physical impossibility for the people of the State, voting at the polls, to have interpreted the constitution more mischievously than the court of appeals has repeatedly interpreted it during the last quarter of a century, as regards the class of cases which I am now considering.

My proposal is merely to give the people an effective constitutional weapon for use against wrong and injustice. Messrs. Choate and Milburn and their allies, in taking the position they do, nakedly champion vested wrong. They appear as the champions and apologists[5] of privilege as against the mass of our people—the farmers, the working men, the small shopkeeper, the decent hard-working citizens of every grade. They defend the courts because the courts in these cases I have mentioned have done injustice, have decided against the people, have decided in favor of the special interests and in favor of privilege. I do not question the good intentions of most of the great lawyers who take this attitude. But the only alternative to questioning their good intentions is to admit that their life-long association with corporations, the habits they have contracted by acting as highly paid special pleaders for privilege, for special interests and for vested wrong, and their utter ignorance of real life and of the needs of the people as a whole, have rendered them unfit to act as advisers of the public, unfit to know what justice is.

Messrs. Choate and Milburn and their associates in effect take the position that the people have not the right to secure workmen's compensation laws, or laws limiting the hours of labor for women in factories, or laws protecting workers from dangerous machinery, or laws making conditions decent in tenement-houses. It is a mere sham for any man to say that he approves of such laws so long as he upholds the courts in declaring them unconstitutional, so long as he fails to approve thoroughgoing action which will give the people power, with reasonable speed, to upset such court decision and to secure real and substantial justice. Messrs. Choate and Milburn say that we are "putting the axe to the root of the tree of well-ordered freedom," when we ask that New York—and every other State where there is need—take effective steps to provide such legislation as many other States of the Union already possess, and as almost every other civilized country outside of the United States has on the statute-books. A more absurd plea was never made than this plea that "well-ordered freedom" will be destroyed by doing justice to men, women, and children who are ground down by excessive toil under conditions ruinous to life and limb; and this, and precisely this, and nothing but this, is what our opponents say when their statement is stripped of verbiage [the use of too many words]. In this matter Messrs. Choate and Milburn and their associates appear as the attorneys of privilege, as special pleaders for special interests, and as the representatives of those great corporations that deny justice to small competitors and to their employees and their customers; and they appear against the people as a whole, and are hostile to the essentials of justice.

Vermont is a State in which "well-ordered freedom" certainly obtains. Are Messrs. Choate and Milburn aware that in Vermont the actual practice about the judges is that they are appointed practically for life, but subject to recall, and therefore to a referendum on their actions, every two years? In that State, the judges are elected by the legislature,

5 An "apologist" is one who argues in defense of a person or cause.

and in practice the legislature always re-elects the judge as long as he wishes to serve, unless he proves unfaithful, when the principle of the recall is applied by the simple process of not re-electing him. In the last twenty or thirty years this has been done in but one case. In Vermont the judges are as upright and independent as any judges in the Union; but in constitutional cases such as those I have mentioned they do really represent, and not misrepresent, the people.

In short, Messrs. Choate and Milburn and their associates, if their language is to be accepted as sincere, know nothing of the position taken by courts and legislatures in other lands as regards these constitutional questions, know little as to what has been done in certain of our own States thereon, and know practically nothing about the needs of the immense bulk of their countrymen. They do not even know what is elementary knowledge among the men specially trained in constitutional law in their country; men like Dean Lewis, of the University of Pennsylvania Law School, and Professor Scaffold, professor of law at the Northwestern Law School. In a recent article Professor Scaffold has shown that the State courts of Illinois have behaved no better than the State courts of New York in these matters. He quotes the emphatic criticisms of these decisions of which I complain by the late Dean Thayer, of the Harvard Law School. He says that these decisions make of the law a weapon with which the strong can strike down the weak, that they make of the law not a shield to protect the people, but a sword to smite [strike] down the people; that they are arbitrary, and that our protest against them represents one phase of the struggle against arbitrary power[6] and in favor of the law of the land, and he sees that my proposal is merely to use a constitutional method to restore to the State law-making bodies the power which the Supreme Court of this nation says belongs to them.

There are sincere and well-meaning men of timid nature who are frightened by the talk of tyranny of the majority. Those worthy gentlemen are nearly a century behind the times. It is true that De Tocqueville, writing about eighty years ago, said that in this country there was great tyranny by the majority. This statement may have been true then, although certainly not to the degree he insisted, but it is not true now. That profound and keen thinker, Mr. James Bryce, in "The American Commonwealth" treats of this in his chapter on the "Tyranny of the Majority" by saying that it does not exist. His own words are that:

"It is no longer a blemish on the American system, and the charges against democracy from the supposed example of America are groundless. The fact that the danger once dreaded has now disappeared is no small evidence of the recuperative forces of the American Government, and the healthy tone of the American people."

I wish that our opponents... who so dread and distrust the American people, would in this matter copy the good faith and sanity of the learned and able ambassador from Great Britain.

I shall protest against the tyranny of the majority whenever it arises, just as I shall protest against every other form of tyranny. But at present we are not suffering in any way from the tyranny of the majority. We suffer from the tyranny of the bosses and of the special interests, that is, from the tyranny of minorities. Mr. Choate, Mr. Milburn, and their allies are acting as the servants and spokesmen of the special interests and are standing cheek by jowl with the worst representatives of politics when they seek to keep the courts in the grasp of privilege and of the politicians; for this is all they accomplish when they prevent them from being responsible in proper fashion to the people. These worthy gentlemen speak as if the judges were somehow imposed on us by Heaven, and were responsible only to Heaven. As a matter of fact judges are human just like other people, and in this country they will either be chosen by the people and responsible to the people, or they will be chosen by, and responsible to, the bosses and the special interests and the political and financial beneficiaries of privilege. It is this last system which Mr. Choate and Mr. Milburn and their allies are by their actions upholding. In the course they are

6 Here, "arbitrary power" refers to tyrannical power that is based upon one's own will or opinion, rather than upon the rule of law.

taking, they and the respectable men associated with them, are, in some cases certainly unconsciously, and in other cases I fear consciously, acting on behalf of the special interests, political and financial, and in favor of privilege, and against the interest of the plain people and against the cause of justice and of human right. In the long run this country will not be a good place for any of us to live in unless it is a reasonably good place for all of us to live in; and it will neither become nor remain a good place for all of us to live in if we permit our government to be turned aside from its original purpose and to become a government . . . by corporation attorneys on the bench and off the bench; and this without regard . . . whether they are or are not conscious of the fact that they are really serving the cause of special privilege and not the cause of the people.

CHAPTER 7

Core Question: What do our persistent debates over religion, citizenship, and law reveal about the nature of American democracy?

Based on what we have read in the preceding six chapters, we should be ready to fully apply the point-counterpoint mode of presentation to three issues that have given rise to vigorous debates from the Founding to this day: (1) the place of religion, (2) the rights of citizenship, and (3) the status of the law.

It is common knowledge that a good number of the early, and not-so-early, immigrants to this country were motivated primarily by the desire to settle in a land where they would be able to practice their religious beliefs without fear of government persecution. As discussed in chapter one, the American "credo," as articulated in the Declaration of Independence, makes no demands regarding religious belief when it comes to the issue of American citizenship. At the same, it explicitly says that our inalienable rights are "endowed by our Creator." "Americanism" is defined as adherence to the moral and political principles found in the Declaration: human equality, inalienable rights, government instituted by consent, and the right of revolution. But if the Declaration liberates the concept of citizenship from the Old World ties of state-sanctioned religion and aristocratic birth, it also produces a potential problem: As you will read, its right of revolution has been interpreted to encourage lawlessness.

On the subject of the status of religion in American democracy, all are agreed that the Constitution seeks to establish religious liberty. Indeed, the very first clause of the First Amendment guarantees that Congress shall neither establish a national religion (as was the case in some of the European countries from which the colonists emigrated) nor interfere with religious worship. But powerful disagreement exists regarding whether religion might be better understood as a political institution in, or as a political problem for, American democracy. In tracking this debate, we turn to expositions on this subject by George Washington, Tocqueville, Thomas Jefferson, the

Supreme Court opinion in *Everson v. Board of Education*, Ronald Reagan, and Walter Mondale. As you will read, Washington, Tocqueville, and Reagan stress the role that religion plays as a political institution in America, whereas Jefferson, *Everson*, and Mondale tend to focus more on the problem that religion can pose for democratic liberty.

What makes one an American citizen? Although the Declaration revolutionized the concept of citizenship, it has also given rise to unresolved questions that are still as powerfully present with us today as at the time of the Founding. We begin the chapter's examination of this debate with the 14th Amendment to the U.S. Constitution, which was ratified in 1868. We then turn to some key precursors to the passage of the Amendment, beginning with the issue of race and citizenship as offered in the course of the Lincoln–Douglas debates. In these debates, we encounter the deepest dialogue over American identity in our history. In the course of their seven debates over the summer and fall of 1858, Lincoln and Douglas both addressed, with opposing conclusions, the infamous Supreme Court decision in *Dred Scott v. Sandford* (1857). This decision interpreted the Declaration of Independence to assert that blacks "had no rights which the white man was bound to respect." Accordingly, we conclude this section of the chapter with Chief Justice Taney's opinion for the Court in *Dred Scott*.

Third and last, we turn to the debate concerning whether the principles underlying American democracy encourage or discourage law-abidingness. We begin with the full text of the Declaration of Independence, wherein is found the assertion of the natural or inalienable right to rebel against despotic government. We then compare Lincoln's and Frederick Douglass's answers to the question "What is law-abidingness?," which are offered in the course of their biting critiques of the *Dred Scott v. Sandford* decision. Finally, we consult Lincoln, Tocqueville, and the Reverend Dr. Martin Luther King Jr. for their differing takes on the questions of whether and why American citizens have a duty to obey the law.

The debate over whether religion is a problem for, or an essential institution of, American democracy

How can religion be understood to be a "political institution" in American democracy?

GEORGE WASHINGTON, "FAREWELL ADDRESS" (1796)

The original Constitution was criticized by the anti-Federalists for, among other things, a lack of what later came to be called a "Bill of Rights" (which refers today primarily to the first ten amendments to the Constitution). Hamilton's Publius strenuously objected to the addition of such, arguing that a Bill of Rights was not only "unnecessary" but also "dangerous." "[T]he Constitution is itself, in every rational sense, and to every useful purpose, A BILL OF RIGHTS" (*Federalist 84*). Nevertheless, fearing that the proposed Constitution would not be ratified, its defenders agreed to consider the proposed amendments *after* the Constitution was approved. As a result, in 1791, the first ten amendments to the Constitution were ratified. The First Amendment, among other things, prohibits Congress from establishing a government-supported religion (the "Establishment Clause") and from infringing on the exercise of any religion (the

"Free Exercise" Clause): "Congress shall make no law respecting an establishment of religion, or prohibiting the free exercise thereof; or abridging the freedom of speech, or of the press; or the right of the people peaceably to assemble, and to petition the Government for a redress of grievances."

Washington's "Farewell Address" speaks in part to the question of the place of religion in American democracy. In 1796, Washington decided that he would not accept a nomination for a third term as president. His Farewell Address was written with the substantial aid of Alexander Hamilton, who had served as Washington's secretary of the Treasury.

WHY THIS READING?

Washington focuses on religion's place as a political institution of American democracy. This arises in the context of his warning to his country to combat the "spirit of party," which he uses synonymously with "faction." (Recall that Madison's Publius, in *Federalist 10*, argues that faction is the "mortal disease" of "popular government." A faction is any group united by an interest or passion adverse either to the common good or to private rights.) It is here that Washington offers his praise of religion, which he deems indispensable to public morality: "[L]et us with caution entertain the supposition that morality can be maintained without religion."

Questions to guide you as you read:

- What does Washington regard as the key elements accounting for the political utility of religion in American democracy?
- Is Washington's argument on behalf of the utility of religion such that one must be a religious believer to accept it? If so, why? If not, why not?

Friends and Citizens:

The period for a new election of a citizen to administer the executive government of the United States being not far distant, and the time actually arrived when your thoughts must be employed in designating the person who is to be clothed with that important trust, it appears to me proper, especially as it may conduce to a more distinct expression of the public voice, that I should now apprise you of the resolution I have formed, to decline being considered among the number of those out of whom a choice is to be made....

...I rejoice that the state of your concerns, external as well as internal, no longer renders the pursuit of inclination incompatible with the sentiment of duty or propriety, and am persuaded, whatever partiality may be retained for my services, that, in the present circumstances of our country, you will not disapprove my determination to retire....

...In looking forward to the moment which is intended to terminate the career of my public life, my feelings do not permit me to suspend the deep acknowledgment of that debt of gratitude which I owe to my beloved country for the many honors it has conferred upon me; still more for the steadfast confidence with which it has supported me; and for the opportunities I have thence enjoyed of manifesting my inviolable [sacred, unbreakable] attachment, by services faithful and persevering, though in usefulness unequal to my zeal [enthusiasm]....Here, perhaps, I ought to stop. But a solicitude [concern] for your welfare, which cannot end but with my life, and the apprehension [fear] of danger, natural to that solicitude, urge me, on an occasion like the present, to offer to your solemn contemplation, and to recommend to your frequent review, some sentiments which are the result of much reflection, of no inconsiderable observation, and which appear to me all-important to the permanency of your felicity [happiness] as a people. These will be offered to you with the more freedom, as you can only see in them the disinterested [unbiased] warnings of a parting friend, who can possibly have no personal motive to bias his counsel....

Interwoven as is the love of liberty with every ligament [muscle] of your hearts, no recommendation of mine is necessary to fortify or confirm the attachment.

The unity of government which constitutes you one people is also now dear to you. It is justly so, for it is a main pillar in the edifice of your real independence, the support of your tranquility at home, your peace abroad; of your safety; of your prosperity; of that very liberty which you so highly prize. But as it is easy to foresee that, from different causes and from different quarters, much pains will be taken, many artifices employed to weaken in your minds the conviction of this truth; as this is the point in your political fortress against which the batteries of internal and external enemies will be most constantly and actively (though often covertly and insidiously) directed, it is of infinite moment that you should properly estimate the immense value of your national union to your collective and individual happiness; that you should cherish a cordial, habitual, and immovable attachment to it; accustoming yourselves to think and speak of it as of the palladium [safeguard] of your political safety and prosperity; watching for its preservation with jealous anxiety; discountenancing [discouraging] whatever may suggest even a suspicion that it can in any event be abandoned; and indignantly frowning upon the first dawning of every attempt to alienate any portion of our country from the rest, or to enfeeble the sacred ties which now link together the various parts.

For this you have every inducement [incentive] of sympathy and interest. Citizens, by birth or choice, of a common country, that country has a right to concentrate your affections. The name of American, which belongs to you in your national capacity, must always exalt the just pride of patriotism more than any appellation [title] derived from local discriminations. With slight shades of difference, you have the same religion, manners, habits, and political principles. You have in a common cause fought and triumphed together; the independence and liberty you possess are the work of joint counsels, and joint efforts of common dangers, sufferings, and successes.

But these considerations, however powerfully they address themselves to your sensibility, are greatly outweighed by those which apply more immediately to your interest. Here every portion of our country finds the most commanding motives for carefully guarding and preserving the union of the whole.

The North, in an unrestrained intercourse [association] with the South, protected by the equal laws of a common government, finds in the productions of the latter great additional resources of maritime and commercial enterprise and precious materials of manufacturing industry. The South, in the same intercourse, benefiting by the agency [activity] of the North, sees its agriculture grow and its commerce expand.... While, then, every part of our country thus feels an immediate and particular interest in union, all the parts combined cannot fail to find in the united mass of means and efforts greater strength, greater resource, proportionably greater security from external danger, a less frequent interruption of their peace by foreign nations; and, what is of inestimable value, they must derive from union an exemption from those broils [brawls] and wars between themselves, which so frequently afflict neighboring countries not tied together by the same governments, which their own rival ships alone would be sufficient to produce, but which opposite foreign alliances, attachments, and intrigues would stimulate and embitter. Hence, likewise, they will avoid the necessity of those overgrown military establishments which, under any form of government, are inauspicious [unfavorable] to liberty, and which are to be regarded as particularly hostile to republican liberty. In this sense it is that your union ought to be considered as a main prop of your liberty, and that the love of the one ought to endear to you the preservation of the other.

These considerations speak a persuasive language to every reflecting and virtuous mind, and exhibit the continuance of the Union as a primary object of patriotic desire. Is there a doubt whether a common government can embrace so large a sphere? Let experience solve it. To listen to mere speculation in such a case were criminal. We are authorized to hope that a proper organization of the whole with the auxiliary [supporting] agency of governments for the respective subdivisions, will afford a happy issue to the experiment. It is well worth a fair and full experiment. With such powerful and obvious motives to union, affecting all parts of our country, while experience shall not have demonstrated its impracticability, there will always be reason to distrust the patriotism of those who in any quarter may endeavor to weaken its bands.

In contemplating the causes which may disturb our Union, it occurs as matter of serious concern that any ground should have been furnished for characterizing parties by geographical discriminations, Northern and Southern, Atlantic and Western; whence designing men may endeavor to excite a belief that there is a real difference of local interests and views. One of the expedients of party to acquire influence within particular districts is to misrepresent the opinions and aims of other districts. You cannot shield yourselves too much against the jealousies and heart-burnings which spring from these misrepresentations; they tend to render alien to each other those who ought to be bound together by fraternal affection....

To the efficacy and permanency of your Union, a government for the whole is indispensable. No alliance, however strict, between the parts can be an adequate substitute; they must inevitably experience the infractions and interruptions which all alliances in all times have experienced. Sensible of this momentous [historic] truth, you have improved upon your first essay, by the adoption of a constitution of government better calculated than your former for an intimate union, and for the efficacious management of your common concerns. This government, the offspring of our own choice, uninfluenced and un-awed, adopted upon full investigation and mature deliberation, completely free in its principles, in the distribution of its powers, uniting security with energy, and containing within itself a provision for its own amendment, has a just claim to your confidence and your support. Respect for its authority, compliance with its laws, acquiescence in its measures, are duties enjoined by the fundamental maxims of true liberty. The basis of our political systems is the right of the people to make and to alter their constitutions of government. But the Constitution which at any time exists, till changed by an explicit and authentic act of the whole people, is sacredly obligatory upon all. The very idea of the power and the right of the people to establish government presupposes the duty of every individual to obey the established government.

All obstructions to the execution of the laws, all combinations and associations, under whatever plausible character, with the real design to direct, control, counteract, or awe the regular deliberation and action of the constituted authorities, are destructive of this fundamental principle, and of fatal tendency. They serve to organize faction, to give it an artificial and extraordinary force; to put, in the place of the delegated will of the nation the will of a party, often a small but artful and enterprising minority of the community; and, according to the alternate triumphs of different parties, to make the public administration the mirror of the ill-concerted and incongruous projects of faction, rather than the organ of consistent and wholesome plans digested by common counsels and modified by mutual interests.

However combinations or associations of the above description may now and then answer popular ends, they are likely, in the course of time and things, to become potent engines, by which cunning, ambitious, and unprincipled men will be enabled to subvert the power of the people and to usurp for themselves the reins of government, destroying afterwards the very engines which have lifted them to unjust dominion.

Towards the preservation of your government, and the permanency of your present happy state, it is requisite, not only that you steadily discountenance irregular oppositions to its acknowledged authority, but also that you resist with care the spirit of innovation upon its principles, however specious the pretexts. One method of assault may be to effect, in the forms of the Constitution, alterations which will impair the energy of the system, and thus to undermine what cannot be directly overthrown. In all the changes to which you may be invited, remember that time and habit are at least as necessary to fix the true character of governments as of other human institutions; that experience is the surest standard by which to test the real tendency of the existing constitution of a country; that facility in changes, upon the credit of mere hypothesis and opinion, exposes to perpetual change, from the endless variety of hypothesis and opinion; and remember, especially, that for the efficient management of your common interests, in a country so extensive as ours, a government of as much vigor as is consistent with the perfect security of liberty is indispensable. Liberty itself will find in such a government, with powers properly distributed and adjusted, its surest guardian. It is, indeed, little else than a name, where the government is too feeble to withstand the enterprises of faction, to confine each member of the society within the limits prescribed by the laws, and to maintain all in the secure and tranquil enjoyment of the rights of person and property.

I have already intimated to you the danger of parties in the State, with particular reference to the founding of them on geographical discriminations. Let me now take a more comprehensive view, and warn you in the most solemn manner against the baneful effects of the spirit of party generally.

This spirit, unfortunately, is inseparable from our nature, having its root in the strongest passions of the human mind. It exists under different shapes in all governments, more or less stifled, controlled, or repressed; but, in those of the popular form, it is seen in its greatest rankness, and is truly their worst enemy.

The alternate domination of one faction over another, sharpened by the spirit of revenge, natural to party dissension, which in different ages and countries has perpetrated the most horrid enormities, is itself a frightful despotism. But this leads at length to a more formal and permanent despotism. The disorders and miseries which result gradually incline the minds of men to seek security and repose in the absolute power of an individual; and sooner or later the chief of some prevailing faction, more able or more fortunate than his competitors, turns this disposition to the purposes of his own elevation, on the ruins of public liberty.

Without looking forward to an extremity of this kind (which nevertheless ought not to be entirely out of sight), the common and continual mischiefs of the spirit of party are sufficient to make it the interest and duty of a wise people to discourage and restrain it.

It serves always to distract the public councils and enfeeble the public administration. It agitates the community with ill-founded jealousies and false alarms, kindles the animosity of one part against another, foments [stirs up] occasionally riot and insurrection. It opens the door to foreign influence and corruption, which finds a facilitated access to the government itself through the channels of party passions. Thus the policy and the will of one country are subjected to the policy and will of another.

There is an opinion that parties in free countries are useful checks upon the administration of the government and serve to keep alive the spirit of liberty. This within certain limits is probably true; and in governments of a monarchical cast, patriotism may look with indulgence, if not with favor, upon the spirit of party. But in those of the popular character, in governments purely elective, it is a spirit not to be encouraged. From their natural tendency, it is certain there will always be enough of that spirit for every salutary purpose. And there being constant danger of excess, the effort ought to be by force of public opinion, to mitigate and assuage it. A fire not to be quenched, it demands a uniform vigilance to prevent its bursting into a flame, lest, instead of warming, it should consume.

It is important, likewise, that the habits of thinking in a free country should inspire caution in those entrusted with its administration, to confine themselves within their respective constitutional spheres, avoiding in the exercise of the powers of one department to encroach upon another. The spirit of encroachment tends to consolidate the powers of all the departments in one, and thus to create, whatever the form of government, a real despotism. A just estimate of that love of power, and proneness to abuse it, which predominates in the human heart, is sufficient to satisfy us of the truth of this position. The necessity of reciprocal checks in the exercise of political power, by dividing and distributing it into different depositaries, and constituting each the guardian of the public weal against invasions by the others, has been evinced by experiments ancient and modern; some of them in our country and under our own eyes. To preserve them must be as necessary as to institute them. If, in the opinion of the people, the distribution or modification of the constitutional powers be in any particular wrong, let it be corrected by an amendment in the way which the Constitution designates. But let there be no change by usurpation; for though this, in one instance, may be the instrument of good, it is the customary weapon by which free governments are destroyed. The precedent must always greatly overbalance in permanent evil any partial or transient benefit, which the use can at any time yield.

Of all the dispositions and habits which lead to political prosperity, religion and morality are indispensable supports. In vain would that man claim the tribute of patriotism, who should labor to subvert these great pillars of human happiness, these firmest props of the duties of men and citizens. The mere politician, equally with the pious man, ought to respect and to cherish them. A volume could not trace all their connections with private and public felicity. Let it simply be asked: Where is the security for property, for reputation, for life, if the sense of religious obligation desert the oaths which are the instruments of investigation in courts of justice? And let us with caution indulge the supposition that morality can be maintained without religion. Whatever may be conceded to the influence of refined education on minds of peculiar structure, reason and experience both forbid us to expect that national morality can prevail in exclusion of religious principle.

It is substantially true that virtue or morality is a necessary spring of popular government. The rule, indeed, extends with more or less force to every species of free government. Who that is a sincere friend to it can look with indifference upon attempts to shake the foundation of the fabric?

Promote then, as an object of primary importance, institutions for the general diffusion of knowledge. In proportion as the structure of a government gives force to public opinion, it is essential that public opinion should be enlightened....

...Observe good faith and justice towards all nations; cultivate peace and harmony with all. Religion and morality enjoin this conduct; and can it be, that good policy does not equally enjoin it? It will be worthy of a free, enlightened, and at no distant period, a great nation, to give to mankind the magnanimous and too novel example of a people always guided by an exalted justice and benevolence. Who can doubt that, in the course of time and things, the fruits of such a plan would richly repay any temporary advantages which might be lost by a steady adherence to it? Can it be that Providence has not connected the permanent felicity of a nation with its virtue? The experiment, at least, is recommended by every sentiment which ennobles human nature. Alas! is it rendered impossible by its vices?

...Though, in reviewing the incidents of my administration, I am unconscious of intentional error, I am nevertheless too sensible of my defects not to think it probable that I may have committed many errors. Whatever they may be, I fervently beseech the Almighty to avert or mitigate the evils to which they may tend. I shall also carry with me the hope that my country will never cease to view them with indulgence; and that, after forty five years of my life dedicated to its service with an upright zeal, the faults of incompetent abilities will be consigned to oblivion, as myself must soon be to the mansions of rest.

Relying on its kindness in this as in other things, and actuated by that fervent love towards it, which is so natural to a man who views in it the native soil of himself and his progenitors for several generations, I anticipate with pleasing expectation that retreat in which I promise myself to realize, without alloy, the sweet enjoyment of partaking, in the midst of my fellow-citizens, the benign influence of good laws under a free government, the ever-favorite object of my heart, and the happy reward, as I trust, of our mutual cares, labors, and dangers.

ALEXIS DE TOCQUEVILLE, *DEMOCRACY IN AMERICA*, "ON RELIGION AS A POLITICAL INSTITUTION" (1835)

Here, Tocqueville advances the proposition that religion is, in practice, a "political institution" that enhances American democracy.

WHY THIS READING?

Tocqueville does not argue from the standpoint of a religious believer, but rather with a view to the "political utility [usefulness]" of religion in maintaining a democratic republic. He finds this utility to grow out of the fact that religion and politics are institutionally separated in the United States. When religion joins itself directly to politics, he argues, citizens lose respect for it, because it has traded "immortal" concerns for a voice in day-to-day political squabbles. Religion best teaches citizens "the art of living free" precisely when it refrains from speaking directly about politics. This separation accounts for the fact, says Tocqueville, that "there is no country in the world where the Christian religion retains a greater influence over the souls of men than in America." By restricting itself to other-worldly concerns, religion combats the tendencies of democratic citizens to focus solely on material well-being, to retreat within themselves and their small, private circles. In the absence of such faith-based instruction, democratic liberty will, he fears, degenerate into license: "Despotism may govern without faith, but liberty cannot." Because the institutional separation of church and state is indispensable if religion is to safeguard liberty and equality, he expresses concerns about Islam, which does not separate church and state. Instead, Islam prescribes "not only religious doctrines, but political maxims, civil and criminal laws, and theories of science."

Questions to guide you as you read:

- What does Tocqueville mean when he speaks of religion's "successful struggle with that spirit of individual independence which is her most dangerous opponent"?

- What does Tocqueville mean in stating that the Americans brought to the New World a form of Christianity that is "democratic and republican"?

"Religion Considered as a Political Institution and How It Powerfully Contributes to the Maintenance of a Democratic Republic Among the Americans"

By the side of every religion is to be found a political opinion, which is connected with it by affinity. If the human mind be left to follow its own bent, it will regulate the temporal [worldly] and spiritual institutions of society in a uniform manner, and man will endeavor, if I may so speak, to harmonize earth with heaven.

The greatest part of British America was peopled by men who, after having shaken off the authority of the Pope, acknowledged no other religious supremacy: they brought with them into the New World a form of Christianity which I cannot better describe than by styling it a democratic and republican religion. This contributed powerfully to the establishment of a republic and a democracy in public affairs; and from the beginning, politics and religion contracted an alliance which has never been dissolved....

...It may be asserted, then, that in the United States no religious doctrine displays the slightest hostility to democratic and republican institutions. The clergy of all the different sects there hold the same language; their opinions are in agreement with the laws, and the human mind flows onwards, so to speak, in one undivided current....

"Indirect Influence of Religious Opinions upon Political Society in the United States"

I have just shown what the direct influence of religion upon politics is in the United States; but its indirect influence appears to me to be still more considerable [significant], and it never instructs the Americans more fully in the art of being free than when it says nothing of freedom.

The sects that exist in the United States are innumerable [numerous]. They all differ in respect to the worship which is due to the Creator; but they all agree in respect to the duties which are due from man to man. Each sect adores the Deity in its own peculiar manner, but all sects preach the same moral law in the name of God. If it be of the highest importance to man, as an individual, that his religion should be true, it is not so to society. Society has no future life to hope for or to fear; and provided the citizens profess a religion, the peculiar [individual] tenets [doctrines] of that religion are of little importance to its interests. Moreover, all the sects of the United States are comprised within the great unity of Christianity, and Christian morality is everywhere the same.

It may fairly be believed that a certain number of Americans pursue a peculiar form of worship from habit more than from conviction. In the United States the sovereign authority is religious, and consequently hypocrisy must be common; but there is no country in the world where the Christian religion retains a greater influence over the souls of men than in America; and there can be no greater proof of its utility and of its conformity to human nature than that its influence is powerfully felt over the most enlightened and free nation of the earth.

I have remarked that the American clergy in general, without even excepting [excluding] those who do not admit religious liberty, are all in favor of civil freedom; but they do not support any particular political system. They keep aloof from parties and from public affairs. In the United States religion exercises but little influence upon the laws and upon the details of public opinion; but it directs the customs of the community, and, by regulating domestic life, it regulates the state.

I do not question that the great austerity [strictness] of manners that is observable in the United States arises, in the first instance, from religious faith. Religion is often unable to restrain man from the numberless temptations which chance offers; nor can it check that passion for gain which everything contributes to arouse; but its influence over the mind of woman is supreme, and women are the protectors of morals. There is certainly no country in the world where the tie of marriage is more respected than in America or where conjugal happiness is more highly or worthily appreciated. In Europe almost all the disturbances of society arise from the irregularities of domestic life. To despise the natural bonds and legitimate pleasures of home is to contract [become infected with] a taste for excesses, a restlessness of heart, and fluctuating desires. Agitated by the tumultuous [chaotic] passions that frequently disturb his dwelling, the European is galled by the obedience which the legislative powers of the state exact. But when the American retires from the turmoil of public life to the bosom of his family, he finds in it the image of order and of peace. There his pleasures are simple and natural, his joys are innocent and calm; and as he finds that an orderly life is the surest path to happiness, he accustoms himself easily to moderate his opinions as well as his tastes. While the European endeavors to forget his domestic troubles by agitating society, the American derives from his own home that love of order which he afterwards carries with him into public affairs.

In the United States the influence of religion is not confined to the manners, but it extends to the intelligence of the people. Among the Anglo-Americans some profess the doctrines of Christianity from a sincere belief in them, and others do the same because they fear to be suspected of unbelief. Christianity, therefore, reigns without obstacle, by universal consent; the consequence is, as I have before observed, that every principle of the moral world is fixed and determinate, although the political world is abandoned to the debates and the experiments of men. Thus the human mind is never left to wander over a boundless field; and whatever may be its pretensions, it is checked from time to time by barriers that it cannot surmount....

The imagination of the Americans, even in its greatest flights, is circumspect [cautious] and undecided; its impulses are checked and its works unfinished. These habits of restraint recur [reappear] in political society and are singularly [exceptionally] favorable both to the tranquillity of the people and to the durability of the institutions they have established. Nature and circumstances have made the inhabitants of the United States bold, as is sufficiently attested by the enterprising spirit with which they seek for fortune. If the mind of the Americans were free from all hindrances, they would shortly become the most daring innovators and the most persistent disputants in the world. But the revolutionists of America are obliged to profess an ostensible respect for Christian morality and equity [justice], which does not permit them to violate wantonly [excessively] the laws that oppose their designs; nor would they find it easy to surmount the scruples of their partisans even if they were able to get over their own. Hitherto no one in the United States has dared to advance the maxim that everything is permissible for the interests of society, an impious [sinful] adage [proverb] which seems to have been invented in an age of freedom to shelter all future tyrants. Thus, while the law permits the Americans to do what they please, religion prevents them from conceiving, and forbids them to commit, what is rash or unjust.

Religion in America takes no direct part in the government of society, but it must be regarded as the first of their political institutions; for if it does not impart a taste for freedom, it facilitates [eases] the use of it. Indeed, it is in this same point of view that the inhabitants of the United States themselves look upon religious belief. I do not know whether all Americans have a sincere faith in their religion—for who can search the human heart?—but I am certain that they hold it to be indispensable to the maintenance of republican institutions.... In the United States, if a politician attacks a sect, this may not prevent the partisans of that very sect from supporting him; but if he attacks all the sects together, everyone abandons him, and he remains alone....

...Despotism may govern without faith, but liberty cannot. Religion is much more necessary in the republic which they set forth in glowing colors than in the monarchy which they attack; it is more needed in democratic republics than in any others. How is it possible that society should escape destruction if the moral tie is not strengthened in proportion as the political tie is relaxed? And what can be done with a people who are their own masters if they are not submissive to the Deity?

"Principle Causes Which Render Religion Powerful in America"

The philosophers of the eighteenth century explained in a very simple manner the gradual decay of religious faith. Religious zeal, said they, must necessarily fail the more generally liberty is established and knowledge diffused [spread]. Unfortunately, the facts by no means accord with their theory. There are certain populations in Europe whose unbelief is only equaled by their ignorance and debasement; while in America, one of the freest and most enlightened nations in the world, the people fulfill with fervor [enthusiasm] all the outward duties of religion.

On my arrival in the United States the religious aspect of the country was the first thing that struck my attention; and the longer I stayed there, the more I perceived the great political consequences resulting from this new state of things. In France I had almost always seen the spirit of religion and the spirit of freedom marching in opposite directions. But in America I found they were intimately united and that they reigned in common over the same country. My desire to discover the causes of this phenomenon increased from day to day. In order to satisfy it I questioned the members of all the different sects; I sought especially the society of the clergy.... To each of these men I expressed my astonishment and explained my doubts. I found that they differed upon matters of detail alone, and that they all attributed the peaceful dominion of religion in their country mainly to the separation of church and state....

This led me to examine more attentively than I had hitherto done the station which the American clergy occupy in political society. I learned with surprise that they filled no public appointments; I did not see one of them in the administration, and they are not even represented in the legislative assemblies. In several states the law excludes them from political life; public opinion excludes them in all. And when I came to inquire into the prevailing spirit of the clergy, I found that most of its members seemed to retire of their own accord from the exercise of power, and that they made it the pride of their profession to abstain from politics.

...These facts convinced me that what I had been told was true; and it then became my object to investigate their causes and to inquire how it happened that the real authority of religion was increased by a state of things which diminished its apparent force. These causes did not long escape my researches.

The short space of threescore [sixty] years can never content the imagination of man; nor can the imperfect joys of this world satisfy his heart. Man alone, of all created beings, displays a natural contempt of existence, and yet a boundless desire to exist; he scorns life, but he dreads annihilation. These different feelings incessantly urge his soul to the contemplation of a future state, and religion directs his musings [thoughts] thither [in that direction]. Religion, then, is simply another form of hope, and it is no less natural to the human heart than hope itself. Men cannot abandon their religious faith without a kind of aberration [deviation] of intellect and a sort of violent distortion of their true nature; they are invincibly brought back to more pious sentiments. Unbelief is an accident, and faith is the only permanent state of mankind. If we consider religious institutions merely in a human point of view, they may be said to derive an inexhaustible element of strength from man himself, since they belong to one of the constituent principles of human nature....

...Religions intimately united with the governments of the earth have been known to exercise sovereign power founded on terror and faith; but when a religion contracts an alliance of this nature, I do not hesitate to affirm that it commits the same error as a man who should sacrifice his future to his present welfare; and in obtaining a power to which it has no claim, it risks that authority which is rightfully its own. When a religion founds its empire only upon the desire of immortality that lives in every human heart, it may aspire to universal dominion; but when it connects itself with a government, it must adopt maxims which are applicable only to certain nations. Thus, in forming an alliance with a political power, religion augments [increases] its authority over a few and forfeits the hope of reigning over all.

As long as a religion rests only upon those sentiments which are the consolation [comfort] of all affliction, it may attract the affections of all mankind. But if it be mixed up with the bitter passions of the world, it may be constrained to defend allies whom its interests, and not the principle of love, have given to it; or to repel as antagonists men who are still attached to it, however opposed they may be to the powers with which it is allied. The church cannot share the temporal power of the state without being the object of a portion of that animosity which the latter excites....

...As long as a religion is sustained by those feelings, propensities [tendencies], and passions which are found to occur under the same forms at all periods of history, it may defy the efforts of time; or at least it can be destroyed only by another religion. But when religion clings to the interests of the world, it becomes almost as fragile a thing as the powers of earth....

...In proportion as a nation assumes a democratic condition of society and as communities display democratic propensities, it becomes more and more dangerous to connect religion with political institutions; for the time is coming when authority will be bandied [tossed casually] from hand to hand, when political theories will succeed one another, and when men, laws, and constitutions will disappear or be modified from day to day, and this not for a season only, but unceasingly. Agitation and mutability [changeableness] are inherent in the nature of democratic republics, just as stagnation and sleepiness are the law of absolute monarchies.

If the Americans, who change the head of the government once in four years, who elect new legislators every two years, and renew the state officers every twelve months; if the Americans, who have given up the political world to the attempts of innovators, had not placed religion beyond their reach, where could it take firm hold in the ebb and flow of human opinions? Where would be that respect which belongs to it, amid the struggles of faction? And what would become of its immortality, in the midst of universal decay? The American clergy were the first to perceive this truth and to act in conformity with it. They saw that they must renounce their religious influence if they were to strive for political power, and they chose to give up the support of the state rather than to share its vicissitudes [unexpected changes]....

"How Religion in the United States Avails Itself of Democratic Tendencies"

I have shown in a preceding chapter that men cannot do without dogmatic [inflexible] belief, and even that it is much to be desired that such belief should exist among them. I now add that, of all the kinds of dogmatic belief, the most desirable appears to me to be dogmatic belief in matters of religion; and this is a clear inference, even from no higher consideration than the interests of this world.

There is hardly any human action, however particular it may be, that does not originate in some very general idea men have conceived of the Deity, of his relation to mankind, of the nature of their own souls, and of their duties to their fellow creatures. Nor can anything prevent these ideas from being the common spring from which all the rest emanates.

Men are therefore immeasurably interested in acquiring fixed ideas of God, of the soul, and of their general duties to their Creator and their fellow men; for doubt on these first principles would abandon all their actions to chance and would condemn them in some way to disorder and impotence.

This, then, is the subject on which it is most important for each of us to have fixed ideas; and unhappily it is also the subject on which it is most difficult for each of us, left to himself, to settle his opinions by the sole force of his reason. None but minds singularly free from the ordinary cares of life, minds at once penetrating, subtle, and trained by thinking, can, even with much time and care, sound [measure] the depths of these truths that are so necessary. And, indeed, we see that philosophers are themselves almost always surrounded with uncertainties; that at every step the natural light which illuminates their path grows dimmer and less secure, and that, in spite of all their efforts, they have discovered as yet only a few conflicting notions, on which the mind of man has been tossed about for thousands of years without ever firmly grasping the truth or finding novelty even in its errors. Studies of this nature are far above the average capacity of men; and, even if the majority of mankind were capable of such pursuits, it is evident that leisure to cultivate them would still be wanting. Fixed ideas about God and human nature are indispensable to the daily practice of men's lives; but the practice of their lives prevents them from acquiring such ideas....

...General ideas respecting God and human nature are therefore the ideas above all others which it is most suitable to withdraw from the habitual action of private judgment and in which there is most to gain and least to lose by recognizing a principle of authority. The first object and one of the principal [chief] advantages of religion is to furnish to each of these fundamental questions a solution that is at once clear, precise, intelligible, and lasting, to the mass of mankind. There are religions that are false and very absurd, but it may be affirmed that any religion which remains within the circle I have just traced, without pretending to go beyond it (as many religions have attempted to do, for the purpose of restraining on every side the free movement of the human mind), imposes a salutary [beneficial] restraint on the intellect; and it must be admitted that, if it does not save men in another world, it is at least very conducive to their happiness and their greatness in this.

This is especially true of men living in free countries. When the religion of a people is destroyed, doubt gets hold of the higher powers of the intellect and half paralyzes all the others. Every man accustoms himself to having only confused and changing notions on the subjects most interesting to his fellow creatures and himself. His opinions are ill-defended and easily abandoned; and, in despair of ever solving by himself the hard problems respecting the destiny of man, he ignobly [dishonorably] submits to think no more about them.

Such a condition cannot but enervate [weaken] the soul, relax the springs of the will, and prepare a people for servitude. Not only does it happen in such a case that they allow their freedom to be taken from them; they frequently surrender it themselves. When there is no longer any principle of authority in religion any more than in politics, men are speedily frightened at the aspect of this unbounded independence. The constant agitation of all surrounding things alarms and exhausts them. As everything is at sea in the sphere of the mind, they determine at least that the mechanism of society shall be firm and fixed; and as they cannot resume their ancient belief, they assume a master.

For my own part, I doubt whether man can ever support at the same time complete religious independence and entire political freedom. And I am inclined to think that if faith be wanting in him, he must be subject; and if he be free, he must believe.

Perhaps, however, this great utility of religions is still more obvious among nations where equality of conditions prevails than among others. It must be acknowledged that equality, which brings great benefits into the world, nevertheless suggests to men (as will be shown hereafter) some very dangerous propensities. It tends to isolate them from one another, to concentrate every man's attention upon himself; and it lays open the soul to an inordinate [immoderate] love of material gratification.

The greatest advantage of religion is to inspire diametrically [absolutely] contrary principles There is no religion that does not place the object of man's desires above and beyond the treasures of earth and that does not naturally raise his soul to regions far above those of the senses. Nor is there any which does not impose on man some duties towards his kind and thus draw him at times from the contemplation of himself. This is found in the most false and dangerous religions.

Religious nations are therefore naturally strong on the very point on which democratic nations are weak; this shows of what importance it is for men to preserve their religion as their conditions become more equal.

...I am at this moment considering religions in a purely human point of view; my object is to inquire by what means they may most easily retain their sway in the democratic ages upon which we are entering.

It has been shown that at times of general culture and equality the human mind consents only with reluctance to adopt dogmatic opinions and feels their necessity acutely only in spiritual matters. This proves, in the first place, that at such times religions ought more cautiously than at any other to confine themselves within their own precincts; for in seeking to extend their power beyond religious matters, they incur a risk of not being believed at all. The circle within which they seek to restrict the human intellect ought therefore to be carefully traced, and beyond its verge the mind should be left entirely free to its own guidance.

Mohammed [the founder of Islam] professed to derive from Heaven, and has inserted in the Koran, not only religious doctrines, but political maxims, civil and criminal laws, and theories of science. The Gospel, on the contrary, speaks only of the general relations of men to God and to each other, beyond which it inculcates and imposes no point of faith. This alone, besides a thousand other reasons, would suffice to prove that the former of these religions [Islam] will never long predominate in a cultivated and democratic age, while the latter is destined to retain its sway at these as at all other periods....

...The preceding observation, that equality leads men to very general and very vast ideas, is principally to be understood in respect to religion. Men who are similar and equal in the world readily conceive the idea of the one God, governing every man by the same laws and granting to every man future happiness on the same conditions. The idea of the unity of mankind constantly leads them back to the idea of the unity of the Creator; while on the contrary in a state of society where men are broken up into very unequal ranks, they are apt to devise as many deities as there are nations, castes [hereditary classes], classes, or families, and to trace a thousand private roads to heaven.

It cannot be denied that Christianity itself has felt, to some extent, the influence that social and political conditions exercise on religious opinions....

...It seems evident that the more the barriers are removed which separate one nation from another and one citizen from another, the stronger is the bent of the human mind, as if by its own impulse, towards the idea of a single and all-powerful Being, dispensing equal laws in the same manner to every man. In democratic ages, then, it is particularly important not to allow the homage [worship] paid to secondary agents to be confused with the worship due to the Creator alone. Another truth is no less clear, that religions ought to have fewer external observances in democratic periods than at any others....

...We shall see that of all the passions which originate in or are fostered by equality, there is one which it renders peculiarly intense, and which it also infuses into the heart of every man; I mean the love of well-being [comfortable self-preservation]. The taste for well-being is the prominent and indelible feature of democratic times.

It may be believed that a religion which should undertake to destroy so deep-seated a passion would in the end be destroyed by it; and if it attempted to wean men entirely from the contemplation of the good things of this world in order to devote their faculties exclusively to the thought of another, it may be foreseen that the minds of men would at length escape its grasp, to plunge into the exclusive enjoyment of present and material pleasures.

The chief concern of religion is to purify, to regulate, and to restrain the excessive and exclusive taste for well-being that men feel in periods of equality; but it would be an error to attempt to overcome it completely or to eradicate it. Men cannot be cured of the love of riches, but they may be persuaded to enrich themselves by none but honest means.

This brings me to a final consideration, which comprises, as it were, all the others. The more the conditions of men are equalized and assimilated [made alike] to each other, the more important is it for religion, while it carefully abstains from the daily turmoil of secular affairs, not needlessly to run counter to the ideas that generally prevail or to the permanent interests that exist in the mass of the people. For as public opinion grows to be more and more the first and most irresistible of existing powers, the religious principle has no external support strong enough to enable it long to resist its attacks. This is not less true of a democratic people ruled by a despot than of a republic. In ages of equality kings may often command obedience, but the majority always commands belief; to the majority, therefore, deference is to be paid in whatever is not contrary to the faith.

I showed in the first Part of this work how the American clergy stand aloof from secular affairs. This is the most obvious but not the only example of their self-restraint. In America religion is a distinct sphere, in which the priest is sovereign, but out of which he takes care never to go. Within its limits he is master of the mind; beyond them he leaves men to themselves and surrenders them to the independence and instability that belong to their nature and their age. I have seen no country in which Christianity is clothed with fewer forms, figures, and observances than in the United States, or where it presents more distinct, simple, and general notions to the mind. Although the Christians of America are divided into a multitude of sects, they all look upon their religion in the same light. This applies to Roman Catholicism as well as to the other forms of belief....

...All the American clergy know and respect the intellectual supremacy exercised by the majority; they never sustain any but necessary conflicts with it. They take no share in the altercations [heated arguments] of parties, but they readily adopt the general opinions of their country and their age, and they allow themselves to be borne away without opposition in the current of feeling and opinion by which everything around them is carried along. They endeavor to amend [improve] their contemporaries, but they do not quit fellowship with them. Public opinion is therefore never hostile to them; it rather supports and protects them, and their belief owes its authority at the same time to the strength which is its own and to that which it borrows from the opinions of the majority.

Thus it is that by respecting all democratic tendencies not absolutely contrary to herself and by making use of several of them for her own purposes, religion sustains a successful struggle with that spirit of individual independence which is her most dangerous opponent.

How can religion be understood to be a political problem for American democracy?

THOMAS JEFFERSON, "A BILL FOR ESTABLISHING RELIGIOUS FREEDOM" (1786)

In 1784, Patrick Henry sponsored a bill in the Virginia legislature calling for a general "religious assessment [tax]." The proposed tax sought to provide funds for teachers from all Christian denominations. Similar measures previously had been passed in several New England states. The bill allowed Virginians to specify, if they so chose, to which church their tax dollars would go. Justification for the proposed bill echoes in important respects what you previously read in Washington's Farewell Address, written twelve years later: Christianity was of "public utility," because it offered, better than any other sources, to "promote" public "virtue" and "peace." Washington, himself a Virginian, agreed with the principle behind the bill, although he worried about the effect its passage might have on public "tranquility." The Virginians Jefferson and Madison opposed the bill. In opposition, Madison wrote his "Memorial and Remonstrance Against Religious Assessments" (1785). In the end, Henry's bill failed, and Jefferson's bill passed.

WHY THIS READING?

Although there has always been agreement in this country that religious liberty should be considered a fundamental right, there has also been disagreement as to why this should be the case. Here, some historical background will be helpful in understanding Jefferson's arguments. Of those American religions powerfully present in Virginia in the 1600s and 1700s, Protestants of the dissenting tradition sought to keep religion and government separate because they believed that politics, and all human institutions, were corrupt; therefore, to interject government into religion would be to taint it. A key spokesman for this view, Roger Williams, put it thus in 1644:

> [T]he Church of the Jews under the Old Testament...and the Church of the Christians under the New Testament...were both separate from the world...when they have opened a gap in the hedge or wall of Separation between the Garden of the Church and the Wilderness of the world, God hath ever broke down the wall itself, removed the Candlestick, and made his Garden a Wilderness, as at this day....[T]herefore if he will ever please to restore his Garden and Paradise again, it must of necessity be walled in peculiarly unto Himself from the world....

Williams's "wall of separation" language, as you will read later in this chapter, would be repeated in an 1802 letter written by Thomas Jefferson, and in Supreme Court Justice Black's majority opinion in *Everson v. Board of Education* (1947). But Jefferson, who agreed with the goodness and necessity of such a "wall," differed as to why it needed to be erected and maintained. Jefferson was a Deist. Briefly put, deism, a "rational religion," denies knowledge based on faith or revelation; the only genuine knowledge is that acquired through the rational observation of nature. Although it grants God's role as the "Creator" or "Author" of the cosmos, it denies that the Deity takes any subsequent notice of or involvement in human affairs and, accordingly, it denies the possibility of miracles. For Jefferson, then, there must be a wall between church and state, because to interject religion into the affairs of government would be to taint politics.

It should be added that, although Jefferson, Madison, and Washington were Deists, the great majority of the Founding generation believed in the God of revelation. Moreover, the contrasting positions of Washington and Jefferson demonstrate that the debate over separation of church and state cannot be divided simply into believers (who might be assumed to oppose strict separation) versus nonbelievers (who might be assumed to support it). Washington, after all, was also a Deist. Instead the debate centers on the question of whether public morality can be maintained in the absence of government's "nonpreferential" support of "general religion." To this question we shall return later in this chapter, when we examine the *Everson* case.

As you will read below, for Jefferson, religious freedom means that our rights as citizens should not be adversely affected by our religious opinions, unless those religion-based opinions turn into actions that interfere with civil peace and good order.

Questions to guide you as you read:

- For Jefferson, is religious freedom a *natural* or a *religious* right? What is the difference, and how does this affect its relationship to American democracy?
- Jefferson argues that "the opinions of men are not the object of civil government, nor under its jurisdiction. . . . " This passage is often cited by critics of "hate-crime" laws. Such laws add penalties based on the motivation of the perpetrator of a violent crime against a member of a protected class. Do the critics rightly enlist Jefferson to be on their side? If so, why? If not, why not?

(EDITORS' NOTE: *The text reprinted below is Jefferson's draft. The bill, as adopted by the Virginia House of Delegates in 1786, deleted the italicized words.)*

Well aware that the opinions and belief of men depend not on their own will, but follow involuntarily the evidence proposed to their minds; that **Almighty God hath created the mind free,** ***and manifested his supreme will that free it shall remain by making it altogether insusceptible of restraint;*** **that all attempts to influence it by temporal punishments, or burthens, or by civil incapacitations, tend only to beget habits of hypocrisy and meanness, and are a departure from the plan of the holy author of our religion, who being lord both of body and mind, yet chose not to propagate it by coercions on either, as was in his Almighty power to do,** ***but to extend it by its influence on reason alone;*** **that the impious [not showing due reverence for God] presumption of legislators and rulers, civil as well as ecclesiastical, who, being themselves but fallible and uninspired men, have assumed dominion over the faith of others, setting up their own opinions and modes of thinking as the only true and infallible, and as**

such endeavoring to impose them on others hath established and maintained false religions over the greatest part of the world and through all time: That to compel a man to furnish contributions of money for the propagation [spreading] of opinions which he disbelieves *and abhors*, is sinful and tyrannical: that even the forcing him to support this or that teacher of his own religious persuasion, is depriving him of the comfortable liberty of giving his contributions to the particular pastor whose morals he would make his pattern, and whose powers he feels most persuasive to righteousness; and is withdrawing from the ministry those temporary rewards, which proceeding from an approbation of their personal conduct, are an additional incitement to earnest and unremitting labours for the instruction of mankind; that our civil rights have no dependence on our religious opinions, any more than our opinions in physics or geometry; that therefore the proscribing [prohibiting] any citizen as unworthy the public confidence by laying upon him an incapacity of being called to offices of trust and emolument [payment], unless he profess or renounce this or that religious opinion, is depriving him injuriously of those privileges and advantages to which, in common with his fellow citizens he has a natural right; that it tends also to corrupt the principles of that very religion it is meant to encourage, by bribing, with a monopoly of worldly honours and emoluments, chose who will externally profess and conform to it; that though indeed these are criminal who do not withstand such temptation, yet neither are those innocent who lay the bait in their way; *that the opinions of men are not the object of civil government, nor under its jurisdiction;* that to suffer the civil magistrate to intrude his powers into the field of opinion and to restrain the profession or propagation of principles on supposition of their ill tendency is a dangerous fallacy, which at once destroys all religious liberty, because he being of course judge of that tendency will make his opinions the rule of judgment, and approve or condemn the sentiments of others only as they shall square with or differ from his own; that it is time enough for the rightful purposes of civil government for its officers to interfere when principles break out into overt acts against peace and good order; and finally, that truth is great and will prevail if left to herself; that she is the proper and sufficient antagonist to error, and has nothing to fear from the conflict unless by human interposition disarmed of her natural weapons, free argument and debate; errors ceasing to be dangerous when it is permitted freely to contradict them.

We the General Assembly of Virginia do enact that no man shall be compelled to frequent or support any religious worship, place, or ministry whatsoever, nor shall be enforced, restrained, molested, or burthened in his body or goods, nor shall otherwise suffer, on account of his religious opinions or belief; but that all men shall be free to profess, and by argument to maintain, their opinions in matters of religion, and that the same shall in no wise diminish, enlarge, or affect their civil capacities.

And though we well know that this assembly, elected by the people for the ordinary purposes of legislation only, have no power to restrain the aces of succeeding Assemblies, constituted with powers equal to our own, and that therefore to declare this act irrevocable would be of no effect in law; yet we are free to declare, and do declare, that the rights hereby asserted are of the natural rights of mankind, and that if any act shall be hereafter passed to repeal the present or to narrow its operation, such act will be an infringement of natural right.

THOMAS JEFFERSON, "LETTER TO NEHEMIAH DODGE AND OTHERS: A COMMITTEE OF THE DANBURY BAPTIST ASSOCIATION, IN THE STATE OF CONNECTICUT" (1802)

WHY THIS READING?

In this letter to the Danbury Baptists, Jefferson, in his second year as president, employs the metaphor of a "wall of separation" between church and state to make the point that the legislative power of the government may properly be used against actions based on religion, but not against religious opinions themselves. Recall that the first documented use of the phrase "wall of separation" is attributed to Roger Williams, a 17th century dissenting Protestant minister.

Question to guide you as you read:

- What is Jefferson's argument for what may be called his "privatizing" of religious opinions?

GENTLEMEN: The affectionate sentiments of esteem and approbation, which you are so good as to express towards me, on behalf of the Danbury Baptist Association, give me the highest satisfaction. My duties dictate a faithful and zealous pursuit of the interests of my constituents, and in proportion as they are persuaded of my fidelity to those duties; the discharge of them becomes more and more pleasing

Believing with you that religion is a matter which lies solely between man and his God, that he owes account to none other for his faith or his worship, that the legislative powers of government reach actions only, and not opinions, I contemplate with sovereign reverence that act of the whole American people which declared that their legislature should "make no law respecting an establishment of religion, or prohibiting the free exercise whereof," thus building a wall of separation between Church and State. Adhering to this expression of the supreme will of the nation in behalf of the rights of conscience, I shall see with sincere satisfaction the progress of those sentiments which tend to restore to man all his natural rights, convinced he has no natural right in opposition to his social duties.

I reciprocate your kind prayers for the protection and blessing of the common Father and Creator of man, and tender you for yourselves and your religious association, assurances of my high respect and esteem.

JUSTICE HUGO BLACK, OPINION OF THE COURT IN *EVERSON V. BOARD OF EDUCATION* (1947)

Under a New Jersey state statute, the Ewing Township Board of Education allowed parents to be reimbursed for the cost of transporting their children to school by way of public transportation. A portion of this money went to reimburse the parents of children who attended Catholic parochial schools. A local taxpayer, Mr. Everson, filed suit against the Ewing Township Board of Education, arguing that the New Jersey statute violated both the 1st and 14th Amendments to the U.S. Constitution.

WHY THIS READING?

In this decision, the Court offers a revised theory of individual religious freedom in constitutional law. Justice Hugo Black delivered the opinion of the Court, which, although it upholds the constitutionality of the New Jersey statute, nonetheless departs from the Washington-Tocqueville understanding of the place of religion in American public life. Using the language of Thomas Jefferson's "Letter to the Danbury Baptists" (above), Justice Black argues that the 1st Amendment erects a "wall of separation" between church and state that must be kept "high and impregnable."

Questions to guide you as you read:

- To what extent does Black make Jefferson's Virginia Bill for Religious Liberty the standard for the entire nation?
- Does Black recognize, in the manner of Tocqueville and Washington, any benefits conferred upon democracy by religious belief?

A New Jersey statute [law] authorizes its local school districts to make rules and contracts for the transportation of children to and from schools. The appellee [the entity being sued], a township board of education, acting pursuant to [in accordance with] this statute authorized reimbursement [refund] to parents of money expended [spent] by them for the bus transportation of their children on regular busses operated by the public transportation system. Part of this money was for the payment of transportation of some children in the community to Catholic parochial schools. These church schools give their students, in addition to secular [non-religious] education, regular religious instruction conforming to the religious tenets [principles] and modes of worship of the Catholic Faith. The superintendent of these schools is a Catholic priest.

The appellant [the person bringing suit], in his capacity as a direct taxpayer, filed suit in a State court challenging the right of the Board to reimburse [refund] parents of parochial school students. He contended that the statute and the resolution passed pursuant to [in accordance with] it violated both the State and the Federal Constitutions. That court held that the legislature was without power to authorize such payment under the State constitution. The New Jersey Court of Errors and Appeals reversed, holding that neither the statute nor the resolution passed pursuant to it was in conflict with the State constitution or the provisions of the Federal Constitution in issue.

Since there has been no attack on the statute on the ground that a part of its language excludes children attending private schools operated for profit from enjoying state payment for their transportation, we need not consider this exclusionary language; it has no relevancy to any constitutional question here presented. Furthermore, if the exclusion clause had been properly challenged, we do not know whether New Jersey's highest court would construe its statutes as precluding payment of the school transportation of any group of pupils, even those of a private school run for profit. Consequently, we put to one side the question as to the validity of the statute against the claim that it does not authorize payment for the transportation generally of school children in New Jersey.

The only contention here is that the State statute and the resolution, in so far as they authorized reimbursement to parents of children attending parochial [religious] schools, violate the Federal Constitution in these two respects, which to some extent overlap. First, they authorize the State to take by taxation the private property of some and bestow it upon others, to be used for their own private purposes. This, it is alleged, violates the due process clause of the Fourteenth Amendment.[1] Second, the statute and the resolution forced inhabitants to pay faxes to help support and maintain schools which arc dedicated to, and which regularly teach, the Catholic Faith. This is alleged to be a use of State power to support church schools contrary to the prohibition of the First Amendment which the Fourteenth Amendment made applicable to the states.[2]

1. The "Due Process Clause" of the 14th Amendment holds that no person shall be deprived of life, liberty, or property without "due process of law."

2. Traditionally, the first ten amendments to the Constitution were thought to apply only to the general government. However, over time, the Supreme Court began to reinterpret this idea. This becomes known as "incorporation theory," which holds that several of the first ten amendments to the Constitution were made applicable to the states via the "Due Process Clause" of the 14th Amendment. This clause says that no one should be deprived of life, liberty, or property without

First. The due process argument that the State law taxes some people to help others carry out their private purposes is framed in two phases. The first phase is that a state cannot tax A to reimburse B for the cost of transporting his children to church schools. This is said to violate the due process clause because the children are sent to these church schools to satisfy the personal desires of their parents, rather than the public's interest in the general education of all children. This argument, if valid, would apply equally to prohibit state payment for the transportation of children to any non-public school, whether operated by a church, or any other non-government individual or group. But, the New Jersey legislature has decided that a public purpose will be served by using tax-raised funds to pay the bus fares of all school children, including those who attend parochial schools. The New Jersey Court of Errors and Appeals has reached the same conclusion. The fact that a state law, passed to satisfy a public need, coincides with the personal desires of the individuals most directly affected is certainly an inadequate reason for us to say that a legislature has erroneously [mistakenly] appraised the public need.

It is true that this Court has, in rare instances, struck down state statutes on the ground that the purpose for which tax-raised funds were to be expended was not a public one. But the Court has also pointed out that this far-reaching authority must be exercised with the most extreme caution. Otherwise, a state's power to legislate for the public welfare might be seriously curtailed [cut back], a power which is a primary reason for the existence of states. Changing local conditions create new local problems which may lead a state's people and its local authorities to believe that laws authorizing new types of public services are necessary to promote the general well-being of the people. The Fourteenth Amendment did not strip the states of their power to meet problems previously left for individual solution.

It is much too late to argue that legislation intended to facilitate the opportunity of children to get a secular education serves no public purpose. The same thing is no less true of legislation to reimburse needy parents, or all parents, for payment of the fares of their children so that they can ride in public busses to and from schools, rather than run the risk of traffic and other hazards incident to walking or "hitchhiking." Nor does it follow that a law has a private rather than a public purpose because it provides that tax-raised funds will be paid to reimburse [refund] individuals on account of money spent by them in a way which furthers a public program. Subsidies and loans to individuals such as farmers and home owners, and to privately owned transportation systems, as well as many other kinds of businesses, have been commonplace practices in our state and national history.

Insofar as the second phase of the due process argument may differ from the first, it is by suggesting that taxation for transportation of children to church schools constitutes support of a religion by the State. But if the law is invalid for this reason, it is because it violates the First Amendment's prohibition against the establishment of religion by law. This is the exact question raised by appellant's second contention, to consideration of which we now turn.

Second. The New Jersey statute is challenged as a "law respecting an establishment of religion." The First Amendment, as made applicable to the states by the Fourteenth, commands that a state "shall make no law respecting an establishment of religion, or prohibiting the free exercise thereof." These words of the First Amendment reflected in the minds of early Americans a vivid mental picture of conditions and practices which they fervently wished to stamp out in order to preserve liberty for

---

due process of law. But what *is* "liberty"? In the 1920s, the Supreme Court decided that the "liberty" of the 14th Amendment was most likely best understood as the sort of immunities and protections found in the first ten amendments to the Constitution. In *Gitlow v. New York*, 268 U.S. 652 (1925), the Court held that "we may and do assume that freedom of speech . . . and of the press . . . are among the fundamental rights and liberties protected . . . from impairment by the states." By the 1940s, other First Amendment liberties [such as religious freedom] had been assumed to fall under this idea as well.

themselves and for their posterity. Doubtless their goal has not been entirely reached; but so far has the Nation moved toward it that the expression "law respecting an establishment of religion," probably does not so vividly remind present-day Americans of the evils, fears, and political problems that caused that expression to be written into our Bill of Rights. Whether this New Jersey law is one respecting the "establishment of religion" requires an understanding of the meaning of that language, particularly with respect to the imposition of taxes. Once again, therefore, it is not inappropriate briefly to review the background and environment of the period in which that constitutional language was fashioned and adopted.

A large proportion of the early settlers of this country came here from Europe to escape the bondage of laws which compelled them to support and attend government favored churches. The centuries immediately before and contemporaneous with [during] the colonization of America had been filled with turmoil, civil strife, and persecution, generated in large part by established sects determined to maintain their absolute political and religious supremacy. With the power of government supporting them, at various times and places, Catholics had persecuted Protestants, Protestants had persecuted Catholics, Protestant sects had persecuted other Protestant sects. Catholics of one shade of belief had persecuted Catholics of another shade of belief, and all of these had from time to time persecuted Jews. In efforts to force loyalty to whatever religious group happened to be on top and in league with the government of a particular time and place, men and women had been fined, cast in jail, cruelly tortured, and killed. Among the offenses for which these punishments had been inflicted were such things as speaking disrespectfully of the views of ministers of government-established churches, non-attendance at those churches, expressions of non-belief in their doctrines, and failure to pay taxes and tithes to support them.

These practices of the old world were transplanted to and began to thrive in the soil of the new America. The very charters granted by the English Crown to the individuals and companies designated to make the laws which would control the destinies of the colonials authorized these individuals and companies to erect religious establishments which all, whether believers or non-believers, would be required to support and attend. An exercise of this authority was accompanied by a repetition of many of the old-world practices and persecutions. Catholics found themselves hounded and proscribed [condemned] because of their faith; Quakers who followed their conscience went to jail; Baptists were peculiarly obnoxious to certain dominant Protestant sects: men and women of varied faiths who happened to be in a minority in a particular locality were persecuted because they steadfastly persisted in worshiping God only as their own consciences dictated. And all of these dissenters were compelled to pay tithes and taxes to support government-sponsored churches whose ministers preached inflammatory sermons designed to strengthen and consolidate the established faith by generating a burning hatred against dissenters.

These practices became so commonplace as to shock the freedom loving colonials into a feeling of abhorrence. The imposition of taxes to pay ministers' salaries and to build and maintain churches and church property aroused their indignation [anger]; it was these feelings which found expression in the First Amendment. No one locality and no one group throughout the Colonies can rightly be given entire credit for having aroused the sentiment that culminated in adoption of the Bill of Rights' provisions embracing religious liberty. But Virginia, where the established church had achieved a dominant influence in political affairs and where many excesses attracted wide public attention, provided a great stimulus and able leadership for the movement. The people there, as elsewhere, reached the conviction that individual religious liberty could be achieved best under a government which was stripped of all power to tax, to support, or otherwise to assist any or all religions, or to interfere with the beliefs of any religious individual or group.

The movement toward this end reached its dramatic climax in Virginia's tax levy for the support of the established church. Thomas Jefferson and James Madison led the fight against this tax. Madison wrote his great Memorial and Remonstrance against the law. In it, he eloquently argued that a true religion did not need the support of law; that no person, either believer or non-believer, should be taxed to support a religious institution of any kind; that the best interest of a society required that the minds of men always be wholly free; and that cruel persecutions were the inevitable result of government established religions. Madison's Remonstrance received strong support throughout Virginia, and the Assembly postponed consideration of the proposed tax measure until its next session. When the proposal came up for consideration at that session, it not only died in committee, but the Assembly enacted the famous "Virginia Bill for Religious Liberty" originally written by Thomas Jefferson. The preamble to the Bill stated among other things that

> Almighty God hath created the mind free; that all attempts to influence it by temporal [earthly] punishment, or burthens [burdens], or by civil incapacitations [disqualifications], tend only to beget [produce] habits of hypocrisy and meanness, and are a departure from the plan of the Holy author of our religion who being Lord both of body and mind, yet chose not to propagate [spread] it by coercions on either...; that to compel a man to furnish contributions of money for the propagation of opinions which he disbelieves, is sinful and tyrannical; that even the forcing him to support this or that teacher of his own religious persuasion, is depriving him of the comfortable liberty of giving his contributions to the particular pastor, whose morals he would make his pattern. And the statute itself enacted

> That no man shall be compelled to frequent or support any religious worship, place, or ministry whatsoever, nor shall be enforced, restrained, molested, or burthened, in his body or goods, nor shall otherwise suffer on account of his religious opinions or belief....

This Court has previously recognized that the provisions of the First Amendment, in the drafting of which Madison and Jefferson played such leading rolls, had same objective and were intended to provide the same protection against governmental intrusion on religious liberty as the Virginia statute. Prior to the adoption of the Fourteenth Amendment, the First Amendment did not apply as a restraint against the states. Most of them did soon provide similar constitutional protections for religious liberty. But some states persisted for about half a century in imposing restraints upon the free exercise of religion and in discriminating against particular religious groups. In recent years, so far as the provision against the establishment of a religion is concerned, the question has most frequently arisen in connection with proposed state aid to church schools and efforts to carry on religious teachings in the public schools in accordance with the tenets of a particular sect. Some churches have either sought or accepted state financial support for their schools. Here again the efforts to obtain state aid or acceptance of it have not been limited to any one particular faith. The state courts, in the main, have remained faithful to the language of their own constitutional provisions designated to protect religious freedom and to separate religions and governments, Their decisions, however, show the difficulty in drawing the line between tax legislation which provides funds for the welfare of the general public and that which is designed to support institutions which teach religion.

The meaning and scope of the First Amendment, preventing establishment of religion or prohibiting the free exercise thereof, in the light of its history and the evils it was designed forever to suppress, have been several times elaborated by the decisions of this Court prior to the application of the First Amendment to the states by the Fourteenth. The broad meaning given the Amendment by these earlier cases has been accepted by this Court in its decisions concerning an individual's religious freedom rendered since the Fourteenth Amendment was interpreted to make the prohibitions of the First applicable to state action abridging religious freedom. There is every reason to give the same application and broad interpretation to the "establishment of religion" clause. The interrelation of these complementary clauses was well summarized in a statement of the Court of Appeals of South Carolina, quoted with approval by this Court, in *Watson v. Jones,* "The structure of our government has, for the preservation of civil liberty, rescued the temporal institutions from religious interference. On the other hand, it has secured religious liberty from the invasions of the civil authority."

The "establishment of religion" clause of the First Amendment means at least this: Neither a state nor the Federal Government can set up a church. Neither can pass laws which aid one religion, aid all religions, or prefer one religion over another. Neither can force nor influence a person to go to or to remain away from church against his will or force him to profess a belief or disbelief in any religion. No person can be punished for entertaining or professing religious beliefs or disbeliefs, for church attendance or non-attendance. No tax in any amount, large or small, can be levied to support any religious activities or institutions, whatever they may be called, or whatever form they may adopt to teach or practice religion. Neither a state nor the Federal Government can openly or secretly, participate in the affairs of any religious organizations or groups and vice versa. In the words of Jefferson, the clause against establishment of religion by law was to erect a "wall of separation between Church and State."

We must consider the New Jersey statute in accordance with the foregoing limitations imposed by the First Amendment. But we must not strike that state statute down if it is within the state's constitutional power even though it approaches the verge of that power. New Jersey cannot consistently with the "establishment of religion" clause of the First Amendment contribute tax-raised funds to the support of an institution which teaches the tenets and faith of any church. On the other hand, other language of the amendment commands that New Jersey cannot exclude individual Catholics, Lutherans, Muhammadans, Baptists, Jews, Methodists, Non-believers, Presbyterians, or the members of any other faith, because of their faith, or lack of it, from receiving the benefits of public welfare legislation. While we do not mean to intimate that a state could not provide transportation only to children attending public schools, we must be careful, in protecting the citizens of New Jersey against state-established churches, to be sure that we do not inadvertently prohibit New Jersey from extending its general State law benefits to all its citizens without regard to their religious belief.

Measured by these standards, we cannot say that the First Amendment prohibits New Jersey from spending tax-raised funds to pay the bus fares of parochial school pupils as a part of a general program under which it pays the fares of pupils attending public and other schools. It is undoubtedly true that children are helped to get to church schools.... [However], state-paid policemen, detailed to protect children going to and from church schools from the very real hazards of traffic, would serve much the same purpose and accomplish much the same result as state provisions intended to guarantee free transportation of a kind which the state deems to be best for the school children's welfare. And parents might refuse to risk their children to the serious danger of traffic accidents going to and from parochial schools, the approaches to which were not protected by policemen. Similarly, parents might be reluctant to permit their children to attend schools which the state had cut off from such general government services as ordinary police and fire protection, connections for sewage disposal, public highways and sidewalks. Of course, cutting off church schools from these services, so separate and so indisputably marked off from the religious function would make it far more difficult for the schools to operate. But such is obviously not the purpose of the First Amendment. That Amendment requires the state to be a neutral in its relations with groups of religious believers and non-believers; it does not require the state to be their adversary. State power is no more to be used so as to handicap religions, than it is to favor them.

This Court has said that parents may, in the discharge of their duty under state compulsory education laws, send their children to a religious rather than a public school if the school meets the secular educational requirements which the state has power to impose. It appears that these parochial schools meet New Jersey's requirements. The State contributes no money to the schools. It does not support them. Its legislation, as applied,

does no more than provide a general program to help parents get their children, regardless of their religion, safely and expeditiously to and from accredited schools.

The First Amendment has erected a wall between church and state. That wall must be kept high and impregnable. We could not approve the slightest breach. New Jersey has not breached it here.

RONALD REAGAN, "REMARKS AT AN ECUMENICAL PRAYER BREAKFAST AT THE REPUBLICAN NATIONAL CONVENTION" (1984)

During the months leading up to the presidential election of 1984, the place and purpose of religion in American politics became a highly visible issue in the debates between President Ronald Reagan and the Democratic nominee Walter Mondale. (Mondale's 1984 speech on religion follows immediately after this reading.) Of particular importance in this debate was the status of religion under the U.S. Constitution.

WHY THIS READING?

The Reagan–Mondale debate continues along the lines previously discussed, namely over whether religion is better understood as a problem for, or a support of, American democracy. In this speech, Reagan offers a contemporary echo of Washington's treatment of religion in his "Farewell Address." Like Washington and Tocqueville, Reagan deems religion to be a political institution that has enhanced American democracy. He argues that, since the Founding, religion has played a positive role in American political life by providing the moral guidance necessary for sustaining a healthy democracy.

Questions to guide you as you read:

- To what extent are Reagan's arguments asserting the place of religion consistent with what you read earlier by Tocqueville and Washington? To what extent are they different?
- What is Reagan's view of the 1962 Supreme Court case *Engel v. Vitale*, which struck down compulsory prayer in public schools? Based on your reading of Jefferson's "Bill for Establishing Religious Freedom," what would be Jefferson's rejoinder to Reagan?

I don't speak as a theologian or a scholar, only as one who's lived a little more than his three score [and] ten—which has been a source of annoyance to some—and as one who has been active in the political life of the Nation for roughly four decades, and now who's served the past three years in our highest office. I speak, I think I can say, as one who has seen much, who has loved his country, and who's seen it change in many ways.

I believe that faith and religion play a critical role in the political life of our nation—and always has—and that the church—and by that I mean all churches, all denominations—has had a strong influence on the state. And this has worked to our benefit as a nation.

Those who created our country—the Founding Fathers and Mothers understood that there is a divine order which transcends the human order. They saw the state, in fact, as a form of moral order and felt that the bedrock of moral order is religion.

The Mayflower Compact began with the words, "In the name of God, amen." The Declaration of

Independence appeals to "Nature's God" and the "Creator" and 'the Supreme Judge of the world.' Congress was given a chaplain, and the oaths of office are oaths before God.

James Madison in the Federalist Papers admitted that in the creation of our republic he perceived the hand of the Almighty. John Jay, the first Chief Justice of the Supreme Court, warned that we must never forget the God from whom our blessings flowed.

George Washington referred to religion's profound and unsurpassed place in the heart of our nation quite directly in his Farewell Address in 1796. Seven years earlier, France had erected a government that was intended to be purely secular. This new government would be grounded on reason rather than the law of God. By 1796 the French Revolution had known the Reign of Terror.

And Washington voiced reservations about the idea that there could be a wise policy without a firm moral and religious foundation. He said, "Of all the dispositions and habits which lead to political prosperity, Religion and morality are indispensable supports. In vain would that man (call himself a patriot) who (would) labour to subvert these... finest props of the duties of men and citizens. The mere Politician... (and) the pious man ought to respect and to cherish (religion and morality)." And he added, "...let us with caution indulge the supposition, that morality can be maintained without religion."

I believe that George Washington knew the City of Man cannot survive without the City of God; that the Visible City will perish without the Invisible City.

Religion played not only a strong role in our national life; it played a positive role. The abolitionist movement was at heart a moral and religious movement; so was the modern civil rights struggle. And throughout this time, the state was tolerant of religious belief, expression, and practice. Society, too, was tolerant.

But in the 1960's, this began to change. We began to make great steps toward secularizing [removing the religious dimension from] our nation and removing religion from its honored place.

In 1962 the Supreme Court in the New York prayer case banned the compulsory saying of prayers. In 1963 the Court banned the reading of the Bible in our public schools *[Abington School District v. Schempp]*. From that point on, the courts pushed the meaning of the ruling ever outward, so that now our children are not allowed voluntary prayer. We even had to pass a law—we passed a special law in the Congress just a few weeks ago to allow student prayer groups the same access to schoolrooms after classes that a young Marxist society, for example, would already enjoy with no opposition.

The 1962 decision opened the way to a flood of similar suits. Once religion had been made vulnerable, a series of assaults were made in one court after another, on one issue after another. Cases were started to argue against tax exempt status for churches. Suits were brought to abolish the words "under God" from the Pledge of Allegiance and to remove "In God We Trust" from public documents and from our currency. Today, there are those who are fighting to make sure voluntary prayer is not returned to the classrooms. And the frustrating thing for the great majority of Americans who support and understand the special importance of religion in the national life—the frustrating thing is that those who are attacking religion claim they are doing it in the name of tolerance, freedom, and open-mindedness. Question: Isn't the real truth that they are intolerant of religion? They refuse to tolerate its importance in our lives.

If all the children of our country studied together all of the many religions in our country, wouldn't they learn greater tolerance of each other's beliefs? If children prayed together, would they not understand what they have in common, and would this not, indeed, bring them closer, and is this not to be desired? So, I submit to you that those who claim to be fighting for tolerance on this issue may not be tolerant at all.

When John Kennedy was running for President in 1960, he said that his church would not dictate his Presidency any more than he would speak for his church. Just so, and proper. But John Kennedy was speaking in an America in which the role of religion—and by that I mean the role of all churches—was secure. Abortion was not a political issue. Prayer was not a political issue. The right of church schools to operate was not a political issue. And it was broadly acknowledged that religious leaders had a right and a duty to speak out on the issues of the day. They held a place of respect, and a politician who spoke to or of them with a lack of respect would not long survive in the political arena. It was acknowledged then that religion held a special place, occupied a special territory in the hearts of the citizenry. The climate has changed greatly since then. And since it has, it logically follows that religion needs defenders against those who care only for the interests of the state.

There are, these days, many questions on which religious leaders are obliged to offer their moral and theological guidance, and such guidance is a good and necessary thing. To know how a church and its members feel on a public issue expands the parameters of debate. It does not narrow the debate; it expands it.

The truth is, politics and morality are inseparable. And as morality's foundation is religion, religion and politics are necessarily related. We need religion as a guide. We need it because we are imperfect, and our government needs the church, because only those humble enough to admit they're sinners can bring to democracy the tolerance requires in order to survive.

A state is nothing more than a reflection of its citizens; the more decent the citizens, the more decent the state. If you practice a religion, whether you're Catholic, Protestant, Jewish, or guided by some other faith, then your private life will be influenced by a sense of moral obligation, and so, too, will your public life. One affects the other. The churches of America do not exist by the grace of the state; the churches of America are not mere citizens of the state. The churches of America exist apart; they have their own vantage point, their own authority. Religion is its own realm; it makes its own claims.

We establish no religion in this country, nor will we ever. We command no worship. We mandate no belief. But we poison our society when we remove its theological underpinnings. We court corruption when we leave it bereft of belief. All are free to believe or not believe; and are free to practice a faith or not. But those who believe must be free to speak of and act on their belief, to apply moral teaching to public questions

I submit to you that the tolerant society is open to and encouraging of all religion. And this does not weaken us; it strengthens us, it makes us strong. You know, if we look back through history to all those great civilizations, those great nations that rose up to even world dominance and then deteriorated, declined, and fell, we find they all had one thing in common. One of the significant forerunners of their fall was their turning away from their God or gods.

Without God, there is no virtue, because there's no prompting of the conscience. Without God, we're mired in the material, that flat world that tells us only what the senses perceive. Without God, there is a coarsening of the society. And without God, democracy will not and cannot long endure. If we ever forget that we're one nation under God, then we will be a nation gone under.

If I could just make a personal statement of my own—in these 3 years I have understood and known better than ever before the words of Lincoln, when he said that he would be the greatest fool on this footstool called Earth if he ever thought that for one moment he could perform the duties of that office without help from One who is stronger than all.

I thank you, thank you for inviting us here today. Thank you for your kindness and your patience. May God keep you, and may we, all of us, keep God.

Thank you.

WALTER MONDALE, "REMARKS TO THE INTERNATIONAL CONVENTION OF B'NAI B'RITH" (1984)

Walter Mondale served as a U.S. senator from Minnesota prior to becoming vice president during the tenure of President Jimmy Carter (1977–1981). At the time of this speech, he was the Democratic nominee for president, running against the incumbent Ronald Reagan. The international convention of the Jewish service organization B'nai

B'rith hosted speeches by both Mondale and Reagan on the subject of the proper relationship between politics and religion.

WHY THIS READING?

Mondale's remarks were primarily a response to Reagan's speech at the Republican National Convention, in which Reagan argued that religion and politics are necessarily joined, and that opponents of school prayer are intolerant of religion. Reagan's comments sparked intense national debate and led Mondale to defend his own views in this address.

Questions to guide you as you read:

- What does Mondale regard as the beneficial effects that separation of church and state has had on faith?
- What dangers to American democracy does Mondale detect in Reagan's approach to the question of the proper relationship between religion and politics?

I believe in an America where all people have the right to pursue their faith not just freely, but also without insult or embarrassment; where religious freedom is not a passive tolerance, but an active celebration of our pluralism.

I believe in an America that gives, as George Washington wrote to the Touro Synagogue "to bigotry no sanction, to persecution no assistance."

I believe in an America that has been a home and refuge for people from every faith. Our Government is the protector of every faith because it is the exclusive property of none.

I believe in an America that honors what Thomas Jefferson first called the "wall of separation between church and state." That freedom has made our faith unadulterated and unintimidated. It has made Americans the most religious people on earth. Today, the religion clauses of the First Amendment do not need to be fixed; they need to be followed.

No More Uplifting Power

There is no more uplifting power on earth than religious faith which cannot be coerced and is tolerant of other beliefs.

To coerce is to doubt the sturdiness of our faith. To ask the state to enforce the religious life of our people is to betray a telling cynicism about the American people.

Moreover, history teaches us that if that force is unleashed it will corrupt our faith, divide our nation, and embitter our people.

Today that force is being wielded by an extreme fringe poised to capture the Republican Party and tear it from its roots in Lincoln.

It is troubling that Rev. Jimmy Swaggart, who insists that Catholicism is a "false religion, and that Jews are dammed to go to hell," is a welcome policy adviser at the White House.

It is disquieting that a Presidential aide, unsatisfied with the religious purity of some White House staff, has urged her colleagues to "get saved or get out."

It is ominous when Reverend Falwell brags that, if Mr. Reagan is reelected, "We will get at least two more appointments to the Supreme Court."

At the Republican Convention in Dallas, moderates were driven out. An ambitious crowd with fire in its eyes seized control of the platform, the podium and perhaps the future of the party.

And they are not disappointed in the performance of their Presidential candidate.

Religion, Mr. Reagan told a prayer breakfast in Dallas, means defenders against those who care only for the interests of the state. His clear implication was that he welcomed such a role for himself.

The Queen of England, where state religion is established, is called Defender of the Faith. But the President of the United States is the defender of the Constitution, which defends all faiths.

A President has no higher role. Whatever his private beliefs and religious practice, a President must be the guardian of the laws which insure America's religious diversity.

Americas have only one President at a time. He must use his leadership to unify us. He must dispute his opponents with respect. The civility of our public debate depends on our willingness to accept the good faith of those who disagree. Our President must rejoice in the noise of public argument; it is the music of freedom.

The President should not attempt to transform policy debates into theological disputes. He must not let it be thought that political dissent from him is unchristian. And he must not cast opposition to his programs as opposition to America.

Last month in Dallas, Mr. Reagan attacked those of us who are trying to preserve the separation of church and state. He supports a constitutional amendment instituting school prayer, with the prayers chosen by local politicians. In Dallas, he said that anyone who opposed that amendment is "intolerant" of religion,

Tuesday, in Utah, Mr. Reagan attacked again, accusing us of favoring "freedom against religion." Instead of construing dissent from him in good faith, Mr. Reagan has insulted the motives, of those who disagree with him, including me.

I don't doubt Mr. Reagan's faith, his patriotism and his family values. And I call on him and his supporters to accept and respect mine.

I refuse to permit my political opponents to divert the debate from the real questions facing our future by questioning my faith, my patriotism, or my family values.

Citizenship: What makes one an American?

Dispute over the role of race in citizenship

14th AMENDMENT TO THE U.S. CONSTITUTION (1868)

Together with the 13th and 15th Amendments, the 14th Amendment, ratified in 1868, is one of the post-Civil War "Reconstruction Amendments." Reconstruction refers to the post-Civil War reordering of government and society in the defeated South. The Amendment was in part a response to the Supreme Court decision in *Dred Scott v. Sandford* (1857; later in this chapter), which held that blacks were not citizens and therefore enjoyed no constitutional protections. In response, the 14th Amendment defines "citizenship," guarantees due process rights in decisions involving life, liberty, and property, and mandates equal protection under the law.

Question to guide you as you read:

- What group did the framers of the 14th Amendment aim to protect in crafting it?

1. All persons born or naturalized in the United States, and subject to the jurisdiction thereof, are citizens of the United States and of the State wherein they reside. No State shall make or enforce any law which shall abridge the privileges or immunities of citizens of the United States; nor shall any State deprive any person of life, liberty, or property, without due process of law; nor deny to any person within its jurisdiction the equal protection of the laws.

2. Representatives shall be apportioned among the several States according to their respective

numbers, counting the whole number of persons in each State, excluding Indians not taxed. But when the right to vote at any election for the choice of electors for President and Vice-President of the United States, Representatives in Congress, the Executive and Judicial officers of a State, or the members of the Legislature thereof, is denied to any of the male inhabitants of such State, being twenty-one years of age, and citizens of the United States, or in any way abridged, except for participation in rebellion, or other crime, the basis of representation therein shall be reduced in the proportion which the number of such male citizens shall bear to the whole number of male citizens twenty-one years of age in such State.

3. No person shall be a Senator or Representative in Congress, or elector of President and Vice-President, or hold any office, civil or military, under the United States, or under any State, who, having previously taken an oath, as a member of Congress, or as an officer of the United States, or as a member of any State legislature, or as an executive or judicial officer of any State, to support the Constitution of the United States, shall have engaged in insurrection or rebellion against the same, or given aid or comfort to the enemies thereof. But Congress may by a vote of two-thirds of each House, remove such disability.

4. The validity of the public debt of the United States, authorized by law, including debts incurred for payment of pensions and bounties for services in suppressing insurrection or rebellion, shall not be questioned. But neither the United States nor any State shall assume or pay any debt or obligation incurred in aid of insurrection or rebellion against the United States, or any claim for the loss or emancipation of any slave; but all such debts, obligations and claims shall be held illegal and void.

5. The Congress shall have power to enforce, by appropriate legislation, the provisions of this article.

ABRAHAM LINCOLN, "SPEECH IN REPLY TO DOUGLAS AT CHICAGO, ILLINOIS" (1858)

This speech demonstrates that the Lincoln–Douglas Senate campaign started some time before the official Lincoln–Douglas debates. Lincoln's "Speech in Reply to Douglas" came two-and-a-half months before commencement of the formal Lincoln–Douglas debates, which began on August 21, 1858, at Ottawa, Illinois. Lincoln would lose to Douglas in his bid to become a U.S. senator representing Illinois. But two years later, they would square off again, this time for the presidency, which Lincoln would win.

WHY THIS READING?

In his reply to Douglas, Lincoln addresses the question of whether race was intended by the Founders to play a role in deciding who qualifies for American citizenship. Lincoln chose to speak at a Fourth of July celebration, where he articulated his views on the Declaration of Independence and what it means to be an American. This exchange, along with the seven Lincoln–Douglas debates that shortly followed, are generally regarded as the most insightful treatments of the relationship of race to American democracy to be found in this country's political discourse.

Questions to guide you as you read:

- How does Lincoln characterize Stephen Douglas's view of the meaning of the Declaration of Independence?
- Does Lincoln believe that the Declaration of Independence meant to include blacks when it stated that "all men are created equal"? If so, why? If not, why not?

My Fellow Citizens:

Now, it happens that we meet together once every year, some time about the 4th of July, for some reason or other. These 4th of July gatherings I suppose have their uses. If you will indulge [permit] me, I will state what I suppose to be some of them.

We are now a mighty nation, we are thirty—or about thirty millions of people, and we own and inhabit about one-fifteenth part of the dry land of the whole earth. We run our memory back over the pages of history for about eighty-two years and we discover that we were then a very small people in point of numbers, vastly inferior to what we are now, with a vastly less extent of country—with vastly less of everything we deem desirable among men—we look upon the change as exceedingly advantageous to us and to our posterity, and we fix upon something that happened away back, as in some way or other being connected with this rise of prosperity. We find a race of men living in that day whom we claim as our fathers and grandfathers; they were iron men, they fought for the principle that they were contending for; and we understood that by what they then did it has followed that the degree of prosperity that we now enjoy has come to us. We hold this annual celebration to remind ourselves of all the good done in this process of time, of how it was done and who did it, and how we are historically connected with it; and we go from these meetings in better humor with ourselves—we feel more attached the one to the other, and more firmly bound to the country we inhabit. In every way we are better men in the age, and race, and country in which we live for these celebrations. But after we have done all this we have not yet reached the whole. There is something else connected with it.

We have besides these men—descended by blood from our ancestors—among us perhaps half our people who are not descendants at all of these men, they are men who have come from Europe—German, Irish, French and Scandinavian—men that have come from Europe themselves, or whose ancestors have come hither and settled here, finding themselves our equals in all things. If they look back through this history to trace their connection with those days by blood, they find they have none, they cannot carry themselves back into that glorious epoch [time] and make themselves feel that they are part of us, but when they look through that old Declaration of Independence they find that those old men say that "We hold these truths to be self-evident, that all men are created equal" and then they feel that that moral sentiment taught in that day evidences their relation to those men, that it is the father of all moral principle in them, and that they have a right to claim it as though they were blood of the blood, and flesh of the flesh of the men who wrote that Declaration, and so they are. This is the electric cord in that Declaration that links the hearts of patriotic and liberty-loving men together, that will link those patriotic hearts as long as the love of freedom exists in the minds of men throughout the world. Now, sirs, for the purpose of squaring things with this idea "don't care if slavery is voted up or voted down," [3] for sustaining the *Dred Scott* decision, for holding that the Declaration of Independence did not mean anything at all, we have Judge Douglas giving his exposition of what the Declaration of Independence means, and we have him saying that the people of America are equal to the people of England. According to his construction, you Germans are not connected with it. Now I ask you in all soberness, if all these things, if indulged in, if ratified, if confirmed and endorsed, if taught to our children, and repeated to them, do not tend to rub out the sentiment of liberty in the country, and to transform this government into a government of some other form. Those arguments that are made, that the inferior race are to be treated with as much allowance as they are capable of enjoying; that as much is to be done for them as their condition will allow. What are these arguments? They are the arguments that kings have made for enslaving the people in all

3. Stephen Douglas repeatedly said that he did not "care if slavery is voted up or down." This statement expresses Douglas's doctrine of "popular sovereignty," or the view that each state should decide for itself whether to have slavery or not.

ages of the world. You will find that all the arguments in favor of king-craft [the art of ruling as a monarch] were of this class; they always bestrode [to straddle, as one does when riding a horse; to tower over] the necks of the people, not that they wanted to do it, but because the people were better off for being ridden. That is their argument, and this argument of the Judge is the same old serpent that says you work and I eat, you toil and I will enjoy the fruits of it.[4] Turn it whatever way you will—whether it come from the mouth of a king, an excuse for enslaving the people of his country, or from the mouth of men of one race as a reason for enslaving the men of another race, it is all the same old serpent, and I hold if that course of argumentation that is made for the purpose of convincing the public mind that we should not care about this, should be granted, it does not stop with the Negro. I should like to know if taking this old Declaration of Independence, which declares that all men are equal upon principle, and making exceptions to it, where will it stop. If one man says it does not mean a Negro, why may not another man say it does not mean another man? If that Declaration is not the truth, let us get the statute book, in which we find it, and tear it out! Who is so bold as to do it! If it is not true, let us tear it out! Let us stick to it then, let us stand firmly by it then.

It may be argued that there are certain conditions that make necessities and impose them upon us, and to the extent that a necessity is imposed upon a man he must submit to it. I think that was the condition in which we found ourselves when we established this government. We had slavery among us, we could not get our constitution unless we permitted them to remain in slavery, we could not secure the good we did secure if we grasped for more, and having by necessity submitted to that much, it does not destroy the principle that is the charter [written grant of rights] of our liberties. Let that charter stand as our standard.

My friend has said to me that I am a poor hand to quote Scripture.[5] I will try it again, however. It is said in one of the admonitions of the Lord, "As your Father in Heaven is perfect, be ye also perfect." The Savior, I suppose, did not expect that any human creature could be perfect as the Father in Heaven; but He said, "As your Father in Heaven is perfect, be ye also perfect." He set that up as a standard, and he who did most towards reaching that standard, attained the highest degree of moral perfection. So I say in relation to the principle that all men are created equal let it be as nearly reached as we can. If we cannot give freedom to every creature, let us do nothing that will impose slavery upon any other creature. Let us then turn this government back into the channel in which the framers of the Constitution originally placed it.[6] Let us stand firmly by each other. If we do not do so we are turning in the contrary direction, that our friend Judge Douglas proposes—not intentionally—as working in the traces tending to make this one universal slave nation. He is one that runs in that direction, and as such I resist him.

My friends, I have detained [kept] you about as long as I desired to do, and I have only to say, let us discard all this quibbling [fussing] about this man and the other man—this race and that race and the other race being inferior, and therefore they must be placed in an inferior position—discarding our standard that we have left us. Let us discard all these things, and unite as one people throughout this land, until we shall once more stand up declaring that all men are created equal.

My friends... I leave you hoping that the lamp of liberty will burn in your bosoms until there shall no longer be a doubt that all men are created free and equal.

---

4. Lincoln said elsewhere that the serpent's statement perfectly captured the injustice of slavery.

5. Lincoln here makes a joke at his own expense. He was widely rumored to be an atheist (one who does not believe in the existence of God) or a deist (one who believes that God created the world, but does not think that He miraculously intervenes within it).

6. Lincoln believed that the Founders tried to set slavery on a gradual course to extinction.

STEPHEN A. DOUGLAS, "FROM THE FIFTH JOINT DEBATE [WITH LINCOLN]" (1858)

In the seven Lincoln–Douglas debates of 1858, candidate Abraham Lincoln (R-IL) and incumbent Senator Stephen A. Douglas (D-IL) traveled from town to town across Illinois debating one another, with a spot in the U.S. Senate hanging in the balance. Although senators were elected by the state legislatures until 1913, Douglas and Lincoln took their arguments directly to the voters of Illinois, who in turn chose the members of the state legislature.

WHY THIS READING?

The question of race in America is as present and powerful today as it was at the time of the Founding. The Lincoln–Douglas debates are remarkable because the candidates entered into a level of political dialogue second to none in eloquence and complexity of argument. The debates revolved around the question of slavery and its relationship to the Founding principles as articulated in the Declaration of Independence and the U.S. Constitution. Lincoln maintained that, through the Declaration and the Constitution, the Founders intended to put slavery on the course of "ultimate extinction," whereas Douglas argued that the Founders intended to forever leave the question of slavery up to each state to decide for itself. Douglas called his characterization of the Founders' position "state sovereignty" or "popular sovereignty," meaning that the question of slavery was to be decided by the citizens of each individual state. The format of the debates was as follows: One man would speak first, his opponent would respond, and then the first speaker would end with a closing statement and response. Each debate lasted three hours. The fifth of the seven Lincoln–Douglas debates took place in Galesburg on October 7, 1858. Of the seven debates, it attracted the largest crowd, most of whom were Lincoln supporters.

Questions to guide you as you read:

- Douglas argues that because Jefferson, the author of the Declaration of Independence, owned slaves, he could not have meant that "the negro and the white man are made equal by the Declaration of Independence." Recall that Lincoln addressed this point in his July 10, 1858 speech (immediately above). What is Lincoln's rejoinder there?
- What policy regarding slavery does Douglas believe is required to achieve lasting peace between the North and the South?

...I tell you that this Chicago doctrine of Lincoln's—declaring that the negro and the white man are made equal by the Declaration of Independence and by Divine Providence—is a monstrous heresy. The signers of the Declaration of Independence never dreamed of the negro when they were writing that document. They referred to white men, to men of European birth and European descent, when they declared the equality of all men. I see a gentleman there in the crowd shaking his head. Let me remind him that when Thomas Jefferson wrote that document, he was the owner, and so continued until his death, of a large number of slaves. Did he intend to say in that Declaration, that his negro slaves, which he held and treated as property, were created his equals by Divine law, and that he was violating the law of God every day of his life by holding them as slaves? It must be borne in mind that when that Declaration was put forth, every one of the thirteen Colonies were slaveholding Colonies, and every man who signed that instrument represented a slave-holding constituency. Recollect, also, that no one of them emancipated [freed] his slaves, much less put them on an equality with himself, after he signed the Declaration. On the contrary, they all continued to hold their negroes as slaves during the revolutionary war. Now, do you believe—are you willing to have it said—that every man who signed the Declaration of Independence declared the negro his equal, and then was hypocrite enough to continue to hold him as a slave, in violation of what he believed to be the Divine law? And yet when you say that the Declaration of Independence includes the negro, you charge the signers of it with hypocrisy [saying one thing and doing another].

I say to you, frankly, that in my opinion, this Government was made by our fathers on the white basis. It was made by white men for the benefit of white men and their posterity forever, and was intended to be administered by white men in all time to come. But while I hold that under our Constitution and political system the negro is not a citizen, cannot be a citizen, and ought not to be a citizen, it does not follow by any means that he should be a slave. On the contrary it does follow that the negro, as an inferior race, ought to possess every right, every privilege, every immunity which he can safely exercise consistent with the safety of the society in which he lives. Humanity requires, and Christianity commands, that you shall extend to every inferior being, and every dependent being, all the privileges, immunities and advantages which can be granted to them consistent with the safety of society. If you ask me the nature and extent of these privileges, I answer that that is a question which the people of each State must decide for themselves. Illinois has decided that question for herself. We have said that in this State the negro shall not be a slave, nor shall he be a citizen. Kentucky holds a different doctrine. New York holds one different from either, and Maine one different from all. Virginia, in her policy on this question, differs in many respects from the others, and so on, until there is hardly two States whose policy is exactly alike in regard to the relation of the white man and the negro. Nor can you reconcile them and make them alike. Each State must do as it pleases. Illinois had as much right to adopt the policy which we have on that subject as Kentucky had to adopt a different policy. The great principle of this Government is, that each State has the right to do as it pleases on all these questions, and no other State, or power on earth has the right to interfere with us, or complain of us merely because our system differs from theirs. In the Compromise Measures of 1850, Mr. Clay declared that this great principle ought to exist in the Territories as well as in the States, and I reasserted his doctrine in the Kansas and Nebraska bill in 1854.

But Mr. Lincoln cannot be made to understand, and those who are determined to vote for him, no matter whether he is a proslavery man in the south and a negro equality advocate in the north, cannot be made to understand how it is that in a Territory the people can do as they please on the slavery question under the *Dred Scott* decision. Let us see whether I cannot explain it to the satisfaction of all impartial men. Chief Justice Taney has said in his opinion in the *Dred Scott* case, that a negro slave being property, stands on an equal footing with other property, and that the owner may carry them into United States territory the same as he does other property. Suppose any two of you, neighbors, should conclude to go to Kansas, one carrying $1,000,000 merchandise, including quantities of liquors. You both agree that under that decision you may carry your property to Kansas, but when you get it there, the merchant who is possessed of the liquors is met by the Maine liquor law, which prohibits the sale or use of his property, and the owner of the slaves is met by equally unfriendly legislation, which makes his property worthless after he gets it there. What is the right to carry your property into the Territory worth to either, when unfriendly legislation in the Territory renders it worthless after you get it there? The slaveholder when he gets his slaves there finds that there is no local law to protect him in holding them, no slave code, no police regulation maintaining and supporting him in his right, and he discovers at once that the absence of such friendly legislation excludes his property from the Territory, just as irresistibly as if there was a positive Constitutional prohibition excluding it. Thus you find it is with any kind of property in a Territory, it depends for its protection on the local and municipal law. If the people of a Territory want slavery, they make friendly legislation to introduce it, but if they do not want it, they withhold all protection from it, and then it cannot exist there. Such was the view taken on the subject by different Southern men when the Nebraska bill passed. See the speech of Mr. Orr, of South Carolina, the present Speaker of the House of Representatives of Congress, made at that time, and there you will find this whole doctrine argued out at full length. Read the speeches of other Southern Congressmen, Senators and Representatives, made in 1854 and you will find that they took the same view of the subject as Mr. Orr—that slavery could never be forced on a people who did not want it. I hold that in this country there is no power on the face of the globe that can force any institution on an unwilling people. The great fundamental principle of our Government is that the people of each State and each Territory shall be left perfectly free to decide for themselves what shall be the nature and character of their institutions. When this Government was made, it was based on that principle. At the time of its formation there were twelve slaveholding States and one free State in this Union. Suppose this doctrine of Mr. Lincoln and the Republicans, of uniformity of laws of all the States on the subject of slavery, had prevailed; suppose Mr. Lincoln himself had been a member of the Convention which framed the Constitution, and that he had risen in that august [impressive] body, and addressing the father of his country, had said as he did at Springfield:

"A house divided against itself cannot stand. I believe this Government cannot endure permanently half slave and half free. I do not expect the Union to be dissolved—I do not expect the house to fall, but I do expect it will cease to be divided. It will become all one thing or all the other."

What do you think would have been the result? Suppose he had made that Convention believe that doctrine and they had acted upon it, what do you think would have been the result? Do you believe that the one free State would have outvoted the twelve slaveholding States, and thus abolish slavery? On the contrary, would not the twelve slaveholding States have outvoted the one free State, and under his doctrine have fastened slavery by an irrevocable [unalterable] Constitutional provision upon every inch of the American Republic? Thus you see that the doctrine he now advocates, if proclaimed at the beginning of the Government, would have established slavery everywhere throughout the American continent, and are you willing, now that we have the majority section, to exercise a power which we never would have submitted to when we were in the minority? If the Southern States had attempted to control our institutions, and make the States all slave when they had the power, I ask: Would you have submitted to it? If you would not, are you willing now, that we have become the strongest under that great principle of self-government that allows each State to do as it pleases, to attempt to control the Southern institutions? Then, my friends, I say to you that there is but one path of peace in this Republic, and that is to administer this Government as our fathers made it, divided into free and slave States, allowing each State to decide for itself whether it wants slavery or not. If Illinois will settle the slavery question for herself, and mind her own business and let her neighbors alone, we will be at peace with Kentucky, and every other Southern State. If every other State in the Union will do the same there will be peace between the North and the South, and in the whole Union.

ABRAHAM LINCOLN, "REPLY TO DOUGLAS AT THE FIFTH JOINT DEBATE" (1858)

WHY THIS READING?

In his reply to Douglas's arguments at Galesburg, Lincoln defends his reading of the Declaration of Independence against Douglas's charge that he misinterprets the

Founders' intentions regarding race in America. In the course of so doing, he also contests Douglas's argument that "if we do not confess that there is a sort inequality between the white and black races, which justifies us in making them slaves, we must, then, insist that there is a degree of equality that requires us to make them our wives." Lincoln's rejoinder to Douglas on this point differentiates equality of natural rights, which Lincoln advocates, from "perfect social and political equality," which Lincoln deems impossible.

Questions to guide you as you read:

- How does Lincoln attempt to reconcile Jefferson's ownership of slaves with his writing that "all men are created equal" in the Declaration?
- Why does Lincoln think it undemocratic to allow, as Douglas wants, the new territories to decide for themselves whether they will adopt slavery or not? If democracy means that the majority rules, on what basis can Lincoln claim that it is undemocratic to allow the majorities in each of the territories to vote slavery "up or down"?

MY FELLOW CITIZENS: A very large portion of the speech which Judge Douglas has addressed to you has previously been delivered and put in print. I do not mean that for a hit upon the Judge at all. If I had not been interrupted, I was going to say that such an answer as I was able to make to a very large portion of it, had already been more than once made and published. Here has been an opportunity afforded to the public to see our respective views upon the topics discussed in a large portion of the speech which he has just delivered. I make these remarks for the purpose of excusing myself for not passing over the entire ground that the Judge has traversed. I however desire to take up some of the points that he has attended to, and ask your attention to them, and I shall follow him backwards upon some notes which I have taken, reversing the order by beginning where he concluded.

The Judge has alluded to the Declaration of Independence, and insisted that negroes are not included in that Declaration; and that it is a slander upon the framers of that instrument, to suppose that negroes were meant therein; and he asks you: Is it possible to believe that Mr. Jefferson, who penned the immortal paper, could have supposed himself applying the language of that instrument to the negro race, and yet held a portion of that race in slavery? Would he not at once have freed them? I only have to remark upon this part of the Judge's speech (and that, too, very briefly, for I shall not detain myself, or you, upon that point for any great length of time), that I believe the entire records of the world, from the date of the Declaration of Independence up to within three years ago, may be searched in vain for one single affirmation, from one single man, that the negro was not included in the Declaration of Independence; I think I may defy Judge Douglas to show that he ever said so, that Washington ever said so, that any President ever said so, that any member of Congress ever said so, or that any living man upon the whole earth ever said so, until the necessities of the present policy of the Democratic party, in regard to slavery, had to invent that affirmation. And I will remind Judge Douglas and this audience, that while Mr. Jefferson was the owner of slaves, as undoubtedly he was, in speaking upon this very subject, he used the strong language that "he trembled for his country when he remembered that God was just;" and I will offer the highest premium in my power to Judge Douglas if he will show that he, in all his life, ever uttered a sentiment at all akin to that of Jefferson....

Now a few words in regard to these extracts from speeches of mine, which Judge Douglas has read to you, and which he supposes are in very great contrast to each other. [These] speeches have been before the public for a considerable time, and if they have any inconsistency in them, if there is any conflict in them, the public [should] have been able to detect it. When the Judge says, in speaking on this subject, that I make speeches of one sort for the people of the northern end of the State, and of a different sort for the southern people, he assumes that I do not understand that my speeches will be put in print and read north and south. I knew all the while that the speech that I made at Chicago, and the one I made at Jonesboro and the one at Charleston, would all be put in print and all the reading and intelligent men in the community would see them and know all about my opinions. And I have not supposed, and do not now suppose, that there is any conflict whatever between them. But the Judge will have it that if we do not confess that there is a sort of inequality between the white and black races, which justifies us in making them slaves, we must, then, insist that there is a degree of equality that requires us to make them our wives. Now, I have all the while taken a broad distinction in regard to that matter; and that is all there is in these different speeches which he arrays here, and the entire reading of either of the speeches will show that that distinction was made. Perhaps by taking two parts of the same speech, he could have got up as much of a conflict as the one he has found. I have all the while maintained, that in so far as it should be insisted that there was an equality between the white and black races that should produce a perfect social and political equality, it was an impossibility. This you have seen in my printed speeches, and with it I have said, that in their right to "life, liberty and the pursuit of happiness," as proclaimed in that old Declaration, the inferior races are our equals. And these declarations I have constantly made in reference to the abstract moral question, to contemplate and consider when we are legislating about any new country which is not already cursed with the actual presence of the evil—slavery. I have never manifested any impatience with the necessities that spring from the actual presence of black people amongst us, and the actual existence of slavery amongst us where it does already exist; but I have insisted that, in legislating for new countries, where it does not exist, there is no just rule other than that of moral and abstract right. With reference to those new countries, those maxims [rules of conduct] as to the right of a people to "life, liberty and the pursuit of happiness" were the just rules to be constantly referred to. There is no misunderstanding this, except by men interested to misunderstand it. I take it that I have to address an intelligent and reading community, who will peruse [study carefully] what I say, weigh it, and then judge whether I advance improper or unsound [false] views, or whether I advance hypocritical, and deceptive, and contrary views in different portions of the country.

CHIEF JUSTICE ROGER TANEY, OPINION OF THE COURT IN *DRED SCOTT V. SANDFORD* (1857)

Dred Scott, a slave, sued his owner for his freedom under the provisions of the Missouri Compromise (1820), one section of which granted freedom to any slave whose master took him into a free state. This provision of the 1820 law was intended to bar masters from bringing their slaves into free states. Scott had been taken to Illinois, a free state, and to federal territory north of the 36 degrees 30 minutes latitude line, where slavery was outlawed by the Compromise. However, in the *Dred Scott* case, the Supreme Court held this section of the Missouri Compromise to be unconstitutional, in part because, according to the Court, it violated the 5th Amendment's guarantee that citizens shall not "be deprived of life, liberty, or property, without due process of law."

WHY THIS READING?

In what is often cited as the most infamous opinion ever written by a Supreme Court Justice, Taney ruled that blacks, whether slave or free, could not be citizens. Scott sued for his freedom, arguing that he had become a citizen of the state of his home state of Missouri because he had been taken to a free state. In opposition, Taney argued that blacks were not included in the Declaration of Independence's assertion that "All men are created equal." Therefore, although Scott had traveled to a free state, Taney ruled that he could not have become free by doing so. Because he was not a citizen of Missouri, Taney concluded that Scott had no standing to sue. Thus, the case was dismissed.

Questions to guide you as you read:

- Chief Justice Taney asserts that, although the phrase "all men are created equal" "would seem to embrace the whole human family," it does not. Why? Based on your prior reading in this chapter, what would be Lincoln's rejoinder to Taney?
- You have read the 14th Amendment above. Which part of Taney's opinion for the Court does the 14th Amendment overturn?

The words "people of the United States" and "citizens" are synonymous terms, and mean the same thing. They both describe the political body who, according to our republican institutions, form the sovereignty [rulers], and who hold the power and conduct the Government through their representatives. They are what we familiarly call the "sovereign people," and every citizen is one of this people, and a constituent member of this sovereignty. The question before us is, whether the class of negro persons... compose a portion of this people, and are constituent members of this sovereignty? We think they are not, and that they are not included, and were not intended to be included, under the word "citizens" in the Constitution, and can therefore claim none of the rights and privileges which that instrument [the Constitution] provides for and secures to citizens of the United States. On the contrary, they were at that time considered as a subordinate and inferior class of beings, who had been subjugated [enslaved] by the dominant race, and, whether emancipated [freed] or not, yet remained subject to their authority, and had no rights or privileges but such as those who held the power and the Government might choose to grant them.

It is not the province [place] of the court to decide upon the justice or injustice, the policy or impolicy [unwise course of action], of these laws. The decision of that question belonged to the political or law-making power; to those who formed the sovereignty and framed the Constitution. The duty of the court is, to interpret the instrument they have framed; with the best lights we can obtain of the subject, and to administer it as we find it, according to its true intent and meaning when it was adopted.

In discussing this question, we must not confound [confuse] the rights of citizenship which a State may confer within its own limits, and the rights of citizenship as a member of the Union. It does not by any means follow, because he has all the rights and privileges of a citizen of a State, that he must be a citizen of the United States. He may have all of the rights and privileges of the citizen of a State, and yet not be entitled to the rights and privileges of a citizen in any other State. For, previous to the adoption of the Constitution of the United States, every State had the undoubted right to confer on whomsoever it pleased the character of citizen, and to endow him with all its rights. But this character of course was confined to the boundaries of the State, and gave him no rights or privileges in other States beyond those secured to him by the laws of nations and the comity [courtesy] of States. Nor have the several States surrendered the power of conferring these rights and privileges by adopting the Constitution of the United States. Each State may still confer them upon an alien, or any one it think proper, or upon any class or description of persons; yet he would not be a citizen in the sense in which that word is used in the Constitution of the United States, nor entitled to sue as such in one of its courts, nor to the privileges and immunities of a citizen in the other States, The rights which he would acquire would be restricted to the State which gave them. The Constitution has conferred on Congress the right to establish a uniform rule of naturalization, and this right is evidently exclusive, and has always been held by this court to be so. Consequently, no State, since the adoption of the Constitution, can by naturalizing an alien invest him with the rights and privileges secured to a citizen of a State under the Federal Government, although, so far as the State alone was concerned, he would undoubtedly be entitled to the rights of a citizen, and clothed with all the rights and immunities which the Constitution and laws of the State attached to that character.

It is very clear, therefore, that no State can, by any act or law of its own, passed since the adoption of the Constitution, introduce a new member into the political community created by the Constitution of the United States. It cannot make him a member of this community by making him a member of its own. And for the same reason it cannot introduce any person, or description of persons, who were not intended to be embraced in this new political family, which the Constitution brought into existence, but were intended to be excluded from it.

The question then arises, whether the provisions of the Constitution, in relation to the personal rights and privileges to which the citizen of a State should be entitled, embraced the negro African race, at that time in this country, or who might afterwards be imported, who had then or should afterwards be made free in any State; and to put it in the power of a single State to make him a citizen of the United States, and endue [endow] him with the full rights of citizenship in every other State without their consent? Does the Constitution of the United States act upon him whenever he shall be made free under the laws of a state, and raised there to the rank of a citizen, and immediately clothe him with all the privileges of a citizen in every other State, and in its own courts?

The court thinks the affirmative [truth] of these propositions cannot be maintained. And if it cannot, the plaintiff [Scott]...could not be a citizen of the State of Missouri, within the meaning of the Constitution of the United States, and, consequently, was not entitled to sue in its courts.

It is true, every person, and every class and description of persons, who were at the time of the adoption of the Constitution recognized as citizens in the several States, became also *citizens* of this new political body; but none other; it was formed by them, and for them and their posterity, but for no one else. And the personal rights and privileges guaranteed to citizens of this new sovereignty were intended to embrace those only who were then members of the several State communities, or who should afterwards by birthright or otherwise become members, according to the provisions of the Constitution and the principles on which it was founded. It was the union of those who were at that time members of distinct and separate political communities into one political family, whose power, for certain specified purposes, was to extend over the whole territory of the United States. And it gave to each citizen rights and privileges outside of his State which he did not before possess, and placed him in every other State upon a perfect equality with its own citizens as to rights of person and rights of property; it made him a citizen of the United States.

It becomes necessary, therefore, to determine who were citizens of the several States when the Constitution was adopted. And in order to do this, we must recur to the Governments and institutions of the thirteen colonies, when they separated from Great Britain and formed new sovereignties, and took their places in the family of independent nations. We must inquire who, at that time, were recognized as the people or citizens of a State, whose rights and liberties had been outraged by the English Government; and who declared their independence, and assumed the powers of Government to defend their rights by force of arms.

In the opinion of the court, the legislation and histories of the times, and the language used in the Declaration of Independence, show, that neither the class of persons who had been imported as slaves, nor their descendants, whether they had become free or not, were then acknowledged as a part of the people, nor intended to be included in the general words used in that memorable instrument [document].

It is difficult at this day to realize the state of public opinion in relation to that unfortunate race, which prevailed in the civilized and enlightened portion of the world at the time of the Declaration of Independence, and when the Constitution of the United States was framed and adopted. But the public history of every European nation displays it in a manner too plain to be mistaken.

They had for more than a century before been regarded as beings of an inferior order, and altogether unfit to associate with the white race, either in social or political relations; and so far inferior, that they had no rights which the white man was bound to respect; and that the negro might justly and lawfully be reduced to slavery for his benefit. He was bought and sold, and treated as an ordinary article of merchandise and traffic, whenever a profit could be made by it. This opinion was at that time fixed and universal in the civilized portion of the white race. It was regarded as an axiom [truth] in morals as well as in politics, which no one thought of disputing, or supposed to be open to dispute; and men in every grade and position in society daily and habitually acted upon it in their private pursuits, as well as in matters of public concerns, without doubting for a moment the correctness of this opinion.

And in no nation was this opinion more firmly fixed or more uniformly acted upon than by the English Government and English people. They not only seized them on the coast of Africa, and sold them or held them in slavery for their own use; but they took them as ordinary articles of merchandise to every country where they could make a profit on them, and were far more extensively engaged in this commerce than any other nation in the world.

The opinion thus entertained and acted upon in England was naturally impressed upon the colonies they founded on this side of the Atlantic. And, accordingly, a negro of the African race was regarded by them as an article of property, and held, and bought and sold as such, in every one of the thirteen colonies which united in the Declaration of Independence, and afterwards formed the Constitution of the United States. The slaves were more or less numerous in the different colonies, as slave labor was found more or less profitable. But no one seems to have doubted the correctness of the prevailing opinion of the time.

The legislation of the different colonies furnished positive and indisputable proof of this fact. It would he tedious, in this opinion, to enumerate the various laws they passed upon this subject. It will be sufficient, as an example of the legislation which then generally prevailed throughout the British colonies, to give the law of two of them; one being still a large slaveholding State, and the other the first State in which slavery ceased to exist....

The province of Maryland, in 1717...passed a law declaring "that if any free negro or mulatto intermarry with any white woman, or if any white man shall intermarry with any negro or mulatto woman, such negro or mulatto shall become a slave during life, excepting mulattoes born of white women, who, for such intermarriage, shall only become servants for seven years....And any white man or white woman who shall intermarry as aforesaid, with any negro or mulatto, such white man or white woman shall become servants during the term of seven years,..."

The other colonial law to which we refer was passed by Massachusetts in 1705....It is entitled "An act for the better preventing of a spurious and mixed issue," etc.; and it provides, that "if any negro or mulatto shall presume to smite or strike any person of the English or other Christian nation, such negro or mulatto shall be severely whipped, at the discretion of the justices before whom the offender shall be convicted."

And "that none of her Majesty's English or Scottish subjects, nor of any other Christian nation, within this province shall contract matrimony with any negro or mulatto; nor shall any person, duly authorized to solemnize marriage, presume to join any such in marriage...."

We give both of these laws in the words used by the respective legislative bodies, because the language in which they are framed, as well as the provisions contained in them show, too plainly to be misunderstood, the degraded condition of this unhappy race. They were still in force when the Revolution began, and are a faithful index to the state of feeling towards the class of persons of whom they speak, and of the position they occupied throughout the thirteen colonies, in the eyes and thoughts of the men who framed the Declaration of Independence and established the State Constitutions and Governments. They show that a perpetual and impassable barrier was intended to be erected between the white race and the one which they had reduced to slavery and governed as subjects with absolute and despotic power and which they then looked upon as so far below them in the scale of created beings, that intermarriage between white persons and negroes or mulattoes were regarded as unnatural and immoral, and punished as crimes....And no distinction in this respect was made between the free negro or mulatto and the slave but this stigma, of the deepest degradation, was fixed upon the whole race.

We refer to these historical facts for the purpose of showing the fixed opinions concerning that race, upon which the statesman of that day spoke and acted. It is necessary to do this, in order to determine whether the general terms used in the Constitution of the United States as to the rights of man and the rights of the people, was intended to include them or to give to them or their posterity the benefit of any of its provisions.

The language of the Declaration of Independence is equally conclusive:

It begins by declaring that, "when in the course of human events it becomes necessary for one people to dissolve the political bonds which have connected them with another, and to assume among, the powers of the earth the separate and equal station to which the laws of nature and natures God entitles them, a decent respect for the opinions of mankind requires that they should declare the causes which impel them to the separation."

It then proceeds to say: "We hold these truths to be self-evident: that all men are created equal; that they are endowed by their Creator with certain unalienable rights; that among them is life, liberty, and the pursuit of happiness; that to secure these rights, Governments are instituted deriving their just powers from the consent of the governed."

The general words above quoted would seem to embrace the whole human family, and if they were used in a similar instrument [document] at this day would be so understood. But it is too clear for dispute, that the enslaved African race were not intended to be included, and formed no part of the people who framed and adopted this declaration; for if the language, as understood in that day, would embrace them, the conduct of the distinguished men who framed the Declaration of Independence would have been utterly and flagrantly inconsistent with the principles they asserted; and instead of the sympathy of mankind, to which they so confidently appealed, they would have deserved and received universal rebuke [criticism] and reprobation.

Yet the men who framed this declaration were great men—high in literary acquirement, high in their sense of honor, and incapable of asserting principles inconsistent with those on which they were acting. They perfectly understood the meaning of the language they used, and how it would be understood by others; and they knew that it would not in any part of the civilized world be supposed to embrace the negro race, which, by common consent, had been excluded from civilized Governments and the family of nations, and doomed to slavery. They spoke and acted according to the then established doctrines and principles, and in the ordinary language of the day, and no one misunderstood them. The unhappy black race were separated from the white by indelible [permanent] marks, and laws long before established, and were never thought of or spoken of except as property, and when the claims of the owner or the profit of the trader were supposed to need protection.

This state of public opinion had undergone no change when the Constitution was adopted, as is equally evident from its provisions and language.

The brief preamble sets forth by whom it was formed, for what purposes, and for whose benefit and protection. It declares that it is formed by the *people* of the United States; that is to say, by those who were members of the different political communities in the several States; and its great object is declared to be to secure the blessings of liberty to themselves and their posterity. It speaks in general terms of the *people* of the United States, and of citizens of the several States, when it is providing for the exercise of the powers granted or the privileges secured to the citizen. It does not define what description of persons are intended to be included under these terms, or who shall be regarded as a citizen and one of the people. It uses them as terms so well understood, that no further description or definition was necessary.

But there are two clauses in the Constitution which point directly and specifically to the negro race as a separate class of persons, and show clearly that they were not regarded as a portion of the people or citizens of the Government then formed.

One of three clauses reserves to each of the thirteen States the right to import slaves until the year 1808, if it think proper. And the importation which it thus sanctions was unquestionably of persons of the race of which we are speaking, as the traffic in slaves in the United States had always been confined to them. And by the other provision the States pledged themselves to each other to maintain the right of property of the master, by delivering up to him any slave who may have escaped from his service, and be found within their respective territories. By the first above-mentioned clause, therefore, the right to purchase and hold this property is directly sanctioned and authorized for twenty years by the people who framed the Constitution. And by the second, they pledge themselves to maintain and uphold the right of the master in the manner specified, as long as the Government they then formed should endure. And these two provisions show, conclusively, that neither the description of persons therein referred to, nor their descendants, were embraced in any of the other provisions of the Constitution; for certainly these two clauses were not intended to confer on them or their posterity the blessings of liberty, or any of the personal rights so carefully provided for the citizen.

No one of that race had over migrated to the United States voluntarily; all of them had been brought here as articles of merchandise. The number that had been emancipated [freed] at that time were but few in comparison with those held in slavery; and they were identified in the public mind with the race to which they belonged, and regarded as part of the slave population rather than the free. It is obvious that they were not even in the minds of the framers of the Constitution when they were conferring special rights and privileges upon the citizens of a state in every other part of the Union.

Indeed, when we look to the condition of this race in the several States at the time, it is impossible to believe that these rights and privileges were intended to be extended to them.

It is very true, that in that portion of the Union where the labor of the negro race was found to be unsuited to the climate and unprofitable to the master, but few slaves were held at the time of the Declaration of Independence; and when the Constitution was adopted, it had entirely worn out in one of them, and measures had been taken for its gradual abolition in several others. But this change had not been produced by any change of opinion in relation to this race; but because it was discovered, from experience, that slave labor was unsuited to the climate and production of these

States: for some of the States, where it had ceased or nearly ceased to exist, were actively engaged in the slave trade, procuring cargoes on the coast of Africa, and transporting them for sale to those parts of the Union where their labor was found to be profitable, and suited to the climate and productions. And this traffic was openly carried on, and fortunes accumulated by it, without reproach [protest] from the people of the States where they resided. And it can hardly be supposed that, in the States where it was then countenanced [seen] in its worst form—that is, in the seizure and transportation—the people would have regarded those who were emancipated as entitled to equal rights with themselves.

And we may here again refer, in support of this proposition, to the plain and unequivocal [unambiguous] language of the laws of the several States, some passed after the Declaration of Independence and before the Constitution was adopted, and some since the Government went into operation.

We need not refer, on this point, particularly to the laws of the present slaveholding States. Their statute books are full of provisions in relation to this class, in the same spirit with the Maryland law which we have before quoted. They have continued to treat them as an inferior class, and to subject them to strict police regulations, drawing a broad line of distinction between the citizen and the slave races, and legislating in relation to them upon the same principle which prevailed at the time of the Declaration of Independence. As relates to these States, it is too plain for argument, that they have never been regarded as a part of the people or citizens of the State, nor supposed to possess any political rights which the dominant race might not withhold or grant at their pleasure. And as long ago as 1822, the Court of Appeals of Kentucky decided that free negroes and mulattoes were not citizens within the meaning of the Constitution of the United States; and the correctness of this decision is recognized, and the same doctrine affirmed, in Tennessee.

And if we turn to the legislation of the States where slavery had worn out, or measures taken for its speedy abolition, we shall find the same opinions and principles equally fixed and equally acted upon.

Thus, Massachusetts, in 1786, passed a law similar to the colonial one of which we have spoken. The law of 1786, like the law of 1706, forbids the marriage of any white person with any negro, Indian, or mulatto, and inflicts a penalty of fifty pounds upon any who join them in marriage; and declares all such marriages absolutely null and void, and degrades thus the unhappy issue of the marriage by fixing upon it the stain of bastardy. And this mark of degradation was renewed, and again impressed upon the race in the careful and deliberate preparation of their revised code published in 1836. This code forbids any person from joining in marriage any white person with any Indian, negro, or mulatto, and subjects the party who shall offend in this respect, to imprisonment not exceeding six months, in the common jail, or to hard labor, and to a fine of not less than fifty nor more than two hundred dollars; and, like the law of 1786, it declares the marriage to be absolutely null and void. It will be seen that the punishment is increased by the code upon the person who shall marry them, by adding imprisonment to a pecuniary [monetary] penalty.

So, too, in Connecticut. We refer more particularly to the legislation of this State, because it was not only among the first to put an end to slavery within its own territory, but was the first to fix a mark of reprobation upon the African slave trade. The law last mentioned was passed in October, 1788, about nine months after the State had ratified and adopted the present Constitution of the United States; and by that law it prohibited its own citizens, under severe penalties, from engaging in the trade, and declared all policies of insurance on the vessel or cargo made in the State to be null and void. But, up to the time of the adoption of the Constitution, there is nothing in the legislation of the state indicating any change of opinion as to the relative rights and position of the white and black races in this country, or indicating that it meant to place the latter, when free, upon a level with its citizens.

The status of law under American principles

Is lawlessness built into the very foundations of American political life?

THE DECLARATION OF INDEPENDENCE (1776)

The 4th of July holiday commemorates the signing of the Declaration of Independence in 1776. Its claims are addressed not only to King George III, but to humankind, because its principles are meant to apply to all human beings in every epoch and every land. The moral core of the Declaration is the theory of justice it presents, which consists of four truths that it holds to be "self-evident" to those who reason rightly about what it means to be a human being. ("Self-evident" does not mean evident to *everyone;* certainly King George III and, later, Hitler, Stalin, and Mao Tse Tung did not regard its principles as "evident.")

WHY THIS READING?

From the time of Jefferson and continuing through the speeches and deeds of Lincoln, Martin Luther King Jr., Ronald Reagan, and Barack Obama, the Declaration of Independence has served as the moral and political beacon by which Americans articulate both their aspirations and their concrete achievements. The four self-evident truths of the Declaration begin with the premise of human equality. Equality is, in fact, the more fundamental truth, from which the other three follow. Because all human beings are "created equal," they possess the "unalienable" rights to "life, liberty, and the pursuit of happiness (the "unalienable"—today "inalienable"—rights constitute the second of the four truths). Equality—understood in the sense that no one has a natural right to rule others without their consent—disposes of the older claim that some individuals deserve to rule over others because of a divine or hereditary right. Accordingly, the only legitimate method by which to institute government is through the "consent" of those to be ruled. Institution of government through consent, then, forms the third truth. Finally, because government is the creation of the sovereign people—rather than the other way around—should the government become destructive of the limited ends for which it was established, it is the people's "right" as well as "duty to throw off such Government, and to provide new Guards for their future security."

This final self-evident truth, the natural right of revolution, has since 1776 served to inspire a number of revolutions around the world (see, e.g., Czech President Vaclav Havel, chapter eight).

Questions to guide you as you read:

- The Declaration is not meant to be a governing document—that is the role of the Constitution. Instead, the Declaration provides the justification for government. What is that justification? What criteria must a government satisfy to be legitimate?

- Should the people decide that government is no longer exercising its power justly, it is their right, says the Declaration, "to alter or abolish to it, and to institute new government." What rationale does Jefferson offer to explain why he is unafraid that the people will overthrow a government that does not deserve to be overthrown?
- Based on your earlier reading of Jefferson's "Bill for Establishing Religious Freedom," is there a difference between the "Nature's God" of the Declaration and the God of revelation? If so, what might it be?

When in the Course of human events it becomes necessary for one people to dissolve the political bands which have connected them with another and to assume among the powers of the earth, the separate and equal station to which the Laws of Nature and of Nature's God entitle them, a decent respect to the opinions of mankind requires that they should declare the causes which impel them to the separation.

We hold these truths to be self-evident, that all men are created equal, that they are endowed by their Creator with certain unalienable Rights, that among these are Life, Liberty and the pursuit of Happiness.—That to secure these rights, Governments are instituted among Men, deriving their just powers from the consent of the governed,—That whenever any Form of Government becomes destructive of these ends, it is the Right of the People to alter or to abolish it, and to institute new Government, laying its foundation on such principles and organizing its powers in such form, as to them shall seem most likely to effect their Safety and Happiness. Prudence, indeed, will dictate that Governments long established should not be changed for light and transient causes; and accordingly all experience hath shewn that mankind are more disposed to suffer, while evils are sufferable than to right themselves by abolishing the forms to which they are accustomed. But when a long train of abuses and usurpations [use without right], pursuing invariably the same Object evinces a design to reduce them under absolute Despotism, it is their right, it is their duty, to throw off such Government, and to provide new Guards for their future security.—Such has been the patient sufferance of these Colonies; and such is now the necessity which constrains them to alter their former Systems of Government. The history of the present King of Great Britain is a history of repeated injuries and usurpations, all having in direct object the establishment of an absolute Tyranny over these States. To prove this, let Facts be submitted to a candid world.

He has refused his Assent to Laws, the most wholesome and necessary for the public good.

He has forbidden his Governors to pass Laws of immediate and pressing importance, unless suspended in their operation till his Assent should be obtained; and when so suspended, he has utterly neglected to attend to them.

He has refused to pass other Laws for the accommodation of large districts of people, unless those people would relinquish the right of Representation in the Legislature, a right inestimable to them and formidable to tyrants only.

He has called together legislative bodies at places unusual, uncomfortable, and distant from the depository of their Public Records, for the sole purpose of fatiguing them into compliance with his measures.

He has dissolved Representative Houses repeatedly, for opposing with manly firmness his invasions on the rights of the people.

He has refused for a long time, after such dissolutions, to cause others to be elected, whereby the Legislative Powers, incapable of Annihilation, have returned to the People at large for their exercise; the State remaining in the mean time exposed to all the dangers of invasion from without, and convulsions within.

He has endeavoured to prevent the population of these States; for that purpose obstructing the Laws for Naturalization of Foreigners; refusing to pass others to encourage their migrations hither, and raising the conditions of new Appropriations of Lands.

He has obstructed the Administration of Justice by refusing his Assent to Laws for establishing Judiciary Powers.

He has made Judges dependent on his Will alone for the tenure of their offices, and the amount and payment of their salaries.

He has erected a multitude of New Offices, and sent hither swarms of Officers to harass our people and eat out their substance.

He has kept among us, in times of peace, Standing Armies without the Consent of our legislatures.

He has affected to render the Military independent of and superior to the Civil Power.

He has combined with others to subject us to a jurisdiction foreign to our constitution, and unacknowledged by our laws; giving his Assent to their Acts of pretended Legislation:

For quartering large bodies of armed troops among us:

For protecting them, by a mock Trial from punishment for any Murders which they should commit on the Inhabitants of these States:

For cutting off our Trade with all parts of the world:

For imposing Taxes on us without our Consent:

For depriving us in many cases, of the benefit of Trial by Jury:

For transporting us beyond Seas to be tried for pretended offences:

For abolishing the free System of English Laws in a neighbouring Province, establishing therein an Arbitrary government, and enlarging its Boundaries so as to render it at once an example and fit instrument for introducing the same absolute rule into these Colonies.

For taking away our Charters, abolishing our most valuable Laws and altering fundamentally the Forms of our Governments:

For suspending our own Legislatures, and declaring themselves invested with power to legislate for us in all cases whatsoever.

He has abdicated Government here, by declaring us out of his Protection and waging War against us.

He has plundered our seas, ravaged our coasts, burnt our towns, and destroyed the lives of our people.

He is at this time transporting large Armies of foreign Mercenaries to compleat the works of death, desolation, and tyranny, already begun with circumstances of Cruelty & Perfidy [treachery] paralleled in the most barbarous ages, and totally unworthy the Head of a civilized nation.

He has constrained our fellow Citizens taken Captive on the high Seas to bear Arms against their Country, to become the executioners of their friends and Brethren, or to fall themselves by their Hands.

He has excited domestic insurrections amongst us, and has endeavoured to bring on the inhabitants of our frontiers, the merciless Indian Savages whose known rule of warfare, is an undistinguished destruction of all ages, sexes and conditions.

In every stage of these Oppressions We have Petitioned for Redress in the most humble terms: Our repeated Petitions have been answered only by repeated injury. A Prince, whose character is thus marked by every act which may define a Tyrant, is unfit to be the ruler of a free people.

Nor have We been wanting in attentions to our British brethren. We have warned them from time to time of attempts by their legislature to extend an unwarrantable jurisdiction over us. We have reminded them of the circumstances of our emigration and settlement here. We have appealed to their native justice and magnanimity, and we have conjured them by the ties of our common kindred to disavow these usurpations, which would inevitably interrupt our connections and correspondence. They too have been deaf to the voice of justice and of consanguinity [relationship by descent from the same ancestors; a close connection]. We must, therefore, acquiesce in the necessity, which denounces our Separation, and hold them, as we hold the rest of mankind, Enemies in War, in Peace Friends.

We, therefore, the Representatives of the united States of America, in General Congress, Assembled, appealing to the Supreme Judge of the world for the rectitude of our intentions, do, in the Name, and by Authority of the good People of these Colonies, solemnly publish and declare, That these united Colonies are, and of Right ought to be Free and Independent States, that they are Absolved from all Allegiance to the British Crown, and that all political connection between them and the State of Great Britain, is and ought to be totally dissolved; and that as Free and Independent States, they have full Power to levy War, conclude Peace, contract Alliances, establish Commerce, and to do all other Acts and Things which Independent States may of right do.—And for the support of this Declaration, with a firm reliance on the protection of Divine Providence, we mutually pledge to each other our Lives, our Fortunes, and our sacred Honor.

What is law-abidingness in the American context?

ABRAHAM LINCOLN, "SPEECH ON THE *DRED SCOTT* DECISION" (1857)

This speech predated the Lincoln–Douglas debates by just over one year. In it, Lincoln attacks the recently announced decision in *Dred Scott v. Sandford.*

WHY THIS READING?

Recall the immediately preceding chapter's examination of the Federalist–anti-Federalist debate over separation-of-powers doctrine. There, we saw that one of the concerns of the anti-Federalists was that the federal courts under the proposed Constitution would effectively come to exercise a veto over the actions of Congress, arrogating to themselves the "legislative power" and thereby undermining democratic government. We also read *Federalist 78*, in which Hamilton's Publius denies that such fears are warranted. Whereas the Congress possesses the power of the "purse," and the president that of the "sword," the federal courts "have neither FORCE nor WILL, but merely judgment" (capitalization in original).

But what is to be done in the event that the Supreme Court's "judgment" errs? Even worse still, what is to be done if that error strikes at the heart of the meaning and purpose of American democracy? This was the question Lincoln believed the country faced with the *Dred Scott* decision. Here, in the course of criticizing Chief Justice Taney's opinion for the majority, he articulates his view of the proper function of the judicial branch in American democracy. He also defends himself against the charge, made by Douglas and others, that he is promoting lawlessness by questioning the Supreme Court's interpretation of the law.

Questions to guide you as you read:

- You have read Jefferson's "Against Judicial Review." Which arguments of Jefferson's does Lincoln employ here in addressing the place and power of the U.S. Supreme Court?
- In contesting the decision in *Dred Scott*, Lincoln claims that he shall offer no "resistance" to it. What does he mean by "resistance," and why does he forego it?

. . . And now as to the *Dred Scott* decision. That decision declares two propositions—first, that a negro cannot sue in the U.S. Courts; and secondly, that Congress cannot prohibit slavery in the Territories. It was made by a divided court—dividing differently on the different points. Judge [Stephen] Douglas does not discuss the merits of the decision; and, in that respect, I shall follow his example, believing I could no more improve on McLean and Curtis, than he could on Taney.

He denounces all who question the correctness of that decision, as offering violent resistance to it. But who resists it? Who has, in spite of the decision, declared Dred Scott free, and resisted the authority of his master over him?

Judicial decisions have two uses—first, to absolutely determine the case decided, and secondly, to indicate to the public how other similar cases will be decided when they arise. For the latter use, they are called "precedents" and "authorities."

We believe, as much as Judge Douglas (perhaps more) in obedience to, and respect for the judicial department of government. We think its decisions on Constitutional questions, when fully settled, should control, not only the particular cases decided, but the general policy of the country, subject to be disturbed only by amendments of the Constitution as provided in that instrument itself. More than this would be revolution. But we think the *Dred Scott* decision is erroneous. We know the court that made it, has often over-ruled its own decisions, and we shall do what we can to have it to over-rule this. We offer no *resistance* to it.

Judicial decisions are of greater or less authority as precedents, according to circumstances. That this should be so, accords both with common sense, and the customary understanding of the legal profession.

If this important decision had been made by the unanimous concurrence [agreement] of the judges, and without any apparent partisan bias, and in accordance with legal public expectation, and with the steady practice of the departments throughout our history, and had been in no part, based on assumed historical facts which are not really true; or, if wanting in some of these, it had been before the court more than once, and had there been affirmed and re-affirmed through a course of years, it then might be, perhaps would be, factious [quarrelsome], nay [no], even revolutionary, to not acquiesce in it as a precedent.

But when, as it is true we find it wanting in all these claims to the public confidence, it is not resistance, it is not factious, it is not even disrespectful, to treat it as not having yet quite established a settled doctrine for the country—But Judge Douglas considers this view awful. Hear him:

"The courts are the tribunals prescribed by the Constitution and created by the authority of the people to determine, expound and enforce the law. Hence, whoever resists the final decision of the highest judicial tribunal, aims a deadly blow to our whole Republican system of government—a blow, which if successful would place all our rights and liberties at the mercy of passion, anarchy and violence. I repeat, therefore, that if resistance to the decisions of the Supreme Court of the United States, in a matter like the points decided in the *Dred Scott* case, clearly within their jurisdiction as defined by the Constitution, shall be forced upon the country as a political issue, it will become a distinct and naked issue between the friends and the enemies of the Constitution—the friends and the enemies of the supremacy of the laws."

Why this same Supreme Court once decided a national bank to be constitutional; but Gen. [Andrew] Jackson, as President of the United States, disregarded the decision, and vetoed a bill for a re-charter, partly on constitutional ground, declaring that each public functionary must support the Constitution, *"as he understands it."* But hear the General's [Jackson's] own words. Here they are, taken from his veto message:

"It is maintained by the advocates of the bank, that its constitutionality, in all its features, ought to be considered as settled by precedent, and by the decision of the Supreme Court. To this conclusion I cannot assent. Mere precedent is a dangerous source of authority, and should not be regarded as deciding questions of constitutional power, except where the acquiescence [agreement] of the people and the States can be considered as well settled. So

far from this being the case on this subject, an argument against the bank might be based on precedent. One Congress in 1791, decided in favor of a bank; another in 1811, decided against it. One Congress in 1815 decided against a bank; another in 1816 decided in its favor. Prior to the present Congress, therefore, the precedents drawn from that source were equal. If we resort to the States, the expressions of legislative, judicial and executive opinions against the bank have been probably to those in its favor as four to one; There is nothing in precedent, therefore, which if its authority were admitted, ought to weigh in favor of the act before me."

I drop the quotations merely to remark that all there ever was, in the way of precedent up to the *Dred Scott* decision, on the points therein decided, had been against that decision. But hear Gen. Jackson further:

"If the opinion of the Supreme Court covered the whole ground of this act, it ought not to control the co-ordinate [other] authorities [branches] of this Government. The Congress, the executive and the court, must each for itself be guided by its own opinion of the Constitution. Each public officer, who takes an oath to support the Constitution, swears that he will support it as he understands it, and not as it is understood by others. . . . "

FREDERICK DOUGLASS, "ON THE *DRED SCOTT* DECISION" (1857)

Douglass's speech on the *Dred Scott* decision predated Lincoln's remarks on the same subject (immediately above) by about one-and-a-half months. Although no less appalled than Lincoln by the Court's reasoning and conclusion, Douglass nonetheless saw in it a cause for optimism, remarking, "my hopes were never brighter." In his view, precisely because the Court's arguments were so flawed, and its decision so horrendous, it would catapult slavery to the forefront of the country's attention; this, in turn, he hoped, would expedite slavery's destruction. Douglass's prediction proved true, although not in the manner that he expected. The *Dred Scott* decision further inflamed the already-hot dispute over slavery; the Civil War would follow four years later in 1861 and, with the South's defeat, slavery would be abolished in 1865 by the 13th Amendment.

WHY THIS READING?

Comparison of Lincoln and Douglass's critiques of *Dred Scott* reveals their contrasting approaches to the question of whether America's principles require obedience to an unjust law. Like Lincoln, Douglass regards the *Dred Scott* decision as anathema. Not only can Douglass find no express or implied endorsements of slavery in either the Declaration or the original Constitution, but he also locates in both documents a number of straightforward denunciations of the South's "peculiar institution." ("Peculiar" here means "our own." Recall Alexander Stephens's use of this phrase in his "Cornerstone Speech" in chapter two.) Unlike Lincoln, Douglass is more prone to point to the role that law-abidingness can play in the perpetuation of injustice, in this case, that of slavery.

Questions to guide you as you read:

- What are the refutations Douglass offers when reviewing the historical analysis offered by Taney in *Dred Scott*? How would Taney, as well as Stephen Douglas, respond?

- Does Frederick Douglass believe that one has a duty to obey even an unjust law? If so, why? If not, why not?
- Douglass lumps Taney together with the abolitionist William Lloyd Garrison (whose 1843 "Resolution" you read in chapter two). Why?

Mr. Chairman, Friends, and Fellow Citizens:

...I come now to the great question as to the constitutionality of slavery. The recent slaveholding decision [*Dred Scott*], as well as the teachings of antislavery men, make this a fit time to discuss the constitutional pretensions of slavery.

The people of the North are a law-abiding people. They love order and respect the means to that end. This sentiment has sometimes led them to the folly and wickedness of trampling upon the very life of law, to uphold its dead form. This was so in the execution of that thrice [three times] accursed Fugitive Slave Bill.... The people permitted this outrage in obedience to the popular sentiment of reverence [respect] for law. While men thus respect law, it becomes a serious matter so to interpret the law as to make it operate against liberty. I have a quarrel with those who fling the Supreme Law of this land between the slave and freedom. It is a serious matter to fling the weight of the Constitution against the cause of human liberty, and those who do it, take upon them a heavy responsibility....

...When I admit that slavery is constitutional, I must see slavery recognized in the Constitution. I must see that it is there plainly stated that one man of a certain description has a right of property in the body and soul of another man of a certain description. There must be no room for a doubt. In a matter so important as the loss of liberty, everything must be proved beyond all reasonable doubt....

...Now let us approach the Constitution from the standpoint thus indicated, and instead of finding in it a warrant for the stupendous [amazing] system of robbery, comprehended in the term slavery, we shall find it strongly against that system.

"We, the people of the United States, in order to form a more perfect Union, establish justice, insure domestic tranquility, provide for the common defense, promote the general welfare, and secure the blessings of liberty to ourselves and our posterity, do ordain and establish this Constitution for the United States of America."

Such are the objects announced by the instrument itself, and they are in harmony with the Declaration of Independence, and the principles of human well-being.

Six objects are here declared, "Union," "defense," "welfare," "tranquility," "justice," and "liberty."

Neither in the preamble nor in the body of the Constitution is there a single mention of the term *slave* or *slave holder, slave master* or *slave state*, neither is there any reference to the color, or the physical peculiarities [characteristics] of any part of the people of the United States. Neither is there anything in the Constitution standing alone, which would imply the existence of slavery in this country.

"We, the people"—not we, the white people; not we, the citizens, or the legal voters; not we, the privileged class, and excluding all other classes but we, the people; not we, the horses and cattle, but we the people—the men and women, the human inhabitants of the United States, do ordain and establish this Constitution.

I ask, then, any man to read the Constitution, and tell me where, if he can, in what particular that instrument affords the slightest sanction of [justification for] slavery?

Where will he find a guarantee for slavery? Will he find it in the declaration that no person shall be deprived of life, liberty, or property, without due process of law? Will he find it in the declaration that the Constitution was established to secure the blessing of liberty? Will he find it in the right of the people to be secure in their persons and papers, and houses, and effects? Will he find it in the clause prohibiting the enactment by any State of a bill of attainder?

These all strike at the root of slavery, and any one of them, but faithfully carried out, would put an end to slavery in every State in the American Union.

Take, for example, the prohibition of a bill of attainder. That is a law entailing on the child the misfortunes of the parent. This principle would destroy slavery in every State of the Union.

The law of slavery is a law of attainder [a bill that punishes a particular person or group; such bills are outlawed by the Constitution]. The child is property because its parent was property, and suffers as a slave because its parent suffered as a slave. Thus the very essence of the whole slave code is in open violation of a fundamental provision of the Constitution, and is in open and flagrant violation of all the objects set forth in the Constitution....

...How is the constitutionality of slavery made out, or attempted to be made out?

First, by discrediting and casting away as worthless the most beneficent [generous or kind] rules of legal interpretation; by disregarding the plain and common sense reading of the instrument itself; by showing that the Constitution does not mean what it says, and says what it does not mean, by assuming that the written Constitution is to be interpreted in the light of a secret and unwritten understanding of its framers, which understanding is declared to be in favor of slavery. It is in this mean, contemptible, underhand method that the Constitution is pressed into the service of slavery.

They do not point us to the Constitution itself, for the reason that there is nothing sufficiently explicit for their purpose; but they delight in supposed intentions—intentions nowhere expressed in the Constitution, and everywhere contradicted in the Constitution.

Judge Taney lays down this system of interpreting in this wise [way]:

> The general words above quoted would seem to embrace the whole human family, and, if they were used in a similar instrument at this day, would be so understood. But it is too clear for dispute that the enslaved African race were not intended to be included, and formed no part of the people who framed and adopted this Declaration; for if the language, as understood in that day, would embrace them, the conduct of the distinguished men who framed the Declaration of Independence would have been utterly and flagrantly inconsistent with the principles they asserted; and instead of the sympathy of mankind, to which they appealed, they would have deserved and received universal rebuke and reprobation.
>
> [Taney continues:] It is difficult, at this day, to realize the state of public opinion respecting that unfortunate class with the civilized and enlightened portion of the world at the time of the Declaration of Independence and the adoption of the Constitution; but history shows they had, for more than a century, been regarded as beings of an inferior order, and unfit associates for the white race, either socially or politically, and had no rights which white men are bound to respect; and the black man might be reduced to slavery, bought and sold, and treated as an ordinary article of merchandise. This opinion, at that time, was fixed and universal with the civilized portion of the white race. It was regarded as an axiom [universal truth] of morals, which no one thought of disputing, and everyone habitually acted upon it, without doubting, for a moment, the correctness of the opinion. And in no nation was this opinion more fixed, and generally acted upon, than in England; the subjects of which government not only seized them on the coast of Africa, but took them, as ordinary merchandise, to where they could make a profit on them. The opinion, thus entertained, was universally maintained on the colonies this side of the Atlantic; accordingly, Negroes of the African race were regarded by

> them as property, and held and bought and sold as such in every one of the thirteen colonies, which united in the Declaration of Independence, and afterwards formed the Constitution.

The argument here is, that the Constitution comes down to us from a slave holding period and a slave holding people; and that, therefore, we are bound to suppose that the Constitution recognizes colored persons of African descent, the victims of slavery at that time, as debarred forever from all participation in the benefit of the Constitution and the Declaration of Independence, although the plain reading of both includes them in their beneficent range.

As a man, an American, a citizen, a colored man of both Anglo-Saxon and African descent, I denounce this representation as a most scandalous and devilish perversion of the Constitution, and a brazen [reckless] misstatement of the facts of history.

But I will not content myself with mere denunciation; I invite attention to the facts.

It is a fact, a great historic fact, that at the time of the adoption of the Constitution, the leading religious denominations in this land were antislavery, and were laboring for the emancipation [freedom] of the colored people of African descent.

The church of a country is often a better index of the state of opinion and feeling than is even the government itself.

The Methodists, Baptists, Presbyterians, and the denomination of Friends, were actively opposing slavery, denouncing the system of bondage, with language as burning and sweeping as we employ at this day.

Take the Methodists. In 1780, that denomination said: "The Conference acknowledges that slavery is contrary to the laws of God, man, and nature, and hurtful to society—contrary to the dictates of conscience and true religion, and doing to others that we would not do unto us." In 1784, the same church declared, "that those who buy, sell or give slaves away, except for the purpose to free them, shall be expelled immediately." In 1785, it spoke even more stringently [forcefully] on the subject. It then said: "We hold in the deepest abhorrence the practice of slavery, and shall not cease to seek its destruction by all wise and proper means."

So much for the position of the Methodist Church in the early history of the Republic, in those days of darkness to which Judge Taney refers.

Let us now see how slavery was regarded by the Presbyterian Church at that early date.

In 1794, the General Assembly of that body pronounced the following judgment in respect to slavery, slaveholders, and slaveholding:

"St. Timothy, 1st chapter, 10th verse: 'The law was made for man stealers.' 'This crime among the Jews exposed the perpetrators of it to capital punishment.' Exodus, xxi, 15.—And the apostle here classes them with sinners of the first rank. The word he uses in its original import [sense], comprehends all who are concerned in bringing any of the human race into slavery, or in retaining them in it. Stealers of men are all those who bring off slaves or freemen, and keep, sell, or buy them. 'To steal a freeman,' says Grotius, 'is the highest kind of theft.' In other instances, we only steal human property, but when we steal or retain men in slavery, we seize those who, in common with ourselves, are constituted, by the original grant, lords of the earth."

I might quote at length, from the sayings of the Baptist Church and the sayings of eminent divines at this early period, showing that Judge Taney has grossly falsified history, but will not detain you with these quotations.

The testimony of the church, and the testimony of the founders of this Republic, from the Declaration downward, prove Judge Taney false; as false to history as he is to law.

Washington and Jefferson, and Adams, and Jay, and Franklin, and Rush, and Hamilton, and a host of others, held no such degrading views on the subject of slavery as are imputed by Judge Taney to the Fathers of the Republic.

All, at that time, looked for the gradual but certain abolition [ending] of slavery, and shaped the constitution with a view to this grand result.

George Washington can never be claimed as a fanatic, or as the representative of fanatics. The slaveholders impudently [in a manner showing a lack of respect] use his name for the base purpose of giving respectability to slavery. Yet, in a letter to Robert Morris, Washington uses this language—language which, at this day, would make him a terror of the slaveholders, and the natural representative of the Republican party.

"There is not a man living, who wishes more sincerely than I do, to see some plan adopted for the abolition of slavery; but there is only one proper and effectual mode by which it can be accomplished, and that is by Legislative authority; and this, as far as my suffrage will go, shall not be wanting [lacking]."

Washington only spoke the sentiment of his times. There were, at that time, Abolition societies in the slave States—Abolition societies in Virginia, in North Carolina, in Maryland, in Pennsylvania, and in Georgia—all slaveholding States. Slavery was so weak, and liberty so strong, that free speech could attack the monster to its teeth. Men were not mobbed and driven out of the presence of slavery, merely because they condemned the slave system. The system was then on its knees imploring to be spared, until it could get itself decently out of the world. In the light of these facts, the Constitution was framed, and framed in conformity to it.

It may, however, be asked, if the Constitution were so framed that the rights of all the people were naturally protected by it, how happens it that a large part of the people have been held in slavery ever since its adoption? Have the people mistaken the requirements of their own Constitution?

The answer is ready. The Constitution is one thing, its administration is another, and, in this instance, a very different and opposite thing. I am here to vindicate [show the goodness of] the law, not the administration of the law. It is the written Constitution, not the unwritten Constitution, that is now before us. If, in the whole range of the Constitution, you can find no warrant for slavery, then we may properly claim it for liberty.

Good and wholesome laws are often found dead on the statute book. We may condemn the practice under them and against them, but never the law itself. To condemn the good law with the wicked practice, is to weaken, not to strengthen our testimony.

It is no evidence that the Bible is a bad book, because those who profess to believe the Bible are bad. The slaveholders of the South, and many of their wicked allies at the North, claim the Bible for slavery; shall we, therefore, fling the Bible away as a pro-slavery book? It would be as reasonable to do so as it would be to fling away the Constitution.

We are not the only people who have illustrated the truth, that a people may have excellent law, and detestable [hateful] practices. Our Savior denounces the Jews, because they made void the law by their traditions. We have been guilty of the same sin.

The American people have made void our Constitution by just such traditions as Judge Taney and Mr. Garrison have been giving to the world of late, as the true light in which to view the Constitution of the United States. I shall follow neither. It is not what Moses allowed for the hardness of heart, but what God requires, ought to be the rule.

It may be said that it is quite true that the Constitution was designed to secure the blessings of liberty and justice to the people who made it, and to the posterity [descendants] of the people who made it, but was never designed to do any such thing for the colored people of African descent. This is Judge Taney's argument, and it is Mr. Garrison's argument, but it is not the argument of the Constitution. The Constitution imposes no such mean and satanic limitations upon its own beneficent [generous] operation. And, if the Constitution makes none, I beg to know what right has anybody, outside of the Constitution, for the special accommodation of slaveholding villainy, to impose such a construction upon the Constitution?

The Constitution knows all the human inhabitants of this country as "the people." It makes, as I have said before, no discrimination in favor of, or against, any class of the people, but is fitted to protect and preserve the rights of all, without reference to color, size, or any physical peculiarities. Besides, it has been shown by William Goodell and others, that in eleven out of the old thirteen States, colored men were legal voters at the time of the adoption of the Constitution.

In conclusion, let me say, all I ask of the American people is, that they live up to the Constitution, adopt its principles, imbibe [drink from] its spirit, and enforce its provisions.

When this is done, the wounds of my bleeding people will be healed, the chain will no longer rust on their ankles, their backs will no longer be torn by the bloody lash, and liberty, the glorious birthright of our common humanity, will become the inheritance of all the inhabitants of this highly favored country.

Why should we obey the law?

ALEXIS DE TOCQUEVILLE, *DEMOCRACY IN AMERICA,* "RESPECT FOR LAW IN THE UNITED STATES" (1835)

WHY THIS READING?

In this selection, Tocqueville displays confidence (a confidence that Lincoln, in the next reading, does not share) in the law-abidingness of the people under American democracy. Because the people (or rather a majority thereof) make the law under democracy, they respect and love their "creation." Even those who oppose a certain law respect it, Tocqueville argues, because they hope, by the same process, to bring the majority over to their side in the next legislative go-round. American law-abidingness, he concludes, is less the result of the citizens' selfless devotion to the common good, and more the result of their identification with the law as self-imposed and, with such identification, their calculation that obedience to the law is in their interest.

Questions to guide you as you read:

- In this reading, Tocqueville observes that "the poor rule" in the United States. His assertion strikes our modern ears as strange. What evidence does he provide for his argument? How would Theodore and Franklin Roosevelt (whom you read in chapter two) respond?
- What is the source and character of the "natural anxiety of the rich" that Tocqueville locates in American democracy?

It is not always feasible to consult the whole people, either directly or indirectly, in the formation of law; but it cannot be denied that, when this is possible, the authority of law is much augmented. This popular origin, which impairs the excellence and the wisdom of legislation, contributes much to increase its power. There is an amazing strength in the expression of the will of a whole people; and when it declares itself, even the imagination of those who would wish to contest it is overawed. The truth of this fact is well known by parties, and they consequently strive to make out a majority whenever they can. If they have not the greater number of voters on their side, they assert that the true majority abstained from voting; and if they are foiled even there, they have recourse to those persons who had no right to vote.

In the United States, except slaves, servants, and paupers supported by the townships, there is no class of persons who do not exercise the elective franchise and who do not indirectly contribute to make the laws. Those who wish to attack the laws must consequently either change the opinion of the nation or trample upon its decision.

A second reason, which is still more direct and weighty, may be adduced: in the United States everyone is personally interested in enforcing the obedience of the whole community to the law; for as the minority may shortly rally the majority to its principles, it is interested in professing that respect for the decrees of the legislator which it may soon have occasion to claim for its own. However irksome an enactment may be, the citizen of the United States complies with it, not only because it is the work of the majority, but because it is his own, and he regards it as a contract to which he is himself a party.

In the United States, then, that numerous and turbulent multitude does not exist who, regarding the law as their natural enemy, look upon it with fear and distrust. It is impossible, on the contrary, not to perceive that all classes display the utmost reliance upon the legislation of their country and are attached to it by a kind of parental affection.

I am wrong, however, in saying all classes; for as in America the European scale of authority is inverted, there the wealthy are placed in a position analogous to that of the poor in the Old World, and it is the opulent classes who frequently look upon law with suspicion. I have already observed that the advantage of democracy is not, as has been sometimes asserted, that it protects the interests of all, but simply that it protects those of the majority. In the United States, where the poor rule, the rich have always something to fear from the abuse of their power. This natural anxiety of the rich may produce a secret dissatisfaction, but society is not disturbed by it, for the same reason that withholds the confidence of the rich from the legislative authority makes them obey its mandates: their wealth, which prevents them from making the law, prevents them from withstanding it. Among civilized nations, only those who have nothing to lose ever revolt; and if the laws of a democracy are not always worthy of respect, they are always respected; for those who usually infringe the laws cannot fail to obey those which they have themselves made and by which they are benefited; while the citizens who might be interested in their infraction are induced, by their character and station, to submit to the decisions of the legislature, whatever they may be. Besides, the people in America obey the law, not only because it is their own work, but because it may be changed if it is harmful; a law is observed because, first, it is a self-imposed evil, and, secondly, it is an evil of transient duration.

ABRAHAM LINCOLN, "THE PERPETUATION OF OUR POLITICAL INSTITUTIONS" (1838)

Lincoln delivered this remarkable speech two weeks short of turning only 29 years old. In his address to the Young Men's Lyceum of Springfield, Illinois, he predicts and laments the decline of reverence for American's experiment in free government. To a certain extent, he argues, this was the natural effect of the passage of time: For those who lived during Revolutionary War, as well as for their children, that struggle had an immediacy that impressed upon them the principles for which they sacrificed. But, as memories faded with time, so too, he feared, would Americans' capacity to preserve their hard-fought liberties by governing themselves in accordance with the rule of law.

WHY THIS READING?

This speech, roughly contemporaneous with Tocqueville's writing of *Democracy in America*, seeks, as does Tocqueville (immediately above), to anchor American law-abidingness in self-interest rightly understood. Now that the Revolutionary generation is gone and with it, its passionate attachment to the new government it helped to found, a new foundation of liberty needs to be established, one built, not of passion, but of "reason, cold, [and] calculating." His hope is that this new, rational foundation would end the lawlessness that he sees engulfing the nation. To accomplish this task, the new foundation must give birth to a new reverence: "a reverence for the constitution and the laws," which should become the "political religion of the nation."

Questions to guide you as you read:

- What does Lincoln mean when he states that free peoples either live forever "or die by suicide"?
- What does Lincoln regard as "the strongest bulwark [safeguard] of any government"? Why?

...In the great journal of things happening under the sun, we, the American People, find our account running, under date of the nineteenth century of the Christian era. We find ourselves in the peaceful possession, of the fairest portion of the earth, as regards extent of territory, fertility of soil, and salubrity [pleasantness] of climate. We find ourselves under the government of a system of political institutions, conducing more essentially to the ends [goals] of civil and religious liberty, than any of which the history of former times tells us. We, when mounting the stage of existence, found ourselves the legal inheritors of these fundamental blessings. We toiled [worked] not in the acquirement or establishment of them—they are a legacy bequeathed [given to] us, by a *once* hardy, brave, and patriotic, but *now* lamented [deeply missed] and departed race of ancestors. Theirs was the task (and nobly they performed it) to possess themselves, and through themselves, us, of this goodly [good] land; and to uprear [erect] upon its hills and its valleys, a political edifice [monument] of liberty and equal rights; 'tis [it is] ours only, to transmit these, the former, unprofaned [not ruined] by the foot of an invader; the latter, undecayed by the lapse of time, and untorn by usurpation [being conquered]—to the latest generation that fate shall permit the world to know. This task of gratitude to our fathers, justice to ourselves, duty to posterity [future generations], and love for our species in general, all imperatively [urgently] require us faithfully to perform.

How, then, shall we perform it? At what point shall we expect the approach of danger? By what means shall we fortify [strengthen] against it? Shall we expect some transatlantic military giant, to step the Ocean, and crush us at a blow? Never! All the armies of Europe, Asia and Africa combined, with all the treasure of the earth (our own excepted) in their military chest; with a [Napoleon] Bonaparte for a commander, could not by force, take a drink from the Ohio, or make a track on the Blue Ridge, in a trial of a thousand years.

At what point then is the approach of danger to be expected? I answer, if it ever reach us, it must spring up amongst us. It cannot come from abroad [overseas]. If destruction be our lot [fate], we must ourselves be its author and finisher. As a nation of freemen, we must live through all time, or die by suicide.

I hope I am over wary [cautious]; but if I am not, there is, even now, something of ill-omen [bad fate] amongst us. I mean the increasing disregard for law which pervades [spreads through] the country; the growing disposition to substitute the wild and furious passions, in lieu [instead] of the sober judgment of Courts; and the worse than savage mobs, for the executive ministers of justice. This disposition is awfully fearful in any community; and that it now exists in ours, though grating [harsh] to our feelings to admit, it would be a violation of truth, and an insult to our intelligence, to deny. Accounts of outrages committed by mobs, form the every-day news of the times. They have pervaded [spread through] the country, from New England to Louisiana;—they are neither peculiar to the eternal snows of the former, nor the burning suns of the latter;—they are not the creature of climate—neither are they confined to the slaveholding, or the non-slave holding States. Alike, they spring up among the pleasure hunting masters of Southern slaves, and the order loving citizens of the land of steady habits. Whatever, then, their cause may be, it is common to the whole country.

It would be tedious [tiresome], as well as useless, to recount the horrors of all of them. Those happening in the State of Mississippi, and at St. Louis, are, perhaps, the most dangerous in example, and revolting [disgusting] to humanity. In the Mississippi case, they first commenced by hanging the regular gamblers: a set of men, certainly not following for a livelihood [job], a very useful, or very honest occupation, but one which, so far from being forbidden by the laws, was actually licensed by an act of the Legislature, passed but a single year before. Next, Negroes, suspected of conspiring to raise an insurrection [rebellion], were caught up and hanged in all parts of the State: then, white men, supposed to be leagued [united] with the Negroes; and finally, strangers, from neighboring States, going thither [there] on business, were, in many instances, subjected to the same fate. Thus went on this process of hanging, from gamblers to Negroes, from Negroes to white citizens, and from these to strangers; till, dead men were seen literally dangling [hanging] from the boughs of trees upon every road side; and in numbers almost sufficient, to rival the native Spanish moss of the country, as a drapery of the forest.

Turn, then, to that horror-striking scene at St. Louis. A single victim was only sacrificed there. His story is very short; and is, perhaps, the most highly tragic, of any thing of its length, that has ever been witnessed in real life. A mulatto man, by the name of Mcintosh, was seized in the street dragged to the suburbs of the city, chained to a tree, and actually burned to death; and all within a single hour from the time he had been a freeman, attending to his own business, and at peace with the world

Such are the effects of mob law; and such are the scenes, becoming more and more frequent in this land so lately famed for love of law and order; and the stories of which, have even now grown too familiar, to attract anything more, than an idle remark.

But you are, perhaps, ready to ask, "What has this to do with the perpetuation [continuing] of our political institutions?" I answer, it has much to do with it. Its direct consequences are, comparatively speaking, but a small evil; and much of its danger consists, in the proneness of our minds, to regard its direct [consequences], as its only consequences. Abstractly considered, the hanging of the gamblers at Vicksburg, was of but little consequence. They constitute a portion of population, that is worse than useless in any community; and their death, if no pernicious [wicked] example be set by it, is never matter of reasonable regret with any one. If they were annually [yearly] swept, from the stage of existence, by the plague or small pox, honest men would, perhaps, be much profited, by the operation. Similar too, is the correct reasoning, in regard to the burning of the negro at St. Louis. He had forfeited his life, by the perpetration [committing] of an outrageous murder, upon one of the most worthy and respectable citizens of the city; and had he not died as he did, he must have died by the sentence of the law, in a very short time afterwards. As to him alone, it was as well the way it was, as it could otherwise have been. But the example in either case, was fearful. When men take it in their heads today, to hang gamblers, or burn murderers, they should recollect, that, in the confusion usually attending such transactions, they will be as likely to hang or burn some one, who is neither a gambler nor a murderer as one who is; and that, acting upon the example they set, the mob of tomorrow, may, and probably will, hang or burn some of them, by the very same mistake. And not only so; the innocent, those who have ever set their faces against violations of law in every shape, alike with the guilty, fall victims to the ravages [angry consequences] of mob law; and thus it goes on, step by step; till all the walls erected for the defense of the persons and property of individuals, are trodden down, and disregarded. But all this even, is not the full extent of the evil. By such examples, by instances of the perpetrators of such acts going unpunished, the lawless in spirit, are encouraged to become lawless in practice; and having been used to no restraint, but dread of punishment, they thus become, absolutely unrestrained. Having ever regarded Government as their deadliest bane, they make a jubilee [celebration] of the suspension of its operations; and pray for nothing so much, as its total annihilation [destruction]. While, on the other hand, good men, men who love tranquility [peace], who desire to abide by the laws, and enjoy their benefits, who would gladly spill their blood in the defense of their country; seeing their property destroyed; their families insulted, and their lives endangered; their persons injured; and seeing nothing in prospect that forebodes a change for the better; become tired of, and disgusted with, a Government that offers them no protection; and are not much averse to [against] a change in which they imagine they have nothing to lose. Thus, then, by the operation of this mobocratic [mob rule] spirit, which all must admit, is now abroad in the land, the strongest bulwark [support] of any Government, and particularly of those constituted like ours, may effectually be broken down and destroyed—I mean the *attachment* of the People. Whenever this effect shall be produced among us; whenever the vicious portion of population shall be permitted to gather in bands of hundreds and thousands, and burn churches, ravage and rob provision stores, throw printing presses into rivers, shoot editors,[7] and hang and burn obnoxious persons at pleasure, and with impunity [no punishment]; depend on it, this Government cannot last. By such things, the feelings of the best citizens will become more or less alienated from it; and thus it will be left without friends, or with too few, and those few too weak, to make their friendship effectual. At such a time and under such circumstances, men of sufficient talent and ambition will not be wanting to seize the opportunity, strike the blow, and overturn that fair [beautiful] fabric, which for the last half century, had been the fondest hope, of the lovers of freedom, throughout the world.

I know the American People are *much* attached to their Government;—I know they would suffer *much* for its sake;—I know they would endure evils long and patiently, before they would ever think of exchanging it for another. Yet, notwithstanding all this, if the laws be continually despised [hated] and disregarded, if their rights to be secure in their persons and property, are held by no better tenure [length of time] than the caprice of a mob, the alienation of their affections from the Government is the natural consequence; and to that, sooner or later, it must come. Here then, is one point at which danger may be expected.

The question recurs "how shall we fortify [guard] against it?" The answer is simple. Let every American, every lover of liberty, every well wisher to his posterity, swear by the blood of the Revolution, never to violate in the least particular, the laws of the country; and never to tolerate their violation by others. As the patriots of seventy-six [1776] did to the support of the Declaration of Independence, so to the support of the Constitution and Laws, let every American pledge his life, his property, and his sacred honor;—let every man remember that to violate the law, is to trample on the blood of his father, and to tear the charter of his own, and his children's liberty. Let reverence [respect] for the laws, be breathed by every American mother, to the lisping [speaking with a lisp] babe, that prattles on her lap—let it be taught in schools, in seminaries, and in colleges;—let it be written in Primers, spelling books, and in Almanacs;—let it be preached from the pulpit, proclaimed in legislative halls, and enforced in courts of justice. And, in short, let it become the *political religion* of the nation; and let the old and the young, the rich and the poor, the grave and the gay [happy], of all sexes and tongues, and colors and conditions, sacrifice unceasingly [without ceasing] upon its altars.

While ever a state of feeling, such as this, shall universally, or even, very generally prevail throughout the nation, vain will be every effort, and fruitless every attempt, to subvert [undermine] our national freedom.

When I so pressingly urge a strict observance of all the laws, let me not be understood as saying

---

7. On November 7, 1837, the Abolitionist newspaper editor Elijah Parish Lovejoy was lynched at Alton, Illinois.

there are no bad laws, nor that grievances may not arise, for the redress [remedy] of which, no legal provisions have been made. I mean to say no such thing. But I do mean to say, that, although bad laws, if they exist, should be repealed as soon as possible, still while they continue in force, for the sake of example, they should be religiously observed. So also in unprovided cases. If such arise, let proper legal provisions be made for them with the least possible delay; but, till then, let them if not too intolerable, be borne with.

There is no grievance that is a fit object of redress [remedy] by mob law. In any case that arises, as for instance, the promulgation of abolitionism, one of two positions is necessarily true; that is, the thing is right within itself, and therefore deserves the protection of all law and all good citizens; or, it is wrong, and therefore proper to be prohibited by legal enactments; and in neither case, is the interposition of mob law, either necessary, justifiable, or excusable.

But, it may be asked, why suppose danger to our political institutions? Have we not preserved them for more than fifty years? And why may we not for fifty times as long?

We hope there is no *sufficient* reason. We hope all dangers may be overcome; but to conclude that no danger may ever arise, would itself be extremely dangerous. There are now, and will hereafter be, many causes, dangerous in their tendency, which have not existed heretofore; and which are not too insignificant to merit attention. That our government should have been maintained in its original form from its establishment until now, is not much to be wondered at. It had many props to support it through that period, which now are decayed, and crumbled away. Through that period, it was felt by all, to be an undecided experiment; now, it is understood to be a successful one. Then, all that sought celebrity and fame, and distinction, expected to find them in the success of that experiment. Their *all* was staked upon it:—their destiny was *inseparably* linked with it. Their ambition aspired to display before an admiring world, a practical demonstration of the truth of a proposition, which had hitherto been considered, at best no better, than problematical; namely, *the capability of a people to govern themselves.* If they succeeded, they were to be immortalized; their names were to be transferred to counties and cities, and rivers and mountains; and to be revered and sung, and toasted through all time. If they failed, they were to be called knaves and fools, and fanatics for a fleeting hour; then to sink and be forgotten. They succeeded. The experiment is successful; and thousands have won their deathless names in making it so. But the game is caught; and I believe it is true, that with the catching, end the pleasures of the chase. This field of glory is harvested, and the crop is already appropriated. But new reapers will arise, and *they,* too, will seek a field. It is to deny, what the history of the world tells us is true, to suppose that men of ambition and talents will not continue to spring up amongst us. And, when they do, they will as naturally seek the gratification [satisfaction] of their ruling passion, as others have so done before them. The question then, is, can that gratification be found in supporting and maintaining an edifice [building] that has been erected by others? Most certainly it cannot. Many great and good men sufficiently qualified for any task they should undertake, may ever be found, whose ambition would aspire to nothing beyond a seat in Congress, a gubernatorial [governor] or a presidential chair; *but such belong not to the family of the lion, or the tribe of the eagle.* What! Think you these places would satisfy an Alexander, a Caesar, or a Napoleon? Never! Towering genius disdains a beaten path. It seeks regions hitherto unexplored. It sees *no distinction* in adding story to story, upon the monuments of fame, erected to the memory of others. It *denies* that it is glory enough to serve under any chief. It *scorns* to tread in the footsteps of *any* predecessor, however illustrious. It thirsts and burns for distinction; and, if possible, it will have it, whether at the expense of emancipating slaves, or enslaving freemen. Is it unreasonable then to expect, that some man possessed of the loftiest [highest] genius, coupled with ambition sufficient to push it to its utmost stretch, will at some time, spring up among us? And when such a one does, it will require the people to be united with each other, attached to the government and laws, and generally intelligent, to successfully frustrate his designs.

Distinction [recognition] will be his paramount object; and although he would as willingly, perhaps more so, acquire it by doing good as harm; yet, that opportunity being past, and nothing left to be done in the way of building up, he would set boldly to the task of pulling down.

Here then, is a probable case, highly dangerous, and such a one as could not have well existed heretofore.

Another reason which *once was;* but which, to the same extent, is *now no more,* has done much in maintaining our institutions thus far. I mean the powerful influence which the interesting scenes of the revolution had upon the *passions* of the people as distinguished from their judgment. By this influence, the jealousy, envy, and avarice, incident to our nature, and so common to a state of peace, prosperity, and conscious strength, were, for the time, in a great measure smothered and rendered inactive; while the deep rooted principles of *hate,* and the powerful motive of *revenge,* instead of being turned against each other, were directed exclusively against the British nation. And thus, from the force of circumstances, the basest principles of our nature, were either made to lie dormant, or to become the active agents in the advancement of the noblest of causes—that of establishing and maintaining civil and religious liberty.

But this state of feeling *must fade, is fading, has faded,* with the circumstances that produced it.

I do not mean to say, that the scenes of the revolution *are now or ever will be* entirely forgotten; but that like every thing else, they must fade upon the memory of the world, and grow more and more dim by the lapse of time. In history, we hope, they will be read of, and recounted, so long as the bible shall be read;—but even granting that they will, their influence *cannot be* what it heretofore has been. Even then, they *cannot be so* universally known, nor so vividly felt, as they were by the generation just gone to rest. At the close of that struggle, nearly every adult male had been a participator in some of its scenes. The consequence was, that of those scenes, in the form of a husband, a father, a son or a brother, a *living history was* to be found in every family—a history bearing the indubitable [undoubted] testimonies of its own authenticity, in the limbs mangled, in the scars of wounds received, in the midst of the very scenes related—a history, too, that could be read and understood alike by all, the wise and the ignorant, the learned and the unlearned. But *those* histories are gone. They *can* be read no more forever. They *were* a fortress of strength; but, what invading foemen could *never do,* the silent artillery of time *has done;* the leveling [tearing down] of its walls. They are gone. They *were* a forest of giant oaks; but the all-resistless hurricane has swept over them, and left only, here and there, a lonely trunk, despoiled of its verdure, shorn of its foliage; unshading and unshaded, to murmur in a few more gentle breezes, and to combat with its mutilated limbs, a few more ruder storms, then to sink, and be no more.

They *were* pillars of the temple of liberty; and now, that they have crumbled away, that temple must fall, unless we, their descendants, supply their places with other pillars, hewn [made] from the solid quarry of sober reason. Passion has helped us, but can do so no more. It will in future be our enemy. Reason, cold, calculating, unimpassioned reason, must furnish all the materials for our future support and defense. Let those materials be molded into *general intelligence, sound morality* and, in particular, a *reverence [respect] for the constitution and laws;* and, that we improved to the last; that we remained free to the last; that we revered his name to the last; that, during his long sleep, we permitted no hostile foot to pass over or desecrate [spoil] his resting place; shall be that which to learn and last trump shall awaken our WASHINGTON.

Upon these let the proud fabric of freedom rest, as the rock of its basis; and as truly as has been said of the only greater institution, "*the gates of hell shall not prevail against it.*"

The case for civil disobedience

REV. DR. MARTIN LUTHER KING JR., "LETTER FROM BIRMINGHAM JAIL" (1963)

On April 12, 1963, in Birmingham, Alabama, Dr. King led a group marching to protest the city's segregationist policies. All were arrested, with King spending eight days in solitary confinement. When he learned of King's arrest, President John F. Kennedy telephoned King to offer support. When Kennedy learned that the Birmingham jailers had denied King his right to make phone calls, the President sent F.B.I. agents there to assure King's legal rights. During his confinement, King composed his "Letter from Birmingham Jail." The immediate purpose for his letter was to respond to a published statement written by eight Alabama clergymen. The clergymen's statement, which appeared in a local newspaper, urged King not to disobey the law. As King would write later, "This response to a published statement by eight fellow clergymen from Alabama...was composed under somewhat constricting circumstance. Begun on the margins of the newspaper in which the statement appeared while I was in jail, the letter was continued on scraps of writing paper supplied by a friendly Negro trusty, and concluded on a pad my attorneys were eventually permitted to leave me."

WHY THIS READING?

In responding to his fellow clergymen's admonition to obey the law, King defends his notion of civil disobedience, which involves "constructive, nonviolent tension which is necessary for growth." He also makes a distinction between just and unjust laws, arguing that only the former should be obeyed, and that "an unjust law is no law at all," for an unjust law undermines the very purposes for which laws are established—and for which they ought to be obeyed—in the first place.

Questions to guide you as you read:

- How does Dr. King's view of law-abidingness agree and disagree with that expressed by Frederick Douglass in "On the *Dred Scott* Decision"?
- By what standards does Dr. King distinguish a just law from an unjust law? To what extent does his distinction rely upon the Declaration of Independence?

My Dear Fellow Clergymen:

While confined here in the Birmingham city jail, I came across your recent statement calling my present activities "unwise and untimely." Seldom do I pause to answer criticism of my work and ideas. If I sought to answer all the criticisms that cross my desk, my secretaries would have little time for anything other than such correspondence in the course of the day, and I would have no time for constructive work. But since I feel that you are men of genuine good will and that your criticisms are sincerely set forth, I want to try to answer your statement in what I hope will be patient and reasonable terms.

I think I should indicate why I am here in Birmingham, since you have been influenced by the view which argues against "outsiders coming in." I have the honor of serving as president of the Southern Christian Leadership Conference, an organization operating in every southern state, with headquarters in Atlanta, Georgia. We have some eighty-five affiliated [allied] organizations across the South, and one of them is the Alabama Christian Movement for Human Rights. Frequently we share staff, educational and financial resources with our affiliates. Several months ago the affiliate here in Birmingham asked us to be on call to engage in a nonviolent direct-action program if such were deemed necessary. We readily consented, and when the hour came we lived up to our promise. So I, along with several members of my staff, am here because I was invited here. I am here because I have organizational ties here.

But more basically, I am in Birmingham because injustice is here. Just as the prophets of the eighth century B.C. left their villages and carried their "thus saith the Lord" far beyond the boundaries of their home towns, and just as the Apostle Paul left his village of Tarsus and carried the gospel of Jesus Christ to the far corners of the Greco-Roman world, so am I compelled to carry the gospel of freedom beyond my own home town. Like Paul, I must constantly respond to the Macedonian call for aid.

Moreover, I am cognizant [aware] of the interrelatedness of all communities and states. I cannot sit idly by [doing nothing] in Atlanta and not be concerned about what happens in Birmingham. Injustice anywhere is a threat to justice everywhere. We are caught in an inescapable network of mutuality, tied in a single garment of destiny. Whatever affects one directly, affects all indirectly. Never again can we afford to live with the narrow, provincial [short-sighted] "outside agitator" idea. Anyone who lives inside the United States can never be considered an outsider anywhere within its bounds.

You deplore [find very bad] the demonstrations taking place in Birmingham. But your statement, I am sorry to say, fails to express a similar concern for the conditions that brought about the demonstrations. I am sure that none of you would want to rest content with the superficial kind of social analysis that deals merely with effects and does not grapple with underlying causes. It is unfortunate that demonstrations are taking place in Birmingham, but it is even more unfortunate that the city's white power structure left the Negro community with no alternative.

In any nonviolent campaign there are four basic steps: collection of the facts to determine whether injustices exist; negotiation; self-purification; and direct action. We have gone through all these steps in Birmingham. There can be no gainsaying [denying] the fact that racial injustice engulfs [drowns] this community. Birmingham is probably the most thoroughly segregated city in the United States. Its ugly record of brutality is widely known. Negroes have experienced grossly unjust treatment in the courts. There have been more unsolved bombings of Negro homes and churches in Birmingham than in any other city in the nation. These are the hard, brutal facts of the case. On the basis of these conditions, Negro leaders sought to negotiate with the city fathers. But the latter consistently refused to engage in good-faith negotiation. Then, last September, came the opportunity to talk with leaders of Birmingham's economic community. In the course of the negotiations, certain promises were made by the merchants—for example, to remove the stores' humiliating racial signs. On the basis of these promises, the Reverend Fred Shuttlesworth and the leaders of the Alabama Christian Movement for Human Rights agreed to a moratorium on all demonstrations. As the weeks and months went by, we realized that we were the victims of a broken promise. A few signs, briefly removed, returned; the others remained.

As in so many past experiences, our hopes had been blasted, and the shadow of deep disappointment settled upon us. We had no alternative except to prepare for direct action, whereby we would present our very bodies as a means of having our case before the conscience of the local and the national community. Mindful of the difficulties involved, we decided to undertake a process of self-purification. We began a series of workshops on nonviolence, and we repeatedly asked ourselves: "Are you able to accept blows without retaliating?" "Are you able to endure the ordeal of jail?" We decided to schedule our direct-action program for the Easter season, realizing that except for Christmas, this is the main shopping period of the year. Knowing that a strong economic-withdrawal program would be the by-product of direct action, we felt that this would be the best time to bring pressure to bear on the merchants for the needed change.

Then it occurred to us that Birmingham's mayoralty [mayor] election was coming up in March, and we speedily decided to postpone action until after election day. When we discovered that the Commissioner of Public Safety, Eugene "Bull" Connor, had piled up enough votes to be in the run-off, we decided again to postpone action until the day after the run-off so that the demonstrations could not be used to cloud the issues. Like many others, we waited to see Mr. Connor defeated, and to this end we endured postponement after postponement. Having aided in this community need, we felt that our direct-action program could be delayed no longer.

You may well ask: "Why direct action? Why sit-ins, marches and so forth? Isn't negotiation a better path?" You are quite right in calling for negotiation. Indeed, this is the very purpose of direct action. Nonviolent direct action seeks to create such a crisis and foster such a tension that a community which has constantly refused to negotiate is forced to confront the issue. It seeks so to dramatize the issue that it can no longer be ignored. My citing the creation of tension as part of the work of the nonviolent-resister may sound rather shocking. But I must confess that I am not afraid of the word "tension." I have earnestly [sincerely] opposed violent tension, but there is a type of constructive, nonviolent tension which is necessary for growth. Just as Socrates felt that it was necessary to create a tension in the mind so that individuals could rise from the bondage of myths and half-truths to the unfettered realm of creative analysis and objective appraisal [analysis], so must we see the need for nonviolent gadflies[8] to create the kind of tension in society that will help men rise from the dark depths of prejudice and racism to the majestic heights of understanding and brotherhood.

The purpose of our direct-action program is to create a situation so crisis-packed that it will inevitably [unavoidably] open the door to negotiation. I therefore concur [agree] with you in your call for negotiation. Too long has our beloved Southland been bogged down in a tragic effort to live in monologue rather than dialogue.

One of the basic points in your statement is that the action that I and my associates have taken in Birmingham is untimely. Some have asked: "Why didn't you give the new city administration time to act?" The only answer that I can give to this query [question] is that the new Birmingham administration must be prodded [pushed] about as much as the outgoing one, before it will act. We are sadly mistaken if we feel that the election of Albert Boutwell as mayor will bring the millennium to Birmingham. While Mr. Boutwell is a much more gentle person than Mr. Connor, they are both segregationists, dedicated to maintenance of the status quo. I have hope that Mr. Boutwell will be reasonable enough to see the futility of massive resistance to desegregation. But he will not see this without pressure from devotees [supporters] of civil rights. My friends, I. must say to you that we have not made a single gain in civil rights without determined legal and nonviolent pressure. Lamentably, [sadly] it is an historical fact that privileged groups seldom give up their privileges voluntarily. Individuals may see the moral light and voluntarily give up their unjust posture; but, as Reinhold Niebuhr has reminded us, groups tend to be more immoral than individuals.

We know through painful experience that freedom is never voluntarily given by the oppressor; it must be demanded by the oppressed. Frankly, I have yet to engage in a direct-action campaign that was "well-timed" in the view of those who have not suffered unduly from the disease of segregation. For years now I have heard the word "Wait!" It rings in the ear of every Negro with piercing familiarity. This "Wait" has almost always meant "Never." We must come to see, with one of our distinguished jurists, that "justice too long delayed is justice denied."

We have waited for more than 340 years for our constitutional and God-given rights. The nations of Asia and Africa are moving with jet-like speed toward gaining political independence but we still creep at horse-and-buggy pace toward gaining a

8. Socrates compared himself to a gadfly or horsefly that had landed on Athens to awaken her from a deep sleep.

cup of coffee at a lunch counter. Perhaps it is easy for those who have never felt the stinging darts of segregation to say, "Wait." But when you have seen vicious mobs lynch your mothers and fathers at will and drown your sisters and brothers at whim; when you have seen hate-filled policemen curse, kick and even kill your black brothers and sisters; when you see the vast majority of your twenty million Negro brothers smothering in an airtight cage of poverty in the midst of an affluent society; when you suddenly find your tongue twisted and your speech stammering as you seek to explain to your six-year-old daughter why she can't go to the public amusement park that has just been advertised on television, and see tears welling up in her eyes when she is told that Fantan is closed to colored children, and see ominous [threatening] clouds of inferiority beginning to form in her little mental sky, and see her beginning to distort her personality by developing an unconscious bitterness toward white people; when you have to concoct [invent] an answer for a five-year-old son who is asking: "Daddy, why do white people treat colored people so mean?"; when you take a cross-country drive and find it necessary to sleep night after night in the uncomfortable corners of your automobile because no motel will accept you; when you are humiliated day in and day out by nagging signs reading "white" and "colored"; when your first name becomes "nigger," your middle name becomes "boy" (however old you are) and your last name becomes "John," and your wife and mother are never given the respected title "Mrs."; when you are harried [harassed] by day and haunted by night by the fact that you are a Negro, living constantly at tiptoe stance, never quite knowing what to expect next, and are plagued with inner fears and outer resentments; when you are forever fighting a degenerating sense of "nobodiness"—then you will understand why we find it difficult to wait. There comes a time when the cup of endurance runs over, and men are no longer willing to be plunged into the abyss [depth] of despair. I hope, sirs, you can understand our legitimate and unavoidable impatience.

You express a great deal of anxiety over our willingness to break laws. This is certainly a legitimate concern. Since we so diligently urge people to obey the Supreme Court's decision of 1954 outlawing segregation in the public schools, at first glance it may seem rather paradoxical for us consciously to break laws. One may well ask: "How can you advocate breaking some laws and obeying others?" The answer lies in the fact that there are two types of laws: just and unjust. I would be the first to advocate obeying just laws. One has not only a legal but a moral responsibility to obey just laws. Conversely, one has a moral responsibility to disobey unjust laws. I would agree with St. Augustine that "an unjust law is no law at all."

Now, what is the difference between the two? How does one determine whether a law is just or unjust? A just law is a man-made code that squares with the moral law or the law of God. An unjust law is a code that is out of harmony with the moral law. To put it in the terms of St. Thomas Aquinas: An unjust law is a human law that is not rooted in eternal law and natural law. Any law that uplifts human personality is just. Any law that degrades human personality is unjust. All segregation statutes are unjust because segregation distorts the soul and damages the personality. It gives the segregator a false sense of superiority and the segregated a false sense of inferiority. Segregation, to use the terminology of the Jewish philosopher Martin Buber, substitutes an "I-it" relationship for an "I-thou" relationship and ends up relegating persons to the status of things. Hence segregation is not only politically, economically and sociologically unsound, it is morally wrong and sinful. Paul Tillich has said that sin is separation. Is not segregation an existential expression of man's tragic separation, his awful estrangement, his terrible sinfulness? Thus it is that I can urge men to obey the 1954 decision of the Supreme Court, for it is morally right; and I can urge them to disobey segregation ordinances, for they are morally wrong.

Let us consider a more concrete example of just and unjust laws. An unjust law is a code that a numerical or power majority group compels [forces] a minority group to obey but does not make binding on itself. This is *difference* made legal. By the same token, a just law is a code that a majority compels a minority to follow and that it is willing to follow itself. This is *sameness* made legal.

Let me give another explanation. A law is unjust if it is inflicted on a minority that, as a result of being denied the right to vote, had no part in enacting or devising the law. Who can say that the legislature of Alabama which set up that state's segregation laws was democratically elected? Throughout Alabama all sorts of devious methods are used to prevent Negroes from becoming registered voters, and there are some counties in which, even though Negroes constitute a majority of the population, not a single Negro is registered. Can any law enacted under such circumstances be considered democratically structured?

Sometimes a law is just on its face and unjust in its application. For instance, I have been arrested on a charge of parading without a permit. Now, there is nothing wrong in having an ordinance [law] which requires a permit for a parade. But such an ordinance becomes unjust when it is used to maintain segregation and to deny citizens the First Amendment privilege of peaceful assembly and protest.

I hope you are able to see the distinction I am trying to point out. In no sense do I advocate evading [avoiding] or defying the law, as would the rabid segregationist. That would lead to anarchy. One who breaks an unjust law must do so openly, lovingly, and with a willingness to accept the penalty. I submit that an individual who breaks a law that conscience tells him is unjust, and who willingly accepts the penalty of imprisonment in order to arouse the conscience of the community over its injustice, is in reality expressing the highest respect for law

Of course, there is nothing new about this kind of civil disobedience. It was evidenced sublimely [perfectly] in the refusal of Shadrach, Mesick [Meshach] and Abednego [as told in the Old Testament, the three young Jews risked death to obey God rather than the Babylonian king] to obey the laws of Nebuchadnezzar, on the ground that a higher moral law was at stake. It was practiced superbly by the early Christians, who were willing to face hungry lions and the excruciating pain of chopping blocks rather than submit to certain unjust laws of the Roman Empire. To a degree, academic freedom is reality today because Socrates practiced civil disobedience. In our own nation, the Boston Tea Party represented a massive act of civil disobedience.

We should never forget that everything Adolf Hitler did in Germany was "legal" and everything the Hungarian freedom fighters did in Hungary was "illegal." It was "illegal" to aid and comfort a Jew in Hitler's Germany. Even so, I am sure that had I lived in Germany at the time, I would have aided and comforted my Jewish brothers. If today I lived in a Communist country where certain principles dear to the Christian faith are suppressed, I would openly advocate disobeying that country's antireligious laws.

I must make two honest confessions to you, my Christian and Jewish brothers. First, I must confess that over the past few years I have been gravely [seriously] disappointed with the white moderate. I have almost reached the regrettable conclusion that the Negro's great stumbling block in his stride toward freedom is not the White Citizen's Councilor or the Ku Klux Klanner, but the white moderate, who is more devoted to "order" than to justice; who prefers a negative peace which is the absence of tension to a positive peace which is the presence of justice; who constantly says: "I agree with you in the goal you seek, but I cannot agree with your methods of direct action"; who paternalistically [condescendingly] believes he can set the timetable for another man's freedom; who lives by a mythical concept of time and who constantly advises the Negro to wait for a "more convenient season." Shallow understanding from people of good will is more frustrating than absolute misunderstanding from people of ill will. Lukewarm [half-hearted] acceptance is much more bewildering than outright rejection.

I had hoped that the white moderate would understand that law and order exist for the purpose of establishing justice and that when they fail in this purpose they become the dangerously structured dams that block the flow of social progress. I had hoped that the white moderate would understand that the present tension in the South is a necessary phase of the transition from an obnoxious negative peace, in which the Negro passively accepted his unjust plight, to a substantive and positive peace, in which all men will respect the dignity and worth of human personality. Actually, we who engage in nonviolent direct action are not the creators of tension. We merely bring to the surface the hidden tension that is already alive. We bring it out in the open, where it can be seen and dealt with. Like a boil [sore] that can never be cured so long as it is covered up but must be opened with all its ugliness to the natural medicines of air and light, injustice must be exposed, with all the tension its exposure creates, to the light of human conscience and the air of national opinion before it can be cured.

In your statement you assert that our actions, even though peaceful, must be condemned because they precipitate [cause] violence. But is this a logical assertion? Isn't this like condemning a robbed man because his possession of money precipitated the evil act of robbery? Isn't this like condemning Socrates because his unswerving commitment to truth and his philosophical inquiries precipitated the act by the misguided populace in which they made him drink hemlock [poison]? Isn't this like condemning Jesus because his unique God-consciousness and never-ceasing devotion to God's will precipitated the evil act of Crucifixion? We must come to see that, as the federal courts have consistently affirmed, it is wrong to urge an individual to cease his efforts to gain his basic constitutional rights because the quest may precipitate violence. Society must protect the robbed and punish the robber.

I had also hoped that the white moderate would reject the myth concerning time in relation to the struggle for freedom. I have just received a letter from a white brother in Texas. He writes: "All Christians know that the colored people will receive equal rights eventually, but it is possible that you are in too great a religious hurry. It has taken Christianity almost two thousand years to accomplish what it has. The teachings of Christ take time to come to earth." Such an attitude stems from a tragic misconception of time, from the strangely irrational notion that there is something in the very flow of time that will inevitably cure all ills. Actually, time itself is neutral; it can be used either destructively or constructively. More and more I feel that the people of ill will have used time much more effectively than have the people of good will. We will have to repent in this generation not merely for the hateful words and actions of the bad people but for the appalling [horrifying] silence of the good people. Human progress never rolls in on wheels of inevitability; it comes through the tireless efforts of men willing to be co-workers with God, and without this hard work, time itself becomes an ally of the forces of social stagnation [motionlessness]. We must use time creatively, in the knowledge that the time is always ripe to do right. Now is the time to make real the promise of democracy and transform our pending national elegy [song of sadness] into a creative psalm of brotherhood. Now is the time to lift our national policy from the quicksand of racial injustice to the solid rock of human dignity.

You speak of our activity in Birmingham as extreme. At first I was rather disappointed that fellow clergymen would see my nonviolent efforts as those of an extremist. I began thinking about the fact that I stand in the middle of two opposing forces in the Negro community. One is a force of complacency [acceptance], made up in part of Negroes who, as a result of long years of oppression, are so drained of self-respect and a sense of "somebodiness" that they have adjusted to segregation; and in part of a few middle-class Negroes who, because of a degree of academic and economic security and because in some ways they profit by segregation, have become insensitive to the problems of the masses. The other force is one of bitterness and hatred, and it comes perilously [dangerously] close to advocating violence. It is expressed in the various black nationalist groups that are springing up across the nation, the largest and best-known being Elijah Muhammad's Muslim movement. Nourished by the Negro's frustration over the continued existence of racial discrimination, this movement is made up of people who have lost faith in America, who have absolutely repudiated [given up] Christianity, and who have concluded that the white man is an incorrigible "devil."

I have tried to stand between these two forces, saying that we need emulate neither the "do-nothingism" of the complacent nor the hatred and despair of the Black Nationalist. For there is the more excellent way of love and nonviolent protest. I am grateful to God that, through the influence of the Negro church, the way of nonviolence became an integral part of our struggle.

If this philosophy had not emerged, by now many streets of the South would, I am convinced, be flowing with blood. And I am further convinced that if our white brothers dismiss as "rabble-rousers" and "outside agitators" those of us who employ nonviolent direct action, and if they refuse to support our nonviolent efforts, millions of Negroes will, out of frustration and despair, seek solace and security in black-nationalist ideologies—a development that would inevitably lead to a frightening racial nightmare.

Oppressed people cannot remain oppressed forever. The yearning for freedom eventually manifests itself, and that is what has happened to the American Negro. Something within has reminded him of his birthright of freedom, and something without has reminded him that it can be gained. Consciously or unconsciously, he has been caught up by the *Zeitgeist* [spirit of the times], and with his black brothers of Africa and his brown and yellow brothers of Asia, South America and the Caribbean, the United States Negro is moving with a sense of great urgency toward the promised land of racial justice. If one recognizes this vital urge that has engulfed the Negro community, one should readily understand why public demonstrations are taking place. The Negro-has many pent-up [suppressed] resentments and latent [unexpressed] frustrations, and he must release them. So let him march; let him make prayer pilgrimages to the city hall; let him go on freedom rides—and try to understand why he must do so. If his repressed emotions are not released in nonviolent ways, they will seek expression through violence; this is not a threat hut a fact of history. So I have not said to my people: "Get rid of your discontent." Rather, I have tried to say that this normal and healthy discontent can be channeled into the creative outlet of nonviolent direct action. And now this approach is being termed extremist.

But though I was initially disappointed at being categorized as an extremist, as I continued to think about the matter I gradually gained a measure of satisfaction from the label. Was not Jesus an extremist for love: "Love your enemies, bless them that curse you, do good to them that hate you, and pray for them which despitefully use you, and persecute you." Was not Amos an extremist for justice: "Let justice roll down like waters and righteousness like an ever-flowing stream." Was not Paul an extremist for the Christian gospel: "I bear in my body the marks of the Lord Jesus." Was not Martin Luther an extremist: "Here I stand; I cannot do otherwise, so help me God." And John Bunyan: "I will stay in jail to the end of my days before I make a butchery of my conscience." And Abraham Lincoln: "This nation cannot survive half slave and half free." And Thomas Jefferson: "We hold these truths to be self-evident, that all men are created equal. . . ." So the question is not whether we will be extremists, but what kind of extremists we will be. Will we be extremists for hate or for love? Will we be extremists for the preservation of injustice or for the extension of justice? In that dramatic scene on Calvary's hill three men were crucified. We must never forget that all three were crucified for the same crime—the crime of extremism. Two were extremists for immorality, and thus fell below their environment. The other, Jesus Christ, was an extremist for love, truth and goodness, and thereby rose above his environment. Perhaps the South, the nation and the world are in dire [desperate] need of creative extremists.

I had hoped that the white moderate would see this need. Perhaps I was too optimistic; perhaps I expected too much. I suppose I should have realized that few members of the oppressor race can understand the deep groans and passionate yearnings of the oppressed race, and still fewer have the vision to see that injustice must be rooted out by strong, persistent and determined action. I am thankful, however, that some of our white brothers in the South have grasped the meaning of this social revolution and committed themselves to it. They are still all too few in quantity, but they are big in quality. Some—such as Ralph McGill, Lillian Smith, Harry Golden, James McBride Dabbs, Ann Braden and Sarah Patton Boyle—have written about our struggle in eloquent and prophetic terms. Others have marched with us down nameless streets of the South. They have languished in filthy, roach infested jails, suffering the abuse and brutality of policemen who view them as "dirty nigger-lovers." Unlike so many of their moderate brothers and sister, they have recognized the urgency of the moment and sensed the need for powerful "action" antidotes to combat the disease of segregation.

Let me take note of my other major disappointment. I have been so greatly disappointed with the white church and its leadership. Of course, there are some notable exceptions. I am not unmindful of the fact that each of you has taken some significant stands on this issue. I commend you, Reverend Stallings, for your Christian stand on this past Sunday, in welcoming Negroes to your worship service on a nonsegregated basis. I commend the Catholic leaders of this state for integrating Spring Hill College several years ago.

But despite these notable exceptions, I must honestly reiterate that I have been disappointed with the church. I do not say this as one of those negative critics who can always find something wrong with the church. I say this as a minister of the gospel, who loves the church; who was nurtured in its bosom; who has been sustained by its spiritual blessings and who will remain true to it as long as the cord of life shall lengthen.

When I was suddenly catapulted [launched] into the leadership of the bus protest in Montgomery, Alabama, a few years ago, I felt we would be supported by the white church. I felt that the white ministers, priests and rabbis of the South would be among our strongest allies. Instead, some have been outright opponents, refusing to understand the freedom movement and misrepresenting its leaders; all too many others have been more cautious than courageous and have remained silent behind the anesthetizing [drug-induced painkilling] security of stained-glass windows.

In spite of my shattered dreams, I came to Birmingham with the hope that the white religious leadership of this community would see the justice of our cause and, with deep moral concern, would serve as the channel through which our just grievances could reach the power structure. I had hoped that each of you would understand. But again I have been disappointed.

I have heard numerous southern religious leaders admonish their worshipers to comply with a desegregation decision because it is the law, but I have longed to hear white ministers declare: "Follow this decree because integration is morally right and because the Negro is your brother." In the midst of blatant [obvious] injustices inflicted upon the Negro, I have watched white churchmen stand on the sideline and mouth pious irrelevancies and sanctimonious [holier-than-thou] trivialities. In the midst of a mighty struggle to rid our nation of racial and economic injustice, I have heard many ministers say: "Those are social issues, with which the gospel has no real concern." And I have watched many churches commit themselves to a completely other-worldly religion which makes a strange, un-Biblical distinction between body and soul, between the sacred and the secular.

I have traveled the length and breadth of Alabama, Mississippi and all the other southern states. On sweltering [hot] summer days and crisp autumn mornings I have looked at the South's beautiful churches with their lofty spires [steeples] pointing heavenward. I have beheld the impressive outlines of her massive religious-education buildings. Over and over I have found myself asking: "What kind of people worship here? Who is their God? Where were their voices when the lips of Governor Barnett dripped with words of interposition [interference] and nullification? Where were they when Governor Wallace gave a clarion [clear] call for defiance and hatred? Where were their voices of support when bruised and weary Negro men and women decided to rise from the dark dungeons of complacency to the bright hills of creative protest?"

Yes, these questions are still in my mind. In deep disappointment I have wept over the laxity [permissiveness] of the church. But be assured that my tears have been tears of love. There can be no deep disappointment where there is not deep love. Yes, I love the church. How could I do otherwise? I am in the rather unique position of being the son, the grandson and the great-grandson of preachers.

Yes, I see the church as the body of Christ. But, oh! How we have blemished and scarred that body through social neglect and through fear of being nonconformists.

There was a time when the church was very powerful—in the time when the early Christians rejoiced at being deemed worthy to suffer for what they believed. In those days the church was not merely a thermometer that recorded the ideas and principles of popular opinion; it was a thermostat that transformed the mores [morals] of society. Whenever the early Christians entered a town, the people in power became disturbed and immediately sought to convict the Christians for being "disturbers of the peace" and "outside agitators." But the Christians pressed on, in the conviction that they were "a colony of heaven," called to obey God rather than man. Small in number, they were big in commitment. They were too God-intoxicated to be "astronomically intimidated." By their effort and example they brought an end to such ancient evils as infanticide and gladiatorial contests.

Things are different now. So often the contemporary church is a weak, ineffectual voice with an uncertain sound. So often it is an arch-defender of the status quo. Far from being disturbed by the presence of the church, the power structure of the average community is consoled by the church's silent—and often even vocal—sanction of things as they are.

But the judgment of God is upon the church as never before. If today's church does not recapture the sacrificial spirit of the early church, it will lose its authenticity, forfeit the loyalty of millions, and be dismissed as an irrelevant social club with no meaning for the twentieth century. Every day I meet young people whose disappointment with the church has turned into outright disgust.

Perhaps I have once again been too optimistic. Is organized religion too inextricably [closely] bound to the status quo [current opinion] to save our nation and the world? Perhaps I must turn my faith to the inner spiritual church, the church within the church, as the true *ekklesia* and the hope of the world. But again I am thankful to God that some noble souls from the ranks of organized religion have broken loose from the paralyzing chains of conformity and joined us as active partners in the struggle for freedom. They have left their secure congregations and walked the streets of Albany, Georgia, with us. They have gone down the highways of the South on tortuous rides for freedom. Yes, they have gone to jail with us. Some have been dismissed from their churches, have lost the support of their bishops and fellow ministers. But they have acted in the faith that right defeated is stronger than evil triumphant. Their witness has been the spiritual salt that has preserved the true meaning of the gospel in these troubled times. They have carved a tunnel of hope through the dark mountain of disappointment.

I hope the church as a whole will meet the challenge of this decisive hour. But even if the church does not come to the aid of justice, I have no despair about the future. I have no fear about the outcome of our struggle in Birmingham, even if our motives are at present misunderstood. We will reach the goal of freedom in Birmingham and all over the nation, because the goal of America is freedom. Abused and scorned though we may be, our destiny is tied up with America's destiny. Before the pilgrims landed at Plymouth, we were here. Before the pen of Jefferson etched the majestic words of the Declaration of Independence across the pages of history, we were here. For more than two centuries our forebears labored in this country without wages; they made cotton king; they built the homes of their masters while suffering gross injustice and shameful humiliation—and yet out of a bottomless vitality they continued to thrive and develop. If the inexpressible cruelties of slavery could not stop us, the opposition we now face will surely fail. We will win our freedom because the sacred heritage of our nation and the eternal will of God are embodied in our echoing demands.

Before closing I feel impelled to mention one other point in your statement that has troubled me profoundly. You warmly commended the Birmingham police force for keeping "order" and "preventing violence." I doubt that you would have so warmly commended the police force if you had seen its dogs sinking their teeth into unarmed, nonviolent

Negroes. I doubt that you would so quickly commend the policemen if you were to observe their ugly and inhumane treatment of Negroes here in the city jail; if you were to watch them push and curse old Negro women and young Negro girls; if you were to see them slap and kick old Negro men and young boys; if you were to observe them, as they did on two occasions, refuse to give us food because we wanted to sing our grace together. I cannot join you in your praise of the Birmingham police department. It is true that the police have exercised a degree of discipline in handling the demonstrators. In this sense they have conducted themselves rather "nonviolently" in public. But for what purpose? To preserve the evil system of segregation. Over the past few years I have consistently preached that nonviolence demands that the means we use must be as pure as the ends we seek. I have tried to make clear that it is wrong to use immoral means to attain moral ends. But now I must affirm that it is just as wrong, or perhaps even more so, to use moral means to preserve immoral ends. Perhaps Mr. Connor and his policemen have been rather nonviolent in public, as was Chief Pritchett in Albany, Georgia, but they have used the moral means of nonviolence to maintain the immoral end of racial injustice. As T. S. Eliot has said: "The last temptation is the greatest treason: To do the right deed for the wrong reason."

I wish you had commended the Negro sit-inners and demonstrators of Birmingham for their sublime courage, their willingness to suffer and their amazing discipline in the midst of great provocation. One day the South will recognize its real heroes. They will be the James Merediths, with the noble sense of purpose that enables them to face jeering and hostile mobs, and with the agonizing loneliness that characterizes the life of the pioneer. They will be old, oppressed, battered Negro women, symbolized in a seventy-two-year-old woman in Montgomery, Alabama, who rose up with a sense of dignity and with her people decided not to ride segregated buses, and who responded with ungrammatical profundity [brilliance] to one who inquired about her weariness: "My feets is tired, but my soul is at rest." They will be the young high school and college students, the young ministers of the gospel and a host of their elders, courageously and nonviolently sitting in at lunch counters and willingly going to jail for conscience's sake. One day the South will know that when these disinherited children of God sat down at lunch counters, they were in reality standing up for what is best in the American dream and for the most sacred values in our Judeo-Christian heritage, thereby bringing our nation back to those great wells of democracy which were dug deep by the founding fathers in their formulation of the Constitution and the Declaration of Independence.

Never before have I written so long a letter. I'm afraid it is much too long to take your precious time. I can assure you that it would have been much shorter if I had been writing from a comfortable desk, but what else can one do when he is alone in a narrow jail cell, other than write long letters, think long thoughts and pray long prayers?

If I have said anything in this letter that overstates the truth and indicates an unreasonable impatience, I beg you to forgive me. If I have said anything that understates the truth and indicates my having a patience that allows me to settle for anything less than brotherhood, I beg God to forgive me.

I hope this letter finds you strong in the faith. I also hope that circumstances will soon make it possible for me to meet each of you, not as an integrationist or a civil-rights leader but as a fellow clergyman and a Christian brother. Let us all hope that the dark clouds of racial prejudice will soon pass away and the deep fog of misunderstanding will be lifted from our fear-drenched communities, and in some not too distant tomorrow the radiant stars of love and brotherhood will shine over our great nation with all their scintillating [sparkling] beauty.

Yours for the cause of Peace and Brotherhood,
Martin Luther King, Jr.

CHAPTER 8

Postscript: Democracy outside America—To what extent might America's experience with democracy provide guidance to countries struggling to establish it?

Chapter one called attention to the fact that the Declaration of Independence did far more than make a case for this country's separation from the reign of a British king. It also offered an argument to the world. It advanced the claim—a revolutionary claim in its day—that human equality, inalienable rights, government instituted by consent, and the right to rebel form the grounds of political justice always and everywhere.

The readings we have examined show that the concrete meaning of these ideas is subject, as circumstances change, to a certain variety of interpretations and applications; that is to say, disagreements. One wonders whether this fact should detract from the power of these ideas. Evidence that it does not is that, since 1776, many countries have been inspired by the Declaration to lead their own democratic revolutions. This chapter concludes this book with an examination of a recent expression of that inspiration by Vaclav Havel. Havel, a poet-philosopher, was the last president of "Czechoslovakia," which threw off communism during the "Velvet" or "Gentle" Revolution of 1989, and subsequently divided into two separate countries: the Czech Republic and Slovakia. Havel then became the first president of the new Czech Republic. This was one of a number of uprisings in Central and Eastern Europe that year, collectively referred to as the "Revolutions of 1989," that led to the dissolution of the Soviet Union in 1991 and the end of the Cold War. That this war came to such a peaceful end was largely if not completely unexpected and, in that way, somewhat mysterious. In retrospect, rational-material (especially economic) explanations have been suggested. But the inspirational force of the Declaration's ideas is a more than material explanation. Havel's expression of that inspiration is in the tradition that, not only guns and armed divisions, but "ideas have consequences."

CZECH PRESIDENT VACLAV HAVEL, "ADDRESS TO A JOINT SESSION OF THE U.S. CONGRESS" (1990)

Vaclav Havel, a Czech playwright, was elected president of Czechoslovakia at the end of 1989. In this address to Congress, he describes his past life under a totalitarian government and then contrasts it with his hopes for what can be achieved under Czechoslovakia's new constitutional democracy. In the course of his remarks, he credits America's Founding documents, as well as its example, with inspiring his and other nations to adopt free institutions.

WHY THIS READING?

Although President Havel is grateful to the United States for the support it has provided to democratic movements, both in his country and elsewhere, he cautions that much work lies ahead if the world is to be successful at achieving Lincoln's vision of the "family of man." More important than material or economic improvements in life, he argues, is the ennobling of the individual conscience: "[W]e still don't know how to put morality ahead of politics, science and economics. We are still incapable of understanding that the only genuine backbone of all our actions, if they are to be moral, is responsibility."

Questions to guide you as you read:

- What reasons does President Havel provide for his assertion that democracy "can never be fully attained"? Is there a basis for this view in the Declaration of Independence? If so, what is it?
- Why does Havel argue that the belief that "man is the pinnacle of creation" is "destructive" and "vain"? How does this view compare to what you have read by Tocqueville and Washington regarding the political utility of religion?

Dear Mr. President, dear Senators and Members of the House, ladies and gentlemen:

My advisers advised me to speak on this important occasion in Czech. I don't know why. Perhaps they wanted you to enjoy the sweet sounds of my mother tongue.

The last time they arrested me, on October 27 of last year, I didn't know whether it was for two days or two years. Exactly one month later, when the rock musician Michael Kocab told me that I would be probably proposed as a presidential candidate, I thought it was one of his usual jokes.

On the 10th of December, 1989, when my actor friend, Jiri Bartoska, in the name of the Civic Forum, nominated me as a candidate for the office of president of the republic, I thought it was out of the question that the parliament we have inherited from the previous regime would elect me.

Nineteen days later, when I was unanimously elected president of my country, I had no idea that, in two months, I would be speaking in front of this famous and powerful assembly and that what I say would be heard by millions of people who have never heard of me and that hundreds of politicians and political scientists would study every word that I say.

When they arrested me on October 27, I was living in a country ruled by the most conservative communist government in Europe, and our society slumbered beneath the pall of a totalitarian system.

Today, less than four months later, I'm speaking to you as the representative of a country that has set out on the road to democracy, a country where there is complete freedom of speech, which is getting ready for free elections and which wants to create a prosperous market economy and its own foreign policy.

It is all very extraordinary. But I have not come here to speak of myself or my feelings, or merely to talk about my own country. I have used this small example of something I know well to illustrate something general and important.

We are living in very extraordinary times. The human face of the world is changing so rapidly that none of the familiar political speedometers are adequate.

We playwrights, who have to cram a whole human life or an entire historical era in a two-hour play, can scarcely understand this rapidity ourselves. And if it gives us trouble, think of the trouble it must give to political scientists who spend their whole life studying the realm of the probable and have less experience with the realm of the improbable than us, the playwrights.

The World in Bipolar Terms

Let me try to explain why I think the velocity of the changes in my country, in Central and Eastern Europe, and of course in the Soviet Union itself, has made such a significant impression on the face of the world today and why it concerns the fate of us all, including you Americans. I would like to look at this first from the political point of view and then from a point of view that we might call philosophical.

Twice in the century, the world has been threatened by a catastrophe. Twice this catastrophe was born in Europe, and twice you Americans, along with others, were called upon to save Europe, the whole world and yourselves. The first rescue mission, among other things, provided significant help to us, Czechs and Slovaks.

Thanks to the great support of your President (Woodrow) Wilson, our first president, Tomas Garrigue Masaryk, founded our modern independent state. He founded it, as you know, on the same principles on which the United States of America had been founded, as Masaryk's manuscripts held by the Library of Congress testify.

In the meantime, the United States made enormous strides. It became the most powerful nation on earth, and it understood the responsibility that flowed from this. Proof of this are the hundreds of thousands of your young citizens who gave their lives for the liberation of Europe and the graves of American airmen and soldiers on Czechoslovak soil.

But something else was happening as well. The Soviet Union appeared, grew and transformed the enormous sacrifices of its people suffering under totalitarian rule into a strength that, after World War II, made it the second most powerful nation in the world.

It was a country that rightly gave people nightmares, because no one knew what would occur to its rulers next and what country they would decide to conquer and drag into its sphere of influence, as it is called in political language.

All of this taught us to see the world in bipolar terms as two enormous forces—one a defender of freedom, the other a source of nightmares. Europe became the point of friction between these two powers, and thus it turned into a single enormous arsenal divided into two parts.

In this process, one half of the arsenal became part of that nightmarish power, while the other, the free part, bordering on the ocean and having no wish to be driven into it, was compelled, together with you, to build a complicated security system to which we probably owe the fact that we still exist.

So you may have contributed to the salvation of us Europeans, of the world and thus of yourselves for a third time. You have helped us to survive until today, without a hot war this time but merely a cold one.

The totalitarian system in the Soviet Union and in most of its satellites is breaking down, and our nations are looking for a way to democracy and independence.

The first act in this remarkable drama began when Mr. (Mikhail) Gorbachev and those around him faced the sad reality of their country, initiated a policy of perestroika ["restructuring"]. Obviously, they had no idea either of what they were setting in motion or how rapidly events would unfold. We knew a lot about the enormous number of growing problems that slumbered beneath the honeyed, unchanging mask of socialism. But I don't think any of us knew how little it would take for these problems to manifest themselves in all their enormity [horror] and for the longings of these nations to emerge in all their strength. The mask fell away so rapidly that, in the flood of work, we have literally no time even to be astonished.

Europe to "Seek Its Own Identity"

What does all this mean for the world in the long run? Obviously, a number of things. This, I am firmly convinced, is a historically irreversible process and, as a result, Europe will begin again to seek its own identity without being compelled to be a divided armory any longer. Perhaps this will create the hope that, sooner or later, your boys will no longer have to stand on guard for freedom in Europe or come to our rescue because Europe will at last be able to stand guard over itself.

But that is still not the most important thing. The main thing is, it seems to me, that these revolutionary changes will enable us to escape from the rather antiquated straitjacket of this bipolar view of the world and to enter at last into an era of multipolarity, that is, into an era in which all of us, large and small, former slaves and former masters, will be able to create what your great President (Abraham) Lincoln called "the family of man."

Can you imagine what a relief this would be to that part of the world which for some reason is called the Third World, even though it is the largest?

One, as you certainly know, most of the big wars and other conflagrations over the centuries have traditionally begun and ended on the territory of modern Czechoslovakia, or else they were somehow related to that area. Let the Second World War stand as the most recent example.

This is understandable: whether we like it or not, we are located in the very heart of Europe and, thanks to this, we have no view of the sea and no real navy. I mention this because political stability in our country has traditionally been important for the whole of Europe. This is still true today. Our government of national understanding, our present Federal Assembly, the other bodies of the state and I, myself, will personally guarantee this stability until we hold free elections, planned for June.

We understand the terribly complex reasons, domestic political reasons, above all, why the Soviet Union cannot withdraw its troops from our territory as quickly as they arrived in 1968. We understand that the arsenals built there over the past 20 years cannot be dismantled and removed overnight.

Nevertheless, in our bilateral negotiations with the Soviet Union, we would like to have as many Soviet units as possible moved out of our country before the elections, in the interests of political stability. The more successful our negotiations, the more those who are elected in our places will be able to guarantee political stability in our country, even after the elections.

Helping Soviets on Road to Democracy

Two, I often hear the question: how can the United States of America help us today? My reply is as paradoxical as the whole of my life has been. You can help us most of all if you help the Soviet Union on its irreversible but immensely complicated road to democracy. It is far more complicated than the road open to its former European satellites. You, yourself, know best how to support as rapidly as possible the nonviolent evolution of this enormous multinational body politic toward democracy and autonomy for all of its people. Therefore, it is not fitting for me to offer you any advice.

I can only say that the sooner, the more quickly, and the more peacefully the Soviet Union begins to move along the road toward genuine political pluralism, respect for the rights of the nations to their own integrity and to a working—that is, a market economy, the better it will be not just for Czechs and Slovaks but for the whole world.

And the sooner you yourselves will be able to reduce the burden of the military budget borne by the American people.

To put it metaphorically, the millions you give to the East today will soon return to you in the form of billions in savings.

Three, it is not true that the Czech writer Vaclav Havel wishes to dissolve the Warsaw Pact tomorrow and NATO the day after that, as some eager journalists have written. Vaclav Havel merely thinks what he has already said here, that for another hundred years American soldiers shouldn't have to be separated from their mothers just because Europe is incapable of being a guarantor of world peace, which it ought to be in order to make some amends, at least, for having given the world two world wars.

Sooner or later, Europe must recover and come into its own and decide for itself how many of whose soldiers it needs so that its own security, and all the wider implications of that security, may radiate peace into the whole world.

Vaclav Havel cannot make decisions about things that are not proper for him to decide. He is merely putting in a good word for genuine peace and for achieving it quickly....

...The borders of the European states, which, by the way, should gradually become less important, should finally be legally guaranteed by a common, regular treaty. It should be more than obvious that the basis for such a treaty would have to be general respect for human rights, genuine political pluralism and genuinely free elections.

Five, naturally we welcome the initiative of President [George H. W.] Bush, which was essentially accepted by Mr. Gorbachev, according to which the number of American and Soviet troops in Europe should be radically reduced. It is a magnificent shot in the arm for the Vienna disarmament talks and creates favorable conditions not only for our own efforts to achieve the quickest possible departure of Soviet troops from Czechoslovakia but indirectly as well for our own intention to make considerable cuts in the Czechoslovak army, which is disproportionately large in relation to our population.

If Czechoslovakia were forced to defend itself against anyone, which we hope will not happen, then it will be capable of doing so with a considerably smaller army, because this time its defense would be, not only after decades but after centuries, supported by the common and indivisible will of both its nations and its leadership.

Our freedom, independence and our newborn democracy have been purchased at great cost, and we shall not surrender them.

For the sake of order, I should add that whatever steps we take are not intended to complicate the Vienna disarmament talks but, on the contrary, to facilitate them.

Sixth, Czechoslovakia is returning to Europe. In the general interest and in its own interests as well, it wants to coordinate its return, both politically and economically, with the other returnees, which means, above all, with its neighbors, the Poles and the Hungarians.

We are doing what we can to coordinate these returns. And at the same time, we are doing what we can so that Europe will be capable of re-accepting us, its wayward children. Which means that it may open itself to us and may begin to transform its structures, which are formally European but de facto Western European, in that direction but in such a way that it will not be to its detriment but rather to its advantage.

Seven, I have already said this in our parliament, and I would like to repeat it here in this Congress, which is architecturally far more attractive.

For many years, Czechoslovakia, as someone's meaningless satellite, has refused to face up honestly to its co-responsibility for the world. It has a lot to make up for. If I dwell on this and so many important things, it is only because I feel, along with my fellow citizens, a sense of culpability for our former reprehensible passivity and a rather ordinary sense of indebtedness.

Eight, we are, of course, delighted that your country is so readily lending its support to our fresh efforts to renew democracy. Both our peoples were deeply moved by the generous offers made a few days ago in Prague at Charles University, one of the oldest in Europe, by your Secretary of State, Mr. James Baker. We are ready to sit down and talk about them.

A Long Way From "Family of Man"

Ladies and gentlemen, I've only been president for two months, and I haven't attended any schools for presidents. My only school was life itself.

Therefore, I don't want to burden you any longer with my political thoughts, but instead I will move on to an area that is more familiar to me, to what I would call the philosophical aspect of these changes that still concern everyone, although they are taking place in our corner of the world.

As long as people are people, democracy, in the full sense of the word, will always be no more than an ideal. One may approach it as one would the horizon in ways that may be better or worse, but it can never be fully attained. In this sense, you, too, are merely approaching democracy. You have thousands of problems of all kinds, as other countries do. But you have one great advantage: you have been approaching democracy uninterruptedly for more than 200 years, and your journey toward the horizon has never been disrupted by a totalitarian system.

Czechs and Slovaks, despite their humanistic traditions that go back to the first millennium, have approached democracy for a mere 20 years, between the two world wars, and now for the three and a half months since the 17th of November last year.

The advantage that you have over us is obvious at once.

The communist type of totalitarian system has left both our nations, Czechs and Slovaks, as it has all the nations of the Soviet Union and the other countries the Soviet Union subjugated in its time, a legacy of countless dead, an infinite spectrum of human suffering, profound economic decline and, above all, enormous human humiliation. It has brought us horrors that fortunately you have not known.

It has given us something positive, a special capacity to look from time to time somewhat further than someone who has not undergone this bitter experience. A person who cannot move and lead a somewhat normal life because he is pinned under a boulder has more time to think about his hopes than someone who is not trapped that way.

What I'm trying to say is this: we must all learn many things from you, from how to educate our offspring, how to elect our representatives, all the way to how to organize our economic life so that it will lead to prosperity and not to poverty. But it doesn't have to be merely assistance from the well-educated, powerful and wealthy to someone who has nothing and therefore has nothing to offer in return.

We, too, can offer something to you: our experience and the knowledge that has come from it.

This is a subject for books, many of which have already been written and many of which are yet to be written. I shall therefore limit myself to a single idea. The specific experience I'm talking about has given me one great certainty: consciousness precedes being, and not the other way around, as the Marxists claim.

For this reason, the salvation of this human world lies nowhere else than in the human heart, in the human power to reflect, in human meekness and in human responsibility.

Without a global revolution in the sphere of human consciousness, nothing will change for the better in the sphere of our being as humans, and the catastrophe toward which this world is headed—be it ecological, social, demographic or a general breakdown of civilization—will be unavoidable. If we are no longer threatened by world war or by the danger that the absurd mountains of accumulated nuclear weapons might blow up the world, this does not mean that we have definitively won. We are, in fact, far from the final victory.

We are still a long way from that "family of man." In fact, we seem to be receding from the ideal rather than growing closer to it. Interests of all kinds—personal, selfish, state, nation, group, and, if you like, company interests—still considerably outweigh genuinely common and global interests. We are still under the sway of the destructive and vain belief that man is the pinnacle of creation and not just a part of it and that therefore everything is permitted.

There are still many who say they are concerned not for themselves but for the cause, while they are demonstrably out for themselves and not for the cause at all. We are still destroying the planet that was entrusted to us and its environment. We still close our eyes to the growing social, ethnic and cultural conflicts in the world. From time to time, we say that the anonymous mega-machinery we have created for ourselves no longer serves us but rather has enslaved us, yet we still fail to do anything about it.

In other words, we still don't know how to put morality ahead of politics, science and economics. We are still incapable of understanding that the only genuine backbone of all our actions, if they are to be moral, is responsibility.

Responsibility to something higher than my family, my country, my company, my success—responsibility to the order of being where all our actions are indelibly recorded and where and only where they will be properly judged.

The interpreter or mediator between us and this higher authority is what is traditionally referred to as human conscience.

If I subordinate my political behavior to this imperative, mediated to me by my conscience, I can't go far wrong. If, on the contrary, I were not guided by this voice, not even 10 presidential schools with 2,000 of the best political scientists in the world could help me.

This is why I ultimately decided, after resisting for a long time, to accept the burden of political responsibility.

I am not the first, nor will I be the last, intellectual to do this. On the contrary, my feeling is that there will be more and more of them all the time. If the hope of the world lies in human consciousness, then it is obvious that intellectuals cannot go on forever avoiding their share of responsibility for the world and hiding their distaste for politics under an alleged need to be independent.

It is easy to have independence in your program and then leave others to carry that program out. If everyone thought that way, pretty soon no one would be independent.

I think that you Americans should understand this way of thinking. Wasn't it the best minds of your country, people you could call intellectuals, who wrote your famous Declaration of Independence, your bill of human rights and your Constitution and who, above all, took upon themselves practical responsibility for putting them into practice? The worker from Branik in Prague that your president referred to in his State of the Union message this year is far from being the only person in Czechoslovakia, let alone in the world, to be inspired by those great documents. They inspire us all; they inspire us despite the fact that they are over 200 years old. They inspire us to be citizens.

When Thomas Jefferson wrote that "governments are instituted among men, deriving their just powers from the consent of the governed," it was a simple and important act of the human spirit. What gave meaning to that act, however, was the fact that the author backed it up with his life. It was not just his words; it was his deeds as well.

I will end where I began: history has accelerated. I believe that once again it will be the human mind that will notice this acceleration, give it a name and transform those words into deeds.

Thank you.

Concluding Reflections from the Editors

One need not suppose that the end of the cold war beginning in the late 1980s marked a permanent end to the danger, either to democracy everywhere or to the principles of the Declaration. Abraham Lincoln long ago noted that democratic countries inspired by the Declaration's principles seem permanently in danger both from internal collapse and from dissolution owing to external dangers. His question at the beginning of the supreme crisis of the Declaration's principles in the United States, remains a question, we think, wherever and whenever those principles have inspired people to replace despotism with free self-government.

> . . . this issue embraces more than the fate of these United States. It presents to the whole family of man, the question, whether a constitutional republic, or a democracy—a government of the people, by the same people—can, or cannot, maintain its territorial integrity, against its own domestic foes. It presents the question, whether discontented individuals, too few in numbers to control administration, according to organic law, in any case, can always, upon the pretences made in this case, or on any other pretences, or arbitrarily, without any pretence, break up their Government, and thus practically put an end to free government upon the earth. It forces us to ask: "Is there, in all republics, this inherent, and fatal weakness?" "Must a government, of necessity, be too strong for the liberties of its own people, or too weak to maintain its own existence?" (Message to Congress in Special Session, July 4, 1861, in Roy P. Basler ed., *Collected Works of Abraham Lincoln* (New Brunswick, NJ: Rutgers University Press, 1953) Vol. 4, p. 427)

Later, in the struggle to defend the right of self-government in World War I, the 142nd anniversary of the Declaration moved Winston Churchill to remind the English-speaking peoples that

> The Declaration of Independence is not only an American document. It follows on the Magna Carta and the [English] Bill of Rights as the third great title-deed on which the liberties of the English-speaking peoples are founded. . . . The political conceptions embodied in the Declaration of Independence are the same as those expressed at that time by Lord Chatham and Mr. Burke and handed down to them by John Hampden and Algernon Sidney. They spring from the same source; they come from the same well of practical truth. . . . (Winston Churchill, "The Declaration of Independence and the War," July 4, 1918)

In 1946, Churchill famously repeated this theme of the Declaration's continuing relevance beyond the United States after the successful defense of its principles against perhaps the gravest external threat it had faced up to that time, namely that of Hitler's Nazism. That success had been, in no small part, owing to Churchill's inspirational wartime leadership.

> We cannot be blind to the fact that the liberties enjoyed by individual citizens throughout the British Empire are not valid in a considerable number of countries, some of which are very powerful. In these States control is enforced upon the common people by various kinds of all-embracing police governments. The power of the State is exercised without restraint, either by dictators or by compact oligarchies operating through a privileged party and a political police.... [W]e must never cease to proclaim in fearless tones the great principles of freedom and the rights of man which are the joint inheritance of the English-speaking world and which through Magna Carta, the Bill of Rights, the Habeas Corpus, trial by jury, and the English common law find their most famous expression in the American Declaration of Independence. (Winston Churchill, "The Sinews of Power," speech at Westminster College, Fulton, Missouri, March 5, 1946, more commonly known as "The Iron Curtain Speech")

We judge that it marks the Declaration's continuing relevance in world politics that Churchill would appeal to it in order to help the world understand the emergence of this new danger to which he gave the name the "Iron Curtain." The subsequent "cold war" between the Western Democracies and the Soviet Union, arguably the great world political struggle of the second half of the 20th century, receded when the Iron Curtain dissolved, in the late 1980s, from popular uprisings in the countries of Eastern Europe. When President Havel made his 1990 speech to Congress, he was restating what, as far as we know, is an uncontroverted position about the Declaration's continuing relevance to democratic government everywhere.

REFERENCES

Addams, Jane. 1915. "Why Women Should Vote." In *Woman Suffrage: History, Arguments, and Results*. Eds. Frances M. Borkman and Annie G. Poritt. New York: National Women Suffrage Publishing.

Alexander, Lamar. 1994. "Cut Their Pay and Send Them Home." At www.heritage.org/research/lecture

Ashcroft, John. 2003. "Address Before the Federalist Society." At www.justice.gov/archive

"Brutus I." 1981. In *The Complete Anti-Federalist*. Eds. Herbert Storing and Murray Dry. Chicago: University of Chicago Press.

Bush, George, W. 2008. "Speech to the Knesset." In *Public Papers of the Presidents of the United States: George W. Bush*. Office of the Federal Register.

"Centinel I." 1981. In *The Complete Anti-Federalist*. Eds. Herbert Storing and Murray Dry. Chicago: University of Chicago Press.

Cleveland, Henry. 1866. *Alexander H. Stephens, in Public and Private*. Philadelphia: National Publishing Co.

Clinton, Bill. 1995. "Mend It, Don't End It." *Public Papers of the Presidents of the United States: Bill Clinton*. Office of the Federal Register.

Diamond, Martin. 1981. *The Founding of the Democratic Republic*. Itasca, IL: F. E. Peacock.

Douglass, Frederick. 1982, 1985. *The Frederick Douglass Papers, Series One*. Volumes II and III. Ed. John W. Blassingame. New Haven, CT: Yale University Press. (Unless otherwise indicated, all Douglass reading selections are from *Douglass Papers.)*

Dred Scott v. Sandford. 1857. 60 U.S. 393.

Everson v. Board of Education. 1947. 330 U.S. 1.

Feingold, Russ. 2001. "On the Anti-Terrorism Bill." At U.S. Senate website: www.senate.gov

Goldwin, Robert. 1990. "Why Blacks, Women, and Jews Are Not Mentioned in the Constitution." In *Why Blacks, Women, and Jews Are Not Mentioned in the Constitution, and Other Unorthodox Views*. Washington, D.C.: AEI Press.

Grutter v. Bollinger. 2003. 539 U.S. 306.

Guinier, Lani. 1993. "Groups, Representation, and Race-Conscious Districting: A Case of the Emperor's Clothes," 71 *Texas Law Review* 1589.

Hamilton, Alexander, James Madison, and John Jay. 1788. *The Federalist*. New York: Modern Library

Hamilton, Alexander. 1904. *The Works of Alexander Hamilton*. Ed. Henry Cabot Lodge. New York: G. P. Putnam's Sons. (Unless otherwise indicated, all Hamilton reading selections are found in *The Works*.)

Havel, Vaclav. 1990. "Address to a Joint Session of the U.S. Congress." At the Library of Congress website: http://thomas.loc.gov

Jefferson, Thomas. 1861. *The Writings of Thomas Jefferson*. Ed. H. A. Washington. New York: H.W. Derby (Unless otherwise indicated, all Jefferson reading selections are found in *The Writings*.)

Johnson, Lyndon B. *Public Papers of the Presidents of the United States: Lyndon B. Johnson*. Office of the Federal Register. (Unless otherwise indicated, all Johnson reading selections are found in the *Public Papers*.)

Jordan, Barbara. 1992. "Change: From What to What?" At http://www.americanrhetoric.com/speeches/barbarajordan1992dnc.html

Kent, James. 1912. "On Universal Suffrage." In *Readings in American Constitutional History, 1776–1876*. Ed. Allen Johnson. New York: Cambridge University Press.

King, Martin Luther. 1963. "I Have a Dream Speech." Permission to reprint received from Intellectual

Properties Management (IPM), Licensing Manager of the Estate of Dr. Martin Luther King, Jr. (Atlanta, GA).

———. 1963. "Letter from Birmingham Jail." Permission to reprint received from Intellectual Properties Management (IPM), Licensing Manager of the Estate of Dr. Martin Luther King, Jr. (Atlanta, GA).

Lincoln, Abraham, and Stephen A. Douglas. 1894. *Political Debates Between Abraham Lincoln and Stephen A. Douglas.* Cleveland, OH: Burrows Brothers.

Lincoln, Abraham. 1953. *The Collected Works of Abraham Lincoln.* Ed. Roy P. Basler. New Brunswick, NJ: Rutgers University Press. (Unless otherwise indicated, all Lincoln reading selections are found in *The Collected Works.*)

Marshall, Thurgood. 1987. "Remarks at the Annual Seminar of the San Francisco Patent and Trademark Law Association." At www.thurgoodmarshall.com/speeches

Miller v. Johnson. 1995. 512 U.S. 622.

Minor v. Happersett. 1875. *88 U.S. 162.*

Moseley-Braun, Carol. 1994. "Speech on the Motor-Voter Bill." At U.S. Senate website: www.senate.gov

Myers v. United States. 1926. 272 U.S. 52.

Obama, Barack. 2008. "A More Perfect Union." At www.nytimes.com/2008/03/18/us/politics/18text-obama.html

Reagan, Ronald. 1982. *Public Papers of the Presidents of the United States: Ronald Reagan.* Office of the Federal Register. (Unless otherwise indicated, all Reagan reading selections are found in the *Public Papers.*)

Reynolds v. Sims. 1964. 377 U.S. 533.

Roosevelt, Franklin D. 1938–1950. The *Public Papers and Addresses of Franklin D. Roosevelt.* Comp. Samuel I. Rosenman. New York, NY: Random House.

———. 1937. "Interview by Arthur Krock." *The New York Times Magazine.*

Roosevelt, Theodore. 1906–1920. *The Works of Theodore Roosevelt.* New York: Charles Scribner's Sons. (Unless otherwise indicated, all Theodore Roosevelt reading selections are found in *The Works.*)

South Carolina v. Katzenbach. 1966. 383 U.S. 301.

Stanton, Elizabeth Cady. 1848. "Seneca Falls Declaration of Sentiments and Resolutions." At www.nps.gov.

Tocqueville, Alexis de. 1835. *Democracy in America.* Trans. Henry Reeve.

Washington, George. 1796. "Farewell Address." At the Library of Congress website: http://www.loc.gov/rr/program/bib/ourdocs/farewell.html

West Virginia v. Barnette. 1943. 319 U.S. 624.

INDEX

CPSIA information can be obtained
at www.ICGtesting.com
Printed in the USA
BVHW011624260921
617491BV00001B/1

9 780195 392111